Henry Thomas Buckle

History of civlization in England VOL I

Henry Thomas Buckle

History of civlization in England VOL I

ISBN/EAN: 9783741167256

Manufactured in Europe, USA, Canada, Australia, Japa

Cover: Foto ©ninafisch / pixelio.de

Manufactured and distributed by brebook publishing software (www.brebook.com)

Henry Thomas Buckle

History of civlization in England VOL I

HISTORY

OF

CIVILIZATION IN ENGLAND.

BY

HENRY THOMAS BUCKLE.

IN THREE VOLUMES.

VOL. I.

NEW EDITION

LONDON:
LONGMANS, GREEN, AND CO.
1873.

ANALYTICAL TABLE OF CONTENTS.

CHAPTER I.

STATEMENT OF THE RESOURCES FOR INVESTIGATING HISTORY, AND PROOFS OF THE REGULARITY OF HUMAN ACTIONS. THESE ACTIONS ARE GOVERNED BY MENTAL AND PHYSICAL LAWS: THEREFORE BOTH SETS OF LAWS MUST BE STUDIED, AND THERE CAN BE NO HISTORY WITHOUT THE NATURAL SCIENCES.

	PAGE
Materials for writing history	1–3
Narrow range of knowledge possessed by historians	–5
Object of the present work	6
Human actions, if not the result of fixed laws, must be due to chance or to supernatural interference	8
Probable origin of free-will and predestination	9–12
Theological basis of predestination, and metaphysical basis of free-will	12–18
The actions of men are caused by their antecedents, which exist either in the human mind or in the external world	18–20
Therefore history is the modification of man by nature, and of nature by man	20–21
Statistics prove the regularity of actions in regard to murder and other crimes	22–26
Similar proof respecting suicides	27–29
Also respecting the number of marriages annually contracted	31–32
And respecting the number of letters sent undirected	32
The historian must ascertain whether mind or nature has most influenced human actions; and therefore there can be no history without physical science	33–35
NOTE A. Passages from Kant on free-will and necessity	35–36

CHAPTER II.

INFLUENCE EXERCISED BY PHYSICAL LAWS OVER THE ORGANIZATION OF SOCIETY AND OVER THE CHARACTER OF INDIVIDUALS.

Man is affected by four classes of physical agents; namely, climate, food, soil, and the general aspect of nature	39–41
Operation of these agents on the accumulation of wealth	41–51

	PAGE
Their operation on the distribution of wealth	51–64
Illustrations of these principles from Ireland	64–67
From Hindustan	69–82
From Egypt	82–93
From Central America	93–94
And from Mexico and Peru	95
Operation of physical laws in Brazil	101–108
Influence of the general aspects of nature upon the imagination and the understanding	118–119
Under some aspects, nature is more prominent than man; under others, man more than nature	120
In the former case the imagination is more stimulated than the understanding, and to this class all the earliest civilisations belong	120–121
The imagination is excited by earthquakes and volcanoes	122–124
And by danger generally	125–128
Also by an unhealthy climate making life precarious	128–130
From these causes the civilisations exterior to Europe are mainly influenced by the imagination, those in Europe by the understanding	130–132
This proposition illustrated by a comparison between Hindustan and Greece	132–147
Further illustration from Central America	147–148
Chemical and physiological note on the connection between food and animal heat	148–151

CHAPTER III.

EXAMINATION OF THE METHOD EMPLOYED BY METAPHYSICIANS FOR DISCOVERING MENTAL LAWS.

In the last chapter, two leading facts have been established, which broadly separate Europe from other parts of the world	154–156
Hence it appears that of the two classes of mental and physical laws the mental are the more important for the history of Europe	156–157
Examination of the two metaphysical methods of generalising mental laws	156–165
Failure of these methods	165–167

CHAPTER IV.

MENTAL LAWS ARE EITHER MORAL OR INTELLECTUAL. COMPARISON OF MORAL AND INTELLECTUAL LAWS, AND INQUIRY INTO THE EFFECT PRODUCED BY EACH ON THE PROGRESS OF SOCIETY.

The historical method of studying mental laws is superior to the metaphysical method	168–174

ANALYTICAL TABLE OF CONTENTS. vii

	PAGE
The progress of society is twofold, moral and intellectual	174–175
Comparison of the moral with the intellectual element	175
There is no evidence that the natural faculties of man improve	176–177
Progress, therefore, depends on an improvement in the circumstances under which the faculties come into play	178
The standard of action having varied in every age, the causes of action must be variable	179
But moral truths have not changed	179
And intellectual truths are constantly changing	181
Intellectual truths are the cause of progress	182
Ignorant men are mischievous in proportion to their sincerity	183–185
Illustrations of this from Rome and Spain	185–188
The diminution of religious persecution is owing to the progress of knowledge	188–190
The diminution of the warlike spirit is owing to the same cause	190–192
Illustrations from Russia and Turkey	195–197
As civilization advances, men of intellect avoid becoming soldiers	198
Illustrations of this from ancient Greece and modern Europe	198–202
The three principal ways in which the progress of knowledge has lessened the warlike spirit are:	
1. The invention of gunpowder	203–209
2. The discoveries made by political economists	210–211
3. The application of steam to purposes of travelling	219–223
Inference to be drawn as to the causes of social progress	224–226

CHAPTER V.

INQUIRY INTO THE INFLUENCE EXERCISED BY RELIGION, LITERATURE, AND GOVERNMENT.

Recapitulation of preceding arguments	227
Moral feelings influence individuals, but do not affect society in the aggregate	228–229
This being as yet little understood, historians have not collected proper materials for writing history	230
Reasons why the present history is restricted to England	231–235
Comparison of the history of England with that of France	235–236
With that of Germany	237–240
With that of the United States of America	240–242
Necessity of ascertaining the fundamental laws of intellectual progress	243
Much may be gained in that respect from studying the histories of Germany, America, France, Spain, and Scotland	244–246

viii ANALYTICAL TABLE OF CONTENTS.

	PAGE
Deductive spirit in Scotland	246–252
Influence of religion on the progress of society	253–256
Illustration from the efforts of missionaries	254–256
Illustration from the Hebrews	257–258
Illustration from the early history of Christianity	259–262
And from Sweden and Scotland	263–266
Influence of literature on the progress of society	268–272
Influence of government on the progress of society	272–287
Illustrated by repeal of the corn-laws	273–274
The best legislation abrogates former legislation	275
The interference of politicians with trade has injured trade	275–278
Legislators have caused smuggling with all its attendant crimes	278–280
They have also increased hypocrisy and perjury	281–283
By their laws against usury they have increased usury	283–284
By other laws they have hindered the advance of knowledge	284–285
England has been less interfered with in these ways than other nations, and is therefore more prosperous than they	286–287

CHAPTER VI

ORIGIN OF HISTORY, AND STATE OF HISTORICAL LITERATURE DURING THE MIDDLE AGES.

Conclusions arrived at by the preceding investigations	288
An inquiry into the changes in historical researches will throw light on the changes in society	289–290
The earliest histories are ballads	291–295
One cause of error in history was the invention of writing	296–300
A change of religion in any country also tends to corrupt its early history	300–307
But the most active cause of all was the influence of the clergy	307–308
Absurdities which were consequently believed	309–317
Illustration of this from the history of Charlemagne by Turpin	318–321
And from the history of the Britons by Geoffrey	321–325
The first improvement in writing history began in the fourteenth and fifteenth centuries	326
But credulity was still prevalent, as is seen in Comines	327–329
And in the predictions of Stoeffler respecting the Deluge	330
Also in the work of Dr. Horst on the Golden Tooth	331–332

CHAPTER VII.

OUTLINE OF THE HISTORY OF THE ENGLISH INTELLECT FROM THE MIDDLE OF THE SIXTEENTH TO THE END OF THE EIGHTEENTH CENTURY.

This absurd way of writing history was the natural result of the state of the age	333

ANALYTICAL TABLE OF CONTENTS.

	PAGE
The spirit of doubt was a necessary precursor of improvement	334
Hence the supreme importance of scepticism	335–336
Origin of religious toleration in England	337
Hooker contrasted with Jewel	339–343
Scepticism and spirit of inquiry on other subjects	343–346
This tendency displayed in Chillingworth	347–350
Chillingworth compared with Hooker and Jewel	350
Subsequent movement in the same direction, and increasing indifference to theological matters	352–355
Great advantage of this	356–358
Under James I. and Charles I. this opposition to authority assumes a political character	359–361
Under Charles II. it takes a frivolous form at court	363
Influence of this spirit upon Sir Thomas Browne	365–367
Its influence upon Boyle	367–370
It causes the establishment of the Royal Society	371
Impetus now given to physical science, and attempts of the clergy to oppose it	372
The clergy are naturally hostile to physical science, because it lessens their own power	372–373
Illustration of this by the superstition of sailors and agriculturists as compared with soldiers and mechanics	375–380
Legislative improvements in the reign of Charles II. in spite of political degradation	380–386
These improvements were due to the sceptical and inquiring spirit	387–388
Aided by the vices of the king	388
And by his dislike of the church	389
He encouraged Hobbes, and neglected the ablest of the clergy	390–393
The clergy, to recover their ground, allied themselves with James II.	394–396
This alliance was dissolved by the Declaration of Indulgence	397–399
The clergy then united with the dissenters and brought about the Revolution of 1688	399–400
Importance of the Revolution	401–403
But the clergy regretted it, and repented of their own act	403
Hostility between them and William III.	405–410
Hence a schism in the church	410–413
Fresh encouragement thus given to scepticism	413–414
Convocation first despised, and then abolished	414–415
After the Revolution the ablest men confine themselves to secular professions, and avoided entering the church	415
The clergy lost all offices out of the church, and their numbers diminished in both Houses of Parliament	416–418
The church rallied for a moment under Anne	418–420
But was weakened by the dissenters, headed by Wesley and Whitefield	420–424

ANALYTICAL TABLE OF CONTENTS.

	PAGE
Theology separated from morals and from politics	424–426
Rapid succession of sceptical controversies	427–429
Knowledge begins to be diffused, and takes a popular form	430–433
Political meetings, and publication of parliamentary debates	433–434
Doctrine of personal representation, and idea of independence	435
Corresponding change in the style of authors	436–439
Hence great reforms became inevitable	439–440
This tendency was aided by George I. and George II.	441–443
But discouraged by George III., under whom began a dangerous political reaction	444–446
Ignorance of George III.	446
Subserviency of Pitt	446–449
Incompetence of other statesmen, and the king's hatred of great men	449–451
Deterioration of the House of Lords	451–455
Ability and accomplishments of Burke	456–461
He opposed the views of George III., and was neglected by him	462–467
Burke's subsequent hallucinations and violence	467–476
The king now favoured him	476–477
Policy of George III. respecting America	478–482
This policy reacted upon England	482–483
Policy in regard to France	483–486
This also reacted upon England	486
And produced arbitrary laws against the liberties of England	487–493
Which were zealously enforced by the executive	494–496
Gloomy political prospects of England late in the eighteenth century	496–498
But, owing to the progress of knowledge, a counter reaction was preparing	498–502
To which, and to the increasing power of public opinion, England owes her great reforms of the nineteenth century	502–505

LIST OF AUTHORS QUOTED.

[In order to assist those who wish to verify my references, and also with the view of indicating the nature and extent of the materials which I have used, I have drawn up the following list of the principal works quoted. When no edition is mentioned, the size is 8vo et infra. When the name of the author is enclosed between brackets, the book is anonymous; but in such cases I have usually subjoined some authority who gives evidence of the authorship.]

[Aarsens de Sommerdyck] Voyage d'Espagne, fait en l'année 1655. Paris, 1665. 4to. Barbier (*Dictionnaire des Ouvrages Anonymes*, vol. ii. p. 468, Paris, 1806) refers to an edition of 1656.
Abd-Allatif, Relation de l'Egypte, traduite par Silvestre de Sacy. Paris, 1810. 4to.
Aberdeen: Extracts from the Council Register of the Burgh of Aberdeen, from 1398 to 1570, printed for the Spalding Club. Aberdeen, 1844. 4to.
Ibid., from 1570 to 1625, printed for the Spalding Club. Aberdeen, 1848. 4to.
Abernethy (J.) The Hunterian Oration for the year 1819. London, 1819.
Abernethy (M. L) Physicke for the Soule. London, 1622. 4to.
Acts of the Parliaments of Scotland from 1124 to 1707. London, 1814–1844. 11 vols. folio.
Acts and Proceedings of the General Assemblies of the Kirk of Scotland, from 1560 to 1618. Edinburgh, 1839–1845. 3 vols. 4to.
Acts of the General Assembly of the Church of Scotland, from 1638 to 1842. Edinburgh, 1843.
Adams (J.) Memoirs of the Life and Doctrines of John Hunter. 2nd edit. London, 1818.
Adolphus (J.) History of England from the accession of George III. London, 1840–1845. 7 vols.
Aguesseau (Chancelier d') Lettres inédites. Paris, 1823. 2 vols.
Aikin (L.) Life of Addison. London, 1843. 2 vols.
Albemarle (Earl of) Memoirs of the Marquis of Rockingham. Lond. 1852. 2 vols.
Alberoni (Cardinal) The History of. London, 1719.
Alison (Sir A.) History of Europe, from the commencement of the French Revolution to 1815. Edinburgh, 1849, 1850. 14 vols.
Allen (J.) Rise and Growth of the Royal Prerogative in England. London, 1849.

Anderson (J.) Prize Essay on the State of Society and Knowledge in the Highlands of Scotland. Edinburgh, 1827.
Antequera (D. J. M.) Historia de la Legislacion Española. Madrid, 1849.
Argyll (The Duke of) Presbytery Examined. London, 1848.
Arnold (Dr.) Lectures on Modern History. London, 1842.
Arnot (H.) The History of Edinburgh. Edinburgh, 1788. 4to.
Asiatic Researches. London and Calcutta, 1799–1836. 20 vols. 4to.
Aubrey (J.) Letters and Lives of Eminent Men. London, 1813. 2 vols.
Andigier (M.) L'Origine des François. Paris, 1676. 2 vols.
Azara (F.) Voyages dans l'Amérique Méridionale. Paris, 1809. 4 vols.

Bacallar (V.) Commentarios de la Guerra de España, e Historia de su Rey Phelipe V. Genova. 2 vols. 4to (no date).
Bacon (J. F.) Six Years in Biscay. London, 1838.
Baillie (R.) Letters and Journals from 1637 to 1662, edited by D. Laing. Edinburgh, 1841–1842. 3 vols.
Bain (A.) The Senses and the Intellect. London, 1855.
Bakewell (R.) Introduction to Geology. London, 1838.
Balfour (Sir J.) Historical Works, containing the Annals of Scotland. London, 1825. 4 vols.
Balfour (J. H.) A Manual of Botany. London, 1849.
Bancroft (G.) History of the American Revolution. London, 1852–1854. 3 vols.
Bannatyne (J.) Journal of Transactions in Scotland, from 1570 to 1573. Edinburgh, 1806.
Barante (M.) Tableau de la Littérature Française au XVIIIe Siècle. Paris, 1847.
Barrington (D.) Observations on the Statutes. 5th edit. London, 1796. 4to.
Barruel (L'Abbé) Mémoires pour l'Histoire du Jacobinisme. Hambourg, 1803. 5 vols.
Barry (G.) History of the Orkney Islands. Edinburgh, 1805. 4to.
Bassompierre (Maréchal de) Mémoires. Paris, 1822, 1823. 3 vols.
Bates (G.) Account of the late Troubles in England. London, 1685. 2 vols.
Baxter (R.) Life and Times, by himself. Published by M. Sylvester. London, 1696. Folio. 3 parts.
Bazin (M. A.) Histoire de France sous Louis XIII. Paris, 1838. 4 vols.
Beausobre (M.) Histoire Critique de Manichée et du Manichéisme. Amsterdam, 1734–9. 2 vols. 4to.
Béclard (P. A.) Éléments d'Anatomie Générale. Paris, 1852.
Bedford Correspondence, edited by Lord J. Russell. 1842–1846. 3 vols.
Beechey (F. W.) Voyage to the Pacific. London, 1831. 2 vols.

LIST OF AUTHORS QUOTED.

Belsham (W.) History of Great Britain, from 1688 to 1802. London, 1805. 12 vols. [Of this work I have used only the last seven volumes, which refer to a period for which Belsham was a contemporary authority. The earlier volumes are worthless.]
[Benoist] Histoire de l'Édit de Nantes. Delft, 1693–1695. 5 vols. 4to.
Berkeley (Bishop of Cloyne) Works. London, 1843. 2 vols.
Berwick (Maréchal de) Mémoires écrits par lui-même. Paris, 1778. 2 vols.
Bichat (X.) Traité des Membranes. Paris, 1802.
Bichat (X.) Anatomie Générale. Paris, 1821. 4 vols.
Bichat (X.) Recherches sur la Vie et la Mort, édit. Magendie. Paris, 1829.
Binning (H.) Sermons, edited by J. Cochrane. Edinburgh, 1839, 1840. 3 vols.
Biographie Universelle. Paris, 1811–1828. 52 vols.
Birch (T.) Life of Tillotson, Archbishop of Canterbury. London, 1753.
Bisset (R.) Life of Edmund Burke. 2nd edit. London, 1800. 2 vols.
Black (J.) Lectures on Chemistry, edited by John Robison. Edinburgh, 1803. 2 vols. 4to.
Blackstone's Commentaries on the Laws of England. London, 1809. 4 vols.
Blainville (D.) Physiologie Générale et Comparée. Paris, 1833. 3 vols.
Blair (R.) Autobiography, from 1593 to 1636; with a continuation to 1680, by W. Row, edited by T. M'Crie for the Wodrow Society. Edinburgh, 1848.
Blanqui (M.) Histoire de l'Économie Politique en Europe. Paris, 1845. 2 vols.
Bogue (D.) and Bennett (J.) History of the Dissenters, from 1688 to 1808. London, 1808–1812. 4 vols.
Bohlen (P.) Das alte Indien, mit besonderer Rücksicht auf Aegypten. Königsberg, 1830. 2 vols.
[Boisel] Journal du Voyage d'Espagne. Paris, 1669. 4to. See Barbier, Dict. des Ouvr. Anonymes, vol. ii. p. 621, Paris, 1806.
Bordas-Demoulin, Le Cartésianisme. Paris, 1843. 2 vols.
Bossuet (Évêque de Meaux) Discours sur l'Histoire Universelle. Paris, 1844.
Boston (T.) Sermons. Glasgow, 1752.
Boston (T.) Human Nature in its Four-fold State. Reprinted, London, 1809.
Bouillaud (J.) Philosophie Médicale. Paris, 1836.
Bouillé (M. de) Mémoires sur la Révolution Française. Paris, 1801–9. 2 vols.
Bouillier (M.) Histoire des divers Corps de la Maison Militaire des Rois de France. Paris, 1818.
Boulainvilliers (Comte) Histoire de l'Ancien Gouvernement de la France. La Haye, 1727. 3 vols.

LIST OF AUTHORS QUOTED.

Bourgoing (J. F.) Tableau de l'Espagne Moderne, quatrième édition. Paris, 1807. 3 vols.
Bouterwek (F.) History of Spanish and Portuguese Literature. London, 1823. 2 vols.
Bowdich (T. E.) Mission to Ashantee. London, 1819. 4to.
Bower (A.) History of the University of Edinburgh. Edinburgh, 1817-1830. 3 vols.
Bowles (G.) Introduccion á la Historia Natural y á la Geografía Física de España. Tercera edicion. Madrid, 1789. 4to.
Bowles (W. L.) Life of Bishop Ken. London, 1830, 1831. 2 vols.
Boyle (R.) Works. London, 1744. 5 vols. folio.
Brand (A.) Description of Orkney, Zetland, Pightland-Firth, and Caithness. Edinburgh, 1701.
Brande (W. T.) A Manual of Chemistry. London, 1848. 2 vols.
Brewster (Sir D.) Memoirs of Sir Isaac Newton. Edinburgh, 1855. 2 vols.
Brienne (L. H. de Loménie) Mémoires inédits. Paris, 1828. 2 vols.
Brissot (J. P.) Mémoires. Paris, 1830. 2 vols.
British Association for Advancement of Science, Reports of. London, 1833-1853. 21 vols.
Brodie (Sir B.) Lectures on Pathology and Surgery. London, 1846.
Brodie (Sir B.) Physiological Researches. London, 1851.
Brougham (Lord) Sketches of Statesmen in the time of George III. London, 1845. 6 vols.
Brougham (Lord) Lives of Men of Letters and Science in the time of George III. London, 1845-1847. 2 vols.
Brougham (Lord) Political Philosophy. 2nd edit. London, 1849. 3 vols.
Broussais (F. J. V.) Examen des Doctrines Médicales. Paris, 1829-1834. 4 vols.
Broussais (F. J. V.) Cours de Phrénologie. Paris, 1836.
Brown (A.) History of Glasgow. Glasgow, 1795, and Edinburgh, 1797. 2 vols.
Brown (T.) Lectures on the Philosophy of the Mind. Edinburgh, 1838.
Browne (J.) History of the Highlands and of the Highland Clans. Glasgow, 1838. 4 vols.
Browne (Sir Thomas) Works and Correspondence, by S. Wilkin. London, 1836. 4 vols.
Buchanan (F.) Journey through Mysore, Canara, and Malabar. London, 1807. 3 vols. 4to.
Buchanan (G.) Rerum Scoticarum Historia, cura Man. Abredonim, 1762.
Buchanan (J.) Sketches of the North-American Indians. London, 1824.
Buckingham (Duke of) Memoirs of George III. London, 1853. 2 vols.
Bullock (W.) Travels in Mexico. London, 1824.

LIST OF AUTHORS QUOTED.

Bulstrode (Sir R.) Memoirs of Charles I. and Charles II. London, 1721.
Bunbury (Sir H.) Correspondence of Sir Thomas Hanmer. London, 1838.
Bunsen (C. C. J.) Egypt's Place in Universal History. London, 1848-1854. 2 vols.
Burckhardt (J. L.) Travels in Arabia. London, 1829. 2 vols.
Burdach (C. F.) Traité de Physiologie considérée comme Science d'Observation. Paris, 1837-1841. 9 vols.
Burke (E.) Correspondence with Laurence. London, 1827.
Burke (E.) Works, by H. Rogers. London, 1841. 2 vols.
Burke (E.) Correspondence between 1744 and 1797. London, 1844. 4 vols.
Burnes (Sir A.) Travels into Bokhara. London, 1834. 3 vols.
Burnet (Bishop G.) History of his own Time. Oxford, 1823. 6 vols.
Burnet (Bishop G.) Lives and Characters, edit. Jebb. London, 1833.
Burnet (Bishop G.) Memoirs of the Lives of James and William, Dukes of Hamilton and Castle-Herald. Oxford, 1852.
Burton (J. H.) Life and Correspondence of David Hume. Edinburgh, 1846. 2 vols.
Burton (J. H.) Lives of Simon Lord Lovat, and Duncan Forbes of Culloden. London, 1847.
Burton (J. H.) Narratives from Criminal Trials in Scotland. London, 1852. 2 vols.
Burton (J. H.) History of Scotland, from 1689 to 1748. London, 1853. 2 vols.
Burton (R. F.) Sindh, and the Races in the Valley of the Indus. London, 1851.
Burton (T.) Diary, from 1655 to 1659. London, 1828. 4 vols.
Butler (C.) Memoirs of the English, Irish, and Scottish Catholics. London, 1822. 4 vols.
Butler (C.) Reminiscences. London, 1824-1827. 2 vols.

Cabanis (P. J. G.) Rapports du Physique et du Moral de l'Homme. Paris, 1843.
Cabarrus (D. F.) Elogio de Carlos III. Madrid, 1789. 4to.
Cabarrus (Conde de) Cartas sobre los Obstaculos que la Naturaleza, la Opinion, y las Leyes oponen à la Felicidad Publica. Madrid, 1813.
Calamy (E.) Account of my own Life, 1631-1731. London, 1829. 2 vols.
Calderwood (D.) History of the Kirk of Scotland, edited by T. Thomson for the Wodrow Society. Edinburgh, 1842-1849. 8 vols.
Campan (Madame) Mémoires sur Marie-Antoinette. Paris, 1826. 3 vols.
Campbell (Lord) Lives of the Lord Chancellors of England. 3rd edit. London, 1848-1850. 7 vols.

Campbell (Lord) Lives of the Chief Justices of England. London, 1849. 2 vols.
Campion (H. de) Mémoires. Paris, 1807.
[Campomanes] Discurso sobre la Educacion Popular de los Artesanos. Madrid, 1775.
[Campomanes] Apéndice á la Educacion Popular. Madrid, 1775-1777. 4 vols.
Capefigue (M.) Histoire de la Réforme, de la Ligue et du Règne de Henri IV. Bruxelles, 1834, 1835. 8 vols.
Capefigue (M.) Richelieu, Mazarin et la Fronde. Paris, 1844. 2 vols.
Capefigue (M.) Louis XIV. Paris, 1844. 2 vols.
Capmany (A de) Qüestiones Criticas sobre varios Puntos de Historia economica, &c. Madrid, 1807.
Cappe (C.) Memoirs, written by herself. London, 1822.
Carlyle (Rev. Dr. Alexander) Autobiography. 2nd edit. Edinburgh, 1860.
Carlyle (T.) Letters and Speeches of Cromwell. 2nd edit. London, 1846. 3 vols.
Carpenter (W. B.) Principles of Human Physiology. 3rd edit. London, 1846.
Cartwright (Major) Life and Correspondence. London, 1826. 2 vols.
Carus (C. G.) Comparative Anatomy of Animals. London, 1827. 2 vols.
Carwithen (J. B. S.) History of the Church of England. Oxford, 1849. 2 vols.
Cassagnac (M. A. G. de) Causes de la Révolution Française. Paris, 1850. 3 vols.
Castro (A.) Examen Filosofico sobre las principales causas de la Decadencia de España. Cadiz, 1852.
Catlin (G.) Letters on the North-American Indians. London, 1841. 2 vols.
Chalmers (G.) Caledonia. London, 1807-1824. 3 vols. 4to.
Chalmers (P.) Historical and Statistical Account of Dunfermline. Edinburgh, 1844.
Chambers (R.) Domestic Annals of Scotland, from the Reformation to the Revolution. Edinburgh, 1858. 2 vols.
Charron (P.) De la Sagesse. Amsterdam, 1782. 2 vols.
Chatham (Earl of) Correspondence. London, 1838-1840. 4 vols.
Chillingworth (W.) The Religion of Protestants. London, 1846.
Chronicle of Perth (The) from 1210 to 1668. Edinburgh, 1831. 4to. Published by the Maitland Club.
Circourt (A. de) Histoire des Arabes d'Espagne. Paris, 1846. 3 vols.
Clapperton (H.) Second Expedition into the Interior of Africa. London, 1829. 4to.
Clarendon (Earl of) State Papers. Oxford, 1767-1786. 3 vols. folio.

LIST OF AUTHORS QUOTED. xvii

Clarendon (Earl of) The History of the Rebellion and Civil Wars in England; also his Life, written by Himself. Oxford, 1843.
Clarendon's Correspondence and Diary, by S. W. Singer. London, 1828. 2 vols. 4to.
Clarke (C.) An Examination of the Internal State of Spain. London, 1818.
Clarke (E.) Letters concerning the Spanish Nation, written at Madrid in 1760 and 1761. London, 1763. 4to.
Cloncurry (Lord) Recollections and Correspondence. Dublin, 1849.
Clot-Bey (A. B.) De la Peste observée en Égypte. Paris, 1840.
Cloud (A) of Witnesses for the Royal Prerogatives of Jesus Christ. 10th edit. Glasgow, 1779.
Cockburn (J.) Jacob's Vow, or Man's Felicity and Duty. Edinburgh, 1696.
Colebrooke (H. T.) A Digest of Hindu Law. Calcutta, 1801. 3 vols.
Coleman (C.) Mythology of the Hindus. London, 1832. 4to.
Coleridge (S. T.) Literary Remains. London, 1836-1839. 4 vols.
Coleridge (S. T.) The Friend. London, 1844. 3 vols.
Combe (G.) Notes on the United States of North America. Edinburgh, 1841. 3 vols.
Comines (P. de) Mémoires, édit. Petitot. 1826. 3 vols.
Comte (A.) Cours de Philosophie Positive. Paris, 1830-1842. 6 vols.
Comte (C.) Traité de Législation. Paris, 1835. 4 vols.
Conde (J. A.) Historia de la Dominacion de los Arabes en España. Paris, 1840.
Condillac (E. B.) Traité des Sensations. Paris, 1798.
Condorcet (Marquis de) Vie de Turgot. Londres, 1786.
Condorcet (Marquis de) Vie de Voltaire, in vol. i. of Œuvres de Voltaire. Paris, 1820.
Conrart (V.) Mémoires. Paris, 1825.
Cook (J.) Three Voyages round the World. London, 1821. 7 vols.
Cook (S. S.) Sketches in Spain, from 1829 to 1832. London, 1834. 2 vols.
Cooke (G. W.) History of Party. London, 1836, 1837. 3 vols.
Copleston (E.) Inquiry into the Doctrines of Necessity and Predestination. London, 1821.
Costa y Borras (J. D. Obispo de Barcelona) Observaciones sobre el Presente y el Porvenir de la Iglesia en España. Segunda edicion. Barcelona, 1857.
Cousin (V.) Cours de l'Histoire de la Philosophie moderne, I™ série. Paris, 1846. 5 vols.
Cousin (V.) Cours de l'Histoire de la Philosophie moderne, II° série. Paris, 1847. 3 vols.
Cowper (W.) Heaven Opened. London, 1631. 4to.
Coxe (W.) Memoirs of the Kings of Spain of the House of Bourbon. 2nd edit. London, 1815. 5 vols.
Crantz (D.) History of Greenland. London, 1767. 2 vols.

LIST OF AUTHORS QUOTED.

Crawfurd (G.) The History of the Shire of Renfrew. Paisley 1782. 3 parts, 4to.
Crawfurd (J.) History of the Indian Archipelago. Edinburgh, 1820. 3 vols.
Crichton (A.) The Life and Diary of Lieut.-Col. J. Blackader. Edinburgh, 1824.
Croker (R.) Travels through several Provinces of Spain and Portugal. London, 1799.
Crookshank (W.) History of the Church of Scotland, from 1660 to 1688. Edinburgh, 1812. 2 vols.
Cudworth (R.) The True Intellectual System of the Universe. London, 1820. 4 vols.
Cullen (W.) Works. Edinburgh, 1827. 2 vols.
Currie (J.) Life and Correspondence, by his Son. London, 1831. 2 vols.
Custine (Marquis de) La Russie en 1839. Paris, 1843. 4 vols.
Cuvier (G.) Recueil des Éloges Historiques. Paris, 1819-1827. 3 vols.
Cuvier (G.) Le Règne Animal. Paris, 1829. 5 vols.
Cuvier (G.) Histoire des Sciences Naturelles depuis leur Origine. Paris, 1831.
Cuvier (G.) Histoire des Progrès des Sciences Naturelles depuis 1789. Bruxelles, 1837, 1838. 2 vols.

Dabistan (The) translated from the Persian, by D. Shea and A. Troyer. Paris, 1843. 3 vols.
Dacier (M.) Rapport sur les Progrès de l'Histoire et de la Littérature depuis 1789. Paris, 1810. 4to.
Dalrymple (Sir D.) Annals of Scotland, from 1057 to 1371. 3rd edit. Edinburgh, 1819. 3 vols.
Dalrymple (J.) History of Feudal Property in Great Britain. London, 1758.
Dalrymple (J.) Memoirs of Great Britian and Ireland. London, 1790. 3 vols.
Dalrymple (W.) Travels through Spain and Portugal in 1774. London, 1777. 4to.
Daniel (G.) Histoire de la Milice Françoise. Paris, 1721. 2 vols. 4to.
Daniell (J. F.) Meteorological Essays. London, 1827.
Darwin (C.) Journal of Researches in Geology and Natural History. London, 1840.
[D'Aulnoy (Madame)] Relation du Voyage d'Espagne. Lyon, 1693. 2 vols. See Ticknor's *History of Spanish Literature*, vol. ii. pp. 320, 321.
Davies (C. M.) History of Holland. London, 1841-1844. 3 vols.
Davila (G. G.) Historia de la Vida y Hechos del Inclito Monarca Amado y Santo D. Felipe Tercero. Reprinted, Madrid, 1771. Folio.
Davis (J. F.) The Chinese. London, 1844. 3 vols.
De Foe (D.) The History of the Union between England and Scotland. London, 1786. 4to.
De Lisle (Romé) Essai de Cristallographia. Paris, 1772.

De Lisle (Romé) Cristallographie. Paris, 1783. 4 vols. 8vo.
Denham (D.) Travels in Northern and Central Africa. London, 1826. 4to.
Denholm (J.) The History of the City of Glasgow and Suburbs. 3rd edition. Glasgow, 1804.
Descartes (R.) Œuvres, par V. Cousin. Paris, 1824–1826. 11 vols.
Des Maizeaux (P.) Life of Chillingworth. London, 1725.
Des Réaux (Tallemant) Les Historiettes. Paris, 1840. 10 vols.
De Staël (Madame) Considérations sur la Révolution Françoise. Paris, 1820. 3 vols.
De Thou (J. A.) Histoire Universelle, depuis 1543 jusqu'en 1607. Londres, 1734. 16 vols. 4to.
Dickson (D.) A Brief Explication of the first Fifty Psalms. London, 1653.
Dickson (D.) Truth's Victory over Error. Reprinted, Glasgow, 1772.
Diderot (D.) Mémoires et Correspondance. Paris, 1830, 1831. 4 vols.
Dillon (J. T.) Travels through Spain. Dublin, 1781.
Diodori Siculi Bibliotheca Historica; recensione Wesselingii. Bipont. 1793–1807. 11 vols.
Diogenes Laertius, De Vitis Philosophorum, edit. Meibomius. Amstel. 1692. 2 vols. 4to.
Disney (J.) Life of Dr. John Jebb, in vol. i. of Jebb's Works. London, 1787.
Diurnal (A) of Remarkable Occurrents that have passed within the Country of Scotland, since the Death of James IV. till the year 1575. Published by the Bannatyne Club. Edinburgh, 1833. 4to.
Dobell (P.) Travels in Kamtchatka and Siberia. London, 1830. 2 vols.
Doblado's Letters from Spain (by Rev. B. White). London, 1822.
Doddridge (P.) Correspondence and Diary. London, 1829–1831. 5 vols.
Doubleday (T.) The True Law of Population. London, 1847.
Dowling (J. G.) Introduction to the Study of Ecclesiastical History. London, 1838.
D'Oyly (G.) Life of Sancroft, Archbishop of Canterbury. London, 1840.
Duclos (M.) Mémoires secrets sur Louis XIV et Louis XV. Paris, 1791. 2 vols.
Du Deffand (Madame) Correspondance inédite. Paris, 1800. 2 vols.
Du Deffand (Madame) Lettres à H. Walpole. Paris, 1827. 4 vols.
Dufau (P. A.) Traité de Statistique. Paris, 1840.
Du Mesnil (M.) Mémoires sur le Prince Le Brun. Paris, 1828.
Dumont (E.) Souvenirs sur Mirabeau. Londres, 1832.
[Dunham] History of Spain and Portugal. London, 1832. 5 vols. See Prescott's *Ferdinand and Isabella*, vol. iii. p. 214.
Dunlop (J.) Memoirs of Spain, from 1621 to 1700. Edinburgh, 1834. 2 vols.

Duplessis-Mornay (P.) Mémoires et Correspondance. Paris, 1824, 1825. 12 vols.
Durham (J.) Exposition of the Song of Solomon. 1669. Reprinted, Glasgow, 1788.
Durham (J.) The Law Unsealed. 1675. Reprinted, Glasgow, 1798.
Durham (J.) A Commentarie upon the Book of the Revelation. Glasgow, 1680. 4to.
Dutens (L.) Mémoires d'un Voyageur qui se repose. Londres, 1806. 3 vols.
Duvernet (J.) Vie de Voltaire. Genève, 1786.
Duvernet (J.) Histoire de la Sorbonne. Paris, 1791. 2 vols.

Eccleston (J.) Introduction to English Antiquities. London, 1847.
Edwards (M.) Zoologie. Paris, 1841, 1842. 2 parts.
Elliotson (J.) Human Physiology. London, 1840.
Ellis Correspondence (The) 1686-1688, edited by G. A. Ellis. London, 1829. 2 vols.
Ellis (Sir H.) Original Letters of Literary Men. Camden Soc. 1843. 4to.
Ellis (W.) A Tour through Hawaii. London, 1827.
Ellis (W.) Polynesian Researches. London, 1831. 4 vols.
Ellis (W.) History of Madagascar. London, 1838. 2 vols.
Elphinstone (M.) The History of India. London, 1849.
Encyclopædia of the Medical Sciences. London, 1847. 4to.
Épinay (Madame d') Mémoires et Correspondance. Paris, 1818. 3 vols.
Erichsen (J.) The Science and Art of Surgery. 2nd edit. London, 1857.
Erman (A.) Travels in Siberia. London, 1848. 2 vols.
Eschbach (M.) Introduction à l'Étude du Droit. Paris, 1846.
Esquirol (E.) Des Maladies Mentales. Paris, 1838. 2 vols.
Estat (L') de l'Espagne. Genève, 1681.
Evelyn (J.) Diary and Correspondence. London, 1827. 5 vols.
Extracts from the Presbytery Book of Strathbogie, from 1631 to 1664. Printed for the Spalding Club. Aberdeen, 1843. 4to.
Extracts from the Registers of the Presbytery of Glasgow, and of the Kirk Sessions of the Parishes of Cambusnethan, Humbie, and Stirling. 4to (no date).

Fairfax Correspondence (The) edited by G. W. Johnson and R. Bell. London, 1848, 1849. 4 vols.
Fanshawe (Lady) Memoirs, written by herself. London, 1830.
Faraday (M.) Discourse on the Conservation of Force. London, 1857.
Fauriel (M.) Histoire de la Gaule Méridionale sous la Domination des conquérants Germains. Paris, 1836. 4 vols.
Felice (G.) History of the Protestants of France. London, 1853.
Fergusson (J.) A Brief Exposition of the Epistles of Paul. London, reprinted from the original editions, 1656-1674.

Feuchtersleben (E.) The Principles of Medical Psychology. Sydenham Soc. 1847.
Flassan (M.) Histoire de la Diplomatie Française. Paris, 1811. 7 vols.
[Fleming (R.)] The Fulfilling of the Scripture, 1681. See Fleming's *Rise and Fall of Rome*, edit. London, 1848, p. xi.
Fletcher (A. of Saltoun) Political Works. Glasgow, 1749.
Fleury (M.) Histoire Ecclésiastique. Paris, 1758–1761. 36 vols.
Flores (F. H.) Memorias de las Reynas Catholicas. Madrid, 1761. 2 vols. 4to.
Flourens (P.) Histoire des Travaux de Cuvier. Paris, 1845.
Fontenay-Mareuil (Marquis de) Mémoires. Paris, 1826. 2 vols.
Fontenelle (B. de) Éloges, in vols. v. and vi. of Œuvres. Paris, 1766.
Foot (J.) The Life of John Hunter. London, 1794.
Forbes (J.) Oriental Memoirs. London, 1834. 2 vols.
Forbes (J.) Certaine Records touching the Estate of the Kirk, in 1605 and 1606. Published by the Wodrow Society. Edinburgh, 1846.
Ford (R.) Hand-Book for Spain. 2nd edit. London, 1847.
Fordun (J.) Scotichronicon, cum Supplementis et Continuatione W. Boweri, cura W. Goodall. Edinburgi, 1775. 2 vols. folio.
Forner (J. P.) Oracion Apologética por la España y su Mérito Literario. Madrid, 1786.
Forry (S.) Climate of the United States, and its Endemic Influences. New York, 1842.
Forster (J.) Life and Times of Goldsmith. 2nd edit. London, 1854. 2 vols.
Fountainhall (Lord) Notes of Scottish Affairs, from 1680 till 1701. Edinburgh, 1822. 4to.
Fox (C. J.) History of the Early Part of the Reign of James II. London, 1808. 4to.
Franck (R.) Northern Memoirs, writ in the year 1658. A new edition. Edinburgh, 1821.
Franklin (B.) Private Correspondence. London, 1817. 2 vols.
Franklin (B.) Life, by himself. London, 1818. 2 vols.

Galfridus Monumetensis, Historia Britonum, edit. Giles. London, 1844.
Gardner (G.) Travels in the Interior of Brazil. London, 1849.
Geddes (M.) Miscellaneous Tracts. 3rd edit. London, 1730. 3 vols.
Genlis (Madame de) Mémoires sur le XVIII° Siècle. Paris, 1825. 10 vols.
Gent (T.) Life, by himself. London, 1832.
Geoffroy Saint-Hilaire (I.) Histoire des Anomalies de l'Organisation chez l'Homme et les Animaux. Bruxelles, 1837. 3 vols.
Georgel (L'A·bé) Mémoires. Paris, 1817, 1818. 6 vols.
Georget (M.) De la Folie. Paris, 1820.
Gibson (J.) History of Glasgow. Glasgow, 1777.

Gillespie (G.) Aaron's Rod Blossoming, or the Divine Ordinance of Church Government Vindicated. London, 1646. 4to.
Giraud (C.) Précis de l'Ancien Droit coutumier français. Paris, 1852.
Godoy (Prince of the Peace) Memoirs, written by himself. London, 1836. 2 vols.
Godwin (W.) Of Population; or the Power of Increase in Mankind. London, 1820.
Gordon (P.) A Short Abridgement of Britane's Distemper, from 1639 to 1649. Printed for the Spalding Club. Aberdeen, 1844. 4to.
Göthe (J. W.) Wahrheit und Dichtung, in vol. ii. of Werke. Stuttgart, 1837.
Government (The) and Order of the Church of Scotland. 1641. Reprinted, Edinburgh, 1690.
Gramont (Le Maréchal de) Mémoires, édit. Petitot et Monmerqué. Paris, 1826, 1827. 2 vols.
Grant (R.) History of Physical Astronomy. London, 1852.
Grant (R. E.) Comparative Anatomy. London, 1841.
Gray (A.) Great and Precious Promises. Glasgow, 1740.
Gray (A.) The Spiritual Warfare, or Sermons concerning the Nature of Mortification. Glasgow, 1840.
Green (J. H.) Vital Dynamics. London, 1840.
Grégoire (M.) Histoire des Confesseurs. Paris, 1824.
Gregory (D.) History of the Western Highlands and Isles of Scotland, from 1493 to 1625. Edinburgh, 1836.
Grenville Papers (The) edited by W. J. Smith. London, 1852, 1853. 4 vols.
Grierson (Dr.) History of St. Andrews. Cupar, 1838.
Grieve (J.) The History of Kamtschatka, translated from the Russian. Gloucester, 1764. 4to.
Grimm et Diderot, Correspondance Littéraire. Paris, 1813, 1814. 17 vols. [This important work consists of three parts, besides a supplement; but in quoting it I have always followed the ordinary lettering, making the supplement vol. xvii.]
Grose (F.) Military Antiquities; a History of the English Army. London, 1812. 2 vols. 4to.
Grosley (M.) A Tour to London. London, 1772. 2 vols.
Grote (G.) History of Greece. London, 1846-1856. 12 vols. 1st edit. of vols. i. ii. iii. iv. ix. x. xi. xii.; 2nd edit. of vols. v. vi. vii. viii.
Grove (W. R.) The Correlation of Physical Forces. 3rd edit. London, 1855.
Guizot (M.) Histoire de la Civilisation en France. Paris, 1846. 4 vols.
Guizot (M.) Histoire de la Civilisation en Europe. Paris, 1846.
Guizot (M.) Essais sur l'Histoire de France. Paris, 1847.
Guthrie (J.) Considerations contributing unto the Discovery of the Dangers that threaten Religion in the Church of Scotland. Reprint, Edinburgh, 1846.

Guthry (H. Bishop of Dunkeld) Memoirs. London, 1702.
Halhed (N. B.) Code of Gentoo Laws. London, 1777.
Halkett (J.) Notes respecting the Indians of North America. London, 1825.
Hallam (H.) Constitutional History of England. London, 1842. 2 vols.
Hallam (H.) Introduction to the Literature of Europe. London, 1843. 3 vols.
Hallam (H.) Europe during the Middle Ages. London, 1846. 2 vols.
Hallam (H.) Supplemental Notes to Europe during the Middle Ages. London, 1848.
Halyburton (T.) The Great Concern of Salvation. Edinburgh, 1722.
Hamilton (W.) Ægyptiaca. London, 1809. 4to.
Hamilton (Sir W.) Notes and Dissertations to Reid. Edinburgh, 1852.
Hamilton (Sir W.) Discussions on Philosophy and Literature. London, 1852.
Hare's Guesses at Truth. First and second series. London, 1847, 1848. 2 vols.
Harford (J. S.) Life of T. Burgess, Bishop of Salisbury. London, 1841.
Harris (G.) Life of Lord Chancellor Hardwicke. London, 1847. 3 vols.
Harris (W.) Lives of James I., Charles I., Cromwell, and Charles II. London, 1814. 5 vols.
Hasse (C. E.) An Anatomical Description of the Diseases of the Organs of Circulation and Respiration. Sydenham Society. London, 1846.
Hausset (Madame du) Mémoires. Paris, 1824.
Haüy (R. J.) Traité de Minéralogie. Paris, 1801. 5 vols.
Hawkins (B.) Elements of Medical Statistics. London, 1829.
Heber (Bishop) Life of Jeremy Taylor, in vol. i. of Taylor's Works. London, 1828.
Heber (Bishop) Journey through the Upper and Southern Provinces of India. London, 1828. 3 vols.
Heeren (A. H. L.) Politics, Intercourse, and Trade of the African Nations. Oxford, 1838. 2 vols.
Heeren (A. H. L.) Politics, Intercourse, and Trade of the Asiatic Nations. London, 1846. 2 vols.
Helvétius (C. A.) De l'Esprit. Amsterdam, 1759. 2 vols.
Henderson (J.) History of Brazil. London, 1821. 4to.
Henle (J.) Traité d'Anatomie Générale. Paris, 1843. 2 vols.
Henslow (J. S.) Descriptive and Physiological Botany. London, 1837.
Herder (J. G.) Ideen zur Geschichte der Menschheit. Stuttgart, 1827, 1828. 4 vols.
Herodoti Musæ, edit. Baehr. Lipsiæ, 1830-1835. 4 vols.

Haron (R.) Observations made in a Journey through the Western Counties of Scotland, in 1792. 2nd edit. Perth, 1799. 2 vols.
Herschel (Sir J.) Discourse on the Study of Natural Philosophy. London, 1831.
Hewson (W.) Works, edited by G. Gulliver for the Sydenham Society. London, 1846.
Historie (The) and Life of King James the Sext, from 1566 to 1596. Published by the Bannatyne Club. Edinburgh, 1825. 4to.
Hitchcock (E.) The Religion of Geology. London, 1851.
Hodgson (J.) The Hunterian Oration, delivered at the Royal College of Surgeons in 1855. London (no date).
Hodgson (R.) Life of Porteus, Bishop of London. London, 1811.
Holcroft (T.) Memoirs, by himself: continued by Hazlitt. London, 1816. 3 vols.
Holland (Sir H.) Medical Notes. London, 1839.
Holland (Lord) Memoirs of the Whig Party. London, 1852–1854. 2 vols.
Holles (Lord) Memoirs. London, 1699.
Hollinshead (R.) The Scottish Chronicle. Arbroath, 1805. 2 vols. 4to.
Home (J.) The History of the Rebellion in the year 1745. London, 1802. 4to.
Hooker (R.) Ecclesiastical Polity. London, 1830. 3 vols.
Hoskins (G. A.) Spain as it is. London, 1851. 2 vols.
Howell (J.) Letters. Eleventh edition. London, 1754.
Howie (J.) Biographia Scoticana. 2nd edit. Glasgow, 1781.
Huetius (P. D.) Commentarius de Rebus ad eum portinentibus. Amstel. 1718.
Humboldt (A.) Essai sur la Nouvelle Espagne. Paris, 1811. 2 vols. 4to.
Humboldt (A.) Cosmos. London, 1846–1852. 4 vols.
Hume (D.) Commentaries on the Law of Scotland respecting Crimes. Edinburgh, 1797. 2 vols. 4to.
Hume (D.) Philosophical Works. Edinburgh, 1826. 4 vols.
Hume (D.) Letters of Eminent Persons to. Edinburgh, 1849.
Hume (D. of Godscroft) The History of the House and Race of Douglas and Angus. Edinburgh, 1743. 2 vols.
Hunt (F. K.) History of Newspapers. London, 1850. 2 vols.
Hunter (J.) Works, edited by J. F. Palmer. London, 1835–1837. 4 vols.
Hunter (J.) Essays and Observations on Natural History, &c. edited by R. Owen. London, 1861. 2 vols.
Hutcheson (F.) An Inquiry into the Original of our Ideas of Beauty and Virtue. 4th edit. London, 1738.
Hutcheson (F.) A System of Moral Philosophy; with the Life of Hutcheson, by W. Leechman. London, 1755. 2 vols. 4to.
Hutcheson (F.) An Essay on the Nature and Conduct of the Passions and Affections. 3rd edit. Glasgow, 1769.

LIST OF AUTHORS QUOTED.

Hutcheson (G.) Exposition on the Twelve Small Prophets. London, 1654, 1655. 3 vols.
Hutcheson (G.) An Exposition of the Book of Job, being the sum of 316 Sermons preached in the City of Edenburgh. London, 1669. Folio.
Hutchinson (Colonel) Memoirs of, by his Widow. London, 1846.
Hutton (J.) Theory of the Earth. Edinburgh, 1795. 2 vols.
Hutton (W.) Life of, by himself. London, 1816.

Ibn Batuta, Travels in the Fourteenth Century, translated from Arabic by S. Lee. London, 1829. 4to.
Inglis (H. D.) Spain in 1830. London, 1831. 2 vols.
Interest (The) of Scotland considered with regard to Police, Trade, &c. Edinburgh, 1733.
Irving (J.) The History of Dumbartonshire. 2nd edit. Dumbarton, 1860. 4to.
Ixtlilxochitl, Histoire des Chichimèques ou des anciens Rois de Tezcuco. Paris, 1840. 2 vols.

Jacobite Memoirs of the Rebellion of 1745, edited, from the Manuscripts of the late Bishop Forbes, by R. Chambers. Edinburgh, 1834.
James II., The Life of, from Memoirs by his own hand, by J. S. Clarke. London, 1816. 2 vols. 4to.
Janer (F.) Condition Social de los Moriscos de España. Madrid, 1857.
Jefferson (T.) Memoirs and Correspondence, by Randolph. London, 1829. 4 vols.
Jehangueir (The Emperor) Memoirs, by himself, translated from Persian by D. Price. London, 1829. 4to.
Jewel (J.) Apologia Ecclesiæ Anglicanæ. London, 1581.
Jobert (A. C. G.) Ideas or Outlines of a New System of Philosophy. London, 1848, 1849. 2 vols.
Johnston (L. F. C.) Institutes of the Civil Law of Spain. London, 1825.
Johnstone (The Chevalier de) Memoirs of the Rebellion in 1715 and 1746. 3rd edit. London, 1822.
Joly (G.) Mémoires. Paris, 1825.
Jones (C. H.) and Sieveking (E. H.) Pathological Anatomy. London, 1854.
Jones (R.) Organization of the Animal Kingdom. London, 1855.
Jones (W.) Life of G. Horne, Bishop of Norwich. London, 1795.
Jones (Sir W.) Works. London, 1799. 6 vols. 4to.
Journal Asiatique. Paris, 1822-1827. 11 vols.
Journal of the Asiatic Society. London, 1834-1851. 14 vols.
Journal of the Geographical Society. London, 1833 (2nd edit. of vol. i.) to 1853. 23 vols.
Jussieu's Botany, by J. H. Wilson. London, 1849.

xxvi   LIST OF AUTHORS QUOTED.

Kaemtz (L. F.) Course of Meteorology. London, 1845.
Kant (J.) Werke. Leipzig, 1838, 1839. 10 vols.
Kay (J.) Condition and Education of the People in England and Europe. London, 1850. 2 vols.
Keith (R.) A Catalogue of the Bishops of Scotland. Edinburgh, 1755. 4to.
Keith (R.) History of the Affairs of Church and State in Scotland, from the beginning of the Reformation to 1568. Published by the Spottiswoode Society. Edinburgh, 1844–1850. 3 vols.
Kemble (J. M.) The Saxons in England. London, 1849. 2 vols.
Ken (Bishop of Bath and Wells) Life of, by a Layman. London, 1854. 2 vols.
Kennedy (W.) Annals of Aberdeen. London, 1818. 2 vols. 4to.
King (Lord) Life of J. Locke. London, 1830. 2 vols.
Kirkton (J.) The Secret and True History of the Church of Scotland, from the Restoration to 1678, edited from the MSS. by C. K. Sharpe. Edinburgh, 1817. 4to.
Klimrath (H.) Travaux sur l'Histoire du Droit Français. Paris, 1843. 2 vols.
Knox (J.) History of the Reformation in Scotland, edited by D. Laing, for the Wodrow Society. Edinburgh, 1846–1848. 2 vols.
Koch (M.) Tableau des Révolutions de l'Europe. Paris, 1823. 3 vols.
Kohl (J. G.) Russia. London, 1842.

Labat (P.) Voyages en Espagne et en Italie. Paris, 1730. Vol. I. containing his travels in Spain.
Laborde (A.) A View of Spain. London, 1809. 5 vols.
Lacretelle (C.) Histoire de France pendant le XVIII° Siècle. Bruxelles, 1819. 3 vols.
Lafayette (Général) Mémoires, Correspondance et Manuscrits. Bruxelles, 1837–1839. 2 vols.
Lafuente (M.) Historia General de España. Madrid, 1850–1857. 19 vols.
Laing (M.) The History of Scotland, from 1603 to 1707. 3rd edit. London, 1819. 4 vols.
Laing (S.) Sweden in 1838. London, 1839.
Laing (S.) Notes on the Social and Political State of Europe. London, 1842.
Laing (S.) Second Series of Notes on Europe. London, 1850.
Laing (S.) Denmark, being the Third Series of Notes. London, 1852.
Laird (M.) Memoirs of the Life and Experiences, with a Preface by the Rev. Mr. Cock. 2nd edit. Glasgow, 1781.
Lamartine (A. de) Histoire des Girondins. Bruxelles, 1847. 8 vols.
Lamont (J. of Newton) Diary, from 1649 to 1671. Edinburgh, 1830. 4to.

LIST OF AUTHORS QUOTED. xxvii

Lankester (E.) Memorials of John Ray. Ray Society, 1846.
Larenaudière (M. de) Mexique et Guatemala. Paris, 1843.
Lathbury (T.) History of the Convocation of the Church of England. London, 1842.
Lathbury (T.) History of the Nonjurors. London, 1845.
Lavallée (T.) Histoire des Français. Paris, 1847. 4 vols.
Lawrence (W.) Lectures on Comparative Anatomy, and the Natural History of Man. London, 1844.
Lawson (J. P.) The Roman Catholic Church in Scotland. Edinburgh, 1836.
Lawson (J. P.) The Book of Perth. Edinburgh, 1847.
Le Blanc (L'Abbé) Lettres d'un François. Lyon, 1758. 3 vols.
Ledwich (E.) Antiquities of Ireland. Dublin, 1804. 4to.
Le Long (J.) Bibliothèque Historique de la France. Paris, 1768-1778. 5 vols. folio.
Lémontey (P. E.) L'Établissement Monarchique de Louis XIV. Paris, 1818.
Lenet (P.) Mémoires. Paris, 1826. 2 vols.
Lepan (M.) Vie de Voltaire. Paris, 1837.
Lepelletier (A.) Physiologie Médicale. Paris, 1831-1833. 4 vols.
Lerminier (E.) Philosophie du Droit. Paris, 1831. 2 vols.
Lesley (J.) The History of Scotland, from 1436 to 1561. Published by the Bannatyne Club. Edinburgh, 1830. 4to.
Leslie (J.) An Experimental Inquiry into the Nature and Propagation of Heat. London, 1804.
Leslie (Sir J.) Treatises on Natural and Chemical Philosophy. Edinburgh, 1838.
Letters from Spain, &c. by an English Officer. London, 1788. 2 vols.
Letters from a Gentleman in the North of Scotland. London, 1815. 2 vols.
Letters of Queen Elizabeth and James VI. of Scotland, edited by J. Bruce, for the Camden Society. London, 1849. 4to.
Lettice (I.) Letters on a Tour through Various Parts of Scotland in 1792. Edinburgh, 1794.
Le Vassor (M.) Histoire du Règne de Louis XIII. Amst. 1701-1711. 10 vols.
Lewes (G. H.) The Spanish Drama. London, 1846.
Liebig (J.) Animal Chemistry. London, 1846.
Liebig (J.) Letters on Chemistry in its relation to Physiology. London, 1851.
Liebig and Kopp's Reports of the Progress of Chemistry and the allied Sciences. London, 1849-1853. 4 vols.
Lindley (J.) The Vegetable Kingdom. London 1847.
Lindley (J.) An Introduction to Botany. London, 1848. 2 vols.
Lindsay (R. of Pitscottie) The Chronicles of Scotland. Edinburgh, 1814. 2 vols.
Lingard (J.) History of England. Paris, 1840. 8 vols.

LIST OF AUTHORS QUOTED.

Lister (M.) An Account of Paris at the close of the Seventeenth Century. Shaftesbury (no date).
Lister (T. H.) Life and Correspondence of the first Earl of Clarendon. London, 1837, 1838. 3 vols.
Llorente (D. J. A.) Histoire Critique de l'Inquisition d'Espagne. Paris, 1817, 1818. 4 vols.
Locke (J.) Works. London, 1794. 9 vols.
Lockhart Papers (The). London, 1817. 2 vols. 4to.
Longchamp et Wagnière, Mémoires sur Voltaire. Paris, 1826. 2 vols.
London (J. C.) An Encyclopædia of Agriculture. London, 1844.
Louville (Marquis de) Mémoires. Paris, 1818. 2 vols.
Low (H.) Sarawak; its Inhabitants and Productions. London, 1835.
Ludlow (E.) Memoirs. Edinburgh, 1751. 3 vols.
Lyell (Sir C.) Principles of Geology. 9th edit. London, 1853.
Lyon (C. J.) History of St. Andrews. Edinburgh, 1843. 2 vols.

Mably (L'Abbé) Observations sur l'Histoire de France. Paris, 1823. 3 vols.
Macaulay (T. B.) History of England. London, 1849-1855. 1st edit. 4 vols.
Mackay (R. W.) The Progress of the Intellect in the Religious Development of the Greeks and Hebrews. London, 1850. 2 vols.
Mackenzie (Sir G.) The Laws and Customs of Scotland in Matters Criminal. Edinburgh, 1699. Folio.
Mackintosh (Sir J.) History of the Revolution in England in 1688. London, 1834. 4to.
Mackintosh (Sir J.) Memoirs, by his Son. London, 1835. 2 vols.
Mackintosh (Sir J.) Dissertation on the Progress of Ethical Philosophy. Edinburgh, 1837.
[Macky (J.)] A Journey though Scotland. 2nd edit. London, 1732. See Watt's *Bibliotheca Britannica*, vol. ii. p. 631, m.
Macpherson (D.) Annals of Commerce. London, 1805. 4 vols. 4to.
Macpherson (J.) Original Papers, from the Restoration to the Accession of the House of Hanover. London, 1775. 2 vols. 4to.
M'Crie (T.) The Life of Andrew Melville. Edinburgh, 1819. 2 vols.
M'Crie (T.) History of the Progress and Suppression of the Reformation in Spain in the Sixteenth Century. Edinburgh, 1829.
M'Crie (T.) The Life of John Knox, edited by A. Crichton. 2nd edit. Edinburgh, 1841.
M'Culloch (J. R.) The Principles of Political Economy. Edinburgh, 1843.
M'Culloh (J. H.) Researches concerning the Aboriginal History of America. Baltimore, 1829.
M'Ure (J.) The History of Glasgow. A new edition. Glasgow, 1830.

M'William (J. O.) Medical History of the Expedition to the Niger. London, 1843.
Mahon (Lord) Spain under Charles II., or Extracts from the Correspondence of A. Stanhope, 1690–1699. London, 1840.
Mahon (Lord) History of England, from 1713 to 1783. London, 1853, 1854. 7 vols.
Maintenon (Madame de) Lettres inédites de, et de la Princesse des Ursins. Paris, 1826. 4 vols.
Malcolm (Sir J.) History of Persia. London, 1829. 2 vols.
Mallet's Northern Antiquities, edit. Blackwell. London, 1847.
Mallet du Pan, Memoirs and Correspondence. London, 1852. 2 vols.
Mallet (Messrs. R. and J. W.) The Earthquake Catalogue of the British Association. From the Transactions of the British Association for the Advancement of Science. London, 1858.
Malthus (T. R.) An Essay on the Principles of Population. London, 1826. 2 vols.
Manning (W. O.) Commentaries on the Law of Nations. London, 1839.
Marchant (J.) The History of the Present Rebellion. London, 1746.
Marchmont Papers, from 1685 to 1750. London, 1831. 3 vols.
Mariana (P. J.) Historia General de España, y la Continuacion por Miniana. Madrid, 1794, 1795. 10 vols.
Mariner (W.) An Account of the Natives of the Tonga Islands. London, 1818. 2 vols.
Marmontel (J. F.) Mémoires. Paris, 1805. 4 vols.
Marsden (W.) History of Sumatra. London, 1783. 4to.
Martinez de la Mata, Dos Discursos, los publica J. A. Canga. Madrid, 1794. This author wrote in the middle of the seventeenth century, and supplies some extremely curious information respecting the economical state of Spain.
Matter (M.) Histoire du Gnosticisme. Paris, 1828. 2 vols.
Matter (M.) Histoire de l'École d'Alexandrie. Paris, 1840–1844. 2 vols.
Matthæi Paris Historia Major, edit. Wats. London, 1684. Folio.
Matthæi Westmonasteriensis Flores Historiarum. London, 1570. 2 vols. folio.
Maury (L. F. A.) Légendes Pieuses du Moyen Age. Paris, 1843.
May (T.) History of the Long Parliament. London, 1647. 3 books, folio.
Mayo (H.) Outlines of Human Physiology. London, 1837.
Meadley (G. W.) Memoirs of W. Paley. Edinburgh, 1810.
Meiners (E.) Betrachtungen über die Fruchtbarkeit &c. der Länder in Asien. Lübeck, 1795, 1796. 2 vols.
Melvill (J.) Autobiography and Diary, edited by R. Pitcairn for the Wodrow Society. Edinburgh, 1842.
Mendoza (D. H.) Guerra de Granada que hizo al Rei D. Felipe II. contra los Moriscos. Valencia, 1776. 4to.
Mercer (A.) The History of Dunfermline. Dunfermline, 1828.

Mercier (M.) J. J. Rousseau considéré comme l'un des premiers Auteurs de la Révolution. Paris, 1791. 2 vols.
Meyen (F. J. F.) Outlines of the Geography of Plants. London, 1846.
Meyer (J. D.) Esprit, Origine et Progrès des Institutions Judiciaires. Paris, 1823. 5 vols.
Mezeray (F. E.) Histoire de France. Paris, 1643-1651. 3 vols. folio.
Michelet (M.) Origines du Droit Français, in vol. ii. of Œuvres. Bruxelles, 1840.
Mignet (M.) Négociations relatives à la Succession d'Espagne sous Louis XIV. Paris, 1835-1842. 4 vols. 4to.
Mill (J.) Analysis of the Phenomena of the Human Mind. London, 1829. 2 vols.
Mill (J.) The History of British India, edited by H. H. Wilson. London, 1848 (the first two vols. only).
Mill (J. S.) Principles of Political Economy. London, 1849. 2 vols.
Mills (C.) History of Chivalry. London, 1825. 2 vols.
Miscellany (The) of the Wodrow Society, edited by D. Laing. Edinburgh, 1844.
Moffat (R.) Southern Africa. London, 1842.
Monconys (M. de) Voyages de. Paris, 1695. 5 vols.
Monk (Bishop of Gloucester) Life of R. Bentley. London, 1833. 2 vols.
Monro (A.) Sermons. London, 1693.
Montaigne (M.) Essais. Paris, 1843.
Montbarey (Prince de) Mémoires. Paris, 1826, 1827. 3 vols.
Monteil (A. A.) Histoire des Français des divers États. Bruxelles, 1843. 8 vols.
Montesquieu (C.) Œuvres complètes. Paris, 1835.
Montglat (Marquis de) Mémoires. Paris, 1825, 1826. 3 vols.
Montlosier (Comte de) La Monarchie Française. Paris, 1814. 3 vols.
Montucla (J. F.) Histoire des Mathématiques. Paris, 1799-1802. 4 vols. 4to.
Morellet (L'Abbé) Mémoires. Paris, 1821. 2 vols.
[Morer (T.)] A Short Account of Scotland. London, 1702. This work is anonymous. The author was 'chaplain to a Scotch Regiment.' See *Records of the Kirk Session, &c., of Aberdeen*, edit. Spalding Club; Aberdeen, 1846, 4to, pp. lxi. lxv.
Mosheim (J. L.) Ecclesiastical History. London, 1839. 2 vols.
Motley (J. L.) History of the Rise of the Dutch Republic. London, 1858. 3 vols.
Motteville (Mme.) Mémoires, édit. Petitot. Paris, 1824. 5 vols.
Moysie (D.) Memoirs of the Affairs of Scotland, from 1577 to 1603. Printed by the Bannatyne Club. Edinburgh, 1830. 4to.
Muirhead (J. P.) The Life of James Watt. 2nd edit. London, 1859.
Müller (J.) Elements of Physiology. London, 1840-1842. 2 vols.

Murchison (Sir R.) Siluria. London, 1854.
Mure (W.) History of the Language and Literature of Ancient Greece. London, 1850–1853. 4 vols.
Muriel (A.) Gobierno del Señor Rey Don Carlos III. Madrid, 1839.
Murray (A.) Life of J. Bruce. Edinburgh, 1808. 4to.
Musset-Pathay (V. D.) Vie de J. J. Rousseau. Paris, 1822. 2 vols.

Naphtali, or the Wrestling of the Church of Scotland for the Kingdom of Christ. Printed in the year 1667.
Napier (M.) The Life and Times of Montrose, illustrated from original Manuscripts. Edinburgh, 1840.
Navarrete (M. F.) Vida de Cervantes, prefixed to Don Quijote. Barcelona, 1839.
Navarrete (M. F.) Noticia Biográfica del Marques de la Ensenada, in vol. ii. of Navarrete Opúsculos. Madrid, 1848.
Neal (D.) History of the Puritans, from 1517 to 1688. London, 1822. 5 vols.
Neander (A.) History of the Christian Religion and Church. London, 1850–1852. 8 vols.
Newman (F. W.) Natural History of the Soul, as the Basis of Theology. London, 1849.
Newman (F. W.) Phases of Faith. London, 1850.
Newman (J. H.) Essay on the Development of Christian Doctrine. London, 1845.
Newton (Bishop of Bristol) Life of, by himself. London, 1816.
Nicholls (J.) Recollections. London, 1822. 2 vols.
Nichols (J.) Literary Anecdotes of the Eighteenth Century. London, 1812–1815. 9 vols.
Nichols (J.) Illustrations of Literary History of the Eighteenth Century. London, 1817–1848. 7 vols.
Nicoll (J.) Diary, from January 1650 to June 1667. Published by the Bannatyne Club. Edinburgh, 1836. 4to.
Niebuhr (C.) Description de l'Arabie. Amsterdam, 1774. 4to.
Nimmo (W.) History of Stirlingshire. Edinburgh, 1777.
Noailles (Duc de) Mémoires par l'Abbé Millot, édit. Petitot et Monmerqué. Paris, 1828, 1829. 4 vols.
Noble (D.) The Brain and its Physiology. London, 1846.
Noble (M.) Memoirs of the House of Cromwell. Birmingham, 1784. 2 vols.
Noble (M.) Lives of the English Regicides. London, 1798. 2 vols.
North (R.) The Lives of the Norths. London, 1826. 3 vols.

Orme (W.) Life of John Owen. London, 1820.
Ortiz y Sans (D. J.) Compendio Cronologico de la Historia de España. Madrid, 1795–1803. 7 vols.
Otter (W.) Life of E. D. Clarke. London, 1825. 2 vols.

LIST OF AUTHORS QUOTED.

Owen (R.) Lectures on the Comparative Anatomy and Physiology of the Invertebrate Animals. 2nd edit. London, 1855.

Paget (J.) Lectures on Surgical Pathology. London, 1853. 2 vols.
Palgrave (Sir F.) Rise and Progress of the English Commonwealth. London, 1832. 2 vols. 4to.
Palissot (M.) Mémoires pour l'Histoire de notre Littérature. Paris, 1803. 2 vols.
Pallme (I.) Travels in Kordofan. London, 1844.
Palmer (W.) A Treatise on the Church. London, 1839. 2 vols.
Park (Mungo) Travels in Africa. London, 1817. 2 vols.
Parker (Bishop) History of his own Time. London, 1727.
Parliamentary History of England, to 1803. London. 36 vols.
Parr (S.) Works. London, 1828. 8 vols.
Patin (G.) Lettres. Paris, 1846. 3 vols.
Patten (R.) The History of the Late Rebellion. London, 1717.
Peignot (G.) Dictionnaire des Livres condamnés au feu. Paris, 1806. 2 vols.
Pellew (G.) Life and Correspondence of Lord Sidmouth. London, 1847. 3 vols.
Pennant (T.) Tour in Scotland. 4th edit. Dublin, 1775. 2 vols.
Penny (G.) Traditions of Perth. Perth, 1836.
Pepys (S.) Diary, from 1659 to 1669. London, 1828. 5 vols.
Percival (R.) Account of the Island of Ceylon. London, 1805. 4to.
Peterborough (C. M. Earl of) Memoir of, with Selections from his Correspondence. London, 1853. 2 vols.
Petrie (G.) Ecclesiastical Architecture and Round Towers of Ireland. Dublin, 1845.
Phillimore (R.) Memoirs of Lord Lyttelton, from 1734 to 1773. London, 1845. 2 vols.
Phillips (B.) Scrofula, its Nature, Causes, and Prevalence. London, 1846.
Pinel (P.) Traité sur l'Aliénation Mentale. 2nd edit. Paris, 1809.
Pinkerton (J.) History of Scotland, from the Accession of the House of Stuart to that of Mary. London, 1797. 2 vols. 4to.
Pinkerton (J.) An Enquiry into the History of Scotland, preceding the year 1056. Edinburgh, 1814. 2 vols.
Pitcairn (R.) Criminal Trials in Scotland, from 1488 to 1624. Edinburgh, 1833. 3 vols. 4to in four parts.
Playfair (J.) Works. Edinburgh, 1822; the first and fourth volumes, containing Illustrations of the Huttonian Theory, and the Life of Hutton.
Pontchartrain (P. de) Mémoires. Paris, 1822. 2 vols.
Porter (G. R.) The Progress of the Nation. London, 1836–1843. 3 vols.
Pouillet (M.) Élémens de Physique. Paris, 1832. 2 vols.
Presbytery Displayd, 1644. Reprinted, London, 1663. 4to.

Prescott (W. H.) History of the Reign of Ferdinand and Isabella. Paris, 1842. 3 vols.
Prescott (W. H.) History of the Conquest of Mexico. London, 1850. 3 vols.
Prescott (W. H.) History of the Conquest of Peru. London, 1850. 3 vols.
Prescott (W. H.) History of the Reign of Philip II. London, 1857-1859. 3 vols.
Prichard (J. C.) A Treatise on Insanity. London, 1835.
Prichard (J. C.) Insanity in relation to Jurisprudence. London, 1842.
Prichard (J. C.) Researches into the Physical History of Mankind. London, 1841-1847. 5 vols.
Priestley (J.) Memoirs by himself, continued by his Son. London, 1806, 1807. 2 vols.
Prior (J.) Life of O. Goldsmith. London, 1837. 2 vols.
Prior (J.) Memoir of E. Burke. London, 1839.
Prout (W.) Bridgewater Treatise on Chemistry, &c. London, 1845.
Pulteney (R.) Historical Sketches of the Progress of Botany in England. London, 1790. 2 vols.

Quatremère (E.) Recherches sur la Langue et la Littérature de l'Égypte. Paris, 1808.
Quérard (J. M.) La France Littéraire. Paris, 1827-1839. 10 vols.
Quetelet (A.) Sur l'Homme et le Développement de ses Facultés. Paris, 1835. 2 vols.
Quetelet (A.) La Statistique Morale, in vol. xxi. of Mém. de l'Acad. de Belgique. Bruxelles, 1848. 4to.
Quick (J.) Synodicon in Gallia; the Acts, &c. of the Councils of the Reformed Churches in France. London, 1692. 2 vols. folio.
Quin (M. J.) Memoirs of Ferdinand VII. King of the Spains. London, 1824.

Rabelais (F.) Œuvres. Amsterdam, 1725. 5 vols.
Rae (P.) The History of the Rebellion against George I. 2nd edit. London, 1746.
Raffles (Sir T. S.) History of Java. London, 1830. 2 vols.
Rammohun Roy, Translations from the Veds and works on Brahmanical Theology. London, 1832.
Rammohun Roy on the Judicial and Revenue Systems of India. London, 1832.
Ramsay (E. B. Dean of Edinburgh) Reminiscences of Scottish Life and Character. 5th edit. Edinburgh, 1859.
Ranke (L.) Die Römischen Päpste. Berlin, 1838, 1839. 3 vols.
Ranke (L.) The Ottoman and the Spanish Empires in the Sixteenth and Seventeenth Centuries. London, 1843.
Ranke (L.) Civil Wars and Monarchy in France in 16th and 17th Centuries. London, 1852. 2 vols.

LIST OF AUTHORS QUOTED.

Raumer (F. von) History of the Sixteenth and Seventeenth Centuries, illustrated by original Documents. London. 1835. 2 vols.
Ray (J.) Second Itinerary in 1661, in Memorials of Ray, edited by E. Lankester for the Ray Society. London, 1846.
Ray (J.) Correspondence, edited by E. Lankester. Ray Society, 1848.
Reid (T.) Essays on the Powers of the Human Mind. Edinburgh, 1808. 3 vols.
Reid (T.) An Inquiry into the Human Mind on the Principles of Common Sense. 7th edit. Edinburgh, 1814.
Relations des Ambassadeurs Vénitiens sur les Affaires de France au XVI⁰ Siècle. Paris, 1838. 2 vols. 4to.
Renouard (P. V.) Histoire de la Médecine. Paris, 1846. 2 vols.
Reports on Botany by the Ray Society. London, 1846.
Reresby (Sir J.) Travels and Memoirs during the Time of Cromwell, Charles II. and James II. London, 1831.
Retz (Cardinal de) Mémoires. Paris, 1844. 2 vols.
Revelations of Spain in 1845, by an English Resident. London, 1845. 2 vols.
Rey (J. A.) Théorie et Pratique de la Science Sociale. Paris, 1842. 3 vols.
Reynier (L.) De l'Économie Publique et Rurale des Arabes et des Juifs. Genève, 1820.
Reynolds (Sir J.) Literary Works. London, 1846. 2 vols.
Rhode (J. G.) Religiöse Bildung, Mythologie und Philosophie der Hindus. Leipzig, 1827. 2 vols.
Ricardo (D.) Works. London, 1846.
Richard (A.) Nouveaux Éléments de Botanique. Paris, 1846.
Richardson (J.) Travels in the Desert of Sahara. London, 1848. 2 vols.
Richardson (J.) A Mission to Central Africa. London, 1853. 2 vols.
Richardson (Sir J.) Arctic Searching Expedition. London, 1851. 2 vols.
Richelieu (Cardinal) Mémoires sur le Règne de Louis XIII. Paris, 1823. 10 vols.
Ridpath (G.) The Border History of England and Scotland. Berwick, 1848. 4to.
Rig-Veda-Sanhita, translated from Sanscrit by H. H. Wilson. London, 1850-1854. 2 vols.
Rio (A. F.) Historia del Reinado de Carlos III. en España. Madrid, 1856. 4 vols.
Ripperda (Duke de) Memoirs of. 2nd edit. London, 1740.
Ritchie (T. E.) Life of David Hume. London, 1807.
Ritter (H.) History of Ancient Philosophy. London, 1838-1846. 4 vols.
Rivarol (M.) Mémoires. Paris, 1824.
Robe (J.) Narratives of the Extraordinary Work of the Spirit of God. Glasgow, 1790.
Robertson (W.) Works. London, 1831.

Robertson (W.) History of Scotland, in Robertson's Works. London, 1831.
Robertson (W.) History of the Reign of Charles V. with additions by W. H. Prescott. London, 1857.
Robin (C.) et Verdeil (F.) Traité de Chimie Anatomique. Paris, 1853. 3 vols.
Rochefoucauld (Duc de la) Mémoires. Paris, 1826. 2 vols.
Rohan (H. Duc de) Mémoires. Paris, 1822.
Rokitansky (C.) A Manual of Pathological Anatomy. Published by the Sydenham Society. London, 1849-1854. 4 vols.
Roland (Mme.) Mémoires. Paris, 1827. 2 vols.
Romilly (Sir S.) Life, written by himself. London, 1842. 2 vols.
Roscoe (H.) The Life of W. Roscoe. London, 1833. 2 vols.
Row (J.) The History of the Kirk of Scotland, from 1558 to 1637, with a Continuation to July 1639. Published by the Wodrow Society. Edinburgh, 1842.
Russell (Lord J.) Memorials and Correspondence of C. J. Fox. London, 1853, 1854. 3 vols.
Russell (M.) History of the Church in Scotland. London, 1834. 2 vols.
Rutherford (S.) Christ Dying. London, 1647. 4to.
Rutherford (S.) A Free Disputation against Pretended Liberty of Conscience. London, 1649. 4to.
Rutherford (S.) Three Hundred and Fifty-Two Religious Letters, between 1638 and 1649. Reprinted, Glasgow, 1824.

Sadler (M. T.) The Law of Population. London, 1830. 2 vols.
Sadler (Sir R.) State Papers and Letters, edited by R. Clifford, with Notes by W. Scott. Edinburgh, 1809. 2 vols. 4to.
Sainte-Aulaire (Le Comte de) Histoire de la Fronde. Paris, 1843. 2 vols.
Sainte-Palaye (De la Curne) Mémoires sur l'Ancienne Chevalerie. Paris, 1759-1781. 3 vols.
Schlosser (F. C.) History of the Eighteenth Century. London, 1843-5. 6 vols.
Scot (J.) The Staggering State of the Scots Statesmen, from 1550 to 1650. Edinburgh, 1754.
Scot (W.) An Apologetical Narration of the State and Government of the Kirk of Scotland, since the Reformation. Published by the Wodrow Society. Edinburgh, 1846.
Scotch Presbyterian Eloquence. 3rd edit. London, 1719.
Scotland: Reasons for Improving the Fisheries and Linnen Manufacture of Scotland. London, 1727.
Scotland, a Modern Account of, written from thence by an English Gentleman, printed in the year 1670, in vol. vi. of the Harleian Miscellany. 1810. 4to.
Scriptores post Bedam Rerum Anglicarum. London, 1596. Folio.
Ségur (Le Comte de) Mémoires ou Souvenirs. Paris, 1825-1827. 3 vols.

Select Biographies, edited for the Wodrow Society by the Rev. W. K. Tweedie. Edinburgh, 1845–1847. 2 vols.
Selections from the Minutes of the Synod of Fife, from 1611 to 1687. Printed for the Abbotsford Club. Edinburgh, 1837. 4to.
Selections from the Minutes of the Presbyteries of St. Andrews and Cupar, from 1641 to 1698. Printed for the Abbotsford Club. Edinburgh, 1837. 4to.
Selections from the Registers of the Presbytery of Lanark, from 1623 to 1709. Printed for the Abbotsford Club. Edinburgh, 1839. 4to.
Selections from the Records of the Kirk Session, Presbytery, and Synod of Aberdeen. Printed for the Spalding Club. Aberdeen, 1846. 4to.
Sempere (M.) Histoire des Cortès d'Espagne. Bordeaux, 1815.
Sempere (M.) Considérations sur les Causes de la Grandeur et de la Décadence de la Monarchie Espagnole. Paris, 1826. 2 vols.
Sermons by Eminent Divines in the two last Centuries. Edinburgh, 1814.
Sevigné (Madame de) Lettres. Paris, 1843. 6 vols.
Sewell (W.) Christian Politics. London, 1845.
Sharp (Archbishop of York) Life, edited by T. Newcome. London, 1825. 2 vols.
[Sharp, Sir C.] Memorials of the Rebellion of 1569. London, 1840.
Sharpe (S.) History of Egypt. London, 1852. 2 vols.
[Shields (A.)] A Hind let loose. Printed in the year 1687. See Howie's *Biographia Scoticana*, p. 576.
Shields (A.) The Scots Inquisition. Edinburgh, 1745.
Shields (A.) An Enquiry into Church Communion. 2nd edit. Edinburgh, 1747.
Short (Bishop of St. Asaph) History of the Church of England, to 1688. London, 1847.
Simon (Duc de) Mémoires publiés sur le Manuscrit original. Paris, 1842. 40 vols.
Simon (J.) Lectures on General Pathology. London, 1850.
Simon (J. F.) Animal Chemistry. London, 1845, 1846. 2 vols.
Simpson (T.) Discoveries on the North Coast of America. London, 1843.
Sinclair (G.) Satan's Invisible World Discovered. Reprinted, Edinburgh, 1780.
Sinclair (Sir J.) Statistical Account of Scotland. Edinburgh, 1791–1799. 21 vols.
Sinclair (Sir J.) History of the Public Revenue of the British Empire. London, 1803, 1804. 3 vols.
Sinclair (Sir J.) The Correspondence of. London, 1831. 2 vols.
Sismondi (J. C. L.) Historical View of the Literature of the South of Europe, with Notes by T. Roscoe. London, 1846. 2 vols.
Sismondi (J. C. L. S. de) Histoire des Français. Paris, 1821–1844. 31 vols.

Skene (W. F.) The Highlanders of Scotland, their Origin, History, and Antiquities. London, 1837. 2 vols.
Smedley (E.) History of the Reformed Religion in France. London, 1832-1834. 3 vols. 8vo.
Smith (A.) The Theory of Moral Sentiments. London, 1822. 2 vols.
Smith (A.) An Inquiry into the Nature and Causes of the Wealth of Nations. Edinburgh, 1839.
Smith (Sir J. E.) Memoir and Correspondence of. London, 1832. 2 vols.
Somers Tracts, edited by Sir W. Scott. London, 1809-1815. 13 vols. 4to.
Somerville (Lord) Memorie of the Somervilles. Edinburgh, 1815. 2 vols.
Somerville (M.) Connexion of the Physical Sciences. London, 1849.
Somerville (M.) Physical Geography. London, 1851. 2 vols.
Sorbière (M.) A Voyage to England. London, 1709.
Sorel (M. C.) La Bibliothèque Française. Paris, 1667.
Soulavie (J. L.) Mémoires du Règne de Louis XVI. Paris, 1801. 6 vols.
Southey (R.) Letters written in Spain and Portugal. 2nd edit. Bristol, 1799.
Southey (R.) History of Brasil. London, 1819-1822. 3 vols. 4to (2nd edit. of vol. i.).
Southey (R.) The Life of Wesley. London, 1846. 2 vols.
Southey (R.) Chronicle of the Cid. Lowell, 1846.
Spain, by an American. London, 1831. 2 vols.
Spalding (J.) The History of the Troubles in Scotland and England, from 1624 to 1645. Edinburgh, 1828-1829. 2 vols. 4to.
Spalding Club Miscellany. Aberdeen, 1841-1852. 5 vols. 4to.
Spence (G.) Origin of the Laws and Political Institutions of Europe. London, 1826.
Spencer (H.) First Principles. London, 1860-1861. Only three parts have yet appeared of this able and remarkable work.
Spix (J. B.) and Martius (C. F.) Travels in Brazil. London, 1824. 2 vols.
Spottiswoode (J. Archbishop of St. Andrews) History of the Church of Scotland. Edinburgh, 1851. 3 vols.
Spottiswoode Miscellany (The) A Collection of Original Papers and Tracts illustrative of the History of Scotland. Edinburgh, 1844, 1845. 2 vols.
Sprengel (K.) Histoire de la Médecine. Paris, 1815-1820. 9 vols.
Squier (E. G.) Travels in Central America. New York, 1853. 2 vols.
State Papers of the Reign of Henry VIII. London, 1836. 4to; vols. iv. and v. containing the Correspondence relative to Scotland and the Borders.
Statistical Society (Journal of). London, 1839-1855. 18 vols.
Stäudlin (C. F.) Geschichte der theologischen Wissenschaften, Göttingen, 1810, 1811. 2 vols.

LIST OF AUTHORS QUOTED.

Stephens (A.) Memoirs of J. H. Tooke. London, 1813. 2 vols.
Stephens (J. L.) Travels in Central America. London, 1842, 1843. 4 vols.
Stevenson (A.) History of the Church and State of Scotland, from the Accession of Charles I. to 1649. Reprinted, Edinburgh, 1840.
Stevenson (J.) A Rare Soul-strengthening and Comforting Cordial for Old and Young Christians. Edited, in 1729, by the Rev. William Cupples. Paisley, 1786.
Stewart (D.) Biographical Memoirs of Smith, Robertson, and Reid. Edinburgh, 1811. 4to.
Stewart (D.) Elements of the Philosophy of the Human Mind. London, 1792-1827. 3 vols.
Story (J.) Commentaries on the Conflict of Laws. London, 1841.
Sully (Duc de) Mémoires des Sages et Royales Œconomies, édit. Petitot. Paris, 1820, 1821. 9 vols.
Swainson (W.) Discourse on the Study of Natural History. London, 1834.
Swainson (W.) Geography and Classification of Animals. London, 1835.
Swinburne (H.) Travels through Spain in 1775 and 1776. 2nd edit. London, 1787. 2 vols.
Swinburne (H.) The Courts of Europe at the close of the last Century. London, 1841. 2 vols.
Symes (M.) Embassy to the Kingdom of Ava. 2nd edit. London, 1800. 3 vols.

Talon (Omer) Mémoires. Paris, 1827. 3 vols.
Talvi's Historical View of the Languages and Literature of the Slavic Nations. New York, 1850.
Tapia (E. de) Historia de la Civilizacion Española. Madrid, 1840. 4 vols.
Taylor (A. S.) Manual of Medical Jurisprudence. London, 1846.
Temple (Sir W.) Works. London, 1814. 4 vols.
Tennemann (W. G.) Geschichte der Philosophie. Leipzig, 1798-1819. 11 vols.
Thirlwall (Bishop of St. David's) History of Greece. London, 1835-1850. 8 vols.
Thomson (J.) Life of William Cullen. Edinburgh, 1832.
Thomson (Mrs.) Memoirs of the Jacobites of 1715 and 1745. London, 1845, 1846. 3 vols.
Thomson (T.) History of the Royal Society. London, 1812. 4to.
Thomson (T.) Chemistry of Vegetables. London, 1838.
Thomson (T.) Chemistry of Animal Bodies. Edinburgh, 1843.
Thomson (T.) History of Chemistry. 2 vols. (no date).
Thornton (W. T.) Over-Population, and its Remedy. London, 1846.
Ticknor (G.) History of Spanish Literature. London, 1849. 3 vols.

LIST OF AUTHORS QUOTED.   xxxix

Timour's Political and Military Institutes, edited by Davy and White. Oxford, 1783. 4to.
Tocqueville (A. de) De la Démocratie en Amérique. Bruxelles, 1840. 5 vols. in 2 parts.
Tocqueville (A. de) L'Ancien Régime et la Révolution. Paris, 1850.
Tocqueville (Le Comte de) Histoire Philosophique du Règne de Louis XV. Paris, 1847. 2 vols.
Tomline (Bishop of Winchester) Life of W. Pitt. London, 1821. 2 vols. 4to.
Torcy (Le Marquis de) Mémoires, édit. Petitot et Monmerqué. Paris, 1828. 2 vols.
Townsend (J.) A Journey through Spain in 1786 and 1787. 2nd edit. London, 1792. 3 vols.
Trail (W.) Account of the Life and Writings of Robert Simson. London, 1812. 4to.
Transactions of the Literary Society of Bombay. London, 1819-1823. 3 vols. 4to.
Transactions of the Royal Asiatic Society. London, 1827-1835. 3 vols. 4to.
Travels through Portugal, Spain, &c. by a Gentleman. London, 1702.
Trotter (J. B.) Memoirs of the Latter Years of C. J. Fox. London, 1811.
Tschudi (J. J.) Travels in Peru. London, 1847.
Tucker (G.) The Life of T. Jefferson. London, 1837. 2 vols.
Tuckey (J. K.) Expedition to the Zaire, in South Africa. 1818. 4to.
Turgot (M.) Œuvres. Paris, 1811. 9 vols.
Turner (E.) Elements of Chemistry. London, 1847. 2 vols.
Turner (Sir J.) Memoirs of his own Life, from 1632 to 1670. Edinburgh 1829. 4to.
Turner (Samuel) An Embassy to Tibet. London, 1800. 4to.
Turner (Sharon) History of England. London, 1839. 12 vols.
Turpinus, De Vita Caroli Magni, edit. S. Ciampi. Florent. 1822.
Twiss (H.) The Life of Lord Chancellor Eldon. London, 1846. 2 vols.
Twiss (T.) Progress of Political Economy in Europe. London, 1847.
Tytler (P. F.) History of Scotland. 3rd edit. Edinburgh, 1845. 7 vols.

Udal ap Rhys, A Tour through Spain and Portugal. 2nd edit. London, 1760.
Ulloa (A.) A Voyage to South America. London, 1772. 2 vols.
Ustariz (G.) Theorica y Practica de Comercio y de Marina. Tercera impression. Madrid, 1757. Folio.

Vander Hammen (L.) Don Filipe el Prudente, segundo deste Nombre. Madrid, 1632. 4to.

LIST OF AUTHORS QUOTED.

Vattel (M. de) Le Droit des Gens. Paris, 1820. 2 vols.
Vaughan (R.) The Protectorate of Cromwell. London, 1839. 2 vols.
Velazquez (L. J.) Orígenes de la Poesia Castellana. Malaga, 1754. 4to.
Vernon (J.) Letters, from 1696 to 1708. London, 1841. 3 vols.
Villars (Madame de) Lettres. Amsterdam, 1759. These letters were written from Madrid, between 1679 and 1681, by the wife of the French Ambassador.
Villemain (M.) De la Littérature au XVIIIe Siècle. Paris, 1846. 4 vols.
Villemarqué (T. H.) Chants Populaires de la Bretagne. Paris, 1846. 2 vols. [Introduction only quoted.]
Vishnu Purana; a System of Hindu Mythology, translated from the Sanscrit by H. H. Wilson. London, 1840. 4to.
Vogel (J.) The Pathological Anatomy of the Human Body. London, 1847.
Volney (C. F.) Voyage en Syrie et en Égypte. Paris, an VII. 2 vols.
Voltaire, Œuvres complètes. Paris, 1820-1826. 70 vols.
Voltaire, Lettres inédites. Paris, 1856. 2 vols.
Voyages faits en Divers Temps en Espagne, &c. par Monsieur M****. Amsterdam, 1700.
Vyse (H.) Operations at the Pyramids. London, 1840-1842. 3 vols.

Wagner (R.) Elements of Physiology. London, 1841.
Wakefield (G.) Life of, by himself. London, 1804. 2 vols.
Walker (C.) The History of Independency. London, 1660, 1661. 4 parts, 4to.
Walker (Sir E.) A Journal of Affairs in Scotland in 1650, in Walker's Historical Discourses. London, 1705. Folio.
Walker (P.) Biographia Presbyteriana. Reprinted, Edinburgh, 1827. 2 vols.
Walpole (H.) Letters, from 1735 to 1797. London, 1840. 6 vols.
Walpole (H.) Memoirs of the Reign of George III. London, 1845. 4 vols.
Walpole (H.) Memoirs of George II. London, 1847. 3 vols.
Walsh (R.) Notices of Brazil. London, 1830. 2 vols.
Walton (W.) The Revolutions of Spain, from 1808 to the end of 1836. London, 1837. 2 vols.
Warburton's Letters to Hurd. London, 1809.
Ward (H. G.) Mexico. London, 1829. 2 vols.
Ward (W.) A View of the History, Literature, and Religion of the Hindoos. London, 1817-1820. 4 vols.
Ward (W. G.) The Ideal of a Christian Church. London, 1844.
Warwick (Sir P.) Memoirs of the Reign of Charles I. London, 1702.
West (E.) Memoirs, written by her own hand. Edinburgh, 1724.

Watson (R.) Historicall Collections of Ecclesiastick Affairs in Scotland. London, 1657.
Watson (R. Bishop of Llandaff) Life, by himself. London, 1818. 2 vols.
Watson (R.) Observations on Southey's Life of Wesley. London, 1821.
Watson (R.) The History of the Reign of Philip II. King of Spain. 7th edit. London, 1839.
Watson (R.) The History of the Reign of Philip III. King of Spain. 3rd edit. London, 1839.
Watson (T.) Lectures on the Principles and Practice of Physic. 4th edit. London, 1857. 2 vols.
Watt (J.) Correspondence, on his Discovery of the Theory of the Composition of Water, edited by J. P. Muirhead. London, 1846.
Wellsted (J. R.) Travels in Arabia. London, 1838. 2 vols.
Wesley (John) The Journals of. London, 1851.
Whately (Archbishop of Dublin) The Errors of Romanism traced to their Origin in Human Nature. London, 1830.
Whately (Archbishop of Dublin) Essays on some of the Dangers to Christian Faith. London, 1839.
Wheaton (H.) History of the Northmen, to the Conquest of England by William of Normandy. London, 1831.
Whewell (W.) History of the Inductive Sciences. London, 1847. 3 vols.
Whewell (W.) Philosophy of the Inductive Sciences, founded upon their History. London, 1847. 2 vols.
Whewell (W.) Bridgewater Treatise. London, 1852.
Whewell (W.) Lectures on the History of Moral Philosophy in England. London, 1852.
Whiston (W.) Memoirs, written by himself. London, 1749.
[White (B.)] Doblado's Letters from Spain. London, 1822.
White (Blanco) Practical and Internal Evidence against Catholicism. London, 1826.
Whitelocke (Commissioner) Journal of the Swedish Embassy in 1653 and 1654. London, 1772. 2 vols. 4to.
Wilberforce (W.) Life, by his Sons. London, 1838. 5 vols.
Wilkinson (Sir J. G.) Manners and Customs of the Ancient Egyptians. 1st series, edit. 1842; 2nd series, edit. 1841. 5 vols.
Williams (C. J. B.) Principles of Medicine. 2nd edit. London, 1848.
Wilson (H.) Account of the Pelew Islands. 2nd edit. London, 1788. 4to.
Wilson (H. H.) Specimens of the Theatre of the Hindus, translated from the Sanscrit. Calcutta, 1827. 3 vols.
Wilson (W.) Memoirs of Daniel Defoe. London, 1830. 3 vols.
Winckler (E.) Geschichte der Botanik. Frankfurt-am-M. 1854.
Winstanley (W.) The Loyal Martyrology. London, 1665.
Winwood (Sir R.) Memorials of Affairs of State, from his Papers. London, 1725. 3 vols. folio.

LIST OF AUTHORS QUOTED.

Wishart (G.) Memoirs of James Graham, Marquis of Montrose. Edinburgh, 1819.
Wodrow (R.) Collections upon the Lives of the Reformers and Ministers of the Church of Scotland. Edit. Maitland Club. Glasgow, 1834–1848. 4to. 4 vols. in 2.
Wodrow (R.) History of the Church of Scotland. Glasgow, 1838. 4 vols.
Wodrow (R.) Analecta, or Materials for a History of Remarkable Providences. Edit. Maitland Club. 1842, 1843. 4 vols. 4to.
Wodrow (R.) Life of the Rev. Robert Bruce, prefixed to Bruce's Sermons. Edit. Wodrow Society. Edinburgh, 1843.
Wodrow (R.) Correspondence. Edit. Wodrow Society. Edinburgh, 1842, 1843. 3 vols.
Wordsworth (C.) Ecclesiastical Biography. London, 1839. 4 vols.
Wrangel (F.) Narrative of an Expedition to the Polar Sea. London, 1840.
Wright (T.) Biographia Britannica Literaria; Anglo-Saxon and Anglo-Norman Periods. London, 1842-1846. 2 vols.

Ximenez (F. J.) Vida y Virtudes del Venerable Siervo de Dios D. J. de Ribera, Arçobispo de Valencia. Roma, 1734. 4to.

Yañez (J.) Memorias para la Historia de Don Felipe III. Madrid, 1723. 4to.
Yonge (W.) Diary, from 1604 to 1628, edited by G. Roberts. Camd. Soc. 1848. 4to.

HISTORY
OF
CIVILIZATION IN ENGLAND.

GENERAL INTRODUCTION.

CHAPTER I.

STATEMENT OF THE RESOURCES FOR INVESTIGATING HISTORY, AND PROOFS OF THE REGULARITY OF HUMAN ACTIONS. THESE ACTIONS ARE GOVERNED BY MENTAL AND PHYSICAL LAWS; THEREFORE BOTH SETS OF LAWS MUST BE STUDIED, AND THERE CAN BE NO HISTORY WITHOUT THE NATURAL SCIENCES.

Of all the great branches of human knowledge, history is that upon which most has been written, and which has always been most popular. And it seems to be the general opinion that the success of historians has, on the whole, been equal to their industry; and that if on this subject much has been studied, much also is understood.

This confidence in the value of history is very widely diffused, as we see in the extent to which it is read, and in the share it occupies in all plans of education. Nor can it be denied that, in a certain point of view, such confidence is perfectly justifiable. It cannot be denied that materials have been collected which, when looked at in the aggregate, have a rich and imposing appearance. The political and military annals of all the great countries in Europe, and of most of those out of Europe, have been carefully compiled, put together in a convenient form, and the evidence on which they rest has been tolerably well sifted. Great attention has been paid to the history of legislation, also to that of religion: while considerable, though inferior, labour has been employed in tracing the progress of science, of literature, of the fine arts, of useful inventions, and, latterly, of the manners and comforts of the people. In order to increase our knowledge of the past, antiquities of every kind have been examined; the sites of ancient cities have been laid bare, coins dug up and deciphered, inscriptions copied, alphabets restored, hieroglyphics interpreted, and, in some instances, long-forgotten languages reconstructed and re-arranged. Several of the laws which regulate the changes of human speech have been discovered, and, in the hands of philologists, have been made to elucidate even the most obscure periods in the early migration of nations. Political economy has been raised to a science, and by it much light has been thrown on the causes of that unequal distribution of wealth which is the most fertile source of social disturbance. Statistics have been so sedulously cultivated, that we have the most extensive information, not only respecting the material interests of men, but also respecting their moral peculiarities; such as, the amount of different crimes, the proportion they bear to each other, and the influence exercised over them by age, sex, education, and the like. With this great movement physical geography has kept pace: the phenomena of climate have been registered, mountains measured, rivers surveyed and tracked to their source, natural productions of all kinds carefully studied, and their hidden properties unfolded: while every food which sustains life has been chemically analysed, its constituents numbered and weighed, and the nature of the connexion between them and the human frame has, in many cases, been satisfactorily ascertained. At the same time, and that nothing should be left undone which might enlarge our knowledge of the events by which man is affected, there have been instituted circumstantial researches in many other departments; so that in regard to the most civilized people, we are now acquainted with the rate of their mortality, of their marriages, the proportion of their births, the character of their employments, and the fluctuations both in their wages and in the prices of the commodities necessary to their existence. These and similar facts have been collected, methodized, and are ripe for use. Such results, which form, as it were, the anatomy of a nation, are remarkable for their minuteness; and to them there have been joined other results less minute, but more extensive. Not only have the actions and characteristics of the great nations been recorded, but a prodigious number of different tribes in all the parts of the known world have been visited and described by travellers, thus enabling us to compare the condition of mankind in every stage of civilization, and under every variety of circumstance. When we moreover add, that this curiosity respecting our fellow-creatures is apparently insatiable; that it is constantly increasing; that the means of gratifying it are also increasing, and that most of the observations which have been made are still preserved;—when we put all these things together, we may form a faint idea of the immense value of that vast body of facts which we now possess, and by the aid of which the progress of mankind is to be investigated.

But if, on the other hand, we are to describe the use that has been made of these materials, we must draw a very different picture. The unfortunate peculiarity of the history of man is, that although its separate parts have been examined with considerable ability, hardly any one has attempted to combine them into a whole, and ascertain the way in which they are connected with each other. In all the other great fields of inquiry, the necessity of generalization is universally admitted, and noble efforts are being made to rise from particular facts in order to discover the laws by which those facts are governed. So far, however, is this from being the usual course of historians, that among them a strange idea prevails, that their business is merely to relate events, which they may occasionally enliven by such moral and political reflections as seem likely to be useful. According to this scheme, any author who from indolence of thought, or from natural incapacity, is unfit to deal with the highest branches of knowledge, has only to pass some years in reading a certain number of books, and then he is qualified to be an historian; he is able to write the history of a great people, and his work becomes an authority on the subject which it professes to treat.

The establishment of this narrow standard has led to results very prejudicial to the progress of our knowledge. Owing to it, historians, taken as a body, have never recognized the necessity of such a wide and preliminary study as would enable them to grasp their subject in the whole of its natural relations. Hence the singular spectacle of one historian being ignorant of political economy; another knowing nothing of law; another nothing of ecclesiastical affairs and changes of opinion; another neglecting the philosophy of statistics, and another physical science: although these topics are the most essential of all, inasmuch as they comprise the principal circumstances by which the temper and character of mankind have been affected, and in which they are displayed. These important pursuits being, however, cultivated, some by one man, and some by another, have been isolated rather than united: the aid which might be derived from analogy and from mutual illustration has been lost; and no disposition has been shown to concentrate them upon history, of which they are, properly speaking, the necessary components.

Since the early part of the eighteenth century, a few great thinkers have indeed arisen, who have deplored the backwardness of history, and have done everything in their power to remedy it. But these instances have been extremely rare: so rare, that in the whole literature of Europe there are not more than three or four really original works which contain a systematic attempt to investigate the history of man according to those exhaustive methods which in other branches of knowledge have proved successful, and by which alone empirical observations can be raised to scientific truths.

Among historians in general, we find, after the sixteenth century, and especially during the last hundred years, several indications of an increasing comprehensiveness of view, and of a willingness to incorporate into their works subjects which they would formerly have excluded. By this means their assemblage of topics has become more diversified, and the mere collection and relative position of parallel facts has occasionally suggested generalizations no traces of which can be found in the earlier literature of Europe. This has been a great gain, in so far as it has familiarized historians with a wider range of thought, and encouraged those habits of speculation, which, though liable to abuse, are the essential condition of all real knowledge, because without them no science can be constructed.

But, notwithstanding that the prospects of historical literature are certainly more cheering now than in any former age, it must be allowed that, with extremely few exceptions, they are only prospects, and that as yet scarcely anything has been done towards discovering the principles which govern the character and destiny of nations. What has been actually effected I shall endeavour to estimate in another part of this introduction: at present it is enough to say, that for all the higher purposes of human thought history is still miserably deficient, and presents that confused and anarchical appearance natural to a subject of which the laws are unknown, and even the foundation unsettled.[1]

Our acquaintance with history being so imperfect, while our materials are so numerous, it seems desirable that something should be done on a scale far larger than has hitherto been attempted, and that a strenuous effort should be made to bring up this great department of inquiry to a level with other departments, in order that we may maintain the balance and harmony of our knowledge. It is in this spirit that the present

---

[1] A living writer, who has done more than any other to raise the standard of history, contemptuously notices 'l'incohérente compilation de faits déjà improprement qualifiée d'histoire.' Comte, Philosophie Positive, vol. v. p. 18. There is much in the method and in the conclusions of this great work with which I cannot agree; but it would be unjust to deny its extraordinary merits.

work has been conceived. To make the execution of it fully equal to the conception is impossible: still I hope to accomplish for the history of man something equivalent, or at all events analogous, to what has been effected by other inquirers for the different branches of natural science. In regard to nature, events apparently the most irregular and capricious have been explained, and have been shown to be in accordance with certain fixed and universal laws. This has been done because men of ability, and, above all, men of patient, untiring thought, have studied natural events with the view of discovering their regularity: and if human events were subjected to a similar treatment, we have every right to expect similar results. For it is clear that they who affirm that the facts of history are incapable of being generalized, take for granted the very question at issue. Indeed they do more than this. They not only assume what they cannot prove, but they assume what in the present state of knowledge is highly improbable. Whoever is at all acquainted with what has been done during the last two centuries, must be aware that every generation demonstrates some events to be regular and predictable, which the preceding generation had declared to be irregular and unpredictable: so that the marked tendency of advancing civilization is to strengthen our belief in the universality of order, of method, and of law. This being the case, it follows that if any facts, or class of facts, have not yet been reduced to order, we, so far from pronouncing them to be irreducible, should rather be guided by our experience of the past, and should admit the probability that what we now call inexplicable will at some future time be explained. This expectation of discovering regularity in the midst of confusion is so familiar to scientific men, that among the most eminent of them it becomes an article of faith: and if the same expectation is not generally found among historians, it must be ascribed partly to their being of inferior ability to the investigators of nature, and partly to the greater complexity of those social phenomena with which their studies are concerned.

Both these causes have retarded the creation of the science of history. The most celebrated historians are manifestly inferior to the most successful cultivators of physical science:[a] no one having devoted himself to history who in point of intellect is at all to be compared with Kepler, Newton, or many others that might be named.[2] And as to the greater complexity of the phenomena, the philosophic historian is opposed by difficulties far more formidable than is the student of nature; since, while on the one hand, his observations are more liable to those causes of error which arise from prejudice and passion, he, on the other hand, is unable to employ the great physical resource of experiment, by which we can often simplify even the most intricate problems in the external world.

It is not, therefore, surprising that the study of the movements of Man should be still in its infancy, as compared with the advanced state of the study of the movements of Nature. Indeed the difference between the progress of the two pursuits is so great, that while in physics the regularity of events, and the power of predicting them, are often taken for granted even in cases still unproved, a similar regularity is in history not only not taken for granted, but is actually denied. Hence it is that whoever wishes to raise history to a level with other branches of knowledge, is met by a preliminary obstacle; since he is told that in the affairs of men there is something mysterious and providential, which makes them impervious to our investigations, and which will always hide from us their future course. To this it might be sufficient to reply, that such an assertion is gratuitous; that it is by its nature incapable of proof; and that it is moreover opposed by the notorious fact that everywhere else increasing knowledge is accompanied by an increasing confidence in the uniformity with which, under the same circumstances,

---

[a] I speak merely of those who have made history their main pursuit. Bacon wrote on it, but only as a subordinate object; and it evidently cost him nothing like the thought which he devoted to other subjects.

the same events must succeed each other. It will, however, be more satisfactory to probe the difficulty deeper, and inquire at once into the foundation of the common opinion that history must always remain in its present empirical state, and can never be raised to the rank of a science. We shall thus be led to one vast question, which indeed lies at the root of the whole subject, and is simply this: Are the actions of men, and therefore of societies, governed by fixed laws, or are they the result either of chance or of supernatural interference? The discussion of these alternatives will suggest some speculations of considerable interest.

For, in reference to this matter, there are two doctrines, which appear to represent different stages of civilization. According to the first doctrine, every event is single and isolated, and is merely considered as the result of a blind chance. This opinion, which is most natural to a perfectly ignorant people, would soon be weakened by that extension of experience which supplies a knowledge of those uniformities of succession and of co-existence that nature constantly presents. If, for example, wandering tribes, without the least tincture of civilization, lived entirely by hunting and fishing, they might well suppose that the appearance of their necessary food was the result of some accident which admitted of no explanation. The irregularity of the supply, and the apparent caprice with which it was sometimes abundant and sometimes scanty, would prevent them from suspecting anything like method in the arrangements of nature; nor could their minds even conceive the existence of those general principles which govern the order of events, and by a knowledge of which we are often able to predict their future course. But when such tribes advance into the agricultural state, they, for the first time, use a food of which not only the appearance, but the very existence, seems to be the result of their own act. What they sow, that likewise do they reap. The provision necessary for their wants is brought more immediately under their own control, and is more palpably the consequence of their own labour. They perceive a distinct plan, and a regular uniformity of sequence, in the relation which the seed they put into the ground bears to the corn when arrived at maturity. They are now able to look to the future, not indeed with certainty, but with a confidence infinitely greater than they could have felt in their former and more precarious pursuits.[1] Hence there arises a dim idea of the stability of events; and for the first time there begins to dawn upon the mind a faint conception of what at a later period are called the Laws of Nature. Every step in the great progress will make their view of this more clear. As their observations accumulate, and as their experience extends over a wider surface, they meet with uniformities that they had never suspected to exist, and the discovery of which weakens that doctrine of chance with which they had originally set out. Yet a little further, and a taste for abstract reasoning springs up; and then some among them generalize the observations that have been made, and despising the old popular opinion, believe that every event is linked to its antecedent by an inevitable connexion, that such antecedent is connected with a preceding fact; and that thus the whole world forms a necessary chain, in which indeed each man may play his part, but can by no means determine what that part shall be.

Thus it is that, in the ordinary march of society, an increasing perception of the regularity of nature destroys the doctrine of Chance, and replaces it by that of Necessary Connexion. And it is, I think, highly probable that out of these two doctrines of Chance and Necessity there have respectively arisen the subsequent dogmas of Free Will and Predestination. Nor is it difficult to understand the manner in which, in a more advanced state of society, this metamorphosis would occur. In every country, as soon as the accumulation

---

[1] Some of the moral consequences of thus diminishing the precariousness of food are noticed by M. Charles Comte in his *Traité de Législation*, vol. ii. pp. 273-275. Compare *Mill's History of India*, vol. i. pp. 180-181. But both these able writers have omitted to observe that the change facilitates a perception of the regularity of phenomena.

of wealth has reached a certain point, the produce of each man's labour becomes more than sufficient for his own support: it is therefore no longer necessary that all should work; and there is formed a separate class, the members of which pass their lives for the most part in the pursuit of pleasure; a very few, however, in the acquisition and diffusion of knowledge. Among these last there are always found some who, neglecting external events, turn their attention to the study of their own minds;⁴ and such men, when possessed of great abilities, become the founders of new philosophies

---

⁴ On the relation between this and the previous creation of wealth, see *Tennemann, Geschichte der Philosophie*, vol. i. p. 30; 'Ein gewisser Grad von Cultur und Wohlstand ist eine nothwendige äussere Bedingung der Entwickelung des philosophischen Geistes. So lange der Mensch noch mit den Mitteln seiner Existenz und der Befriedigung seiner thierischen Bedürfnisse beschäftiget ist, so lange gehet die Entwickelung und Bildung seiner Geisteskräfte nur langsam von statten, und er nähert sich nur Schritt vor Schritt einer freiern Vernunftthätigkeit.' . . . 'Daher finden wir, dass man nur in denen Nationen anfing zu philosophiren, welche sich zu einer beträchtlichen Stufe des Wohlstandes und der Cultur emporgehoben hatten.' Hence, as I shall endeavour to prove in the next chapter, the immense importance of the physical phenomena which precede and often control the metaphysical. In the history of the Greek mind we can distinctly trace the passage from physical to metaphysical inquiries. See *Grote's History of Greece*, vol. iv. p. 519, edit. 1847. That the atomic doctrine, in its relation to chance, was a natural precursor of Platonism, is remarked in *Broussais, Examen des Doctrines Médicales*, vol. i. pp. 53, 54, an able though one-sided work. Compare, respecting the Chance of the atomists, *Ritter's History of Ancient Philosophy*, vol. i. p. 553; an hypothesis, as Ritter says, 'destructive of all inner energy;' consequently antagonistic to the psychological hypothesis which subsequently sprang up and conquered it. That physical researches came first, is moreover attested by Diogenes Laertius: Μέρη δὲ Φιλοσοφίας τρία, φυσικὸν, ἠθικὸν, διαλεκτικόν· φυσικὸν μὲν, τὸ περὶ κόσμου, καὶ τῶν ἐν αὐτῷ· ἠθικὸν δὲ, τὸ περὶ βίου καὶ τῶν πρὸς ἡμᾶς· διαλεκτικὸν δὲ, τὸ ἀμφοτέρων τοὺς λόγους πρεσβεῦον· καὶ μέχρι μὲν 'Αρχελάου τὸ φυσικὸν εἶδος ἦν· ἀπὸ δὲ Σωκράτους, ὡς προείρηται, τὸ ἠθικόν· ἀπὸ δὲ Ζήνωνος τοῦ Ἐλεάτου, τὸ διαλεκτικόν. *De Vitis Philosophorum Proœm.* segm. 18, vol. i. p. 12: compare lib. ii. segm. 16, vol i. p. 89.

and new religions, which often exercise immense influence over the people who receive them. But the authors of these systems are themselves affected by the character of the age in which they live. It is impossible for any man to escape the pressure of surrounding opinions; and what is called a new philosophy or a new religion is generally not so much a creation of fresh ideas, but rather a new direction given to ideas already current among contemporary thinkers.[5] Thus, in the case now before us, the doctrine of Chance in the external world corresponds to that of Free Will in the internal: while the other doctrine of Necessary Connexion is equally analogous to that of Predestination; the only difference being that the first is a development by the metaphysician, the second by the theologian. In the first instance, the metaphysician setting out with the doctrine of Chance, carries into the study of the mind this arbitrary and irresponsible principle, which in its new field becomes Free Will; an expression by which all difficulties seem to be removed, since perfect freedom, itself the cause of all actions, is caused by none, but, like the doctrine of Chance, is an ultimate fact admitting of no further explanation.[6] In the second instance, the theologian taking up the doctrine of Necessary Connexion recasts it into a religious shape; and his mind being already full of conceptions of order and of uniformity, he naturally ascribes such undeviating

---

[5] Beausobre has some good remarks on this in his learned work *Histoire Critique de Manichée*, vol. i. p. 179, where he says that the great religious heresies have been founded on previous philosophies. Certainly no one acquainted with the history of opinions will admit the sweeping assertion of M. Stahl that 'la philosophie d'un peuple a sa racine dans sa théologie.' *Klimrath, Travaux*, vol. ii. p. 454, Paris, 1843.

[6] 'Also ist ein Wille, dem die blosse gesetzgebende Form der Maxime allein zum Gesetze dienen kann, ein freier Wille.' *Kritik der praktischen Vernunft* in *Kant's Werke*, vol. iv. p. 128. 'Hat selber für sich eigentlich keinen Bestimmungsgrund.' *Metaphysik der Sitten* in *Werke*, vol. v. p. 12. 'Die unbedingte Causalität der Ursache.' *Kritik der reinen Vernunft* in *Werke*, vol. ii. p. 339. See also *Prolegomena zu jeder künftigen Metaphysik* in vol. iii. p. 268.

regularity to the prescience of Supreme Power; and thus to the magnificent notion of One God there is added the dogma that by Him all things have from the beginning been absolutely pre-determined and pre-ordained.

These opposite doctrines of free will and predestination[7] do, no doubt, supply a safe and simple solution of the obscurities of our being; and as they are easily understood, they are so suited to the average capacity of the human mind, that even at the present day an immense majority of men are divided between them; and they have not only corrupted the sources of our knowledge, but have given rise to religious sects, whose mutual animosities have disturbed society, and too often embittered the relations of private life. Among the more advanced European thinkers there is, however, a growing opinion that both doctrines are wrong or, at all events, that we have no sufficient evidence of their truth. And as this is a matter of great moment, it is important, before we proceed further, to clear up as much of it as the difficulties inherent in these subjects will enable us to do.

Whatever doubts may be thrown on the account which I have given of the probable origin of the ideas

---

[7] That these doctrines, when treated according to the ordinary methods of reasoning, not only oppose but exclude each other, would be universally admitted if it were not for a desire generally felt to save certain parts of each: it being thought dangerous to give up free will on account of weakening moral responsibility, and equally dangerous to give up predestination on account of impugning the power of God. Various attempts have therefore been made to reconcile liberty with necessity, and make the freedom of man harmonize with the foreknowledge of the Deity. Compare on this point a remarkable letter from Locke to Molyneux (*Locke's Works*, vol. viii. p. 305), with the argument in one of Bentley's Sermons (*Monk's Life of Bentley*, vol. ii. pp. 7, 8); also *Ritter's Hist. of Ancient Philosophy*, vol. iv. pp. 143, 144; *Tennemann, Gesch. der Philosophie*, vol. iv. pp. 301-304; *Copleston's Inquiry into the Doctrines of Necessity and Predestination*, pp. 6, 7, 46, 69, 70, 85, 92, 108, 136; *Mosheim's Ecclesiastical Hist.*, vol. i. p. 207, vol. ii. p. 96; *Neander's Hist. of the Church*, vol. iv. pp. 294, 389-391; *Bishop of Lincoln on Tertullian*, 1845, p. 323; *Hodgson on Buddhism*, in *Transac. of Asiatic Society*, vol. ii. p. 232.

of free will and predestination, there can, at all events, be no dispute as to the foundation on which those ideas are now actually based. The theory of predestination is founded on a theological hypothesis; that of free will on a metaphysical hypothesis. The advocates of the first proceed on a supposition for which, to say the least of it, they have as yet brought forward no good evidence. They require us to believe that the Author of Creation, whose beneficence they at the same time willingly allow, has, notwithstanding His supreme goodness, made an arbitrary distinction between the elect and the non-elect; that He has from all eternity doomed to perdition millions of creatures yet unborn, and whom His act alone can call into existence: and that He has done this, not in virtue of any principle of justice, but by a mere stretch of despotic power.[8] This doctrine owes its authority among Protestants to the dark though powerful mind of Calvin; but in the early Church it was first systematically methodized by Augustin, who appears to have borrowed it from the Manicheans.[9] At all events, and putting aside its incompatibility with other notions which are supposed to be fundamental,[10]

[8] Even Ambrose, who never went so far as Augustin, states this principle in its repulsive nakedness: 'Deus quos dignat vocat, quos vult religiosos facit.' *Neander*, vol. iv. p. 287. Calvin declares 'that God, in predestinating from all eternity one part of mankind to everlasting happiness, and another to endless misery, was led to make this distinction by no other motive than His own good pleasure and free will.' *Mosheim's Eccles. Hist.*, vol. ii. p. 103, see also p. 100; and *Carwithen's Hist. of the Church of England*, vol. i. p. 552.

[9] On the Manichæan origin of Augustin's opinions, compare *Potter, Esprit de l'Église*, vol. ii. p. 171, Paris, 1821; *Tomline's Refutation of Calvinism*, 1817, pp. 571-576; *Southey's Book of the Church*, 1824, vol. i. pp. 301, 302; *Matter, Hist. du Gnosticisme*, 1828, vol. i. p. 325. However, Beausobre (*Histoire de Manichée*, vol. ii. pp. 33-40) seems to have proved a difference between the election of Augustin and that of Basilides.

[10] On the absurdity of 'an omnipotent arbitrary Deity,' and on the incongruity of such a combination with φύσει καλὸν καὶ δίκαιον, see *Cudworth's Intellect. Syst.*, vol. i. pp. 45, 419, vol. iii. p. 241, vol. iv. p. 160. See also *Theodicee* in *Kant's Werke*, vol. vi. pp. 141, 142, and *Metaphysik der Sitten* in vol. v. p. 332, upon 'den göttlichen Zweck in Ansehung des menschlichen Geschlechts.'

it must, in a scientific investigation, be regarded as a barren hypothesis, because, being beyond the province of our knowledge, we have no means of ascertaining either its truth or its falsehood.

The other doctrine, which has long been celebrated under the name of Free Will, is connected with Arminianism; but it in reality rests on the metaphysical dogma of the supremacy of human consciousness. Every man, it is alleged, feels and knows that he is a free agent: nor can any subtleties of argument do away with our consciousness of possessing a free will.[11] Now the existence of this supreme jurisdiction, which is thus to set at defiance all the ordinary methods of reasoning, involves two assumptions: of which the first, though possibly true, has never been proved; and the other is unquestionably false. These assumptions are, that there is an independent faculty called consciousness, and that the dictates of that faculty are infallible. But, in the first place, it is by no means certain that consciousness is a faculty; and some of the ablest thinkers have been of opinion that it is merely a state or condition of the mind.[12] Should this turn out to be the case, the argu-

---

[11] Johnson said to Boswell, 'Sir, we *know* our will is free, and there's an end on't.' *Boswell's Life of Johnson*, edit. Croker, 1848, p. 203. 'La question: Sommes-nous libres? me paraît au-dessous de la discussion. Elle est résolue par le témoignage de la conscience attestant que dans certains cas nous pourrions faire le contraire de ce que nous faisons.' *Cousin, Hist. de la Philosophie*, I. Série, vol. i. pp. 190, 191. 'Die Freiheit des Menschen, als moralischen Wesens, gründet sich auf das sittliche Bewusstseyn.' *Tennemann, Gesch. der Philosophie*, vol. v. p. 161. That this is the only ground for believing in the freedom of the will is so evident, that we need not notice the mystical proof of Philo (*Ritter's Ancient Philosophy*, vol. iv. p. 447); nor the physical one of the Basilidian monads (*Beausobre, Hist. de Manichée*, vol. ii. p. 23); still less the argument of Bardesanes, who thought to demonstrate freedom by the variety of human customs! *Matter, Hist. du Gnosticisme*, vol. i. p. 323, which should be compared with *Burdach's Physiologie comme Science d'Observation*, vol. v. p. 60, Paris, 1839.

[12] Mr. James Mill (*Analysis of the Mind*, vol. i. pp. 171, 172) says that consciousness and belief are the same, and that great error has arisen from calling 'consciousness a feeling distinct

ment falls to the ground; since, even if we admit that all the faculties of the mind, when completely exercised, are equally accurate, no one will make the same claim for every condition into which the mind itself may be casually thrown. However, waiving this objection, we may, in the second place, reply, that even if consciousness is a faculty, we have the testimony of all history to prove its extreme fallibility.[13] All the great stages

---

from all other feelings.' According to Locke (*Essay concerning Human Understanding*, book ii. chap. i., *Works*, vol. i. p. 89), 'consciousness is the perception of what passes in a man's own mind.' Brown (*Philosophy of the Mind*, pp. 67, 68) denies that consciousness is a faculty: and Sir W. Hamilton complains of 'Reid's degradation of consciousness into a special faculty.' *Notes to Reid's Works*, pp. 223, 297, 373. M. Cousin (*Hist. de la Philosophie*, II. Série, vol. i. p. 131) pronounces consciousness to be 'phénomène complexe;' and at p. 94, 'la *condition* nécessaire de l'intelligence c'est la conscience:' while a still later writer (*Jobert's New System of Philosophy*, vol. i. p. 25) declares that 'we have the consciousness of our consciousness—this is certain.' The statement in Alciphron, Dialogue vii. (*Berkeley's Works*, vol. i. pp. 505, 506) is equally unsatisfactory: and what still further perplexes the question is the existence of what is now recognised as 'double consciousness.' See on this extraordinary phenomenon *Elliotson's Physiology*, pp. 367–369, 1165; *Mayo's Physiology*, pp. 195, 196; *Prichard's Treatise on Insanity*, pp. 450, 451; *Carpenter's Human Physiology*, p. 379.

[13] This requires explanation. Consciousness is infallible as to the *fact* of its testimony; but fallible as to the *truth*. That we are conscious of certain phenomena, is a proof that those phenomena exist in the mind, or are presented to it; but to say that this demonstrates the truth of the phenomena is to go a step further, and not only offer a testimony, but also pass a judgment. The moment we do this, we introduce the element of fallibility; because consciousness and judgment put together cannot be always right, inasmuch as judgment is often wrong.

The late Blanco White, a thinker of considerable subtlety, says: 'The important distinction between *libertas a necessitate* and *libertas a coactione*, is seldom attended to. Nothing whatever can *force* my will: every man is more or less conscious of that fact: but at the same time we are, or may be, equally conscious that we are never decided without a motive.' *Life of B. White, by Himself*, 1845, vol. iii. p. 90. But how can a man be conscious 'that nothing whatever can force his will'? This is not consciousness, but judgment: it is a judgment of what may be, not a consciousness of what is. If

through which, in the progress of civilization, the human race has successively passed, have been characterized by certain mental peculiarities or convictions, which have left their impress upon the religion, the philosophy, and the morals of the age. Each of these convictions has been to one period a matter of faith, to another a matter for derision;[14] and each of them has, in its own epoch, been as intimately bound up with the minds of men, and become as much a part of their consciousness, as is that opinion which we now term freedom of the will. Yet it is impossible that all these products of consciousness can be true, because many of them contradict each other. Unless, therefore, in different ages there are different standards of truth, it is clear that the testimony of a man's consciousness is no proof of an opinion being true; for if it were so, then two propositions diametrically opposed to each other might both be equally accurate. Besides this, another view may be drawn from the common operations of ordinary life. Are we not in certain circumstances conscious of the existence of spectres and phantoms; and yet is it not generally admitted that such beings have no existence at all? Should it be attempted to refute this argument by saying that such consciousness is apparent and not real, then I ask, What is it that judges between the consciousness which is genuine and that which is spurious?[15] If this boasted faculty

---

there is any meaning in the word 'consciousness,' it must refer solely to the present, and can never include future contingencies as to what may be or can be.

[14] As Herder says, ' Was diese Nation ihrem Gedankenkreise unentbehrlich hält, daran hat jene nie gedacht oder hält es gar für schädlich.' *Ideen zur Gesch. der Menschheit*, vol. ii. p. 130.

[15] Plato was struck by the extreme difficulty of finding a standard in the human mind whereby we may test the truth or falsehood of spectral phenomena and dreams. And the only conclusion to which this consummate thinker could arrive, was that whatever appears true to the individual mind is true for him: which, however, is an evasion of the problem, not a solution of it. See the Theætetus, where Plato, as usual, puts his own speculations into the mouth of Socrates. He opens the question at the beginning of sec. 39 (*Platonis Opera*.

deceives us in some things, what security have we that it will not deceive us in others? If there is no security, the faculty is not trustworthy. If there is a security, then, whatever it may be, its existence shows the necessity for some authority to which consciousness is subordinate, and thus does away with that doctrine of the supremacy of consciousness, on which the advocates of free will are compelled to construct the whole of their theory. Indeed, the uncertainty as to the existence of consciousness as an independent faculty, and the manner in which that faculty, if it exists, has contradicted its own suggestions, are two of the many reasons which have long since convinced me that metaphysics will never be raised to a science by the ordinary method of observing individual minds; but that its study can only be successfully prosecuted by the deductive application

---

vol. iii. p. 426, edit. Bekker, Lond. 1826). Μὴ τοίνυν ἀκολλώμεν ὅσον ἐλλεῖπον αὐτοῦ. λείπεται δὲ ἐνινλίων τε πέρι καὶ νόσων, τῶν τε ἄλλων καὶ μανίας, &c. These are the supposed sources of error; but Socrates, after discussing them, and entangling Theætetus in a maze, sums up at the end of sec. 45, p. 434, ἀληθὴς ἄρα ἐμοὶ ἡ ἐμὴ αἴσθησις. See further, p. 515, on the formation of erroneous judgments; and respecting the assertions made by many of the Greeks that πᾶσα φαντασία ἀληθὴς and πᾶσα δόξα ἀληθὴς, compare Cudworth, vol. iii. p. 379, vol. iv. p. 118. For physiological considerations concerning the preservation of consciousness in dreams and in insanity, see Broussais, Examen des Doctrines Médicales, vol. i. p. 406; his Cours de Phrénologie, p. 49; Esquirol, Maladies Mentales, vol. i. p. 97, vol. ii. p. 790; Simon's Pathology, p. 204; Holland's Medical Notes, p. 434; Henle, Anatomie Générale, vol. ii. p. 287; Burdach, Traité de Physiologie, vol. v. p. 223. See, too, the passages in Tennemann which connect this difficulty with the theory of representation (Geschichte der Philosophie, vol. i. p. 357, vol. ii. pp. 119, 159, vol. iii. p. 406, vol. iv. p. 418); and the attempt of Berkeley (Works, vol. i. pp. 93, 101, 176) to turn it into a defence of his own system, on the ground that our belief respecting the external world may be as false when we are awake as when we dream. The solution offered by the Stoics is merely a verbal and unproved distinction: διαφέρει δὲ φαντασία καὶ φάντασμα. φάντασμα μὲν γάρ ἐστι δόκησις διανοίας οἷα γίνεται κατὰ τοὺς ὕπνους· φαντασία δέ ἐστι τύπωσις ἐν ψυχῇ τουτέστιν ἀλλοίωσις, ὡς ὁ Χρύσιππος ἐν τῇ δωδεκάτῃ περὶ ψυχῆς ὑφίσταται. Diog. Laert. de Vitis Philos. lib. vii. segm. 50, vol. i. p. 395.

of laws which must be discovered historically, that is to say, which must be evolved by an examination of the whole of those vast phenomena which the long course of human affairs presents to our view.

Fortunately, however, for the object of this work, the believer in the possibility of a science of history is not called upon to hold either the doctrine of predestined events, or that of freedom of the will;[16] and the only positions which, in this stage of the inquiry, I shall expect him to concede are the following: That when we perform an action, we perform it in consequence of some motive or motives; that those motives are the results of some antecedents; and that, therefore, if we were acquainted with the whole of the antecedents, and with all the laws of their movements, we could with unerring certainty predict the whole of their immediate results. This, unless I am greatly mistaken, is the view which must be held by every man whose mind is unbiased by system, and who forms his opinions according to the evidence actually before him.[17] If, for example, I am intimately acquainted with the character of any person, I can frequently tell how he will act

---

[16] Meaning by free will, a cause of action residing in the mind, and exerting itself independently of motives. If any one says that we have this power of acting without motives, but that in the practical exercise of the power we are always guided by motives either conscious or unconscious—if any one says this, he asserts a barren proposition, which does not interfere with my views, and which may or may not be true, but which most assuredly no one has ever yet succeeded in proving.

[17] That is, according to the phenomenal evidence presented to the understanding, and estimated by the ordinary logic with which the understanding is conversant. But Kant has made a most remarkable attempt to avoid the practical consequences of this, by asserting that freedom, being an idea produced by the reason, must be referred to transcendental laws of the reason; that is, to laws which are removed from the domain of experience, and cannot be verified by observation. In regard, however, to the scientific conceptions of the understanding (as distinguished from the Reason) he fully admits the existence of a Necessity destructive of Liberty. In Note A, at the end of this chapter, I shall put together the most important passages in which Kant unfolds this view.

under some given circumstances. Should I fail in this prediction, I must ascribe my error not to the arbitrary and capricious freedom of his will, nor to any supernatural pre-arrangement, for of neither of these things have we the slightest proof; but I must be content to suppose either that I had been misinformed as to some of the circumstances in which he was placed, or else that I had not sufficiently studied the ordinary operations of his mind. If, however, I were capable of correct reasoning, and if, at the same time, I had a complete knowledge both of his disposition and of all the events by which he was surrounded, I should be able to foresee the line of conduct which, in consequence of those events, he would adopt.[18]

Rejecting, then, the metaphysical dogma of free will, and the theological dogma of predestined events,[19] we

---

[18] This is, of course, an hypothetical case, merely given as an illustration. We never can know the whole of any man's antecedents, or even the whole of our own; but it is certain that the nearer we approach to a complete knowledge of the antecedent, the more likely we shall be to predict the consequent.

[19] The doctrine of providential interference is bound up with that of predestination, because the Deity, foreseeing all things, must have foreseen His own Intention to interfere. To deny this foresight, is to limit the omniscience of God. Those, therefore, who hold that, in particular cases, a special providence interrupts the ordinary course of events, must also hold that in each case the interruption had been predestined; otherwise they impeach one of the Divine attributes. For, as Thomas Aquinas puts it (*Neander's History of the Church*, vol. viii. p. 176), 'knowledge, as knowledge, does not imply, indeed, causality; but in so far as it is a knowledge belonging to the artist who forms, it stands in the relation of causality to that which is produced by his art.'

The same argument is stated by Alciphron, though not quite so conclusively; *Dialogue* vii. sec. 20 in *Berkeley's Works*, vol. i. p. 515: and as to the impossibility of Omniscience having new knowledge or an afterthought, see *Hitchcock's Religion of Geology*, 1851, pp. 267, 328; an ingenious work, but one which leaves all the real difficulties untouched. Compare *Ritter's Hist. of Ancient Philos.* vol. iv. pp. 326, 327, with *Tennemann, Gesch. der Philos.* vol. vi. pp. 151, 342-345, vol. ix. pp. 81-94, vol. xi. p. 178; and in particular, the question raised (vol. viii. p. 242), 'Ob das Vorherwissen Gottes die Ursache der künftigen Dinge sey, oder nicht.' It was to meet all this, that some asserted the

are driven to the conclusion that the actions of men, being determined solely by their antecedents, must have a character of uniformity, that is to say, must, under precisely the same circumstances, always issue in precisely the same results. And as all antecedents are either in the mind or out of it, we clearly see that all the variations in the results, in other words, all the changes of which history is full, all the vicissitudes of the human race, their progress or their decay, their happiness or their misery, must be the fruit of a double action; an action of external phenomena upon the mind, and another action of the mind upon the phenomena.

These are the materials out of which a philosophic history can alone be constructed. On the one hand, we have the human mind obeying the laws of its own existence, and, when uncontrolled by external agents, developing itself according to the conditions of its organization. On the other hand, we have what is called Nature, obeying likewise its laws; but incessantly coming into contact with the minds of men, exciting their passions, stimulating their intellect, and therefore giving to their actions a direction which they would not have taken without such disturbance. Thus we have man modifying nature, and nature modifying man; while out of this reciprocal modification all events must necessarily spring.

The problem immediately before us, is to ascertain the method of discovering the laws of this double modification: and this, as we shall presently see, leads us into a preliminary inquiry as to which of the two modifications is the more important; that is to say, whether the thoughts and desires of men are more influenced by physical phenomena, or whether the physical phenomena are more influenced by them. For it is evident that whichever class is the more active, should if possible be studied before the other; and this, partly because its results will be more prominent,

---

eternity of matter, and others the existence of two original principles, one good and one evil.

Beausobre, Histoire de Manichée, vol. ii. pp. 145, 146, 252, 336.

and therefore more easy to observe; and partly because by first generalizing the laws of the greater power we shall leave a smaller residue of unexplained facts than if we had begun by generalizing the laws of the lesser power. But, before entering into this examination, it will be convenient to state some of the most decisive proofs we now possess of the regularity with which mental phenomena succeed each other. By this means the preceding views will be considerably strengthened; and we shall, at the same time, be able to see what those resources are which have been already employed in elucidating this great subject.

That the results actually effected are extremely valuable is evident, not only from the wide surface which the generalizations cover, but also from the extraordinary precautions with which they have been made. For while most moral inquiries have depended on some theological or metaphysical hypothesis, the investigations to which I allude are exclusively inductive; they are based on collections of almost innumerable facts, extending over many countries, thrown into the clearest of all forms, the form of arithmetical tables; and finally, they have been put together by men who, being for the most part mere government officials,[20] had no particular theory to maintain, and no interest in distorting the truth of the reports they were directed to make.

The most comprehensive inferences respecting the actions of men, which are admitted by all parties as incontestable truths, are derived from this or from analogous sources; they rest on statistical evidence, and are expressed in mathematical language. And whoever is aware of how much has been discovered by this single method, must not only recognize the uniformity with which mental phenomena succeed each other, but must, I think, feel sanguine that still more important discoveries will be made, so soon as there are brought into play those other powerful resources which even the present state of knowledge will abun-

---

[20] *Dufau, Traité de Statistique,* pp. 75, 148.

dantly supply. Without, however, anticipating future inquiries, we are, for the moment, only concerned with those proofs of the existence of a uniformity in human affairs which statisticians have been the first to bring forward.

The actions of men are by an easy and obvious division separated into two classes, the virtuous and the vicious; and as these classes are correlative, and when put together compose the total of our moral conduct, it follows that whatever increases the one, will in a relative point of view diminish the other; so that if we can in any period detect a uniformity and a method in the vices of a people, there must be a corresponding regularity in their virtues; or if we could prove a regularity in their virtues, we should necessarily infer an equal regularity in their vices; the two sets of actions being, according to the terms of the division, merely supplementary to each other.[21] Or, to express this proposition in another way, it is evident that if it can be demonstrated that the bad actions of men vary in obedience to the changes in the surrounding society, we shall be obliged to infer that their good actions, which are, as it were, the residue of their bad ones, vary in the same manner; and we shall be forced to the further conclusion, that such variations are the result of large and general causes, which, working upon the aggregate of society, must produce certain con-

---

[21] Some moralists have also established a third class of actions, which they call indifferent, as belonging neither to virtue nor to vice; and hence there arose the famous doctrine of probability, set up by several eminent Romish casuists, and hotly attacked by Pascal. But this, if we put aside its worst feature, namely its practical bearings, is merely a question of definition; inasmuch as every indifferent act must lean on the side either of evil or of good, and may therefore be referred to the category to which it inclines; and certainly every increase of vice diminishes virtue relatively, though not always absolutely. Among the Greek philosophers there was a schism on this point: 'Ἀρέσκει δὲ αὐτοῖς (i.e. the Stoics) μηδὲν μέσον εἶναι ἀρετῆς καὶ κακίας· τῶν περιπατητικῶν μεταξὺ ἀρετῆς καὶ κακίας εἶναι λεγόντων τὴν προκοπήν. Diog. Laert. de Vitis Philosophorum, lib. vii. segm. 127, vol. i. p. 445.

sequences, without regard to the volition of those particular men of whom the society is composed.

Such is the regularity we expect to find, if the actions of men are governed by the state of the society in which they occur; while, on the other hand, if we can find no such regularity, we may believe that their actions depend on some capricious and personal principle peculiar to each man, as free will or the like. It becomes, therefore, in the highest degree important to ascertain whether or not there exists a regularity in the entire moral conduct of a given society; and this is precisely one of those questions for the decision of which statistics supply us with materials of immense value.

For the main object of legislation being to protect the innocent against the guilty, it naturally followed that European governments, so soon as they became aware of the importance of statistics, should begin to collect evidence respecting the crimes they were expected to punish. This evidence has gone on accumulating, until it now forms of itself a large body of literature, containing, with the commentaries connected with it, an immense array of facts, so carefully compiled, and so well and clearly digested, that more may be learned from it respecting the moral nature of Man than can be gathered from all the accumulated experience of preceding ages.[71] But as it will be impossible

---

[71] I say this advisedly: and whoever has examined these subjects must be aware of the way in which writers on morals repeat the commonplace and hackneyed notions of their predecessors; so that a man, after reading everything that has been written on moral conduct and moral philosophy, will find himself nearly as much in the dark as when his studies first began. The most accurate investigators of the human mind have hitherto been the poets, particularly Homer and Shakespeare; but these extraordinary observers mainly occupied themselves with the concrete phenomena of life; and if they analyzed, as they probably did, they have concealed the steps of the process, so that now we can only verify their conclusions empirically. The great advance made by the statisticians consists in applying to these inquiries the doctrine of averages, which no one thought of doing before the eighteenth century.

in this Introduction to give anything like a complete statement of those inferences which, in the actual state of statistics, we are authorized to draw, I shall content myself with examining two or three of the most important, and pointing out the connexion between them.

Of all offences, it might well be supposed that the crime of murder is one of the most arbitrary and irregular. For when we consider that this, though generally the crowning act of a long career of vice, is often the immediate result of what seems a sudden impulse; that when premeditated, its committal, even with the least chance of impunity, requires a rare combination of favourable circumstances for which the criminal will frequently wait; that he has thus to bide his time, and look for opportunities he cannot control; that when the time has come his heart may fail him; that the question whether or not he shall commit the crime may depend on a balance of conflicting motives, such as fear of the law, a dread of the penalties held out by religion, the prickings of his own conscience, the apprehension of future remorse, the love of gain, jealousy, revenge, desperation;—when we put all these things together, there arises such a complication of causes, that we might reasonably despair of detecting any order or method in the result of those subtle and shifting agencies by which murder is either caused or prevented. But now, how stands the fact? The fact is, that murder is committed with as much regularity, and bears as uniform a relation to certain known circumstances, as do the movements of the tides, and the rotations of the seasons. M. Quetelet, who has spent his life in collecting and methodizing the statistics of different countries, states, as the result of his laborious researches, that 'in everything which concerns crime, the same numbers re-occur with a constancy which cannot be mistaken; and that this is the case even with those crimes which seem quite independent of human foresight, such, for instance, as murders, which are generally committed after quarrels arising from circumstances apparently casual. Nevertheless, we know from experience that every year there not only take place nearly the same number of murders, but that even the instruments by which they are committed are employed in the same proportion.'[23] This was the language used in 1835 by confessedly the first statistician in Europe, and every subsequent investigation has confirmed its accuracy. For later inquiries have ascertained the extraordinary fact that the uniform reproduction of crime is more clearly marked, and more capable of being predicted, than are the physical laws connected with the disease and destruction of our bodies. Thus, for instance, the number of persons accused of crime in France between 1826 and 1844 was, by a singular coincidence, about equal to the male deaths which took place in Paris during the same period, the difference being that the fluctuations in the amount of crime were actually smaller than the fluctuations in the mortality; while a similar regularity was observed in each separate offence, all of which obeyed the same law of uniform and periodical repetition.[24]

---

[23] 'Dans tout ce qui se rapporte aux crimes, les mêmes nombres se reproduisent avec une constance telle, qu'il serait impossible de la méconnaître, même pour ceux des crimes qui sembleraient devoir échapper le plus à toute prévision humaine, tels que les meurtres, puisqu'ils se commettent, en général, à la suite de rixes qui naissent sans motifs, et dans les circonstances, en apparence, les plus fortuites. Cependant l'expérience prouve que non-seulement les meurtres sont annuellement à peu près en même nombre, mais encore que les instrumens qui servent à les commettre sont employés dans les mêmes proportions.' *Quetelet sur l'Homme*, Paris, 1835, vol. i. p. 7; see also vol. ii. pp. 164, 247.

[24] 'Thus in twenty years' observations, the number of persons accused of various crimes in France, and registered under their respective ages, scarcely varies at any age from year to year, comparing the proportion per cent. under each age with the totals. The number of persons accused in all France, in the years 1826 to 1844, was about equal to the deaths of males registered in Paris; but singularly enough, the former results are more regular than the latter, notwithstanding the accidental causes which might affect them;—notwithstanding even a revolution in Paris, which convulsed society and brought in a new dynasty.' *Brown on the Uniform Action of the Human Will*, in *The Assurance Magazine*, no. viii., July 1852, pp. 349, 350. That the variations

26 RESOURCES FOR INVESTIGATING HISTORY.

This, indeed, will appear strange to those who believe that human actions depend more upon the peculiarities of each individual than on the general state of society. But another circumstance remains behind still more striking. Among public and registered crimes there is none which seems so completely dependent on the individual as suicide. Attempts to murder or to rob may be, and constantly are, successfully resisted; baffled sometimes by the party attacked, sometimes by the officers of justice. But an attempt to commit suicide is much less liable to interruption. The man who is determined to kill himself is not prevented at the last moment by the struggles of an enemy; and, as he can easily guard against the interference of the civil power,[25] his act becomes as it were isolated; it is cut off from foreign disturbances, and seems more clearly the product of his own volition than any other offence could possibly be. We may also add that, unlike crimes in general, it is rarely caused by the instigation of confederates; so that men, not being goaded into it by their companions, are uninfluenced by one great

---

in crime are less than those of mortality, is also noticed in *Statistique Morale*, pp. 18, 34, in *Mémoires de l'Académie de Belgique*, vol. xxi., Bruxelles, 1848, 4to.

[25] The folly of lawgivers thinking that by their enactments they can diminish suicide, is exposed by M. C. Comte in his *Traité de Législation*, vol. i. p. 486. See also some good remarks by Jefferson, in his observations on criminal law in *Appendix to Jefferson's Memoirs, by Randolph*, vol. i. pp. 126, 127. Heber (*Journey through India*, vol. i. pp. 389, 390) found that the English Government had vainly attempted to check the suicides frequently committed at Benares by drowning: and in our country the interference of legislators is met by the perjury of jurors, since, as Bentham says, English juries do not hesitate to violate their oaths by declaring the suicide to be *non compos*. *Principles of Penal Law*, in *Bentham's Works*, edit. Bowring, 1843, vol. i. pp. 479, 480. In regard to the determination of the individual, and the impossibility of baffling his intention, there are cases recorded of persons who, being deprived of the ordinary means of destruction, put an end to life by holding their breath; while others effected their purpose by turning back the tongue so as to exclude air from the larynx. *Elliotson's Human Physiology*, pp. 491, 492.

class of external associations which might hamper what is termed the freedom of their will. It may, therefore, very naturally be thought impracticable to refer suicide to general principles, or to detect anything like regularity in an offence which is so eccentric, so solitary, so impossible to control by legislation, and which the most vigilant police can do nothing to diminish. There is also another obstacle that impedes our view: this is, that even the best evidence respecting suicide must always be very imperfect. In cases of drowning, for example, deaths are liable to be returned as suicides which are accidental; while, on the other hand, some are called accidental which are voluntary.[26] Thus it is, that self-murder seems to be not only capricious and uncontrollable, but also very obscure in regard to proof; so that on all these grounds it might be reasonable to despair of ever tracing it to those general causes by which it is produced.

These being the peculiarities of this singular crime, it is surely an astonishing fact, that all the evidence we possess respecting it points to one great conclusion, and can leave no doubt on our minds that suicide is merely the product of the general condition of society, and that the individual felon only carries into effect what is a necessary consequence of preceding circumstances.[27]

---

[26] This also applies to other cases besides those of drowning. See *Taylor's Medical Jurisprudence*, 1846, pp. 587, 597; and on the difficulty of always distinguishing a real suicide from an apparent one, see *Esquirol, Maladies Mentales*, vol. i. p. 575. From a third to a half of all suicides are by drowning. Compare *Dufau, Traité de Statistique*, p. 304; *Winslow's Anatomy of Suicide*, 1840, p. 277; *Quetelet, Statistique Morale*, p. 66. But among these, many are no doubt involuntary; and it is certain that popular opinion grossly exaggerates the length of time during which it is possible to remain under water. *Brodie's Surgery*, 1846, pp. 89-92.

[27] 'Tout semble dépendre de causes déterminées. Ainsi, nous trouvons annuellement à peu près le même nombre de suicides, non-seulement en général, mais encore en faisant la distinction des sexes, celle des âges, ou même celle des instruments employés pour se détruire. Une année reproduit si fidèlement les chiffres de l'année qui a précédé, qu'on peut prévoir ce qui doit arriver dans l'année qui va suivre.' *Quetelet, Statistique Morale*, 1848, p. 35; see also p. 40.

In a given state of society, a certain number of persons must put an end to their own life. This is the general law; and the special question as to who shall commit the crime depends, of course, upon special laws; which, however, in their total action, must obey the large social law to which they are all subordinate. And the power of the larger law is so irresistible, that neither the love of life nor the fear of another world can avail anything towards even checking its operation. The causes of this remarkable regularity I shall hereafter examine; but the existence of the regularity is familiar to whoever is conversant with moral statistics. In the different countries for which we have returns, we find year by year the same proportion of persons putting an end to their own existence; so that, after making allowance for the impossibility of collecting complete evidence, we are able to predict, within a very small limit of error, the number of voluntary deaths for each ensuing period; supposing, of course, that the social circumstances do not undergo any marked change. Even in London, notwithstanding the vicissitudes incidental to the largest and most luxurious capital in the world, we find a regularity greater than could be expected by the most sanguine believer in social laws; since political excitement, mercantile excitement, and the misery produced by the dearness of food, are all causes of suicide, and are all constantly varying.[20] Nevertheless, in this vast metropolis, about 240 persons every year make away with themselves; the annual suicides oscillating, from the pressure of temporary causes, between 266, the highest, and 213, the lowest. In 1846, which was the great year of excitement caused by the railway panic, the suicides in London were 266; in 1847 began a slight improvement, and they fell to 256; in 1848 they were

---

[20] On the causes of suicides, see *Burdach's Traité de Physiologie*, vol. v. pp. 476–478; and *Forry's Climate and its Endemic Influences*, p. 329. The latest researches of M. Casper confirm the statement of earlier statisticians, that suicide is more frequent among Protestants than among Catholics. Casper, *Denkwürdigkeiten zur medicinischen Statistik*, Berlin, 1846, p. 139.

247; in 1849 they were 213; and in 1850 they were 229.[19]

Such is some, and only some, of the evidence we now possess respecting the regularity with which, in the same state of society, the same crimes are necessarily reproduced. To appreciate the full force of this evidence, we must remember that it is not an arbitrary selection of particular facts, but that it is generalized from an exhaustive statement of criminal statistics, consisting of many millions of observations, extending over countries in different grades of civilization, with different laws, different opinions, different morals, different habits. If we add to this, that these statistics have been collected by persons specially employed for that purpose, with every means of arriving at the truth, and with no interest to deceive, it surely must be admitted that the existence of crime according to a fixed and uniform scheme, is a fact more clearly attested than any other in the moral history of man. We have here parallel chains of evidence formed with extreme care, under the most different circumstances, and all pointing in the same direction; all of them forcing us to the conclusion, that the offences of men are the result not so much of the vices of the individual offender as of the state of society into which that individual is thrown.[50] This is an inference resting on broad and tangible proofs accessible to all the world; and as such cannot be overturned, or even impeached, by any of those hypotheses with which metaphysicians and

---

[19] See the tables in the *Assurance Magazine*, no. iv. p. 309, no. v. p. 34, no. viii. p. 350. These are the only complete consecutive returns of London suicides yet published; those issued by the police being imperfect. *Assurance Magazine*, no. v. p. 53. From inquiries made for me at the General Register Office, in January 1856, I learnt that there was an intention of completing the yearly returns, but I do not know if this has since been done.

[50] 'L'expérience démontre en effet, avec toute l'évidence possible, cette opinion, qui pourra sembler paradoxale au premier abord, que *c'est la société qui prépare le crime, et que le coupable n'est que l'instrument qui l'exécute*.' *Quetelet sur l'Homme*, vol. ii. p. 325.

theologians have hitherto perplexed the study of past events.

Those readers who are acquainted with the manner in which in the physical world the operations of the laws of nature are constantly disturbed, will expect to find in the moral world disturbances equally active. Such aberrations proceed, in both instances, from minor laws, which at particular points meet the larger laws, and thus alter their normal action. Of this, the science of mechanics affords a good example in the instance of that beautiful theory called the parallelogram of forces; according to which the forces are to each other in the same proportion as is the diagonal of their respective parallelograms.[31] This is a law pregnant with great results; it is connected with those important mechanical resources, the composition and resolution of forces; and no one acquainted with the evidence on which it stands, ever thought of questioning its truth. But the moment we avail ourselves of it for practical purposes, we find that in its action it is warped by other laws, such as those concerning the friction of air, and the different density of the bodies on which we operate, arising from their chemical composition, or, as some suppose, from their atomic arrangement. Perturbations being thus let in, the pure and simple action of the mechanical law disappears. Still, and although the results of the law are incessantly disturbed, the law itself remains intact.[32] Just in the same way, the great

---

[31] The diagonal always giving the resultant when each side represents a force; and if we look on the resultant as a compound force, a comparison of diagonals becomes a comparison of compounds.

[32] A law of nature being merely a generalization of relations, and having no existence except in the mind, is essentially intangible; and therefore, however small the law may be, it can never admit of exceptions, though its operation may admit of innumerable exceptions. Hence, as Dugald Stewart (*Philosophy of the Mind*, vol. ii. p. 211) rightly says, we can only refer to the laws of nature 'by a sort of figure or metaphor.' This is constantly lost sight of even by authors of repute; some of whom speak of laws as if they were causes, and therefore liable to interruption by larger causes; while other writers pronounce them to be 'delegated agencies'

social law, that the moral actions of men are the product not of their volition, but of their antecedents, is itself liable to disturbances which trouble its operation without affecting its truth. And this is quite sufficient to explain those slight variations which we find from year to year in the total amount of crime produced by the same country. Indeed, looking at the fact that the moral world is far more abundant in materials than the physical world, the only ground for astonishment is that these variations should not be greater; and from the circumstance that the discrepancies are so trifling, we may form some idea of the prodigious energy of those vast social laws, which, though constantly interrupted, seem to triumph over every obstacle, and which, when examined by the aid of large numbers, scarcely undergo any sensible perturbation.[22]

---

from the Deity. Compare *Prout's Bridgewater Treatise*, pp. 318, 435, 495; *Sadler's Law of Population*, vol. ii. p. 67; *Burdach's Physiologie*, vol. i. p. 160. Mr. Paget, in his able work, *Lectures on Pathology*, vol. i. p. 481, vol. ii. p. 542, with much greater accuracy calls such cases 'apparent exceptions' to laws; but it would be better to say, 'exceptions to the operations of laws.' The context clearly proves that Mr. Paget distinctly apprehends the difference; but a slight alteration of this kind would prevent confusion in the minds of ordinary readers.

[23] Mr. Rawson, in his *Inquiry into the Statistics of Crime in England and Wales* (published in the *Journal of the Statistical Society*, vol. ii. pp. 316–341), says, p. 327, 'No greater proof can be given of the possibility of arriving at certain constants with regard to crime, than the fact which appears in the following table, that the greatest variation which has taken place during the last three years, in the proportion of any class of criminals at the same period of life, has not exceeded a half per cent.' See also *Report of British Association for 1839, Transac. of Sec.*, p. 118. Indeed, all writers who have examined the evidence are forced to admit this regularity, however they may wish to explain it. M. Dufau (*Traité de Statistique*, p. 144) says, 'Les faits de l'ordre moral sont, aussi bien que ceux de l'ordre naturel, le produit de causes constantes et régulières,' &c.; and at p. 367, 'C'est ainsi que le monde moral se présente à nous, de ce point de vue, comme offrant, de même que le monde physique, un ensemble continu d'effets dus à des causes constantes et régulières, dont il appartient surtout à la statistique de constater l'action.' See to the same effect *Moreau-Christophe des Prisons en France*, Paris, 1838, pp. 53, 189.

Nor is it merely the crimes of men which are marked by this uniformity of sequence. Even the number of marriages annually contracted, is determined, not by the temper and wishes of individuals, but by large general facts, over which individuals can exercise no authority. It is now known that marriages bear a fixed and definite relation to the price of corn;[34] and in England the experience of a century has proved that, instead of having any connexion with personal feelings, they are simply regulated by the average earnings of the great mass of the people:[35] so that this immense social and religious institution is not only swayed, but is completely controlled, by the price of food and by the rate of wages. In other cases, uniformity has been detected, though the causes of the uniformity are still unknown. Thus, to give a curious instance, we are now able to prove that even the aberrations of memory are marked by this general character of necessary and invariable order. The post-offices of London and of Paris have latterly published returns of the number of letters which the writers, through forgetfulness, omitted to direct; and, making allowance for the difference of circumstances, the returns are year after year copies of each other. Year after year the same proportion of letter-writers forget this simple act; so that for each successive period we can actually foretell the number of persons whose

---

[34] 'It is curious to observe how intimate a relation exists between the price of food and the number of marriages.' . . . . 'The relation that subsists between the price of food and the number of marriages is not confined to our own country; and it is not improbable that, had we the means of ascertaining the facts, we should see the like result in every civilized community. We possess the necessary returns from France; and these fully bear out the view that has been given.' *Porter's Progress of the Nation*, vol. ii. pp. 244, 245, London, 1838.

[35] 'The marriage returns of 1850 and 1851 exhibit the excess which since 1750 has been invariably observed when the substantial earnings of the people are above the average.' *Journal of Statistical Society*, vol. xv. p. 185.

memory will fail them in regard to this trifling and, as it might appear, accidental occurrence.[36]

To those who have a steady conception of the regularity of events, and have firmly seized the great truth that the actions of men, being guided by their antecedents, are in reality never inconsistent, but, however capricious they may appear, only form part of one vast scheme of universal order, of which we in the present state of knowledge can barely see the outline—to those who understand this, which is at once the key and the basis of history, the facts just adduced, so far from being strange, will be precisely what would have been expected and ought long since to have been known. Indeed, the progress of inquiry is becoming so rapid and so earnest, that I entertain little doubt that before another century has elapsed, the chain of evidence will be complete, and it will be as rare to find an historian who denies the undeviating regularity of the moral world, as it now is to find a philosopher who denies the regularity of the material world.

It will be observed, that the preceding proofs of our actions being regulated by law, have been derived from statistics; a branch of knowledge which, though still in its infancy,[37] has already thrown more light on

---

[36] See *Somerville's Physical Geography*, vol. ii. pp. 409–411, which, says this able writer, proves that 'forgetfulness as well as free will is under constant laws.' But this is using the word 'free will' in a sense different from that commonly employed.

[37] Achenwall, in the middle of the eighteenth century, is usually considered to be the first systematic writer on statistics, and is said to have given them their present name. See *Lewis, Methods of Observation and Reasoning in Politics*, 1852, vol. i. p. 72; *Biographie Universelle*, vol. i. p. 140; *Dufau, Traité de Statistique*, pp. 9, 10. Even so late as 1800, the Bishop of Llandaff wrote to Sir John Sinclair, 'I must think the kingdom is highly indebted to you for bringing forward a species of knowledge (statistics) wholly new in this country, though not new in other parts of Europe.' *Sinclair's Correspondence*, vol. i. p. 230. Sinclair, notwithstanding his industry, was a man of slender powers, and did not at all understand the real importance of statistics, of which, indeed, he took a mere practical view. Since then statistics have been

the study of human nature than all the sciences put together. But although the statisticians have been the first to investigate this great subject by treating it according to those methods of reasoning which in other fields have been found successful; and although they have, by the application of numbers, brought to bear upon it a very powerful engine for eliciting truth— we must not, on that account, suppose that there are no other resources remaining by which it may likewise be cultivated: nor should we infer that because the physical sciences have not yet been applied to history, they are therefore inapplicable to it. Indeed, when we consider the incessant contact between man and the external world, it is certain that there must be an intimate connexion between human actions and physical laws; so that if physical science had not hitherto been brought to bear upon history, the reason is, either that historians have not perceived the connexion, or else that, having perceived it, they have been destitute of the knowledge by which its workings can be traced. Hence there has arisen an unnatural separation of the two great departments of inquiry, the study of the internal and that of the external: and although, in the present state of European literature, there are some unmistakable symptoms of a desire to break down this artificial barrier, still it must be admitted that as yet nothing has been actually accomplished towards effecting so great an end. The moralists, the theologians, and the metaphysicians, continue to prosecute their studies without much respect for what they deem the inferior labours of scientific men; whose inquiries, indeed, they frequently attack, as dangerous to the interests of religion, and as inspiring us with an

---

applied extensively to medicine; and still more recently, and on a smaller scale, to philology and to jurisprudence. Compare Bouillaud, *Philosophie Médicale*, pp. 96, 186; Renouard, *Hist. de la Médecine*, vol. ii. pp. 474, 475; Esquirol, *Maladies Mentales*, vol. ii. pp. 665–667; Holland's *Medical Notes*, pp. 5, 472; Vogel's *Pathological Anatomy*, pp. 15–17; Simon's *Pathology*, p. 180; Phillips on *Scrofula*, pp. 70, 118, &c.; Prichard's *Physical Hist. of Mankind*, vol. iv. p. 414; Eschbach, *Étude du Droit*, pp. 392–394.

undue confidence in the resources of the human understanding. On the other hand, the cultivators of physical science, conscious that they are an advancing body, are naturally proud of their own success; and, contrasting their discoveries with the more stationary position of their opponents, are led to despise pursuits the barrenness of which has now become notorious.

It is the business of the historian to mediate between these two parties, and reconcile their hostile pretensions by showing the point at which their respective studies ought to coalesce. To settle the terms of this coalition, will be to fix the basis of all history. For since history deals with the actions of men, and since their actions are merely the product of a collision between internal and external phenomena, it becomes necessary to examine the relative importance of those phenomena; to inquire into the extent to which their laws are known; and to ascertain the resources for future discovery possessed by these two great classes, the students of the mind and the students of nature. This task I shall endeavour to accomplish in the next two chapters: and if I do so with anything approaching to success, the present work will at least have the merit of contributing something towards filling up that wide and dreary chasm, which, to the hindrance of our knowledge, separates subjects that are intimately related, and should never be disunited.

Note A.

'Der Begriff der Freiheit ist ein reiner Vernunftbegriff, der eben darum für die theoretische Philosophie transcendent, d. L ein solcher ist, dem kein angemessenes Beispiel in irgend einer möglichen Erfahrung gegeben werden kann, welcher also keinen Gegenstand einer uns möglichen theoretischen Erkenntniss ausmacht, und schlechterdings nicht für ein constitutives, sondern lediglich als regulatives, und zwar nur bloss negatives Princip der speculativen Vernunft gelten kann, im praktischen Gebrauche der selben aber seine Realität durch praktische Grundsätze beweist, die, als Gesetze, eine Causalität der reinen Vernunft, unabhängig von allen empirischen Bedingungen (dem Sinnlichen überhaupt), die Willkühr zu bestimmen, und einen reinen Willen in uns beweisen, in welchem die sittlichen Begriffe und Gesetze ihren Ursprung haben.' *Metaphysik der Sitten*, in *Kant's Werke*, vol. v. pp. 20, 21. 'Würden die Gegenstände der Sinnenwelt für Dinge an sich selbst genommen, und die oben angeführten Naturgesetze für Gesetze der Dinge an sich selbst, so wäre der Widerspruch' (*i. e.* between Liberty and Necessity) 'unvermeidlich. Ebenso, wenn das Subject der Freiheit gleich den übrigen Gegenständen als blosse Erscheinung vorgestellt würde, so könnte ebensowohl der Widerspruch nicht vermieden werden; denn es würde ebendasselbe von einerlei Gegenständen in derselben Bedeutung zugleich bejaht und verneint werden. Ist aber Naturnothwendigkeit blos auf Erscheinungen bezogen, und Freiheit bloss auf Dinge an sich selbst, so entspringt kein Widerspruch, wenn man gleich beide Arten von Causalität annimmt oder zugibt, so schwer oder unmöglich es auch sein möchte, die von der letzteren Art begreiflich zu machen.' .... 'Natur also und Freiheit eben demselben Dinge, aber in verschiedener Beziehung, einmal als Erscheinung, das andre Mal als einem Dinge an sich selbst ohne Widerspruch beigelegt werden können.' .... 'Nun kann ich ohne Widerspruch sagen: alle Handlungen vernünftiger Wesen, sofern sie Erscheinungen sind (in irgend einer Erfahrung angetroffen werden), stehen unter der Naturnothwendigkeit; eben dieselben Handlungen aber, bloss respective auf das vernünftige Subject und dessen Vermögen, nach blosser Vernunft zu handeln, sind frei.' *Prolegomena zu jeder künftigen Metaphysik*, in *Kant's Werke*, vol. iii. pp. 268–270. 'Denn ein Geschöpf zu sein und als Naturwesen bloss dem Willen seines Urhebers zu folgen; dennoch aber als freihandelndes Wesen (welches seinen vom äusseren Einfluss unabhängigen Willen hat, der dem ersteren vielfältig zuwider sein kann), der Zurechnung fähig zu sein, und seine eigne That doch auch zugleich als die Wirkung eines höheren Wesens anzusehen: ist eine Vereinbarung von Begriffen, die wir zwar in der Idee einer Welt, als des höchsten Gutes, zusammen denken müssen; die aber nur der einsehen kann, welcher bis zur Kenntniss der übersinnlichen (intelligiblen) Welt durchdringt und die Art einsieht, wie sie der Sinnenwelt zum Grunde liegt.' *Theodicee*, in *Kant's Werke*, vol. vi. p. 149. 'Nun wollen wir annehmen, die durch unsere Kritik nothwendig gemachte Unterscheidung der Dinge, als Gegenstände der Erfahrung, von eben denselben, als Dingen an sich selbst, wäre gar nicht gemacht, so müsste der Grundsatz der Causalität und mithin der Naturmechanismus in Bestimmung derselben durchaus von allen Dingen überhaupt als wirkenden Ursachen gelten. Von eben demselben Wesen also, z. B. der menschlichen Seele, würde ich nicht sagen können, ihr Wille sei frei, und er sei doch zugleich der Naturnothwendigkeit unterworfen, d. i. nicht frei, ohne in einen offenbaren Widerspruch zu gerathen; weil ich die Seele in beiden Sätzen in eben derselben Bedeutung, nämlich als Ding überhaupt (als Sache an sich selbst), genommen habe und, ohne vorhergehende Kritik, auch nicht anders nehmen konnte. Wenn aber die Kritik nicht geirrt hat, da sie das Object in zweierlei Bedeutung nehmen lehrt, nämlich als Erscheinung, oder als Ding an sich selbst; wenn die Deduction ihrer Verstandesbegriffe richtig ist, mithin auch der Grundsatz der Causalität nur auf Dinge im ersten Sinne genommen, nämlich so fern sie Gegenstände der Erfahrung sind, geht, eben dieselben aber nach der zweiten Bedeutung ihm nicht unterworfen sind, so wird eben derselbe Wille in der Erscheinung (den sichtbaren Handlungen) als dem Naturgesetze nothwendig gemäss und so fern nicht frei, und doch andererseits, als einem Dinge an sich selbst angehörig, jenem nicht unterworfen, mithin als frei gedacht, ohne dass hiebei ein Widerspruch vorgeht.' *Kritik der reinen Vernunft*, in *Kant's Werke*, vol. ii. p. 24. ' Und hier zeigt die zwar gemeine, aber betrügliche Voraussetzung der absoluten Realität der Erscheinungen sogleich ihren nachtheiligen Einfluss, die Vernunft zu verwirren. Denn sind Erscheinungen Dinge an sich selbst, so ist Freiheit nicht zu retten. Alsdann ist Natur die vollständige und an sich hinreichend bestimmende Ursache jeder Begebenheit, und die Bedingung derselben ist jederzeit nur in der Reihe der Erscheinungen enthalten, die sammt ihrer Wirkung unter dem Naturgesetze nothwendig sind. Wenn dagegen Erscheinungen für Nichts mehr gelten, als sie in der That sind, nämlich nicht für Dinge an sich, sondern blosse Vorstellungen, die nach empirischen Gesetzen zusammenhängen, so müssen sie selbst noch Gründe haben, die nicht Erscheinungen sind.' . . . . 'Hier habe ich nur die Anmerkung machen wollen, dass, da der durchgängige Zusammenhang aller Erscheinungen in einem Context der Natur ein unnachlässliches Gesetz ist, dieses alle Freiheit nothwendig umstürzen müsste, wenn man der Realität der Erscheinungen hartnäckig anhängen wollte. Daher auch diejenigen, welche hierin der gemeinen Meinung folgen, niemals dahin haben gelangen können, Natur und Freiheit mit einander zu vereinigen.' *Kritik*, in *Werke*, vol. ii. pp. 419, 420. Finally, at p. 433, 'Man muss wohl bemerken, dass wir hiedurch nicht die Wirklichkeit der Freiheit, als eines der Vermögen, welche die Ursache von den Erscheinungen unserer Sinnenwelt enthalten, haben darthun wollen. Denn ausser dass dieses gar keine transcendentale Betrachtung, die bloss mit Begriffen zu thun hat, gewesen sein würde, so könnte es auch nicht gelingen, indem wir aus der Erfahrung niemals auf Etwas, was gar nicht nach Erfahrungsgesetzen gedacht werden muss, schliessen können. Ferner haben wir auch gar nicht einmal die Möglichkeit der Freiheit beweisen wollen; denn dieses wäre auch nicht gelungen, weil wir überhaupt von keinem Realgrunde und keiner Causalität aus blossen Begriffen *a priori* die Möglichkeit erkennen können. Die Freiheit wird hier nur als transcendentale Idee behandelt, wodurch die Vernunft die Reihe der Bedingungen in der Erscheinung durch das sinnlich Unbedingte schlechthin aufzuheben denkt, dabei sich in eine Antinomie mit ihren eigenen Gesetzen, welche sie dem empirischen Gebrauche des Verstandes vorschreibt, verwickelt. Dass nun diese Antinomie auf einem blossen Scheine beruhe, und dass Natur der Causalität aus Freiheit wenigstens nicht widerstreite, das war das

Einzige, was wir leisten konnten, und woran es uns auch einzig und allein gelegen war.'

These passages prove that Kant saw that the phenomenal reality of Free Will is an indefensible doctrine: and as the present work is an investigation of the laws of phenomena, his transcendental philosophy does not affect my conclusions. According to Kant's view (and with which I am inclined to agree) the ordinary metaphysical and theological treatment of this dark problem is purely empirical, and therefore has no value. The denial of the supremacy of consciousness follows as a natural consequence, and is the result of the Kantian philosophy, and not, as is often said, the base of it.

CHAPTER II.

INFLUENCE EXERCISED BY PHYSICAL LAWS OVER THE ORGANIZATION OF SOCIETY AND OVER THE CHARACTER OF INDIVIDUALS.

If we inquire what those physical agents are by which the human race is most powerfully influenced, we shall find that they may be classed under four heads: namely, Climate, Food, Soil, and the General Aspect of Nature; by which last, I mean those appearances which, though presented chiefly to the sight, have, through the medium of that or other senses, directed the association of ideas, and hence in different countries have given rise to different habits of national thought. To one of these four classes, may be referred all the external phenomena by which Man has been permanently affected. The last of these classes, or what I call the General Aspect of Nature, produces its principal results by exciting the imagination, and by suggesting those innumerable superstitions which are the great obstacles to advancing knowledge. And as, in the infancy of a people, the power of such superstitions is supreme, it has happened that the various Aspects of Nature have caused corresponding varieties in the popular character, and have imparted to the national religion peculiarities which, under certain circumstances, it is impossible to efface. The other three agents, namely, Climate, Food, and Soil, have, so far as we are aware, had no direct influence of this sort; but they have, as I am about to prove, originated the most important consequences in regard to the general organization of society, and from them there have followed many of those large and conspicuous differences between nations, which are often ascribed to some fundamental difference in the various races into which mankind is divided. But while such original distinctions of race are altogether hypothetical,[1] the discrepancies which are caused by difference of climate, food, and soil, are capable of a satisfactory explanation, and, when understood, will be found to clear up many of the difficulties which still obscure the study of history. I purpose, therefore, in the first place, to examine the laws of these three vast agents in so far as they are connected with Man in his social condition; and having traced the working of those laws with as much precision as the present state of physical knowledge will allow, I shall then examine the remaining agent, namely, the General Aspect of Nature, and shall endeavour to point out the most important divergencies to which its variations have, in different countries, naturally given rise.

Beginning, then, with climate, food, and soil, it is evident that these three physical powers are in no small degree dependent on each other: that is to say, there is a very close connexion between the climate of a country and the food which will ordinarily be grown in that country; while at the same time the food is itself influenced by the soil which produces it, as also by the elevation or depression of the land, by the state of the atmosphere, and, in a word, by all those conditions to the assemblage of which the name of Physical Geography is, in its largest sense, commonly given.[2]

---

[1] I cordially subscribe to the remark of one of the greatest thinkers of our time, who says of the supposed differences of race, 'of all vulgar modes of escaping from the consideration of the effect of social and moral influences on the human mind, the most vulgar is that of attributing the diversities of conduct and character to inherent natural differences.' *Mill's Principles of Political Economy*, vol. i. p. 390. Ordinary writers are constantly falling into the error of assuming the existence of this difference, which may or may not exist but which most assuredly has never been proved. Some singular instances of this will be found in *Alison's History of Europe*, vol. ii. p. 336, vol. vi. p. 136. vol. viii. pp. 525, 526, vol. xiii. p. 347; where the historian thinks that by a few strokes of his pen he can settle a question of the greatest difficulty, connected with some of the most intricate problems in physiology. On the supposed relation between race and temperament, see *Comte, Philosophie Positive*, vol. iii. p.355.

[2] As to the proper limits of physical geography, see *Prichard*

The union between these physical agents being thus intimate, it seems advisable to consider them not under their own separate heads, but rather under the separate heads of the effects produced by their united action. In this way we shall rise at once to a more comprehensive view of the whole question; we shall avoid the confusion that would be caused by artificially separating phenomena which are in themselves inseparable; and we shall be able to see more clearly the extent of that remarkable influence, which, in an early stage of society, the powers of Nature exercise over the fortunes of Man.

Of all the results which are produced among a people by their climate, food, and soil, the accumulation of wealth is the earliest, and in many respects the most important. For although the progress of knowledge eventually accelerates the increase of wealth, it is nevertheless certain that, in the first formation of society, the wealth must accumulate before the knowledge can begin. As long as every man is engaged in collecting the materials necessary for his own subsistence, there will be neither leisure nor taste for higher pursuits; no science can possibly be created, and the utmost that can be effected will be an attempt to economise labour by the contrivance of such rude and imperfect instruments as even the most barbarous people are able to invent.

In a state of society like this, the accumulation of wealth is the first great step that can be taken, because without wealth there can be no leisure, and without leisure there can be no knowledge. If what a people consume is always exactly equal to what they possess, there will be no residue, and therefore, no capital being

---

on *Ethnology*, in *Report of the British Association for* 1847, p. 235. The word 'climate' I always use in the narrow and popular sense. Dr. Forry and many previous writers make it nearly coincide with 'physical geography:' 'Climate constitutes the aggregate of all the external physical circumstances appertaining to each locality in its relation to organic nature.' *Forry's Climate of the United States and its Endemic Influences*, New York, 1842, p. 127.

accumulated, there will be no means by which the
unemployed classes may be maintained.* But if the
produce is greater than the consumption, an overplus
arises, which, according to well-known principles, increases itself, and eventually becomes a fund out of
which, immediately or remotely, every one is supported
who does not create the wealth upon which he lives.
And now it is that the existence of an intellectual class
first becomes possible, because for the first time there
exists a previous accumulation, by means of which men
can use what they did not produce, and are thus enabled to devote themselves to subjects for which at an
earlier period the pressure of their daily wants would
have left them no time.

Thus it is that of all the great social improvements
the accumulation of wealth must be the first, because
without it there can be neither taste nor leisure for that
acquisition of knowledge on which, as I shall hereafter
prove, the progress of civilization depends. Now, it is
evident that among an entirely ignorant people, the
rapidity with which wealth is created will be solely
regulated by the physical peculiarities of their country.
At a later period, and when the wealth has been
capitalized, other causes come into play; but until this
occurs, the progress can only depend on two circumstances: first on the energy and regularity with which
labour is conducted, and secondly on the returns made
to that labour by the bounty of nature. And these two
causes are themselves the result of physical antecedents.
The returns made to labour are governed by the fertility of the soil, which is itself regulated partly by the
admixture of its chemical components, partly by the
extent to which, from rivers or from other natural
causes, the soil is irrigated, and partly by the heat and
humidity of the atmosphere. On the other hand, the
energy and regularity with which labour is conducted,

---

* By unemployed classes, I mean what Adam Smith calls the unproductive classes; and though both expressions are strictly speaking inaccurate, the word 'unemployed' seems to convey more clearly than any other the idea in the text.

will be entirely dependent on the influence of climate. This will display itself in two different ways. The first, which is a very obvious consideration, is, that if the heat is intense, men will be indisposed, and in some degree unfitted, for that active industry which in a milder climate they might willingly have exerted. The other consideration, which has been less noticed, but is equally important, is, that climate influences labour not only by enervating the labourer or by invigorating him, but also by the effect it produces on the regularity of his habits.* Thus we find that no people living in a very northern latitude have ever possessed that steady and unflinching industry for which the inhabitants of temperate regions are remarkable. The reason of this becomes clear, when we remember that in the more northern countries the severity of the weather, and, at some seasons, the deficiency of light, render it impossible for the people to continue their usual out-of-door employments. The result is, that the working classes being compelled to cease from their ordinary pursuits, are rendered more prone to desultory habits; the chain of their industry is as it were broken, and they lose that impetus which long-continued and uninterrupted practice never fails to give. Hence there arises a national character more fitful and capricious than that possessed by a people whose climate permits the regular exercise of their ordinary industry. Indeed, so powerful is this principle, that we may perceive its operation even under the most opposite circumstances. It would be difficult to conceive a greater difference in government, laws, religion, and manners, than that which distinguishes Sweden and Norway on the one hand, from Spain and Portugal on the other. But those four countries have one great point in common. In all of them, continued agricultural industry is impracticable. In the two southern countries, labour is

---

* This has been entirely neglected by the three most philosophical writers on climate: Montesquieu, Hume, and M. Charles Comte in his *Traité de Législation*. It is also omitted in the remarks of M. Guizot on the influence of climate, *Civilisation en Europe*, p. 97.

interrupted by the heat, by the dryness of the weather, and by the consequent state of the soil. In the two northern countries, the same effect is produced by the severity of the winter and the shortness of the days. The consequence is, that these four nations, though so different in other respects, are all remarkable for a certain instability and fickleness of character; presenting a striking contrast to the more regular and settled habits which are established in countries whose climate subjects the working classes to fewer interruptions, and imposes on them the necessity of a more constant and unremitting employment.[5]

These are the great physical causes by which the creation of wealth is governed. There are, no doubt, other circumstances which operate with considerable force, and which, in a more advanced state of society, possess an equal, and sometimes a superior, influence. But this is at a later period; and looking at the history of wealth in its earliest stage, it will be found to depend entirely on soil and climate: the soil regulating the returns made to any given amount of labour; the climate regulating the energy and constancy of the labour itself. It requires but a hasty glance at past events, to prove the immense power of these two great physical conditions. For there is no instance in history of any country being civilized by its own efforts, unless it has possessed one of these conditions in a very favourable form. In Asia, civilization has always been confined to that vast tract where a rich and alluvial soil has secured to man that wealth without some share of which no intellectual progress can begin. This great region extends, with a few interruptions, from the east of Southern China to the western coasts of Asia Minor, of Phœnicia, and of Palestine. To the north of this

---

[5] See the admirable remarks in *Laing's Denmark*, 1852, pp. 204, 366, 367; though Norway appears to be a better illustration than Denmark. In *Rey's Science Sociale*, vol. i. pp. 195, 196, there are some calculations respecting the average loss to agricultural industry caused by changes in the weather; but no notice is taken of the connexion between these changes, when abrupt, and the tone of the national character.

immense belt, there is a long line of barren country which has invariably been peopled by rude and wandering tribes, who are kept in poverty by the ungenial nature of the soil, and who, as long as they remained on it, have never emerged from their uncivilized state. How entirely this depends on physical causes, is evident from the fact that these same Mongolian and Tartarian hordes have, at different periods, founded great monarchies in China, in India, and in Persia, and have, on all such occasions, attained a civilization nowise inferior to that possessed by the most flourishing of the ancient kingdoms. For in the fertile plains of Southern Asia,[6] nature has supplied all the materials of wealth; and there it was that these barbarous tribes acquired for the first time some degree of refinement, produced a national literature, and organized a national polity; none of which things they, in their native land, had been able to effect.[7] In the same way, the Arabs in their own country have, owing to the extreme aridity of their soil,[8] always been a rude and uncultivated people; for in their case, as in all

[6] This expression has been used by different geographers in different senses; but I take it in its common acceptation, without reference to the more strictly physical view of Ritter and his followers in regard to Central Asia. See *Prichard's Physical History of Mankind*, vol. iv. p. 278, edit. 1844. At p. 92, Prichard makes the Himalaya the southern boundary of Central Asia.

[7] There is reason to believe that the Tartars of Thibet received even their alphabet from India. See the interesting Essay on Tartarian Coins in *Journal of Asiatic Society*, vol. iv. pp. 276, 277; and on the Scythian Alphabet, see vol. xii. p. 336.

[8] In *Somerville's Physical Geo-* graphy, vol. i. p. 132, it is said that in Arabia there are 'no rivers;' but Mr. Wallsted (*Travels in Arabia*, vol. ii. p. 409) mentions one which empties itself into the sea five miles west of Aden. On the streams in Arabia, see *Meiners über die Fruchtbarkeit der Länder*, vol. i. pp. 149, 150. That the sole deficiency is want of irrigation appears from Burckhardt, who says (*Travels in Arabia*, vol. i. p. 240), 'In Arabia, wherever the ground can be irrigated by wells, the sands may be soon made productive.' And for a striking description of one of the oases of Oman, which shows what Arabia might have been with a good river system, see *Journal of Geographical Society*, vol. vii. pp. 106, 107.

others, great ignorance is the fruit of great poverty. But in the seventh century they conquered Persia ;[9] in the eighth century they conquered the best part of Spain ;[10] in the ninth century they conquered the Punjaub, and eventually nearly the whole of India.[11] Scarcely were they established in their fresh settlements, when their character seemed to undergo a great change. They, who in their original land were little else than roving savages, were now for the first time able to accumulate wealth, and, therefore, for the first time did they make some progress in the arts of civilization. In Arabia they had been a mere race of wandering shepherds ;[12] in their new abodes they became the founders of mighty empires—they built cities, endowed schools,

---

[9] Mr. Morier (*Journal of Geog. Soc.* vol. vii. p. 230) says, 'the conquest of Persia by the Saracens A.D. 651.' However, the fate of Persia was decided by the battles of Kudseah and Nahavand, which were fought in 638 and 641: see *Malcolm's History of Persia*, vol. i. pp. xvi. 139, 142.

[10] In 712. *Hallam's Middle Ages*, vol. i. p. 369.

[11] They were established in the Punjaub early in the ninth century, but did not conquer Guzerat and Malwa until five hundred years later. Compare Wilson's note in the *Vishnu Purana*, pp. 481, 482, with *Asiatic Researches*, vol. ix. pp. 187, 188, 203. On their progress in the more southern part of the Peninsula, see *Journal of Asiatic Society*, vol. iii. pp. 222, 223, vol. iv. pp. 28–30.

[12] 'A race of pastoral barbarians.' *Dickinson on the Arabic Language*, in *Journal of Asiat. Society*, vol. v. p. 323. Compare *Reynier, Economie des Arabes*, pp. 27, 28 ; where, however, a very simple question is needlessly complicated. The old Persian writers bestowed on them the courteous appellation of 'a band of naked lizard-eaters.' *Malcolm's Hist. of Persia*, vol. i. p. 133. Indeed, there are few things in history better proved than the barbarism of a people whom some writers wish to invest with a romantic interest. The eulogy passed on them by Meiners is rather suspicious, for he concludes by saying, 'die Eroberungen der Araber waren höchst selten so blutig und zerstörend, als die Eroberungen der Tataren, Persen, Türken. u. s. w. in ältern und neuern Zeiten waren.' *Fruchtbarkeit der Länder*, vol. i. p. 153. If this is the best that can be said, the comparison with Tartars and Turks does not prove much ; but it is singular that this learned author should have forgotten a passage in Diodorus Siculus which gives a pleasant description of them nineteen centuries ago on the eastern side : *Bibliothec. Hist.* lib. ii. vol. ii. p. 137. Ἔχουσι

collected libraries; and the traces of their power are still to be seen at Cordova, at Bagdad, and at Delhi.[13] Precisely in the same manner, there is adjoining Arabia at the north, and only separated from it elsewhere by the narrow waters of the Red Sea, an immense sandy plain, which, covering the whole of Africa in the same latitude, extends westward until it reaches the shores of the Atlantic.[14] This enormous tract is, like Arabia,

---

δὲ βίον λῃστρικὸν, καὶ πολλὴν τῆς ὁμόρου χώρας κατατρέχοντες λῃστεύουσιν, &c.

[13] The only branch of knowledge which the Arabians ever raised to a science was astronomy, which began to be cultivated under the caliphs about the middle of the eighth century, and went on improving until 'la ville de Bagdad fut, pendant le dixième siècle, le théâtre principal de l'astronomie chez les orientaux.' *Montucla, Histoire des Mathématiques*, vol. i. pp. 355, 364. The old Pagan Arabs, like most barbarous people living in a clear atmosphere, had such an empirical acquaintance with the celestial phenomena as was used for practical purposes; but there is no evidence to justify the common opinion that they studied this subject as a science. Dr. Dorn (*Transactions of the Asiatic Society*, vol. ii. p. 371) says, ' of a scientific knowledge of astronomy among them no traces can be discovered.' Beausobre (*Histoire de Manichée*, vol. i. p. 20) is quite enthusiastic about the philosophy of the Arabs in the time of Pythagoras! and he tells us, that 'ces peuples ont toujours cultivé les sciences.' To establish this fact, he quotes a long passage from a life of Mohammed written early in the eighteenth century by Boulainvilliers, whom he calls, ' un des plus beaux génies de France.' If this is an accurate description, those who have read the works of Boulainvilliers will think that France was badly off for men of genius; and as to his life of Mohammed, it is little better than a romance: the author was ignorant of Arabic, and knew nothing which had not been already communicated by Maracci and Pococke. See *Biographie Universelle*, vol. v. p. 321.

In regard to the later Arabian astronomers, one of their great merits was to approximate to the value of the annual precession much closer than Ptolemy had done. See *Grant's History of Physical Astronomy*, 1852, p. 319.

[14] Indeed it goes beyond it: ' the trackless sands of the Sahara desert, which is even prolonged for miles into the Atlantic Ocean in the form of sandbanks.' *Somerville's Physical Geography*, vol. i. p. 149. For a singular instance of one of these sandbanks being formed into an island, see *Journal of Geograph. Society*, vol. ii. p. 284. The Sahara desert, exclusive of Bornou and Darfour, covers an area of 194,000 square leagues; that is, nearly three times the

a barren waste;[15] and therefore, as in Arabia, the inhabitants have always been entirely uncivilized, acquiring no knowledge, simply because they have accumulated no wealth.[16] But this great desert is, in its eastern part, irrigated by the waters of the Nile, the overflowing of which covers the sand with a rich alluvial deposit, that yields to labour the most abundant, and indeed the most extraordinary, returns.[17] The consequence is, that in that spot, wealth was

---

size of France, or twice the size of the Mediterranean. Compare Lyell's *Geology*, p. 694, with Somerville's *Connexion of the Sciences*, p. 294. As to the probable southern limits of the plateau of the Sahara, see *Richardson's Mission to Central Africa*, 1853, vol. ii. pp. 146, 156; and as to the part of it adjoining the Mandingo country, see *Mungo Park's Travels*, vol. i. pp. 237, 238. Respecting the country south of Mandara, some scanty information was collected by Denham in the neighbourhood of Lake Tchad. *Denham's Northern and Central Africa*, pp. 121, 122, 144-146.

[15] Richardson, who travelled through it south of Tripoli, notices its 'features of sterility, of unconquerable barrenness.' *Richardson's Sahara*, 1848, vol. i. p. 86; and see the striking picture at p. 409. The long and dreary route from Mourzouk to Yeou, on Lake Tchad, is described by Denham, one of the extremely few Europeans who have performed that hazardous journey. *Denham's Central Africa*, pp. 2-60. Even on the shore of the Tchad there is hardly any vegetation, 'a coarse grass and a small bell-flower being the only plants that I could discover,' p. 90. Compare his remark on Bornou, p. 317. The condition of part of the desert in the fourteenth century is described in the *Travels of Ibn Batuta*, p. 233, which should be compared with the account given by Diodorus Siculus of the journey of Alexander to the temple of Ammon. *Bibliothec. Historic.* lib. xvii. vol. vii. p. 348.

[16] Richardson, who travelled in 1850 from Tripoli to within a few days of Lake Tchad, was struck by the stationary character of the people. He says, 'neither in the desert nor in the kingdoms of Central Africa is there any march of civilization. All goes on according to a certain routine established for ages past.' *Mission to Central Africa*, vol. i. pp. 304, 305. See similar remarks in *Pallme's Travels in Kordofan*, pp. 108, 109.

[17] Abd-Allatif, who was in Egypt early in the thirteenth century, gives an interesting account of the rising of the Nile, to which Egypt owes its fertility. *Abd-Allatif, Relation de l'Égypte*, pp. 329-340, 374-376, and Appendix, p. 504. See also on these periodical inundations. *Wilkinson's Ancient Egyptians*, vol. iv. pp. 101-104; and on the

rapidly accumulated, the cultivation of knowledge quickly followed, and this narrow strip of land[18] became the seat of Egyptian civilization; a civilization which, though grossly exaggerated,[19] forms a striking contrast to the barbarism of the other nations of Africa, none of which have been able to work out their own progress, or emerge, in any degree, from the ignorance to which the penury of nature has doomed them.

---

half-astronomical half theological notions connected with them, pp. 372-377, vol. v. pp. 291, 292. Compare on the religious importance of the Nile *Bunsen's Egypt*, vol. i. p. 409. The expression, therefore, of Herodotus (book ii. chap. v. vol. i. p. 484), ὕπερ τοῦ ποταμοῦ is true in a much larger sense than he intended; since to the Nile Egypt owes all the physical peculiarities which distinguish it from Arabia and the great African desert. Compare *Heeren's African Nations*, vol. ii. p. 68; *Reynier, Economie des Arabes*, p. 3; *Postan's on the Nile and Indus*, in *Journal of Asiatic Society*, vol. vii. p. 275; and on the difference between the soil of the Nile and that of the surrounding desert, see *Volney, Voyage en Syrie et en Egypte*, vol. i. p. 14.

[18] 'The average breadth of the valley from one mountain-range to the other, between Cairo in Lower, and Edfoo in Upper Egypt, is only about seven miles; and that of the cultivable land, whose limits depend on the inundation, scarcely exceeds five and a half.' *Wilkinson's Ancient Egyptians*, vol. i. p. 216. According to Gerard, ' the mean width of the valley between Syene and Cairo is about nine miles.' Note in *Heeren's African Nations*, vol. ii. p. 62.

[19] I will give one instance of this from an otherwise sensible writer, and a man too of considerable learning: 'As to the physical knowledge of the Egyptians, their cotemporaries gave them credit for the astonishing power of their magic; and as we cannot suppose that the instances recorded in Scripture were to be attributed to the exertion of supernatural powers, we must conclude that they were in possession of a more intimate knowledge of the laws and combinations of nature than what is professed by the most learned men of the present age.' *Hamilton's Egyptiaca*, pp. 61, 62. It is a shame that such nonsense should be written in the nineteenth century: and yet a still more recent author (*Vyse on the Pyramids*, vol. i. p. 28) assures us that ' the Egyptians, for especial purposes, were endowed with great wisdom and science.' Science properly so called, the Egyptians had none; and as to their wisdom, it was considerable enough to distinguish them from barbarous nations like the old Hebrews, but it was inferior to that of the Greeks, and it was of course immeasurably below that of modern Europe.

These considerations clearly prove that of the two primary causes of civilization, the fertility of the soil is the one which in the ancient world exercised most influence. But in European civilization, the other great cause, that is to say, climate, has been the most powerful; and this, as we have seen, produces an effect partly on the capacity of the labourer for work, partly on the regularity or irregularity of his habits. The difference in the result has curiously corresponded with the difference in the cause. For, although all civilization must have for its antecedent the accumulation of wealth, still what subsequently occurs will be in no small degree determined by the conditions under which the accumulation took place. In Asia, and in Africa, the condition was a fertile soil, causing an abundant return; in Europe, it was a happier climate, causing more successful labour. In the former case, the effect depends on the relation between the soil and its produce; in other words, the mere operation of one part of external nature upon another. In the latter case, the effect depends on the relation between the climate and the labourer; that is, the operation of external nature not upon itself, but upon man. Of these two classes of relations, the first, being the less complicated, is the less liable to disturbance, and therefore came sooner into play. Hence it is, that, in the march of civilization, the priority is unquestionably due to the most fertile parts of Asia and Africa. But although their civilization was the earliest, it was very far, indeed, from being the best or most permanent. Owing to circumstances which I shall presently state, the only progress which is really effective depends, not upon the bounty of nature, but upon the energy of man. Therefore it is, that the civilization of Europe, which, in its earliest stage, was governed by climate, has shown a capacity of development unknown to those civilizations which were originated by soil. For the powers of nature, notwithstanding their apparent magnitude, are limited and stationary; at all events, we have not the slightest proof that they have ever increased, or that they will ever be able to increase. But the powers of man, so far as experience and analogy can guide us, are unlimited; nor are we possessed of any evidence which authorizes us to assign even an imaginary boundary at which the human intellect will, of necessity, be brought to a stand. And as this power which the mind possesses of increasing its own resources, is a peculiarity confined to man, and one eminently distinguishing him from what is commonly called external nature, it becomes evident that the agency of climate, which gives him wealth by stimulating his labour, is more favourable to his ultimate progress than the agency of soil, which likewise gives him wealth, but which does so, not by exciting his energies, but by virtue of a mere physical relation between the character of the soil and the quantity or value of the produce that it almost spontaneously affords.

Thus far as to the different ways in which climate and soil affect the creation of wealth. But another point of equal, or perhaps of superior, importance remains behind. After the wealth has been created, a question arises as to how it is to be distributed; that is to say, what proportion is to go to the upper classes, and what to the lower. In an advanced stage of society, this depends upon several circumstances of great complexity, and which it is not necessary here to examine.[20] But in a very early stage of society, and

---

[20] Indeed many of them are still unknown; for, as M. Rey justly observes, most writers pay too exclusive an attention to the production of wealth, and neglect the laws of its distribution. *Rey, Science Sociale*, vol. iii. p. 271. In confirmation of this, I may mention the theory of rent, which was only discovered about half a century ago, and which is connected with so many subtle arguments that it is not yet generally adopted; and even some of its advocates have shown themselves unequal to defending their own cause. The great law of the ratio between the cost of labour and the profits of stock, is the highest generalization we have reached respecting the distribution of wealth; but it cannot be consistently admitted by any one who holds that rent enters into price.

before its later and refined complications have begun, it may, I think, be proved that the distribution of wealth is, like its creation, governed entirely by physical laws; and that those laws are moreover so active as to have invariably kept a vast majority of the inhabitants of the fairest portion of the globe in a condition of constant and inextricable poverty. If this can be demonstrated, the immense importance of such laws is manifest. For since wealth is an undoubted source of power, it is evident that, supposing other things equal, an inquiry into the distribution of wealth is an inquiry into the distribution of power, and, as such, will throw great light on the origin of those social and political inequalities, the play and opposition of which form a considerable part of the history of every civilized country.

If we take a general view of this subject, we may say that after the creation and accumulation of wealth have once fairly begun, it will be distributed among two classes, those who labour, and those who do not labour; the latter being, as a class, the more able, the former the more numerous. The fund by which both classes are supported is immediately created by the lower class, whose physical energies are directed, combined, and as it were economized, by the superior skill of the upper class. The reward of the workmen is called their wages; the reward of the contrivers is called their profits. At a later period, there will arise what may be called the saving class; that is, a body of men who neither contrive nor work, but lend their accumulations to those who contrive, and in return for the loan, receive a part of that reward which belongs to the contriving class. In this case, the members of the saving class are rewarded for their abstinence in refraining from spending their accumulations, and this reward is termed the interest of their money; so that there is made a threefold division—Interest, Profits, and Wages. But this is a subsequent arrangement, which can only take place to any extent when wealth has been considerably accumulated; and in the stage of society we are now considering, this third, or saving

class, can hardly be said to have a separate existence."¹
For our present purpose, therefore, it is enough to
ascertain what those natural laws are, which, as soon as
wealth is accumulated, regulate the proportion in
which it is distributed to the two classes of labourers
and employers.

Now, it is evident that wages being the price paid
for labour, the rate of wages must, like the price of all
other commodities, vary according to the changes in
the market. If the supply of labourers outstrips the
demand, wages will fall; if the demand exceeds the
supply, they will rise. Supposing, therefore, that in
any country there is a given amount of wealth to be
divided between employers and workmen, every increase
in the number of the workmen will tend to lessen the
average reward each can receive. And if we set aside
those disturbing causes by which all general views are
affected, it will be found that, in the long-run, the
question of wages is a question of population; for
although the total sum of the wages actually paid
depends upon the largeness of the fund from which
they are drawn, still the amount of wages received by
each man must diminish as the claimants increase,
unless, owing to other circumstances, the fund itself
should so advance as to keep pace with the greater
demands made upon it."²

---

⁸¹ In a still more advanced stage, there is a fourth division of wealth, and part of the produce of labour is absorbed by rent. This, however, is not an element of price, but a consequence of it; and in the ordinary march of affairs, considerable time must elapse before it can begin. Rent, in the proper sense of the word, is the price paid for using the natural and indestructible powers of the soil, and must not be confused with rent commonly so called; for this last also includes the profits of stock. I notice this, because several of the opponents of Ricardo have placed the beginning of rent too early, by overlooking the fact that apparent rent is very often profits disguised.

⁸² ' Wages depend, then, on the proportion between the number of the labouring population, and the capital or other funds devoted to the purchase of labour; we will say, for shortness, the capital. If wages are higher at one time or place than at another, if the subsistence and comfort of the class of hired labourers are more ample, it is, and can be, for no other reason than because

To know the circumstances most favourable to the increase of what may be termed the wages-fund is a matter of great moment, but is one with which we are not immediately concerned. The question we have now before us, regards not the accumulation of wealth, but its distribution; and the object is, to ascertain what those physical conditions are, which, by encouraging a rapid growth of population, over-supply the labour market, and thus keep the average rate of wages at a very low point.

Of all the physical agents by which the increase of the labouring classes is affected, that of food is the most active and universal. If two countries, equal in all other respects, differ solely in this—that in one the national food is cheap and abundant, and in the other scarce and dear, the population of the former country will inevitably increase more rapidly than the population of the latter.[83] And, by a parity of reasoning, the average rate of wages will be lower in the former than in the latter, simply because the labour-market will be more amply stocked.[24] An inquiry, therefore,

---

capital bears a greater proportion to population. It is not the absolute amount of accumulation or of production that is of importance to the labouring class; it is not the amount even of the funds destined for distribution among the labourers; it is the proportion between those funds and the numbers among whom they are shared. The condition of the class can be bettered in no other way than by altering that proportion to their advantage; and every scheme for their benefit which does not proceed on this as its foundation, is, for all permanent purposes, a delusion.' *Mill's Principles of Political Economy*, 1849, vol. i. p. 425. See also vol. ii. pp. 264, 265, and *M'Culloch's Political Economy*, pp. 379, 380. Ricardo, in his *Essay on the Influence of a Low Price of Corn*, has stated, with his usual terseness, the three possible forms of this question: 'The rise or fall of wages is common to all states of society, whether it be the stationary, the advancing, or the retrograde state. In the stationary state, it is regulated wholly by the increase or falling-off of the population. In the advancing state, it depends on whether the capital or the population advance at the more rapid course. In the retrograde state, it depends on whether population or capital decrease with the greater rapidity. *Ricardo's Works*, p. 379.

[23] The standard of comfort being of course supposed the same.

[24] 'No point is better established, than that the supply of

into the physical laws on which the food of different countries depends, is, for our present purpose, of the greatest importance; and fortunately it is one respecting which we are able, in the present state of chemistry and physiology, to arrive at some precise and definite conclusions.

The food consumed by man produces two, and only two, effects necessary to his existence. These are, first to supply him with that animal heat without which the functions of life would stop; and secondly, to repair the waste constantly taking place in his tissues, that is, in the mechanism of his frame. For each of these separate purposes there is a separate food. The temperature of our body is kept up by substances which contain no nitrogen, and are called non-azotized; the incessant decay in our organism is repaired by what are known as azotized substances, in which nitrogen is always found.[25] In the former case, the carbon of non-azotized food combines with the oxygen we take in, and gives rise to that internal combustion by which our animal heat is renewed. In the latter case, nitrogen having little affinity for oxygen,[26] the nitrogenous or

---

labourers will always ultimately be in proportion to the means of supporting them.' *Principles of Political Economy*, chap. xxi. in *Ricardo's Works*, p. 176. Compare *Smith's Wealth of Nations*, book i. chap. xi. p. 86, and *M'Culloch's Political Economy*, p. 222.

[25] The division of food into azotized and non-azotized is said to have been first pointed out by Magendie. See *Müller's Physiology*, vol. i. p. 525. It is now recognised by most of the best authorities. See, for instance, *Liebig's Animal Chemistry*, p. 134; *Carpenter's Human Physiology*, p. 685; *Brande's Chemistry*, vol. ii. pp. 1218, 1870. The first tables of food constructed according to it were by Boussingault; see an elaborate essay by Messrs. Lawes and Gilbert on *The Composition of Foods*, in *Report of British Association for 1852*, p. 323: but the experiments made by these gentlemen are neither numerous nor diversified enough to establish a general law; still less can we accept their singular assertion, p. 346, that the comparative prices of different foods are a test of the nutriment they comparatively contain.

[26] 'Of all the elements of the animal body, nitrogen has the feeblest attraction for oxygen; and, what is still more remarkable, it deprives all combustible elements with which it combines,

azotized food is, as it were, guarded against combustion;[27] and being thus preserved, is able to perform its duty of repairing the tissues, and supplying those losses which the human organism constantly suffers in the wear and tear of daily life.

These are the two great divisions of food;[28] and if we inquire into the laws which regulate the relation they bear to man, we shall find that in each division the most important agent is climate. When men live in a hot country, their animal heat is more easily kept up than when they live in a cold one; therefore they require a smaller amount of that non-azotized food, the sole business of which is to maintain at a certain point the temperature of the body. In the same way, they, in the hot country, require a smaller amount of azotized food, because on the whole their bodily exertions are less frequent, and on that account the decay of their tissues is less rapid.[29]

---

to a greater or less extent, of the power of combining with oxygen, that is, of undergoing combustion.' *Liebig's Letters on Chemistry*, p. 372.

[27] The doctrine of what may be called the protecting power of some substances is still imperfectly understood, and until late in the eighteenth century, its existence was hardly suspected. It is now known to be connected with the general theory of poisons. See *Turner's Chemistry*, vol. i. p. 516. To this we must probably ascribe the fact that several poisons which are fatal when applied to a wounded surface, may be taken into the stomach with impunity. *Brodie's Physiological Researches*, 1851, pp. 137, 138. It seems more reasonable to refer this to chemical laws than to hold, with Sir Benjamin Brodie, that some poisons 'destroy life by paralysing the muscles of respiration without immediately affecting the action of the heart.'

[28] Prout's well-known division into saccharine, oily, and albuminous, appears to me of much inferior value, though I observe that it is adopted in the last edition of *Elliotson's Human Physiology*, pp. 65, 160. The division by M. Lepelletier into 'les alimens solides et les boissons' is of course purely empirical. *Lepelletier, Physiologie Médicale*, vol. ii. p. 100, Paris, 1832. In regard to Prout's classification, compare *Burdach's Traité de Physiologie*, vol. ix. p. 240, with *Wagner's Physiology*, p. 452.

[29] The evidence of an universal connexion in the animal frame between exertion and decay, is now almost complete. In regard to the muscular system, see *Carpenter's Human*

Since, therefore, the inhabitants of hot climates do, in their natural and ordinary state, consume less food than the inhabitants of cold ones, it inevitably follows that, provided other things remain equal, the growth of population will be more rapid in countries which are hot than in those which are cold. For practical purposes, it is immaterial whether the greater plenty of a substance by which the people are fed arises from a larger supply, or whether it arises from a smaller consumption. When men eat less, the result will be just the same as if they had more; because the same amount of nutriment will go further, and thus population will gain a power of increasing more quickly than it could do in a colder country, where, even if provisions were equally abundant, they, owing to the climate, would be sooner exhausted.

This is the first point of view in which the laws of climate are, through the medium of food, connected with the laws of population, and therefore with the laws of the distribution of wealth. But there is also another point of view, which follows the same line of thought, and will be found to strengthen the argument just stated. This is, that in cold countries, not only are men compelled to eat more than in hot ones, but

---

Physiology, pp. 440, 441, 581, edit. 1846: 'there is strong reason to believe the waste or decomposition of the muscular tissue to be in exact proportion to the degree in which it is exerted.' This perhaps would be generally anticipated even in the absence of direct proof; but what is more interesting, is that the same principle holds good of the nervous system. The human brain of an adult contains about one and a half per cent. of phosphorus; and it has been ascertained, that after the mind has been much exercised, phosphates are excreted, and that in the case of inflammation of the brain their excretion (by the kidneys) is very considerable. See Paget's Lectures on Surgical Pathology, 1853, vol. i: pp. 6, 7, 434; Carpenter's Human Physiology, pp. 192, 193, 222; Simon's Animal Chemistry, vol. ii. p. 426; Henle, Anatomie Générale, vol. ii. p. 172. The reader may also consult respecting the phosphorus of the brain the recent very able work of MM. Robin et Verdeil, Chimie Anatomique, vol. i. p. 215, vol. ii. p. 348, Paris, 1853. According to these writers (vol. iii. p. 445), its existence in the brain was first announced by Hensing, in 1779.

their food is dearer, that is to say, to get it is more difficult, and requires a greater expenditure of labour. The reason of this I will state as briefly as possible, without entering into any details beyond those which are absolutely necessary for a right understanding of this interesting subject.

The objects of food are, as we have seen, only two: namely, to keep up the warmth of the body, and repair the waste in the tissues.[30] Of these two objects, the former is effected by the oxygen of the air entering our lungs, and, as it travels through the system, combining with the carbon which we take in our food.[31] This

---

[30] Though both objects are equally essential, the former is usually the more pressing; and it has been ascertained by experiment, what we should expect from theory, that when animals are starved to death, there is a progressive decline in the temperature of their bodies; so that the proximate cause of death by starvation is not weakness, but cold. See *Williams's Principles of Medicine*, p. 36; and on the connexion between the loss of animal heat and the appearance of *rigor mortis* in the contractile parts of the body, see *Vogel's Pathological Anatomy of the Human Body*, p. 532. Compare the important and thoughtful work of Burdach, *Physiologie comme Science d'Observation*, vol. v. pp. 144, 436, vol. ix. p. 231.

[31] Until the last twenty or five-and-twenty years, it used to be supposed that this combination took place in the lungs; but more careful experiments have made it probable that the oxygen unites with the carbon in the circulation, and that the blood-corpuscules are the carriers of the oxygen. Compare *Liebig's Animal Chemistry*, p. 78; *Letters on Chemistry*, pp. 335, 336; *Turner's Chemistry*, vol. ii. p. 1319; *Müller's Physiology*, vol. i. pp. 92, 159. That the combination does not take place in the air-cells is moreover proved by the fact that the lungs are not hotter than other parts of the body. See *Müller*, vol. i. p. 348; *Thomson's Animal Chemistry*, p. 633; and *Brodie's Physiol. Researches*, p. 33. Another argument in favour of the red corpuscules being the carriers of oxygen, is that they are most abundant in those classes of the vertebrata which maintain the highest temperature; while the blood of invertebrata contains very few of them; and it has been doubted if they even exist in the lower articulata and mollusca. See *Carpenter's Human Physiol.* pp. 109, 532; *Grant's Comparative Anatomy*, p. 472; *Elliotson's Human Physiol.* p. 159. In regard to the different dimensions of corpuscules, see *Henle, Anatomie Générale*, vol. i. pp. 457-467, 494, 495; *Blainville, Physiologie Comparée*, vol. i. pp. 298, 299, 301-304; *Milne Edwards, Zoologie*,

combination of oxygen and carbon never can occur without producing a considerable amount of heat, and it is in this way that the human frame is maintained at its necessary temperature.[21] By virtue of a law familiar to chemists, carbon and oxygen, like all other elements, will only unite in certain definite proportions;[22] so that to keep up a healthy balance, it is

---

part i. pp. 54-56; *Fourth Report of British Association*, pp. 117, 118; *Simon's Animal Chemistry*, vol. i. pp. 103, 104; and, above all, the important observations of Mr. Gulliver (*Carpenter*, pp. 105, 106). These additions to our knowledge, besides being connected with the laws of animal heat and of nutrition, will, when generalized, assist speculative minds in raising pathology to a science. In the mean time I may mention the relation between an examination of the corpuscules and the theory of inflammation which Hunter and Broussais were unable to settle: this is, that the proximate cause of inflammation is the obstruction of the vessels by the adhesion of the pale corpuscules. Respecting this striking generalization, which is still on its trial, compare *Williams's Principles of Medicine*, 1848, pp. 258-265, with *Paget's Surgical Pathology*, 1853, vol. i. pp. 313-317; *Jones and Sieveking's Pathological Anatomy*, 1854, pp. 28, 105, 106. The difficulties connected with the scientific study of inflammation are evaded in *Vogel's Pathological Anatomy*, p. 418; a work which appears to me to have been greatly overrated.

[21] On the amount of heat disengaged by the union of carbon and oxygen, see the experiments of Dulong, in *Liebig's Animal Chemistry*, p. 44; and those of Despretz, in *Thomson's Animal Chemistry*, p. 634. Just in the same way, we find that the temperature of plants is maintained by the combination of oxygen with carbon: see *Balfour's Botany*, pp. 231, 232, 322, 323. As to the amount of heat caused generally by chemical combination, there is an essay well worth reading by Dr. Thomas Andrews in *Report of British Association for* 1849, pp. 63-78. See also *Report for* 1852, *Transac. of Sec.* p. 40, and *Liebig and Kopp's Reports on the Progress of Chemistry*, vol. i. p. 34, vol. iii. p. 16, vol. iv. p. 20; also *Pouillet, Élémens de Physique*, Paris, 1832, vol. i. part i. p. 411.

[22] The law of definite proportions, which, since the brilliant discoveries by Dalton, is the corner-stone of chemical knowledge, is laid down with admirable clearness in *Turner's Elements of Chemistry*, vol. i. pp. 146-151. Compare *Brande's Chemistry*, vol. i. pp. 139-144; *Cuvier, Progrès des Sciences*, vol. ii. p. 255; *Somerville's Connexion of the Sciences*, pp. 120, 121. But none of these writers have considered the law so philosophically as M. A. Comte, *Philosophie Positive*, vol. iii. pp. 133-176, one of the best chapters in his very profound, but ill-understood work.

needful that the food which contains the carbon should vary according to the amount of oxygen taken in: while it is equally needful that we should increase the quantity of both of these constituents whenever a greater external cold lowers the temperature of the body. Now it is obvious that in a very cold climate, this necessity of providing a nutriment more highly carbonized will arise in two distinct ways. In the first place, the air being denser, men imbibe at each inspiration a greater volume of oxygen than they would do in a climate where the air is rarefied by heat.[34] In the second place, cold accelerates their respiration, and thus obliging them to inhale more frequently than the inhabitants of hot countries, increases the amount of oxygen which they on an average take in.[35] On both these

---

[34] 'Ainsi, dans des temps égaux, la quantité d'oxygène consommée par le même animal est d'autant plus grande que la température ambiante est moins élevée.' *Robin et Verdeil, Chimie Anatomique*, vol. ii. p. 44. Compare *Simon's Lectures on Pathology*, 1850, p. 188, for the diminished quantity of respiration in a high temperature; though one may question Mr. Simon's inference that *therefore* the blood is more venous in hot countries than in cold ones. This is not making allowance for the difference of diet, which corrects the difference of temperature.

[35] 'The consumption of oxygen in a given time may be expressed by the number of respirations.' *Liebig's Letters on Chemistry*, p. 314; and see *Thomson's Animal Chemistry*, p. 611. It is also certain that exercise increases the number of respirations; and birds, which are the most active of all animals, consume more oxygen than any others. *Milne Edwards, Zoologie*, part i. p. 88, part ii. p. 371; *Flourens, Travaux de Cuvier*, pp. 153, 154, 265, 266. Compare, on the connexion between respiration and the locomotive organs, *Beclard, Anatomie Générale*, pp. 39, 44; *Burdach, Traité de Physiologie*, vol. ix. pp. 485, 556-559; *Carus' Comparative Anatomy*, vol. i. pp. 99, 164, 358, vol. ii. pp. 142, 160; *Grant's Comparative Anatomy*, pp. 455, 495, 522, 529, 537; *Rymer Jones's Animal Kingdom*, pp. 369, 440, 692, 714, 720; *Owen's Invertebrata*, pp. 322, 345, 366, 505. Thus too it has been experimentally ascertained, that in human beings exercise increases the amount of carbonic-acid gas. *Mayo's Human Physiology*, p. 64; *Liebig and Kopp's Reports*, vol. iii. p. 359.

If we now put these facts together, their bearing on the propositions in the text will become evident; because, on the whole, there is more exercise taken in cold climates than in hot ones, and there must therefore be an increased respiratory action.

grounds the consumption of oxygen becomes greater: it is therefore requisite that the consumption of carbon should also be greater; since by the union of these two elements in certain definite proportions, the temperature of the body and the balance of the human frame can alone be maintained.[36]

Proceeding from these chemical and physiological principles, we arrive at the conclusion, that the colder the country is in which a people live, the more highly carbonized will be their food. And this, which is a purely scientific inference, has been verified by actual experiment. The inhabitants of the polar regions consume large quantities of whale-oil and blubber; while within the tropics such food would soon put an end to life, and therefore the ordinary diet consists almost entirely of fruit, rice, and other vegetables. Now it has been ascertained by careful analysis, that in the polar food there is an excess of carbon; in the tropical food an excess of oxygen. Without entering into details, which to the majority of readers would be distasteful, it may be said generally, that the oils contain about six times as much carbon as the fruits, and that they have in them very little oxygen;[37] while starch,

---

For proof that greater exercise is both taken and required, compare *Wrangel's Polar Expedition*, pp. 79, 102; *Richardson's Arctic Expedition*, vol. i. p. 365; *Simpson's North Coast of America*, pp. 49, 88, which should be contrasted with the contempt for such amusements in hot countries. Indeed, in polar regions all this is so essential to preserve a normal state, that scurvy can only be kept off in the northern part of the American continent by taking considerable exercise: see *Cranz, History of Greenland*, vol. i. pp. 46, 62, 338.

[36] See the note at the end of this chapter.

[37] 'The fruits used by the inhabitants of southern climes do not contain, in a fresh state, more than 12 per cent. of carbon; while the blubber and train-oil which feed the inhabitants of polar regions contain 66 to 80 per cent. of that element.' *Liebig's Letters on Chemistry*, p. 320; see also p. 375, and *Turner's Chemistry*, vol. ii. p. 1315. According to Prout (*Mayo's Human Physiol.* p. 136), 'the proportion of carbon in oily bodies varies from about 60 to 80 per cent.' The quantity of oil and fat habitually consumed in cold countries is remarkable. Wrangel (*Polar Expedition*, p. 21) says of the tribes in the north-east of Siberia, 'fat is their greatest delicacy.

which is the most universal, and, in reference to nutrition, the most important constituent in the vegetable world,[38] is nearly half oxygen.[39]

The connexion between this circumstance and the subject before us is highly curious: for it is a most remarkable fact, and one to which I would call particular attention, that owing to some more general law, of which we are ignorant, highly carbonized food is more costly than food in which comparatively little carbon is found. The fruits of the earth, of which oxygen is the most active principle, are very abundant; they may be obtained without danger, and almost without trouble. But that highly carbonized food, which in a very cold climate is absolutely necessary to life, is not produced in so facile and spontaneous a manner. It is not, like vegetables, thrown up by the soil; but it consists of the fat, the blubber, and the oil[40] of powerful and ferocious animals. To procure it, man must incur great risk and expend great labour. And although this is undoubtedly a contrast of extreme cases, still it is evident that the nearer a people approach

---

They eat it in every possible shape; raw, melted, fresh, or spoilt.' See also *Simpson's Discoveries on the North Coast of America*, pp. 147, 404.

[38] 'So common, that no plant is destitute of it.' *Lindley's Botany*, vol. i. p. 111; and at p. 121, 'starch is the most common of all vegetable productions.' Dr. Lindley adds (vol. i. p. 292), that it is difficult to distinguish the grains of starch secreted by plants from cytoblasts. See also on the starch-granules, first noticed by M. Link, *Reports on Botany by the Ray Society*, pp. 223, 370; and respecting its predominance in the vegetable world, compare *Thomson's Chemistry of Vegetables*, pp. 650-652, 875; *Brande's Chemistry*, vol. ii. p. 1160; *Turner's Chemistry*, vol. ii. p. 1236; *Liebig and Kopp's Reports*, vol. ii. pp. 97, 98, 122.

[39] The oxygen is 49·39 out of 100. See the table in *Liebig's Letters on Chemistry*, p. 379. Amidin, which is the soluble part of starch, contains 53·33 per cent. of oxygen. See *Thomson's Chemistry of Vegetables*, p. 654, on the authority of Prout, who has the reputation of being an accurate experimenter.

[40] Of which a single whale will yield 'cent vingt tonneaux.' *Cuvier, Règne Animal*, vol. i. p. 297. In regard to the solid food, Sir J. Richardson (*Arctic Expedition*, 1851, vol. i. p. 243) says that the inhabitants of the Arctic regions only maintain themselves by chasing whales and 'consuming blubber.'

to either extremity, the more subject will they be to the conditions by which that extremity is governed. It is evident that, as a general rule, the colder a country is, the more its food will be carbonized; the warmer it is, the more its food will be oxidized.[41] At the same time, carbonized food, being chiefly drawn from the animal world, is more difficult to obtain than oxidized food, which is drawn from the vegetable world.[42] The result has been that among nations where the coldness of the climate renders a highly carbonized diet essential, there is for the most part displayed, even in the infancy of society, a bolder and more adventurous character, than we find among those other nations whose ordinary nutriment, being highly oxidized, is easily obtained, and indeed is supplied to them, by the bounty of nature, gratuitously and without a struggle.[43] From this

---

[41] It is said, that to keep a person in health, his food, even in the temperate parts of Europe, should contain 'a full eighth more carbon in winter than in summer.' *Liebig's Animal Chemistry*, p. 16.

[42] The most highly carbonized of all foods are undoubtedly yielded by animals; the most highly oxidized by vegetables. In the vegetable kingdom there is, however, so much carbon, that its predominance, accompanied with the rarity of nitrogen, has induced chemical botanists to characterize plants as carbonized, and animals as azotized. But we have here to attend to a double antithesis. Vegetables are carbonized in so far as they are non-azotized; but they are oxidized in opposition to the highly carbonized animal food of cold countries. Besides this, it is important to observe that the carbon of vegetables is most abundant in the woody and un-nutritious part, which is not eaten; while the carbon of animals is found in the fatty and oily parts, which are not only eaten, but are, in cold countries, greedily devoured.

[43] Sir J. Malcolm (*History of Persia*, vol. ii. p. 380), speaking of the cheapness of vegetables in the East, says, 'in some parts of Persia fruit has hardly any value.' Cuvier, in a striking passage (*Règne Animal*, vol. i. pp. 73, 74), has contrasted vegetable with animal food, and thinks that the former, being so easily obtained, is the more natural. But the truth is that both are equally natural: though when Cuvier wrote scarcely anything was known of the laws which govern the relation between climate and food. On the skill and energy required to obtain food in cold countries, see *Wrangel's Polar Expedition*, pp. 70, 71, 191, 192; *Simpson's Discoveries on the North Coast of America*,

original divergence there follow many other consequences, which, however, I am not now concerned to trace; my present object being merely to point out how this difference of food affects the proportion in which wealth is distributed to the different classes.

The way in which this proportion is actually altered has, I hope, been made clear by the preceding argument; but it may be useful to recapitulate the facts on which the argument is based. The facts, then, are simply these. The rate of wages fluctuates with the population; increasing when the labour-market is under-supplied, diminishing when it is over-supplied. The population itself, though affected by many other circumstances, does undoubtedly fluctuate with the supply of food; advancing when the supply is plentiful, halting or receding when the supply is scanty. The food essential to life is scarcer in cold countries than in hot ones; and not only is it scarcer, but more of it is required;[44] so that on both grounds smaller encouragement is given to the growth of that population from whose ranks the labour-market is stocked. To express, therefore, the conclusion in its simplest form, we may say, that there is a strong and constant tendency in hot countries for wages to be low, in cold countries for them to be high.

---

p. 249; *Crantz, History of Greenland*, vol. i. pp. 22, 32, 105, 131, 154, 155, vol. ii. pp. 203, 265, 324.

[44] 'Cabanis (*Rapports du Physique et du Moral*, p. 313) says, 'Dans les temps et dans les pays froids on mange et l'on agit davantage.' That much food is eaten in cold countries, and little in hot ones, is mentioned by numerous travellers, none of whom are aware of the cause. See *Simpson's Discov. on North Coast of America*, p. 218; *Custine's Russie*, vol. iv. p. 66; *Wrangel's Expedition*, pp. 21, 327; *Crantz, History of Greenland*, vol. i. pp. 145, 360; *Richardson's Central Africa*, vol. ii. p. 46; *Richardson's Sahara*, vol. i. p. 137; *Denham's Africa*, p. 37; *Journal of Asiatic Society*, vol. v. p. 144, vol. viii. p. 186; *Burckhardt's Travels in Arabia*, vol. ii. p. 265; *Niebuhr, Description de l'Arabie*, p. 45; *Ulloa' Voyage to South America*, vol. i. pp. 403, 408; *Journal of Geograph. Society*, vol. iii. p. 283, vol. vi. p. 85, vol. xix. p. 121; *Spix and Martius's Travels in Brasil*, vol. i. p. 164; *Southey's History of Brazil*, vol. iii. p. 848; *Volney, Voyage en Syrie et en Egypte*, vol. i. pp. 379, 380, 460; *Low's Sarawak*, p. 140.

Applying now this great principle to the general course of history, we shall find proofs of its accuracy in every direction. Indeed, there is not a single instance to the contrary. In Asia, in Africa, and in America, all the ancient civilizations were seated in hot climates; and in all of them the rate of wages was very low, and therefore the condition of the labouring classes very depressed. In Europe, for the first time, civilization arose in a colder climate: hence the reward of labour was increased, and the distribution of wealth rendered more equal than was possible in countries where an excessive abundance of food stimulated the growth of population. This difference produced, as we shall presently see, many social and political consequences of immense importance. But before discussing them, it may be remarked that the only apparent exception to what has been stated is one which strikingly verifies the general law. There is one instance, and only one, of a great European people possessing a very cheap national food. This people, I need hardly say, are the Irish. In Ireland the labouring classes have for more than two hundred years been principally fed by potatoes, which were introduced into their country late in the sixteenth, or early in the seventeenth century.[45] Now, the peculiarity of the potato is, that until the appearance of the late disease, it was and perhaps still is, cheaper than any other food equally wholesome. If we compare its reproductive power with the amount of nutriment contained in it, we find that one acre of average land sown with potatoes will support twice as many persons as the same quantity of land sown with wheat.[46] The consequence is, that in a country

---

[45] Meyen (*Geography of Plants*, 1846, p. 313) says that the potato was introduced into Ireland in 1586; but according to Mr. M'Culloch (*Dictionary of Commerce*, 1849, p. 1048), 'potatoes, it is commonly thought, were not introduced into Ireland till 1610, when a small quantity was sent by Sir Walter Raleigh to be planted in a garden on his estate in the vicinity of Youghall.' Compare *Loudon's Encyclop. of Agriculture*, p. 845: 'first planted by Sir Walter Raleigh on his estate of Youghall, near Cork.'

[46] Adam Smith (*Wealth of Nations*, book i. chap. xi. p. 67)

where men live on potatoes, the population will, if other things are tolerably equal, increase twice as fast as in a country where they live on wheat. And so it has actually occurred. Until a very few years ago, when the face of affairs was entirely altered by pestilence and emigration, the population of Ireland was, in round numbers, increasing annually three per cent.; the population of England during the same period increasing one and a half per cent.[47] The result was, that in these two countries the distribution of wealth was altogether different. Even in England the growth of population is somewhat too rapid; and the labour-market being overstocked, the working classes are not sufficiently paid for their labour.[48] But their condition is one of sumptuous splendour, compared to that in which only a few years ago the Irish were forced to live. The misery in which they were plunged has no doubt always been aggravated by the ignorance of their rulers, and by that scandalous misgovernment which, until very recently, formed one of the darkest blots on

---

supposes that it will support three times as many; but the statistics of this great writer are the weakest part of his work, and the more careful calculations made since he wrote bear out the statement in the text. 'It admits of demonstration that an acre of potatoes will feed double the number of people that can be fed from an acre of wheat.' *Loudon's Encyclop. of Agriculture*, 5th edit. 1844, p. 845. So, too, in *M'Culloch's Dict.* p. 1048, 'an acre of potatoes will feed double the number of individuals that can be fed from an acre of wheat.' The daily average consumption of an able-bodied labourer in Ireland is estimated at nine and a half pounds of potatoes for men, and seven and a half for women. See *Phillip's on Scrofula*, 1846, p. 177.

[47] *Malthus, Essay on Population*, vol. i. pp. 424, 425, 431, 435, 441, 442; *M'Culloch's Political Economy*, pp. 381, 382.

[48] The lowest agricultural wages in our time have been in England about 1s. a day; while from the evidence collected by Mr. Thornton in 1845, the highest wages then paid were in Lincolnshire, and were rather more than 13s. a week; those in Yorkshire and Northumberland being nearly as high. *Thornton on Over-Population*, pp. 12-15, 24, 25. Godwin, writing in 1820, estimates the average at 1s. 6d. a day. *Godwin on Population*, p. 574. Mr. Phillips, in his work *On Scrofula*, 1846, p. 345, says, 'at present the ratio of wages is from 9s. to 10s.'

INFLUENCE OF PHYSICAL LAWS. 67

the glory of England. The most active cause, however, was, that their wages were so low as to debar them, not only from the comforts, but from the common decencies of civilized life; and this evil condition was the natural result of that cheap and abundant food, which encouraged the people to so rapid an increase, that the labour-market was constantly gorged.[49] So far was this carried, that an intelligent observer who travelled through Ireland twenty years ago, mentioned that at that time the average wages were fourpence a day, and that even this wretched pittance could not always be relied upon for regular employment.[50]

Such have been the consequences of cheap food in a country which, on the whole, possesses greater natural resources than any other in Europe.[51] And if we inves-

---

[49] The most miserable part, namely Connaught, in 1733, contained 242,160 inhabitants; and in 1821, 1,110,229. See *Sadler's Law of Population*, vol. ii. p. 490.

[50] Mr. Inglis, who in 1834 travelled through Ireland with a particular view to its economical state, says, as the result of very careful inquiries, 'I am quite confident, that if the whole yearly earnings of the labourers of Ireland were divided by the whole number of labourers, the result would be under this sum — *Fourpence a day for the labourers of Ireland.*' *Inglis, Journey throughout Ireland in 1834*, Lond. 1835, 2nd edit. vol. ii. p. 300. At Balinasloe, in the county of Galway, 'A gentleman with whom I was accidentally in company offered to procure, on an hour's warning, a couple of hundred labourers at fourpence even for temporary employment.' *Inglis*, vol. ii. p. 17. The same writer says (vol. i. p. 263), that at Tralee 'it often happens that the labourers, after working in the canal from five in the morning until eleven in the forenoon, are discharged for the day with the pittance of twopence.' Compare, in *Cloncurry's Recollections*, Dublin, 1849, p. 310, a letter from Dr. Doyle written in 1829, describing Ireland as 'a country where the market is always overstocked with labour, and in which a man's labour is not worth, at an average, more than threepence a day.'

[51] It is singular that so acute a thinker as Mr. Kay should, in his otherwise just remarks on the Irish, entirely overlook the effect produced on their wages by the increase of population. *Kay's Social Condition of the People*, vol. i. pp. 8, 9, 92, 223, 306–334. This is the more observable, because the disadvantages of cheap food have been noticed not only by several common writers, but by the highest of all authorities on population, Mr. Malthus: see the sixth edition of his *Essay on Population*,

tigate on a larger scale the social and economical condition of nations, we shall see the same principle everywhere at work. We shall see that, other things remaining equal, the food of a people determines the increase of their numbers, and the increase of their numbers determines the rate of their wages. We shall moreover find, that when the wages are invariably low,[52] the distribution of wealth being thus very unequal, the distribution of political power and social influence will also be very unequal; in other words, it will appear that the normal and average relation between the upper and lower classes will, in its origin, depend upon those peculiarities of nature, the operations of which I have endeavoured to indicate.[53] After

---

[51] vol. i. p. 469, vol. ii. pp. 123, 124, 383, 384. If these things were oftener considered, we should not hear so much about the idleness and levity of the Celtic race; the simple fact being, that the Irish are unwilling to work, not because they are Celts, but because their work is badly paid. When they go abroad, they get good wages, and therefore they become as industrious as any other people. Compare *Journal of Statistical Society*, vol. vii. p. 24, with *Thornton on Over-Population*, p. 425; a very valuable work. Even in 1799, it was observed that the Irish as soon as they left their own country became industrious and energetic. See *Parliamentary History*, vol. xxxiv. p. 222. So too, in North America, 'they are most willing to work hard.' *Lyell's Second Visit to the United States*, 1849, vol. i. p. 187.

[52] By low wages, I mean low reward of labour, which is of course independent both of the cost of labour and of the money-rate of wages.

[53] In a recent work of considerable ingenuity (*Doubleday's True Law of Population*, 1847, pp. 25-29, 69, 78, 123, 124, &c.) it is noticed that countries are more populous when the ordinary food is vegetable than when it is animal; and an attempt is made to explain this on the ground that a poor diet is more favourable to fecundity than a rich one. But though the fact of the greater increase of population is indisputable, there are several reasons for being dissatisfied with Mr. Doubleday's explanation.

1st. That the power of propagation is heightened by poor living, is a proposition which has never been established physiologically; while the observations of travellers and of governments are not sufficiently numerous to establish it statistically.

2nd. Vegetable diet is as generous for a hot country as animal diet is for a cold country; and since we know that, notwithstanding the difference of food and climate, the tempera-

putting all these things together, we shall, I trust, be able to discern, with a clearness hitherto unknown, the intimate connexion between the physical and moral world; the laws by which that connexion is governed; and the reasons why so many ancient civilizations reached a certain stage of development, and then fell away, unable to resist the pressure of nature, or make head against those external obstacles by which their progress was effectually retarded.

If, in the first place, we turn to Asia, we shall see an admirable illustration of what may be called the collision between internal and external phenomena. Owing to circumstances already stated, Asiatic civilization has always been confined to that rich tract where alone wealth could be easily obtained. This immense zone comprises some of the most fertile parts of the globe; and of all its provinces, Hindostan is certainly the one which for the longest period has possessed the greatest civilization.[54] And as the materials for forming an

---

ture of the body varies little between the equator and the poles (compare *Liebig's Animal Chemistry*, p. 18; *Holland's Medical Notes*, p. 473; *Pouillet, Élémens de Physique*, vol. i. part i. p. 414; *Burdach's Traité de Physiologie*, vol. ix. p. 663), we have no reason to believe that there is any other normal variation, but should rather suppose that, in regard to all essential functions, vegetable diet and external heat are equivalent to animal diet and external cold.

3rd. Even conceding, for the sake of argument, that vegetable food increases the procreative power, this would only affect the number of births, and not the density of population; for a greater number of births may be, and often are, remedied by a greater mortality; a point in regard to which Godwin, in trying to refute Malthus, falls into serious error. *Godwin on Population*, p. 317.

Since writing the above, I have found that these views of Mr. Doubleday's were in a great measure anticipated by Fourier. See *Rey, Science Sociale*, vol. i. p. 185.

[54] I use the word 'Hindostan' in the popular sense, as extending south to Cape Comorin; though, properly speaking, it only includes the country north of the Nerbudda. Compare *Mill's History of India*, vol. ii. p. 178; *Bohlen, das alte Indien*, vol. i. p. 11; *Meiners über die Länder in Asien*, vol. i. p. 224. The word itself is not found in the old Sanscrit, and is of Persian origin. *Halhed's Preface to the Gentoo Laws*, pp. xx. xxi.; *Asiatic Researches*, vol. iii. pp. 368, 369.

opinion respecting India are more ample than those respecting any other part of Asia,[55] I purpose to select it as an example, and use it to illustrate those laws which, though generalized from political economy, chemistry, and physiology, may be verified by that more extensive survey, the means of which history alone can supply.

In India, the great heat of the climate brings into play that law already pointed out, by virtue of which the ordinary food is of an oxygenous rather than of a carbonaceous character. This, according to another law, obliges the people to derive their usual diet not from the animal, but from the vegetable world, of which starch is the most important constituent. At the same time the high temperature, incapacitating men for arduous labour, makes necessary a food of which the returns will be abundant, and which will contain much nutriment in a comparatively small space. Here, then, we have some characteristics, which, if the preceding views are correct, ought to be found in the ordinary food of the Indian nations. So they all are. From the earliest period the most general food in India has been rice,[56] which is the most nutritive of all the

---

[55] So that, in addition to works published on their philosophy, religion, and jurisprudence, a learned geographer stated several years ago, that 'kein anderes Asiatisches Reich ist in den letzten drey Jahrhunderten von so vielen und so einsichtsvollen Europäern durchreist und beschrieben worden, als Hindostan.' *Meiners Länder in Asien*, vol. i. p. 225. Since the time of Meiners, such evidence has become still more precise and extensive; and is, I think, too much neglected by M. Rhode in his valuable work on India: 'Dem Zwecke dieser Arbeit gemäss, betrachten wir hier nur Werke der Hindus selbst, oder Auszüge aus denselben als Quellen.' *Rhode, Religiöse Bildung der Hindus*, vol. i. p. 43.

[56] This is evident from the frequent and familiar mention of it in that remarkable relic of antiquity, the Institutes of Menu. See the *Institutes*, in *Works of Sir W. Jones*, vol. iii. pp. 87, 132, 156, 200, 215, 366, 400, 403, 434. Thus too, in the enumeration of Foods in *Vishnu Purana*, pp. 46, 47, rice is the first mentioned. See further evidence in *Bohlen, das alte Indien*, vol. i. p. 22, vol. ii. pp. 159, 160; *Wilson's Theatre of the Indus*, vol. i. part ii. pp. 15, 16, 37, 92, 95, vol. ii. part ii. p. 35, part iii. p. 64; *Notes on the Mu-*

cerealia;[57] which contains an enormous proportion of starch;[58] and which yields to the labourer an average return of at least sixty fold.[59]

Thus possible is it, by the application of a few physical laws, to anticipate what the national food of a country will be, and therefore to anticipate a long train of ulterior consequences. What in this case is no less remarkable, is that though in the south of the peninsula, rice is not so much used as formerly, it has been replaced, not by animal food, but by another grain called ragi.[60] The original rice, however, is so suited to the circumstances I have described, that it is still the most general food of nearly all the hottest countries of Asia,[61]

---

habharata, in *Journal of Asiatic Society*, vol. vii. p. 141; *Travels of Ibn Batuta in Fourteenth Century*, p. 164; *Colebrooke's Digest of Hindu Law*, vol. i. p. 499, vol. ii. pp. 44, 48, 436, 569, vol. iii. pp. 11, 148, 205, 206, 207, 266, 364, 530; *Asiatic Researches*, vol. vii. pp. 299, 302; *Ward on the Hindoos*, vol. i. p. 209, vol. iii. p. 105.

[57] 'It contains a greater proportion of nutritious matter than any of the cerealia.' *Somerville's Physical Geography*, vol. ii. p. 220.

[58] It contains from 63·8 to 85·07 per cent. of starch. *Brande's Chemistry*, vol. ii. p. 1624; *Thomson's Chemistry of Organic Bodies*, p. 883.

[59] It is difficult to collect sufficient evidence to strike an average; but in Egypt, according to Savary, rice 'produces eighty bushels for one.' *Loudon's Encyclop. of Agriculture*, p. 173. In Tenasserim, the yield is from 80 to 100. *Low's History of Tenasserim*, in *Journal of Asiatic Society*, vol. iii. p. 29. In South America, 250 fold, according to Spix and Martius (*Travels in Brazil*, vol. ii. p. 79); or from 200 to 300, according to Southey (*History of Brazil*, vol. iii. pp. 658, 806). The lowest estimate given by M. Meyen is forty fold; the highest, which is marsh rice in the Philippine Islands, 400 fold. *Meyen's Geography of Plants*, 1846, p. 301.

[60] *Elphinstone's History of India*, p. 7. Ragi is the Cynosurus Corocanus of Linnæus; and, considering its importance, it has been strangely neglected by botanical writers. The best account I have seen of it is in *Buchanan's Journey through the Countries of Mysore, Canara, and Malabar*, vol. i. pp. 100-104, 285, 286, 375, 376, 403, vol. ii. pp. 103, 104, vol. iii. pp. 239, 240, 296, 297. In the large cities, millet is generally used; of which 'a quantity sufficient for two meals may be purchased for about a halfpenny.' *Gibson on Indian Agriculture*, in *Journal of Asiatic Society*, vol. viii. p. 100.

[61] *Marsden's History of Sumatra*, pp. 56, 59; *Raffles' History of Java*, vol. i. pp. 39, 106, 119,

from which at different times it has been transplanted to other parts of the world.[62]

In consequence of these peculiarities of climate, and of food, there has arisen in India that unequal distribution of wealth which we must expect to find in countries where the labour-market is always redundant.[63] If we examine the earliest Indian records which have been preserved—records between two and three thousand years old—we find evidence of a state of things similar to that which now exists, and which, we may rely upon it, always has existed ever since the

---

129, 240; *Perceval's Ceylon*, pp. 337, 364; *Transac. of Society of Bombay*, vol. ii. p. 155; *Transac. of Asiatic Society*, vol. i. p. 510; *Journal of Asiatic Society*, vol. L pp. 228, 247, vol. ii. pp. 44, 64, 251, 257, 262, 336, 344, vol. iii. pp. 8, 25, 300, 340, vol. iv. pp. 82, 83, 104, vol. v. pp. 241, 246; *Asiatic Researches*, vol. v. pp. 124, 229, vol. xii. p. 148, vol. xvi. pp. 171, 172; *Journal of Geograph. Society*, vol. ii. p. 88, vol. iii. pp. 124, 295, 300, vol. v. p. 263, vol. viii. pp. 341, 359, vol. xix. pp. 132, 137.

[62] Rice, so far as I have been able to trace it, has travelled westward. Besides the historical evidence, there are philological probabilities in favour of its being indigenous to Asia, and the Sanscrit name for it has been very widely diffused. Compare *Humboldt's Cosmos*, vol. ii. p. 472, with *Crawfurd's History of the Indian Archipelago*, vol. i. p. 358. In the fourteenth century, it was the common food on the Zanguebar Coast; and is now universal in Madagascar. *Travels of Ibn Batuta in Fourteenth Century*, p. 56; *Ellis's History of Madagascar*, vol. i. pp. 39, 297–304, vol. ii. p. 292; *Journal of Geograph. Society*, vol iii. p. 212. From Madagascar its seeds were, according to *M'Culloch's Dictionary of Commerce*, p. 1105, carried to Carolina late in the seventeenth century. It is now cultivated in Nicaragua (*Squier's Central America*, vol. i. p. 38) and in South America (*Henderson's Hist. of Brazil*, pp. 292, 307, 395, 440, 468), where it is said to grow wild. Compare *Meyen's Geography of Plants*, pp. 291, 297, with *Azara, Voyages dans l'Amérique Méridionale*, vol. i. p. 100, vol. ii. p. 80. The ancient Greeks, though acquainted with rice, did not cultivate it; and its cultivation was first introduced into Europe by the Arabs. See *Humboldt, Nouvelle Espagne*, vol. ii. pp. 409, 410.

[63] So far as food is concerned, Diodorus Siculus notices the remarkable fertility of India, and the consequent accumulation of wealth. See two interesting passages in *Bibliothec. Hist.* lib. ii. vol ii. pp. 49, 50, 108, 109. But of the economical laws of distribution he, like all the ancient writers, was perfectly ignorant.

accumulation of capital once fairly began. We find the upper classes enormously rich, and the lower classes miserably poor. We find those by whose labour the wealth is created, receiving the smallest possible share of it; the remainder being absorbed by the higher ranks in the form either of rent or of profit. And as wealth is, after intellect, the most permanent source of power, it has naturally happened that a great inequality of wealth has been accompanied by a corresponding inequality of social and political power. It is not, therefore, surprising that from the earliest period to which our knowledge of India extends, an immense majority of the people, pinched by the most galling poverty, and just living from hand to mouth, should always have remained in a state of stupid debasement, broken by incessant misfortune, crouching before their superiors in abject submission, and only fit either to be slaves themselves or to be led to battle to make slaves of others.[64]

To ascertain the precise value of the average rate of wages in India for any long period, is impossible; because, although the amount might be expressed in money, still the value of money, that is, its purchasing power, is subject to incalculable fluctuations, arising from changes in the cost of production.[65] But, for our present purpose, there is a method of investigation which will lead to results far more accurate than any statement could be that depended merely on a collection

---

[64] An able and very learned apologist for this miserable people says, 'The servility so generally ascribed to the Hindu is never more conspicuous than when he is examined as an evidence. But if it be admitted that he acts as a slave, why blame him for not possessing the virtues of a free man? *The oppression of ages has taught him implicit submission.*' Vans Kennedy, in *Transactions of the Society of Bombay*, vol. iii. p. 141. Compare the observations of Charles Hamilton in *Asiatic Researches*, vol. i. p. 305.

[65] The impossibility of having a standard of value, is clearly pointed out in *Turgot's Réflexions sur la Formation et la Distribution des Richesses*, in *Œuvres*, vol. v. pp. 51, 52. Compare *Ricardo's Works*, pp. 11, 28–30, 46, 166, 253, 270, 401, with *M'Culloch's Principles of Political Economy*, pp. 298, 299, 307.

of evidence respecting the wages themselves. The method is simply this: that inasmuch as the wealth of a country can only be divided into wages, rent, profits, and interest, and inasmuch as interest is on an average an exact measure of profits,[66] it follows that if among any people rent and interest are both high, wages must be low.[67] If, therefore, we can ascertain the current interest of money, and the proportion of the produce of the soil which is absorbed by rent, we shall get a perfectly accurate idea of the wages; because wages are the residue, that is, they are what is left to the labourers after rent, profits, and interest have been paid.

Now it is remarkable, that in India both interest and rent have always been very high. In the *Institutes of Menu*, which were drawn up about B.C. 900,[68] the lowest

---

[66] *Smith's Wealth of Nations*, book i. chap. ix. p. 37; where, however, the proposition is stated rather too absolutely, since the risks arising from an insecure state of society must be taken into consideration. But that there is an average ratio between interest and profits is obvious, and is distinctly laid down by the Sanscrit jurists. See *Colebrooke's Digest of Hindu Law*, vol. i. pp. 72, 81.

[67] Ricardo (*Principles of Political Economy*, chap. vi. in *Works*, p. 65) says, 'whatever increases wages, necessarily reduces profits.' And in chap. xv. p. 122, 'whatever raises the wages of labour, lowers the profits of stock.' In several other places he makes the same assertion, very much to the discomfort of the ordinary reader, who knows that in the United States, for instance, wages and profits are both high. But the ambiguity is in the language, not in the thought; and in these and similar passages Ricardo by wages meant cost of labour, in which sense the proposition is quite accurate. If by wages we mean the reward of labour, then there is no relation between wages and profits; for when rent is low, both of them may be high, as is the case in the United States. That this was the view of Ricardo is evident from the following passage: 'Profits, it cannot be too often repeated, depend on wages; not on nominal but real wages; not on the number of pounds that may be annually paid to the labourer, but on the number of days' work necessary to obtain those pounds.' *Political Economy*, chap. vii., *Ricardo's Works*, p. 82. Compare *Mill's Principles of Political Economy*, vol. i. p. 509, vol. ii. p. 225.

[68] I take the estimate of Mr. Elphinstone (*History of India*, pp. 225-228) as midway between Sir William Jones (*Works*, vol. iii. p. 56) and Mr. Wilson (*Rig Veda Sanhita*, vol. i. p. xlvii.).

INFLUENCE OF PHYSICAL LAWS. 75

legal interest for money is fixed at fifteen per cent., the highest at sixty per cent.[69] Nor is this to be considered as a mere ancient law now fallen into disuse. So far from that, the *Institutes of Menu* are still the basis of Indian jurisprudence;[70] and we know on very good authority, that in 1810 the interest paid for the use of money varied from thirty-six to sixty per cent.[71]

Thus much as to one of the elements of our present calculation. As to the other element, namely, the rent, we have information equally precise and trustworthy. In England and Scotland, the rent paid by the cultivator for the use of land is estimated in round numbers, taking one farm with another, at a fourth of the gross produce.[72] In France, the average proportion is about a third;[73] while in the United States of North America

---

[69] *Institutes of Menu*, chap. viii. sec. 140–142, in *Works of Sir W. Jones*, vol. iii. p. 295. The subsequent Sanscrit commentators recognize nearly the same rate of interest, the minimum being fifteen per cent. See *Colebrooke's Digest of Hindu Law*, vol. i. pp. 29, 36, 43, 98, 99, 237, vol. ii. p. 70.

[70] In *Colebrooke's Digest*, vol. i. p. 454, and vol. iii. p. 229, Menu is called 'the highest authority of memorial law,' and 'the founder of memorial law.' The most recent historian of India, Mr. Elphinstone, says (*Hist. of India*, p. 83) 'the code of Menu is still the basis of the Hindu jurisprudence; and the principal features remain unaltered to the present day.' This remarkable code is also the basis of the laws of the Burmese, and even of those of the Laos. *Journal of the Asiatic Society*, vol. ii. p. 271, vol. iii. pp. 28, 296, 332, vol. v. p. 232.

[71] See, in *Mill's History of India*, vol. i. p. 317, the report of a committee of the House of Commons in 1810, in which it is stated that the ryots paid 'the heavy interest of three, four, and five per cent. per month.' Ward, writing about the same time, mentions as much as seventy-five per cent. being given, and this apparently without the lender incurring any extraordinary risk. *Ward on the Hindoos*, vol. ii. p. 190.

[72] Compare the table in *London's Encyclopædia of Agriculture*, p. 778, with *Mavor's note in Tusser's Five Hundred Points of Husbandry*, p. 195, Lond. 1812, and *M'Culloch's Statistical Account of the British Empire*, 1847, vol. i. p. 560.

[73] This is the estimate I have received from persons well acquainted with French agriculture. The rent, of course, varies in each separate instance, according to the natural powers of the soil, according to the extent to which those powers have been improved, and according to the facilities for bringing the produce to mar-

it is well known to be much less, and, indeed, in some parts, to be merely nominal.[74] But in India the legal rent, that is, the lowest rate recognized by the law and usage of the country, is one-half of the produce; and even this cruel regulation is not strictly enforced, since in many cases rents are raised so high, that the cultivator not only receives less than half the produce, but receives so little as to have scarcely the means of providing seed to sow the ground for the next harvest.[75]

The conclusion to be drawn from these facts is manifest. Rent and interest being always very high, and interest varying, as it must do, according to the rate of profits, it is evident that wages must have been very low; for since there was in India a specific amount of wealth to be divided into rent, interest, profits, and wages, it is clear that the first three could only have been increased at the expense of the fourth; which is saying, in other words, that the reward of the labourers was very small in proportion to the reward received by the upper classes. And though this, being an inevitable inference, does not require extraneous support, it may be mentioned that in modern times, for which alone we have direct evidence, wages have in India always been excessively low, and the people have been, and still are,

---

ket. But, notwithstanding these variations, there must be in every country an average rent, depending upon the operation of general causes.

[74] "Owing to the immense supply of land preventing the necessity of cultivating those inferior soils which older countries are glad to use, and are therefore willing to pay a rent for the right of using. In the United States, profits and wages (i.e. the reward of the labourer, not the cost of labour) are both high, which would be impossible if rent were also high."

[75] See *Rammohun Roy on the Judicial and Revenue Systems of India*, 1832, pp. 59–61, 63, 69, 92, 94. At p. 69, this high authority says of the agricultural peasantry of Bengal: 'In an abundant season, when the price of corn is low, the sale of their whole crops is required to meet the demands of the landholder, leaving little or nothing for seed or subsistence to the labourer or his family.' In Cashmere, the sovereign received half the produce of the rice-crop, leaving the other half to the cultivator. *Moorcroft's Notices of Cashmere*, in *Journal of Geog. Society*, vol. ii. p. 266.

obliged to work for a sum barely sufficient to meet the exigencies of life.[76]

This was the first great consequence induced in India by the cheapness and abundance of the national food.[77]

---

[76] Heber (*Journey through India*, vol. i. pp. 209, 356, 357, 359) gives some curious instances of the extremely low rate at which the natives are glad to work. As to the ordinary wages in India in the present century, see *Journal of Asiatic Society*, vol. i. p. 255, vol. v. p. 171; *Rammohun Roy on the Judicial and Revenue Systems*, pp. 105, 106; *Sykes's Statistics of the Deccan Reports of the British Association*, vol. vi. p. 321; *Ward's View of the Hindoos*, vol. iii. p. 207; *Colebrooke's Digest of Hindu Law*, vol. ii. p. 184. On wages in the south of India, the fullest information will be found in Buchanan's valuable work, *Journey through the Mysore, Canara, and Malabar*, vol. i. pp. 124, 125, 133, 171, 175, 216, 217, 298, 390, 415, vol. ii. pp. 12, 19, 22, 37, 90, 108, 132, 217, 218, 315, 481, 523, 525, 562, vol. iii. pp. 35, 181, 226, 298, 321, 349, 363, 398, 428, 555. I wish that all travellers were equally minute in recording the wages of labour; a subject of far greater importance than those with which they usually fill their books.

On the other hand, the riches possessed by the upper classes have, owing to this mal-distribution of wealth, been always enormous, and sometimes incredible. See *Forbes's Oriental Memoirs*, vol. ii. p. 297; *Bohlen, das alte Indien*, vol. ii. p. 119; *Travels of Ibn Batuta*, p. 41; *Ward's Hindoos*, vol. iii. p. 176. The autobiography of the Emperor Jehaungeir contains such extraordinary statements of his immense wealth, that the Editor, Major Price, thinks that some error must have been made by the copyist; but the reader will find in *Grote's History of Greece* (vol. xii. pp. 229, 245) evidence of the treasures which it was possible for Asiatic rulers to collect in that state of society. The working of this unequal distribution is thus stated by Mr. Glyn (*Transac. of Asiatic Society*, vol. i. p. 482): 'The nations of Europe have very little idea of the actual condition of the inhabitants of Hindustan; they are more wretchedly poor than we have any notion of. Europeans have hitherto been too apt to draw their opinions of the wealth of Hindustan from the gorgeous pomp of a few emperors, sultans, nawabs, and rajahs; whereas a more intimate and accurate view of the real state of society would have shown that these princes and nobles were engrossing all the wealth of the country, whilst the great body of the people were earning but a bare subsistence, groaning under intolerable burdens, and hardly able to supply themselves with the necessaries of life, much less with its luxuries.'

[77] Turner, who travelled in 1783 through the north-east of Bengal, says: 'Indeed, the extreme poverty and wretchedness

But the evil by no means stopped there. In India, as in every other country, poverty provokes contempt, and wealth produces power. When other things are equal, it must be with classes of men as with individuals, that the richer they are, the greater the influence they will possess. It was therefore to be expected, that the unequal distribution of wealth should cause an unequal distribution of power; and as there is no instance on record of any class possessing power without abusing it, we may easily understand how it was that the people of India, condemned to poverty by the physical laws of their climate, should have fallen into a degradation from which they have never been able to escape. A few instances may be given to illustrate, rather than to prove, a principle which the preceding arguments have, I trust, placed beyond the possibility of dispute.

To the great body of the Indian people the name of Sudras is given;[78] and the native laws respecting them contain some minute and curious provisions. If a member of this despised class presumed to occupy the

---

of these people will forcibly appear, when we recollect how little is necessary for the subsistence of a peasant in these regions. The value of this can seldom amount to more than one penny per day, even allowing him to make his meal of two pounds of boiled rice, with a due proportion of salt, oil, vegetables, fish, and chili.' *Turner's Embassy to Tibet*, p. 11. Ibn Batuta, who travelled in Hindostan in the fourteenth century, says: 'I never saw a country in which provisions were so cheap.' *Travels of Ibn Batuta*, p. 194.

[78] The Sudras are estimated by Ward (*View of the Hindoos*, vol. iii. p. 281) at 'three-fourths of the Hindoos.' At all events, they comprise the whole of the working classes; the Vaisyas not being husbandmen, as they are often called, but landlords, owners of cattle, and traders. Compare *Institutes of Menu*, chap. ix. sec. 326-333, in *Works of Sir W. Jones*, vol. iii. pp. 380, 381, with *Colebrooke's Digest*, vol. i. p. 15, from which it appears that the Vaisyas were always the masters, and that the Sudra was to 'rely on agriculture for his subsistence.' The division, therefore, between 'the industrious and the servile' (*Elphinstone's History of India*, p. 12) is too broadly stated, and we must, I think, take the definition of M. Rhode: 'Die Kaste der Sudras umfasst die ganze arbeitende, oder um Lohn dienende Classe des Volks.' *Relig. Bildung der Hindus*, vol. ii. p. 561.

same seat as his superiors, he was either to be exiled or to suffer a painful and ignominious punishment.[78] If he spoke of them with contempt, his mouth was to be burned;[80] if he actually insulted them, his tongue was to be slit;[81] if he molested a Brahmin, he was to be put to death;[82] if he sat on the same carpet with a Brahmin, he was to be maimed for life;[83] if, moved by the desire of instruction, he even listened to the reading of the sacred books, burning oil was to be poured into his ears;[84] if, however, he committed them to memory, he was to be killed;[85] if he were guilty of a crime, the punishment for it was greater than that inflicted on his superiors;[86] but if he himself were murdered, the penalty was the same as for killing a dog, a cat, or a crow.[87] Should he marry his daughter to a Brahmin, no retribution that could be exacted in this world was sufficient; it was therefore announced that the Brahmin must go to hell, for having suffered contamination from a woman immeasurably his in-

---

[79] 'Either be banished with a mark on his hinder parts, or the king shall cause a gash to be made on his buttock.' *Institutes of Menu*, chap. viii. sec. 281, in *Works of Sir W. Jones*, vol. iii. p. 315. See also *Ward's View of the Hindoos*, vol. iii. p. 67.

[80] *Menu*, chap. viii. sec. 271, in *Jones's Works*, vol. iii. p. 314.

[81] *Menu*, chap. viii. sec. 270.

[82] 'If a Sudra gives much and frequent molestation to a Brahmin, the magistrate shall put him to death.' *Halhed's Code of Gentoo Laws*, p. 202.

[83] *Halhed's Code of Gentoo Laws*, p. 207. As to the case of striking a Brahmin, see *Rammohun Roy on the Veds*, p. 227, 2nd edit. 1832.

[84] 'And if a Sooder listens to the Beids of the Shaster, then the oil, heated as before, shall be poured into his ears; and araeca and wax shall be melted together, and the orifice of his ears shall be stopped up therewith.' *Halhed*, p. 262. Compare the prohibition in *Menu*, chap. iv. sec. 99, chap. x. sec. 109-111, in *Jones's Works*, vol. iii. pp. 174. 398.

[85] *Halhed*, p. 262: 'the magistrate shall put him to death.' In Mrichchakati, the judge says to a Sudra, 'If you expound the Vedas, will not your tongue be cut out?' *Wilson's Theatre of the Hindus*, vol. i. part ii. p. 170.

[86] *Ward's View of the Hindoos*, vol. iv. p. 306. To this the only exception was in the case of theft. *Mill's History of India*, vol. i. pp. 193, 260. A Brahmin could 'on no account be capitally punished.' *Asiatic Researches*, vol. xv. p. 44.

[87] *Menu*, chap. xi. sec. 132, in *Works of Sir W. Jones*, vol. iii. p. 422.

ferior.⁸⁸ Indeed, it was ordered that the mere name of a labourer should be expressive of contempt, so that his proper standing might be immediately known.⁸⁹ And lest this should not be enough to maintain the subordination of society, a law was actually made forbidding any labourer to accumulate wealth;⁹⁰ while another clause declared, that even though his master should give him freedom, he would in reality still be a slave; 'for,' says the lawgiver—'for of a state which is natural to him, by whom can he be divested?'⁹¹

By whom, indeed, could he be divested? I ween not where that power was by which so vast a miracle could be worked. For in India, slavery, abject, eternal slavery, was the natural state of the great body of the people; it was the state to which they were doomed by physical laws utterly impossible to resist. The energy of those laws is, in truth, so invincible, that wherever they have come into play, they have kept the productive classes in perpetual subjection. There is no instance on record of any tropical country, in

---

⁸⁸ 'A Brahmin, if he take a Sudra to his bed as his first wife, sinks to the regions of torment.' *Institutes of Menu,* chap. iii. sec. 17, in *Jones,* vol. iii. p. 121. Compare the denial of funeral rites, in *Colebrooke's Digest of Hindu Law,* vol. iii. p. 329. And on the different hells invented by the Hindu clergy, see *Vishnu Purana,* p. 207; *Ward's View of the Hindoos,* vol. ii. pp. 182, 183; *Coleman's Mythology of the Hindus,* p. 113. The curious details in *Rhode, die Religiöse Bildung der Hindus,* vol. i. pp. 392, 393, rather refer to Buddhism, and should be compared with *Journal Asiatique,* I. série, vol. viii. pp. 80, 81, Paris, 1826.

⁸⁹ *Menu,* chap. ii. sec. 31, in *Jones,* vol. iii. p. 87; also noticed in *Rhode, Relig. Bildung,* vol. ii. p. 561: 'sein Name soll schon Verachtung ausdrücken.' So, too, Mr. Elphinstone (*History of India,* p. 17): 'the proper name of a Sudra is directed to be expressive of contempt.' Compare *Origines du Droit,* in *Œuvres de Michelet,* vol. ii. p. 387, Bruxelles, 1840.

⁹⁰ *Menu,* chap. x. sec. 129, in *Jones,* vol. iii. p. 401. This law is pointed out by Mill (*History of India,* vol. i. p. 195) as an evidence of the miserable state of the people, which, Mr. Wilson (note in p. 213) vainly attempts to evade.

⁹¹ 'A Sudra, though emancipated by his master, is not released from a state of servitude; for of a state which is natural to him, by whom can he be divested?' *Institutes of Menu,* chap. viii. sec. 414, in *Works of Sir W. Jones,* vol. iii. p. 333.

which wealth having been extensively accumulated, the people have escaped their fate; no instance in which the heat of the climate has not caused an abundance of food, and the abundance of food caused an unequal distribution, first of wealth, and then of political and social power. Among nations subjected to these conditions, the people have counted for nothing; they have had no voice in the management of the state, no control over the wealth their own industry created. Their only business has been to labour; their only duty to obey. Thus there has been generated among them, those habits of tame and servile submission, by which, as we know from history, they have always been characterized. For it is an undoubted fact, that their annals furnish no instance of their having turned upon their rulers, no war of classes, no popular insurrections, not even one great popular conspiracy. In those rich and fertile countries there have been many changes, but all of them have been from above, not from below. The democratic element has been altogether wanting. There have been in abundance, wars of kings, and wars of dynasties. There have been revolutions in the government, revolutions in the palace, revolutions on the throne; but no revolutions among the people;[92] no mitigation of that hard lot which nature, rather than man, assigned to them. Nor was it until civilization arose in Europe, that other physical laws came into operation, and therefore other results were produced. In Europe, for the first time, there was some approach to equality, some tendency to correct that enormous disproportion of wealth and power, which formed the essential

---

[92] An intelligent observer says, 'It is also remarkable how little the people of Asiatic countries have to do in the revolutions of their governments. They are never guided by any great and common impulse of feeling, and take no part in events the most interesting and important to their country and their own prosperity.' *M'Murdo on the Country of Sindh*, in *Journal of Asiatic Society*, vol. i. p. 250. Compare similar remarks in *Herder's Ideen sur Geschichte*, vol. iii. p. 114; and even in *Alison's History of Europe*, vol. x. pp. 419, 420.

weakness of the greatest of the more ancient countries. As a natural consequence, it is in Europe that everything worthy of the name of civilization has originated; because there alone have attempts been made to preserve the balance of its relative parts. There alone has society been organized according to a scheme, not indeed sufficiently large, but still wide enough to include all the different classes of which it is composed, and thus, by leaving room for the progress of each, to secure the permanence and advancement of the whole.

The way in which certain other physical peculiarities confined to Europe, have also accelerated the progress of Man by diminishing his superstition, will be indicated towards the end of this chapter; but as that will involve an examination of some laws which I have not yet noticed, it seems advisable, in the first place, to complete the inquiry now before us; and I therefore purpose proving that the line of argument which has been just applied to India, is likewise applicable to Egypt, to Mexico, and to Peru. For by thus including in a single survey, the most conspicuous civilizations of Asia, Africa, and America, we shall be able to see how the preceding principles hold good of different and distant countries; and we shall be possessed of evidence sufficiently comprehensive to test the accuracy of those great laws which, without such precaution, I might be supposed to have generalized from scanty and imperfect materials.

The reasons why, of all the African nations, the Egyptians alone were civilized, have been already stated, and have been shown to depend on those physical peculiarities which distinguish them from the surrounding countries, and which, by facilitating the acquisition of wealth, not only supplied them with material resources that otherwise they could never have obtained, but also secured to their intellectual classes the leisure and the opportunity of extending the boundaries of knowledge. It is, indeed, true that, notwithstanding these advantages, they effected nothing of much moment; but this was owing to circumstances which will be hereafter explained; and it must, at all events, be admitted that they raised themselves far above every other people by whom Africa was inhabited.

The civilization of Egypt being, like that of India, caused by the fertility of the soil, and the climate being also very hot,[93] there were in both countries brought into play the same laws; and there naturally followed the same results. In both countries we find the national food cheap and abundant: hence the labour-market over-supplied; hence a very unequal division of wealth and power; and hence all the consequences which such inequality will inevitably produce. How this system worked in India, I have just attempted to examine; and although the materials for studying the former condition of Egypt are much less ample, they are still sufficiently numerous to prove the striking analogy between the two civilizations, and the identity of those great principles which regulated the order of their social and political development.

If we inquire into the most important circumstances which concerned the people of ancient Egypt, we shall see that they are exactly the counterpart of those that have been noticed in India. For, in the first place, as regards their ordinary food, what rice is to the most fertile parts of Asia, that are dates to Africa. The palm-tree is found in every country from the Tigris to the Atlantic;[94] and it supplies millions of human beings with their daily food in Arabia,[95] and in nearly

---

[93] Volney (*Voyage en Egypte*, vol. i. pp. 58–63) has a good chapter on the climate of Egypt.

[94] It is, however, unknown in South Africa. See the account of the Palmaceæ in *Lindley's Vegetable Kingdom*, 1847, p. 136, and *Meyen's Geog. of Plants*, p. 337.

[95] 'Of all eatables used by the Arabs, dates are the most favourite.' *Burckhardt's Travels in Arabia*, vol. i. p. 58. See also, for proof of their abundance in the west of Arabia, vol. i. pp. 103, 157, 238, vol. ii. pp. 91, 100, 105, 118, 209, 210, 214, 253, 300, 331. And on the dates of Oman and the east of Arabia, see *Wellsted's Travels in Arabia*, vol. i. pp. 188, 189, 236, 276, 290, 349. Compare *Niebuhr, Description de l'Arabie*, pp. 142, 296. Indeed, they are so important, that the Arabs have different names for them according to the stages of their growth. Djewhari says, 'La dénomina-

84   INFLUENCE OF PHYSICAL LAWS.

the whole of Africa north of the equator.⁹⁶ In many parts of the great African desert it is indeed unable to bear fruit; but naturally it is a very hardy plant, and produces dates in such profusion, that towards the north of the Sahara they are eaten not only by man, but also by domestic animals.⁹⁷ And in Egypt, where the palm is said to be of spontaneous growth,⁹⁸ dates,

---

⁹⁶ tion *balah* précède le nom *boer;* car la datte se nomme d'abord *tala,* en suite *khalal,* puis *balah,* puis *boer,* puis *rotab,* et enfin *tamr.*' De *Sacy's note to Abd-Allatif, Relation, de l'Egypte,* p. 74, and see p. 118. Other notices of the dates of Arabia will be found in *Travels of Ibn Batuta in Fourteenth Century,* p. 66; *Journal of Asiatic Soc.* vol. viii. p. 285; *Journal of Geograph. Soc.* vol. iv. p. 201, vol. vi. pp. 53, 55, 58, 66, 68, 74, vol. vii. p. 32, vol. ix. pp. 147, 151.

⁹⁶ Heeren (*Trade of the African Nations,* vol. i. p. 182) supposes that in Africa, dates are comparatively little known south of 26° north lat. But this learned writer is certainly mistaken; and a reference to the following passages will show that they are common as far down as the parallel of Lake Tchad, which is nearly the southern limit of our knowledge of Central Africa; *Denham's Central Africa,* p. 295; *Clapperton's Journal,* in *Appendix to Denham,* pp. 34, 59; *Clapperton's Second Expedition,* p. 159. Further east they are somewhat scarcer, but are found much more to the south than is supposed by Heeren: see *Pallme's Kordofan,* p. 230.

⁹⁷ 'Dates are not only the principal growth of the Fezzan oases, but the main subsistence of their inhabitants. All live on dates; men, women, and children, horses, asses, and camels, and sheep, fowls, and dogs.' *Richardson's Travels in the Sahara,* vol. ii. p. 323, and see vol. i. p. 343: as to those parts of the desert where the palm will not bear, see vol. i. pp. 387, 405, vol. ii. pp. 291, 363. Respecting the dates of western Africa, see *Journal of Geograph. Society,* vol. xii. p. 204.

⁹⁸ 'It flourished spontaneously in the valley of the Nile.' *Wilkinson's Ancient Egyptians,* vol. ii. p. 372. As further illustration of the importance to Africa of this beautiful plant, it may be mentioned, that from the high-palm there is prepared a peculiar beverage, which in some parts is in great request. On this, which is called palm-wine, see *M'William's Medical Expedition to the Niger,* pp. 71, 116; *Meredith's Gold Coast of Africa,* 1812, pp. 55, 56; *Laird and Oldfield's Expedition into the Interior of Africa,* 1837, vol. ii. pp. 170, 213; *Bowditch, Mission to Ashantee,* pp. 69, 100, 152, 293, 386, 392. But I doubt if this is the same as the palm-wine mentioned in *Balfour's Botany,* 1849, p. 532. Compare *Tuckey's Expedition to the Zaire,* pp. 155, 216, 224, 356.

besides being the chief sustenance of the people, are so plentiful, that from a very early period they have been given commonly to camels, the only beasts of burden generally used in that country.[99]

From these facts, it is evident that, taking Egypt as the highest type of African civilization, and India as the highest type of Asiatic civilization, it may be said that dates are to the first civilization what rice is to the second. Now it is observable, that all the most important physical peculiarities found in rice are also found in dates. In regard to their chemistry, it is well known that the chief principle of the nutriment they contain is the same in both; the starch of the Indian vegetable being merely turned into the sugar of the Egyptian. In regard to the laws of climate, their affinity is equally obvious; since dates, like rice, belong to hot countries, and flourish most in or near the tropics.[100] In regard to their increase, and the laws of their connexion with the soil, the analogy is also exact; for dates, just the same as rice, require little labour, and yield abundant returns, while they occupy so small a space of land in comparison with the nutriment they afford, that upwards of two hundred palm-trees are sometimes planted on a single acre.[101]

Thus striking are the similarities to which, in different countries, the same physical conditions naturally give rise. At the same time, in Egypt, as in India, the attainment of civilization was preceded by the possession of a highly fertile soil; so that, while the exuberance of the land regulated the speed with which wealth was

---

[99] *Wilkinson's Ancient Egyptians*, vol. ii. pp. 175-178. See also on the abundance of dates, the extracts from an Arabian geographer in Quatremère, *Recherches sur l'Égypte*, pp. 220, 221.

[100] On their relation to the laws of climate, see the remarks respecting the geographical limits of their power of ripening, in Jussieu's *Botany*, edit. Wilson, 1849, p. 734.

[101] 'In the valley of the Nile, a feddan (1¼ acre) is sometimes planted with 400 trees.' *Wilkinson's Ancient Egyptians*, vol. ii. p. 178. At Mourzuk an entire date-palm is only worth about a shilling. *Richardson's Central Africa*, vol. i. p. 111.

created, the abundance of the food regulated the proportions into which the wealth was divided. The most fertile part of Egypt is the Said;[103] and it is precisely there that we find the greatest display of skill and knowledge, the splendid remains of Thebes, Carnac, Luxor, Dendera, and Edfou.[103] It is also in the Said, or as it is often called the Thebaid, that a food is used which multiplies itself even more rapidly than either dates or rice. This is the dhourra, which until recently was confined to Upper Egypt,[104] and of which the reproductive power is so remarkable, that it yields to the labourer a return of two hundred and forty for one.[105] In Lower Egypt the dhourra was formerly

---

[103] On the remarkable fertility of the Said, see *Abd-Allatif, Relation de l'Egypte*, p. 3.

[103] The superiority of the ruins in Southern Egypt over those in the northern part is noticed by Heeren (*African Nations*, vol. ii. p. 69), and must, indeed, be obvious to whoever has studied the monuments. In the Said the Coptic was preserved longer than in Lower Egypt, and is known to philologists by the name of Misr. See *Quatremère, Recherches sur la Langue de l'Egypte*, pp. 20, 41, 42. See also on the Saidic, pp. 134-140, and some good remarks by Dr. Prichard (*Physical Hist.* vol. ii. p. 202); who, however, adopts the paradoxical opinion of Georgi respecting the origin of the language of the Thebaid.

[104] Abd-Allatif (*Relation de l'Egypte*, p. 32) says, that in his time it was only cultivated in the Said. This curious work by Abd-Allatif was written in A.D. 1203. *Relation*, p. 423. Meiners thinks that Herodotus and other ancient writers refer to the dhourra without mentioning it: 'diese Durra muss daher im Herodot wie in andern alten Schriftstellern vorzüglich verstanden werden, wenn von hundert, zwey hundert, und mehrfältigen Früchten, welche die Erde trage, die Rede ist.' *Meiners, Fruchtbarkeit der Länder*, vol. i. p. 139. According to Volney, it is the Holcus Arundinaceus of Linnæus, and appears to be similar to millet; and though that accurate traveller distinguishes between them, I observe that Captain Haines, in a recent memoir, speaks of them as being the same. Compare Haines in *Journal of Geog. Soc.* vol. xv. p. 118, with *Volney, Voyage en Egypte*, vol. i. p. 195.

[105] 'The return is in general not less than 240 for one; and the average price is about 3s. 9d. the ardeb, which is scarcely 3d. per bushel.' *Hamilton's Ægyptiaca*, p. 420. In Upper Egypt, 'the doura constitutes almost the whole subsistence of the peasantry,' p. 419. At p. 96, Hamilton says, 'I have frequently counted 3,000 grains in one ear of doura, and each stalk has in general four or five ears.' For an account of

INFLUENCE OF PHYSICAL LAWS.   87

unknown; but, in addition to dates, the people made a sort of bread from the lotos, which sprang spontaneously out of the rich soil of the Nile.¹⁰⁶ This must have been a very cheap and accessible food; while to it there was joined a profusion of other plants and herbs, on which the Egyptians chiefly lived.¹⁰⁷ Indeed so inexhaustible was the supply, that at the time of the Mohammedan invasion there were, in the single city of Alexandria, no less than four thousand persons occupied in selling vegetables to the people.¹⁰⁸

From this abundance of the national food, there resulted a train of events strictly analogous to those which took place in India. In Africa generally, the growth of population, though on the one hand stimulated by the heat of the climate, was on the other hand checked by the poverty of the soil. But on the banks of the Nile this restraint no longer existed,¹⁰⁹ and therefore

---

the dhourra bread, see *Volney, Voyage en Egypte*, vol. i. p. 161.

¹⁰⁶ 'Επεὰν πλήρης γένηται ὁ ποταμὸς, καὶ τὰ πεδία πελαγίσῃ, φύεται ἐν τῷ ὕδατι κρίνεα πολλὰ, τὰ Αἰγύπτιοι καλέουσι λωτόν· ταῦτα ἐπεὰν δρέψωσι, αὐαίνουσι πρὸς ἥλιον· καὶ ἔπειτα τὸ ἐκ τοῦ μέσου τοῦ λωτοῦ τῇ μήκωνι ἴδε ἰμφερὶς, πτίσαντες ποιεῦνται ἐξ αὐτοῦ ἄρτους ὀπτοὺς πυρί. *Herodot.* ii. 92, vol. i. p. 688.

¹⁰⁷ *Wilkinson's Ancient Egyptians*, vol. ii. pp. 370-372, 400, vol. iv. p. 50. Abd-Allatif gives a curious account of the different vegetables grown in Egypt early in the thirteenth century. *Relation*, pp. 16-36, and the notes of De Sacy, pp. 37-134. On the κύαμος of Herodotus there are some botanical remarks worth reading in the *Correspondence of Sir J. E. Smith*, vol. ii. pp. 224-232; but I doubt the assertion, p. 227, that Herodotus 'knew nothing of any other kind of κύαμος in Egypt than that of the ordinary bean.'

¹⁰⁸ 'When Alexandria was taken by Amer, the lieutenant of the Caliph Omer, no less than 4,000 persons were engaged in selling vegetables in that city.' *Wilkinson's Ancient Egyptians*, vol. ii. p. 372, and see vol. i. p 277, vol. iv. p. 60. Niebuhr (*Description de l'Arabie*, p. 136) says that the neighbourhood of Alexandria is so fertile, that 'le froment y rend le centuple.' See also on its rich vegetation, *Matter, Histoire de l'École d'Alexandrie*, vol. i. p. 52.

¹⁰⁹ The encouragement given to the increase of population by the fertility arising from the inundation of the Nile, is observed by many writers, but by none so judiciously as Malthus; *Essay on Population*, vol. i. pp. 161-163. This great work, the principles of which have been grossly misrepresented, is still the best

the laws already noticed came into uncontrolled operation. By virtue of those laws, the Egyptians were not only satisfied with a cheap food, but they required that food in comparatively small quantities; thus by a double process, increasing the limit to which their numbers could extend. At the same time the lower orders were able to rear their offspring with the greater ease, because, owing to the high rate of temperature, another considerable source of expense was avoided; the heat being such that, even for adults, the necessary clothes were few and slight, while the children of the working classes were entirely naked; affording a striking contrast to those colder countries where, to preserve ordinary health, a supply of warmer and more costly covering is essential. Diodorus Siculus, who travelled in Egypt nineteen centuries ago, says, that to bring up a child to manhood did not cost more than twenty drachmas, scarcely thirteen shillings English money; a circumstance which he justly notices as a cause of the populousness of the country.[110]

To compress into a single sentence the preceding remarks, it may be said that in Egypt the people multiplied rapidly, because while the soil increased their supplies, the climate lessened their wants. The result was, that Egypt was not only far more thickly peopled than any other country in Africa, but probably more so than any in the ancient world. Our information upon this point is indeed somewhat scanty, but it is derived from sources of unquestioned credibility. Herodotus, who the more he is understood the more accurate he is

---

which has been written on the important subject of population, though the author, from a want of sufficient reading, often errs in his illustrations; while he, unfortunately, had no acquaintance with those branches of physical knowledge which are intimately connected with economical inquiries.

[110] Τρέφουσι δὲ τὰ παιδία μετὰ τινος εὐχερείας ἀδαπάνου,

καὶ παντελῶς ἀπίστου.... ὑποδήματων δὲ τῶν πλείστων καὶ γυμνῶν τρεφομένων διὰ τὴν εὐκρασίαν τῶν τόπων, τὴν πᾶσαν δαπάνην οἱ γονεῖς, ἄχρις ἂν εἰς ἡλικίαν ἔλθῃ τὸ τέκνον, οὐ πλείω ποιοῦσι δραχμῶν εἴκοσι. δι' ἃς αἰτίας μάλιστα τὴν Αἴγυπτον συμβαίνει πολυανθρωπίᾳ διαφέρειν, καὶ διὰ τοῦτο πλείστας ἔχειν μεγάλων ἔργων κατασκευάς. Bibliothec. Hist. book i. chap. lxxx. vol. i. p. 238.

found to be,[111] states that in the reign of Amasis there were said to have been twenty thousand inhabited cities.[112] This may, perhaps, be considered an exaggeration; but what is very observable is, that Diodorus Siculus, who travelled in Egypt four centuries after Herodotus, and whose jealousy of the reputation of his great predecessor made him anxious to discredit his statements,[113] does nevertheless, on this important point, confirm them. For he not only remarks that Egypt was at that time as densely inhabited as any existing country, but he adds, on the authority of records which were then extant, that it was formerly the most populous in the world, having contained, he says, upwards of eighteen thousand cities.[114]

These were the only two ancient writers who, from personal knowledge, were well acquainted with the state of Egypt;[115] and their testimony is the more

---

[111] Frederick Schlegel (*Philos. of Hist.* p. 247, London, 1846) truly says, 'The deeper and more comprehensive the researches of the moderns have been on ancient history, the more have their regard and esteem for Herodotus increased.' His minute information respecting Egypt and Asia Minor is now admitted by all competent geographers; and I may add, that a recent and very able traveller has given some curious proofs of his knowledge even of the western parts of Siberia. See Erman's valuable work, *Travels in Siberia*, vol. i. pp. 211, 297-301.

[112] Ἐπ' Ἀμάσιος δὲ βασιλέος λέγεται Αἴγυπτος μάλιστα δὴ τότε εὐδαιμονῆσαι, καὶ τὰ ἀπὸ τοῦ ποταμοῦ τῇ χώρῃ γινόμενα, καὶ τὰ ἀπὸ τῆς χώρης τοῖσι ἀνθρώποισι, καὶ πόλις ἐν αὐτῇ γενέσθαι τὰς ἁπάσας τότε δισμυρίας τὰς οἰκεομένας. *Herodot.* book ii. chap. clxxvii. vol. i. pp. 881, 882.

[113] Diodorus, who, though an honest and painstaking man, was in every respect inferior to Herodotus, says, impertinently enough, ὅσα μὲν οὖν Ἡρόδοτος καί τινες τῶν τὰς Αἰγυπτίων πράξεις συνταξαμένων ἐσχεδιάκασιν, ἑκουσίως προκρίναντες τῆς ἀληθείας τὸ παραδοξολογεῖν, καὶ μύθους πλάττειν ψυχαγωγίας ἕνεκα, παρήσομεν. *Biblioth. Hist.* book i. chap. lxix. vol. i. p. 207. In other places he alludes to Herodotus in the same tone, without actually mentioning him.

[114] Πολυανθρωπία δὲ τὸ μὲν παλαιὸν πολὺ προέσχε πάντων τῶν γνωριζομένων τόπων κατὰ τὴν οἰκουμένην, καὶ καθ' ἡμᾶς δὲ οὐδενὸς τῶν ἄλλων δοκεῖ λείπεσθαι. ἐπὶ μὲν γὰρ τῶν ἀρχαίων χρόνων ἔσχε κώμας ἀξιολόγους, καὶ πόλεις πλείους τῶν μυρίων καὶ ὀκτακισχιλίων, ὡς ἐν ταῖς ἀναγραφαῖς ὁρᾶν ἔστι κατακεχωρισμένον. *Diod. Sic. Biblioth Hist.* book i. chap. xxxi. vol. i. p. 89.

[115] Notwithstanding the positive assertions of M. Matter

valuable because it was evidently drawn from different sources; the information of Herodotus being chiefly collected at Memphis, that of Diodorus at Thebes.[116] And whatever discrepancies there may be between these two accounts, they are both agreed respecting the rapid increase of the people, and the servile condition into which they had fallen. Indeed, the mere appearance of those huge and costly buildings, which are still standing, are a proof of the state of the nation that erected them. To raise structures so stupendous,[117] and yet so useless,[118] there must have been tyranny on the part of the rulers, and slavery on the part of the

---

(*Hist. de l'Ecole d'Alexandrie*, vol. ii. p. 286; compare *Hist. du Gnosticisme*, vol. i. p. 48), there is no good evidence for the supposed travels in Egypt of the earlier Greeks, and it is even questionable if Plato ever visited that country. ('Whether he ever was in Egypt is doubtful.' *Bunsen's Egypt*, vol. i. p. 60.) The Romans took little interest in the subject (*Bunsen*, vol. i. pp. 152-158); and, says M. Bunsen, p. 152, 'with Diodorus all systematic inquiry into the history of Egypt ceases, not only on the part of the Greeks, but of the ancients in general.' Mr. Leake, in an essay on the Quorra, arrives at the conclusion, that after the time of Ptolemy, the ancients made no additions to their knowledge of African geography. *Journal of Geographical Society*, vol. ii. p. 9.

[116] See on this some good remarks in *Heeren's African Nations*, vol. ii. pp. 202-207; and as to the difference between the traditions of Thebes and Memphis, see *Matter, Histoire de l'Ecole d'Alexandrie*, vol. i. p. 7. The power and importance of the two cities fluctuated, both being at different periods the capital. *Bunsen's Egypt*, vol. ii. pp. 54, 55, 244, 445, 446; *Vyse on the Pyramids*, vol. iii. pp. 27, 100; *Sharpe's History of Egypt*, vol. i. pp. 9, 19, 24, 34, 187, 185.

[117] Sir John Herschel (*Disc. on Natural Philosophy*, p. 60) calculates that the great pyramid weighs twelve thousand seven hundred and sixty million pounds. Compare *Lyell's Principles of Geology*, p. 459, where the still larger estimate of six million tons is given. But according to Perring, the present quantity of masonry is 6,316,000 tons, or 82,110,000 cubic feet. See *Bunsen's Egypt*, vol. ii. p. 155, London, 1854, and *Vyse on the Pyramids*, 1840, vol. ii. p. 113.

[118] Many fanciful hypotheses have been put forward as to the purpose for which the pyramids were built; but it is now admitted that they were neither more nor less than tombs for the Egyptian kings! See *Bunsen's Egypt*, vol. ii. pp. xvii. 88, 105, 372, 389; and *Sharpe's History of Egypt*, vol. i. p. 21.

people. No wealth, however great, no expenditure, however lavish, could meet the expense which would have been incurred, if they had been the work of free men, who received for their labour a fair and honest reward.[119] But in Egypt, as in India, such considerations were disregarded, because everything tended to favour the upper ranks of society and depress the lower. Between the two there was an immense and impassable gap.[120] If a member of the industrious classes changed his usual employment, or was known to pay attention to political matters, he was severely punished;[121] and under no circumstances was the possession of land allowed to an agricultural labourer, to a mechanic, or indeed to any one except the king, the clergy, and the army.[122] The people at large were little better than beasts of burden; and all that was expected from them was an unremitting and unrequited labour. If they neglected their work, they were flogged; and the same punishment was frequently inflicted upon domestic servants, and even upon women.[123] These and similar regulations were well conceived; they were admirably suited to that vast social system, which, because it was based on despotism, could only be upheld by cruelty. Hence it was that, the industry of the whole nation

---

[119] For an estimate of the expense at which one of the pyramids could be built in our time by European workmen, see *Vyse on the Pyramids*, vol. ii. p. 268. On account, however, of the number of disturbing causes, such calculations have little value.

[120] Those who complain that in Europe this interval is still too great, may derive a species of satisfaction from studying the old extra-European civilizations.

[121] *Wilkinson's Ancient Egyptians*, vol. ii. pp. 8, 9. 'Nor was any one permitted to meddle with political affairs, or to hold any civil office in the state.' . . 'If any artizan meddled with political affairs, or engaged in any other employment than the one to which he had been brought up, a severe punishment was instantly inflicted upon him.' Compare *Diod. Sic. Bibliothec. Hist.* book i. chap. lxxiv. vol. i. p. 223.

[122] *Wilkinson's Ancient Egyptians*, vol. i. p. 263, vol. ii. p. 2; *Sharpe's History of Egypt*, vol. ii. p. 24.

[123] *Wilkinson's Ancient Egyptians*, vol. ii. pp. 41, 42, vol. iii. p. 69, vol. iv. p. 131. Compare Ammianus Marcellinus, in *Hamilton's Ægyptiaca*, p. 309.

being at the absolute command of a small part of it, there arose the possibility of rearing those vast edifices, which inconsiderate observers admire as a proof of civilization,[124] but which, in reality, are evidence of a state of things altogether depraved and unhealthy; a state in which the skill and the arts of an imperfect refinement injured those whom they ought to have benefited; so that the very resources which the people had created were turned against the people themselves.

That in such a society as this, much regard should be paid to human suffering, it would indeed be idle to expect.[125] Still, we are startled by the reckless prodigality with which, in Egypt, the upper classes squandered away the labour and the lives of the people. In this respect, as the monuments yet remaining abundantly prove, they stand alone and without a rival. We may form some idea of the almost incredible waste, when we hear that two thousand men were occupied for three years in carrying a single stone from Elephantine to Sais;[126] that the Canal of the Red Sea alone,

[121] *Vyse on the Pyramids*, vol. i. p. 61, vol. ii. p. 92.

[125] 'Ein König ahmte den andern nach, oder suchte ihn zu übertreffen; indess das gutmüthige Volk seine Lebenstage am Baue dieser Monumente verzehren musste. So entstanden wahrscheinlich die Pyramiden und Obelisken Aegyptons. Nur in den ältesten Zeiten wurden sie gebauet: denn die spätere Zeit und jede Nation, die ein nützliches Gewerbe treiben lernte, bauete keine Pyramiden mehr. Weit gefehlt also, dass Pyramiden ein Kennzeichen von der Glückseligkeit und Aufklärung des alten Aegyptens seyn sollten, sind sie ein unwidersprechliches Denkmal von dem Aberglauben und der Gedankenlosigkeit sowohl der Armen, die da baueten, als der Ehrgeizigen, die den Bau befahlen.' *Herder's Ideen zur Geschichte*, vol. iii. pp. 103, 104: see also p. 293, and some admirable remarks in *Volney's Voyage en Egypte*, vol. i. pp. 240, 241. Even M. Bunsen, notwithstanding his admiration, says of one of the pyramids, 'the misery of the people, already grievously oppressed, was aggravated by the construction of this gigantic building. . . . . . The bones of the oppressors of the people who for two whole generations harassed hundreds of thousands from day to day,' &c. *Bunsen's Egypt*, vol. ii. p. 176, a learned and enthusiastic work.

[126] Καὶ τοῦτο ἐθαύμαζον μὲν ἐν' ἔτεα τρία διοχίλιοι δὲ οἱ προσετετάχατο ἄνδρες ἀγωγέες. *Herodot.* book ii. chap. clxxv. vol. i. p. 807. On the enormous weight of

cost the lives of a hundred and twenty thousand
Egyptians;[127] and that to build one of the pyramids
required the labour of three hundred and sixty thousand
men for twenty years.[128]

If, passing from the history of Asia and Africa, we
now turn to the New World, we shall meet with fresh
proof of the accuracy of the preceding views. The
only parts of America which before the arrival of the
Europeans were in some degree civilized, were Mexico
and Peru;[129] to which may probably be added that
long and narrow tract which stretches from the south
of Mexico to the Isthmus of Panama. In this latter
country, which is now known as Central America, the
inhabitants, aided by the fertility of the soil,[130] seem to
have worked out for themselves a certain amount of
knowledge; since the ruins still extant, prove the possession of a mechanical and architectural skill too
considerable to be acquired by any nation entirely
barbarous.[131] Beyond this, nothing is known of their

---

the stones which the Egyptians sometimes carried, see *Bunsen's Egypt*, vol. i. p. 379; and as to the machines employed, and the use of inclined roads for the transit, see *Vyse on the Pyramids*, vol. i. p. 197, vol. iii. pp. 14, 38.

[128] *Wilkinson's Ancient Egyptians*, vol. i. p. 70: but this learned writer is unwilling to believe a statement so adverse to his favourite Egyptians. It is likely enough that there is some exaggeration; still no one can dispute the fact of an enormous and unprincipled waste of human life.

[128] Τριάκοντα μὲν γὰρ καὶ ἓξ μυριάδες ἀνδρῶν, ὥς φασι, ταῖς τῶν ἔργων λειτουργίαις προσήδρευσαν, τὸ δὲ πᾶν κατασκεύασμα τέλος ἔσχε μόγις ἐτῶν εἴκοσι διελθόντων. Diod. Sic. *Bibliothec. Hist.* book i. ch. lxiii. vol. i. p. 188.

[129] 'When compared with other parts of the New World, Mexico and Peru may be considered as polished states.' *History of America*, book vii. in *Robertson's Works*, p. 904. See, to the same effect, *Journal of Geograph. Society*, vol. v. p. 365.

[130] Compare *Squier's Central America*, vol. i. pp. 34, 244, 358, 421, vol. ii. p. 307, with *Journal of Geograph. Society*, vol. iii. p. 59, vol. viii. pp. 319, 323.

[131] Mr. Squier (*Central America*, vol. ii. p. 68), who explored Nicaragua, says of the statues, 'the material, in every case, is a black basalt, of great hardness, which, with the best of modern tools, can only be cut with difficulty.' Mr. Stephens (*Central America*, vol. ii. p. 355) found at Palenque 'elegant specimens of art and models for study.' See also vol. iii. pp. 276, 369,

history; but the accounts we have of such buildings as Copan, Palenque, and Uxmal, make it highly probable that Central America was the ancient seat of a civilization, in all essential points similar to those of India and Egypt; that is to say, similar to them in respect to the unequal distribution of wealth and power, and the thraldom in which the great body of the people consequently remained.[133]

But although the evidence from which we might estimate the former condition of Central America is almost entirely lost,[133] we are more fortunate in regard

---

[133] 406, vol. iv. p. 293. Of the paintings at Chichen he says (vol. iv. p. 311), 'they exhibit a freedom of touch which could only be the result of discipline and training under masters.' At Copan (vol. i. p. 151), 'it would be impossible, with the best instruments of modern times, to cut stones more perfectly.' And at Uxmal (vol. ii. p. 431), throughout, the laying and polishing of the stones are as perfect as under the rules of the best modern masonry.' Our knowledge of Central America is almost entirely derived from these two writers; and although the work of Mr. Stephens is much the more minute, Mr. Squier says (vol. ii. p. 306), what I believe is quite true, that until the appearance of his own book in 1853, the monuments in Nicaragua were entirely unknown. Short descriptions of the remains in Guatemala and Yucatan will be found in *Larenaudière's Mexique et Guatemala*, pp. 308–327, and in *Journal of Geograph. Society*, vol. iii. pp. 60–63.

[133] See the remarks on Yucatan in *Prichard's Physical History of Mankind*, vol. v. p. 348:

'a great and industrious, though perhaps, as the writer above cited (Gallatin) observes, an enslaved population. Splendid temples and palaces attest the power of the priests and nobles, while as usual no trace remains of the huts in which dwelt the mass of the nation.'

[133] Dr. M'Culloh (*Researches concerning the Aboriginal History of America*, pp. 272–340) has collected from the Spanish writers some meagre statements respecting the early condition of Central America; but of its social state and history, properly so called, nothing is known; nor is it even certain to what family of nations the inhabitants belonged, though a recent author can find 'la civilisation guatemalienne ou misteco-zapotèque et muysquiche vivante pour nous encore dans les ruines de Mitla et de Palenque.' *Mexique et Guatemala, par Larenaudière*, p. 8, Paris, 1843. Dr. Prichard, too, refers the ruins in Central America to 'the Mayan race:' see *Prichard on Ethnology*, in *Report of British Association for 1847*, p. 252. But the evidence for these and similar statements is very unsatisfactory.

to the histories of Mexico and Peru. There are still existing considerable and authentic materials, from which we may form an opinion on the ancient state of those two countries, and on the nature and extent of their civilization. Before, however, entering upon this subject, it will be convenient to point out what those physical laws were which determined the localities of American civilization; or, in other words, why it was that in these countries alone, society should have been organized into a fixed and settled system, while the rest of the New World was peopled by wild and ignorant barbarians. Such an inquiry will be found highly interesting, as affording further proof of the extraordinary, and indeed irresistible, force with which the powers of nature have controlled the fortunes of man.

The first circumstance by which we must be struck, is that in America, as in Asia and Africa, all the original civilizations were seated in hot countries; the whole of Peru proper being within the southern tropic, the whole of Central America and Mexico within the northern tropic. How the heat of the climate operated on the social and political arrangements of India and Egypt, I have attempted to examine; and it has, I trust, been proved that the result was brought about by diminishing the wants and requirements of the people, and thus producing a very unequal distribution of wealth and power. But, besides this, there is another way in which the average temperature of a country affects its civilization, and the discussion of which I have reserved for the present moment, because it may be more clearly illustrated in America than elsewhere. Indeed, in the New World, the scale on which Nature works, being much larger than in the Old, and her forces being more overpowering, it is evident that her operations on mankind may be studied with greater advantage than in countries where she is weaker, and where, therefore, the consequences of her movements are less conspicuous.

If the reader will bear in mind the immense influence which an abundant national food has been shown to exercise, he will easily understand how, owing to the pressure of physical phenomena, the civilization of America was, of necessity, confined to those parts where alone it was found by the discoverers of the New World. For, setting aside the chemical and geognostic varieties of soil, it may be said that the two causes which regulate the fertility of every country are heat and moisture.[134] Where these are abundant, the land will be exuberant; where they are deficient, it will be sterile. This rule is, of course, in its application subject to exceptions, arising from physical conditions which are independent of it; but if other things are equal, the rule is invariable. And the vast additions which, since the construction of isothermal lines, have been made to our knowledge of geographical botany, enable us to lay this down as a law of nature, proved not only by arguments drawn from vegetable physiology, but also by a careful study of the proportions in which plants are actually distributed in different countries.[135]

---

[134] Respecting the connection between the vegetable productions of a country and its geognostic peculiarities, little is yet known; but the reader may compare *Meyen's Geography of Plants*, p. 64, with *Reports on Botany by the Ray Society*, 1846, pp. 70, 71. The chemical laws of soil are much better understood, and have a direct practical bearing on the use of manures. See *Turner's Chemistry*, vol. ii. pp. 1310-1314; *Brande's Chemistry*, vol. i. p. 691, vol. ii. pp. 1887-1869; *Balfour's Botany*, pp. 116-122; *Liebig and Kopp's Reports*, vol. ii. pp. 315, 326, vol. iii. p. 463, vol. iv. pp. 438, 442, 446.

[135] As to the influence of heat and moisture on the geographical distribution of plants, see *Henslow's Botany*, pp. 295-300, and *Balfour's Botany*, pp. 560-563.

Meyen (*Geog. of Plants*, p. 263) says, 'I, therefore, after allowing for local circumstances, bring the vegetation of islands also under the law of nature, according to which the number of species constantly increases with increasing heat and corresponding humidity.' On the effect of temperature alone, compare a note in *Erman's Siberia*, vol. i. pp. 64, 65, with *Reports on Botany by the Ray Society*, pp. 339, 340. In the latter work, it is supposed that heat is the most important of all single agents; and though this is probably true, still the influence of humidity is immense. I may mention as an instance of this, that it has been recently ascertained that the oxygen used by seeds during germination, is not always taken from the air, but is obtained by decomposing

A general survey of the continent of America will illustrate the connexion between this law and the subject now before us. In the first place, as regards moisture, all the great rivers in the New World are on the eastern coast, none of them on the western. The causes of this remarkable fact are unknown;[136] but it is certain that neither in North, nor in South America, does one considerable river empty itself into the Pacific; while on the opposite side there are numerous rivers, some of enormous magnitude, all of great importance, as the Negro, the La Plata, the San Francisco, the Amazon, the Orinoco, the Mississippi, the Alabama, the Saint John, the Potomac, the Susquehannah, the Delaware, the Hudson, and the Saint Lawrence. By this vast water-system the soil is towards the east constantly irrigated;[137] but towards the west there is in North America only one river of value, the Oregon;[138] while

---

water. See the curious experiments of Edwards and Colin in *Lindley's Botany*, vol. ii. pp. 261, 262, London, 1848; and on the direct nourishment which water supplies to vegetables, see Burdach's great work, *Traité de Physiologie*, vol. ix. pp. 254, 398.

[136] There is a difference between the watersheds of the eastern and western ranges, which explains this in part, but not entirely; and even if the explanation were more satisfactory than it is, it is too proximate to the phenomenon to have much scientific value, and must itself be referred to higher geological considerations.

[137] Of this irrigation some idea may be formed from an estimate that the Amazon drains an area of 2,500,000 square miles; that its mouth is 96 miles wide; and that it is navigable 2,200 miles from its mouth. *Somerville's Physical Geography*, vol. i. p. 423. Indeed, it is said in an essay on the Hydrography of South America (*Journal of Geograph. Society*, vol. ii. p. 250), that ' with the exception of one short portage of three miles, water flows, and is for the most part navigable, between Buenos Ayres, in 35° south latitude, to the mouth of the Orinoco, in nearly 9° north. See also on this river-system, vol. v. p. 93, vol. x. p. 267. In regard to North America, Mr. Rogers (*Geology of North America*, p. 8, *Brit. Assoc. for 1834*) says, ' the area drained by the Mississippi and all its tributaries is computed at 1,099,000 square miles.' Compare *Richardson's Arctic Expedition*, vol. ii. p. 164.

[138] The Oregon, or Columbia as it is sometimes called, forms a remarkable botanical line, which is the boundary of the Californian flora. See *Reports on Botany by the Ray Society*, p. 113.

in South America, from the Isthmus of Panama to the Straits of Magellan, there is no great river at all.

But as to the other main cause of fertility, namely heat, we find in North America a state of things precisely the reverse. There we find that while the irrigation is on the east, the heat is on the west.[139] This difference of temperature between the two coasts is probably connected with some great meteorological law; for in the whole of the northern hemisphere, the eastern part of continents and of islands is colder than the western.[140] Whether, however, this is owing to some large and comprehensive cause, or whether each instance has a cause peculiar to itself, is an alternative, in the present state of knowledge, impossible to decide; but the fact is unquestionable, and its influence upon the early history of America is extremely curious. In consequence of it, the two great conditions of fertility have not been united in any part of the continent north of Mexico. The countries on the one side have wanted heat; those on the other side have wanted irrigation. The accumulation of wealth being thus impeded, the progress of society was stopped; and until, in the sixteenth century, the knowledge of Europe was brought to bear upon America, there is no instance of any people north of the twentieth parallel, reaching even that

---

[139] For proof that the mean temperature of the western coast of North America is higher than that of the eastern coast, see *Journal of Geograph. Society*, vol. ix. p. 380, vol. xi. pp. 168, 216; Humboldt, *la Nouvelle Espagne*, vol. i. pp. 42, 336; *Richardson's Arctic Expedition*, vol. ii. pp. 214, 218, 219, 259, 260. This is well illustrated by the botanical fact, that on the west coast the Coniferæ grow as high as 68° or 70° north latitude; while on the east their northern limit is 60°. See an Essay on the Morphology of the Coniferæ, in *Reports on Botany by the Ray Society*, p. 8, which should be compared with *Forry on the Climate of the United States and its Endemic Influences*, New York, 1842, p. 89.

[140] 'Writers on climate have remarked that the eastern coasts of continents in the northern hemisphere have a lower mean temperature than the western coasts.' *Richardson on North American Zoology*, p. 129, *Brit. Assoc. for* 1836: see also *Report for* 1841, *Sections*, p. 28; *Davis's China*, vol. iii. pp. 140, 141; *Journal of Geograph. Society*, vol. xxii. p. 176.

imperfect civilization to which the inhabitants of India and of Egypt easily attained.[141] On the other hand, south of the twentieth parallel, the continent suddenly changes its form, and, rapidly contracting, becomes a small strip of land, until it reaches the Isthmus of Panama. This narrow tract was the centre of Mexican civilization; and a comparison of the preceding arguments will easily show why such was the case; for the peculiar configuration of the land secured a very large amount of coast, and thus gave to the southern part of North America the character of an island. Hence there arose one of the characteristics of an insular climate, namely, an increase of moisture caused by the watery vapour which springs from the sea.[142] While, therefore, the position of Mexico near the equator gave it heat,

---

[141] The little that is known of the early state of the North-American tribes has been brought together by Dr. M'Culloh in his learned work, *Researches concerning America*, pp. 119-146. He says, p. 121, that they 'lived together without laws and civil regulations.' In that part of the world, the population has probably never been fixed; and we now know that the inhabitants of the north-east of Asia have at different times passed over to the north-west of America, as in the case of the Tschuktschi, who are found in both continents. Indeed, Dobell was so struck by the similarity between the North-American tribes and some he met with nearly as far west as Tomsk, that he believed their origin to be the same. See *Dobell's Travels in Kamtschatka and Siberia*, 1830, vol. ii. p. 112. And on this question of intercourse between the two continents, compare *Crantz's History of Greenland*, vol. i. pp. 259, 260, with *Richardson's Arctic Expedition*, vol. i. pp. 362, 363, and *Prichard's Physical History of Mankind*, vol. iv. pp. 458, 463, vol. v. pp. 371, 378.

[142] From general physical considerations, we should suppose a relation between amount of rain and extent of coast; and in Europe, where alone we have extensive meteorological records, the connexion has been proved statistically. 'If the quantity of rain that falls in different parts of Europe is measured, it is found to be less, other things being equal, as we recede from the sea-shore.' *Kaemtz's Meteorology*, 1845, p. 139. Compare pp. 91, 94. Hence, no doubt, the greater rarity of rain as we advance north from Mexico. 'Au nord du 20°, surtout depuis les 22° au 30° de latitude, les pluies, que ne durent que pendant les mois de juin, de juillet, d'août, et de septembre, sont peu fréquentes dans l'intérieur du pays.' *Humboldt, la Nouvelle Espagne*, vol. i. p. 46.

the shape of the land gave it humidity; and this being the only part of North America in which these two conditions were united, it was likewise the only part which was at all civilized. There can be no doubt that if the sandy plains of California and southern Columbia, instead of being scorched into sterility, had been irrigated by the rivers of the east, or if the rivers of the east had been accompanied by the heat of the west, the result of either combination would have been that exuberance of soil by which, as the history of the world decisively proves, every early civilization was preceded. But inasmuch as, of the two elements of fertility, one was deficient in every part of America north of the twentieth parallel, it followed that, until that line was passed, civilization could gain no resting-place; and there never has been found, and we may confidently assert never will be found, any evidence that even a single ancient nation, in the whole of that enormous continent, was able to make much progress in the arts of life, or organize itself into a fixed and permanent society.

Thus far as to the physical agents which controlled the early destinies of North America. But in reference to South America, a different train of circumstances came into play; for the law by virtue of which the eastern coasts are colder than the western, is not only inapplicable to the southern hemisphere, but is replaced by another law precisely the reverse. North of the equator, the east is colder than the west; south of the equator, the east is hotter than the west.[143] If now, we connect this fact with what has been noticed respecting the vast river-system which distinguishes the east of America from the west, it becomes evident that in South America there exists that coöperation of heat and humidity in which North America is deficient.

---

[143] 'The difference between the climates of the east and west coasts of continents and islands, has also been observed in the southern hemisphere but here the west coasts are colder than the east, while in the northern hemisphere the east coasts are the colder.' *Meyen's Geography of Plants*, 1846, p. 21.

The result is, that the soil in the eastern part of South America is remarkable for its exuberance, not only within the tropic, but considerably beyond it; the south of Brazil, and even part of Uruguay, possessing a fertility not to be found in any country of North America situated under a corresponding latitude.

On a hasty view of the preceding generalizations, it might be expected that the eastern side of South America, being thus richly endowed by nature,[144] would have been the seat of one of those civilizations, which, in other parts of the world, similar causes produced. But if we look a little further, we shall find that what has just been pointed out, by no means exhausts even the physical bearings of this subject, and that we must take into consideration a third great agent, which has sufficed to neutralize the natural results of the other two, and to retain in barbarism the inhabitants of what otherwise would have been the most flourishing of all the countries of the New World.

The agent to which I allude is the trade-wind; a striking phenomenon, by which, as we shall hereafter see, all the civilizations anterior to those of Europe were greatly and injuriously influenced. This wind covers no less than 56° of latitude; 28° north of the equator, and 28° south of it.[145] In this large tract, which comprises some of the most fertile countries in

---

[144] Mr. Darwin, who has written one of the most valuable works ever published on South America, was struck by this superiority of the eastern coast; and he mentions that 'fruits which ripen well and are very abundant, such as the grape and fig, in latitude 41° on the east coast, succeed very poorly in a lower latitude on the opposite side of the continent.' *Darwin's Journal of Researches*, Lond. 1840, p. 263. Compare *Meyen's Geog. of Plants*, pp. 25, 188. So that the proposition of Daniell (*Meteorological Essays*, p. 104, sec. xiv.) is expressed too generally, and should be confined to continents north of the equator.

[145] The trade-winds sometimes reach the thirtieth parallel. See *Daniell's Meteorological Essays*, p. 469. Dr. Traill (*Physical Geography*, Edin. 1838, p. 200), says, 'they extend to about 30° on each side of the equator:' but I believe they are rarely found so high; though Robertson is certainly wrong in supposing that they are peculiar to the tropics; *History of America*, book iv. in *Robertson's Works*, p. 781.

the world, the trade-wind blows, during the whole year, either from the north-east or from the south-east.[146] The causes of this regularity are now well understood, and are known to depend partly on the displacement of air at the equator, and partly on the motion of the earth; for the cold air from the poles is constantly flowing towards the equator, and thus producing northerly winds in the northern hemisphere, and southerly winds in the southern. These winds are, however, deflected from their natural course by the movement of the earth, as it revolves on its axis from west to east. And as the rotation of the earth is, of course, more rapid at the equator than elsewhere, it happens that in the neighbourhood of the equator the speed is so great as to outstrip the movements of the atmosphere from the poles, and forcing them into another direction, gives rise to those easterly currents which are called trade-winds.[147] What, however, we

---

[146] 'In the northern hemisphere the trade-wind blows from the north-east, and in the southern from the south-east.' *Meyen's Geog. of Plants*, p. 42. Compare *Walsh's Brazil*, vol. i. p. 112, vol. ii. p. 494; and on the 'tropical east-wind' of the Gulf of Mexico, see *Forry's Climate of the United States*, p. 206. Dr. Forry says that it has given to the growth of the trees ' an inclination from the sea.'

[147] Respecting the causes of the trade-winds, see *Somerville's Connexion of the Physical Sciences*, pp. 136, 137; *Leslie's Natural Philosophy*, p. 518; *Daniell's Meteorological Essays*, pp. 44, 102, 478–481; *Kaemtz's Meteorology*, pp. 37–39; *Prout's Bridgewater Treatise*, pp. 254–256. The discovery of the true theory is often ascribed to Mr. Daniell; but Hadley was the real discoverer. *Note in Prout*, p. 257.

The monsoons, which popular writers frequently confuse with the trade-winds, are said to be caused by the predominance of land, and by the difference between its temperature and that of the sea: see *Kaemtz*, pp. 42–45. On what may be called the conversion of the trades into monsoons, according to the laws very recently promulgated by M. Dove, see *Report of British Association for* 1847 (*Transac. of Sections*, p. 30) and *Report for* 1848, p. 94. The monsoons are noticed in *Humboldt's Cosmos*, vol. ii. p. 485; *Asiatic Researches*, vol. xviii. part i. p. 261; *Thirlwall's History of Greece*, vol. vii. pp. 13, 55; *Journal of Geograph. Society*, vol. ii. p. 90, vol. iv. pp. 8, 9, 148, 149, 169, vol. xi. p. 162, vol. xv. pp. 146–149, vol. xvi. p. 185, vol. xviii. pp. 67, 68, vol. xxiii. p. 112; *Low's Sarawak*, p. 30.

INFLUENCE OF PHYSICAL LAWS. 103

are now rather concerned with, is not so much an explanation of the trade-winds, as an account of the way in which this great physical phenomenon is connected with the history of South America.

The trade-wind, blowing on the eastern coast of South America, and proceeding from the east, crosses the Atlantic Ocean, and therefore reaches the land surcharged with the vapours accumulated in its passage. These vapours, on touching the shore, are, at periodical intervals, condensed into rain; and as their progress westward is checked by that gigantic chain of the Andes, which they are unable to pass,[148] they pour the whole of their moisture on Brazil, which, in consequence, is often deluged by the most destructive torrents.[149] This abundant supply, being aided by that vast river-system peculiar to the eastern part of America, and being also accompanied by heat, has stimulated the soil into an activity unequalled in any other part of the world.[150] Brazil, which is nearly as large as the whole of Europe, is covered with a vege-

---

[148] *Lyell's Principles of Geology*, pp. 201, 714, 715; see also *Somerville's Physical Geography*, vol. ii. p. 71. And on this confining power of the Cordillera of the Andes, see Azara, *Voyages dans l'Amérique Méridionale*, vol. i. p. 33. According to Dr. Tschudi, the eastern chain is properly the Andes, and the western the Cordillera; but this distinction is rarely made. *Tschudi's Travels in Peru*, p. 290.

[149] On the rain of Brazil, see *Daniell's Meteorological Essays*, p. 335; *Darwin's Journal*, pp. 11, 83; *Spix and Martius's Travels in Brazil*, vol. ii. p. 113, *Gardner's Travels in Brazil*, pp. 53, 99, 114, 175, 233, 394.

[150] Dr. Gardner, who looked at these things with the eye of a botanist, says that near Rio de Janeiro the heat and moisture are sufficient to compensate even the poorest soil; so that 'rocks, on which scarcely a trace of earth is to be observed, are covered with vellozias, tillandsias, melastomaceæ, cacti, orchideæ, and ferns, and all in the vigour of life.' *Gardner's Travels in Brazil*, p. 9. See also on this combination, *Walsh's Brazil*, vol. ii. pp. 297, 298, a curious description of the rainy season: 'For eight or nine hours a day, during some weeks, I never had a dry shirt on me; and the clothes I divested myself of at night, I put on quite wet in the morning. When it did not rain, which was very rare, there shone out in some places a burning sun; and we went smoking along, the wet exhaling by the heat, as if we were dissolving into vapour.'

tation of incredible profusion. Indeed, so rank and luxuriant is the growth, that Nature seems to riot in the very wantonness of power. A great part of this immense country is filled with dense and tangled forests, whose noble trees, blossoming in unrivalled beauty, and exquisite with a thousand hues, throw out their produce in endless prodigality. On their summit are perched birds of gorgeous plumage, which nestle in their dark and lofty recesses. Below, their base and trunks are crowded with brushwood, creeping plants, innumerable parasites, all swarming with life. There, too, are myriads of insects of every variety; reptiles of strange and singular form; serpents and lizards, spotted with deadly beauty: all of which find means of existence in this vast workshop and repository of Nature. And that nothing may be wanting to this land of marvels, the forests are skirted by enormous meadows, which, reeking with heat and moisture, supply nourishment to countless herds of wild cattle, that browse and fatten on their herbage; while the adjoining plains, rich in another form of life, are the chosen abode of the subtlest and most ferocious animals, which prey on each other, but which it might almost seem no human power can hope to extirpate.[161]

Such is the flow and abundance of life by which Brazil is marked above all the other countries of the earth.[162] But, amid this pomp and splendour of

---

[161] On the natural history of Brazil, I have compared a few notices in *Swainson's Geography of Animals*, pp. 75-87, with *Cuvier, Règne Animal*, vol. i. p. 460, vol. ii. pp. 28, 65, 66, 89, vol. iv. pp. 51, 75, 258, 320, 394, 486, 561, vol. v. pp. 40, 195, 272, 334, 553; *Azara, Amérique Méridionale*, vol. i. pp. 244-388, and the greater part of vols. iii. and iv.; *Winckler, Geschichte der Botanik*, pp. 378, 576-678; *Southey's History of Brazil*, vol. i. p. 27, vol. iii. pp. 315, 823; *Gardner's Brazil*, pp. 18, 32-34, 41-44, 131, 330; *Spix and Martius's Brazil*, vol. i. pp. 207-209, 238-248, vol. ii. pp. 131, 160-163. And as to the forests, which are among the wonders of the world, *Somerville's Physical Geog.* vol. ii. pp. 204-206; *Prichard's Physical History*, vol. v. p. 497; *Darwin's Journal*, pp. 11, 24; *Walsh's Brazil*, vol. i. p. 146, vol. ii. pp. 29, 30, 253.

[162] This extraordinary richness has excited the astonishment of all who have seen it. Mr. Walsh,

Nature, no place is left for Man. He is reduced to insignificance by the majesty with which he is surrounded. The forces that oppose him are so formidable that he has never been able to make head against them, never able to rally against their accumulated pressure. The whole of Brazil, notwithstanding its immense apparent advantages, has always remained entirely uncivilized; its inhabitants wandering savages, incompetent to resist those obstacles which the very bounty of Nature had put in their way. For the natives, like every people in the infancy of society, are averse to enterprise; and being unacquainted with the arts by which physical impediments are removed, they have never attempted to grapple with the difficulties that stopped their social progress. Indeed, those difficulties are so serious, that during more than three hundred years the resources of European knowledge have been vainly employed in endeavouring to get rid of them. Along the coast of Brazil, there has been introduced from Europe a certain amount of that civilization, which the natives by their own efforts could never have reached. But such civilization, in itself very imperfect, has never penetrated the recesses of the country; and in the interior there is still found a state of things similar to that which has always existed. The people, ignorant, and therefore brutal, practising no restraint, and recognizing no law, continue to live on in their old and inveterate barbarism.[142] In their

---

who had travelled in some very fertile countries, mentions 'the exceeding fecundity of nature which characterizes Brazil.' *Walsh's Brazil*, vol. ii. p. 19. And a very eminent naturalist, Mr. Darwin, says (*Journal*, p. 29), 'In England, any person fond of natural history enjoys in his walks a great advantage, by always having something to attract his attention; but in those fertile climates, teeming with life, the attractions are so numerous that he is scarcely able to walk at all.'

[143] Azara (*Amérique Méridionale*, vol. ii. pp. 1-168) gives a curious, but occasionally a disgusting account of the savage natives in that part of Brazil south of 16°, to which his observations were limited. And as to the inhabitants of other parts, see *Henderson's History of Brazil*, pp. 28, 29, 107, 173, 248, 315, 473; *M'Culloh's Researches concerning America*, p. 77; and the

country, the physical causes are so active, and do their work on a scale of such unrivalled magnitude, that it has hitherto been found impossible to escape from the effects of their united action. The progress of agriculture is stopped by impassable forests, and the harvests are destroyed by innumerable insects.[154] The mountains are too high to scale, the rivers are too wide to bridge; every thing is contrived to keep back the human mind, and repress its rising ambition. It is thus that the energies of Nature have hampered the spirit of Man. Nowhere else is there so painful a contrast between the grandeur of the external world and the littleness of the internal. And the mind, cowed by this unequal struggle, has not only been unable to advance, but without foreign aid it would undoubtedly have receded. For even at present, with all the improvements constantly introduced from Europe, there are no signs of real progress; while, notwithstanding the frequency of colonial settlements, less than one-fiftieth of the land is cultivated.[155] The habits of the people are as barbarous as ever; and as to their numbers, it is well worthy of remark, that Brazil, the country

---

more recent account of Dr. Martius, in *Journal of Geograph. Society*, vol. ii. pp. 191-199. Even in 1817, it was rare to see a native in Rio de Janeiro (*Spix and Martius's Travels in Brazil*, vol. i. p. 142); and Dr. Gardner (*Travels in Brazil*, pp. 61, 62) says, that 'more than one nation of Indians in Brazil' have returned to that savage life from which they had apparently been reclaimed.

[154] Sir C. Lyell (*Principles of Geology*, p. 682) notices 'the incredible number of insects which lay waste the crops in Brazil;' and Mr. Swainson, who had travelled in that country, says 'The red ants of Brazil are so destructive, and at the same time so prolific, that they frequently dispute possession of the ground with the husbandman, defy all his skill to extirpate their colonies, and fairly compel him to leave his fields uncultivated.' *Swainson on the Geography and Classification of Animals*, p. 87. See more about these insects in *Darwin's Journal*, pp. 37-43; *Southey's History of Brazil*, vol. i. pp. 144, 256, 333-335, 343, vol. ii. pp. 365, 642, vol. iii. p. 876; *Spix and Martius's Travels in Brazil*, vol. i. p. 259, vol. ii. p. 117; *Cuvier, Règne Animal*, vol. iv. p. 320.

[155] The cultivated land is estimated at from 1½ to 2 per cent. See *M'Culloch's Geog. Dict.* 1849, vol. i. p. 430.

where, of all others, physical resources are most powerful, where both vegetables and animals are most abundant, where the soil is watered by the noblest rivers, and the coast studded by the finest harbours—this immense territory, which is more than twelve times the size of France, contains a population not exceeding six millions of people.[156]

These considerations sufficiently explain why it is, that in the whole of Brazil there are no monuments even of the most imperfect civilization; no evidence that the people had, at any period, raised themselves above the state in which they were found when their country was first discovered. But immediately opposite to Brazil there is another country, which, though situated in the same continent, and lying under the same latitude, is subjected to different physical conditions, and therefore was the scene of different social results. This is the celebrated kingdom of Peru, which included the whole of the southern tropic, and which, from the circumstances just stated, was naturally the only part of South America where any thing approaching to civilization could be attained. In Brazil, the heat of the climate was accompanied by a twofold irrigation, arising first from the immense river-system incidental to the eastern coast; and secondly, from the abundant moisture deposited by the trade-winds. From this combination there resulted that unequalled fertility, which, so far as Man was concerned, defeated its own ends, stopping his progress by an exuberance, which, had it been less excessive, it would have aided. For, as we have clearly seen, when the productive

---

[156] During the present century, the population of Brazil has been differently stated at different times; the highest computation being 7,000,000, and the lowest 4,000,000. Comp. *Humboldt, Nouv. Espagne*, vol. ii. p. 855; *Gardner's Brazil*, p. 12; *M'Culloch's Geog. Dict.* 1849, vol. i. pp. 430, 434. Mr. Walsh describes Brazil as 'abounding in lands of the most exuberant fertility, but nearly destitute of inhabitants.' *Walsh's Brazil*, vol. i. p. 248. This was in 1828 and 1829, since which the European population has increased; but, on the whole, 6,000,000 seems to be a fair estimate of what can only be known approximatively. In *Alison's History*, vol. x. p. 229, the number given is 5,000,000; but the area also is rather under-stated.

powers of Nature are carried beyond a certain point, the imperfect knowledge of uncivilized men is unable to cope with them, or in any way turn them to their own advantage. If, however, those powers, being very active, are nevertheless confined within manageable limits, there arises a state of things similar to that noticed in Asia and Africa; where the profusion of Nature, instead of hindering social progress, favoured it, by encouraging that accumulation of wealth, without some share of which progress is impossible.

In estimating, therefore, the physical conditions by which civilization was originally determined, we have to look, not merely at the exuberance, but also at what may be called the manageability of Nature; that is, we have to consider the ease with which the resources may be used, as well as the number of the resources themselves. Applying this to Mexico and Peru, we find that they were the countries of America where this combination most happily occurred. For though their resources were much less numerous than those of Brazil, they were far more easy to control; while at the same time the heat of the climate brought into play those other laws by which, as I have attempted to show, all the early civilizations were greatly influenced. It is a very remarkable fact, which, I believe, has never been observed, that even in reference to latitude, the present limit of Peru to the south corresponds with the ancient limit of Mexico to the north; while, by a striking, but to me perfectly natural coincidence, both these boundaries are reached before the tropical line is passed; the boundary of Mexico being 21° N. lat., that of Peru 21½° S. lat.[167]

Such is the wonderful regularity which history, when comprehensively studied, presents to our view. And if we compare Mexico and Peru with those countries of the Old World which have been already noticed, we shall find,

[167] "Vidaca being the most southerly point of the present Peruvian coast; though the conquests of Peru, incorporated with the empire, extended far into Chili, and within a few degrees of Patagonia. In regard to Mexico, the northern limit of the empire was 21° on the Atlantic coast, and 19° on the Pacific. *Prescott's History of Mexico*, vol. i. p. 2.

as in all the civilizations anterior to those of Europe, that their social phenomena were subordinate to their physical laws. In the first place, the characteristics of their national food were precisely those met with in the most flourishing parts of Asia and Africa. For although few of the nutritious vegetables belonging to the Old World were found in the New, their place was supplied by others exactly analogous to rice and dates; that is to say, marked by the same abundance, by the same facility of growth, and by the same exuberant returns; therefore, followed by the same social results. In Mexico and Peru, one of the most important articles of food has always been maize, which, we have every reason to believe, was peculiar to the American continent.[158] This, like rice and dates, is eminently the product of a hot climate; and although it is said to grow at an elevation of upwards of 7,000 feet,[159] it is rarely seen beyond the fortieth parallel,[160] and its exuberance rapidly diminishes with the

---

[158] A question has been raised as to the Asiatic origin of maize: *Reynier, Economie des Arabes*, pp. 94, 95. But later and more careful researches seem to have ascertained beyond much doubt that it was unknown before America was discovered. Compare *Meyen's Geography of Plants*, pp. 44, 303, 304; *Walckenaer's note in Azara, Amérique Méridionale*, vol. i. p. 149; *Cuvier, Progrès des Sciences Naturelles*, vol. ii. p. 354; *Cuvier, Éloges Historiques*, vol. ii. p. 178; *Loudon's Encyclopædia of Agriculture*, p. 829; *M'Culloch's Dict. of Commerce*, 1849, p. 831. The casual notices of maize by Ixtlilxochitl, the native Mexican historian, show its general use as an article of food before the arrival of the Spaniards: see *Ixtlilxochitl, Histoire des Chichimèques*, vol. i. pp. 53, 64, 240, vol. ii. p. 19.

[159] 'Maize, indeed, grows to the height of 7,200 feet above the level of the sea, but only predominates between 3,000 and 6,000 of elevation. *Lindley's Vegetable Kingdom*, 1847, p. 112. This refers to the tropical parts of South America; but the Zea Mais is said to have been raised on the slopes of the Pyrenees 'at an elevation of 3,000 to 4,000 feet.' See *Austen on the Forty Days' Maize*, in *Report of Brit. Assoc. for* 1849, *Trans. of Sec.* p. 68.

[160] M. Meyen (*Grog. of Plants*, p. 302) and Mr. Balfour (*Botany*, p. 567) suppose that in America 40° is about its limit; and this is the case in regard to its extensive cultivation; but it is grown certainly as high as 52°, perhaps as high as 54°, north latitude: see *Richardson's Arctic Expedition*, 1851, vol. ii. pp. 49, 234.

diminution of temperature. Thus, for example, in New California, its average yield is seventy or eighty fold ;[161] but in Mexico Proper the same grain yields three or four hundred fold, and, under very favourable circumstances, even eight hundred fold.[162]

A people who derived their sustenance from a plant of such extraordinary fecundity, had little need to exercise their industrious energies; while at the same time they had every opportunity of increasing their numbers, and thus producing a train of social and political consequences similar to those which I have noticed in India and in Egypt. Besides this, there were, in addition to maize, other kinds of food to which the same remarks are applicable. The potato, which, in Ireland, has brought about such injurious effects by stimulating the growth of population, is said to be indigenous to Peru; and although this is denied by a very high authority,[163] there is, at all events, no doubt that it was found there in great abundance when the country was first discovered by the Europeans.[164] In Mexico, potatoes were unknown till the

[161] 'Sous la zone tempérée, entre les 33 et 38 degrés de latitude, par exemple dans la Nouvelle Californie, le maïs ne produit, en général, année commune, que 70 à 80 grains pour un.' *Humboldt, la Nouvelle Espagne,* vol. ii. p. 375.

[162] 'La fécondité du Tlaolli, ou maïs mexicain, est au-delà de tout ce que l'on peut imaginer en Europe. La plante, favorisée par de fortes chaleurs et par beaucoup d'humidité, acquiert une hauteur de deux à trois mètres. Dans les belles plaines qui s'étendent depuis San Juan del Rio à Queretaro, par exemple dans les terres de la grande métairie de l'Esperanza, une fanègue de maïs en produit quelquefois huit cents. Des terrains fertiles en donnent, année commune, trois à quatre cents.' *Humboldt, Nouv. Espagne,* vol. ii. p. 374. Nearly the same estimate is given by Mr. Ward: see *Ward's Mexico,* vol. i. p. 32, vol. ii. p. 230. In Central America (Guatemala), maize returns three hundred for one. *Mexique et Guatemala, par Larenaudière,* p. 257.

[163] 'La pomme de terre n'est pas indigène au Pérou.' *Humboldt, Nouv. Espagne,* vol. ii. p. 400. On the other hand, Cuvier (*Histoire des Sciences Naturelles,* part ii. p. 183) peremptorily says, 'il est impossible de douter qu'elle ne soit originaire du Pérou:' see also his *Éloges Historiques,* vol. ii. p. 171. Compare *Winckler, Gesch. der Botanik,* p. 92: 'Von einem gewissen Carnot unter den Gewächsen Peru's mit dem Namen papas aufgeführt.'

[164] And has been used ever

arrival of the Spaniards; but both Mexicans and Peruvians lived to a great extent on the produce of the banana; a vegetable whose reproductive powers are so extraordinary, that nothing but the precise and unimpeachable testimony of which we are possessed could make them at all credible. This remarkable plant is, in America, intimately connected with the physical laws of climate; since it is an article of primary importance for the subsistence of man whenever the temperature passes a certain point.[165] Of its nutritive powers, it is enough to say, that an acre sown with it will support more than fifty persons; whereas the same amount of land sown with wheat in Europe will only support two persons.[166] As to the exuberance of its growth, it is calculated that, other circumstances remaining the same, its produce is forty-four times greater than that of potatoes, and a hundred and thirty-three times greater than that of wheat.[167]

It will now be easily understood why it was that, in all important respects, the civilizations of Mexico and Peru were strictly analogous to those of India and Egypt. In these four countries, as well as in a few others in

---

since for food. On the Peruvian potato compare *Tschudi's Travels in Peru*, pp. 178, 368, 386; *Ulloa's Voyage to South America*, vol. i. pp. 287, 288. In Southern Peru, at the height of 13,000 or 14,000 feet, a curious process takes place, the starch of the potato being frozen into saccharine. See a valuable paper by Mr. Bollaert in *Journal of Geograph. Society*, vol. xxi. p. 119.

[166] Humboldt (*Nouv. Espagne*, vol. ii. p. 359) says, 'partout où la chaleur moyenne de l'année excède vingt-quatre degrés centigrades, le fruit du bananier est un objet de culture du plus grand intérêt pour la subsistance de l'homme.' Compare *Bullock's Mexico*, p. 281.

[166] *M'Culloch's Geograph. Dict.*, 1849, vol. ii. p 315.

[167] 'Je doute qu'il existe une autre plante sur le globe, qui, sur un petit espace de terrain, puisse produire une masse de substance nourrissante aussi considérable.' . . . . 'Le produit des bananes est par conséquent à celui du froment comme 133 : 1 —à celui des pommes de terre comme 44 : 1.' *Humboldt, Nouvelle Espagne*, vol. ii. pp. 362, 363. See also *Prout's Bridgewater Treatise*, p. 333, edit. 1845; *Prescott's Peru*, vol. i. pp. 131, 132; *Prescott's Mexico*, vol. i. p. 114. Earlier notices, but very imperfect ones, of this remarkable vegetable may be found in *Ulloa's South America*, vol. i. p. 74; and in *Boyle's Works*, vol. iii. p. 590.

Southern Asia and Central America, there existed an amount of knowledge, despicable indeed if tried by an European standard, but most remarkable if contrasted with the gross ignorance which prevailed among the adjoining and cotemporary nations. But in all of them there was the same inability to diffuse even that scanty civilization which they really possessed; there was the same utter absence of any thing approaching to the democratic spirit; there was the same despotic power on the part of the upper classes, and the same contemptible subservience on the part of the lower. For, as we have clearly seen, all these civilizations were affected by certain physical causes, which, though favourable to the accumulation of wealth, were unfavourable to a just subdivision of it. And as the knowledge of men was still in its infancy,[166] it was found impossible to struggle against these physical agents, or prevent them from producing those effects on the social organization which I have attempted to trace. Both in Mexico and in Peru, the arts, and particularly those branches of them which minister to the luxury of the wealthy classes, were cultivated with great success. The houses of the higher ranks were filled with ornaments and utensils of admirable workmanship; their chambers were hung with splendid tapestries; their dresses and their personal decorations betrayed an almost incredible expense; their jewels of exquisite and varied form; their rich and flowing robes embroidered with the rarest feathers, collected from the most distant parts of the empire: all supplying evidence of the possession of unlimited wealth, and of the ostentatious prodigality with which that wealth was

---

[166] The only science with which they had much acquaintance was astronomy, which the Mexicans appear to have cultivated with considerable success. Compare the remark of La Place, in Humboldt, Nouvelle Espagne, vol. i. p. 92, with Prichard's Physical History, vol. v. pp. 323, 329; M'Culloch's Researches, pp. 201-225. Larenaudière's Mexique, pp. 51, 52; Humboldt's Cosmos, vol. iv. p. 456; Journal of Geog. Society, vol. vii. p. 3. However, their astronomy, as might be expected, was accompanied by astrology: see Ixtlilxochitl, Histoire des Chichimèques, vol. i. p.168, vol. ii. pp. 94, 111.

wasted.[169] Immediately below this class came the people; and what their condition was, may be easily imagined. In Peru the whole of the taxes were paid by them; the nobles and the clergy being altogether exempt.[170] But as, in such a state of society, it was impossible for the people to accumulate property, they were obliged to defray the expenses of government by their personal labour, which was placed under the entire command of the state.[171] At the same time, the rulers of the country were well aware that, with a system like this, feelings of personal independence were incompatible; they therefore contrived laws by which, even in the most minute matters, freedom of action was controlled. The people were so shackled, that they could neither change their residence, nor alter their clothes, without permission from the governing powers.

---

[169] The works of art produced by the Mexicans and Peruvians are under-rated by Robertson: who, however, admits that he had never seen them. *History of America*, book vii., in *Robertson's Works*, pp. 909, 920. But during the present century considerable attention has been paid to this subject: and in addition to the evidence of skill and costly extravagance collected by Mr. Prescott, *History of Peru*, vol. i. pp. 28, 142; *History of Mexico*, vol. i. pp. 27, 28, 122, 256, 270, 307, vol. ii. pp. 115, 116), I may refer to the testimony of M. Humboldt, the only traveller in the New World who has possessed a competent amount of physical as well as historical knowledge. *Humboldt, Nouvelle Espagne*, vol. ii. p. 483, and elsewhere. Compare Mr. Pentland's observations on the tombs in the neighbourhood of Titicaca (*Jour. of Geog. Soc.* vol. x. p. 554) with *M'Culloh's Researches*, pp. 364-366; *Mexique par Larenaudière*, pp. 41, 42, 66; *Ulloa's South America*, vol. i. pp. 465, 466.

[170] 'The members of the royal house, the great nobles, even the public functionaries, and the numerous body of the priesthood, were all exempt from taxation. The whole duty of defraying the expenses of the government belonged to the people.' *Prescott's History of Peru*, vol. i. p. 56

[171] Ondegardo emphatically says, 'Solo el trabajo de las personas era el tributo que se dava, porque ellos no poseian otra cosa.' *Prescott's Peru*, vol. i. p. 57. Compare *M'Culloh's Researches*, p. 359. In Mexico the state of things was just the same: 'Le petit peuple, qui ne possédait point de biens-fonds, et qui ne faisait point de commerce, payait sa part des taxes en travaux de différents genres; c'était par lui que les terres de la couronne étaient cultivées, les ouvrages publics exécutés, et les diverses maisons appartenantes à l'empereur construites ou entretenues.' *Larenaudière's Mexique*, p. 39.

To each man the law prescribed the trade he was to follow, the dress he was to wear, the wife he was to marry, and the amusements he was to enjoy.[172] Among the Mexicans the course of affairs was similar; the same physical conditions being followed by the same social results. In the most essential particular for which history can be studied, namely, the state of the people, Mexico and Peru are the counterpart of each other. For though there were many minor points of difference,[173] both were agreed in this, that there were only two classes—the upper class being tyrants, and the lower class being slaves. This was the state in which Mexico was found when it was discovered by the Europeans,[174] and towards which it must have been tending from the earliest period. And so insupportable had all this become, that we know, from the most decisive evidence, that the general disaffection it produced among the people was one of the causes which, by facilitating the progress of the Spanish invaders, hastened the downfall of the Mexican empire.[175]

---

[172] Mr. Prescott notices this with surprise, though, under the circumstances, it was in truth perfectly natural. He says (*Hist. of Peru*, vol. i. p. 159), 'Under this extraordinary polity, a people, advanced in many of the social refinements, well skilled in manufactures and agriculture, were unacquainted, as we have seen, with money. They had nothing that deserved to be called property. They could follow no craft, could engage in no labour, no amusement, but such as was specially provided by law. They could not change their residence or their dress without a licence from the government. They could not even exercise the freedom which is conceded to the most abject in other countries—that of selecting their own wives.'

[173] The Mexicans being, as Prichard says (*Physical History*, vol. v. p. 467), of a more cruel disposition than the Peruvians; but our information is too limited to enable us to determine whether this was mainly owing to physical causes or to social ones. Herder preferred the Peruvian civilization: 'der gebildetste Staat dieses Welttheils, Peru.' *Ideen zur Geschichte der Menschheit*, vol. i. p. 39.

[174] See in *Humboldt's Nouvelle Espagne*, vol. i. p. 101, a striking summary of the state of the Mexican people at the time of the Spanish Conquest: see also *History of America*, book vii., in *Robertson's Works*, p. 907.

[175] *Prescott's History of the Conquest of Mexico*, vol. i. p. 34. Compare a similar remark on the invasion of Egypt in *Bunsen's Egypt*, vol. ii. p. 414.

The further this examination is carried, the more striking becomes the similarity between those civilizations which flourished anterior to what may be called the European epoch of the human mind. The division of a nation into castes would be impossible in the great European countries; but it existed from a remote antiquity in Egypt, in India, and apparently in Persia.[176] The very same institution was rigidly enforced in Peru;[177] and what proves how consonant it was to that stage of society, is, that in Mexico, where castes were not established by law, it was nevertheless a recognised custom that the son should follow the occupation of his father.[178] This was the political symptom of that stationary and conservative spirit, which, as we shall hereafter see, has marked every country in which the upper classes have monopolized power. The religious symptom of the same spirit was displayed in that inordinate reverence for antiquity, and in that hatred of change, which the greatest of all the writers on America has well pointed out as an analogy between the natives of Mexico and those of Hindostan.[179] To this

---

[176] That there were castes in Persia is stated by Firdousi; and his assertion, putting aside its general probability, ought to outweigh the silence of the Greek historians, who, for the most part, knew little of any country except their own. According to Malcolm, the existence of caste in the time of Jemsheed, is confirmed by some 'Mahomedan authors;' but he does not say who they were. *Malcolm's History of Persia*, vol. i. pp. 505, 506. Several attempts have been made, but very unsuccessfully, to ascertain the period in which castes were first instituted. Compare *Asiatic Researches*, vol. vi. p. 251; *Heeren's African Nations*, vol. ii. p. 121; *Bunsen's Egypt*, vol. ii. p. 410; *Rammohun Roy on the Veds*, p. 269.

[177] *Prescott's History of Peru*, vol. i. pp. 143, 156.
[178] *Prescott's History of Mexico*, vol. i. p. 124.
[179] 'Les Américains, comme les habitans de l'Indoustan, et comme tous les peuples qui ont gémi long-temps sous le despotisme civil et religieux, tiennent avec une opiniâtreté extraordinaire à leurs habitudes, à leurs mœurs, à leurs opinions. . . . . Au Mexique, comme dans l'Indoustan, il n'étoit pas permis aux fidèles de changer la moindre chose aux figures des idoles. Tout ce qui appartenoit au rite des Aztèques et des Hindous étoit assujéti à des lois immuables.' *Humboldt, Nouv. Espagne*, vol. i. pp. 95, 97. Turgot (*Œuvres*, vol. ii. pp. 226, 313, 314) has some admirable remarks on this fixity

may be added, that those who have studied the history of the ancient Egyptians, have observed among that people a similar tendency. Wilkinson, who is well known to have paid great attention to their monuments, says that they were more unwilling than any other nation to alter their religious worship;[160] and Herodotus, who travelled in their country two thousand three hundred years ago, assures us that, while they preserved old customs, they never acquired new ones.[161] In another point of view, the similarity between these distant countries is equally interesting, since it evidently arises from the causes already noticed as common to both. In Mexico and Peru, the lower classes being at the disposal of the upper, there followed that frivolous waste of labour which we have observed in Egypt, and evidence of which may also be seen in the re-

---

of opinion natural to certain states of society. See also *Herder's Ideen zur Geschichte*, vol. iii. pp. 34, 35; and for other illustrations of this unpliancy of thought, and adherence to old customs, which many writers suppose to be an eastern peculiarity but which is far more widely spread, and is, as Humboldt clearly saw, the result of an unequal distribution of power, compare *Turner's Embassy to Tibet*, p. 41; *Forbes's Oriental Memoirs*, vol. I. pp. 15, 164, vol. ii. p. 236; *Mill's History of India*, vol. ii. p. 214; *Elphinstone's History of India*, p. 48; *Otter's Life of Clarke*, vol. ii. p. 109; *Transac. of Asiatic Society*, vol. ii. p. 84; *Journal of Asiat. Society*, vol. viii. p. 116.

[160] 'How scrupulous the Egyptians were, above all people, in permitting the introduction of new customs in matters relating to the gods.' *Wilkinson's Ancient Egyptians*, vol. iii. p. 262. Compare p. 275. Thus, too, M. Bunsen notices the 'tenacity with which the Egyptians adhered to old manners and customs.' *Bunsen's Egypt*, vol. ii. p. 64. See also some remarks on the difference between this spirit and the love of novelty among the Greeks, in *Ritter's History of Ancient Philosophy*, vol. iv. pp. 625, 626.

[161] *Herodot.* book ii. chap. 79: πατρίοισι δὲ χρεώμενοι νόμοισι, ἄλλον οὐδένα ἐπικτῶνται: and see the note in *Bachr*, vol. i. p. 660: 'νόμους priores interpretes explicarunt *cantilenas, hymnos*; Schweighæuserus rectius intellexit *instituta ac mores*.' In the same way, in Timæus, Plato represents an Egyptian priest saying to Solon, "Ἕλληνες ἀεὶ παῖδές ἐστε, γέρων δὲ Ἕλλην οὐκ ἔστιν. And when Solon asked what he meant, Νέοι ἐστε, was the reply, τὰς ψυχὰς πάντες· οὐδεμίαν γὰρ ἐν αὐταῖς ἔχετε δι' ἀρχαίαν ἀκοὴν παλαιὰν δόξαν οὐδὲ μάθημα χρόνῳ πολιὸν οὐδέν. Chap. v. in *Platonis Opera*, vol. vii. p. 242, edit. Bekker, Lond. 1826.

mains of those temples and palaces which are still found in several parts of Asia. Both Mexicans and Peruvians erected immense buildings, which were as useless as those of Egypt, and which no country could produce, unless the labour of the people were ill-paid and ill-directed.[102] The cost of these monuments of vanity is unknown; but it must be been enormous; since the Americans, being ignorant of the use of iron,[103] were unable to employ a resource by which, in the construction of large works, labour is greatly abridged. Some particulars, however, have been preserved, from which an idea may be formed on this subject. To take, for instance, the palaces of their kings: we find that in Peru, the erection of the royal residence occupied, during fifty years, 20,000 men;[104] while that of Mexico cost the labour of no less than 200,000: striking facts, which, if all other testimonies had perished, would enable us to appreciate the condition of countries in which, for such insignificant purposes, such vast power was expended.[105]

The preceding evidence, collected from sources of

---

[102] The Mexicans appear to have been even more wantonly prodigal than the Peruvians. See, respecting their immense pyramids, one of which, Cholula, had a base 'twice as broad as the largest Egyptian pyramid,' *M'Culloh's Researches*, pp. 252-256; *Bullock's Mexico*, pp. 111-115, 414; *Humboldt's Nouvelle Espagne*, vol. i. pp. 240, 241.

[103] *Prescott's History of Mexico*, vol. i. p. 117, vol. iii. p. 341; and *Prescott's History of Peru*, vol. i. p. 145. See also *Haüy, Traité de Minéralogie*, Paris, 1801, vol. iv. p. 372.

[104] *Prescott's History of Peru*, vol. i. p. 13.

[105] Mr. Prescott (*History of Mexico*, vol. i. p. 153) says, 'We are not informed of the time occupied in building this palace; but 200,000 workmen, it is said, were employed on it. However this may be, it is certain that the Tezcucan monarchs, like those of Asia and ancient Egypt, had the control of immense masses of men, and would sometimes turn the whole population of a conquered city, including the women, into the public works. The most gigantic monuments of architecture which the world has witnessed would never have been reared by the hands of freemen.' The Mexican historian, Ixtlilxochitl, gives a curious account of one of the royal palaces. See his *Histoire de Chichimèques*, translated by Ternaux-Compans, Paris, 1840, vol. i. pp. 257-262, chap. xxxvii.

unquestioned credibility, proves the force of those great physical laws, which, in the most flourishing countries out of Europe, encouraged the accumulation of wealth, but prevented its dispersion; and thus secured to the upper classes a monopoly of one of the most important elements of social and political power. The result was, that in all those civilizations the great body of the people derived no benefit from the national improvements; hence, the basis of the progress being very narrow, the progress itself was very insecure.[186] When, therefore, unfavourable circumstances arose from without, it was but natural that the whole system should fall to the ground. In such countries, society, being divided against itself, was unable to stand. And there can be no doubt that long before the crisis of their actual destruction, these one-sided and irregular civilizations had begun to decay; so that their own degeneracy aided the progress of foreign invaders, and secured the overthrow of those ancient kingdoms, which, under a sounder system, might have been easily saved.

Thus far as to the way in which the great civilizations exterior to Europe have been affected by the peculiarities of their food, climate, and soil. It now remains for me to examine the effect of those other physical agents to which I have given the collective name of Aspects of Nature, and which will be found suggestive of some very wide and comprehensive inquiries into the influence exercised by the external world in predisposing men to certain habits of thought, and thus giving a particular tone to religion, arts, literature, and, in a word, to all the principal manifestations of the human mind. To ascertain how this is brought

---

[186] This may be illustrated by a good remark of M. Matter, to the effect that when the Egyptians had once lost their race of kings, it was found impossible for the nation to reconstruct itself. *Matter, Histoire de l'École d'Alexandrie*, vol. i. p. 68; a striking passage. In Persia, again, when the feeling of loyalty decayed, so also did the feeling of national power. *Malcolm's History of Persia*, vol. ii. p. 130. The history of the most civilized parts of Europe presents a picture exactly the reverse of this.

about, forms a necessary supplement to the investigations just concluded. For, as we have seen that climate, food, and soil mainly concern the accumulation and distribution of wealth, so also shall we see that the Aspects of Nature concern the accumulation and distribution of thought. In the first case, we have to do with the material interests of Man; in the other case with his intellectual interests. The former I have analyzed as far as I am able, and perhaps as far as the existing state of knowledge will allow.[187] But the other, namely, the relation between the Aspects of Nature and the mind of Man, involves speculations of such magnitude, and requires such a mass of materials drawn from every quarter, that I feel very apprehensive as to the result; and I need hardly say, that I make no pretensions to anything approaching an exhaustive analysis, nor can I hope to do more than generalize a few of the laws of that complicated, but as yet unexplored, process by which the external world has affected the human mind, has warped its natural movements, and too often checked its natural progress.

The Aspects of Nature, when considered from this point of view, are divisible into two classes: the first class being those which are most likely to excite the imagination; and the other class being those which address themselves to the understanding commonly so called, that is, to the mere logical operations of the intellect. For although it is true that, in a complete and well-balanced mind, the imagination and the understanding each play their respective parts, and are auxiliary to each other, it is also true that, in a majority of instances, the understanding is too weak to curb the imagination and restrain its dangerous licence. The tendency of advancing civilization is to remedy this disproportion, and invest the reasoning powers with that authority, which, in an early stage of

---

[187] I mean in regard to the physical and economical generalizations. As to the literature of the subject, I am conscious of many deficiencies, particularly in respect to the Mexican and Peruvian histories.

society, the imagination exclusively possesses. Whether or not there is ground for fearing that the reaction will eventually proceed too far, and that the reasoning faculties will in their turn tyrannize over the imaginative ones, is a question of the deepest interest; but, in the present condition of our knowledge, it is probably an insoluble one. At all events, it is certain that nothing like such a state has yet been seen; since, even in this age, when the imagination is more under control than in any preceding one, it has far too much power; as might be easily proved, not only from the superstitions which in every country still prevail among the vulgar, but also from that poetic reverence for antiquity, which, though it has been long diminishing, still hampers the independence, blinds the judgment, and circumscribes the originality of the educated classes.

Now, so far as natural phenomena are concerned, it is evident, that whatever inspires feelings of terror, or of great wonder, and whatever excites in the mind an idea of the vague and uncontrollable, has a special tendency to inflame the imagination, and bring under its dominion the slower and more deliberate operations of the understanding. In such cases, Man, contrasting himself with the force and majesty of Nature, becomes painfully conscious of his own insignificance. A sense of inferiority steals over him. From every quarter innumerable obstacles hem him in, and limit his individual will. His mind, appalled by the indefined and indefinable, hardly cares to scrutinize the details of which such imposing grandeur consists.[168] On the

---

[168] The sensation of fear, even when there is no danger, becomes strong enough to destroy the pleasure that would otherwise be felt. See, for instance, a description of the great mountain boundary of Hindostan, in *Asiatic Researches*, vol. xi. p. 469: 'It is necessary for a person to place himself in our situation before he can form a just conception of the scene. The depth of the valley below, the progressive elevation of the intermediate hills, and the majestic splendour of the cloud-capped Himalaya, formed so grand a picture, that the mind was impressed with a sensation of dread rather than of pleasure.' Compare vol. xiv. p. 116, Calcutta, 1822. In the Tyrol, it has been observed, that the grandeur of the mountain

other hand, where the works of Nature are small and feeble, Man regains confidence; he seems more able to rely on his own power; he can, as it were, pass through and exercise authority in every direction. And as the phenomena are more accessible, it becomes easier for him to experiment on them, or to observe them with minuteness; an inquisitive and analytic spirit is encouraged, and he is tempted to generalize the appearances of Nature, and refer them to the laws by which they are governed.

Looking in this way at the human mind as affected by the Aspects of Nature, it is surely a remarkable fact, that all the great early civilizations were situated within and immediately adjoining the tropics, where those aspects are most sublime, most terrible, and where Nature is, in every respect, most dangerous to Man. Indeed, generally, in Asia, Africa, and America, the external world is more formidable than in Europe. This holds good not only of the fixed and permanent phenomena, such as mountains, and other great natural barriers, but also of occasional phenomena, such as earthquakes, tempests, hurricanes, pestilences; all of which are in those regions very frequent and very disastrous. These constant and serious dangers produce effects analogous to those caused by the sublimity of Nature, in so far, that in both cases there is a tendency to increase the activity of the imagination. For the peculiar province of the imagination being to deal with the unknown, every event which is unexplained, as well as important, is a direct stimulus to our imaginative faculties. In the tropics, events of this kind are more numerous than elsewhere; it therefore follows that in the tropics the imagination is most likely to triumph. A few illustrations of the working of this principle will place it in a clearer light, and will prepare the reader for the arguments based upon it.

Of those physical events which increase the insecurity

---

scenery imbues the minds of the natives with fear, and has caused the invention of many superstitious legends. *Alison's Europe*, vol. ix. pp. 79, 80.

of Man, earthquakes are certainly among the most
striking, in regard to the loss of life which they cause,
as also in regard to their sudden and unexpected occurrence. There is reason to believe that they are always
preceded by atmospheric changes which strike immediately at the nervous system, and thus have a direct
physical tendency to impair the intellectual powers.[189]
However this may be, there can be no doubt as to the
effect they produce in encouraging particular associations and habits of thought. The terror which they
inspire excites the imagination even to a painful extent,
and, overbalancing the judgment, predisposes men to
superstitious fancies. And what is highly curious, is,
that repetition, so far from blunting such feelings,
strengthens them. In Peru, where earthquakes appear
to be more common than in any other country,[190] every
succeeding visitation increases the general dismay; so
that, in some cases, the fear becomes almost insupportable.[191] The mind is thus constantly thrown into a

---

[189] 'Une augmentation d'élec-
tricité s'y manifeste aussi presque
toujours, et ils sont généralement
annoncés par le mugissement
des bestiaux, par l'inquiétude
des animaux domestiques, et
dans les hommes par cette sorte
de malaise qui, en Europe,
précède les orages dans les
personnes nerveuses.' Cuvier,
Prog. des Sciences, vol. i. p. 205.
See also, on this 'Vorgefühl,' the
observation of Von Hoff, in Mr.
Mallet's valuable essay on earthquakes (Brit. Assoc. for 1850, p.
68; and the 'foreboding' in
Tschudi's Peru, p. 165; and a
letter in Nichols's Illustrations of
the Eighteenth Century, vol. iv.
p. 504. The probable connexion
between earthquakes and electricity is noticed in Bakewell's
Geology, p. 434.

[190] 'Peru is more subject
perhaps than any other country
to the tremendous visitation of
earthquakes.' M'Culloch's Geog.
Dict. 1849. vol. ii. p. 499. Dr.
Tschudi (Travels in Peru, p.
162) says of Lima, 'at an
average forty-five shocks may
be counted on in the year.' See
also on the Peruvian earthquakes, pp. 43, 75, 87, 90.

[191] A curious instance of
association of ideas conquering
the deadening effect of habit.
Dr. Tschudi (Peru, p. 170),
describing the panic, says, 'no
familiarity with the phenomenon
can blunt this feeling.' Beale
(South-Sea Whaling Voyage,
Lond. 1839, p. 205) writes, 'it
is said at Peru, that the oftener
the natives of the place feel
those vibrations of the earth,
instead of becoming habituated
to them, as persons do who
are constantly exposed to other
dangers, they become more filled

timid and anxious state: and men witnessing the most serious dangers, which they can neither avoid nor understand, become impressed with a conviction of their own inability, and of the poverty of their own resources.[192] In exactly the same proportion, the imagination is aroused, and a belief in supernatural interference actively encouraged. Human power failing, superhuman power is called in; the mysterious and the invisible are believed to be present; and there grow up among the people those feelings of awe and of helplessness, on which all superstition is based, and without which no superstition can exist.[193]

Further illustration of this may be found even in Europe, where such phenomena are, comparatively speaking, extremely rare. Earthquakes and volcanic eruptions are more frequent and more destructive in Italy, and in the Spanish and Portuguese peninsula, than in any other of the great countries; and it is pre-

---

with dismay every time the shock is repeated, so that aged people often find the terror a slight shock will produce almost insupportable.' Compare *Darwin's Journal*, pp. 422, 423. So, too, in regard to Mexican earthquakes, Mr. Ward observes, that 'the natives are both more sensible than strangers of the smaller shocks, and more alarmed by them.' *Ward's Mexico*, vol. ii. p. 55. On the physiological effects of the fear caused by earthquakes, see the remarkable statement by Oriander in *Burdach's Physiologie comme Science d' Observation*, vol. ii. pp. 223, 224. That the fear should be not deadened by familiarity, but increased by it, would hardly be expected by speculative reasoners unacquainted with the evidence; and we find, in fact, that the Pyrrhonists asserted that οἱ γοῦν σεισμὰ παρ' οἷς συνεχὲς ἀνατελοῦνται, οὐ θαυμάζονται· οὐδ' ὁ ἥλιος, ὅτι καθ' ἡμέραν ὁρᾶται. *Diog. Laert. de Vitis Philos.* lib. ix. segm. 67, vol. i. p. 591.

[192] Mr. Stephens, who gives a striking description of an earthquake in Central America, emphatically says, 'I never felt myself so feeble a thing before.' *Stephens's Central America*, vol. i. p. 383. See also the account of the effects produced on the mind by an earthquake, in *Transac. of Soc. of Bombay*, vol. iii. p. 98, and the note at p. 105.

[193] The effect of earthquakes in encouraging superstition, is noticed in Lyell's admirable work, *Principles of Geology*, p. 492. Compare a myth on the origin of earthquakes in Beausobre, *Histoire Critique de Manichée*, vol. i. p. 243.

cisely there that superstition is most rife, and the
superstitious classes most powerful. Those were the
countries where the clergy first established their
authority, where the worst corruptions of Christianity
took place, and where superstition has during the
longest period retained the firmest hold. To this may
be added another circumstance, indicative of the connexion between these physical phenomena and the
predominance of the imagination. Speaking generally,
the fine arts are addressed more to the imagination;
the sciences to the intellect.[184] Now it is remarkable,
that all the greatest painters, and nearly all the greatest
sculptors, modern Europe has possessed, have been
produced by the Italian and Spanish peninsulas. In
regard to science, Italy has no doubt had several men
of conspicuous ability; but their numbers are out of
all proportion small when compared with her artists
and poets. As to Spain and Portugal, the literature of
those two countries is eminently poetic, and from their
schools have proceeded some of the greatest painters
the world has ever seen. On the other hand, the
purely reasoning faculties have been neglected, and the
whole Peninsula, from the earliest period to the present
time, does not supply to the history of the natural
sciences a single name of the highest merit; not one
man whose works form an epoch in the progress of
European knowledge.[185]

---

[184] The greatest men in science, and in fact all very great men, have no doubt been remarkable for the powers of their imagination. But in art the imagination plays a far more conspicuous part than in science; and this is what I mean to express by the proposition in the text. Sir David Brewster, indeed, thinks that Newton was deficient in imagination: 'the weakness of his imaginative powers.' *Brewster's Life of Newton*, 1855, vol. ii. p. 133.

It is impossible to discuss so large a question in a note; but to my apprehension, no poet, except Dante and Shakespeare, ever had an imagination more soaring and more audacious than that possessed by Sir Isaac Newton.

[185] The remarks made by Mr. Ticknor on the absence of science in Spain, might be extended even further than he has done. See *Ticknor's History of Spanish Literature*, vol. iii. pp. 222, 223. He says, p. 237, that in 1771,

The manner in which the Aspects of Nature, when they are very threatening, stimulate the imagination,[196] and by encouraging superstition discourage knowledge, may be made still more apparent by one or two additional facts. Among an ignorant people, there is a direct tendency to ascribe all serious dangers to supernatural intervention; and a strong religious sentiment being thus aroused,[197] it constantly happens, not only that the danger is submitted to, but that it is actually worshipped. This is the case with some of the Hindus in the forest of Malabar;[198] and many similar instances will occur to whoever has studied the condition of barbarous tribes.[199] Indeed, so far is this carried, that in some countries the inhabitants, from feelings of reverential fear, refuse to destroy

---

the University of Salamanca being urged to teach the physical sciences, replied, 'Newton teaches nothing that would make a good logician or metaphysician, and Gassendi and Descartes do not agree so well with revealed truth as Aristotle does.'

[196] In *Asiatic Researches*, vol. vi. pp. 35, 36, there is a good instance of an earthquake giving rise to a theological fiction. See also vol. i. pp. 154-157; and compare *Coleman's Mythology of the Hindus*, p. 17.

[197] See for example, *Asiatic Researches*, vol. iv. pp. 56, 57, vol. vii. p. 94; and the effect produced by a volcano, in *Journal of Geograph. Society*, vol. v. p. 388. See also vol. xx. p. 8, and a practical recognition of the principle by Sextus Empiricus, in *Tennemann's Geschichte der Philosophie*, vol. i. p. 292. Compare the use the clergy made of a volcanic eruption in Iceland (*Wheaton's History of the Northmen*, p. 42); and see further *Raffles' History of Java*, vol. i. pp. 29, 274, and *Tschudi's Peru*, pp. 64, 167, 171.

[198] The Hindus in the Iruuri forests, says Mr. Edye, 'worship and respect everything from which they apprehend danger.' *Edye on the Coast of Malabar*, in *Journal of Asiatic Society*, vol. ii. p. 337.

[199] Dr. Prichard (*Physical History*, vol. iv. p. 501) says 'The tiger is worshipped by the Bajm tribe in the vicinity of the Garrows or Garrodus. Compare *Transactions of Asiatic Society*, vol. iii. p. 66. Among the Garrows themselves, this feeling is so strong, that 'the tiger's nose strung round a woman's neck is considered as a great preservative in childbirth.' *Coleman's Mythology of the Hindus*, p. 321. The Seiks have a curious superstition respecting wounds inflicted by tigers (*Burne's Bokhara*, 1834, vol. iii. p. 140); and the Malasir believe that these animals are sent as a punishment for irreligion. *Buchanan's Journey through the Mysore*, vol. ii. p. 385.

wild-beasts and noxious reptiles; the mischief these animals inflict being the cause of the impunity they enjoy.[200]

It is in this way, that the old tropical civilizations had to struggle with innumerable difficulties unknown to the temperate zone, where European civilization has long flourished. The devastations of animals hostile to man, the ravages of hurricanes, tempests, earthquakes,[201] and similar perils, constantly pressed upon them, and affected the tone of their national character. For the mere loss of life was the smallest part of the inconvenience. The real mischief was, that there were engendered in the mind, associations which made the imagination predominate over the understanding; which infused into the people a spirit of reverence instead of a spirit of inquiry; and which encouraged a disposition to neglect the investigation of natural causes, and ascribe events to the operation of supernatural ones.

Everything we know of those countries proves how active this tendency must have been. With extremely few exceptions, health is more precarious, and disease more

---

[200] The inhabitants of Sumatra are, for superstitious reasons, most unwilling to destroy tigers, though they commit frightful ravages. *Marsden's History of Sumatra*, pp. 149, 254. The Russian account of the Kamtschatkans says, 'besides the above-mentioned gods, they pay a religious regard to several animals from which they apprehend danger.' *G. irve's History of Kamtschatka*, p. 205. Bruce mentions that in Abyssinia, hyænas are considered 'enchanters;' and the inhabitants 'will not touch the skin of a hyæna till it has been prayed over and exorcised by a priest.' *Murray's Life of Bruce*, p. 472. Allied to this, is the respect paid to bears (*Erman's Siberia*, vol. i. p. 492, vol. ii. pp. 42, 43); also the extensively-diffused worship of the serpent, whose wily movements are well calculated to inspire fear, and therefore rouse the religious feelings. The danger apprehended from noxious reptiles is connected with the Dews of the Zendavesta. See *Matter's Histoire du Gnosticisme*, vol. i. p. 380, Paris, 1828.

[201] To give one instance of the extent to which these operate, it may be mentioned, that in 1815 an earthquake and volcanic eruption broke forth in Sumbawa, which shook the ground 'through an area of 1,000 miles in circumference,' and the detonations of which were heard at a distance of 970 geographical miles. *Somerville's Connexion of the Physical Sciences*, p. 283; *Hitchcock's Religion of Geology*, p. 190; *Low's Sarawak*, p. 10; *Bakewell's Geology*, p. 438.

common, in tropical climates than in temperate ones. Now, it has been often observed, and indeed is very obvious, that the fear of death makes men more prone to seek supernatural aid than they would otherwise be. So complete is our ignorance respecting another life, that it is no wonder if even the stoutest heart should quail at the sudden approach of that dark and untried future. On this subject the reason is perfectly silent; the imagination, therefore, is uncontrolled. The operation of natural causes being brought to an end, supernatural causes are supposed to begin. Hence it is, that whatever increases in any country the amount of dangerous disease, has an immediate tendency to strengthen superstition, and aggrandize the imagination at the expense of the understanding. This principle is so universal, that, in every part of the world, the vulgar ascribe to the intervention of the Deity those diseases which are peculiarly fatal, and especially those which have a sudden and mysterious appearance. In Europe it used to be believed that every pestilence was a manifestation of the divine anger;[202] and this opinion, though it has long been dying away, is by no means extinct, even in the most civilized countries.[203]

---

[202] In the sixteenth century, 'Les différentes sectes s'accordèrent néanmoins à regarder les maladies graves et dangereuses comme un effet immédiat de la puissance divine; idée que Fernel contribua encore à répandre davantage. On trouve dans Paré plusieurs passages de la Bible, cités pour prouver que la colère de Dieu est la seule cause de la peste, qu'elle suffit pour provoquer ce fléau, et que sans elle les causes éloignées ne sauraient agir.' *Sprengel, Histoire de la Médecine*, vol. iii. p. 112. The same learned writer says of the Middle Ages (vol. ii. p. 372), 'D'après l'esprit généralement répandu dans ces siècles de barbarie, on croyait la lèpre envoyée d'une manière immédiate par Dieu.' See also pp. 145, 346, 431. Bishop Heber says that the Hindus deprive lepers of caste and of the right of possessing property, because they are objects of 'Heaven's wrath.' *Heber's Journey through India*, vol. ii. p. 330. On the Jewish opinion, see *Le Clerc, Bibliothèque Universelle*, vol. iv. p. 402, Amsterdam, 1702. And as to the early Christians, see *Maury, Légendes Pieuses*, p. 68, Paris, 1843: though M. Maury ascribes to 'les idées orientales reçues par le christianisme,' what is due to the operation of a much wider principle.

[203] Under the influence of the inductive philosophy, the theo-

Superstition of this kind will of course be strongest, either where medical knowledge is most backward, or

logical theory of disease was seriously weakened before the middle of the seventeenth century; and by the middle, or at all events the latter half, of the eighteenth century, it had lost all its partisans among scientific men. At present it still lingers on among the vulgar; and traces of it may be found in the writings of the clergy, and in the works of other persons little acquainted with physical knowledge. When the cholera broke out in England, attempts were made to revive the old notion; but the spirit of the age was too strong for such efforts to succeed; and it may be safely predicted that men will never return to their former opinions, unless they first return to their former ignorance. As a specimen of the ideas which the cholera tended to excite, and of their antagonism to all scientific investigation, I may refer to a letter written in 1832 by Mrs. Grant, a woman of some accomplishments, and not devoid of influence (*Correspondence of Mrs. Grant*, London, 1844, vol. iii. pp. 216, 217), where she states that 'it appears to me great presumption to indulge so much as people do in speculation and conjecture about a disease so evidently a peculiar infliction, and different from all other modes of suffering hitherto known.' This desire to limit human speculation is precisely the feeling which long retained Europe in darkness; since it effectually prevented those free inquiries to which we are indebted for all the real knowledge we possess. The doubts of Boyle upon this subject supply a curious instance of the transitory state through which the mind was passing in the seventeenth century, and by which the way was prepared for the great liberating movement of the next age. Boyle, after stating both sides of the question, namely, the theological and the scientific, adds, 'and it is the less likely that these sweeping and contagious maladies should be always sent for the punishment of impious men, because I remember to have read in good authors, that as some plagues destroyed both men and beasts, so some other did peculiarly destroy brute animals of very little consideration or use to men, as cats,' &c.

'Upon these and the like reasons, I have sometimes suspected that in the controversy about the origin of the plague, namely, whether it be natural or supernatural, neither of the contending parties is altogether in the right; since it is very possible that some pestilences may not break forth without an extraordinary, though perhaps not immediate, interposition of Almighty God, provoked by the sins of men; and yet other plagues may be produced by a tragical concourse of merely natural causes.' *Discourse on the Air*, in *Boyle's Works*, vol. iv. pp. 288, 289. 'Neither of the contending parties is altogether in

where disease is most abundant. In countries where both these conditions are fulfilled, the superstition is supreme; and even where only one of the conditions exists, the tendency is so irresistible, that, I believe, there are no barbarous people who do not ascribe to their good or evil deities, not only extraordinary diseases, but even many of the ordinary ones to which they are liable.[304]

Here, then, we have another specimen of the unfavourable influence, which, in the old civilizations, external phenomena exercised over the human mind. For those parts of Asia where the highest refinement was reached, are, from various physical causes, much more unhealthy

---

the right!'—an instructive passage towards understanding the compromising spirit of the seventeenth century; standing midway, as it did, between the credulity of the sixteenth, and the scepticism of the eighteenth.

[304] To the historian of the human mind, the whole question is so full of interest, that I shall refer in this note to all the evidence I have been able to collect: and whoever will compare the following passages may satisfy himself that there is in every part of the world an intimate relation between ignorance respecting the nature and proper treatment of a disease, and the belief that such disease is caused by supernatural power, and is to be cured by it. *Burton's Sindh,* p. 146, London, 1851; *Ellis's Polynesian Researches,* vol. i. p. 395, vol. iii. pp. 36, 41, vol. iv. pp. 293, 334, 375; *Cullen's Works,* Edinb. 1827, vol. ii. pp. 414, 434; *Esquirol, Maladies Mentales,* vol. i. pp. 274, 482; *Cabanis, Rapports du Physique et du Moral,* p. 277; *Volney, Voyage en Syrie,* vol. i. p. 426; *Turner's Embassy to Tibet,* p. 104; *Syme's Embassy to Ava,* vol. ii. p. 211; *Ellis's Tour through Hawaii,* pp. 282, 283, 332, 333; *Renouard, Histoire de la Médecine,* vol. i. p. 398; *Broussais, Examen des Doctrines Médicales,* vol. i. pp. 261, 262; *Grote's History of Greece,* vol. i. p. 485 (compare p. 251, and vol. vi. p. 213); *Grieve's History of Kamtschatka,* p. 217; *Journal of Statist. Soc.* vol. x. p. 10; *Buchanan's North American Indians,* pp. 256, 257; *Halkett's North American Indians,* pp. 36, 37, 388, 393, 394; *Catlin's North American Indians,* vol. i. pp. 35–41; *Briggs on the Aboriginal Tribes of India,* in *Report of Brit. Assoc. for* 1850, p. 172; *Transactions of Soc. of Bombay,* vol. ii. p. 30; *Percival's Ceylon,* p. 201; *Buchanan's Journey through the Mysore,* vol. ii. pp. 27, 152, 266, 528, vol. iii. pp. 23, 188, 253 (so, too, M. Geoffroy Saint Hilaire, *Anomalies de l'Organisation,* vol. iii. p. 380, says that when we were quite ignorant of the cause of monstrous births, the phenomenon was ascribed to the Deity,—' de là aussi l'intervention supposée de la divinité;'

than the most civilized parts of Europe.²⁰⁴ This fact alone must have produced a considerable effect on the national character,²⁰⁶ and the more so, as it was aided by those other circumstances which I have pointed out, all tending in the same direction. To this may be added, that the great plagues by which Europe has at different periods been scourged, have, for the most part, proceeded from the East, which is their natural birthplace, and where they are most fatal. Indeed, of those cruel diseases now existing in Europe, scarcely one is indigenous; and the worst of them were imported from tropical countries in and after the first century of the Christian era.²⁰⁷

Summing up these facts, it may be stated, that in the

---

and for an exact verification of this, compare *Burdach, Traité de Physiologie*, vol. ii. p. 247, with *Journal of Geog. Soc.* vol. xvi. p. 113); *Ellis's History of Madagascar*, vol. i. pp. 224, 225; *Prichard's Physical History*, vol. i. p. 207, vol. v. p. 492: *Journal of Asiatic Society*, vol. iii. p. 230, vol. iv. p. 158; *Asiatic Researches*, vol. iii. pp. 29, 156, vol. iv. pp. 56, 58, 74, vol. xvi. pp. 215, 280; *Neander's History of the Church*, vol. iii. p. 119; *Crawfurd's History of the Indian Archipelago*, vol. i. p. 328; *Low's Sarawak*, pp. 174, 261; *Cook's Voyages*, vol. i. p. 229; *Mariner's Tonga Islands*, vol. i. pp. 194, 350-360, 374, 438, vol. ii. pp. 172, 230; *Hue's Travels in Tartary and Thibet*, vol. i. pp. 74-77; *Richardson's Travels in the Sahara*, vol. i. p. 27; *M'Culloh's Researches*, p. 105; *Journal of Geog. Soc.* vol. i. p. 41; vol. iv. p. 260, vol. xiv. p. 37. And in regard to Europe, compare *Spence, Origin of the Laws of Europe*, p. 322; *Turner's Hist. of England*, vol. iii. p. 443; *Phillips on Scrofula*, p. 255; *Otter's Life of Clarke*, vol. i. pp.

265, 268, which may be illustrated by the 'sacred' disease of Cambyses, no doubt epilepsy; see *Herodot.* lib. iii. chap. xxxiv. vol. ii. p. 63.

²⁰⁶ Heat, moisture, and consequent rapid decomposition of vegetable matter, are certainly among the causes of this; and to them may perhaps be added the electrical state of the atmosphere in the tropics. Compare *Holland's Medical Notes*, p. 477; *M'William's Medical Expedition to the Niger*, pp. 157, 183; *Simon's Pathology*, p. 269; *Forry's Climate and its Endemic Influences*, p. 168. M. Lepelletier says, rather vaguely (*L'hygiologie Médicale*, vol. iv. p. 527), that the temperate zones are 'favorables à l'exercice complet et régulier des phénomènes vitaux.'

²⁰⁶ And must have strengthened the power of the clergy; for, as Charlevoix says with great frankness, 'pestilences are the harvests of the ministers of God.' *Southey's History of Brazil*, vol. ii. p. 254.

²⁰⁷ For evidence of the extra-European origin of European

civilizations exterior to Europe, all nature conspired to increase the authority of the imaginative faculties, and weaken the authority of the reasoning ones. With the materials now existing, it would be possible to follow this vast law to its remotest consequences, and show how in Europe it is opposed by another law diametrically opposite, and by virtue of which the tendency of natural phenomena is, on the whole, to limit the imagination, and embolden the understanding: thus inspiring Man with confidence in his own resources, and facilitating the increase of his knowledge, by encouraging that bold, inquisitive, and scientific spirit, which is constantly advancing, and on which all future progress must depend.

It is not to be supposed that I can trace in detail the way in which, owing to these peculiarities, the civilization of Europe has diverged from all others that preceded it. To do this, would require a learning and a reach of thought to which hardly any single man ought to pretend; since it is one thing to have a perception of a large and general truth, and it is another thing to follow out that truth in all its ramifications, and prove it by such evidence as will satisfy ordinary readers. Those, indeed, who are accustomed to speculations of this character, and are able to discern in the history of man something more than a mere relation of events, will at once understand that in these complicated subjects, the wider any generalization is, the greater will be the chance of apparent exceptions; and that when the theory covers a very large space, the exceptions may be innumerable, and yet the theory remain perfectly accurate. The two fundamental propositions

---

diseases, some of which, such as the small-pox, have passed from epidemics into endemics, compare *Encyclop. of the Medical Sciences*, 4to, 1847, p. 728; *Transactions of Asiatic Society*, vol. ii. pp. 54, 55; *Michaelis on the Laws of Moses*, vol. iii. p. 313; *Sprengel, Histoire de la Médecine*, vol. ii. pp. 33, 195; *Wallace's Dissertation on the Numbers of Mankind*, pp. 81, 82; *Huetiana*, Amst. 1723, pp. 132–135; *Sandrra on the Small Pox*, Edinb. 1813, pp. 3–4; *Wilks's Hist. of the South of India*, vol. iii. pp. 16–21; *Clot-Bey de la Peste*, Paris, 1840, p. 227.

which I hope to have demonstrated, are, 1st, That there are certain natural phenomena which act on the human mind by exciting the imagination; and 2dly, That those phenomena are much more numerous out of Europe than in it. If these two propositions are admitted, it inevitably follows, that in those countries where the imagination has received the stimulus, some specific effects must have been produced; unless, indeed, the effects have been neutralized by other causes. Whether or not there have been antagonistic causes, is immaterial to the truth of the theory, which is based on the two propositions just stated. In a scientific point of view, therefore, the generalization is complete; and it would perhaps be prudent to leave it as it now stands, rather than attempt to confirm it by further illustrations, since all particular facts are liable to be erroneously stated, and are sure to be contradicted by those who dislike the conclusions they corroborate. But in order to familiarize the reader with the principles I have put forward, it does seem advisable that a few instances should be given of their actual working: and I will, therefore, briefly notice the effects they have produced in the three great divisions of Literature, Religion, and Art. In each of these departments, I will endeavour to indicate how the leading features have been affected by the Aspects of Nature; and with a view of simplifying the inquiry, I will take the two most conspicuous instances on each side, and compare the manifestations of the intellect of Greece with those of the intellect of India: these being the two countries respecting which the materials are most ample, and in which the physical contrasts are most striking.

If, then, we look at the ancient literature of India, even during its best period, we shall find the most remarkable evidence of the uncontrolled ascendency of the imagination. In the first place, we have the striking fact that scarcely any attention has been paid to prose composition; all the best writers having devoted themselves to poetry, as being most congenial to the national habits of thought. Their works on grammar, on law, on history, on medicine, on mathematics, on geography, and on metaphysics, are nearly all poems, and are put together according to a regular system of versification.[208] The consequence is, that while prose writing is utterly despised, the art of poetry has been cultivated so assiduously, that the Sanscrit can boast of metres more numerous and more complicated than have ever been possessed by any of the European languages.[209]

---

[208] 'So verwandelt das geistige Leben des Hindu sich in wahre Poesie, und das bezeichnende Merkmal seiner ganzen Bildung ist: Herrschaft der Einbildungskraft über den Verstand; im geraden Gegensatz mit der Bildung des Europäers, deren allgemeiner Charakter in der Herrschaft des Verstandes über die Einbildungskraft besteht. Es wird dadurch begreiflich, dass die Literatur der Hindus nur eine poetische ist; dass sie überreich an Dichterwerken, aber arm am wissenschaftlichen Schriften sind; dass ihre heiligen Schriften, ihre Gesetze und Sagen poetisch, und grösstentheils in Versen geschrieben sind; ja dass Lehrbücher der Grammatik, der Heilkunde, der Mathematik und Erdbeschreibung in Versen verfasst sind.' *Rhode, Religiöse Bildung der Hindus*, vol ii. p. 626. Thus, too, we are told respecting one of their most celebrated metaphysical systems, that 'the best text of the Sanchya is a short treatise in verse.' *Colebrooke on the Philosophy of the Hindus*, in *Transactions of Asiatic Society*, vol. i. p. 23. And in another place the same high authority says (*Asiatic Researches*, vol. x. p. 439), 'the metrical treatises on law and other sciences are almost entirely composed in this easy verse.' M. Klaproth, in an analysis of a Sanscrit history of Cashmere, says, 'comme presque toutes les compositions hindoues, il est écrit en vers.' *Journal Asiatique*, I. série, vol. vii. p. 8, Paris, 1825. See also, in vol. vi. pp. 175, 176, the remarks of M. Burnouf: 'Les philosophes indiens, comme s'ils ne pouvaient échapper aux influences poétiques de leur climat, traitent les questions de la métaphysique le plus abstraite par similitudes et métaphores.' Compare vol. vi. p. 4, 'le génie indien si poétique et si religieux;' and see *Cousin, Hist. de la Philosophie*, II. série, vol. i. p. 27.

[209] Mr. Yates says of the Hindus, that no other people have ever 'presented an equal variety of poetic compositions. The various metres of Greece and Rome have filled Europe with astonishment; but what are these, compared with the extensive range of Sanscrit metres under its three classes of poetical writing?' *Yates on Sanscrit Alliteration*, in *Asiatic Researches*, vol. xx. p. 159, Calcutta, 1836. See also on the Sanscrit metres, p. 321, and an Essay by Colebrooke, vol. x. pp. 389-474. On the metrical system of the Vedas, see Mr. Wilson's note in the *Rig Veda Sankita*, vol. ii. p. 135.

This peculiarity in the form of Indian literature is accompanied by a corresponding peculiarity in its spirit. For it is no exaggeration to say, that in that literature every thing is calculated to set the reason of man at open defiance. An imagination, luxuriant even to disease, runs riot on every occasion. This is particularly seen in those productions which are most eminently national, such as the Ramayana, the Muhabharat, and the Puranas in general. But we also find it even in their geographical and chronological systems, which of all others might be supposed least liable to imaginative flights. A few examples of the statements put forward in the most authoritative books, will supply the means of instituting a comparison with the totally opposite condition of the European intellect, and will give the reader some idea of the extent to which credulity can proceed, even among a civilized people.[210]

Of all the various ways in which the imagination has distorted truth, there is none that has worked so much harm as an exaggerated respect for past ages. This reverence for antiquity is repugnant to every maxim of reason, and is merely the indulgence of a poetic sentiment in favour of the remote and unknown. It is, therefore, natural that, in periods when the intellect was comparatively speaking inert, this sentiment should have been far stronger than it now is; and there can be little doubt that it will continue to grow weaker, and that in the same proportion the feeling of progress will gain ground; so that veneration for the past will be succeeded by hope for the future. But formerly the veneration was supreme, and innumerable traces of it may be found in the literature and popular creed of every country. It is this, for instance, which inspired

---

[210] In Europe, as we shall see in the sixth chapter of this volume, the credulity was at one time extraordinary; but the age was then barbarous, and barbarism is always credulous. On the other hand, the examples gathered from Indian literature will be taken from the works of a lettered people, written in a language extremely rich, and so highly polished, that some competent judges have declared it equal, if not superior, to the Greek.

the poets with their notion of a golden age, in which the world was filled with peace, in which evil passions were stilled, and crimes were unknown. It is this, again, which gave to theologians their idea of the primitive virtue and simplicity of man, and of his subsequent fall from that high estate. And it is this same principle which diffused a belief that in the olden times, men were not only more virtuous and happy, but also physically superior in the structure of their bodies; and that by this means they attained to a larger stature, and lived to a greater age, than is possible for us, their feeble and degenerate descendants.

Opinions of this kind, being adopted by the imagination in spite of the understanding, it follows that the strength of such opinions becomes, in any country, one of the standards by which we may estimate the predominance of the imaginative faculties. Applying this test to the literature of India, we shall find a striking confirmation of the conclusions already drawn. The marvellous feats of antiquity with which the Sanscrit books abound, are so long and so complicated, that it would occupy too much space to give even an outline of them; but there is one class of these singular fictions which is well worth attention, and admits of being briefly stated. I allude to the extraordinary age which man was supposed to have attained in former times. A belief in the longevity of the human race, at an early period of the world, was the natural product of those feelings which ascribed to the ancients an universal superiority over the moderns; and this we see exemplified in some of the Christian, and in many of the Hebrew writings. But the statements in these works are tame and insignificant when compared with what is preserved in the literature of India. On this, as on every subject, the imagination of the Hindus distanced all competition. Thus, among an immense number of similar facts, we find it recorded that in ancient times the duration of the life of common men was 80,000 years,[211] and that holy men lived to be upwards of

---

[211] 'The limit of life was vol. xvi. p. 456, Calcutta, 1828. 80,000 years.' *Asiatic Researches* This was likewise the estimate

100,000.[212] Some died a little sooner, others a little later; but in the most flourishing period of antiquity, if we take all classes together, 100,000 years was the average.[213] Of one king, whose name was Yudhishthir, it is casually mentioned that he reigned 27,000 years; [214] while another, called Alarka, reigned 66,000.[215] They were cut off in their prime, since there are several instances of the early poets living to be about half-a-million.[216] But the most remarkable case is that of a very shining character in Indian history, who united in his single person the functions of a king and a saint. This eminent man lived in a pure and virtuous age, and his days were, indeed, long in the land; since, when he was made king, he was two million years old: he then reigned 6,300,000 years; having done which, he resigned his empire, and lingered on for 100,000 years more.[217]

---

[212] of the Tibetan divines, according to whom men formerly 'parvenaient à l'âge de 80,000 ans.' *Journal Asiatique*, I. séria, vol. iii. p. 199, Paris, 1823.

[213] 'Den Hindu macht dieser Widerspruch nicht verlegen, da er seine Heiligen 100,000 Jahre und länger leben lässt.' *Rhode, Relig. Bildung der Hindus*, vol. i. p. 175.

[214] In the *Dabistan*, vol. ii. p. 47, it is stated of the earliest inhabitants of the world, that 'the duration of human life in this age extended to one hundred thousand common years.'

[215] Wilford (*Asiatic Researches*, vol. v. p. 242) says, 'When the Puranics speak of the kings of ancient times, they are equally extravagant. According to them, King Yudhishthir reigned seven-and-twenty thousand years.'

[216] 'For sixty thousand and sixty hundred years no other youthful monarch except Alarka reigned over the earth.' *Vishnu Purana*, p. 408.

[217] 'And sometimes more. In the Essay on Indian Chronology in *Works of Sir W. Jones*, vol. i. p. 325, we hear of 'a conversation between Valmic and Vyasa, ... two bards whose ages were separated by a period of 864,000 years.' This passage is also in *Asiatic Researches*, vol. ii. p. 399.

[217] 'He was the first king, first anchoret, and first saint; and is therefore entitled Prathama-Raja, Prathama Bhicshacara, Prathama Jina, and Prathama Tirthancara. At the time of his inauguration as king, his age was 2,000,000 years. He reigned 6,300,000 years, and then resigned his empire to his sons: and having employed 100,000 years in passing through the several stages of austerity and sanctity, departed from this

The same boundless reverence for antiquity made the Hindus refer every thing important to the most distant periods; and they frequently assign a date which is absolutely bewildering.²¹⁸ Their great collection of laws, called the *Institutes of Menu*, is certainly less than 3,000 years old; but the Indian chronologists, so far from being satisfied with this, ascribe to them an age that the sober European mind finds a difficulty even in conceiving. According to the best native authorities, these Institutes were revealed to man about two thousand million years before the present era.²¹⁹

All this is but a part of that love of the remote, that straining after the infinite, and that indifference to the present, which characterizes every branch of the Indian intellect. Not only in literature, but also in religion and in art, this tendency is supreme. To subjugate the understanding, and exalt the imagination, is the universal principle. In the dogmas of their theology, in the character of their gods, and even in the forms of their temples, we see how the sublime and threatening aspects of the external world have filled the mind of the people with those images of the grand and the terrible, which they strive to reproduce in a visible form, and to which they owe the leading peculiarities of their national culture.

Our view of this vast process may be made clearer by comparing it with the opposite condition of Greece. In Greece, we see a country altogether the reverse of India. The works of nature, which in India are of startling magnitude, are in Greece far smaller, feebler, and in every way less threatening to man. In the

---

world on the summit of a mountain named Ashtapada.' *Asiatic Researches*, vol. ix. p. 305.

²¹⁸ Speculationen über Zahlen sind dem Inder so geläufig, dass selbst die Sprache einen Ausdruck hat für eine Unität mit 63 Nullen, nämlich Asanke, eben weil die Berechnung der Weltperioden diese enorme Grössen nothwendig machte; denn jene einfachen 12,000 Jahre schienen einem Volke, welches so gerne die höchstmögliche Potenz auf seine Gottheit übertragen mögte, viel zu geringe zu sayn.' Bohlen, *das alte Indien*, vol. ii. p. 298.

²¹⁹ *Elphinstone's History of India*, p. 136, 'a period exceeding 4,320,000 multiplied by six times seventy-one.'

great centre of Asiatic civilization, the energies of the human race are confined, and as it were intimidated, by the surrounding phenomena. Besides the dangers incidental to tropical climates, there are those noble mountains, which seem to touch the sky, and from whose sides are discharged mighty rivers, which no art can divert from their course, and which no bridge has ever been able to span. There, too, are impassable forests, whole countries lined with interminable jungle, and beyond them, again, dreary and boundless deserts; all teaching Man his own feebleness, and his inability to cope with natural forces. Without, and on either side, there are great seas, ravaged by tempests far more destructive than any known in Europe, and of such sudden violence, that it is impossible to guard against their effects. And, as if in those regions every thing combined to cramp the activity of Man, the whole line of coast, from the mouth of the Ganges to the extreme south of the peninsula, does not contain a single safe and capacious harbour, not one port that affords a refuge, which is perhaps more necessary there than in any other part of the world.[290]

But in Greece, the aspects of nature are so entirely different, that the very conditions of existence are changed. Greece, like India, forms a peninsula; but while in the Asiatic country every thing is great and terrible, in the European country every thing is small and feeble. The whole of Greece occupies a space somewhat less than the kingdom of Portugal,[291] that is

---

[290] Symes (*Embassy to Ava*, vol. iii. p. 278) says: 'From the mouth of the Ganges to Cape Comorin, the whole range of one continental territory, there is not a single harbour capable of affording shelter to a vessel of 500 tons burden.' Indeed, according to Parcival, there is with the exception of Bombay, no harbour, 'either on the Coromandel or Malabar coasts, in which ships can moor in safety at all seasons of the year.' *Percival's Account of Ceylon*, pp. 2, 16, 66.

[291] 'Altogether its area is somewhat less than that of Portugal.' *Grote's History of Greece*, vol. ii. p. 302; and the same remark in *Thirlwall's History of Greece*, vol. i. p. 2, and in *Heeren's Ancient Greece*, 1845, p. 16. M. Heeren says, 'But

about a fortieth part of what is now called Hindostan.[223] Situated in the most accessible part of a narrow sea, it had easy contact on the east with Asia Minor, on the west with Italy, on the south with Egypt. Dangers of all kinds were far less numerous than in the tropical civilizations. The climate was more healthy;[223] earthquakes were less frequent; hurricanes were less disastrous; wild-beasts and noxious animals less abundant. In regard to the other great features, the same law prevails. The highest mountains in Greece are less than one-third of the Himalaya, so that nowhere do they reach the limit of perpetual snow.[224] As to rivers, not only is there nothing approaching those imposing volumes which are poured down from the mountains of Asia, but nature is so singularly sluggish, that neither in Northern nor in Southern Greece do we find any thing beyond a few streams, which are easily forded, and which, indeed, in the summer season, are frequently dried up.[225]

These striking differences in the material phenomena

---

even if we add all the islands, its square contents are a third less than those of Portugal.'

[222] The area of Hindostan being, according to Mr. M'Culloch (*Geog. Dict.* 1849, vol. i. p. 993), 'between 1,200,000 and 1,300,000 square miles.'

[223] In the best days of Greece, those alarming epidemics, by which the country was subsequently ravaged, were comparatively little known: see Thirlwall's *History of Greece*, vol. iii. p. 134, vol. viii. p. 471. This may be owing to large cosmical causes, or to the simple fact, that the different forms of pestilence had not yet been imported from the East by actual contact. On the vague accounts we possess of the earlier plagues, see *Clot-Bey de la Peste*, Paris, 1840, pp. 21, 46, 184. The relation even of Thucydides is more satisfactory to scholars than to pathologists.

[224] 'Mount Guino, the highest point in Greece, and near its northern boundary, is 8,239 feet high. . . . . No mountain in Greece reaches the limit of perpetual snow.' *M'Culloch's Geog. Dict.* 1849, vol. i. p. 924. Compare the table of mountains in Baker's Memoir on North Greece, in *Journal of Geographical Society*, vol. vii. p. 94, with *Bakewell's Geology*, pp. 621, 622.

[225] 'Greece has no navigable river.' *M'Culloch's Geog. Dict.* vol. i. p. 924. 'Most of the rivers of Greece are torrents in early spring, and dry before the end of the summer.' *Grote's History of Greece*, vol. ii. p. 286.

of the two countries gave rise to corresponding differences in their mental associations. For as all ideas must arise partly from what are called spontaneous operations in the mind, and partly from what is suggested to the mind by the external world, it was natural that so great an alteration in one of the causes should produce an alteration in the effects. The tendency of the surrounding phenomena was in India to inspire fear; in Greece to give confidence. In India Man was intimidated; in Greece he was encouraged. In India obstacles of every sort were so numerous, so alarming, and apparently so inexplicable, that the difficulties of life could only be solved by constantly appealing to the direct agency of supernatural causes. Those causes being beyond the province of the understanding, the resources of the imagination were incessantly occupied in studying them; the imagination itself was overworked, its activity became dangerous, it encroached on the understanding, and the equilibrium of the whole was destroyed. In Greece opposite circumstances were followed by opposite results. In Greece Nature was less dangerous, less intrusive, and less mysterious than in India. In Greece, therefore, the human mind was less appalled, and less superstitious; natural causes began to be studied; physical science first became possible; and Man, gradually waking to a sense of his own power, sought to investigate events with a boldness not to be expected in those other countries, where the pressure of Nature troubled his independence, and suggested ideas with which knowledge is incompatible.

The effect of these habits of thought on the national religion must be very obvious to whoever has compared the popular creed of India with that of Greece. The mythology of India, like that of every tropical country, is based upon terror, and upon terror, too, of the most extravagant kind. Evidence of the universality of this feeling abounds in the sacred books of the Hindus, in their traditions, and even in the very form and appearance of their gods. And so deeply is all this impressed on the mind, that the most popular deities are invariably those with whom images of fear are most intimately associated. Thus, for example, the worship of Siva is more general than any other; and as to its antiquity, there is reason to believe that it was borrowed by the Brahmins from the original Indians.[226] At all events, it is very ancient, and very popular; and Siva himself forms, with Brahma and Vishnu, the celebrated Hindu Triad. We need not, therefore, be surprised that with this god are connected images of terror, such as nothing but a tropical imagination could conceive. Siva is represented to the Indian mind as a hideous being, encircled by a girdle of snakes, with a human skull in his hand, and wearing a necklace composed of human bones. He has three eyes; the ferocity of his temper is marked by his being clothed in a tiger's skin; he is represented as wandering about like a madman, and over his left shoulder the deadly cobra di capella rears its head. This monstrous creation of an awe-struck fancy has a wife Doorga, called sometimes Kali, and sometimes by other names.[227] She has a body of dark blue; while the palms of her hands are red, to indicate her insatiate appetite for blood. She has four arms,

---

[226] See Stevenson on *The Anti-Brahmanical Religion of the Hindus*, in *Journal of Asiatic Society*, vol. viii. pp. 331, 332, 336, 338. Mr. Wilson (*Journal*, vol. iii. p. 204) says, 'The prevailing form of the Hindu religion in the south of the peninsula was, at the commencement of the Christian era, and some time before it most probably, that of Siva.' See also vol. v. p. 85, where it is stated that Siva 'is the only Hindu god to whom honour is done at Ellora.' Compare *Transac. of Soc. of Bombay*, vol. iii. p. 521; *Heeren's Asiatic Nations*, 1846, vol. ii. pp. 62, 66. On the philosophical relations between the followers of Siva and those of Vishnu, see *Ritter's Hist. of Ancient Philosophy*, vol. iv. pp. 334, 335; and the noticeable fact (*Buchanan's Mysore*, vol. ii. p. 410), that even the Naimar caste, whose 'proper deity' is Vishnu, 'wear on their foreheads the mark of Siva.' As to the worship of Siva in the time of Alexander the Great, see *Thirlwall's History of Greece*, vol. vii. p. 36; and for further evidence of its extent, Bohlen, *das alte Indien*, vol. i. pp. 29, 147, 206, and *Transac. of Asiatic Society*, vol. ii. pp. 50, 204.

[227] So it is generally stated by the Hindu theologians; but, according to Rammohun Roy, Siva had two wives. See *Rammohun Roy on the Veds*, p. 90.

142   INFLUENCE OF PHYSICAL LAWS.

with one of which she carries the skull of a giant; her tongue protrudes, and hangs lollingly from her mouth; round her waist are the hands of her victims; and her neck is adorned with human heads strung together in a ghastly row.[228]

If we now turn to Greece, we find, even in the infancy of its religion, not the faintest trace of any thing approaching to this. For, in Greece, the causes of fear being less abundant, the expression of terror was less common. The Greeks, therefore, were by no means disposed to incorporate into their religion those feelings of dread natural to the Hindus. The tendency of Asiatic civilization was to widen the distance between men and their deities; the tendency of Greek civilization was to diminish it. Thus it is, that in Hindostan all the gods had something monstrous about them; as Vishnu with four hands, Brahma with five heads, and the like.[229] But the gods of Greece were always represented in forms entirely human.[230] In that country, no artist would have gained attention, if he had presumed to portray them in any other shape. He might

---

[228] On these attributes and representations of Siva and Doorga, see *Rhode, Religiöse Bildung der Hindus*, vol. ii. p. 241; *Coleman's Mythology of the Hindus*, pp. 63, 92; *Bohlen, das alte Indien*, vol. i. p. 207; *Ward's Religion of the Hindoos*, vol. i. pp. xxxvii. 27, 143; *Transac. of Society of Bombay*, vol. i. pp. 215, 221. Compare the curious account of an image supposed to represent Mahadeo, in *Journal Asiatique*, L série, vol. i. p. 354, Paris, 1822.

[229] *Ward on the Religion of the Hindoos*, vol. i. p. 35; *Transac. of Society of Bombay*, vol. i. p. 223. Compare the gloss in the *Dabistan*, vol. ii. p. 202.

[230] 'The Greek gods were formed like men, with greatly increased powers and faculties, and acted as men would do if so circumstanced, but with a dignity and energy suited to their nearer approach to perfection. The Hindu gods, on the other hand, though endued with human passions, have always something monstrous in their appearance, and wild and capricious in their conduct. They are of various colours, red, yellow, and blue; some have twelve heads, and most have four hands. They are often enraged without a cause, and reconciled without a motive.' *Elphinstone's History of India*, pp. 96, 97. See also *Erskine on the Temple of Elephanta*, in *Transac. of Society of Bombay* vol. i. p. 246; and the *Dabistan*, vol. i. p. cxl.

make them stronger than men, he might make them more beautiful; but still they must be men. The analogy between God and Man, which excited the religious feelings of the Greeks, would have been fatal to those of the Hindus.

This difference between the artistic expressions of the two religions was accompanied by an exactly similar difference between their theological traditions. In the Indian books, the imagination is exhausted in relating the feats of the gods; and the more obviously impossible any achievement is, the greater the pleasure with which it was ascribed to them. But the Greek gods had not only human forms, but also human attributes, human pursuits, and human tastes.[31] The men of Asia, to whom every object of nature was a source of awe, acquired such habits of reverence, that they never dared to assimilate their own actions with the actions of their deities. The men of Europe, encouraged by the safety and inertness of the material world, did not fear to strike a parallel, from which they would have shrunk had they lived amid the dangers of a tropical country. It is thus

---

[31] 'In the material polytheism of other leading ancient nations, the Egyptians, for example, the incarnation of the Deity was chiefly, or exclusively, confined to animals, monsters, or other fanciful emblems. . . . In Greece, on the other hand, it was an almost necessary result of the spirit and grace with which the deities were embodied in human forms, that they should also be burdened with human interests and passions. Heaven, like earth, had its courts and palaces, its trades and professions, its marriages, intrigues, divorces.' *Mure's History of the Literature of Ancient Greece*, vol. i. pp. 471, 472. So, too, Tennemann (*Geschichte der Philosophie*, vol. iii. p. 419): 'Diese Götter haben Menschengestalt. . . . Haben die Götter aber nicht nur menschliche Gestalt, sondern auch einen menschlichen Körper, so sind sie als Menschen auch denselben Unvollkommenheiten, Krankheiten und dem Tode unterworfen; dieses streitet mit dem Begriffe,' *i.e.* of Epicurus. Compare *Grote's History of Greece*, vol. i. p. 506: 'The mythical age was peopled with a mingled aggregate of gods, heroes, and men, so confounded together, that it was often impossible to distinguish to which class any individual name belonged.' See also the complaint of Xenophanes, in *Müller's Hist. of Lit. of Greece*, London, 1856, p. 261.

that the Greek divinities are so different from those of the Hindus, that in comparing them we seem to pass from one creation into another. The Greeks generalized their observations upon the human mind, and then applied them to the gods.[232] The coldness of women was figured in Diana; their beauty and sensuality in Venus; their pride in Juno; their accomplishments in Minerva. To the ordinary avocations of the gods the same principle was applied. Neptune was a sailor; Vulcan was a smith; Apollo was sometimes a fiddler, sometimes a poet, sometimes a keeper of oxen. As to Cupid, he was a wanton boy, who played with his bow and arrows; Jupiter was an amorous and good-natured king; while Mercury was indifferently represented either as a trustworthy messenger, or else as a common and notorious thief.

Precisely the same tendency to approximate human forces towards superhuman ones, is displayed in another peculiarity of the Greek religion. I mean, that in Greece we for the first time meet with hero-worship, that is, the deification of mortals. According to the principles already laid down, this could not be expected in a tropical civilization, where the Aspects of Nature filled Man with a constant sense of his own incapacity. It is, therefore, natural that it should form no part of the ancient Indian religion;[233] neither was it known to the Egyptians,[234] nor to the Persians,[235] nor, so far as I am aware, to the Ara-

---

[232] The same remark applies to beauty of form, which they first aimed at in the statues of men, and then brought to bear upon the statues of the gods. This is well put in Mr. Grote's important work, *History of Greece*, vol. iv. pp. 133, 134, edit. 1847.

[233] 'But the worship of deified heroes is no part of that system.' *Colebrooke on the Vedas*, in *Asiatic Researches*, vol. viii. p. 495.

[234] *Mackay's Religious Development*, vol. ii. p. 53, Lond. 1850. Compare *Wilkinson's Ancient Egyptians*, vol. iv. pp. 148, 318; and *Matter, Histoire de l'École d'Alexandrie*, vol. i. p. 2; the 'culte des grands hommes,' which afterwards arose in Alexandria (*Matter*, vol. i. p. 54), must have been owing to Greek influence.

[235] There are no indications of it in the Zendavesta; and Herodotus says, that the Persians were unlike the Greeks, in so far as they disbelieved in a god having a human form; book i. chap. cxxxi. vol. i. p. 308: οὐκ ἀνθρωποφυέας ἐνόμισαν τοὺς θεούς, κατάπερ οἱ Ἕλληνες εἶναι.

bians.²³⁶ But in Greece, Man being less humbled, and, as it were, less eclipsed, by the external world, thought more of his own powers, and human nature did not fall into that discredit in which it elsewhere sank. The consequence was, that the deification of mortals was a recognized part of the national religion at a very early period in the history of Greece;²³⁷ and this has been found so natural to Europeans, that the same custom was afterwards renewed with eminent success by the Romish Church. Other circumstances, of a very different character, are gradually eradicating this form of idolatry; but its existence is worth observing, as one of the innumerable illustrations of the way in which European civilization has diverged from all those that preceded it.²³⁸

It is thus, that in Greece every thing tended to exalt the dignity of man, while in India every thing tended to depress it.²³⁹ To sum up the whole, it may be said that

---

²³⁶ I am not acquainted with any evidence connecting this worship with the old Arabian religion; and it was certainly most alien to the spirit of Mohammedanism.

²³⁷ Mure's *History of the Literature of Greece*, vol. i. pp. 28, 500, vol. ii. p. 402: very good remarks on a subject handled unsatisfactorily by Coleridge; *Literary Remains*, vol. i. p. 185. Thirlwall (*History of Greece*, vol. i. p. 207) admits that 'the views and feelings out of which it (the worship of heroes) arose, seem to be clearly discernible in the Homeric poems.' Compare *Cudworth's Intellectual System*, vol. ii. pp. 226, 372. In the Cratylus, chap. xxxiii., Socrates is represented as asking, Οὐκ οἶσθα ὅτι ἡμίθεοι οἱ ἥρωες; *Platonis Opera*, vol. iv. p. 227, edit. Bekker, Lond. 1826. And in the next century, Alexander obtained for his friend, Hephæstion, the right of being 'worshipped as a hero'

Grote's History of Greece, vol. xii. p. 339.

²³⁸ The adoration of the dead, and particularly the adoration of martyrs, was one great point of opposition between the orthodox church and the Manichæans (*Beausobre, Histoire Critique de Manichée*, vol. i. p. 316, vol. ii. pp. 651, 669); and it is easy to understand how abhorrent such a practice must have been to the Persian heretics.

²³⁹ M. Cousin, in his eloquent and ingenious work (*Histoire de la Philosophie*, 3e série, vol. i. pp. 183, 187), has some judicious observations on what he calls 'l'époque de l'infini' of the East, contrasted with that 'du fini,' which began in Europe. But as to the physical causes of this, he only admits the grandeur of nature, overlooking those natural elements of mystery and of danger by which religious sentiments were constantly excited.

the Greeks had more respect for human powers; the Hindus for superhuman. The first dealt more with the known and available; the other with the unknown and mysterious.[240] And by a parity of reasoning, the imagination, which the Hindus, being oppressed by the pomp and majesty of nature, never sought to control, lost its supremacy in the little peninsula of ancient Greece. In Greece, for the first time in the history of the world, the imagination was, in some degree, tempered and confined by the understanding. Not that its strength was impaired, or its vitality diminished. It was broken-in and tamed; its exuberance was checked, its follies were chastised. But that its energy remained, we have ample proof in those productions of the Greek mind which have survived to our own time. The gain, therefore, was complete; since the inquiring and sceptical faculties of the human understanding were cultivated, without destroying the reverential and poetic instincts of the imagination. Whether or not the balance was accurately adjusted, is another question; but it is certain that the adjustment was more nearly arrived at in Greece than in any previous civilization.[241] There can, I think, be little doubt

---

[240] A learned orientalist says, that no people have made such efforts as the Hindus 'to solve, exhaust, comprehend, what is insolvable, inexhaustible, incomprehensible.' *Troyer's Preliminary Discourse on the Dabistan*, vol. i. p. cviii.

[241] This is noticed by Tennemann, who, however, has not attempted to ascertain the cause: 'Die Einbildungskraft des Griechen war schöpferisch, sie schuf in seinem Innern neue Ideenwelten; aber er wurde doch nie verleitet, die idealische Welt mit der wirklichen zu verwechseln, weil sie immer mit einem richtigen Verstande und gesunder Beurtheilungskraft verbunden war.' *Geschichte der Philosophie*, vol. i. p. 8; and vol. vi. p. 490, he says, 'Bei allen diesen Mängeln und Fehlern sind doch die Griechen die einzige Nation der alten Welt, welche Sinn für Wissenschaft hatte, und zu diesem Behufe forschte. Sie haben doch die Bahn gebrochen, und den Weg zur Wissenschaft geebnet.' To the same effect, *Sprengel, Histoire de la Médecine*, vol. i. p. 215. And on this difference between the Eastern and the European mind, see *Matter, Histoire du Gnosticisme*, vol. i. pp. 18, 233, 234. So, too, Kant (*Logik*, in *Kant's Werke*, vol. i. p. 350), 'Unter allen Völkern haben also die Griechen erst angefangen zu philosophiren. Denn sie haben zuerst versucht,

that, notwithstanding what was effected, too much authority was left to the imaginative faculties, and that the purely reasoning ones did not receive, and never have received, sufficient attention. Still, this does not affect the great fact, that the Greek literature is the first in which this deficiency was somewhat remedied, and in which there was a deliberate and systematic attempt to test all opinions by their consonance with human reason, and thus vindicate the right of Man to judge for himself on matters which are of supreme and incalculable importance.

I have selected India and Greece as the two terms of the preceding comparison, because our information respecting those countries is most extensive, and has been most carefully arranged. But every thing we know of the other tropical civilizations confirms the views I have advocated respecting the effects produced by the Aspects of Nature. In Central America extensive excavations have been made; and what has been brought to light proves that the national religion was, like that of India, a system of complete and unmitigated terror.[142] Neither there nor in Mexico, nor in Peru, nor in Egypt, did the people desire to represent their deities in human forms, or ascribe to them human attributes. Even their temples are huge buildings, often constructed with great skill, but showing an evident wish to impress the mind with fear, and offering a striking contrast to the lighter and smaller structures which the Greeks employed for religious purposes. Thus, even in the style of architecture do we see the same principle at work; the dangers of the

---

nicht an dem Leitfaden der Bilder die Vernunfterkenntnisse zu cultiviren, sondern *in abstracto*; statt dass die anderen Völker sich die Begriffe immer nur durch Bilder *in concreto* verständlich zu machen suchten.'

[142] Thus, of one of the idols at Copan, 'The intention of the sculptor seems to have been to excite terror.' *Stephen's Central America*, vol. i. p. 152; at p. 159, 'The form of sculpture most generally used was a death's head.' At Mayapan (vol. iii. p. 133), 'representations of human figures or animals with hideous features and expressions, in producing which the skill of the artist seems to have been expended;' and again, p. 412, 'unnatural and grotesque faces.'

tropical civilization being more suggestive of the infinite, while the safety of the European civilization was more suggestive of the finite. To follow out the consequences of this great antagonism, it would be necessary to indicate how the infinite, the imaginative, the synthetic, and the deductive, are all connected; and are opposed, on the other hand, by the finite, the sceptical, the analytic, and the inductive. A complete illustration of this would carry me beyond the plan of this Introduction and would perhaps exceed the resources of my own knowledge; and I must now leave to the candour of the reader what I am conscious is but an imperfect sketch, but what may, nevertheless, suggest to him materials for future thought, and, if I might indulge the hope, may open to historians a new field, by reminding them that every where the hand of Nature is upon us, and that the history of the human mind can only be understood by connecting with it the history and the aspects of the material universe.

Note 36 to p. 61.

As these views have a social and economical importance quite independent of their physiological value, I will endeavour, in this note, to fortify them still further, by showing that the connexion between carbonized food and the respiratory functions may be illustrated by a wider survey of the animal kingdom.

The gland most universal among the different classes of animals is the liver;[a] and its principal business is to relieve the system of its superfluous carbon, which it accomplishes by secreting bile, a highly carbonized fluid.[b] Now, the connexion between this process and the respiratory functions is highly curious. For, if we take a general view of animal life, we shall find that the liver and lungs are nearly always compensatory; that is to say, when one organ is

---

[a] 'The most constant gland in the animal kingdom is the liver.' *Grant's Comp. Anat.* p. 576. See also *Bérard, Anat. Gén.* p. 18, and *Burdach, Traité de Physiol.* vol. ix. p. 380. Burdach says, 'Il existe dans presque tout le règne animal;' and the latest researches have detected the rudiments of a liver even in the Entozoa and Rotifera. *Rymer Jones's Animal Kingdom*, 1855, p. 183, and *Owen's Invertebrata*, 1855, p. 104.

[b] Until the analysis made by Demarçay in 1837, hardly any thing was known of the composition of bile; but this accomplished chemist ascertained that its essential constituent is cholate of soda, and that the choleic acid contains nearly sixty-three per cent. of carbon. Compare *Thomson's Animal Chemistry*, pp. 59, 60, 412, &c., with *Simon's Chemistry*, vol. ii. pp. 17–21.

small and inert, the other is large and active. Thus, reptiles have feeble lungs, but a considerable liver;[a] and thus, too, in fishes, which have no lungs, in the ordinary sense of the word, the size of the liver is often enormous.[b] On the other hand, insects have a very large and complicated system of air tubes; but their liver is minute, and its functions are habitually sluggish.[c] If, instead of comparing the different classes of animals, we compare the different stages through which the same animal passes, we shall find further confirmation of this wide and striking principle. For the law holds good even before birth; since in the unborn infant the lungs have scarcely any activity, but there is an immense liver, which is full of energy and pours out bile in profusion.[d] And so invariable is this relation, that in man the liver is the first organ which is formed: it is preponderant during the whole period of foetal life; but it rapidly diminishes when, after birth, the lungs come into play, and a new scheme of compensation is established in the system.[e]

---

[a] 'The size of the liver and the quantity of the bile are not proportionate to the quantity of the food and frequency of eating; but inversely to the size and perfection of the lungs. .... The liver is proportionately larger in reptiles, which have lungs with large cells incapable of rapidly decarbonizing the blood.' *Good's Study of Medicine*, 1822, vol. I. pp. 52, 53. See Cuvier, *Règne Animal*, vol. ii. p. 2, on 'la petitesse des vaisseaux pulmonaires' of reptiles.

[b] *Carus's Comparative Anatomy*, vol. ii. p. 230; *Grant's Comp. Anat.* pp. 835, 896; *Rymer Jones's Animal Kingdom*, p. 644.

[c] Indeed it has been supposed by M. Galde that the 'vaisseaux biliares' of some insects were not 'sécréteurs;' but this opinion appears to be erroneous. See Latreille, in Cuvier, *Règne Animal*, vol. iv. pp. 797, 798.

[d] 'La prédominance du foie avant la naissance' is noticed by Bichat (*Anatomie Générale*, vol. ii. p. 272), and by many other physiologists; but Dr. Elliotson appears to have been one of the first to understand a fact, the explanation of which we might vainly seek for in the earlier writers. 'The hypothesis, that one great use of the liver was, like that of the lungs, to remove carbon from the system, with this difference, that the alteration of the capacity of the air caused a reception of caloric into the blood, in the case of the lungs, while the hepatic excretion takes place without introduction of caloric, was, I recollect, a great favourite with me when a student. . . . The Heidelberg professors have adduced many arguments to the same effect. In the foetus, for whose temperature the mother's heat must be sufficient, the lungs perform no function; but the liver is of great size, and bile is secreted abundantly, so that the meconium accumulates considerably during the latter months of pregnancy.' *Elliotson's Human Physiology*, 1840, p. 102. In *Lepelletier's Physiologie Médicale*, vol. i. p. 446, vol. ii. pp. 14, 646, 650, all this is sadly confused.

[e] 'The liver is the first-formed organ in the embryo. It is developed from the alimentary canal, and at about the third week fills the whole abdomen, and is one-half the weight of the entire embryo. . . . . At birth it is of very large size, and occupies the whole upper part of the abdomen. . . . The liver diminishes rapidly after birth, probably from obliteration of the umbilical vein.' *Wilson's Human Anatomy*, 1851, p. 638. Compare *Burdach's Physiologie*, vol. iv. p. 447, where it is said of the liver in childhood, 'Cet organe croit avec lenteur, surtout comparativement aux poumons; le rapport de ceux-ci au foie étant à peu près de 1 : 3 avant la respiration, il était de 1 : 1·85 après l'établissement de cette dernière fonction.' See also p. 91, and vol. iii. p. 443; and on the predominance of the liver in foetal life, see the remarks of Serres (*Geoffroy Saint-Hilaire, Anomalies de l'Organisation*, vol. ii. p. 11), whose generalization is perhaps a little premature.

These facts, interesting to the philosophic physiologist, are of great moment in reference to the doctrines advocated in this chapter. Inasmuch as the liver and lungs are compensatory in the history of their organization, it is highly probable that they are also compensatory in the functions they perform; and that what is left undone by one will have to be accomplished by the other. The liver, therefore, fulfilling the duty, as chemistry teaches us, of decarbonising the system by secreting a carbonized fluid, we should expect, even in the absence of any further evidence, that the lungs would be likewise decarbonizing; in other words, we should expect that if, from any cause, we are surcharged with carbon, our lungs must assist in remedying the evil. This brings us, by another road, to the conclusion that highly carbonized food has a tendency to tax the lungs; so that the connexion between a carbonized diet and the respiratory functions, instead of being, as some assert, a crude hypothesis, is an eminently scientific theory, and is corroborated not only by chemistry, but by the general scheme of the animal kingdom, and even by the observation of embryological phenomena. The views of Liebeg, and of his followers, are indeed supported by so many analogies, and harmonize so well with other parts of our knowledge, that nothing but a perverse hatred of generalization, or an incapacity for dealing with large speculative truths, can explain the hostility directed against conclusions which have been gradually forcing themselves upon us since Lavoisier, seventy years ago, attempted to explain the respiratory functions by subjecting them to the laws of chemical combination.

In this, and previous notes (see in particular notes 30, 31, 35), I have considered the connexion between food respiration, and animal heat, at a length which will appear tedious to readers uninterested in physiological pursuits; but the investigation has become necessary, on account of the difficulties raised by experimenters, who, not having studied the subject comprehensively, object to certain parts of it. To mention what, from the ability and reputation of the author, is a conspicuous instance of this, Sir Benjamin Brodie has recently published a volume (*Physiological Researches*, 1851) containing some ingeniously contrived experiments on dogs and rabbits, to prove that heat is generated rather by the nervous system than by the respiratory organs. Without following this eminent surgeon into all its details, I may be permitted to observe, 1st, That, as a mere matter of history, no great physiological truth has ever yet been discovered, nor has any great physiological fallacy been destroyed, by such limited experiments on a single class of animals; and this is partly because in physiology a crucial instance is impracticable, owing to the fact that we deal with resisting and living bodies, and partly because every experiment produces an abnormal condition, and thus lets in fresh causes, the operation of which is incalculable; unless, as often happens in the inorganic world, we can control the whole phenomenon. 2nd, That the other department of the organic world, namely, the vegetable kingdom, has, so far as we are aware, no nervous system, but nevertheless possesses heat; and we moreover know that the heat is a product of oxygen and carbon (see note 32 to chapter ii.). 3d, That the evidence of travellers respecting the different sorts of food, and the different quantities of food, used in hot countries and in cold ones, is explicable by the respiratory and chemical theories of the origin of animal heat, but is inexplicable by the theory of the nervous origin of heat.

CHAPTER III.

EXAMINATION OF THE METHOD EMPLOYED BY METAPHYSICIANS FOR DISCOVERING MENTAL LAWS.

THE evidence that I have collected seems to establish two leading facts, which, unless they can be impugned, are the necessary basis of universal history. The first fact is, that in the civilizations out of Europe, the powers of nature have been far greater than in those in Europe. The second fact is, that those powers have worked immense mischief; and that while one division of them has caused an unequal distribution of wealth, another division of them has caused an unequal distribution of thought, by concentrating attention upon subjects which inflame the imagination. So far as the experience of the past can guide us, we may say, that in all the extra European civilizations, these obstacles are insuperable: certainly no nation has ever yet overcome them. But Europe, being constructed upon a smaller plan than the other quarters of the world—being also in a colder region, having a less exuberant soil, a less imposing aspect, and displaying in all her physical phenomena much greater feebleness—it was easier for Man to discard the superstitions which Nature suggested to his imagination; and it was also easier for him to effect, not, indeed, a just division of wealth, but something nearer to it, than was practicable in the older countries.

Hence it is that, looking at the history of the world as a whole, the tendency has been, in Europe, to subordinate nature to man; out of Europe, to subordinate man to nature. To this there are, in barbarous countries, several exceptions; but in civilized countries the rule has been universal. The great division, therefore, between European civilization and non-European civilization, is the basis of the philosophy of history, since it suggests the important consideration, that if we would understand, for instance, the history of India, we must make the external world our first study, because it has influenced man more than man has influenced it. If, on the other hand, we would understand the history of a country like France or England, we must make man our principal study, because nature being comparatively weak, every step in the great progress has increased the dominion of the human mind over the agencies of the external world. Even in those countries where the power of man has reached the highest point, the pressure of nature is still immense; but it diminishes in each succeeding generation, because our increasing knowledge enables us not so much to control nature as to foretell her movements, and thus obviate many of the evils she would otherwise occasion. How successful our efforts have been, is evident from the fact, that the average duration of life constantly becomes longer, and the number of inevitable dangers fewer; and what makes this the more remarkable is, that the curiosity of men is keener, and their contact with each other closer, than in any former period; so that while apparent hazards are multiplied, we find from experience that real hazards are, on the whole, diminished.[1]

If, therefore, we take the largest possible view of the history of Europe, and confine ourselves entirely to the primary cause of its superiority over other parts of the world, we must resolve it into the encroach-

---

[1] This diminution of casualties is undoubtedly one cause, though a slight one, of the increased duration of life; but the most active cause is a general improvement in the physical condition of man: see Sir B. Brodie's Lectures on Pathology and Surgery, p. 212; and for proof that civilized men are stronger than uncivilized ones, see Quetelet, sur l'Homme, vol. ii. pp. 67, 272; Lawrence's Lectures on Man, pp. 275, 276; Ellis's Polynesian Researches, vol. i. p. 98; Whately's Lectures on Political Economy, 8vo. 1831, p. 69; Journal of the Statistical Society, vol. xvii. pp. 32, 33; Dufau, Traité de Statistique, p. 107; Hawkins's Medical Statistics, p. 232.

ment of the mind of man upon the organic and inorganic forces of nature. To this all other causes are subordinate.² For we have seen that wherever the powers of nature reached a certain height, the national civilization was irregularly developed, and the advance of the civilization stopped. The first essential was, to limit the interference of these physical phenomena; and that was most likely to be accomplished where the phenomena were feeblest and least imposing. This was the case with Europe; it is accordingly in Europe alone, that man has really succeeded in taming the energies of nature, bending them to his own will, turning them aside from their ordinary course, and compelling them to minister to his happiness, and subserve the general purposes of human life.

All around us are the traces of this glorious and successful struggle. Indeed, it seems as if in Europe there was nothing man feared to attempt. The invasions of the sea repelled, and whole provinces, as in the case of Holland, rescued from its grasp, mountains cut through and turned into level roads; soils of the most obstinate sterility becoming exuberant, from the mere advance of chemical knowledge; while, in regard to electric phenomena, we see the subtlest, the most rapid, and the most mysterious of all forces, made the medium of thought, and obeying even the most capricious behests of the human mind.

---

² The general social consequences of this I shall hereafter consider; but the mere economical consequences are well expressed by Mr. Mill: 'Of the features which characterize this progressive economical movement of civilized nations, that which first excites attention, through its intimate connexion with the phenomena of Production, is the perpetual, and, so far as human foresight can extend, the unlimited, growth of man's power over nature. Our knowledge of the properties and laws of physical objects shows no sign of approaching its ultimate boundaries; it is advancing more rapidly, and in a greater number of directions at once, than in any previous age or generation, and affording such frequent glimpses of unexplored fields beyond, as to justify the belief that our acquaintance with nature is still almost in its infancy.' *Mill's Principles of Polit. Economy*, vol. ii. pp. 246–7.

In other instances, where the products of the external world have been refractory, man has succeeded in destroying what he could hardly hope to subjugate. The most cruel diseases, such as the plague, properly so called, and the leprosy of the Middle Ages,[3] have entirely disappeared from the civilized parts of Europe; and it is scarcely possible that they should ever again be seen there. Wild beasts and birds of prey have been extirpated, and are no longer allowed to infest the haunts of civilised men. Those frightful famines, by which Europe used to be ravaged several times in every century,[4] have ceased; and so successfully have we grappled with them, that there is not the slightest fear of their ever returning with any thing like their former severity. Indeed, our resources are now so great, that we could at worst, only suffer from a slight and temporary scarcity: since, in the present state of knowledge, the evil would be met at the outset by remedies which chemical science could easily suggest.[5]

It is hardly necessary to notice how, in numerous other instances, the progress of European civilization has

---

[3] What this horrible disease once was, may be estimated from the fact, 'qu'au treizième siècle on comptait en France seulement, deux mille léproseries, et que l'Europe entière renfermait environ dix-neuf mille établissemens semblables.' *Sprengel, Histoire de la Médecine*, vol. ii. p. 374. As to the mortality caused by the plague, see *Clot-Bey, de la Peste*, Paris, 1840, pp. 62, 63, 185, 292.

[4] For a curious list of famines, see an essay by Mr. Farr, in *Journal of the Statistical Society*, vol. ix. pp. 159–163. He says, that in the eleventh, twelfth, and thirteenth centuries, the average was, in England, one famine every fourteen years.

[5] In the opinion of one of the highest living authorities, famine is, even in the present state of chemistry, 'next to impossible.' *Herschel's Discourse on Natural Philosophy*, p. 65. Cuvier (*Recueil des Eloges*, vol. i. p. 10) says that we have succeeded 'à rendre toute famine impossible.' See also *Godwin on Population*, p. 500; and for a purely economical argument to prove the impossibility of famine, see *Mill's Principles of Political Economy*, vol. ii. p. 258; and compare a note in *Ricardo's Works*, p. 191. The Irish famine may seem an exception: but it could have been easily baffled except for the poverty of the people, which frustrated our efforts to reduce it to a dearth.

been marked by the diminished influence of the external world: I mean, of course, those peculiarities of the external world which have an existence independent of the wishes of man, and were not created by him. The most advanced nations do, in their present state, owe comparatively little to those original features of nature which, in every civilization out of Europe, exercised unlimited power. Thus, in Asia and elsewhere, the course of trade, the extent of commerce, and many similar circumstances, were determined by the existence of rivers, by the facility with which they could be navigated, and by the number and goodness of the adjoining harbours. But, in Europe, the determining cause is, not so much these physical peculiarities, as the skill and energy of man. Formerly the richest countries were those in which nature was most bountiful; now the richest countries are those in which man is most active. For, in our age of the world, if nature is parsimonious, we know how to compensate her deficiencies. If a river is difficult to navigate, or a country difficult to traverse, our engineers can correct the error, and remedy the evil. If we have no rivers, we make canals; if we have no natural harbours, we make artificial ones. And so marked is this tendency to impair the authority of natural phenomena, that it is seen even in the distribution of the people, since, in the most civilized parts of Europe, the population of the towns is everywhere outstripping that of the country; and it is evident that the more men congregate in great cities, the more they will become accustomed to draw their materials of thought from the business of human life, and the less attention they will pay to those peculiarities of nature, which are the fertile source of superstition, and by which, in every civilization out of Europe, the progress of man was arrested.

From these facts it may be fairly inferred, that the advance of European civilization is characterized by a diminishing influence of physical laws, and an increasing influence of mental laws. The complete proof of this generalization can be collected only from history; and therefore I must reserve a large share of the evidence on which it is founded for the future volumes of this work.

But that the proposition is fundamentally true must be admitted by whoever, in addition to the arguments just adduced, will concede two premisses, neither of which seem susceptible of much dispute. The first premiss is, that we are in possession of no evidence that the powers of nature have ever been permanently increased; and that we have no reason to expect that any such increase can take place. The other premiss is, that we have abundant evidence that the resources of the human mind have become more powerful, more numerous, and more able to grapple with the difficulties of the external world; because every fresh accession to our knowledge supplies fresh means with which we can either control the operations of nature, or, failing in that, can foresee the consequences, and thus avoid what it is impossible to prevent; in both instances, diminishing the pressure exercised on us by external agents.

If these premisses are admitted, we are led to a conclusion which is of great value for the purpose of this Introduction. For, if the measure of civilization is the triumph of the mind over external agents, it becomes clear, that of the two classes of laws which regulate the progress of mankind, the mental class is more important than the physical. This, indeed, is assumed by one school of thinkers as a matter of course, though I am not aware that its demonstration has been hitherto attempted by any thing even approaching an exhaustive analysis. The question, however, as to the originality of my arguments, is one of very trifling moment; but what we have to notice is, that in the present stage of our inquiry, the problem with which we started has become simplified, and a discovery of the laws of European history is resolved, in the first instance, into a discovery of the laws of the human mind. These mental laws, when ascertained, will be the ultimate basis of the history of Europe; the physical laws will be treated as of minor importance, and as merely giving rise to disturbances, the force and the frequency of which have, during several centuries, perceptibly diminished.

If we now inquire into the means of discovering the laws of the human mind, the metaphysicians are ready with an answer; and they refer us to their own labours as supplying a satisfactory solution. It therefore becomes necessary to ascertain the value of their researches, to measure the extent of their resources, and, above all, to test the validity of that method which they always follow, and by which alone, as they assert, great truths can be elicited.

The metaphysical method, though necessarily branching into two divisions, is, in its origin, always the same, and consists in each observer studying the operations of his own mind.⁶ This is the direct opposite of the historical method; the metaphysician studying one mind, the historian studying many minds. Now, the first remark to make on this is, that the metaphysical method is one by which no discovery has ever yet been made in any branch of knowledge. Every thing we at present know has been ascertained by studying phenomena, from which all casual disturbances having been removed, the law remains as a conspicuous residue.⁷ And this can only be done by observations so numerous as to eliminate the disturbances, or else by experiments so delicate as to isolate the phenomena. One of these conditions is essential to all inductive science; but neither of them does the metaphysician obey. To isolate the phenomenon is for him an impossibility; since no man, into whatever state of reverie he may be thrown, can entirely cut himself off from the influence of external events, which must produce an effect on his mind, even when he is unconscious of their presence. As to the other condi-

---

⁶ 'As the metaphysician carries within himself the materials of his reasoning, he is not under a necessity of looking abroad for subjects of speculation or amusement.' *Stewart's Philosophy of the Mind*, vol. i. p. 462; and the same remark, almost literally repeated, at vol. iii. p. 260. Locke makes what passes in each man's mind the sole source of metaphysics, and the sole test of their truth. *Essay concerning Human Understanding*, in *Locke's Works*, vol. i. pp. 16, 76, 79, 121, 146, 152, 287, vol. ii. pp. 141, 243.

⁷ The deductive sciences form, of course, an exception to this; but the whole theory of metaphysics is founded on its inductive character, and on the supposition that it consists of generalized observations, and that from them alone the science of mind can be raised

tion, it is by the metaphysician set at open defiance; for his whole system is based on the supposition that, by studying a single mind, he can get the laws of all minds; so that while he, on the one hand, is unable to isolate his observations from disturbances, he, on the other hand, refuses to adopt the only remaining precaution—he refuses so to enlarge his survey as to eliminate the disturbances by which his observations are troubled.*

This is the first and fundamental objection to which metaphysicians are exposed, even on the threshold of their science. But if we penetrate a little deeper, we shall meet with another circumstance, which, though less obvious, is equally decisive. After the metaphysician has taken for granted that, by studying one mind, he can discover the laws of all minds, he finds himself involved in a singular difficulty as soon as he begins to apply even this imperfect method. The difficulty to which I allude is one which, not being met with in any other pursuit, seems to have escaped the attention of those who are unacquainted with metaphysical controversies. To understand, therefore, its nature, it is requisite to give a short account of those two great schools, to one of which all metaphysicians must necessarily belong.

In investigating the nature of the human mind, according to the metaphysical scheme, there are two methods of proceeding, both of which are equally obvious,

---

* These remarks are only applicable to those who follow the purely metaphysical method of investigation. There is, however, a very small number of metaphysicians, among whom M. Cousin is the most eminent in France, in whose works we find larger views, and an attempt to connect historical inquiries with metaphysical ones; thus recognizing the necessity of verifying their original speculations. To this method there can be no objection, provided the metaphysical conclusions are merely regarded as hypothesis, which require verification to raise them to theories. But, instead of this cautious proceeding, the almost invariable plan is, to treat the hypothesis as if it were a theory already proved, and as if there remained nothing to do but to give historical illustrations of truths established by the psychologist. This confusion between illustration and verification appears to be the universal failing of those who, like Vico and Fichte, speculate upon historical phenomena à priori.

and yet both of which lead to entirely different results. According to the first method, the inquirer begins by examining his sensations. According to the other method, he begins by examining his ideas. These two methods always have led, and always must lead, to conclusions diametrically opposed to each other. Nor are the reasons of this difficult to understand. In metaphysics, the mind is the instrument as well as the material on which the instrument is employed. The means by which the science must be worked out, being thus the same as the object upon which it works, there arises a difficulty of a very peculiar kind. This difficulty is, the impossibility of taking a comprehensive view of the whole of the mental phenomena; because, however extensive such a view may be, it must exclude the state of the mind by which, or in which, the view itself is taken. Hence we may perceive what, I think, is a fundamental difference between physical and metaphysical inquiries. In physics, there are several methods of proceeding, all of which lead to the same results. But in metaphysics, it will invariably be found, that if two men of equal ability, and equal honesty, employ different methods in the study of the mind, the conclusions which they obtain will also be different. To those who are unversed in these matters, a few illustrations will set this in a clearer light. Metaphysicians who begin by the study of ideas observe in their own minds an idea of space. Whence, they ask, can this arise? It cannot, they say, owe its origin to the senses, because the senses only supply what is finite and contingent; whereas the idea of space is infinite and necessary.[9] It is infinite, since we cannot conceive

---

[9] Compare *Stewart's Philosophy of the Mind*, vol. ii. p. 194, with Cousin, *Hist. de la Philosophie*, II. série, vol. ii. p. 92. Among the Indian metaphysicians, there was a sect which declared space to be the cause of all things. *Journal of Asiatic Soc.* vol. vi. pp. 268, 290. See also the *Dabistan*, vol. ii. p. 40 which, however, was contrary to the Vedas. *Rammohun Roy on the Veda*, 1832, pp. 8, 111. In Spain, the doctrine of the infinity of space is heretical. *Doblado's Letters*, p. 96; which should be compared with the objection of Irenæus against the Valentinians, in *Bamsobre, Histoire du Manichée*, vol. ii. p. 275. For the

that space has an end; and it is necessary, since we cannot conceive the possibility of its non-existence. Thus far the idealist. But the sensualist, as he is called,[10]— he who begins, not with ideas, but with sensations, arrives at a very different conclusion. He remarks that we can have no idea of space until we have first had an idea of objects; and that the ideas of objects can only be the results of the sensations which those objects excite. As to the idea of space being necessary, this, he says, only results from the circumstance that we never can perceive an object which does not bear a certain position to some other object. This forms an indissoluble association between the idea of position and the idea of an object; and as this association is constantly repeated before us, we at length find ourselves unable to conceive an object without position, or, in other words, without space.[11] As to space being infinite, this, he says, is a

---

different theories of space, I may, moreover, refer to *Ritter's Hist. of Ancient Philosophy*, vol. i. pp. 451, 473, 477, vol. ii. p. 314, vol. iii. pp. 195–204; *Cudworth's Intellectual System*, vol. i. p. 191, vol. iii. pp. 230, 472; *Kritik der reinen Vernunft*, in *Kant's Werke*, vol. ii. pp. 23, 62, 81, 120, 139, 147, 258, 334, 347; *Tennemann, Geschichte der Philosophie*, vol. i. p. 109, vol. ii. p. 303, vol. iii. pp. 130–137, vol. iv. p. 284, vol. v. pp. 384–387, vol. vi. p. 99, vol. viii. pp. 87, 88, 683, vol. ix. pp. 257, 365, 410, vol. x. p. 79, vol. xi. pp. 195, 385–389.

[10] This is the title conferred by M. Cousin upon nearly all the greatest English metaphysicians, and upon Condillac and all his disciples in France, their system having 'le nom mérité de sensualisme.' *Cousin, Histoire de la Philosophie*, II. série, vol. ii. p. 88. The same name is given to the same school, in *Feuchters-*

leben's Medical Psychology, p. 52, and in *Renouard's Histoire de la Médecine*, vol. i. p. 346, vol. ii. p. 368. In *Jobert's New System of Philosophy*, vol. ii. p. 334, 8vo. 1848, it is called 'sensationalism,' which seems a preferable expression.

[11] This is very ably argued by Mr. James Mill in his *Analysis of the Phenomena of the Human Mind*, vol. ii. pp. 32, 93–95, and elsewhere. Compare *Essay concerning Human Understanding*, in *Locke's Works*, vol. i. pp. 147, 148, 154, 157, and the ingenious distinction, p. 198, 'between the idea of the infinity of space, and the idea of a space infinite.' At p. 208, Locke sarcastically says, 'But yet, after all this, there being men who persuade themselves that they have clear, positive, comprehensive ideas of infinity, it is fit they enjoy their privilege; and I should be very glad (with

notion we get by conceiving a continual addition to lines, or to surfaces, or to bulk, which are the three modifications of extension.[12] On innumerable other points we find the same discrepancy between the two schools. The idealist,[13] for example, asserts that our notions of cause, of time, of personal identity, and of substance, are universal and necessary; that they are simple; and that not being susceptible of analysis, they must be referred to the original constitution of the mind.[14] On the other hand, the sensationalist, so far from recognizing the simplicity of these ideas, considers them to be extremely complex, and looks upon their universality and necessity as merely the result of a frequent and intimate association.[15]

---

some others that I know, who acknowledge they have none such) to be better informed by their communication.'

[12] *Mill's Analysis of the Mind*, vol. ii. pp. 96, 97. See also the *Examination of Malebranche*, in *Locke's Works*, vol. viii. pp. 248, 249; and *Müller's Elements of Physiology*, vol. ii. p. 1081, which should be compared with *Comte, Philosophie Positive*, vol. i. p. 354.

[13] I speak of idealists in opposition to sensationalists; though the word idealist is often used by metaphysicians in a very different sense. On the different kinds of idealism, see *Kritik der reinen Vernunft*, and *Prolegomena zu jeder künftigen Metaphysik*, in *Kant's Werke*, vol. ii. pp. 223, 389, vol. iii. pp. 204, 210, 306, 307. According to him, the Cartesian idealism is empirical.

[14] Thus, Dugald Stewart (*Philosophical Essays*, Edin. 1810, p. 33) tells us of 'the simple idea of personal identity.' And Reid (*Essays on the Powers of the Mind*, vol. i. p. 354) says, 'I know of no ideas or notions that have a better claim to be accounted simple and original than those of space and time.' In the Sanscrit metaphysics, time is 'an independent cause.' See the *Vishnu Purana*, pp. 10, 216.

[15] 'As Space is a comprehensive word, including all positions, or the whole of synchronous order, so Time is a comprehensive word, including all successions, or the whole of successive order.' *Mill's Analysis of the Mind*, vol. ii. p. 100; and on the relation of time to memory, vol. i. p. 252. In *Jobert's New System of Philosophy*, vol. i. p. 33, it is said that 'time is nothing but the succession of events, and we know events by experience only.' See also p. 133, and compare respecting time *Condillac, Traité des Sensations*, pp. 104-114, 222, 223, 331-333. To the same effect is *Essay concerning Human Understanding*, book ii. chap. xiv., in *Locke's Works*, vol. i. p. 163;

This is the first important difference which is inevitably consequent on the adoption of different methods. The idealist is compelled to assert, that necessary truths and contingent truths have a different origin.[16] The sensationalist is bound to affirm that they have the same origin.[17] The further these two great schools advance, the more marked does their divergence become. They are at open war in every department of morals, of philosophy, and of art. The idealists say that all men have essentially the same notion of the good, the true, and the beautiful. The sensationalists affirm that there is no such standard, because ideas depend upon sensations, and because the sensations of men depend upon the changes in their bodies, and upon the external events by which their bodies are affected.

Such is a short specimen of the opposite conclusions to which the ablest metaphysicians have been driven, by the simple circumstance that they have pursued opposite methods of investigation. And this is the more important to observe, because, after these two methods have been employed, the resources of metaphysics

---

and see his second reply to the Bishop of Worcester, in *Works*, vol. iii. pp. 414–416; and as to the idea of substance, see vol. i. pp. 285–290, 292, 308, vol. iii. pp. 6, 10, 17.

[16] Reid (*Essays on the Powers of the Mind*, vol. i. p. 281) says, that necessary truths 'cannot be the conclusions of the senses; for our senses testify only what is, and not what must necessarily be.' See also vol. ii. pp. 53, 204, 239, 240, 281. The same distinction is peremptorily asserted in *Whewell's Philosophy of the Inductive Sciences*, 8vo, 1847, vol. i. pp. 60–73, 140; and see *Dugald Stewart's Philosophical Essays*, pp. 123, 124. Sir W. Hamilton (*Additions to Reid's Works*, p. 754) says, that non-contingent truths 'have their converse absolutely incogitable.' But this learned writer does not mention how we are to know when anything is 'absolutely incogitable.' That we cannot cogitate an idea, is certainly no proof of its being incogitable; for it may be cogitated at some later period, when knowledge is more advanced.

[17] This is asserted by all the followers of Locke; and one of the latest productions of that school declares, that 'to say that necessary truths cannot be acquired by experience, is to deny the most clear evidence of our senses and reason.' *Jobert's New System of Philosophy*, vol. i. p. 58.

are evidently exhausted.[18] Both parties agree that mental laws can only be discovered by studying individual minds, and that there is nothing in the mind which is not the result either of reflection or of sensation. The only choice, therefore, they have to make, is between subordinating the results of sensation to the laws of reflection, or else subordinating the results of reflection to the laws of sensation. Every system of metaphysics has been constructed according to one of these schemes; and this must always continue to be the case, because, when the two schemes are added together, they include the totality of metaphysical phenomena. Each process is equally plausible;[19] the supporters of each are equally confident; and, by the very nature of the dispute, it is impossible that any middle term should be found; nor can there ever be an umpire, because no one can mediate between metaphysical controversies without being a metaphysician, and no one can be a metaphysician without being either a sensationalist or an

---

[18] To avoid misapprehension, I may repeat, that, here and elsewhere, I mean by metaphysics, that vast body of literature which is constructed on the supposition that the laws of the human mind can be generalized *solely* from the facts of individual consciousness. For this scheme, the word 'metaphysics' is rather inconvenient, but it will cause no confusion if this definition of it is kept in view by the reader.

[19] What a celebrated historian of philosophy says of Platonism, is equally true of all the great metaphysical systems: 'Dass sie ein zusammenhängendes harmonisches Ganzes ausmachen (*i.e.* the leading propositions of it) fällt in die Augen.' *Tennemann, Geschichte der Philosophie*, vol. ii. p. 527. And yet he confesses (vol. iii. p. 52) of it and the opposite system: 'und wenn man auf die Beweise sieht, so ist der Empirismus des Aristoteles nicht besser begründet als der Rationalismus des Plato.' Kant admits that there can be only one true system, but is confident that he has discovered what all his predecessors have missed. *Die Metaphysik der Sitten*, in *Kant's Werke*, vol. v. p. 5, where he raises the question, 'ob es wohl mehr, als eine Philosophie geben könne.' In the *Kritik*, and in the *Prolegomena zu jeder künftigen Metaphysik*, he says that metaphysics have made no progress, and that the study can hardly be said to exist. *Werke*, vol. ii. pp. 49, 50, vol. iii. pp. 166, 246.

idealist; in other words, without belonging to one of those very parties whose claims he professes to judge.[20]

On these grounds, we must, I think, arrive at the conclusion, that as metaphysicians are unavoidably, and by the very nature of their inquiry, broken up into two completely antagonistic schools, the relative truth of which there are no means of ascertaining; as they, moreover, have but few resources, and as they use those resources according to a method by which no other science has ever been developed,—we, looking at these things, ought not to expect that they can supply us with sufficient data for solving those great problems which the history of the human mind presents to our view. And whoever will take the pains fairly to estimate the present condition of mental philosophy, must admit that, notwithstanding the influence it has always exercised over some of the most powerful minds, and through them over society at large, there is, nevertheless, no other study which has been so zealously prosecuted, so long continued, and yet remains so barren of

---

[20] We find a curious instance of this, in the attempt made by M. Cousin to found an eclectic school; for this very able and learned man has been quite unable to avoid the one-sided view which is to every metaphysician an essential preliminary; and he adopts that fundamental distinction between necessary ideas and contingent ideas, by which the idealist is separated from the sensationalist: 'la grande division des idées aujourd'hui établie est la division des idées contingentes et des idées nécessaires.' *Cousin, Hist. de la Philosophie*, II. série, vol. i. p. 82: see also vol. ii. p. 92, and the same work, I. série, vol. i. pp. 249, 267, 268, 311, vol. iii. pp. 51-54. M. Cousin constantly contradicts Locke, and then says he has refuted that profound and vigorous thinker; while he does not even state the arguments of James Mill, who, as a metaphysician, is the greatest of our modern sensationalists, and whose views, whether right or wrong, certainly deserve notice from an eclectic historian of philosophy.

Another eclectic, Sir W. Hamilton, announces (*Discussions on Philosophy*, p. 597) 'an undeveloped philosophy, which, I am confident, is founded upon truth. To this confidence I have come, not merely through the convictions of my own consciousness, but by finding in this system a centre and conciliation for the most opposite of philosophical opinions.' But, at p. 589, he summarily disposes of one of the most important of these philosophical opinions as 'the superficial edifice of Locke.'

results. In no other department has there been so much movement, and so little progress. Men of eminent abilities, and of the greatest integrity of purpose, have in every civilized country, for many centuries, been engaged in metaphysical inquiries; and yet at the present moment their systems, so far from approximating towards truth, are diverging from each other with a velocity which seems to be accelerated by the progress of knowledge. The incessant rivalry of the hostile schools, the violence with which they have been supported, and the exclusive and unphilosophic confidence with which each has advocated its own method,—all these things have thrown the study of the mind into a confusion only to be compared to that in which the study of religion has been thrown by the controversies of the theologians.[21] The consequence is, that if we except a very few of the laws of association, and perhaps I may add the modern theories of vision and of touch,[22] there is not to be found in the whole compass of metaphysics a single principle of importance, and at the same time of incontestable truth. Under these circumstances, it is impossible to avoid a suspicion that there is some fundamental error in the manner in which these inquiries have been prosecuted. For my own part, I believe that, by mere observation of our own minds, and even by such rude experiments

---

[21] Berkeley, in a moment of candour, inadvertently confesses what is very damaging to the reputation of his own pursuits: 'Upon the whole, I am inclined to think that the far greater part, if not all, of those difficulties which have hitherto amused philosophers, and blocked up the way to knowledge, are entirely owing to ourselves. That we have first raised a dust, and then complain we cannot see.' *Principles of Human Knowledge,* in *Berkeley's Works,* vol. i. p. 74. Every metaphysician and theologian should get this sentence by heart: 'That we have first raised a dust, and then complain we cannot see.'

[22] Some of the laws of association, as stated by Hume and Hartley, are capable of historical verification, which would change the metaphysical hypothesis into a scientific theory. Berkeley's theory of vision, and Brown's theory of touch, have, in the same way, been verified physiologically; so that we now know what otherwise we could only have suspected.

as we are able to make upon them, it will be impossible to raise psychology to a science; and I entertain very little doubt that metaphysics can only be successfully studied by an investigation of history so comprehensive as to enable us to understand the conditions which govern the movements of the human race.[32]

---

[32] In regard to one of the difficulties stated in this chapter as impeding metaphysicians, it is only just to quote the remarks of Kant: 'Wie aber das Ich, der ich denke, von dem Ich, das sich selbst anschaut, unterschieden (indem ich mir noch and ere Anschauungsart wenigstens als möglich vorstellen kann), und doch mit diesem letzteren als dasselbe Subject einerlei sei, wie ich also sagen könne: Ich als Intelligenz und denkend Subject, erkenne mich selbst als gedachtes Object, so fern ich mir noch über das in der Anschauung gegeben bin, nur, gleich anderen Phänomenen, nicht wie ich vor dem Verstande bin, sondern wie ich mir erscheine, hat nicht mehr auch nicht weniger Schwierigkeit bei sich, als wie ich mir selbst überhaupt ein Object und zwar der Anschauung und innerer Wahrnehmungen sein könne.' *Kritik der reinen Vernunft*, in *Kant's Werke*, vol. ii. p. 144. I am very willing to let the question rest on this: for to me it appears that both cases are not only equally difficult, but, in the present state of our knowledge, are equally impossible.

CHAPTER IV.

MENTAL LAWS ARE EITHER MORAL OR INTELLECTUAL. COMPARISON OF MORAL AND INTELLECTUAL LAWS, AND INQUIRY INTO THE EFFECT PRODUCED BY EACH ON THE PROGRESS OF SOCIETY.

In the preceding chapter, it has, I trust, been made apparent, that, whatever may hereafter be the case, we, looking merely at the present state of our knowledge, must pronounce the metaphysical method to be unequal to the task, often imposed upon it, of discovering the laws which regulate the movements of the human mind. We are, therefore, driven to the only remaining method, according to which mental phenomena are to be studied, not simply as they appear in the mind of the individual observer, but as they appear in the actions of mankind at large. The essential opposition between these two plans is very obvious: but it may perhaps be well to bring forward further illustration of the resources possessed by each for the investigation of truth; and for this purpose, I will select a subject which, though still imperfectly understood, supplies a beautiful instance of the regularity with which, under the most conflicting circumstances, the great Laws of Nature are able to hold their course.

The case to which I refer, is that of the proportion kept up in the births of the sexes; a proportion which if it were to be greatly disturbed in any country, even for a single generation, would throw society into the most serious confusion, and would infallibly cause a great increase in the vices of the people.[1] Now, it has

---

[1] Thus we find that the Crusades, by diminishing the proportion of men to women in Europe, increased licentiousness. See a curious passage in *Sprengel, Histoire de la Médecine,*

always been suspected that, on an average, the male and female births are tolerably equal; but, until very recently, no one could tell whether or not they are precisely equal, or, if unequal, on which side there is an excess.[2] The births being the physical result of physical antecedents, it was clearly seen that the laws of the births must be in those antecedents; that is to say, that the causes of the proportion of the sexes must reside in the parents themselves.[3] Under these circumstances, the question arose, if it was not possible to elucidate this difficulty by our knowledge of animal physiology; for it was plausibly said, 'Since physiology is a study of the laws of the body,[4] and since all births

---

vol. ii. p. 376. In Yucatan, there is generally a considerable excess of women, and the result is prejudicial to morals. *Stephens's Central America*, vol. iii. pp. 380, 429. On the other hand, respecting the state of society produced by an excess of males, see *Mallet's Northern Antiquities*, p. 259; *Journal of Geographical Society*, vol. xv. p. 45, vol. xvi. p. 307; *Southey's Commonplace Book*, third series, p. 579.

[2] On this question a variety of conflicting statements may be seen in the old writers. Goodman, early in the seventeenth century, supposed that more females were born than males. *Southey's Commonplace Book*, third series, p. 696. Turgot (*Œuvres*, vol. ii. p. 247) rightly says, 'il naît un peu plus d'hommes que de femmes;' but the evidence was too incomplete to make this more than a lucky guess; and I find that even Herder, writing in 1785, takes for granted that the proportion was about equal: 'ein ziemliches Gleichmaass in den Geburten beider Geschlechter' (*Ideen zur Geschichte*, vol. ii. p. 149), and was sometimes in favour of girls, 'ja, die Nachrichten mehrerer Reisenden machen es wahrscheinlich, dass in manchen dieser Gegenden wirklich mehr Töchter als Söhne geboren werden.'

[3] A question, indeed, has been raised as to the influence exercised by the state of the mind during the period of orgasm. But whatever this influence may be, it can only affect the subsequent birth through and by physical antecedents, which in every case must be regarded as the proximate cause. If, therefore, the influence were proved to exist, we should still have to search for physical laws: though such laws would of course be considered merely as secondary ones, resolvable into some higher generalization.

[4] Some writers treat physiology as a study of the laws of life. But this, looking at the subject as it now stands, is far too bold a step, and several branches of knowledge will have

are products resulting from the body, it follows that if we know the laws of the body, we shall know the laws of the birth.' This was the view taken by physiologists of our origin;[a] and this is precisely the view taken by metaphysicians of our history. Both parties believed that it was possible at once to rise to the cause of the phenomenon, and by studying its laws predict the phenomenon itself. The physiologist said, 'By studying individual bodies, and thus ascertaining the laws which regulate the union of the parents, I will discover the proportion of the sexes, because the proportion is merely the result to which the union gives rise.' Just in the same way, the metaphysician says, 'By studying individual minds, I will ascertain the laws which govern their movements; and in that way I will predict the movements of mankind, which are obviously compounded of the individual movements.'[b] These are the

---

to be raised from their present empirical state, before the phenomena of life can be scientifically investigated. The more rational mode seems to be, to consider physiology and anatomy as correlative; the first forming the dynamical, and the second forming the statical part of the study of organic structure.

[a] 'Voulez-vous savoir de quoi dépend le sexe des enfants? Fernel vous répond, sur la foi des anciens, qu'il dépend des qualités de la semence du père et de la mère.' *Renouard, Histoire de la Médecine*, Paris, 1846, vol. ii. p. 106; see also, at p. 185, the opinion of Hippocrates, adopted by Galen; and similar views in *Lepelletier, Physiologie Médicale*, vol. iv. p. 332, and *Sprengel, Hist. de la Médecine*, vol. i. pp. 252, 10, vol. ii. p. 115, vol. iv. p. 62. For further information as to the opinions which have been held respecting the origin of sexes, see *Beausobre, Histoire de Manichée*, vol. ii. p. 417; *Asiatic Researches*, vol. iii, pp. 358, 361; *Vishnu Purana*, p. 349; *Works of Sir William Jones*, vol. iii. p. 126; *Ritter's History of Ancient Philosophy*, vol. iii. p. 191; *Denham and Clapperton's Africa*, pp. 323, 324; *Maintenon, Lettres Inédites*, vol. ii. p. 62; and the view of Itohl (*Burdach's Physiologie*, vol. ii. p. 472), 'que les femmes chez lesquelles prédomine le système artériel procréent des garçons, au lieu que celles dont le système veineux a la prédominance mettent au monde des filles.' According to Anaxagoras the question was extremely simple: καὶ ἄῤῥενα μὲν ἀπὸ τῶν δεξιῶν, θήλεα δὲ ἀπὸ τῶν ἀριστερῶν. *Diog. Laert.* ii. 9, vol. L p. 85.

[b] 'Le métaphysicien se voit comme la source de l'évidence et

expectations which have been confidently held out, by physiologists respecting the laws of the sexes, and by metaphysicians respecting the laws of history. Towards the fulfilment, however, of these promises the metaphysicians have done absolutely nothing; nor have the physiologists been more successful, although their views have the support of anatomy, which admits of the employment of direct experiment, a resource unknown to metaphysics. But towards settling the present question, all this availed them nothing; and physiologists are not yet possessed of a single fact which throws any light on this problem: Is the number of male births equal to female births—is it greater, or is it less?

These are questions to which all the resources of physiologists, from Aristotle down to our own time, afford no means of reply.[7] And yet at the present day

---

le confident de la nature: Moi seul, dit-il, je puis généraliser les idées, et découvrir le germe des événements qui se développent journellement dans le monde physique et moral; et c'est par moi seul que l'homme peut être éclairé.' *Helvetius, de l'Esprit*, vol. i. p. 66. Compare *Herder, Ideen zur Geschichte der Menschheit*, vol. ii. p. 105. Thus, too, M. Cousin (*Hist. de la Philosophie*, II. série, vol. i. p. 131) says, 'Le fait de la conscience transporté de l'individu dans l'espèce et dans l'histoire, est la clef de tous les développements de l'humanité.'

[7] Considering the very long period during which physiology has been studied, it is remarkable how little the physiologists have contributed towards the great and final object of all science, namely, the power of predicting events. To me it appears that the two principal causes of this are, the backwardness of chemistry, and the still extremely imperfect state of the microscope, which even now is so inaccurate an instrument, that when a high power is employed, little confidence can be placed in it; and the examination, for instance, of the spermatozoa has led to the most contradictory results. In regard to chemistry, MM. Robin and Verdeil, in their recent great work, have ably proved what manifold relations there are between it and the further progress of our knowledge of the animal frame; though I venture to think that these eminent writers have shown occasionally an undue disposition to limit the application of chemical laws to physiological phenomena. See *Robin et Verdeil, Chimie Anatomique et Physiologique*, Paris, 1853, vol. I. pp. 20, 34, 167, 337, 338, 437, 661, vol. ii. pp. 136, 137, 508, vol. iii. pp. 135, 144, 183, 281,

we, by the employment of what now seems a very natural method, are possessed of a truth which the united abilities of a long series of eminent men failed to discover. By the simple experiment of registering the number of births and their sexes; by extending this registration over several years, in different countries,— we have been able to eliminate all casual disturbances, and ascertain the existence of a law which, expressed in round numbers, is, that for every twenty girls there are born twenty-one boys: and we may confidently say, that although the operations of this law are of course liable to constant aberrations, the law itself is so powerful, that we know of no country in which during a single year the male births have not been greater than the female ones.⁵

The importance and the beautiful regularity of this law make us regret that it still remains an empirical truth, not having yet been connected with the physical

---

283, 351, 547. The increasing tendency of chemistry to bring under its control what are often supposed to be purely organic phenomena, is noticed cautiously in *Turner's Chemistry*, vol. ii. p. 1308, London, 1847; and boldly in *Liebig's Letters on Chemistry*, 1851, pp. 250, 251. The connexion between chemistry and physiology is touched on rather too hastily in *Bouilland, Philosophie Médicale*, pp. 160, 257; *Broussais, Examen des Doctrines Médicales*, vol. iii. p. 166; *Brodie's Lectures on Pathology*, p. 48; *Henle, Traité d'Anatomie*, vol. i. pp. 25, 26; *Feuchtersleben's Medical Psychology*, p. 68; but better in *Holland's Medical Notes*, 1839, p. 270, a thoughtful and suggestive work. On the necessity of chemistry for increasing our knowledge of embryology, compare *Wagner's Physiology*, pp.

131, 132 note, with *Burdach, Traité de Physiologie*, vol. iv. pp. 59, 168.

⁵ It used to be supposed that some of the eastern countries formed an exception to this; but more precise observations have contradicted the loose statements of the earlier travellers, and in no part of the world, so far as our knowledge extends, are more girls born than boys; while in every part of the world for which we have statistical returns, there is a slight excess on the side of male births. Compare *Marsden's History of Sumatra*, p. 234; *Raffles' History of Java*, vol. i. pp. 81, 82; *Sykes on the Statistics of the Deccan*, in *Reports of British Association*, vol. vi. pp. 246, 261, 262; *Niebuhr, Description de l'Arabie*, p. 63; *Humboldt, Nouv. Espagne*, vol. i. p. 139; *M'William, Medical History of Expedition to the*

phenomena by which its operations are caused.* But this is immaterial to my present purpose, which is only to notice the method by which the discovery has been made. For this method is obviously analogous to that by which I propose to investigate the operations of the human mind; while the old and unsuccessful method is analogous to that employed by the metaphysicians. As long as physiologists attempted to ascertain the laws of the proportion of sexes by individual experiments, they effected absolutely nothing towards the end

---

Niger, p. 113; *Elliotson's Human Physiology*, p. 795; *Thomson's Hist. of Royal Society*, p. 531; *Sadler's Law of Population*, vol. i. pp. 507, 511, vol. ii. pp. 324, 335; *Paris and Fonblanque's Medical Jurisprudence*, vol. i. p. 259; *Journal of Statist. Soc.* vol. iii. pp. 263, 264, vol. xvii. pp. 46, 123; *Journal of Geographical Soc.* vol. xx. p. 17; *Fourth Report of British Association*, pp. 687, 689, *Report for* 1842, pp. 144, 145; *Transac. of Sections for* 1840, p. 174, *for* 1847, p. 96, *for* 1849, p. 87; *Dufau, Traité de Statistique*, pp. 24, 209, 210; *Burdach, Traité de Physiologie*, vol. ii. pp. 66, 57, 273, 274, 281, vol. v. p. 373; *Hawkins's Medical Statistics*, pp. 221, 222.

* In *Müller's Physiology*, vol. ii. p. 1657, a work of great authority, it is said, that 'the causes which determine the sex of the embryo are unknown, although it appears that the relative age of the parents has some influence over the sex of the offspring.' That the relative age of the parents does affect the sex of their children, may, from the immense amount of evidence now collected, be considered almost certain; but M. Müller, instead of referring to physiological writers, ought to have mentioned that the statisticians, and not the physiologists, were the first to make this discovery. On this curious question, see *Carpenter's Human Physiology*, p. 746; *Sadler's Law of Population*, vol. ii. pp. 333, 336, 342; *Journal of Statistical Society*, vol. iii. pp. 263, 264. In regard to animals below man, we find from numerous experiments, that among sheep and horses the age of the parents 'has a very great general influence upon the sex' of the offspring. *Elliotson's Physiology*, pp. 708, 709; and see *Cuvier, Progrès des Sciences Naturelles*, vol. ii. p. 406. As to the relation between the origin of sex and the laws of arrested development, compare *Geoffroy Saint-Hilaire, Hist. des Anomalies de l'Organisation*, vol. ii. pp. 33, 34, 73, vol. iii. p. 278, with *Lindley's Botany*, vol. ii. p. 81. In *Esquirol, Maladies Mentales*, vol. i. p. 302, there is a singular case recorded by Lamotte, which would seem to connect this question with pathological phenomena, though it is uncertain whether the epilepsy was an effect or a cognate symptom.

they hoped to achieve. But when men became dissatisfied with these individual experiments, and instead of them, began to collect observations less minute, but more comprehensive, then it was that the great law of nature, for which during many centuries they had vainly searched, first became unfolded to their view. Precisely in the same way, as long as the human mind is only studied according to the narrow and contracted method of metaphysicians, we have every reason for thinking that the laws which regulate its movements will remain unknown. If, therefore, we wish to effect anything of real moment, it becomes necessary that we should discard those old schemes, the insufficiency of which is demonstrated by experience as well as by reason; and that we should substitute in their place such a comprehensive survey of facts as will enable us to eliminate those disturbances which, owing to the impossibility of experiment, we shall never be able to isolate.

The desire that I feel to make the preliminary views of this Introduction perfectly clear, is my sole apology for having introduced a digression which, though adding nothing to the strength of the argument, may be found useful as illustrating it, and will at all events enable ordinary readers to appreciate the value of the proposed method. It now remains for us to ascertain the manner in which, by the application of this method, the laws of mental progress may be most easily discovered.

If, in the first place, we ask what this progress is, the answer seems very simple: that it is a two-fold progress, Moral and Intellectual; the first having more immediate relation to our duties, the second to our knowledge. This is a classification which has been frequently laid down, and with which most persons are familiar. And so far as history is a narration of results, there can be no doubt that the division is perfectly accurate. There can be no doubt that a people are not really advancing, if, on the one hand, their increasing ability is accompanied by increasing vice, or if, on the other hand, while they are becoming more virtuous, they likewise become more ignorant. This double movement, moral and intellectual, is essential to the very idea of civilization, and includes the entire theory of mental progress. To be willing to perform our duty is the moral part; to know how to perform it is the intellectual part: while the closer these two parts are knit together, the greater the harmony with which they work; and the more accurately the means are adapted to the end, the more completely will the scheme of our life be accomplished, and the more securely shall we lay a foundation for the further advancement of mankind.

A question, therefore, now arises of great moment: namely, which of those two parts or elements of mental progress is the most important. For the progress itself being the result of their united action, it becomes necessary to ascertain which of them works more powerfully, in order that we may subordinate the inferior element to the laws of the superior one. If the advance of civilization, and the general happiness of mankind, depend more on their moral feelings than on their intellectual knowledge, we must of course measure the progress of society by those feelings; while if, on the other hand, it depends principally on their knowledge, we must take as our standard the amount and success of their intellectual activity. As soon as we know the relative energy of these two components, we shall treat them according to the usual plan for investigating truth; that is to say, we shall look at the product of their joint action as obeying the laws of the more powerful agent, whose operations are casually disturbed by the inferior laws of the minor agent.

In entering into this inquiry, we are met by a preliminary difficulty, arising from the loose and careless manner in which ordinary language is employed on subjects that require the greatest nicety and precision. For the expression, Moral and Intellectual Progress, is suggestive of a serious fallacy. In the manner in which it is generally used, it conveys an idea that the moral and intellectual faculties of men are, in the advance of civilization, naturally more acute and more trustworthy than they were formerly. But this, though it may possibly be true, has never been proved. It may be that, owing to some physical causes still unknown, the average capacity of the brain is, if we compare long periods of time, becoming gradually greater; and that therefore the mind, which acts through the brain, is, even independently of education, increasing in aptitude and in the general competence of its views.[10] Such, however, is still our ignorance of physical laws, and so completely are we in the dark as to the circumstances which regulate the hereditary transmission of character, temperament,[11] and other personal peculiarities, that

---

[10] That the natural powers of the human brain are improving because they are capable of transmission, is a favourite doctrine with the followers of Gall, and is adopted by M. A. Comte (*Philosophie Positive*, vol. iv. pp. 384, 385); who, however, admits that it has never been sufficiently verified: 'sans que toutefois l'expérience ait encore suffisamment prononcé.' Dr. Prichard, whose habits of thought were very different, seems, nevertheless, inclined to lean in this direction; for his comparison of skulls led him to the conclusion, that the present inhabitants of Britain, 'either as the *result of many ages of greater intellectual cultivation*, or from some other cause, have, as I am persuaded, much more capacious braincases than their forefathers.' *Prichard's Physical History of Mankind*, vol. i. p. 305. Even if this were certain, it would not prove that the contents of the crania were altered, though it might create a presumption; and the general question must, I think, remain unsettled until the researches begun by Blumenbach, and recently continued by Morton, are carried out upon a scale far more comprehensive than has hitherto been attempted. Compare Burdach, *Traité de Physiologie*, vol. ii. p. 253; where, however, the question is not stated with sufficient caution.

[11] None of the laws of hereditary descent connected with the formation of character, have yet been generalized; nor is our knowledge much more advanced respecting the theory of temperaments, which still remains the principal obstacle in the way of the phrenologists. The difficulties attending the study of temperaments, and the obscurity in which this important subject is shrouded, may be estimated by whoever will compare what has been said upon it by the following writers: *Müller's Physiology*, vol. ii. pp. 1406–1410; *Elliotson's Human Physiology*, pp. 1059–1062; *Blainville, Physiologie Générale et Comparée*, vol. i. pp. 168, 264, 265, vol. ii. pp. 43, 130, 214, 328, 329, vol. iii. pp. 54, 74, 118, 148, 149, 284,

we must consider this alleged progress as a very doubtful point; and, in the present state of our knowledge, we cannot safely assume that there has been any permanent improvement in the moral or intellectual faculties of man, nor have we any decisive ground for saying that those faculties are likely to be greater in an infant born in the most civilized part of Europe, than in one born in the wildest region of a barbarous country.[12]

285; *Williams's Principles of Medicine*, pp. 16, 17, 112, 113; Geoffroy Saint Hilaire, *Anomalies de l'Organisation*, vol. i. pp. 186, 100; Broussais, *Examen des Doctrines Médicales*, vol. i. pp. 204, 205, vol. iii. p. 276; Renouard, *Hist. de la Médecine*, vol. i. p. 326; Sprengel, *Hist. de la Médecine*, vol. i. p. 380; vol. ii. p. 468, vol iii. p. 21, vol. v. p. 325, vol. vi. p. 492; Esquirol, *Maladies Mentales*, vol. i. pp. 39, 226, 429, 594, vol. ii. p. 20; Lepelletier, *Physiol. Médicale*, vol. i. pp. 139, 281, vol. iii. pp. 372-429, vol. iv. pp. 93, 123, 133, 143, 146, 177; Henle, *Anatomie Générale*, vol. i. p. 474, vol. ii. pp. 288, 280, 316; Bichat, *Anatomie Générale*, vol. i. p. 207, vol. ii. p. 444, vol. iii. pp. 310, 507, vol. iv. pp. 281, 399, 400, 504; Bichat *sur la Vie*, pp. 80, 61, 234, 235; Phillips on *Scrofula*, p. 9; Feuchtersleben's *Medical Psychology*, pp. 143-145; *Œuvres de Fontenelle*, Paris, 1760, vol. v. p. 110; Cullen's *Works*, Edinb. 1827, vol. i. pp. 214-221; Cabanis, *Rapports du Physique et du Moral*, pp. 76-83, 229-261, 520-533; Noble on the *Brain*, pp. 370-376; Combe's *North America*, vol. i. pp. 126-128. Latterly, attention has been paid to the chemistry of the blood as it varies in the various temperaments; and this seems a more satisfactory method than the old plan of merely describing the obvious symptoms of the temperament. Clark on *Animal Physiology*, in *Fourth Report of the British Association*, p. 126; Simon's *Animal Chemistry*, vol. i. p. 236; Wagner's *Physiology*, p. 262.

[12] We often hear of hereditary talents, hereditary vices, and hereditary virtues; but whoever will critically examine the evidence will find that we have no proof of their existence. The way in which they are commonly proved is in the highest degree illogical; the usual course being for writers to collect instances of some mental peculiarity found in a parent and in his child, and then to infer that the peculiarity was bequeathed. By this mode of reasoning we might demonstrate any proposition; since in all large fields of inquiry there are a sufficient number of empirical coincidences to make a plausible case in favour of whatever view a man chooses to advocate. But this is not the way in which truth is discovered; and we ought to inquire not only how many instances there are of hereditary talents, &c.

Whatever, therefore, the moral and intellectual progress of men may be, it resolves itself not into a progress of natural capacity,[13] but into a progress, if I may so say, of opportunity; that is, an improvement in the circumstances under which that capacity after birth comes into play. Here, then, lies the gist of the whole matter. The progress is one, not of internal power, but of external advantage. The child born in a civilized land is not likely, as such, to be superior to one born among barbarians; and the difference which ensues between the acts of the two children will be caused, so far as we know, solely by the pressure of external circumstances; by which I mean the surrounding opinions, knowledge, associations; in a word, the entire mental atmosphere in which the two children are respectively nurtured.

---

but how many instances there are of such qualities not being hereditary. Until something of this sort is attempted, we can know nothing about the matter inductively: while, until physiology and chemistry are much more advanced, we can know nothing about it deductively.

These considerations ought to prevent us from receiving statements (*Taylor's Medical Jurisprudence*, pp. 644, 678, and many other books) which positively affirm the existence of hereditary madness and hereditary suicide; and the same remark applies to hereditary disease (on which see some admirable observations in *Phillips on Scrofula*, pp. 101–120, London, 1846); and with still greater force does it apply to hereditary vices and hereditary virtues; inasmuch as ethical phenomena have not been registered as carefully as physiological ones, and therefore our conclusions respecting them are even more precarious.

[13] To what has been already stated, I will add the opinions of two of the most profound among modern thinkers. 'Men, I think, have been much the same for natural endowments in all times.' *Conduct of the Understanding*, in *Locke's Works*, vol. ii. p. 361. 'Les dispositions primitives agissent également chez les peuples barbares et chez les peuples policés; ils sont vraisemblablement les mêmes dans tous les lieux et dans tous les toms... Plus il y aura d'hommes, et plus vous aurez de grands hommes ou d'hommes propres à devenir grands.' *Progrès de l'Esprit Humain*, in *Œuvres de Turgot*, vol. ii. p. 264. The remarks of Dr. Brown (*Lectures on the Mind*, p. 57), if I rightly understand his rhetorical language, apply not to natural capacity, but to that which is acquired: see the end of his ninth Lecture.

On this account it is evident, that if we look at mankind in the aggregate, their moral and intellectual conduct is regulated by the moral and intellectual notions prevalent in their own time. There are, of course, many persons who will rise above those notions, and many others who will sink below them. But such cases are exceptional, and form a very small proportion of the total amount of those who are nowise remarkable either for good or for evil. An immense majority of men must always remain in a middle state, neither very foolish nor very able, neither very virtuous nor very vicious, but slumbering on in a peaceful and decent mediocrity, adopting without much difficulty the current opinions of the day, making no inquiry, exciting no scandal, causing no wonder, just holding themselves on a level with their generation, and noiselessly conforming to the standard of morals and of knowledge common to the age and country in which they live.

Now, it requires but a superficial acquaintance with history to be aware that this standard is constantly changing, and that it is never precisely the same even in the most similar countries, or in two successive generations in the same country. The opinions which are popular in any nation vary in many respects almost from year to year; and what in one period is attacked as a paradox or a heresy, is in another period welcomed as a sober truth; which, however, in its turn is replaced by some subsequent novelty. This extreme mutability in the ordinary standard of human actions shows that the conditions on which the standard depends must themselves be very mutable; and those conditions, whatever they may be, are evidently the originators of the moral and intellectual conduct of the great average of mankind.

Here, then, we have a basis on which we can safely proceed. We know that the main cause of human actions is extremely variable; we have only, therefore, to apply this test to any set of circumstances which are supposed to be the cause, and if we find that such circumstances are not very variable, we must infer that they are not the cause we are attempting to discover.

Applying this test to moral motives, or to the dictates of what is called moral instinct, we shall at once see how extremely small is the influence those motives have exercised over the progress of civilization. For there is, unquestionably, nothing to be found in the world which has undergone so little change as those great dogmas of which moral systems are composed. To do good to others; to sacrifice for their benefit your own wishes; to love your neighbour as yourself; to forgive your enemies; to restrain your passions; to honour your parents; to respect those who are set over you: these, and a few others, are the sole essentials of morals; but they have been known for thousands of years, and not one jot or tittle has been added to them by all the sermons, homilies, and text-books which moralists and theologians have been able to produce.[14]

---

[14] That the system of morals propounded in the New Testament contained no maxim which had not been previously enunciated, and that some of the most beautiful passages in the Apostolic writings are quotations from pagan authors, is well known to every scholar; and so far from supplying, as some suppose, an objection against Christianity, it is a strong recommendation of it, as indicating the intimate relation between the doctrines of Christ and the moral sympathies of mankind in different ages. But to assert that Christianity communicated to man moral truths previously unknown, argues, on the part of the asserter, either gross ignorance or else wilful fraud. For evidence of the knowledge of moral truths possessed by barbarous nations, independently of Christianity, and for the most part previous to its promulgation, compare *Mackay's Religious Development*, vol. ii. pp. 376–380; *Mure's Hist. of Greek Literature*, vol. ii. p. 398, vol. iii. p. 380; *Prescott's History of Mexico*, vol. i. p. 31; *Elphinstone's History of India*, p. 47; *Works of Sir W. Jones*, vol. i. pp. 87, 168, vol. iii. pp. 105, 114; *Mill's History of India*, vol. i. p. 419; *Bohlen, das alte Indien*, vol. i. pp. 364–366; *Beausobre, Histoire de Manichée*, vol. i. pp. 318, 319; *Coleman's Mythology of the Hindus*, p. 193; *Transac. of Soc. of Bombay*, vol. iii. p. 198; *Transac. of Asiatic Society*, vol. 1. p. 5, vol. iii. pp. 283, 284; *Asiatic Researches*, vol. vi. p. 271, vol. vii. p. 40, vol. xvi. pp. 130, 277, vol. xx. pp. 460, 461; *The Dabistan*, vol. i. pp. 328, 338; *Catlin's North-American Indians*, vol. ii. p. 243; *Syme's Embassy to Ava*, vol. ii. p. 389; *Davis's Chinese*, vol. i. p. 196, vol. ii. pp. 136, 233; *Journal Asiatique*, I. série, vol. iv. p. 77, Paris, 1824.

But, if we contrast this stationary aspect of moral truths with the progressive aspect of intellectual truths, the difference is indeed startling.[16] All the great moral systems which have exercised much influence have been fundamentally the same; all the great intellectual systems have been fundamentally different. In reference to our moral conduct, there is not a single principle now known to the most cultivated Europeans, which was not likewise known to the ancients. In reference to the conduct of our intellect, the moderns have not only made the most important additions to every department of knowledge that the ancients ever attempted to study, but besides this, they have upset and revolutionized the old methods of inquiry; they have consolidated into one great scheme all those resources of induction which Aristotle alone dimly perceived; and they have created sciences, the faintest idea of which never entered the mind of the boldest thinker antiquity produced.

---

[16] Sir James Mackintosh was so struck by the stationary character of moral principles, that he denies the possibility of their advance, and boldly affirms that no further discoveries can be made in morals: 'Morality admits no discoveries.... More than three thousand years have elapsed since the composition of the Pentateuch; and let any man, if he is able, tell me in what important respect the rule of life has varied since that distant period. Let the Institutes of Menu be explored with the same view; we shall arrive at the same conclusion. Let the books of false religion be opened; it will be found that their moral system is, in all its grand features, the same. . . . The fact is evident that no improvements have been made in practical morality. . . . The facts which lead to the formation of moral rules are as accessible, and must be as obvious, to the simplest barbarian as to the most enlightened philosopher. . . . The case of the physical and speculative sciences is directly opposite. There the facts are remote and scarcely accessible. . . . . . From the countless variety of the facts with which they are conversant, it is impossible to prescribe any bounds to their future improvement. It is otherwise with morals. They have hitherto been stationary; and, in my opinion, they are likely for ever to continue so.' *Life of Mackintosh, edited by his Son*, London, 1835, vol. i. pp. 119–122. Condorcet (*Vie de Turgot*, p. 180) says, 'La morale de toutes les nations a été la même;' and Kant (*Logik*, in *Kant's Werke*, vol. I. p. 356), 'In der Moral-philosophie sind wir nicht weiter gekommen, als die Alten.'

These are, to every educated man, recognized and notorious facts; and the inference to be drawn from them is immediately obvious. Since civilization is the product of moral and intellectual agencies, and since that product is constantly changing, it evidently cannot be regulated by the stationary agent; because, when surrounding circumstances are unchanged, a stationary agent can only produce a stationary effect. The only other agent is the intellectual one; and that this is the real mover may be proved in two distinct ways: first, because being, as we have already seen, either moral or intellectual, and being, as we have also seen, not moral, it must be intellectual; and, secondly, because the intellectual principle has an activity and a capacity for adaptation, which, as I undertake to show, is quite sufficient to account for the extraordinary progress that, during several centuries, Europe has continued to make.

Such are the main arguments by which my view is supported; but there are also other and collateral circumstances which are well worthy of consideration. The first is, that the intellectual principle is not only far more progressive than the moral principle, but is also far more permanent in its results. The acquisitions made by the intellect are, in every civilized country, carefully preserved, registered in certain well-understood formulas, and protected by the use of technical and scientific language; they are easily handed down from one generation to another, and thus assuming an accessible, or, as it were, a tangible form, they often influence the most distant posterity, they become the heirlooms of mankind, the immortal bequest of the genius to which they owe their birth. But the good deeds effected by our moral faculties are less capable of transmission; they are of a more private and retiring character; while, as the motives to which they owe their origin are generally the result of self-discipline and of self-sacrifice, they have to be worked out by every man for himself; and thus, begun by each anew, they derive little benefit from the maxims of preceding experience, nor can they well be stored up for the use of future moralists. The consequence is, that although moral excellence is more amiable, and to most persons more attractive, than intellectual excellence, still, it must be confessed that, looking at ulterior results, it is far less active, less permanent, and, as I shall presently prove, less productive of real good. Indeed, if we examine the effects of the most active philanthropy, and of the largest and most disinterested kindness, we shall find that those effects are, comparatively speaking, short-lived; that there is only a small number of individuals they come in contact with and benefit; that they rarely survive the generation which witnessed their commencement; and that, when they take the more durable form of founding great public charities, such institutions invariably fall, first into abuse, then into decay, and after a time are either destroyed, or perverted from their original intention, mocking the effort by which it is vainly attempted to perpetuate the memory even of the purest and most energetic benevolence.

These conclusions are no doubt very unpalatable; and what makes them peculiarly offensive is, that it is impossible to refute them. For the deeper we penetrate into this question, the more clearly shall we see the superiority of intellectual acquisitions over moral feeling.[16] There is no instance on record of an ignorant man who, having good intentions, and supreme power to enforce them, has not done far more evil than good. And whenever the intentions have been very eager, and the power very extensive, the evil has been enormous. But if you can diminish the sincerity of that man, if you can mix some alloy with his motives, you will likewise diminish the evil which he works. If he is selfish as well as ignorant, it will often happen that you may play off his vice against his ignorance, and by exciting his fears restrain his mischief. If, however, he has no fear, if he is entirely unselfish, if his sole object is the good of others, if he pursues that object

---

[16] One part of the argument is well stated by Cuvier, who says, 'Le bien que l'on fait aux hommes, quelque grand qu'il soit, est toujours passager; les vérités qu'on leur laisse sont éternelles.' *Cuvier, Éloges Historiques*, vol. ii. p. 304

with enthusiasm, upon a large scale, and with disinterested zeal, then it is that you have no check upon him, you have no means of preventing the calamities which, in an ignorant age, an ignorant man will be sure to inflict. How entirely this is verified by experience, we may see in studying the history of religious persecution. To punish even a single man for his religious tenets, is assuredly a crime of the deepest dye; but to punish a large body of men, to persecute an entire sect, to attempt to extirpate opinions, which, growing out of the state of society in which they arise, are themselves a manifestation of the marvellous and luxuriant fertility of the human mind,—to do this is not only one of the most pernicious, but one of the most foolish acts that can possibly be conceived. Nevertheless, it is an undoubted fact that an overwhelming majority of religious persecutors have been men of the purest intentions, of the most admirable and unsullied morals. It is impossible that this should be otherwise. For they are not bad-intentioned men, who seek to enforce opinions which they believe to be good. Still less are they bad men, who are so regardless of temporal considerations as to employ all the resources of their power, not for their own benefit, but for the purpose of propagating a religion which they think necessary to the future happiness of mankind. Such men as these are not bad, they are only ignorant; ignorant of the nature of truth, ignorant of the consequences of their own acts. But, in a moral point of view, their motives are unimpeachable. Indeed, it is the very ardour of their sincerity which warms them into persecution. It is the holy zeal by which they are fired that quickens their fanaticism into a deadly activity. If you can impress any man with an absorbing conviction of the supreme importance of some moral or religious doctrine; if you can make him believe that those who reject that doctrine are doomed to eternal perdition; if you then give that man power, and by means of his ignorance blind him to the ulterior consequences of his own act,—he will infallibly persecute those who deny his doctrine; and the extent of his persecution will be regulated by the extent of his sincerity. Diminish the sincerity, and you will diminish the persecution: in other words, by weakening the virtue you may check the evil. This is a truth of which history furnishes such innumerable examples, that to deny it would be not only to reject the plainest and most conclusive arguments, but to refuse the concurrent testimony of every age. I will merely select two cases, which, from the entire difference in their circumstances, are very apposite as illustrations: the first being from the history of Paganism, the other from the history of Christianity; and both proving the inability of moral feelings to control religious persecution.

I. The Roman emperors, as is well known, subjected the early Christians to persecutions, which, though they have been exaggerated, were frequent and very grievous. But what to some persons must appear extremely strange, is, that among the active authors of these cruelties, we find the names of the best men who ever sat on the throne; while the worst and most infamous princes were precisely those who spared the Christians, and took no heed of their increase. The two most thoroughly depraved of all the emperors were certainly Commodus and Elagabalus; neither of whom persecuted the new religion, or indeed adopted any measures against it. They were too reckless of the future, too selfish, too absorbed in their own infamous pleasures, to mind whether truth or error prevailed; and being thus indifferent to the welfare of their subjects, they cared nothing about the progress of a creed, which they, as Pagan emperors, were bound to regard as a fatal and impious delusion. They, therefore, allowed Christianity to run its course, unchecked by those penal laws which more honest, but more mistaken, rulers would assuredly have enacted.[17] We find,

---

[17] 'The first year of Commodus must be the epocha of the toleration. From all these authorities, it appears beyond exception, that Commodus put a stop to the persecution in the first year of his reign. . . . . . Not one writer, either heathen or Christian, makes Commodus a persecutor.' *Letters concerning*

accordingly, that the great enemy of Christianity was Marcus Aurelius: a man of kindly temper, and of fearless, unflinching honesty, but whose reign was characterized by a persecution from which he would have refrained had he been less in earnest about the religion of his fathers.[16] And to complete the argument, it may be added, that the last and one of the most strenuous of the opponents of Christianity, who occupied the throne of the Cæsars, was Julian: a prince of eminent probity, whose opinions are often attacked, but against whose moral conduct even calumny itself has hardly breathed a suspicion.[19]

---

the Thundering Legion, in *Moyle's Works*, vol. ii. p. 266, London, 1726. 'Heliogabalus also, though in other respects the most infamous of all princes, and perhaps the most odious of all mortals, showed no marks of bitterness or aversion to the disciples of Jesus.' *Mosheim's Eccl. History*, vol. i. p. 66: see also *Milman's Hist. of Christianity*, London, 1840, vol. ii. p. 225.

[18] Dr. Milman (*History of Christianity*, 1840, vol. ii. p. 159) says, 'A blameless disciple in the severest school of philosophic morality, the austerity of Marcus rivalled that of the Christians in its contempt of the follies and diversions of life; yet his native kindliness of disposition was not hardened or embittered by the severity or the pride of his philosophy. With Aurelius, nevertheless, Christianity found not only a fair and high-minded competitor for the command of the human mind; not only a rival in the exaltation of the soul of man to higher views and more dignified motives; but a violent and intolerant persecutor.' M. Guizot compares him with Louis IX. of France; and certainly there was in both an evident connexion between sincarity and persecution: 'Marc Aurèle et saint Louis sont peut-être les deux seuls princes qui, en toute occasion, aient fait de leurs croyances morales la première règle de leur conduite: Marc Aurèle, stoïcien; saint Louis, chrétien.' *Guizot, Civilisation en France*, vol. iv. p. 142. Even Duplessis Mornay (*Mém.* vol. iv. p. 374) calls him 'le meilleur des empereurs payens;' and Ritter (*Hist. of Philos.* vol. iv. p. 222), 'the virtuous and noble emperor.'

[19] Neander (*History of the Church*, vol. i. p. 122) observes, that the best emperors opposed Christianity, and that the worst ones were indifferent to its encroachments. The same remark, in regard to Marcus and Commodus, is made by Gibbon (*Decline and Fall*, chap. xvi. p. 220, Lond. 1838). Another writer, of a very different character, ascribes this peculiarity to the wiles of the devil: 'In the primitive times, it is ob-

II. The second illustration is supplied by Spain; a country of which it must be confessed, that in no other have religious feelings exercised such sway over the affairs of men. No other European nation has produced so many ardent and disinterested missionaries, zealous self-denying martyrs, who have cheerfully sacrificed their lives in order to propagate truths which they thought necessary to be known. Nowhere else have the spiritual classes been so long in the ascendant; nowhere else are the people so devout, the churches so crowded, the clergy so numerous. But the sincerity and the honesty of purpose by which the Spanish people, taken as a whole, have always been marked, have not only been unable to prevent religious persecution, but have proved the means of encouraging it. If the nation had been more lukewarm, it would have been more tolerant. As it was, the preservation of the faith became the first consideration; and everything being sacrificed to this one object, it naturally happened that zeal begat cruelty, and the soil was prepared in which the Inquisition took root and flourished. The supporters of that barbarous institution were not hypocrites, but enthusiasts. Hypocrites are for the most part too supple to be cruel. For cruelty is a stern and unbending passion; while hypocrisy is a fawning and flexible art, which accommodates itself to human feelings, and flatters the weakness of men in order that it may gain its own ends. In Spain, the earnestness of the nation, being concentrated on a single topic, carried everything before it; and hatred of heresy becoming a habit, persecution of heresy was thought a duty. The conscientious energy with which that duty was fulfilled is seen in the history of the Spanish Church. Indeed, that the inquisitors were remarkable for an undeviating and incorruptible integrity, may be proved in a variety of ways, and from different and independent sources of evidence. This is a question to which

---

served that the best emperors were some of them stirred up by Satan to be the bitterest persecutors of the Church.' *Memoirs of Colonel Hutchinson*, p. 85.

I shall hereafter return; but there are two testimonies which I cannot omit, because, from the circumstances attending them, they are peculiarly unimpeachable. Llorente, the great historian of the Inquisition, and its bitter enemy, had access to its private papers; and yet, with the fullest means of information, he does not even insinuate a charge against the moral character of the inquisitors; but while execrating the cruelty of their conduct, he cannot deny the purity of their intentions.[20] Thirty years earlier, Townsend, a clergyman of the Church of England, published his valuable work on Spain;[21] and though, as a Protestant and an Englishman, he had every reason to be prejudiced against the infamous system which he describes, he also can bring no charge against those who upheld it; but having occasion to mention its establishment at Barcelona, one of its most important branches, he makes the remarkable admission, that all its members are men of worth, and that most of them are of distinguished humanity.[22]

These facts, startling as they are, form a very small part of that vast mass of evidence which history contains, and which decisively proves the utter inability of moral feelings to diminish religious persecution. The way in which the diminution has been really effected by the mere progress of intellectual acquirements, will be pointed out in another part of this volume; when we shall see that the great antagonist of intolerance is

---

[20] By which, indeed, he is sorely puzzled. 'On reconnaître mon impartialité dans quelques circonstances où je fais remarquer chez les inquisiteurs des dispositions généreuses; ce qui me porte à croire que les atroces sentences rendues par le Saint-Office, sont plutôt une conséquence de ses lois organiques, qu'un effet du caractère particulier de ses membres.' *Llorente, Histoire Critique de l'Inquisition d'Espagne*, vol. i. p. xxiii.: compare vol. ii. pp. 267, 268, vol. iv. p. 153.

[21] Highly spoken of by the late Blanco White, a most competent judge. See *Doblado's Letters from Spain*, p. 5.

[22] 'It is, however, universally acknowledged, for the credit of the corps at Barcelona, that all its members are men of worth, and most of them distinguished for humanity.' *Townsend's Journey through Spain, in 1786 and 1787*, vol. i. p. 122, Lond. 1792.

not humanity, but knowledge. It is to the diffusion of knowledge, and to that alone, that we owe the comparative cessation of what is unquestionably the greatest evil men have ever inflicted on their own species. For that religious persecution is a greater evil than any other, is apparent, not so much from the enormous and almost incredible number of its known victims,[23] as from the fact that the unknown must be far more numerous, and that history gives no account of those who have been spared in the body, in order that they might suffer in the mind. We hear much of martyrs and confessors—of those who were slain by the sword, or consumed in the fire; but we know little of that still larger number who, by the mere threat of persecution, have been driven into an outward abandonment of their real opinions; and who, thus forced into an apostasy the heart abhors, have passed the remainder of their life in the practice of a constant and humiliating hypocrisy. It is this which is the real curse of religious persecution. For in this way, men being constrained to mask their thoughts, there arises a habit of securing safety by falsehood, and of purchasing impunity with deceit. In this way fraud becomes a necessary of life; insincerity is made a daily custom; the whole tone of public feeling is vitiated, and the gross amount of vice

---

[23] In 1546, the Venetian ambassador at the court of the Emperor Charles V. stated, in an official report to his own government on his return home, 'that in Holland and in Friesland, more than 30,000 persons have suffered death at the hands of justice for Anabaptist errors.' *Correspondence of Charles V. and his Ambassadors,* edited by William Bradford, Lond. 8vo, 1850, p. 471. In Spain, the Inquisition, during the eighteen years of Torquemada's ministry, punished, according to the lowest estimate, upwards of 105,000 persons, of whom 8,800 were burned. *Prescott's History of Ferdinand and Isabella,* vol. i. p. 265. In Andalusia alone, during a single year, the Inquisition put to death 2,000 Jews, 'besides 17,000 who underwent some form of punishment less severe than that of the stake.' *Ticknor's History of Spanish Literature,* vol. i. p. 410. For other statistical evidence on this horrible subject, see Llorente, *Histoire de l'Inquisition,* vol. i. pp. 160, 229, 238, 239, 279, 280, 406, 407, 455, vol. ii. pp. 77, 116, 370, vol. iv. p. 31; and, above all, the summary at pp. 242–273.

and of error fearfully increased. Surely, then, we have reason to say, that, compared to this, all other crimes are of small account; and we may well be grateful for that increase of intellectual pursuits which has destroyed an evil that some among us would even now willingly restore.

The principle I am advocating is of such immense importance in practice as well as in theory, that I will give yet another instance of the energy with which it works. The second greatest evil known to mankind—the one by which, with the exception of religious persecution, most suffering has been caused—is, unquestionably, the practice of war. That this barbarous pursuit is, in the progress of society, steadily declining, must be evident, even to the most hasty reader of European history.[24] If we compare one country with another, we shall find that for a very long period wars have been becoming less frequent; and now so clearly is the movement marked, that, until the late commencement of hostilities, we had remained at peace for nearly forty years: a circumstance unparalleled, not only in our own country, but also in the annals of every other country which has been important enough to play a leading part in the affairs of the world.[25] The question arises, as to what share our moral feelings have had in bringing about this great improvement. And if this question is answered, not according to preconceived opinions, but according to the evidence we possess, the answer will certainly be, that those feelings have had no share at all. For it

---

[24] On the diminished love of war, which is even more marked than the actual diminution of war, see some interesting remarks in *Comte, Philosophie Positive*, vol. iv. pp. 488, 713, vol. vi. pp. 68, 424-436, where the antagonism between the military spirit and the industrial spirit is, on the whole, well worked out; though some of the leading phenomena have escaped the attention of this eminent philosopher, from his want of acquaintance with the history and present state of political economy.

[25] In *Pellew's Life of Sidmouth*, 1847, vol. iii. p. 137, this prolonged peace is gravely ascribed to 'the wisdom of the adjustment of 1815;' in other words, to the proceedings of the Congress of Vienna!

surely will not be pretended that the moderns have made any discoveries respecting the moral evils of war. On this head nothing is now known that has not been known for many centuries. That defensive wars are just, and that offensive wars are unjust, are the only two principles which, on this subject, moralists are able to teach. These two principles were as clearly laid down, as well understood, and as universally admitted, in the Middle Ages, when there was never a week without war, as they are at the present moment, when war is deemed a rare and singular occurrence. Since, then, the actions of men respecting war have been gradually changing, while their moral knowledge respecting it has not been changing, it is palpably evident that the changeable effect has not been produced by the unchangeable cause. It is impossible to conceive an argument more decisive than this. If it can be proved that, during the last thousand years, moralists or theologians have pointed out a single evil caused by war, the existence of which was unknown to their predecessors,—if this can be proved, I will abandon the view for which I am contending. But if, as I most confidently assert, this cannot be proved, then it must be conceded that, no additions having been made on this subject to the stock of morals, no additions can have been made to the result which the morals produce.[26]

---

[26] Unless more zeal has been displayed in the diffusion of moral and religious principles; in which case it would be possible for the principles to be stationary, and yet their effects be progressive. But so far from this, it is certain that in the Middle Ages there were, relatively to the population, more churches than there are now; the spiritual classes were far more numerous, the proselyting spirit far more eager, and there was a much stronger determination to prevent purely scientific inferences from encroaching on ethical ones. Indeed, during the Middle Ages, the moral and religious literature outweighed all the profane literature put together; and surpassed it, not only in bulk, but also in the ability of its cultivators. Now, however, the generalizations of moralists have ceased to control the affairs of men, and have made way for the larger doctrine of expediency, which includes all interests and all classes. Systematic writers on morals reached their zenith in the thir-

Thus far as to the influence exercised by moral feelings in increasing our distaste for war. But if, on the other hand, we turn to the human intellect, in the narrowest sense of the term, we shall find that every great increase in its activity has been a heavy blow to the warlike spirit. The full evidence for this I shall hereafter detail at considerable length; and in this Introduction I can only pretend to bring forward a few of those prominent points, which, being on the surface of history, will be at once understood.

Of these points, one of the most obvious is, that every important addition made to knowledge increases the authority of the intellectual classes, by increasing the resources which they have to wield. Now, the antagonism between these classes and the military class is evident: it is the antagonism between thought and action, between the internal and the external, between argument and violence, between persuasion and force; or, to sum up the whole, between men who live by the pursuits of peace and those who live by the practice of war. Whatever, therefore, is favourable to one class, is manifestly unfavourable to the other. Supposing the remaining circumstances to be the same, it must happen, that as the intellectual acquisitions of a people increase, their love of war will diminish; and if their intellectual acquisitions are very small, their love of war will be very great.[27] In perfectly barbarous countries,

---

teenth century, fell off rapidly after that period, were, as Coleridge well says, opposed by 'the genius of Protestantism:' and, by the end of the seventeenth century, became extinct in the most civilized countries; the *Ductor Dubitantium* of Jeremy Taylor being the last comprehensive attempt of a man of genius to mould society solely according to the maxims of moralists. Compare two interesting passages in *Mosheim's Ecclesiast. Hist.*, vol. i. p. 338, and *Coleridge's Friend*, vol. iii. p. 104.

[27] Herder boldly asserts that man originally, and by virtue of his organization, is peaceably disposed; but this opinion is decisively refuted by the immense additions which, since the time of Herder, have been made to our knowledge of the feelings and habits of savages. 'Indessen ist's wahr, dass der Bau des Menschen vorzüglich auf die Vertheidigung, nicht auf den Angriff gerichtet ist: in diesem

there are no intellectual acquisitions; and the mind being a blank and dreary waste, the only resource is external activity,[19] the only merit personal courage. No account is made of any man, unless he has killed an enemy; and the more he has killed, the greater the reputation he enjoys.[29] This is the purely savage state; and it is the state in which military glory is most esteemed, and military men most respected.[30] From

[19] muss ihm die Kunst zu Hülfe kommen, in jener aber ist er von Natur das kräftigste Geschöpf der Erde. Seine Gestalt selbst lehret ihn also Friedlichkeit, nicht räuberische Mordverwüstung,—der Humanität erstes Merkmal.' *Ideen zur Geschichte*, vol. i. p. 185.

[29] Hence, no doubt, that acuteness of the senses, natural, and indeed necessary, to an early state of society, and which, being at the expense of the reflecting faculties, assimilates man to the lower animals. See *Carpenter's Human Physiology*, p. 404; and a fine passage in *Herder's Ideen zur Geschichte*, vol. ii. p. 12: 'Das abstehende thierische Ohr, das gleichsam immer lauscht und horcht, das kleine scharfe Auge, das in der weitesten Ferne den kleinsten Rauch oder Staub gewahr wird, der weisse hervorbleckende, knochenbenagende Zahn, der dicke Hals und die zurückgebogene Stellung ihres Kopfes auf demselben.' Compare *Prichard's Physical Hist. of Mankind*, vol. i. pp. 292, 293; *Azara, Amérique Méridionale*, vol. ii. p. 18; *Wrangel's Polar Expedition*, p. 384; *Pallme's Travels in Kordofan*, pp. 132, 133.

[30] 'Among some Macedonian tribes, the man who had never slain an enemy was marked by a degrading badge.' *Grote's History of Greece*, vol. xi. p. 397. Among the Dyaks of Borneo, 'a man cannot marry until he has procured a human head; and he that has several may be distinguished by his proud and lofty bearing, for it constitutes his patent of nobility.' *Earl's Account of Borneo*, in *Journal of Asiatic Society*, vol. iv. p. 181. See also *Crawfurd on Borneo*, in *Journal of Geog. Soc.*, vol. xxiii. pp. 77, 80. And for similar instances of this absorption of all other ideas into warlike ones, compare *Journal of Geog. Soc.*, vol. x. p. 357; *Mallet's Northern Antiquities*, pp. 158, 159, 195; *Thirlwall's Hist. of Greece*, vol. i. pp. 226, 284, vol. viii. p. 209; *Henderson's History of Brazil*, p. 475; *Southey's History of Brazil*, vol. i. pp. 126, 248; *Asiatic Researches*, vol. ii. p. 188, vol. vii. p. 193; *Transactions of Bombay Society*, vol. ii. pp. 51, 52; *Hoskins's Travels in Ethiopia*, p. 163; *Origines du Droit*, in *Œuvres de Michelet*, vol. ii. pp. 333, 334 note. So also the Thracians: γῆς δὲ ἐργάτης ἀτιμότατος. τὸ ζῆν ἀπὸ πολέμου καὶ λῃστύος, κάλλιστον. *Herodotus*, book v. chap. 6, vol. iii. p. 10, edit. Baehr.

[30] Malcolm (*History of Persia*,

this frightful debasement, even up to the summit of civilization, there is a long series of consecutive steps; gradations, at each of which something is taken from the dominion of force, and something given to the authority of thought. Slowly, and one by one, the intellectual and pacific classes begin to arise; at first held in great contempt by warriors, but nevertheless gradually gaining ground, increasing in number and in power, and at each increase weakening that old military spirit, in which all other tendencies had formerly been absorbed. Trade, commerce, manufactures, law, diplomacy, literature, science, philosophy,—all these things, originally unknown, became organized into separate studies, each study having a separate class, and each class insisting on the importance of its own pursuit. Of these classes, some are, no doubt, less pacific than others; but even those which are the least pacific, are, of course, more so than men whose associations are entirely military, and who see in every fresh war that chance of personal distinction, from which, during peace, they are altogether debarred.[31]

---

vol. i. p. 204) says of the Tartars, 'There is only one path to eminence, that of military renown.' Thus, too, in the *Institutes of Timour*, p. 269: 'He only is equal to stations of power and dignity, who is well acquainted with the military art, and with the various modes of breaking and defeating hostile armies.' The same turn of mind is shown in the frequency and evident delight with which Homer relates battles—a peculiarity noticed in *Mure's Greek Literature*, vol. ii. pp. 63, 64, where an attempt is made to turn it into an argument to prove that the Homeric poems are all by the same author; though the more legitimate inference would be that the poems were all composed in a barbarous age.

[31] To the prospect of personal distinction there was formerly added that of wealth; and in Europe, during the Middle Ages, war was a very lucrative profession, owing to the custom of exacting heavy ransom for the liberty of prisoners. See Barrington's learned work, *Observations on the Statutes*, pp. 390-393. In the reign of Richard II. 'a war with France was esteemed as almost the only method by which an English gentleman could become rich.' Compare *Turner's Hist. of England*, vol. vi. p. 21. Sainte Palaye (*Mémoires sur l'ancienne Chevalerie*, vol. i. p. 311) says, 'La guerre enrichissoit alors par le butin, et par les rançons, celui qui la faisoit avec le plus de valeur, de vigilance et d'activité.

Thus it is that, as civilization advances, an equipoise is established, and military ardour is balanced by motives which none but a cultivated people can feel. But among a people whose intellect is not cultivated, such a balance can never exist. Of this we see a good illustration in the history of the present war.[82] For the peculiarity of the great contest in which we are engaged is, that it was produced, not by the conflicting interests of civilized countries, but by a rupture between Russia and Turkey, the two most barbarous monarchies now remaining in Europe. This is a very significant fact. It is highly characteristic of the actual condition of society, that a peace of unexampled length should have been broken, not, as former peaces were broken, by a quarrel between two civilized nations, but by the encroachments of the uncivilized Russians on the still more uncivilized Turks. At an earlier period, the influence of intellectual, and therefore pacific, habits was indeed constantly increasing, but was still too weak, even in the most advanced countries, to control the old warlike habits: hence there arose a desire for conquest, which often outweighed all other feelings, and induced great nations like France and England to attack each other on the slightest pretence, and seek every opportunity of gratifying the vindictive hatred with which both contemplated the prosperity of their neighbour. Such, however, is now the progress of affairs, that these two nations, laying aside the peevish and irritable jealousy they once entertained, are united in a common cause, and have drawn the sword, not for selfish purposes, but to protect the civilized world against the incursions of a barbarous foe.

This is the leading feature which distinguishes the present war from its predecessors. That a peace should

---

La rançon étoit, ce semble, pour l'ordinaire, une année des revenus du prisonnier.' For an analogy with this, see *Rig Veda Sanhita*, vol. i. p. 208, sec. 3, and vol. ii. p. 265, sec. 13. In Europe, the custom of paying a ransom for prisoners-of-war survived the Middle Ages, and was only put an end to by the peace of Munster, in 1648. *Manning's Commentaries on the Law of Nations*, 1839, p. 162; and on the profits formerly made, pp. 157, 158.

[83] I wrote this in 1855.

last for nearly forty years, and should then be interrupted, not, as heretofore, by hostilities between civilized states, but by the ambition of the only empire which is at once powerful and uncivilized—is one of many proofs that a dislike to war is a cultivated taste peculiar to an intellectual people. For no one will pretend that the military predilections of Russia are caused by a low state of morals, or by a disregard of religious duties. So far from this, all the evidence we have shows that vicious habits are not more common in Russia than in France or England;[33] and it is certain that the Russians submit to the teachings of the church with a docility greater than that displayed by their civilized opponents.[34] It is, therefore, clear that Russia is a warlike country, not because the inhabitants are immoral, but because they are unintellectual. The fault is in the head, not in the heart. In Russia, the national intellect being little cultivated, the intellectual classes lack influence; the military class, therefore, is supreme. In this early stage of society, there is as yet no middle rank,[35] and consequently the thoughtful and pacific habits which spring from the middle ranks have no existence. The minds of men, deprived of mental pursuits,[36] naturally turn to warlike

---

[33] Indeed some have supposed that there is less immorality in Russia than in Western Europe; but this idea is probably erroneous. See *Stirling's Russia*, Lond. 1841, pp. 59, 60. The benevolence and charitable disposition of the Russians are attested by Pinkerton, who had good means of information, and was by no means prejudiced in their favour. See *Pinkerton's Russia*, Lond. 1833, pp. 335, 336. Sir John Sinclair also says they are 'prone to acts of kindness and charity.' *Sinclair's Correspondence*, vol. ii. p. 241.

[34] The reverence of the Russian people for their clergy has attracted the attention of many observers, and is, indeed, too notorious to require proof.

[35] A very observing and intelligent writer says, 'Russia has only two ranks—the highest and the lowest.' *Letters from the Baltic*, Lond. 1841, vol. ii. p. 185. 'Les marchands, qui formaraient une classe moyenne, sont en si petit nombre qu'ils ne peuvent marquer dans l'état: d'ailleurs presque tous sont étrangers; .... où donc trouver cette classe moyenne qui fait la force des états?' *Custine's Russie*, vol. ii. pp. 125, 126: see also vol. iv. p. 74.

[36] A recent authoress, who had admirable opportunities of studying the society of St. Petersburg.

ones, as the only resource remaining to them. Hence it is that, in Russia, all ability is estimated by a military standard. The army is considered to be the greatest glory of the country: to win a battle, or outwit an enemy, is valued as one of the noblest achievements of life; and civilians, whatever their merits may be, are despised by this barbarous people, as beings of an altogether inferior and subordinate character.[37]

---

which she estimated with that fine tact peculiar to an accomplished woman, was amazed at this state of things among classes surrounded with every form of luxury and wealth: 'a total absence of all rational tastes, or literary topics..... Here it is absolutely *mauvais genre* to discuss a rational subject—mere *pédanterie* to be caught upon any topics beyond dressing, dancing, and a *jolie tournure.*' *Letters from the Baltic*, 1841, vol. ii. p. 233. M. Custine (*La Russie en 1839*, vol. i. p. 321) says 'Règle générale, personne ne profère jamais un mot qui pourrait intéresser vivement quelqu'un.' At vol. ii. p. 195, 'De toutes les facultés de l'intelligence, la seule qu'on estime ici c'est le tact.' Another writer of repute, M. Kohl, contemptuously observes, that in Russia, 'the depths of science are not even guessed at.' *Kohl's Russia*, 1842, Lond. p. 142.

[37] According to Schnitzler, 'Precedence is determined, in Russia, by military rank; and an ensign would take the *pas* of a nobleman not enrolled in the army, or occupying some situation giving military rank.' *M'Culloch's Geog. Dict.* 1849, vol. ii. p. 614. The same thing is stated in *Pinkerton's Russia*, 1833, p. 321. M. Erman, who travelled through great part of the Russian empire, says, 'In the modern language of St. Petersburg, one constantly hears a distinction of the greatest importance, conveyed in the inquiry which is habitually made respecting individuals of the educated class: Is he a plain-coat or a uniform?' *Erman's Siberia*, vol. i. p. 45. See also on this preponderance of the military classes, which is the inevitable fruit of the national ignorance, *Kohl's Russia*, pp. 28, 194; *Stirling's Russia under Nicholas the First*, p. 7.; *Custine's Russie*, vol. i. pp. 147, 152, 252, 266, vol. ii. pp. 71, 128, 309, vol. iii. p. 326, vol. iv. p. 264. Sir A. Alison (*History of Europe*, vol. ii. pp. 301, 302) says, 'The whole energies of the nation are turned towards the army. Commerce, the law, and all civil employments, are held in no esteem; the whole youth of any consideration betake themselves to the profession of arms.' The same writer (vol. x. p. 560) quotes the remark of Bremner, that 'nothing astonishes the Russian or Polish noblemen so much as seeing the estimation in which the civil professions, and especially the bar, are held in Great Britain.'

In England, on the other hand, opposite causes have produced opposite results. With us intellectual progress is so rapid, and the authority of the middle class so great, that not only have military men no influence in the government of the state, but there seemed at one time even a danger lest we should push this feeling to an extreme; and lest, from our detestation of war, we should neglect those defensive precautions which the enmity of other nations makes it advisable to adopt. But this at least we may safely say, that, in our country, a love of war is, as a national taste, utterly extinct. And this vast result has been effected, not by moral teachings, nor by the dictates of moral instinct; but by the simple fact, that in the progress of civilization there have been formed certain classes of society which have an interest in the preservation of peace, and whose united authority is sufficient to control those other classes whose interest lies in the prosecution of war.

It would be easy to conduct this argument further, and to prove how, by an increasing love of intellectual pursuits, the military service necessarily declines, not only in reputation, but likewise in ability. In a backward state of society men of distinguished talents crowd to the army, and are proud to enrol themselves in its ranks. But, as society advances, new sources of activity are opened, and new professions arise, which, being essentially mental, offer to genius opportunities for success more rapid than any formerly known. The consequence is, that in England, where these opportunities are more numerous than elsewhere, it nearly always happens that if a father has a son whose faculties are remarkable, he brings him up to one of the lay professions, where intellect, when accompanied by industry, is sure to be rewarded. If, however, the inferiority of the boy is obvious, a suitable remedy is at hand: he is made either a soldier or a clergyman; he is sent into the army, or hidden in the church. And this, as we shall hereafter see, is one of the reasons why, as society advances, the ecclesiastical spirit and the military spirit never fail to decline. As soon as eminent men grow unwilling to enter any profession, the lustre of that profession will be tarnished:

first its reputation will be lessened, and then its power
will be abridged. This is the process through which
Europe is actually passing, in regard both to the church
and to the army. The evidence, so far as the ecclesiastical profession is concerned, will be found in another
part of this work. The evidence respecting the military
profession is equally decisive. For although that profession has in modern Europe produced a few men of undoubted genius, their number is so extremely small, as
to amaze us at the dearth of original ability. That the
military class, taken as a whole, has a tendency to degenerate, will become still more obvious if we compare
long periods of time. In the ancient world, the leading
warriors were not only possessed of considerable accomplishments, but were comprehensive thinkers in politics
as well as in war, and were in every respect the first
characters of their age. Thus—to give only a few specimens from a single people—we find that the three most
successful statesmen Greece ever produced were Solon,
Themistocles, and Epaminondas,—all of whom were distinguished military commanders. Socrates, supposed by
some to be the wisest of the ancients, was a soldier; and
so was Plato; and so was Antisthenes, the celebrated
founder of the Cynics. Archytas, who gave a new direction to the Pythagorean philosophy; and Melissus, who
developed the Eleatic philosophy—were both of them
well-known generals, famous alike in literature and in
war. Among the most eminent orators, Pericles, Alci-
biades, Andocides, Demosthenes, and Æschines were all
members of the military profession; as also were the
two greatest tragic writers, Æschylus and Sophocles.
Archilochus, who is said to have invented iambic verses,
and whom Horace took as a model, was a soldier; and
the same profession could likewise boast of Tyrtæus, one
of the founders of elegiac poetry, and of Alcæus, one of
the best composers of lyric poetry. The most philosophic
of all the Greek historians was certainly Thucydides;
but he, as well as Xenophon and Polybius, held high
military appointments, and on more than one occasion
succeeded in changing the fortunes of war. In the midst
of the hurry and turmoil of camps, these eminent men

cultivated their minds to the highest point that the knowledge of that age would allow: and so wide is the range of their thoughts, and such the beauty and dignity of their style, that their works are read by thousands who care nothing about the sieges and battles in which they were engaged.

These were among the ornaments of the military profession in the ancient world; and all of them wrote in the same language, and were read by the same people. But in the modern world this identical profession, including many millions of men, and covering the whole of Europe, has never been able, since the sixteenth century, to produce ten authors who have reached the first class either as writers or as thinkers. Descartes is an instance of an European soldier combining the two qualities; he being as remarkable for the exquisite beauty of his style as for the depth and originality of his inquiries. This, however, is a solitary case; and there is, I believe, no second one of a modern military writer thus excelling in both departments. Certainly, the English army, during the last two hundred and fifty years, affords no example of it, and has, in fact, only possessed two authors, Raleigh and Napier, whose works are recognized as models, and are studied merely for their intrinsic merit. Still, this is simply in reference to style; and these two historians, notwithstanding their skill in composition, have never been reputed profound thinkers on difficult subjects, nor have they added anything of moment to the stock of our knowledge. In the same way, among the ancients, the most eminent soldiers were likewise the most eminent politicians, and the best leaders of the army were generally the best governors of the state. But here, again, the progress of society has wrought so great a change, that for a long period instances of this have been excessively rare. Even Gustavus Adolphus and Frederick the Great failed ignominiously in their domestic policy, and showed themselves as short-sighted in the arts of peace as they were sagacious in the arts of war. Cromwell, Washington, and Napoleon are, perhaps, the only first-rate modern warriors of whom it can be fairly said, that they were equally competent to govern a kingdom and command an army. And, if we look at England as furnishing a familiar illustration, we see this remark exemplified in our two greatest generals, Marlborough and Wellington. Marlborough was a man not only of the most idle and frivolous pursuits, but was so miserably ignorant, that his deficiencies made him the ridicule of his contemporaries; and of politics he had no other idea but to gain the favour of the sovereign by flattering his mistress, to desert the brother of that sovereign at his utmost need, and afterwards, by a double treachery, turn against his next benefactor, and engage in a criminal, as well as a foolish, correspondence with the very man whom a few years before he had infamously abandoned. These were the characteristics of the greatest conqueror of his age, the hero of a hundred fights, the victor of Blenheim and of Ramilies. As to our other great warrior, it is indeed true that the name of Wellington should never be pronounced by an Englishman without gratitude and respect: these feelings are, however, due solely to his vast military services, the importance of which it would ill become us to forget. But whoever has studied the civil history of England during the present century knows full well that this military chief, who in the field shone without a rival, and who, to his still greater glory be it said, possessed an integrity of purpose, an unflinching honesty, and a high moral feeling, which could not be surpassed, was nevertheless utterly unequal to the complicated exigencies of political life. It is notorious, that in his views of the most important legislative measures he was always in the wrong. It is notorious, and the evidence of it stands recorded in our Parliamentary Debates, that every great measure which was carried, every great improvement, every great step in reform, every concession to the popular wishes, was strenuously opposed by the Duke of Wellington, became law in spite of his opposition, and after his mournful declarations that by such means the security of England would be seriously imperilled. Yet there is now hardly a forward schoolboy who does not know that to these very measures the present stability of our country is mainly owing. Experience, the great test of wisdom, has amply proved, that those vast schemes of reform, which the Duke of Wellington spent his political life in opposing, were, I will not say expedient or advisable, but were indispensably necessary. That policy of resisting the popular will which he constantly advised is precisely the policy which has been pursued, since the Congress of Vienna, in every monarchy except our own. The result of that policy is written for our instruction: it is written in that great explosion of popular passion, which in the moment of its wrath upset the proudest thrones, destroyed princely families, ruined noble houses, desolated beautiful cities. And if the counsel of our great general had been followed, if the just demands of the people had been refused—this same lesson would have been written in the annals of our own land; and we should most assuredly have been unable to escape the consequence of that terrible catastrophe, in which the ignorance and selfishness of rulers did, only a few years ago, involve a large part of the civilized world.

Thus striking is the contrast between the military genius of ancient times, and the military genius of modern Europe. The causes of this decay are clearly traceable to the circumstance that, owing to the immense increase of intellectual employments, few men of ability will now enter a profession into which, in antiquity, men of ability eagerly crowded, as supplying the best means of exercising those faculties which, in more civilized countries, are turned to a better account. This, indeed, is a very important change; and thus to transfer the most powerful intellects from the arts of war to the arts of peace, has been the slow work of many centuries, the gradual, but constant, encroachments of advancing knowledge. To write the history of those encroachments would be to write the history of the human intellect—a task impossible for any single man adequately to perform. But the subject is one of such interest, and has been so little studied, that though I have already carried this analysis farther than I had intended, I cannot refrain from noticing what appear to me to be the three leading ways in which the warlike spirit of the ancient world has been weakened by the progress of European knowledge.

The first of these arose out of the invention of Gunpowder; which, though a warlike contrivance, has in its results been eminently serviceable to the interests of peace.[38] This important invention is said to have been made in the thirteenth century;[39] but was not in common use until the fourteenth, or even the beginning of the fifteenth, century. Scarcely had it come into operation, when it worked a great change in the whole scheme and practice of war. Before this time, it was considered the duty of nearly every citizen to be prepared to enter the military service, for the purpose either of defending his own country, or of attacking others.[40] Standing armies were entirely unknown; and in their place there existed a rude and barbarous militia, always ready for battle, and always unwilling to engage in those peaceful pursuits which were then universally despised. Nearly every man being a

---

[38] The consequences of the invention of gunpowder are considered very superficially by Frederick Schlegel (*Lectures on the History of Literature*, vol. ii. pp. 37, 38), and by Dugald Stewart (*Philosophy of the Mind*, vol. i. p. 262). They are examined with much greater ability, though by no means exhaustively, in Smith's *Wealth of Nations*, book v. chap. i. pp. 292, 296, 297; Herder's *Ideen zur Geschichte der Menschheit*, vol. iv. p. 301; Hallam's *Middle Ages*, vol. ii. p. 470.

[39] From the following authorities, it appears impossible to trace it further back than the thirteenth century; and it is doubtful whether the Arabs were, as is commonly supposed, the inventors: Humboldt's *Cosmos*, vol. ii. p. 590; Koch, *Tableaux des Révolutions*, vol. i. p. 242; Beckmann's *History of Inventions*, 1846, vol. ii. p. 505; *Histoire Lit. de la France*, vol. xx. p. 236; Thomson's *History of Chemistry*, vol. i. p. 36; Hallam's *Middle Ages*, vol. i. p. 341. The statements in Erman's *Siberia*, vol. i. pp. 370, 371, are more positive than the evidence we are possessed of will justify; but there can be no doubt that a sort of gunpowder was at an early period used in China, and in other parts of Asia.

[40] Vattel, *le Droit des Gens*, vol. ii. p. 129; Lingard's *History of England*, vol. ii. pp. 356, 357. Among the Anglo-Saxons, 'all free men and proprietors of land, except the ministers of religion, were trained to the use of arms, and always held ready to take the field at a moment's warning.' Eccleston's *English Antiquities*, p. 92. 'There was no distinction between the soldier and the citizen.' Palgrave's *Anglo-Saxon Commonwealth*, vol. i. p. 200.

soldier, the military profession, as such, had no separate existence; or, to speak more properly, the whole of Europe composed one great army, in which all other professions were merged. To this the only exception was the ecclesiastical profession; but even that was affected by the general tendency, and it was not at all uncommon to see large bodies of troops led to the field by bishops and abbots, to most of whom the arts of war were in those days perfectly familiar.[41] At all events, between these two professions men were necessarily divided: the only avocations were war and theology; and if you refused to enter the church, you were bound to serve in the army. As a natural consequence, everything of real importance was altogether neglected. There were, indeed, many priests and many warriors, many sermons and many battles.[42] But, on the other hand, there was neither trade, nor commerce, nor manufactures; there was no science, no literature: the useful arts were entirely unknown; and even the highest ranks of society were unacquainted, not only with the most ordinary comforts, but with the commonest decencies of civilized life.

---

[41] On these warlike ecclesiastics, compare *Grose's Military Antiq.* vol. i. pp. 67–8; *Lingard's Hist. of England*, vol. ii. pp. 26, 183, vol. iii. p. 14; *Turner's Hist. of England*, vol. iv. p. 458, vol. v. pp. 92, 402, 406; *Mosheim's Eccl. History*, vol. i. pp. 173, 193, 241; *Crichton's Scandinavia*, Edinb. 1838, vol. i. p. 220. Such opponents were the more formidable, because in those happy days it was sacrilege for a layman to lay hands on a bishop. In 1095 his Holiness the Pope caused a council to declare, 'Quód qui apprehenderit episcopum omnino exlex fiat.' *Matthæi Paris Historia Major*, p. 18. As the context contains no limitation of this, it would follow that a man became spiritually outlawed if he, even in self-defence, took a bishop prisoner.

[42] As Sharon Turner observes of England under the Anglo-Saxon government, 'war and religion were the absorbing subjects of this period.' *Turner's History of England*, vol. iii. p. 263. And a recent scientific historian says of Europe generally: 'alle Künste und Kenntnisse, die sich nicht auf das edle Kriegs-, Rauf- und Raubhandwerk bezogen, waren überflüssig und schädlich. Nur etwas Theologie war vonnöthen, um die Erde mit dem Himmel zu verbinden.' *Winckler, Geschichte der Botanik*, 1854, p. 56.

But so soon as gunpowder came into use, there was laid the foundation of a great change. According to the old system, a man had only to possess, what he generally inherited from his father, either a sword or a bow, and he was ready equipped for the field.[43] According to the new system, new means were required, and the equipment became more costly and more difficult. First, there was the supply of gunpowder;[44]

---

[43] In 1181, Henry II. of England ordered that every man should have either a sword or bow; which he was not to sell, but leave to his heir: 'cæteri autem omnes haberent wanbasiam, capellum ferreum, lanceam et gladium, vel arcum et sagittas: et prohibuit ne aliquis arma sua venderet vel invadiaret; sed cum moreretur, daret illa propinquiori hæredi suo.' *Rog. de Hov. Annal. in Scriptores post Bedam*, p. 343 rev. In the reign of Edward I., it was ordered that every man possessing land to the value of forty shillings should keep 'a sword, bow and arrows, and a dagger... Those who were to keep bows and arrows might have them out of the forest.' *Grose's Military Antiquities*, vol. ii. pp. 301, 302. Compare *Geijer's History of the Swedes*, part i. p. 94. Even late in the fifteenth century, there were at the Universities of Oxford and Cambridge, 'in each from four to five thousand scholars, all grown up, carrying swords and bows, and in great part gentry.' *Sir William Hamilton on the History of Universities*, in *Hamilton's Philosoph. Discussions*, p. 414. One of the latest attempts made to revive archery was a warrant issued by Elizabeth in 1596, and printed by Mr. Collier in the *Egerton Papers*, pp. 217-220, edit. Camden Soc. 1840. In the south-west of England, bows and arrows did not finally disappear from the muster-rolls till 1690; and in the meantime the musket gained ground. See *Yonge's Diary*, edit. Camden Soc. 1848, p. xvii.

[44] It is stated by many writers that no gunpowder was manufactured in England until the reign of Elizabeth. *Camden's Elizabeth*, in *Kennett's History*, vol. ii. p. 388, London, 1719; *Strickland's Queens of England*, vol. vi. p. 223, Lond. 1843; *Grose's Military Antiquities*, vol. i. p. 378. But Sharon Turner (*History of England*, vol. vi. pp. 490, 491, Lond. 1830) has shown, from an order of Richard III. in the Harleian manuscripts, that it was made in England in 1483; and Mr. Eccleston (*English Antiquities*, p. 182, Lond. 1847) states, that the English both made and exported it as early as 1411: compare p. 202. At all events, it long remained a costly article; and even in the reign of Charles I., I find a complaint of its dearness, 'whereby the train-bands are much discouraged in their exercising.' *Parliament. Hist.* vol. ii. p. 655. In 1686, it appears

then there was the possession of muskets, which were expensive weapons, and considered difficult to manage.[45] Then, too, there were other contrivances to which gunpowder naturally gave rise, such as pistols, bombs, mortars, shells, mines, and the like.[46] All these things, by increasing the complication of the military art, increased the necessity of discipline and practice; while, at the same time, the change that was being effected in the ordinary weapons deprived the great majority of men of the possibility of procuring them. To suit these altered circumstances, a new system was organized: and it was found advisable to train up bodies of men

---

from the *Clarendon Correspondence*, vol. i. p. 413, that the wholesale price ranged from about 2*l.* 10*s.* to 3*l.* per barrel. On the expense of making it in the present century, see *Liebig and Kopp's Reports on Chemistry*, vol. iii. p. 325, Lond. 1852.

[45] The muskets were such miserable machines, that, in the middle of the fifteenth century, it took a quarter of an hour to charge and fire one. *Hallam's Middle Ages*, vol. i. p. 342. Grose (*Military Antiquities*, vol. i. p. 146, vol. ii. pp. 292, 337) says, that the first mention of muskets in England is in 1471; and that rests for them did not become obsolete until the reign of Charles I. In the recent edition of *Beckmann's History of Inventions*, Lond. 1846, vol. ii. p. 535, it is strangely supposed that muskets were 'first used at the battle of Pavia.' Compare *Daniel, Histoire de la Milice*, vol. i. p. 404, with *Smythe's Military Discourses*, in *Ellis's Original Letters*, p. 53, edit. Camden Society.

[46] Pistols are said to have been invented early in the sixteenth century. *Grose's Military Antiq.* vol. i. pp. 102, 146. Gunpowder was first employed in mining towns in 1487. *Prescott's Hist. of Ferdinand and Isabella*, vol. ii. p. 32; *Koch, Tableaux des Révolutions*, vol. i. p. 243; *Daniel, Histoire de la Milice Française*, vol. i. p. 574. Daniel (*Milice Française*, vol. i. pp. 580, 581) says that bombs were not invented till 1588; and the same thing is asserted in *Biographie Universelle*, vol. xv. p. 248: but, according to Grose (*Military Antiq.* vol. i. p. 387), they are mentioned by Valturinus in 1472. On the general condition of the French artillery in the sixteenth century, see *Relations des Ambassadeurs Vénitiens*, vol. i. pp. 94, 476, 478, Paris, 1838, 4to: a curious and valuable publication. There is some doubt as to the exact period in which cannons were first known; but they were certainly used in war before the middle of the fourteenth century. See *Bohlen, das alte Indien*, vol. ii. p. 83; *Daniel, Histoire de la Milice*, vol. i. pp. 441, 442.

for the sole purpose of war, and to separate them as much as possible from those other employments in which formerly all soldiers were occasionally engaged. Thus it was that there arose standing armies; the first of which were formed in the middle of the fifteenth century,[47] almost immediately after gunpowder was generally known. Thus, too, there arose the custom of. employing mercenary troops; of which we find a few earlier instances, though the practice was not fully established until the latter part of the fourteenth century.[48]

The importance of this movement was soon seen, by the change it effected in the classification of European society. The regular troops being, from their discipline, more serviceable against the enemy, and also more immediately under the control of the government, it naturally followed that, as their merits became understood, the old militia should fall, first into disrepute, then be neglected, and then sensibly diminish. At the same time, this diminution in the number of undisciplined soldiers deprived the country of a part of its warlike resources, and therefore made it necessary to pay more attention to the disciplined ones, and to confine them more exclusively to their military duties. Thus it was that a division was first broadly established between the soldier and the civilian; and there arose a separate military profession,[49] which, consisting of a comparatively

---

[47] *Blackstone's Commentaries*, vol. i. p. 413; *Daniel, Hist. de la Milice*, vol. i. p. 210, vol. ii. pp. 491, 493; *Œuvres de Turgot*, vol. viii. p. 229.

[48] The leading facts respecting the employment of mercenary troops are indicated with great judgment by Mr. Hallam, in his *Middle Ages*, vol. i. p. 326–337.

[49] Grose (*Military Antiquities*, vol. i. pp. 310, 311) says, that until the sixteenth century, English soldiers had no professional dress, but 'were distinguished by badges of their leaders' arms, similar to those now worn by watermen.' It was also early in the sixteenth century that there first arose a separate military literature. *Daniel, Hist. de la Milice*, vol. l. p. 380: 'Les autours, qui ont écrit en détail sur la discipline militaire: or ce n'est guères que sous François I, et sous l'Empereur Charles V, que les Italiens, les François, las Espagnols et les Allemans ont commencé à écrire sur ce sujet.'

small number of the total amount of citizens, left the remainder to settle in some other pursuit.[50] In this way immense bodies of men were gradually weaned from their old warlike habits; and being, as it were, forced into civil life, their energies became available for the general purposes of society, and for the cultivation of those arts of peace which had formerly been neglected. The result was, that the European mind, instead of being, as heretofore, solely occupied either with war or with theology, now struck out into a middle path, and created those great branches of knowledge to which modern civilization owes its origin. In each successive generation this tendency towards a separate organization was more marked; the utility of a division of labour became clearly recognised; and by this means knowledge itself advanced, the authority of this middle or intellectual class correspondingly increased. Each addition to its power lessened the weight of the other two classes, and checked those superstitious feelings and that love of war, on which, in an early state of society, all enthusiasm is concentrated. The evidence of the growth and diffusion of this intellectual principle is so full and decisive, that it would be possible, by combining all the branches of knowledge, to trace nearly the whole of its consecutive steps. At present, it is enough to say, that, taking a general view, this third, or intellectual, class, first displayed an independent, though still a vague, activity in the fourteenth and fifteenth centuries; that in the sixteenth century, this activity, assuming a distinct form, showed itself in

---

[50] The change from the time when every layman was a soldier, is very remarkable. Adam Smith (*Wealth of Nations*, book v. chap. i. p. 291) says, 'Among the civilized nations of modern Europe, it is commonly computed, that not more than the one-hundredth part of the inhabitants of any country can be employed as soldiers, without ruin to the country which pays the expense of their service.' The same proportion is given in *Sadler's Law of Population*, vol. i. p. 292; and in *Grandeur et Décadence des Romains*, chap. iii.—*Œuvres de Montesquieu*, p. 130: also in *Sharpe's History of Egypt*, vol. i. p. 105; and in *Alison's History of Europe*, vol. xii. p. 318.

religious outbreaks; that in the seventeenth century, its energy, becoming more practical, was turned against the abuses of government, and caused a series of rebellions, from which hardly any part of Europe escaped; and finally, that in the eighteenth and nineteenth centuries, it has extended its aim to every department of public and private life, diffusing education, teaching legislators, controlling kings, and, above all, settling on a sure foundation that supremacy of Public Opinion, to which not only constitutional princes, but even the most despotic sovereigns, are now rendered strictly amenable.

These, indeed, are vast questions; and, without some knowledge of them, no one can understand the present condition of European society, or form the least idea of its future prospects. It is, however, sufficient that the reader can now perceive the way in which so slight a matter as the invention of gunpowder diminished the warlike spirit, by diminishing the number of persons to whom the practice of war was habitual. There were, no doubt, other and collateral circumstances which tended in the same direction; but the use of gunpowder was the most effectual, because, by increasing the difficulty and expense of war, it made a separate military profession indispensable; and thus, curtailing the action of the military spirit, left an overplus, an unemployed energy, which soon found its way to the pursuits of peace, infused into them a new life, and began to control that lust of conquest, which, though natural to a barbarous people, is the great enemy of knowledge, and is the most fatal of those diseased appetites by which even civilized countries are too often afflicted.

The second intellectual movement, by which the love of war has been lessened, is much more recent, and has not yet produced the whole of its natural effects. I allude to the discoveries made by Political Economy: a branch of knowledge with which even the wisest of the ancients had not the least acquaintance, but which possesses an importance it would be difficult to exaggerate, and is, moreover, remarkable, as being the only subject immediately connected with the art of government that has yet been raised to a science. The practical value of this noble study, though perhaps only fully known to the more advanced thinkers, is gradually becoming recognized by men of ordinary education: but even those by whom it is understood seem to have paid little attention to the way in which, by its influence, the interests of peace, and therefore of civilization, have been directly promoted.[51] The manner in which this has been brought about, I will endeavour to explain, as it will furnish another argument in support of that great principle which I wish to establish.

It is well known, that, among the different causes of war, commercial jealousy was formerly one of the most conspicuous; and there are numerous instances of quarrels respecting the promulgation of some particular tariff, or the protection of some favourite manufacture. Disputes of this kind were founded upon the very ignorant, but the very natural notion, that the advantages of commerce depend upon the balance of trade, and that whatever is gained by one country must be lost by another. It was believed that wealth is composed entirely of money; and that it is, therefore, the essential interest of every people to import few commodities and much gold. Whenever this was done, affairs were said to be in a sound and healthy state; but, if this was not done, it was declared that we were being drained of our resources, and that some other country was getting the better of us, and was enriching itself at our expense.[52] For this the only remedy

---

[51] The pacific tendencies of political economy are touched on very briefly in Blanqui, Histoire de l'Economie Politique, vol. ii. p. 207; and in Twiss's Progress of Political Economy, p. 240.

[52] This favourite doctrine is illustrated in a curious 'Discourse,' written in 1578, and printed in Stow's London, in which it is laid down, that if our exports exceed our imports, we gain by the trade; but that, if they are less, we lose. Stow's London, edit. Thoms, 1842, p. 205. Whenever this balance was disturbed, politicians were thrown into an agony of fear. In 1620, James I. said, in one of his long speeches, 'It's strange that my Mint hath not gone this

was to negotiate a commercial treaty, which should oblige the offending nation to take more of our commodities, and give us more of their gold: if, however, they refused to sign the treaty, it became necessary to bring them to reason; and for this purpose an armament was fitted out to attack a people who, by lessening our wealth, had deprived us of that money by which alone trade could be extended in foreign markets.[83]

This misconception of the true nature of barter was

---

eight or nine years; but I think the fault of the want of money is the uneven balancing of trade. *Parl. History*, vol. i. p. 1179; see also the debate 'On the Scarcity of Money,' pp. 1194–1196. In 1620, the House of Commons, in a state of great alarm, passed a resolution, 'That the importation of tobacco out of Spain is one reason of the scarcity of money in this kingdom.' *Parl. Hist.* vol. i. p. 1198. In 1627, it was actually argued in the House of Commons that the Netherlands were being weakened by their trade with the East Indies, because it carried money out of the country! *Parl. Hist.* vol. ii. p. 220. Half a century later, the same principle was advocated by Sir William Temple in his Letters, and also in his Observations upon the United Provinces. *Temple's Works*, vol. i. p. 175, vol. ii. pp. 117, 118.

[83] In 1672, the celebrated Earl of Shaftesbury, then Lord Chancellor, announced that the time had come when the English must go to war with the Dutch; for that it was 'impossible both should stand upon a balance; and that, if we do not master their trade, they will ours. They or we must truckle. One must and will give the law to the other. There is no compounding, where the contest is for the trade of the whole world.' *Somers' Tracts*, vol. viii. p. 39. A few months later, still insisting on the propriety of the war, he gave as one of his reasons that it 'was necessary to the trade of England that there should be a fair adjustment of commerce in the East Indies.' *Parl. Hist.* vol. iv. p. 687. In 1701, Stepney, a diplomatist and one of the lords of trade, published an essay, strongly insisting on the benefits which would accrue to English commerce by a war with France. *Somers' Tracts*, vol. xi. pp. 199, 217; and he says, p. 205, that one of the consequences of peace with France would be 'the utter ruin and destruction of our trade.' See also, in vol. xiii. p. 688, the remarks on the policy of William III. In 1743, Lord Hardwicke, one of the most eminent men of his time, said, in the House of Lords, 'If our wealth is diminished, it is time to ruin the commerce of that nation which has driven us from the markets of the Continent—by sweeping the seas of their ships, and by blockading their ports.' *Campbell's Lives of the Chancellors*, vol. v. p. 89.

formerly universal;[54] and being adopted even by the ablest politicians, was not only an immediate cause of war, but increased those feelings of natural hatred by which war is encouraged; each country thinking that it had a direct interest in diminishing the wealth of its neighbours.[55] In the seventeenth, or even late in the sixteenth century, there were, indeed, one or two eminent thinkers who exposed some of the fallacies upon which this opinion was based.[56] But their arguments found

---

[54] In regard to the seventeenth century, see Mill's *History of India*, vol i. pp. 41, 42. To this I may add, that even Locke had very confused notions respecting the use of money in trade. See *Essay on Money*, in *Locke's Works*, vol. iv.; and in particular pp. 9, 10, 12, 20, 21, 49–52. Berkeley, profound thinker as he was, fell into the same errors, and assumes the necessity of maintaining the balance of trade, and lessening our imports in proportion as we lessen our exports. See the *Querist*, Nos. xcix. clxi., in *Berkeley's Works*, vol. ii. pp. 246, 250: see also his proposal for a sumptuary law, in *Essay towards Preventing the Ruin of Great Britain*, in *Works*, vol. ii. p. 190. The economical views of Montesquieu (*Esprit des Lois*, livre xx. chap. xii. in *Œuvres*, p. 353) are as hopelessly wrong; while Vattel (*Droit des Gens*, vol. i. pp. 111, 117, 118, 206) goes out of his way to praise the mischievous interference of the English government, which he recommends as a pattern to other states.

[55] The Earl of Bristol, a man of some ability, told the House of Lords, in 1642, that it was a great advantage to England for other countries to go to war with each other; because by that means we should get their money, or, as he called it, their 'wealth.' See his speech, in *Parl. History*, vol. ii. pp. 1274–1279.

[56] Serra, who wrote in 1613, is said to have been the first to prove the absurdity of discouraging the exportation of the precious metals. See Twiss *on the Progress of Political Economy*, pp. 8, 12, 13. But I believe that the earliest approach towards modern economical discoveries is a striking essay published in 1581, and ascribed to William Stafford. It will be found in the *Harleian Miscellany*, vol. ix. pp. 139–192, edit. Park, 1812; and the title, *Brief Conceipt of English Policy*, gives an inadequate idea of what is, on the whole, the most important work on the theory of politics which had then appeared: since the author not only displays an insight into the nature of price and value, such as no previous thinker possessed, but he points out clearly the causes of that system of enclosures which is the leading economical fact in the reign of Elizabeth, and is intimately connected with the rise of the poor-laws. Some account of this essay is given by Dr. Twiss;

no favour with those politicians by whom European affairs were then administered. It is doubtful if they were known; and it is certain that, if known, they were despised by statesmen and legislators, who, from the constancy of their practical occupations, cannot be supposed to have sufficient leisure to master each new discovery that is successively made; and who in consequence are, as a body, always in the rear of their age. The result was, that they went blundering on in the old track, believing that no commerce could flourish without their interference, troubling that commerce by repeated and harassing regulations, and taking for granted that it was the duty of every government to benefit the trade of their own people by injuring the trade of others.[57]

But in the eighteenth century, a long course of events, which I shall hereafter trace, prepared the way for a spirit of improvement, and a desire for reform, of which the world had then seen no example. This great movement displayed its energy in every department of knowledge; and now it was that a successful attempt

---

but the original is easily accessible, and should be read by every student of English history. Among other heretical propositions, it recommends free trade in corn.

[57] In regard to the interference of the English legislature, it is stated by Mr. M'Culloch (*Polit. Econ.* p. 260), on the authority of a committee of the House of Commons, that before the year 1820, 'no fewer than two thousand laws with respect to commerce had been passed at different periods.' It may be confidently asserted, that every one of those laws was an unmitigated evil, since no trade, and indeed no interest of any kind, can be protected by government without inflicting immeasurably greater loss upon the unprotected interests and trades; while, if the protection is universal, the loss will be universal. Some striking instances of the absurd laws which have been passed respecting trade, are collected in *Barrington's Observations on the Statutes*, pp. 279–285. Indeed, it was considered necessary that every parliament should do something in this way; and Charles II., in one of his speeches, says, 'I pray, contrive any good short bills which may improve the industry of the nation . . . . and so God bless your councils.' *Parl. History*, vol. iv. p. 291. Compare the remarks on the fishery-trade, in *Somers' Tracts*, vol. xii. p. 33.

was first made to raise Political Economy to a science, by discovering the laws which regulate the creation and diffusion of wealth. In the year 1776, Adam Smith published his *Wealth of Nations;* which, looking at its ultimate results, is probably the most important book that has ever been written, and is certainly the most valuable contribution ever made by a single man towards establishing the principles on which government should be based. In this great work, the old theory of protection as applied to commerce was destroyed in nearly all its parts ;[58] the doctrine of the balance of trade was not only attacked, but its falsehood was demonstrated; and innumerable absurdities, which had been accumulating for ages, were suddenly swept away.[59]

If the *Wealth of Nations* had appeared in any preceding century, it would have shared the fate of the great works of Stafford and Serra; and although the principles which it advocated would, no doubt, have excited the attention of speculative thinkers, they would, in all probability, have produced no effect on practical politicians, or, at all events, would only have exercised an indirect and precarious influence. But the diffusion of knowledge had now become so general, that even our ordinary legislators were, in some degree, prepared for these great truths, which, in a former period, they would have despised as idle novelties. The result was, that the doctrines of Adam Smith soon found their way into the House of Commons ;[60] and, being adopted by a few of the leading

---

[58] To this the only exception of any moment is the view taken of the usury-laws, which Jeremy Bentham has the honour of demolishing.

[59] Before Adam Smith, the principal merit is due to Hume; but the works of that profound thinker were too fragmentary to produce much effect. Indeed, Hume, notwithstanding his vast powers, was inferior to Smith in comprehensiveness as well as in industry.

[60] The first notice I have observed of the *Wealth of Nations* in Parliament is in 1783; and between then and the end of the century it is referred to several times, and latterly with increasing frequency. See *Parliamentary*

members, were listened to with astonishment by that great assembly, whose opinions were mainly regulated by the wisdom of their ancestors, and who were loth to believe that anything could be discovered by the moderns which was not already known to the ancients. But it is in vain that such men as these always set themselves up to resist the pressure of advancing knowledge. No great truth which has once been found has ever afterwards been lost; nor has any important discovery yet been made which has not eventually carried everything before it. Even so, the principles of Free Trade, as demonstrated by Adam Smith, and all the consequences which flow from them, were vainly struggled against by the most overwhelming majorities of both Houses of Parliament. Year by year this great truth made its way; always advancing, never receding.[61] The majority was at first deserted by a few men of ability, then by ordinary men, then it became a minority, then even the minority began to dwindle;

History, vol. xxiii. p. 1152, vol. xxvi. pp. 481, 1035, vol. xxvii. p. 385, vol. xxix. pp. 834, 905 962, 1065, vol. xxx. pp. 330, 333, vol. xxxii. p. 2, vol. xxxiii. pp. 353, 386, 522, 548, 549, 563, 774, 777, 778, 822, 823, 824, 825, 827, 1249, vol. xxxiv. pp. 11, 97, 98, 141, 142, 304, 473, 650, 901, 902, 903. It is possible that one or two passages may have been overlooked; but I believe that these are the only instances of Adam Smith being referred to during seventeen years. From a passage in *Pellew's Life of Sidmouth*, vol. i. p. 51, it appears that even Addington was studying Adam Smith in 1787.

[61] In 1797, Pulteney, in one of his financial speeches, appealed to 'the authority of Dr. Smith, who, it was well said, would persuade the present generation and govern the next.' *Parl. Hist.* vol. xxxiii. p. 778. In 1813, Dugald Stewart (*Philosophy of the Human Mind*, vol. ii. p. 472) announced that the doctrine of free trade 'has now, I believe, become the prevailing creed of thinking men all over Europe.' And in 1816, Ricardo said, 'The reasoning by which the liberty of trade is supported is so powerful, that it is daily obtaining converts. It is with pleasure that I see the progress which this great principle is making amongst those whom we should have expected to cling the longest to old prejudices.' *Proposals for an Economical Currency*, in *Ricardo's Works*, p. 407.

and at the present day, eighty years after the publication of Smith's *Wealth of Nations*, there is not to be found any one of tolerable education who is not ashamed of holding opinions which, before the time of Adam Smith, were universally received.

Such is the way in which great thinkers control the affairs of men, and by their discoveries regulate the march of nations. And truly the history of this one triumph alone should be enough to repress the presumption of statesmen and legislators, who so exaggerate the importance of their craft as to ascribe great results to their own shifting and temporary contrivances. For, whence did they derive that knowledge, of which they are always ready to assume the merit? How did they obtain their opinions? How did they get at their principles? These are the elements of their success; and these they can only learn from their masters—from those great teachers, who, moved by the inspiration of genius, fertilize the world with their discoveries. Well may it be said of Adam Smith, and said, too, without fear of contradiction, that this solitary Scotchman has, by the publication of one single work, contributed more towards the happiness of man, than has been effected by the united abilities of all the statesmen and legislators of whom history has preserved an authentic account.

The result of these great discoveries I am not here concerned to examine, except so far as they aided in diminishing the energy of the warlike spirit. And the way in which they effected this may be easily stated. As long as it was generally believed that the wealth of a country consists of its gold, it was of course also believed that the sole object of trade is to increase the influx of the precious metals; it, therefore, became natural that Government should be expected to take measures by which such influx could be secured. This, however, could only be done by draining other countries of their gold; a result which they, for precisely the same reasons, strenuously resisted. The consequence was, that any idea of real reciprocity was impossible: every commercial treaty was an attempt made by one nation to outwit another;[62] every new tariff was a declaration of hostility; and that which ought to be the most peaceable of all pursuits became one of the causes of those national jealousies and national animosities, by which war is mainly promoted.[63] But when it was once clearly understood that gold and silver are not wealth, but are merely the representatives of wealth; when men began to see that wealth itself solely consists of the value which skill and labour can add to the raw material, and that money is of no possible use to a nation except to measure and circulate their riches; when these great truths were recognized,[64] all the old notions respecting the balance of trade, and the supreme importance of the precious metals, at once fell to the ground. These enormous errors being dispersed, the true theory of barter was easily worked out. It was perceived, that if commerce is allowed to be free, its advantages will be shared by every country which engages in it; that, in the absence of monopoly, the benefits of trade are of

---

[62] Sir Theodore Janson, in his *General Maxims of Trade*, published in 1713, lays it down as a principle universally recognized, that 'All the nations of Europe seem to strive who shall outwit one another in point of trade; and they concur in this maxim, that the less they consume of foreign commodities, the better it is for them.' *Somers' Tracts*, vol. xiii. p. 292. Thus, too, in a *Dialogue between an Englishman and a Dutchman*, published in 1700, the Dutchman is represented as boasting that his government had 'forced treaties of commerce exclusive to all other nations.' *Somers' Tracts*, vol. xi. p. 376. This is the system of 'narrow selfishness' denounced by Dr. Story, in his noble work, *Conflict of Laws*, 1841, p. 32.

[63] 'It cannot, indeed, be denied that mistaken views of commerce, like those so frequently entertained of religion, have been the cause of many wars and of much bloodshed.' *M'Culloch's Principles of Political Economy*, p. 140. See also pp. 37, 38: 'It has made each nation regard the welfare of its neighbours as incompatible with its own: hence the reciprocal desire of injuring and impoverishing each other; and hence that spirit of commercial rivalry, which has been the immediate or remote cause of the greater number of modern wars.'

[64] On the rapid diffusion during the present century of the principles worked out by the economists, compare *Laing's Sweden*, pp. 356–358, with a note to the last edition of *Malthus on Population*, 1826, vol. ii. pp. 354, 355.

necessity reciprocal; and that, so far from depending
on the amount of gold received, they simply arise from
the facility with which a nation gets rid of those commodities which it can produce most cheaply, and receives in return those commodities which it could only
produce at a great expense, but which the other nation
can, from the skill of its workmen, or from the bounty
of nature, afford to supply at a lower rate. From this
it followed, that, in a mercantile point of view, it would
be as absurd to attempt to impoverish a people with
whom we trade, as it would be in a tradesman to wish
for the insolvency of a rich and frequent customer.
The result is, that the commercial spirit, which formerly was often warlike, is now invariably pacific.[65]
And although it is perfectly true that not one merchant
out of a hundred is familiar with the arguments on
which these economical discoveries are founded, that
does not prevent the effect which the discoveries themselves produce on his own mind. The mercantile class is,
like every other, acted upon by causes which only a few
members of that class are able to perceive. Thus, for
instance, of all the innumerable opponents of protection,
there are very few indeed who can give valid reasons
to justify their opposition. But this does not prevent
the opposition from taking place. For an immense
majority of men always follow with implicit submission
the spirit of their own time; and the spirit of the
time is merely its knowledge, and the direction that
knowledge takes. As, in the ordinary avocations of
daily life, everyone is benefited, in the increase of his

[65] 'The feelings of rival tradesmen, prevailing among nations, overruled for centuries all sense of the general community of advantage which commercial countries derive from the prosperity of one another; and that commercial spirit, which is now one of the strongest obstacles to wars, was during a certain period of European history their principal cause.' *Mill's Political Economy*, 1849, vol. ii. p. 221. This great change in the feelings of the commercial classes did not begin before the present century, and has not been visible to ordinary observers until the last five-and-twenty or thirty years; but it was foretold in a remarkable passage written by Herder in 1787; see his *Ideen sur Geschichte*, vol. iii. pp. 292, 293.

comforts, and of his general security, by the progress of many arts and sciences, of which perhaps he does not even know the name, just so is the mercantile class benefited by those great economical discoveries which, in the course of two generations, have already effected a complete change in the commercial legislation of this country, and which are now operating slowly, but steadily, upon those other European states where, public opinion being less powerful, it is more difficult to establish great truths and extirpate old abuses. While, therefore, it is perfectly true, that among merchants, a comparatively small number are acquainted with political economy, it is not the less true that they owe a large part of their wealth to the political economists; who, by removing the obstacles with which the ignorance of successive governments had impeded trade, have now settled on a solid foundation that commercial prosperity which is by no means the least of our national glories. Most assuredly is it also true, that this same intellectual movement has lessened the chance of war, by ascertaining the principles which ought to regulate our commercial relations with foreign countries; by proving, not only the inutility, but the positive mischief, caused by interfering with them; and finally, by exploding those long-established errors, which, inducing men to believe that nations are the natural enemies of each other, encouraged those evil feelings, and fostered those national jealousies, to the strength of which the military spirit owed no small share of its former influence.

The third great cause by which the love of war has been weakened, is the way in which discoveries respecting the application of Steam to the purposes of travelling have facilitated the intercourse between different countries, and thus aided in destroying that ignorant contempt which one nation is too apt to feel for another. Thus, for instance, the miserable and impudent falsehoods which a large class of English writers formerly directed against the morals and private character of the French, and, to their shame be it said, even against the chastity of French women, tended not a little to embitter the angry feelings then existing between the two first countries of Europe; irritating the English against French vices, irritating the French against English calumnies. In the same way, there was a time when every honest Englishman firmly believed that he could beat ten Frenchmen; a class of beings whom he held in sovereign contempt, as a lean and stunted race, who drank claret instead of brandy, who lived entirely off frogs; miserable infidels, who heard mass every Sunday, who bowed down before idols, and who even worshipped the Pope. On the other hand, the French were taught to despise us, as rude unlettered barbarians, without either taste or humanity; surly, ill-conditioned men, living in an unhappy climate, where a perpetual fog, only varied by rain, prevented the sun from ever being seen; suffering from so deep and inveterate a melancholy, that physicians had called it the English spleen; and under the influence of this cruel malady constantly committing suicide, particularly in November, when we were well known to hang and shoot ourselves by thousands.[66]

Whoever has looked much into the older literature of France and England, knows that these were the opinions which the two first nations of Europe, in the ignorance and simplicity of their hearts, held respecting each other. But the progress of improvement, by bringing the two countries into close and intimate contact, has dissipated these foolish prejudices, and taught each people to admire, and, what is still more important, to respect each other. And the greater the

---

[66] That there are more suicides in gloomy weather than in fine weather used always to be taken for granted, and was a favourite topic with the French wits, who were never weary of expatiating on our love of self-murder, and on the relation between it and our murky climate. Unfortunately for such speculations, the fact is exactly opposite to what is generally supposed, and we have decisive evidence that there are more suicides in summer than in winter. See *Quetelet sur l'Homme*, vol. ii. pp. 152, 158; *Tissot de la Manie du Suicide*, Paris, 1840, pp. 50, 149, 150; *Journal of Statistical Society*, vol. i. p. 102; *Winslow's Anatomy of Suicide*, 1840, pp. 131, 132; *Hawkins's Medical Statistics*, p. 170.

contact, the greater the respect. For, whatever theologians may choose to assert, it is certain that mankind at large has far more virtue than vice, and that in every country good actions are more frequent than bad ones. Indeed, if this were otherwise, the preponderance of evil would long since have destroyed the human race, and not even have left a single man to lament the degeneracy of his species. An additional proof of this is the fact, that the more nations associate with each other, and the more they see and know of their fellow-creatures, the more quickly do ancient enmities disappear. This is because an enlarged experience proves that mankind is not so radically bad as we from our infancy are taught to believe. But if vices were really more frequent than virtues, the result would be, that the increasing amalgamation of society would increase our bad opinion of others; because, though we may love our own vices, we do not generally love the vices of our neighbours. So far, however, is this from being the actual consequence, that it has always been found that those whose extensive knowledge makes them best acquainted with the general course of human actions, are precisely those who take the most favourable view of them. The greatest observer and the most profound thinker is invariably the most lenient judge. It is the solitary misanthrope, brooding over his fancied wrongs, who is most prone to depreciate the good qualities of our nature, and exaggerate its bad ones. Or else it is some foolish and ignorant monk, who, dreaming away his existence in an idle solitude, flatters his own vanity by denouncing the vices of others; and thus declaiming against the enjoyments of life, revenges himself on that society from which by his own superstition he is excluded. These are the sort of men who insist most strongly on the corruption of our nature, and on the degeneracy into which we have fallen. The enormous evil which such opinions have brought about, is well understood by those who have studied the history of countries in which they are, and have been, most prevalent. Hence it is that, among the innumerable benefits derived from advancing knowledge, there are few more important than those improved facilities of communication,[67] which, by increasing the frequency with which nations and individuals are brought into contact, have, to an extraordinary extent, corrected their prejudices, raised the opinion which each forms of the other, diminished their mutual hostility, and thus diffusing a more favourable view of our common nature, have stimulated us to develop those boundless resources of the human understanding, the very existence of which it was once considered almost a heresy to assert.

This is precisely what has occurred in modern Europe. The French and English people have, by the mere force of increased contact, learned to think more favourably of each other, and to discard that foolish contempt in which both nations formerly indulged. In this, as in all cases, the better one civilized country is acquainted with another, the more it will find to respect and to imitate. For of all the causes of national hatred, ignorance is the most powerful. When you increase the contact, you remove the ignorance, and thus you diminish the hatred.[68] This is the true bond of charity; and it is worth all the lessons which moralists and divines are able to teach. They have pursued their vocation for centuries, without producing the least effect in lessening the frequency of war. But it may

---

[67] Respecting which I will only mention one fact, in regard to our own country. By the returns of the Board of Trade, it appears that the passengers annually travelling by railway amounted in 1842 to nineteen millions; but in 1852 they had increased to more than eighty-six millions. *Journal of Statistical Society*, vol. xvi. p. 292.

[68] Of this, Mr. Stephens (in his valuable work, *Central America*, vol. i. pp. 247-8) relates an interesting instance in the case of that remarkable man Carrera: 'Indeed, in no particular had he changed more than in his opinion of foreigners; a happy illustration of the effect of personal intercourse in breaking down prejudices against individuals or classes.' Mr. Elphinstone (*History of India*, p. 195) says, 'Those who have known the Indians longest have always the best opinion of them: but *this is rather a compliment to human nature than to them, since it is true of every other people*.' Compare an instructive passage in *Darwin's Journal of Researches*, p. 421, with *Burdach, Traité de Physiologie comme Science d'Observation*, vol. ii. p. 61.

be said without the slightest exaggeration, that every new railroad which is laid down, and every fresh steamer which crosses the Channel, are additional guarantees for the preservation of that long and unbroken peace which, during forty years, has knit together the fortunes and the interests of the two most civilized nations of the earth.

I have thus, so far as my knowledge will permit, endeavoured to indicate the causes which have diminished religious persecution and war: the two greatest evils with which men have yet contrived to afflict their fellow-creatures. The question of the decline of religious persecution I have only briefly noticed, because it will be more fully handled in a subsequent part of this volume. Enough, however, has been advanced to prove how essentially it is an intellectual process, and how little good can be effected on this subject by the operation of moral feelings. The causes of the decline of the warlike spirit I have examined at considerable, and, perhaps, to some readers, at tedious length, and the result of that examination has been, that the decline is owing to the increase of the intellectual classes, to whom the military classes are necessarily antagonistic. In pushing the inquiry a little deeper, we have, by still further analysis, ascertained the existence of three vast though subsidiary causes, by which the general movement has been accelerated. These are— the invention of Gunpowder, the discoveries of Political Economy, and the discovery of improved means of Locomotion. Such are the three great modes or channels by which the progress of knowledge has weakened the old warlike spirit; and the way in which they have effected this has, I trust, been clearly pointed out. The facts and arguments which I have brought forward, have, I can conscientiously say, been subjected to careful and repeated scrutiny; and I am quite unable to see on what possible ground their accuracy is to be impugned. That they will be disagreeable to certain classes, I am well aware; but the unpleasantness of a statement is hardly to be considered a proof of its falsehood. The sources from which the evidence has been derived are fully indicated; and the arguments, I hope, fairly stated. And from them there results a most important conclusion. From them we are bound to infer, that the two oldest, greatest, most inveterate, and most widely-spread evils which have ever been known, are constantly, though, on the whole, slowly, diminishing; and that their diminution has been effected, not at all by moral feelings, nor by moral teachings, but solely by the activity of the human intellect, and by the inventions and discoveries which, in a long course of successive ages, man has been able to make.

Since, then, in the two most important phenomena which the progress of society presents, the moral laws have been steadily and invariably subordinate to the intellectual laws, there arises a strong presumption that in inferior matters the same process has been followed. To prove this in its full extent, and thus raise the presumption to an absolute certainty, would be to write, not an Introduction to history, but the History itself. The reader must, therefore, be satisfied for the present with what, I am conscious, is merely an approach towards demonstration; and the complete demonstration must necessarily be reserved for the future volumes of this work: in which I pledge myself to show that the progress Europe has made from barbarism to civilization is entirely due to its intellectual activity; that the leading countries have now, for some centuries, advanced sufficiently far to shake off the influence of those physical agencies by which in an earlier state their career might have been troubled; and that although the moral agencies are still powerful, and still cause occasional disturbances, those are but aberrations, which, if we compare long periods of time, balance each other, and thus in the total amount entirely disappear. So that, in a great and comprehensive view, the changes in every civilized people are, in their aggregate, dependent solely on three things: first, on the amount of knowledge possessed by their ablest men; secondly, on the direction which that knowledge takes, that is to say, the sort of subjects to which it refers: thirdly, and above all, on the extent to which the knowledge is diffused, and the freedom with which it pervades all classes of society.

These are the three great movers of every civilized country; and although their operation is frequently disturbed by the vices or the virtues of powerful individuals, such moral feelings correct each other, and the average of long periods remains unaffected. Owing to causes of which we are ignorant, the moral qualities do, no doubt, constantly vary; so that in one man, or perhaps even in one generation, there will be an excess of good intentions; in another an excess of bad ones. But we have no reason to think that any permanent change has been effected in the proportion which those who naturally possess good intentions bear to those in whom bad ones seem to be inherent. In what may be called the innate and original morals of mankind, there is, so far as we are aware, no progress. Of the different passions with which we are born, some are more prevalent at one time, some at another; but experience teaches us that, as they are always antagonistic, they are held in balance by the force of their own opposition. The activity of one motive is corrected by the activity of another. For to every vice there is a corresponding virtue. Cruelty is counteracted by benevolence; sympathy is excited by suffering; the injustice of some provokes the charity of others; new evils are met by new remedies, and even the most enormous offences that have ever been known have left behind them no permanent impression. The desolation of countries and the slaughter of men are losses which never fail to be repaired, and at the distance of a few centuries every vestige of them is effaced. The gigantic crimes of Alexander or Napoleon become after a time void of effect, and the affairs of the world return to their former level. This is the ebb and flow of history, the perpetual flux to which by the laws of our nature we are subject. Above all this, there is a far higher movement; and as the tide rolls on, now advancing, now receding, there is, amid its endless fluctuations, one thing, and one alone, which endures for ever. The actions of bad men produce only temporary evil, the actions of good men only temporary good; and eventually the good and the evil altogether subside, are neutralized by subsequent generations, absorbed by the incessant movements of future ages. But the discoveries of great men never leave us; they are immortal, they contain those eternal truths which survive the shock of empires, outlive the struggles of rival creeds, and witness the decay of successive religions. All these have their different measures and their different standards; one set of opinions for one age, another set for another. They pass away like a dream; they are as the fabric of a vision, which leaves not a rack behind. The discoveries of genius alone remain: it is to them we owe all that we now have, they are for all ages and all times; never young, and never old, they bear the seeds of their own life; they flow on in a perennial and undying stream; they are essentially cumulative, and, giving birth to the additions which they subsequently receive, they thus influence the most distant posterity, and after the lapse of centuries produce more effect than they were able to do even at the moment of their promulgation.

CHAPTER V.

INQUIRY INTO THE INFLUENCE EXERCISED BY RELIGION, LITERATURE, AND GOVERNMENT.

By applying to the history of Man those methods of investigation which have been found successful in other branches of knowledge, and by rejecting all preconceived notions which would not bear the test of those methods, we have arrived at certain results, the heads of which it may now be convenient to recapitulate. We have seen that our actions, being solely the result of internal and external agencies, must be explicable by the laws of those agencies; that is to say, by mental laws and by physical laws. We have also seen that mental laws are, in Europe, more powerful than physical laws; and that, in the progress of civilization, their superiority is constantly increasing, because advancing knowledge multiplies the resources of the mind, but leaves the old resources of nature stationary. On this account, we have treated the mental laws as being the great regulators of progress; and we have looked at the physical laws as occupying a subordinate place, and as merely displaying themselves in occasional disturbances, the force and frequency of which have been long declining, and are now, on a large average, almost inoperative. Having, by this means, resolved the study of what may be called the dynamics of society into the study of the laws of the mind, we have subjected these last to a similar analysis; and we have found that they consist of two parts, namely, moral laws and intellectual laws. By comparing these two parts, we have clearly ascertained the vast superiority of the intellectual laws; and we have seen, that as the progress of civilization is marked by the triumph of the mental laws over the physical, just so is it marked by the triumph of the intellectual laws over the moral ones. This important inference rests on two distinct arguments. First, that moral truths being stationary, and intellectual truths being progressive, it is highly improbable that the progress of society should be due to moral knowledge, which for many centuries has remained the same, rather than to intellectual knowledge, which for many centuries has been incessantly advancing. The other argument consists in the fact, that the two greatest evils known to mankind have not been diminished by moral improvement; but have been, and still are, yielding to the influence of intellectual discoveries. From all this it evidently follows, that if we wish to ascertain the conditions which regulate the progress of modern civilization, we must seek them in the history of the amount and diffusion of intellectual knowledge; and we must consider physical phenomena and moral principles as causing, no doubt, great aberrations in short periods, but in long periods correcting and balancing themselves, and thus leaving the intellectual laws to act uncontrolled by these inferior and subordinate agents.

Such is the conclusion to which we have been led by successive analyses, and on which we now take our stand. The actions of individuals are greatly affected by their moral feelings and by their passions; but these being antagonistic to the passions and feelings of other individuals, are balanced by them; so that their effect is, in the great average of human affairs, nowhere to be seen; and the total actions of mankind, considered as a whole, are left to be regulated by the total knowledge of which mankind is possessed. And of the way in which individual feeling and individual caprice are thus absorbed and neutralized, we find a clear illustration in the facts already brought forward respecting the history of crime. For by those facts it is decisively proved, that the amount of crime committed in a country is, year after year, reproduced with the most startling uniformity, not being in the least affected by those capricious and personal feelings to which human actions are too often referred. But if, instead of examining the history of crime year by year, we were to examine it month by month, we should find less regularity; and if we were to examine it hour by hour, we should find no regularity at all; neither would its regularity be seen, if, instead of the criminal records of a whole country, we only knew those of a single street, or of a single family. This is because the great social laws by which crime is governed, can only be perceived after observing great numbers or long periods; but in a small number, and a short period, the individual moral principle triumphs, and disturbs the operation of the larger and intellectual law. While, therefore, the moral feelings by which a man is urged to commit a crime, or to abstain from it, will produce an immense effect on the amount of his own crimes, they will produce no effect on the amount of crimes committed by the society to which he belongs; because, in the long-run, they are sure to be neutralized by opposite moral feelings, which cause in other men an opposite conduct. Just in the same way, we are all sensible that moral principles do affect nearly the whole of our actions; but we have incontrovertible proof that they produce not the least effect on mankind in the aggregate, or even on men in very large masses, provided that we take the precaution of studying social phenomena for a period sufficiently long, and on a scale sufficiently great, to enable the superior laws to come into uncontrolled operation.

The totality of human actions being thus, from the highest point of view, governed by the totality of human knowledge, it might seem a simple matter to collect the evidence of the knowledge, and, by subjecting it to successive generalizations, ascertain the whole of the laws which regulate the progress of civilization. And that this will be eventually done, I do not entertain the slightest doubt. But, unfortunately, history has been written by men so inadequate to the great task they have undertaken, that few of the necessary materials have yet been brought together. Instead of telling us those things which alone have any value,—instead of giving us information respecting the progress of knowledge, and the way in which mankind has been affected by the diffusion of that knowledge,—instead of these things, the vast majority of historians fill their works with the most trifling

and miserable details: personal anecdotes of kings and
courts; interminable relations of what was said by one
minister, and what was thought by another; and, what is
worse than all, long accounts of campaigns, battles, and
sieges, very interesting to those engaged in them, but
to us utterly useless, because they neither furnish new
truths, nor do they supply the means by which new
truths may be discovered. This is the real impediment
which now stops our advance. It is this want of judgment, and this ignorance of what is most worthy of
selection, which deprives us of materials that ought long
since to have been accumulated, arranged, and stored-up
for future use. In other great branches of knowledge,
observation has preceded discovery; first the facts have
been registered, and then their laws have been found.
But in the study of the history of Man, the important
facts have been neglected, and the unimportant ones
preserved. The consequence is, that whoever now attempts to generalize historical phenomena must collect
the facts, as well as conduct the generalization. He finds
nothing ready to his hand. He must be the mason as
well as the architect; he must not only scheme the edifice,
but likewise excavate the quarry. The necessity of performing this double labour entails upon the philosopher
such enormous drudgery, that the limits of an entire life
are unequal to the task; and history, instead of being
ripe, as it ought to be, for complete and exhaustive
generalizations, is still in so crude and informal a state,
that not the most determined and protracted industry
will enable any one to comprehend the really important
actions of mankind, during even so short a period as two
successive centuries.

On account of these things, I have long since abandoned my original scheme; and I have reluctantly determined to write the history, not of general civilization,
but of the civilization of a single people. While, however, by this means, we curtail the field of inquiry, we
unfortunately diminish the resources of which the inquiry
is possessed. For although it is perfectly true, that the
totality of human actions, if considered in long periods,
depends on the totality of human knowledge, it must be

allowed that this great principle, when applied only to one country, loses something of its original value. The more we diminish our observations, the greater becomes the uncertainty of the average; in other words, the greater the chance of the operation of the larger laws being troubled by the operation of the smaller. The interference of foreign governments; the influence exercised by the opinions, literature, and customs of a foreign people; their invasions, perhaps even their conquests; the forcible introduction by them of new religions, new laws, and new manners,—all these things are perturbations, which, in a view of universal history, equalize each other, but which, in any one country, are apt to disturb the natural march, and thus render the movements of civilization more difficult to calculate. The manner in which I have endeavoured to meet this difficulty will be presently stated; but what I first wish to point out, are the reasons which have induced me to select the history of England as more important than any other, and therefore as the most worthy of being subjected to a complete and philosophic investigation.

Now, it is evident that, inasmuch as the great advantage of studying past events consists in the possibility of ascertaining the laws by which they were governed, the history of any people will become more valuable in proportion as their movements have been least disturbed by agencies not arising from themselves. Every foreign or external influence which is brought to bear upon a nation is an interference with its natural development, and therefore complicates the circumstances we seek to investigate. To simplify complications, is, in all branches of knowledge, the first essential of success. This is very familiar to the cultivators of physical science, who are often able, by a single experiment, to discover a truth which innumerable observations had vainly searched; the reason being, that by experimenting on phenomena, we can disentangle them from their complications; and thus isolating them from the interference of unknown agencies, we leave them, as it were, to run their own course, and disclose the operation of their own law.

This, then, is the true standard by which we must

measure the value of the history of any nation. The importance of the history of a country depends, not upon the splendour of its exploits, but upon the degree to which its actions are due to causes springing out of itself. If, therefore, we could find some civilized people who had worked out their civilization entirely by themselves; who had escaped all foreign influence, and who had been neither benefited nor retarded by the personal peculiarities of their rulers,—the history of such a people would be of paramount importance; because it would present a condition of normal and inherent development; it would show the laws of progress acting in a state of isolation; it would be, in fact, an experiment ready-made, and would possess all the value of that artificial contrivance to which natural science is so much indebted.

To find such a people as this is obviously impossible; but the duty of the philosophic historian is, to select for his especial study the country in which the conditions have been most closely followed. Now, it will be readily admitted, not only by ourselves, but by intelligent foreigners, that in England, during, at all events, the last three centuries, this has been done more constantly and more successfully than in any other country. I say nothing of the number of our discoveries, the brilliancy of our literature, or the success of our arms. These are invidious topics; and other nations may perhaps deny to us those superior merits which we are apt to exaggerate. But I take up this single position, that of all European countries, England is the one where, during the longest period, the government has been most quiescent, and the people most active; where popular freedom has been settled on the widest basis; where each man is most able to say what he thinks, and do what he likes; where every one can follow his own bent, and propagate his own opinions; where, religious persecution being little known, the play and flow of the human mind may be clearly seen, unchecked by those restraints to which it is elsewhere subjected; where the profession of heresy is least dangerous, and the practice of dissent most common; where hostile creeds flourish side by side, and rise and decay without disturbance, according to the wants of the people, unaffected by the wishes of the church, and uncontrolled by the authority of the state; where all interests, and all classes, both spiritual and temporal, are most left to take care of themselves; where that meddlesome doctrine called Protection was first attacked, and where alone it has been destroyed; and where, in a word, those dangerous extremes to which interference gives rise having been avoided, despotism and rebellion are equally rare, and concession being recognized as the groundwork of policy, the national progress has been least disturbed by the power of privileged classes, by the influence of particular sects, or by the violence of arbitrary rulers.

That these are the characteristics of English history is notorious; to some men a matter of boast, to others of regret. And when to these circumstances we add, that England, owing to its insular formation,[1] was, until the middle of the last century, rarely visited by foreigners, it becomes evident that, in our progress as a people, we have been less affected than any other by the two main sources of interference, namely, the authority of government, and the influence of foreigners. In the sixteenth century, it became a fashion, among the English nobility, to travel abroad;[2] but it was by no means the fashion for foreign nobility to travel in England. In the seventeenth century, the custom of travelling for amusement spread so much, that, among

---

[1] Coleridge well says, 'it is the chief of many blessings derived from the insular character and circumstances of our country, that our social institutions have formed themselves out of our proper needs and interests.' *Coleridge on the Constitution of the Church and State*, 8vo. 1830, pp. 20, 21. The political consequences of this were much noticed at the time of the French Revolution. See *Mémoires de La Fayette*, vol. i. p. 404, Bruxelles, 1837.

[2] In another place, I shall collect the evidence of the rapidly increasing love of travelling in the sixteenth century; but it is interesting to observe, that during the latter half of the century there was first established the custom of appointing travelling tutors. Compare *Barrington's Observations on the Statutes*, p. 218, with a letter from Beza, written in 1598, in *Mémoires et Correspondance de Du Plessis Mornay*, vol. ix. p. 81.

the rich and idle classes, there were few Englishmen who did not, at least once in their life, cross the Channel; while the same classes in other countries, partly because they were less wealthy, partly from an inveterate dislike to the sea, hardly ever entered our island, unless compelled to do so on some particular business. The result was, that in other countries, and particularly in France and Italy, the inhabitants of the great cities became gradually accustomed to foreigners, and, like all men, were imperceptibly influenced by what they often saw. On the other hand, there were many of our cities in which none but Englishmen ever set their feet;[3] and inhabitants, even of the metropolis, might grow old without having once seen a single foreigner, except, perhaps, some dull and pompous ambassador taking his airing on the banks of the Thames. And although it is often said that, after the restoration of Charles II., our national character began to be greatly influenced by French example,[4] this, as I shall fully prove, was confined to that small and insignificant part of society which hung about the court; nor did it produce any marked effect upon the two most important classes, — the intellectual class, and the industrious class. The movement may, indeed, be traced in the most worthless parts of our literature, — in the shameless productions of Buckingham, Dorset, Etherege, Killigrew, Mulgrave, Rochester, and Sedley. But neither then, nor at a much later period, were any of our great thinkers influenced by the intellect of

---

[3] In regard to the society of women, this was still more observable, even at a much later period; and when the Countess de Boufflers visited England, at the beginning of the reign of George III., 'on lui faisoit un mérite de sa curiosité de voir l'Angleterre; car on remarquoit qu'elle étoit la seule dame françoise de qualité qui fût venue en voyageuse depuis deux cents ans: on ne comprenoit point, dans cette classe, les ambassadrices, ni la duchesse de Mazarin, qui y étoient venues par nécessité.' *Dutens, Mémoires d'un Voyageur*, vol. i. p. 217. Compare *Mémoires de Madame de Genlis*, vol. viii. p. 241.

[4] *Orme's Life of Owen*, p. 288; *Mahon's History of England*, vol. ii. p. 211; and many other writers.

France;⁵ on the contrary, we find in their ideas, and even in their style, a certain rough and native vigour, which, though offensive to our more polished neighbours, has at least the merit of being the indigenous product of our own country.⁶ The origin and extent of that connexion between the French and English intellects which subsequently arose, is a subject of immense importance; but, like most others of real value, it has been entirely neglected by historians. In the present work, I shall attempt to supply this deficiency: in the mean time I may say, that although we have been, and still are, greatly indebted to the French for our improvement in taste, in refinement, in manners,

---

⁵ The only Englishman of genius who, during this period, was influenced by the French mind, was Dryden; but this is chiefly apparent in his plays, the whole of which are now deservedly forgotten. His great works, and, above all, those wonderful satires, in which he distances every competitor, except Juvenal, are thoroughly national, and, as mere specimens of English, are, if I may express my own judgment, to be ranked immediately after Shakspeare. In Dryden's writings there are unquestionably many Gallicisms of expression, but few Gallicisms of thought; and it is by these last that we must estimate the real amount of foreign influence. Sir Walter Scott goes so far as to say, 'It will admit of question, whether any single French word has been naturalized upon the sole authority of Dryden.' *Scott's Life of Dryden*, p. 523, 8vo. 1808. Rather a bold assertion. As to the opinion of Fox, see Lord Holland's preface to *Fox's James II.*, 4to. 1808, p. xxxii.

⁶ Another circumstance which has maintained the independence, and therefore increased the value, of our literature, is, that in no great country have literary men been so little connected with the government, or rewarded by it. That this is the true policy, and that to protect literature is to injure it, are propositions for the proof of which I must refer to chap. xi. of this volume—on the system of Louis XIV. In the mean time, I will quote the following words from a learned and, what is much better, a thoughtful writer: 'Nor must he who will understand the English institutions leave out of view the character of the enduring works which had sprung from the salient energy of the English mind. Literature had been left to develop itself. William of Orange was foreign to it; Anne cared not for it; the first George knew no English; the second not much.' *Bancroft's History of the American Revolution*, vol. ii. p. 48. Compare *Forster's Life of Goldsmith*, 1854, vol. i. pp. 93-96, vol. ii. p. 460.

and indeed in all the amenities of life, we have borrowed from them nothing absolutely essential, nothing by which the destinies of nations are permanently altered. On the other hand, the French have not only borrowed from us some very valuable political institutions, but even the most important event in French history is due, in no small degree, to our influence. Their revolution of 1789 was, as is well known, brought about, or, to speak more properly, was mainly instigated, by a few great men, whose works, and afterwards whose speeches, roused the people to resistance; but what is less known, and nevertheless is certainly true, is, that these eminent leaders learnt in England that philosophy and those principles by which, when transplanted into their own country, such fearful and yet such salutary results were effected.[7]

It will not, I hope, be supposed, that by these remarks I mean to cast any reflection on the French: a great and admirable people; a people in many respects superior to ourselves; a people from whom we have still much to learn, and whose deficiencies, such as they are, arise from the perpetual interference of a long line of arbitrary rulers. But, looking at this matter historically, it is unquestionably true that we have worked out our civilization with little aid from them, while they have worked out theirs with great aid from us. At the same time, it must also be admitted, that our governments have interfered less with us than their governments have interfered with them. And without in the least prejudging the question as to which is the greater country, it is solely on these grounds that I consider our history more important than theirs; and I select for especial study the progress of English civilization, simply because, being less affected by agencies not arising from itself, we can the more clearly discern in it the normal march of society, and the undisturbed operation of those great laws by which the fortunes of mankind are ultimately regulated.

---

[7] See, for evidence of this influence of England, chap. v. of the second volume.

After this comparison between the relative value of French and English history, it seems scarcely necessary to examine the claims which may be put forward for the history of other countries. Indeed, there are only two in whose favour any thing can be said: I mean Germany, considered as a whole, and the United States of North America. As to the Germans, it is undoubtedly true, that since the middle of the eighteenth century they have produced a greater number of profound thinkers than any other country, I might perhaps say, than all other countries put together. But the objections which apply to the French are still more applicable to the Germans. For the protective principle has been, and still is, stronger in Germany than in France. Even the best of the German governments are constantly interfering with the people; never leaving them to themselves, always looking after their interests, and meddling in the commonest affairs of daily life. Besides this, the German literature, though now the first in Europe, owes it origin, as we shall hereafter see, to that great sceptical movement, by which, in France, the Revolution was preceded. Before the middle of the eighteenth century, the Germans, notwithstanding a few eminent names, such as Kepler and Leibnitz, had no literature of real value; and the first impetus which they received, was caused by their contact with the French intellect, and by the influence of those eminent Frenchmen who, in the reign of Frederick the Great, flocked to Berlin,* a city which

---

* The history of this remarkable, though short-lived, union between the French and German intellects will be traced in the next volume; but its first great effect, in stimulating, or rather in creating, the German literature, is noticed by one of the most learned of their own writers: 'Denn einestheils war zu diesen Gegenständen immer die lateinische Sprache gebraucht und die Muttersprache zu wenig cultivirt worden, anderntheils wurden diese Schriften auch meistentheils nur von Gelehrten, und zwar Universitätsgelehrten, für welche sie auch hauptsächlich bestimmt waren, gelesen. Gegen die Mitte des achtzehnten Jahrhunderts, als mehrere englische und französische Werke gelesen und übersetzt wurden, und durch die Vorliebe des Königs von Preussen Friedrichs II., der von Franzosen gebildet wor-

has ever since been the head-quarters of philosophy and science. From this there have resulted some very important circumstances, which I can here only briefly indicate. The German intellect, stimulated by the French into a sudden growth, has been irregularly developed; and thus hurried into an activity greater than the average civilization of the country requires. The consequence is, that there is no nation in Europe in which we find so wide an interval between the highest minds and the lowest minds. The German philosophers possess a learning, and a reach of thought, which places them at the head of the civilized world. The German people are more superstitious, more prejudiced, and, notwithstanding the care which the government takes of their education, more really ignorant, and more unfit to guide themselves, than are the inhabitants either of France or of England.* This

---

den war, französische Gelehrte besonders geehrt und angestellt wurden, entstand ein Wetteifer der Deutschen, auch in dem schriftlichen Vortrage nicht zurück zu bleiben, und die Sprache hub sich bald zu einem hohen Grade von Vollkommenheit.' Tennemann, *Geschichte der Philosophie*, vol. xi. pp. 286, 287.

* A popular view of the system of national education established in Germany will be found in *Kay's Social Condition and Education of the People of Europe*, vol. ii. pp. 1-344. But Mr. Kay, like most literary men, overrates the advantages of literary acquirements, and underrates that education of the faculties which neither books nor schools can impart to a people who are debarred from the exercise of civil and political rights. In the history of the protective spirit (chaps. ix. and x. of the present volume), I shall return to this subject, in connexion with France; and in the next volume I shall examine it in regard to German civilization. In the mean time, I must be allowed to protest against the account Mr. Kay has given of the results of compulsory education; an agreeable picture, drawn by an amiable and intelligent writer, but of the inaccuracy of which I possess decisive evidence. Two points only I will now refer to: 1st. The notorious fact, that the German people, notwithstanding their so-called education, are unfit to take any share in political matters, and have no aptitude for the practical and administrative parts of government. 2nd. The fact, equally notorious to those who have studied the subject, that there are more popular superstitions in Prussia, the most educated part of Germany, than there are in England; and that the tenacity with which

separation and divergence of the two classes is the natural result of that artificial stimulus, which a century ago was administered to one of the classes, and which thus disturbed the normal proportions of society. Owing to this, the highest intellects have, in Germany, so outstripped the general progress of the nation, that there is no sympathy between the two parties; nor are there at present any means by which they may be brought into contact. Their great authors address themselves, not to their country, but to each other. They are sure of a select and learned audience, and they use what, in reality, is a learned language; they turn their mother-tongue into a dialect, eloquent indeed, and very powerful, but so difficult, so subtle, and so full of complicated inversions, that to their own lower classes it is utterly incomprehensible.[10] From

---

men cling to them is greater in Prussia than in England. For illustration of the practical working, in individual cases, of compulsory education, and of the hardship it causes, see a scandalous occurrence, related in *Laing's Notes of a Traveller*, 8vo. 1842, p. 165, first series; and on the physical evils produced by German education, see *Phillips on Scrofula*, London, 1846, pp. 253, 254, where there is some useful evidence of the consequences of 'that great German sin of over-regulation.'

[10] This is well stated by Mr. Laing, by far the ablest traveller who has published observations on European society: 'German authors, both the philosophic and the poetic, address themselves to a public far more intellectual, and more highly cultivated, than our reading public. . . . In our literature, the most obscure and abstruse of metaphysical or philosophical writers *take the public mind in a far lower state,* simply cognisant of the meaning of language, and possessed of the ordinary reasoning powers. . . . The social influence of German literature is, consequently, confined within a narrower circle. It has no influence on the mind of the lower, or even of the middle classes in active life, who have not the opportunity or leisure to screw their faculties up to the pitch-note of their great writers. The reading public must devote much time to acquire the knowledge, tone of feeling, and of imagination, necessary to follow the writing public. The social economist finds accordingly in Germany the most extraordinary dulness, inertness of mind, and ignorance, below a certain level, with the most extraordinary intellectual development, learning, and genius, at or above it.' *Laing's Notes of a Traveller*, first series, pp. 266, 267. The same acute observer says, in a later work (*Notes*, third series, 8vo.

this, there have arisen some of the most marked peculiarities of German literature. For, being deprived of ordinary readers, it is cut off from the influence of ordinary prejudice; and hence, it has displayed a boldness of inquiry, a recklessness in the pursuit of truth and a disregard of traditional opinions, which entitle it to the highest praise. But, on the other hand, this same circumstance has produced that absence of practical knowledge, and that indifference to material and physical interests, for which the German literature is justly censured. As a matter of course, all this has widened the original breach, and increased the distance which separates the great German thinkers from that dull and plodding class, which, though it lies immediately beneath them, still remains uninfluenced by their knowledge, and uncheered by the glow and fire of their genius.

In America, on the other hand, we see a civilization precisely the reverse of this. We see a country, of which it has been truly said, that in no other are there so few men of great learning, and so few men of great ignorance.[11] In Germany, the speculative classes and the practical classes are altogether disunited; in America, they are altogether fused. In Germany, nearly every year brings forward new discoveries, new philosophies, new means by which the boundaries of knowledge are to be enlarged. In America, such inquiries are almost entirely neglected: since the time of Jonathan Edwards no great metaphysician has appeared; little attention has been paid to physical

---

1852, p. 12): 'The two classes speak and think in different languages. The cultivated German language, the language of German literature, is not the language of the common man, nor even of the man far up in the middle ranks of society,—the farmer, tradesman, shopkeeper.' See also pp. 351, 352, 354. It is singular that so clear and vigorous a thinker as Mr. Laing evidently is, should have failed in detecting the cause of this peculiar phenomenon.

[11] 'Je ne pense pas qu'il y ait de pays dans le monde où, proportion gardée avec la population, il se trouve aussi peu d'ignorants et moins de savants qu'en Amérique.' *Tocqueville de la Démocratie en Amérique*, vol. i. p. 91.

science; and, with the single exception of jurisprudence,[12] scarcely anything has been done for those vast subjects on which the Germans are incessantly labouring. The stock of American knowledge is small, but it is spread through all classes; the stock of German knowledge is immense, but it is confined to one class. Which of these two forms of civilization is the more advantageous, is a question we are not now called upon to decide. It is enough for our present purpose, that in Germany, there is a serious failure in the diffusion of knowledge; and, in America, a no less serious one in its accumulation. And as civilization is regulated by the accumulation and diffusion of knowledge, it is evident that no country can even approach to a complete and perfect pattern, if, cultivating one of those conditions to an excess, it neglects the cultivation of the other. Indeed, from this want of balance and equilibrium between the two elements of civilization, there have arisen in America and in Germany those great but opposite evils, which, it is to be feared, will not be easily remedied; and which, until remedied, will certainly retard the progress of both countries,

---

[12] The causes of this exception I shall endeavour to trace in the next volume; but it is interesting to notice, that, as early as 1775, Burke was struck by the partiality of the Americans for works on law. See *Burke's Speech*, in *Parliamentary History*, vol. xviii. p. 495; or in *Burke's Works*, vol. i. p. 188. He says: 'In no country perhaps in the world is the law so general a study. The profession itself is numerous and powerful; and in most provinces it takes the lead. The greater number of the deputies sent to the Congress were lawyers. But all who read—and most do read—endeavour to obtain some smattering in that science. I have been told by an eminent bookseller, that in no branch of his business, after tracts of popular devotion, were so many books as those on the law exported to the plantations. The colonists have now fallen into the way of printing them for their own use. I hear that they have sold nearly as many of Blackstone's Commentaries in America as in England.' Of this state of society, the great works of Kent and Story were, at a later period, the natural result. On the respect at present felt for the legal profession, see *Lyell's Second Visit to the United States*, 1849, vol. i. p. 45; and as to the judges, *Combe's N. America*, vol. ii. p. 329.

notwithstanding the temporary advantages which such one-sided energy does for the moment always procure.

I have very briefly, but I hope fairly, and certainly with no conscious partiality, endeavoured to estimate the relative value of the history of the four leading countries of the world. As to the real greatness of the countries themselves, I offer no opinion; because each considers itself to be first. But, unless the facts I have stated can be controverted, it certainly follows, that the history of England is, to the philosopher, more valuable than any other; because he can more clearly see in it the accumulation and diffusion of knowledge going hand-in-hand; because that knowledge has been less influenced by foreign and external agencies; and because it has been less interfered with, either for good or for evil, by those powerful, but frequently incompetent men, to whom the administration of public affairs is entrusted.

It is on account of these considerations, and not at all from those motives which are dignified with the name of patriotism, that I have determined to write the history of my own country, in preference to that of any other; and to write it in a manner as complete, and as exhaustive, as the materials which are now extant will enable me to do. But, inasmuch as the circumstances already stated, render it impossible to discover the laws of society solely by studying the history of a single nation, I have drawn up the present Introduction in order to obviate some of the difficulties with which this great subject is surrounded. In the earlier chapters, I have attempted to mark out the limits of the subject considered as a whole, and fix the largest possible basis upon which it can rest. With this view, I have looked at civilization as broken into two vast divisions: the European division, in which Man is more powerful than Nature; and the non-European division, in which Nature is more powerful than Man. This has led us to the conclusion, that national progress, in connexion with popular liberty, could have originated in no part of the world except in Europe; where, therefore, the rise of real civilization, and the encroachments of the human mind upon the forces of nature, are alone to be studied. The superiority of the mental laws over the physical, being thus recognized as the groundwork of European history, the next step has been, to resolve the mental laws into moral and intellectual, and prove the superior influence of the intellectual ones in accelerating the progress of Man. These generalizations appear to me the essential preliminaries of history, considered as a science; and, in order to connect them with the special history of England, we have now merely to ascertain the fundamental condition of intellectual progress, as, until that is done, the annals of any people can only present an empirical succession of events, connected by such stray and casual links as are devised by different writers, according to their different principles. The remaining part of this Introduction will, therefore, be chiefly occupied in completing the scheme I have sketched, by investigating the history of various countries in reference to those intellectual peculiarities on which the history of our own country supplies no adequate information. Thus, for instance, in Germany, the accumulation of knowledge has been far more rapid than in England; the laws of the accumulation of knowledge may, on that account, be most conveniently studied in German history, and then applied deductively to the history of England. In the same way, the Americans have diffused their knowledge much more completely than we have done; I, therefore, purpose to explain some of the phenomena of English civilization by those laws of diffusion, of which, in American civilization, the workings may be most clearly seen, and hence the discovery most easily made. Again, inasmuch as France is the most civilized country in which the protective spirit is very powerful, we may trace the occult tendencies of that spirit among ourselves, by studying its obvious tendencies among our neighbours. With this view, I shall give an account of French history, in order to illustrate the protective principle, by showing the injury it has inflicted on a very able and enlightened people. And, in an analysis of the French Revolution,

I shall point out how that great event was a reaction against the protective spirit; while, as the materials for the reaction were drawn from England, we shall also see in it the way in which the intellect of one country acts upon the intellect of another; and we shall arrive at some results respecting that interchange of ideas which is likely to become the most important regulator of European affairs. This will throw much light on the laws of international thought; and, in connexion with it, two separate chapters will be devoted to a History of the Protective Spirit, and an Examination of its relative intensity in France and England. But the French, as a people, have, since the beginning or middle of the seventeenth century, been remarkably free from superstition; and, notwithstanding the efforts of their government, they are very averse to ecclesiastical power: so that, although their history displays the protective principle in its political form, it supplies little evidence respecting its religious form; while, in our own country, the evidence is also scanty. Hence, my intention is, to give a view of Spanish history; because in it we may trace the full results of that protection against error which the spiritual classes are always eager to afford. In Spain, the church has, from a very early period, possessed more authority, and the clergy have been more influential, both with the people and the government, than in any other country; it will, therefore, be convenient to study in Spain the laws of ecclesiastical development, and the manner in which that development affects the national interests. Another circumstance, which operates on the intellectual progress of a nation, is the method of investigation that its ablest men habitually employ. This method can only be one of two kinds; it must be either inductive, or deductive. Each of these belongs to a different form of civilization, and is always accompanied by a different style of thought, particularly in regard to religion and science. These differences are of such immense importance, that, until their laws are known, we cannot be said to understand the real history of past events. Now, the two extremes of the difference are, undoubtedly, Germany and the United States; the Germans being pre-eminently deductive, the Americans inductive. But Germany and America are, in so many other respects, diametrically opposed to each other, that I have thought it expedient to study the operations of the deductive and inductive spirit in countries between which a closer analogy exists; because the greater the similarity between two nations, the more easily can we trace the consequences of any single divergence, and the more conspicuous do the laws of that divergence become. Such an opportunity occurs in the history of Scotland, as compared with that of England. Here we have two nations, bordering on each other, speaking the same language, reading the same literature, and knit together by the same interests. And yet it is a truth, which seems to have escaped attention, but the proof of which I shall fully detail, that, until the last thirty or forty years, the Scotch intellect has been even more entirely deductive than the English intellect has been inductive. The inductive tendencies of the English mind, and the almost superstitious reverence with which we cling to them, have been noticed with regret by a few, and a very few, of our ablest men.[13] On the other hand, in Scotland, particularly during the eighteenth century, the great thinkers, with hardly an exception, adopted the deductive method. Now, the characteristic of deduction, when applied to branches of knowledge not yet ripe for it, is, that it increases the number of hypotheses from which we reason downwards, and brings into disrepute the slow and patient ascent peculiar to inductive inquiry. This desire to grasp at truth by speculative, and, as it were, foregone conclusions, has often led the way to great discoveries; and no one, properly instructed, will deny its immense value. But when it is universally followed, there is

---

[13] Particularly Coleridge and Mr. John Mill. But, with the greatest possible respect for Mr. Mill's profound work on Logic, I must venture to think that he has ascribed too much to the influence of Bacon in encouraging the inductive spirit, and too little to those other circumstances which gave rise to the Baconian philosophy, and to which that philosophy owes its success.

imminent danger lest the observation of mere empirical uniformities should be neglected; and lest thinking men should grow impatient at those small and proximate generalizations which, according to the inductive scheme, must invariably precede the larger and higher ones. Whenever this impatience actually occurs, there is produced serious mischief. For these lower generalizations form a neutral ground, which speculative minds and practical minds possess in common, and on which they meet. If this ground is cut away, the meeting is impossible. In such case, there arises among the scientific classes an undue contempt for inferences which the experience of the vulgar has drawn, but of which the laws seem inexplicable; while, among the practical classes, there arises a disregard of speculations so wide, so magnificent, and of which the intermediate and preliminary steps are hidden from their gaze. The results of this in Scotland are highly curious, and are, in several respects, similar to those which we find in Germany; since in both countries the intellectual classes have long been remarkable for their boldness of investigation and their freedom from prejudice, and the people at large equally remarkable for the number of their superstitions and the strength of their prejudices. In Scotland this is even more striking than in Germany; because the Scotch, owing to causes which have been little studied, are, in practical matters, not only industrious and provident, but singularly shrewd. This, however, in the higher departments of life, has availed them nothing; and, while there is no country which possesses a more original, inquisitive, and innovating literature than Scotland does, so also is there no country, equally civilized, in which so much of the spirit of the Middle Ages still lingers, in which so many absurdities are still believed, and in which it would be so easy to rouse into activity the old feelings of religious intolerance.

The divergence, and indeed the hostility, thus established between the practical and speculative classes, is the most important fact in the history of Scotland, and is partly cause and partly effect of the predominance of the deductive method. For this descending scheme being opposed to the ascending or inductive scheme, neglects those lower generalizations which are the only ones that both classes understand, and, therefore, the only ones where they sympathize with each other. The inductive method, as popularized by Bacon, gave great prominence to these lower or proximate truths; and this, though it has often made the intellectual classes in England too utilitarian, has at all events saved them from that state of isolation in which they would otherwise have remained. But in Scotland the isolation has been almost complete, because the deductive method has been almost universal. Full evidence of this will be collected in the third volume; but, that I may not leave the subject entirely without illustration, I will notice very briefly the principal instances that occurred during those three generations in which Scotch literature reached its highest excellence.

During this period, which comprises nearly a century, the tendency was so unmistakable as to form a striking phenomenon in the annals of the human mind. The first great symptom was a movement begun by Simson, professor at the University of Glasgow, and continued by Stewart, professor at the University of Edinburgh. These able men made strenuous efforts to revive the pure Greek geometry, and depreciate the algebraic or symbolical analysis.[14] Hence there arose

---

[14] Simson was appointed in 1711; and even before he began to lecture, he drew up 'a translation of the three first books of L'Hospital's Conic Sections, in which geometrical demonstrations are substituted for the algebraical of the original, according to Mr. Simson's early taste on this subject.' *Trail's Life and Writings of Robert Simson*, 1812, 4to. p. 4. This was probably the rudiment of his work on Conic Sections, published in 1735. Montucla, *Histoire des Mathématiques*, vol. iii. p. 12. On the difference between the ancient and modern schemes, there are some ingenious, though perhaps scarcely tenable, remarks in Dugald Stewart's *Philosophy of the Mind*, vol. ii. pp. 354 seq. and p. 360. See also Comte, *Philosophie Positive*, vol. i. pp. 383–395. Matthew Stewart, the mathematical professor at Edinburgh, was the father of Dugald. See, respecting him and his crusade against the modern analysis, Bower's *History*

among them, and among their disciples, a love of the most refined methods of solution, and a contempt for those easier, but less elegant ones, which we owe to algebra.[15] Here we clearly see the isolating and esoteric character of a scheme which despises what ordinary understandings can quickly master, and which had rather proceed from the ideal to the tangible, than mount from the tangible to the ideal. Just at the same time, the same spirit was displayed, in another branch of inquiry, by Hutcheson, who, though an Irishman by birth, was educated in the University of Glasgow, and was professor there. In his celebrated moral and æsthetic researches, he, in the place of inductive reasoning from palpable facts, substituted deductive reasoning from impalpable principles; ignoring the immediate and practical suggestions of the senses, and believing that by a hypothetical assumption of certain laws, he could descend upon the facts, instead of rising from the facts in order to learn the laws.[16] His philosophy exercised immense influence among metaphysicians;[17] and his method of working down-

---

of the University of Edinburgh, vol. ii. pp. 357–360, vol. iii. p. 249; and a strange passage in *First Report of the British Association*, p. 59.

[15] One of Simson's great reasons for recommending the old analysis, was that it was 'more elegant' than the comparatively modern practice of introducing algebraic calculations into geometry. See *Trail's Simson*, 1812, 4to. pp. 27, 67; a valuable work, which Lord Brougham, in his hasty life of Simson, calls, 'a very learned and exceedingly ill-written, indeed hardly readable' book. *Brougham's Men of Letters and Science*, vol. i. p. 482, 8vo. 1845. Dr. Trail's style is clearer, and his sentences are less involved, than Lord Brougham's; and he had moreover the great advantage of understanding the subject upon which he wrote.

[16] Sir James Mackintosh (*Dissertation on Ethical Philosophy*, p. 208) says of Hutcheson, 'To him may also be ascribed that proneness to multiply ultimate and original principles in human nature, which characterized the Scottish school till the second extinction of a passion for metaphysical speculation in Scotland.' There is an able view of Hutcheson's philosophy in *Cousin, Histoire de la Philosophie*, I. série, vol. iv. pp. 31 seq.; written with clearness and eloquence, but perhaps overpraising Hutcheson.

[17] On its influence, see a letter from Mackintosh to Parr, in

wards, from the abstract to the concrete, was adopted by another and a still greater Scotchman, the illustrious Adam Smith. How Smith favoured the deductive form of investigation is apparent in his *Theory of Moral Sentiments*, likewise in his *Essay on Language*,[18] and even in his fragment on the *History of Astronomy*, in which he, from general considerations, undertook to prove what the march of astronomical discovery must have been, instead of first ascertaining what it had been.[19] The *Wealth of Nations*, again, is entirely deductive, since in it Smith generalizes the laws of wealth, not from the phenomena of wealth, nor from statistical statements, but from the phenomena of selfishness; thus making a deductive application of one set of

---

Memoirs of Mackintosh, by his Son, vol. i. p. 334. Compare *Letters from Warburton to Hurd*, pp. 37, 82.

[18] Which is added to his *Theory of Moral Sentiments*, edit. 1822, 2 volumes. Compare a letter which Smith wrote in 1763 on the origin of language (in *Nichol's Literary Illustrations of the Eighteenth Century*, vol. iii. pp. 515, 516), which exhibits, on a small scale, the same treatment, as distinguished from a generalization of the facts which are supplied by a comprehensive comparison of different languages. Dr. Arnold speaks slightingly of such investigations. He says, 'Attempts to explain the phenomena of language *a priori* seem to me unwise.' *Arnold's Miscellaneous Works*, p. 365. This would lead into a discussion too long for a note, but it appears to me that these *a priori* inferences are, to the philologist, what hypotheses are to the inductive natural philosopher; and if this be the case, they are extremely important, because no really fruitful experiment ever can be made unless it is preceded by a judicious hypothesis. In the absence of such an hypothesis, men may grope in the dark for centuries, accumulating facts without obtaining knowledge.

[19] See, for instance, his attempt to prove, from general reasonings concerning the human mind, that there was a necessary relation in regard to the order in which men promulgated the system of concentric spheres and that of eccentric spheres and epicycles. *History of Astronomy*, in Smith's *Philosophical Essays*, 1795, 4to. pp. 31, 36, which it may be convenient to compare with *Whewell's Philosophy of the Inductive Sciences*, 1847, vol. ii. pp. 53, 60, 61. This striking fragment of Adam Smith's is probably little read now; but it is warmly praised by one of the greatest living philosophers, M. A. Comte, in his *Philosophie Positive*, vol. vi. p. 319.

mental principles to the whole set of economical facts.[20] The illustrations with which his great book abounds are no part of the real argument: they are subsequent to the conception; and if they were all admitted, the work, though less interesting and perhaps less influential, would, in a scientific point of view, be equally valuable. To give another instance: the works of Hume, his metaphysical essays alone excepted, are all deductive; his profound economical inquiries are essentially *a priori*, and might have been written without any acquaintance with those details of trade and finance from which, according to the inductive scheme, they should have been generalized.[21] Thus, too, in his

---

[20] The two writers who have inquired most carefully into the method which political economists ought to follow, are Mr. John Mill (*Essays on Unsettled Questions of Political Economy*, 1844, pp. 120–164) and Mr. Rae (*New Principles of Political Economy*, 1834, pp. 328–351). Mr. Rae, in his ingenious work, objects to Adam Smith that he transgressed the rules of the Baconian philosophy, and thus prevented his inferences from being as valuable as they would have been if he had treated his subject inductively. But Mr. Mill, with great force of reasoning, has proved that the deductive plan is the only one by which political economy can be raised to a science. He says, p. 143, 'political economy is essentially an *abstract* science, and its method is the method *a priori*;' and at p. 146, that the *a posteriori* method is 'altogether inefficacious.' To this I may add, that the modern theory of rent, which is now the cornerstone of political economy, was got at, not by generalizing economical facts, but by reasoning downwards after the manner of geometricians. Indeed, those who oppose the theory of rent, always do so on the ground that it is contradicted by facts; and then, with complete ignorance of the philosophy of method, they infer that therefore the theory is wrong. See, for instance, Jones *on the Distribution of Wealth*, 8vo. 1831: a book containing some interesting facts, but vitiated by this capital defect of method. See also *Journal of Statistical Society*, vol. i. p. 317, vol. vi. p. 322; where it is said that economical theories should be generalised from statistical facts. Compare vol. xvii. p. 116, vol. xviii. p. 101.

[21] A striking instance has lately come to light of the sagacity with which Hume employed this method. See *Burton's Life and Correspondence of Hume*, vol. ii. p. 486; where we find, that immediately Hume had read the *Wealth of Nations*, he detected Smith's error concerning rent being an element of price: so that it now appears that Hume

Natural History of Religion, he endeavoured simply by reflection, and independently of evidence, to institute a purely speculative investigation into the origin of religious opinions.[22] In the same way, in his *History of England*, instead of first collecting the evidence, and then drawing inferences from it, he began by assuming that the relations between the people and the government must have followed a certain order, and he either neglected or distorted the facts by which this supposition was contradicted.[23] These different writers, though

---

was the first to make this great discovery, as far as the idea is concerned; though Ricardo has the merit of proving it.

[22] The historical facts he introduces are merely illustrations; as any one will see who will read *The Natural History of Religion*, in *Hume's Philos. Works*, Edinb. 1826, vol. iv. pp. 435–513. I may mention, that there is a considerable similarity between the views advocated in this remarkable essay and the religious stages of *Comte's Philosophie Positive*; for Hume's early form of polytheism is evidently the same as M. Comte's fetichism, from which both these writers believe that monotheism subsequently arose, as a later and more refined abstraction. That this was the course adopted by the human mind is highly probable, and is confirmed by the learned researches of Mr. Grote. See his *History of Greece*, vol. i. pp. 462, 497, vol. v. p. 22. The opposite and more popular opinion, of monotheism preceding idolatry, was held by most of the great earlier writers, and is defended by many moderns, and among others by Dr. Whewell (*Bridgewater Treatise*, p. 256),

who expresses himself with considerable confidence: see also *Letters from Warburton to Hurd*, p. 239. Compare *Thirlwall's History of Greece*, vol. i. p. 183, Lond. 1835, with the 'einige Funken des Monotheismus' of Kant, *Kritik der reinen Vernunft*, in *Kant's Werke*, vol. ii. p. 455.

[23] That is to say, he treated historical facts as merely illustrative of certain general principles, which he believed could be proved without the facts; so that, as M. Schlosser (*History of the Eighteenth Century*, vol. ii. p. 76) well says, 'History with Hume was only a subordinate pursuit, only a means by which he might introduce his philosophy,' &c. Considering how little is known of the principles which govern social and political changes, there can be no doubt that Hume was premature in the application of this method; but it is absurd to call the method dishonest, since the object of his History was, not to *prove* conclusions, but to *illustrate* them: and he therefore thought himself justified in selecting the illustrations. I am simply stating his views,

varying in their principles, and in the subjects they studied, were all agreed as to their method; that is to say, they were all agreed to investigate truth rather by descent than by ascent. The immense social importance of this peculiarity I shall examine in the third volume, where I shall endeavour to ascertain how it affected the national civilization, and caused some curious contrasts with the opposite, and more empirical, character of English literature. In the meantime, and merely to state what will be hereafter proved, I may add, that the deductive method was employed, not only by those eminent Scotchmen I have mentioned, but was carried into the speculative *History of Civil Society* by Ferguson; into the study of legislation by Mill; into the study of jurisprudence by Mackintosh; into geology by Hutton; into thermotics by Black and Leslie; into physiology by Hunter, by Alexander Walker, and by Charles Bell; into pathology by Cullen; into therapeutics by Brown and Currie.

This is an outline of the plan I purpose to follow in the present Introduction, and by means of which I hope to arrive at some results of permanent value. For by studying different principles in those countries where they have been most developed, the laws of the principles will be more easily unfolded than if we had studied them in countries where they are very obscure. And, inasmuch as, in England, civilization has followed a course more orderly, and less disturbed, than in any other country, it becomes the more necessary, in writing its history, to use some resources like those which I have suggested. What makes the history of England so eminently valuable is, that nowhere else has the national progress been so little interfered with, either for good or for evil. But the mere fact that our civilization has, by this means, been preserved in a more natural and healthy state, renders it incumbent on us to study the diseases to which it is liable, by observing those other countries where social disease is more rife.

---

without at all defending them; Indeed, I believe that in this respect he was seriously in the wrong.

The security and the durability of civilization must depend on the regularity with which its elements are combined, and on the harmony with which they work. If any one element is too active, the whole composition will be in danger. Hence it is, that although the laws of the composition of the elements will be best ascertained wherever we can find the composition most complete, we must, nevertheless, search for the laws of each separate element wherever we can find the element itself most active. While, therefore, I have selected the history of England, as that in which the harmony of the different principles has been longest maintained, I have, precisely on that account, thought it advisable to study each principle separately in the country where it has been most powerful, and where, by its inordinate development, the equilibrium of the entire structure has been disturbed.

By adopting these precautions, we shall be able to remove many of the difficulties which still beset the study of history. Before, however, entering that wide field which now lies in our way, it will be well to clear up some preliminary points, which I have not yet noticed, and the discussion of which may obviate certain objections that might otherwise be raised. The subjects to which I allude, are Religion, Literature, and Government: three topics of vast importance, and which, in the opinion of many persons, are the prime movers of human affairs. That this opinion is altogether erroneous will be amply proved in the present work; but as the opinion is widely spread, and is very plausible, it is necessary that we should at once come to some understanding respecting it, and inquire into the real nature of that influence, which these three great powers do actually exercise over the progress of civilization.

Now, in the first place, it is evident that if a people were left entirely to themselves, their religion, their literature, and their government would be, not the causes of their civilization, but the effects of it. Out of a certain condition of society certain results naturally follow. Those results may, no doubt, be tampered with by some external agency; but if that is not done, it is impossible that a highly civilized people, accustomed to reason and to doubt, should ever embrace a religion of which the glaring absurdities set reason and doubt at defiance. There are many instances of nations changing their religion, but there is no instance of a progressive country voluntarily adopting a retrogressive religion; neither is there any example of a declining country ameliorating its religion. It is of course true, that a good religion is favourable to civilization, and a bad one unfavourable to it. Unless, however, there is some interference from without, no people will ever discover that their religion is bad until their reason tells them so; but if their reason is inactive, and their knowledge stationary, the discovery will never be made. A country that continues in its old ignorance will always remain in its old religion. Surely nothing can be plainer than this. A very ignorant people will, by virtue of their ignorance, incline towards a religion full of marvels; a religion which boasts of innumerable gods, and which ascribes every occurrence to the immediate authority of those gods. On the other hand, a people whose knowledge makes them better judges of evidence, and who are accustomed to that most difficult task, the practice of doubting, will require a religion less marvellous, less obtrusive; one that taxes their credulity less heavily. But will you, therefore, say, that the badness of the first religion causes the ignorance; and that the goodness of the second religion causes the knowledge? Will you say, that when one event precedes another, the one which comes first is the effect, and the one which follows afterwards is the cause? This is not the way in which men reason on the ordinary affairs of life; and it is difficult to see why they should reason thus respecting the history of past events.

The truth is, that the religious opinions which prevail in any period are among the symptoms by which that period is marked. When the opinions are deeply rooted, they do, no doubt, influence the conduct of men; but before they can be deeply rooted, some intellectual change must first have taken place. We may as well expect that the seed should quicken in the barren rock, as that a mild and philosophic religion should be established among ignorant and ferocious savages. Of this innumerable experiments have been made, and always with the same result. Men of excellent intentions, and full of a fervent though mistaken zeal, have been, and still are, attempting to propagate their own religion among the inhabitants of barbarous countries. By strenuous and unremitting activity, and frequently by promises, and even by actual gifts, they have, in many cases, persuaded savage communities to make a profession of the Christian religion. But whoever will compare the triumphant reports of the missionaries with the long chain of evidence supplied by competent travellers, will soon find that such profession is only nominal, and that these ignorant tribes have adopted, indeed, the ceremonies of the new religion, but have by no means adopted the religion itself. They receive the externals, but there they stop. They may baptize their children; they may take the sacrament; they may flock to the church. All this they may do, and yet be as far removed from the spirit of Christianity as when they bowed the knee before their former idols. The rites and forms of a religion lie on the surface; they are at once seen, they are quickly learned, easily copied by those who are unable to penetrate to that which lies beneath. It is this deeper and inward change which alone is durable; and this the savage can never experience while he is sunk in an ignorance that levels him with the brutes by which he is surrounded. Remove the ignorance, and then the religion may enter. This is the only course by which ultimate benefit can be effected. After a careful study of the history and condition of barbarous nations, I do most confidently assert, that there is no well attested case of any people being permanently converted to Christianity, except in those very few instances where missionaries, being men of knowledge, as well as men of piety, have familiarized the savage with habits of thought, and, by thus stimulating his intellect, have prepared him for the reception of those religious principles, which, without such stimulus, he could never have understood.[24]

It is in this way that, looking at things upon a large scale, the religion of mankind is the effect of their improvement, not the cause of it. But, looking at things upon a small scale, or taking what is called a practical view of some short and special period, circumstances will occasionally occur which disturb this general order, and apparently reverse the natural process. And this, as in all such cases, can only arise from the peculiarities of individual men; who, moved by the minor laws which regulate individual actions, are able, by their genius or their energy, to interfere with the operation of those greater laws which regulate large societies. Owing to circumstances still unknown, there appear, from time to time, great thinkers, who, devoting their lives to a single purpose, are able to anticipate the progress of mankind, and to produce a religion or a philosophy, by which important effects are eventually brought about. But, if we look into history, we shall clearly see that, although the origin of a new opinion may be thus due

---

[24] A writer of great authority has made some remarks on this, which are worth attending to: 'Ce fut alors que les Jésuites pénétrèrent dans la Chine pour y prêcher l'évangile. Ils ne tardèrent pas à s'apercevoir qu'un des moyens les plus efficaces pour s'y maintenir, en attendant le moment que le ciel avoit marqué pour éclairer ce vaste empire, étoit d'étaler des connoissances astronomiques.' Montucla, Histoire des Mathématiques, vol. i. p. 468; and see vol. ii. pp. 586, 587. Cuvier delicately hints at the same conclusion. He says of Emery: 'Il se souvenait que l'époque où le christianisme a fait le plus de conquêtes, et où ses ministres ont obtenu le plus de respect, est celle où ils portaient chez les peuples convertis les lumières des lettres, en même temps que les vérités de la religion, et où ils formaient à la fois dans les nations l'ordre le plus éminent et le plus éclairé. Cuvier, Éloges Historiques, vol. iii. p. 170. Even Southey (History of Brasil, vol. ii. p. 378) says: 'Missionaries have always complained of the fickleness of their converts; and they must always complain of it, till they discover that some degree of civilization must precede conversion, or at least accompany it.' And see to the same effect, Halkett's Notes on the North American Indians, pp. 352, 353; and Combe's North America, vol. i. p. 250, vol. ii. p. 358.

to a single man, the result which the new opinion produces will depend on the condition of the people among whom it is propagated. If either a religion or a philosophy is too much in advance of a nation, it can do no present service, but must bide its time, until the minds of men are ripe for its reception. Of this innumerable instances will occur to most readers. Every science and every creed has had its martyrs; men exposed to obloquy, or even to death, because they knew more than their contemporaries, and because society was not sufficiently advanced to receive the truths which they communicated. According to the ordinary course of affairs, a few generations pass away, and then there comes a period when these very truths are looked upon as commonplace facts; and a little later, there comes another period, in which they are declared to be necessary, and even the dullest intellects wonder how they could ever have been denied. This is what happens when the human mind is allowed to have fair play, and to exercise itself, with tolerable freedom, in the accumulation and diffusion of knowledge. If, however, by violent, and therefore by artificial, means, this same society is prevented from exercising its intellect, then the truths, however important they may be, can never be received. For why should certain truths be rejected in one age, and acknowledged in another? The truths remain the same; their ultimate recognition must, therefore, be due to a change in the society which now accepts what it had before despised. Indeed, history is full of evidence of the utter inefficiency even of the noblest principles, when they are promulgated among a very ignorant nation. Thus it was that the doctrine of One God, taught to the Hebrews of old, remained for many centuries altogether inoperative. The people to whom it was addressed had not yet emerged from barbarism; they were, therefore, unable to raise their minds to so elevated a conception. Like all other barbarians, they craved after a religion which would feed their credulity with incessant wonders; and which, instead of abstracting the Deity to a single essence, would multiply their gods until they covered every field, and swarmed in every forest. This is the idolatry which is the natural fruit of ignorance; and this it is to which the Hebrews were perpetually recurring. Notwithstanding the most severe and unremitting punishments, they, at every opportunity, abandoned that pure theism which their minds were too backward to receive, and relapsed into superstitions which they could more easily understand,—into the worship of the golden calf, and the adoration of the brazen serpent. Now, and in this age of the world, they have long ceased to do these things. And why? Not because their religious feelings are more easily aroused, or their religious fears more often excited. So far from this, they are dissevered from their old associations; they have lost for ever those scenes by which men might well have been moved. They are no longer influenced by those causes which inspired emotions, sometimes of terror, sometimes of gratitude. They no longer witness the pillar of cloud by day, or the pillar of fire by night; they no longer see the Law being given from Sinai, nor do they hear the thunder rolling from Horeb. In the presence of these great appeals, they remained idolaters in their hearts, and whenever an opportunity occurred, they became idolaters in their practice; and this they did because they were in that state of barbarism, of which idolatry is the natural product. To what possible circumstance can their subsequent change be ascribed, except to the simple fact, that the Hebrews, like all other people, as they advanced in civilization, began to abstract and refine their religion, and, despising the old worship of many gods, thus by slow degrees elevated their minds to that steady perception of One Great Cause, which, at an earlier period, it had been vainly attempted to impress upon them?

Thus intimate is the connexion between the opinions of a people and their knowledge; and thus necessary is it that, so far as nations are concerned, intellectual activity should precede religious improvement. If we require further illustrations of this important truth, we shall find them in the events which occurred in

Europe soon after the promulgation of Christianity. The Romans were, with rare exceptions, an ignorant and barbarous race; ferocious, dissolute, and cruel. For such a people, Polytheism was the natural creed; and we read, accordingly, that they practised an idolatry which a few great thinkers, and only a few, ventured to despise. The Christian religion, falling among these men, found them unable to appreciate its sublime and admirable doctrines. And when, a little later, Europe was overrun by fresh immigrations, the invaders, who were even more barbarous than the Romans, brought with them those superstitions which were suited to their actual condition. It was upon the materials arising from these two sources that Christianity was now called to do her work. The result is most remarkable. For after the new religion seemed to have carried all before it, and had received the homage of the best part of Europe, it was soon found that nothing had been really effected. It was soon found that society was in that early stage in which superstition is inevitable; and in which men, if they do not have it in one form, will have it in another. It was in vain that Christianity taught a simple doctrine, and enjoined a simple worship. The minds of men were too backward for so great a step, and required more complicated forms, and a more complicated belief. What followed is well known to the students of ecclesiastical history. The superstition of Europe, instead of being diminished, was only turned into a fresh channel. The new religion was corrupted by the old follies. The adoration of idols was succeeded by the adoration of saints; the worship of the Virgin was substituted for the worship of Cybele;[25] Pagan ceremonies were established in Christian churches; not only the mummeries of idolatry, but

---

[25] This is curiously illustrated by the fact, that the 25th of March, which is now called Lady-day, in honour of the Virgin Mary, was, in Pagan times, called Hilaria, and was dedicated to Cybele, the mother of the gods. Compare *Blunt's Vestiges of Ancient Manners*, 8vo. 1823, pp. 51–55, with *Hampson's Medii Ævi Kalendarium*, 8vo. 1841, vol. i. pp. 56, 177.

likewise its doctrines, were quickly added, and were incorporated and worked into the spirit of the new religion; until, after a lapse of a few generations, Christianity exhibited so grotesque and hideous a form, that its best features were lost, and the lineaments of its earlier loveliness altogether destroyed.[26]

After some centuries were passed, Christianity slowly emerged from these corruptions; many of which, however, even the most civilized countries have not yet been able to throw off.[27] Indeed, it was found impossible to effect even the beginning of a reform, until the European intellect was, in some degree, roused from its lethargy. The knowledge of men, gradually advancing, made them indignant at superstitions which they had formerly admired. The way in which their indignation increased, until, in the sixteenth century, it broke out into that great event which is well called the Reformation, forms one of the most interesting subjects in modern history. But, for our present purpose, it is enough to keep in mind the memorable and important fact that, for centuries after Christianity was the established religion of Europe, it failed to bear its natural fruit, because its lot was cast among a people whose ignorance compelled them to be superstitious, and who, on account of their superstition, defaced a system which, in its original purity, they were unable to receive.[28]

---

[26] On this interesting subject, the two best English books are, *Middleton's Letter from Rome*, and *Priestley's History of the Corruption of Christianity*; the former work being chiefly valuable for ritual corruptions, the latter work for doctrinal ones. *Blunt's Vestiges of Ancient Manners* is also worth reading; but is very inferior to the two treatises just named, and is conceived in a much narrower spirit.

[27] The large amount of Paganism which still exists in every Christian sect, forms an argument against an ingenious distinction which M. Bunsen has made between the change of a religion and that of a language; alterations in a religion being, as he supposes, always more abrupt than those in a language. *Bunsen's Egypt*, vol. i. pp. 358, 359.

[28] It was necessary, says M. Maury, that the church 'so rapprochât davantage de l'esprit grossier, inculte, ignorant du barbare.' *Maury, Légendes Pieuses du Moyen Age*, p. 101. An exactly similar process has

Indeed, in every page of history, we meet with fresh evidence of the little effect religious doctrines can produce upon a people, unless preceded by intellectual culture. The influence exercised by Protestantism, as compared with Catholicism, affords an interesting example of this. The Catholic religion bears to the Protestant religion exactly the same relation that the Dark Ages bear to the sixteenth century. In the Dark Ages, men were credulous and ignorant; they therefore produced a religion which required great belief and little knowledge. In the sixteenth century, their credulity and ignorance, though still considerable, were rapidly diminishing, and it was found necessary to organize a religion suited to their altered circumstances: a religion more favourable to free inquiry; a religion less full of miracles, saints, legends, and idols; a religion of which the ceremonies were less frequent, and less burdensome; a religion which should discourage penance, fasting, confession, celibacy, and those other mortifications which had long been universal. All this was done by the establishment of Protestantism; a mode of worship which, being thus suited to the age, made, as is well known, speedy progress. If this great movement had been allowed to proceed without interruption, it would, in the course of a few generations, have overthrown the old superstition, and established in its place a simpler and less troublesome creed; the rapidity with which this was done, being, of course, proportioned to the intellectual activity of the different countries. But, unfortunately, the European governments, who are always meddling in matters with which they have no concern, thought it their duty to protect the religious interests of the

---

taken place in India, where the Puranas are to the Vedas what the works of the Fathers are to the New Testament. Compare Elphinstone's *History of India*, pp. 87, 88, 98; *Wilson's Preface to the Vishnu Purana*, p. 7; and *Transactions of Bombay Society*, vol. i. p. 205. So that as M. Max Müller well expresses it, the Puranas are 'a secondary formation of Indian mythology.' *Müller on the Languages of India*, in *Reports of British Association for* 1847, p. 324.

people; and making common cause with the Catholic clergy, they, in many instances, forcibly stopped the heresy, and thus arrested the natural development of the age. This interference was, in nearly all cases, well intended, and is solely to be ascribed to the ignorance of rulers respecting the proper limits of their functions; but the evils caused by this ignorance it would be difficult to exaggerate. During almost a hundred and fifty years, Europe was afflicted by religious wars, religious massacres, and religious persecutions; not one of which would have arisen, if the great truth had been recognised, that the state has no concern with the opinions of men, and no right to interfere, even in the slightest degree, with the form of worship which they may choose to adopt. This principle was, however, formerly unknown, or at all events unheeded; and it was not until the middle of the seventeenth century that the great religions contests were brought to a final close, and the different countries settled down into their public creeds; which, in the essential points, have never since been permanently altered; no nation having, for more than two hundred years, made war upon another on account of its religion; and all the great Catholic countries having, during the same period, remained Catholic, all the great Protestant ones remained Protestant.

From this it has arisen, that, in several of the European countries, the religious development has not followed its natural order, but has been artificially forced into an unnatural one. According to the natural order, the most civilized countries should all be Protestants, and the most uncivilized ones Catholics. In the average of instances this is actually the case; so that many persons have been led into the singular error, of ascribing all modern enlightenment to the influence of Protestantism; overlooking the important fact, that until the enlightenment had begun, Protestantism was never required. But although, in the ordinary course of affairs, the advance of the Reformation would have been the measure, and the symptom, of that advance of knowledge by which it was preceded, still, in many cases, the authority of the government and of the church acted as disturbing causes, and frustrated the natural progress of religious improvement. And, after the treaty of Westphalia had fixed the political relations of Europe, the love of theological strife so greatly subsided, that men no longer thought it worth their while to raise a religious revolution, and to risk their lives in an attempt to overturn the creed of the state. At the same time, governments, not being themselves particularly fond of revolutions, have encouraged this stationary condition; and very naturally, and, as it appears to me, very wisely, have made no great alteration, but have left the national establishments as they found them; that is to say, the Protestant ones Protestant, and the Catholic ones Catholic. Hence it is, that the national religion professed by any country at the present moment, is no decisive criterion of the present civilization of the country; because the circumstances which fixed the religion occurred long since, and the religion remains endowed and established by the mere continuance of an impetus which was formerly given.

Thus far as to the origin of the ecclesiastical establishments of Europe. But, in their practical consequences, we see some results which are highly instructive. For many countries owing their national creed, not to their own proper antecedents, but to the authority of powerful individuals, it will be invariably found, that in such countries the creed does not produce the effects which might have been expected from it, and which, according to its terms, it ought to produce. Thus, for instance, the Catholic religion is more superstitious, and more intolerant, than the Protestant; but it by no means follows, that those countries which profess the former creed, must be more superstitious, and more intolerant, than those which profess the latter. So far from this, the French are not only quite as free from those odious qualities as are the most civilized Protestants, but they are more free from them than some Protestant nations, as the Scotch and the Swedes. Of the highly-educated class, I am not here speaking; but of the clergy, and of the people generally, it must be admitted, that in Scotland there is more bigotry, more superstition, and a more thorough contempt for the religion of others, than there is in France. And in Sweden, which is one of the oldest Protestant countries in Europe,[19] there is, not occasionally, but habitually, an intolerance and a spirit of persecution, which would be discreditable to a Catholic country; but which is doubly disgraceful when proceeding from a people who profess to base their religion on the right of private judgment.[20]

These things show, what it would be easy to prove by a wider induction, that when, from special, or, as they are called, accidental causes, any people profess a religion more advanced than themselves, it will not produce

---

[19] The doctrines of Luther were first preached in Sweden in 1519; and, in 1527, the principles of the Reformation were formally adopted in an assembly of the States at Westeraes, which enabled Gustavus Vasa to seize the property of the church. *Geijer's History of the Swedes*, part i. pp. 110, 118, 119; *Mosheim's Ecclesiastical History*, vol. ii. p. 22; *Crichton and Wheaton's History of Scandinavia*, vol. i. pp. 399, 400. The apostasy proceeded so favourably, that De Thou (*Histoire Univ.* vol. xiii. p. 312) says, in 1596, 'Il y avoit déjà si long-tems que ce culte étoit établi en Suède, qu'il étoit comme impossible de trouver, soit parmi le peuple, soit parmi les seigneurs, quelqu'un qui se souvînt d'avoir vu dans ce roïaume l'exercice public de la religion catholique.'

[20] On the state of things in 1838, see some curious, and indeed shameful, details in *Laing's Sweden*, 8vo. London, 1839. Mr. Laing, though himself a Protestant, truly says, that in Protestant Sweden there 'is inquisition law, working in the hands of a Lutheran state-church, as strongly as in Spain or Portugal in the hands of a Roman Catholic Church.' *Laing's Sweden*, p. 324. In the seventeenth century, it was ordered by the Swedish Church, and the order was confirmed by government, that 'if any Swedish subject change his religion, be shall be banished the kingdom, and lose all right of inheritance, both for himself and his descendants.... If any bring into the country teachers of another religion, he shall be fined and banished.' *Burton's Diary*, vol. iii. p. 867, 8vo. 1828. To this may be added, that it was not till 1781 that Roman Catholics were allowed to exercise their religion in Sweden. See *Crichton's History of Scandinavia*, Edinb. 1838, vol. ii. p. 320. See also, on this intolerant spirit, *Whitelocke's Journal of the Swedish Embassy*, vol. i. pp. 164, 412, vol. ii. p. 312.

its legitimate effect.[31] The superiority of Protestantism over Catholicism consists in its diminution of superstition and intolerance, and in the check which it gives to ecclesiastical power. But the experience of Europe teaches us, that when the superior religion is fixed among an inferior people, its superiority is no longer seen. The Scotch and the Swedes,—and to them might be added some of the Swiss cantons,—are less civilized than the French, and are therefore more superstitious. This being the case, it avails them little that they have a religion better than the French. It avails them little that, owing to circumstances which have long since passed away, they, three centuries ago, adopted a creed to which the force of habit, and the influence of tradition, now oblige them to cling. Whoever has travelled in Scotland with sufficient attention to observe the ideas and opinions of the people, and whoever will look into Scotch theology, and read the history of the Scotch Kirk, and the proceedings of the Scotch Assemblies and Consistories, will see how little the country has benefited by its religion, and how wide an interval there is between its intolerant spirit and the natural tendencies of the Protestant Reformation. On the other hand, whoever will subject France to a similar examination,

---

[31] We see a good instance of this in the case of the Abyssinians, who have professed Christianity for centuries; but, as no pains were taken to cultivate their intellect, they found the religion too pure for them: they, therefore, corrupted it, and, down to the present moment, they have not made the slightest progress. The accounts given by Bruce of them are well known; and a traveller, who visited them in 1839, says: 'Nothing can be more corrupt than the nominal Christianity of this unhappy nation. It is mixed up with Judaism, Mahommedanism, and idolatry, and is a mass of rites and superstitions which cannot mend the heart.' *Kraff's Journal at Ankobar*, in *Journal of Geographical Society*, vol. x. p. 488; see also vol. xiv. p. 13: and for a similar state of things in America, see the account of the Quiché Indians, in *Stephens's Central America*, vol. ii. pp. 191, 192. Compare *Squier's Central America*, vol. i. pp. 322, 323, with *Halkett's North-American Indians*, pp. 29, 212, 268. For further confirmation of this view, in another part of the world, see *Tuckey's Expedition to the Zaire*, pp. 79, 80, 165.

will see an illiberal religion accompanied by liberal views, and a creed full of superstitions professed by a people among whom superstition is comparatively rare.

The simple fact is, that the French have a religion worse than themselves; the Scotch have a religion better than themselves. The liberality of France is as ill suited to Catholicism, as the bigotry of Scotland is ill suited to Protestantism. In these, as in all similar cases, the characteristics of the creed are overpowered by the characteristics of the people; and the national faith is, in the most important points, altogether inoperative, because it does not harmonize with the civilization of the country in which it is established. How idle, then, it is to ascribe the civilization to the creed; and how worse than foolish are the attempts of government to protect a religion which, if suited to the people, will need no protection, and, if unsuited to them, will work no good!

If the reader has seized the spirit of the preceding arguments, he will hardly require that I should analyze with equal minuteness the second disturbing cause, namely, Literature. It is evident, that what has already been said respecting the religion of a people, is, in a great measure, applicable to their literature. Literature,[22] when it is in a healthy and unforced state, is simply the form in which the knowledge of a country is registered; the mould in which it is cast. In this, as in the other cases we have considered, individual men may of course take great steps, and rise to a great height above the level of their age. But if they rise beyond a certain point, their present usefulness is impaired; if they rise still higher, it is destroyed.[23] When the interval between

---

[22] I use the word literature, not as opposed to science, but in its larger sense, including everything which is written—'taking the term literature in its primary sense, of an application of letters to the records of facts or opinions.' *Mure's History of the Literature of Greece*, vol. iv. p. 50.

[23] Compare *Tocqueville, Démocratie en Amérique*, vol. ii. p. 130, with some admirable remarks on the Sophists in *Grote's History of Greece*, vol. viii. p. 481. Sir W. Hamilton, whose learning respecting the history of opinions is well known, says, 'Precisely in proportion as an

the intellectual classes and the practical classes is too great, the former will possess no influence, the latter will reap no benefit. This is what occurred in the ancient world, when the distance between the ignorant idolatry of the people and the refined systems of philosophers was altogether impassable;[24] and this is the principal reason why the Greeks and Romans were unable to retain the civilization which they for a short time possessed. Precisely the same process is at the present moment going on in Germany, where the most valuable part of literature forms an esoteric system, which, having nothing in common with the nation itself, produces no effect on the national civilization. The truth is, that although Europe has received great benefit from its literature, this is owing, not to what the literature has originated, but to what it has preserved. Knowledge must be acquired, before it can be written; and the only use of books is, to serve as a storehouse in which the treasures of the intellect are safely kept, and where they

---

author is in advance of his age, is it likely that his works will be neglected.' *Hamilton's Discussions on Philosophy*, p. 186. Thus, too, in regard to the fine arts, Sir Joshua Reynolds (*Fourth Discourse*, in *Works*, vol. i. p. 363) says, 'Present time and future may be considered as rivals; and he who solicits the one, must expect to be discountenanced by the other.'

[24] Hence the intellectually exclusive and, as M. Neander well terms it, 'aristocratic spirit of antiquity.' *Neander's History of the Church*, vol. i. pp. 40, 97, vol. ii. p. 31. This is constantly overlooked by writers who use the word 'democracy' loosely; forgetting that, in the same age, democracies of politics may be very common, while democracies of thought are very rare. For proof of the universal prevalence formerly of this esoteric and aristocratic spirit, see the following passages: *Ritter's History of Ancient Philosophy*, vol. i. p. 338, vol. iii. pp. 9, 17; *Tennemann, Geschichte der Philosophie*, vol. ii, pp. 200, 205, 220; *Beausobre, Histoire Critique de Manichée*, vol. ii. p. 41; *Matter, Histoire du Gnosticisme*, vol. i. p. 13, vol. ii. pp. 83, 370; *Sprengel, Histoire de la Médecine*, vol. i. p. 250; *Grote's History of Greece*, vol. i. p. 561, vol. iv. p. 514; *Thirlwall's History of Greece*, vol. ii. p. 150, vol. vi. p. 95; *Warburton's Works*, vol. vii. pp. 862, 972, 4to. 1788; *Sharpe's History of Egypt*, vol. ii. p. 174; *Cudworth's Intellect. System*, vol. ii. pp. 114, 365, 443, vol. iii. p. 30.

may be conveniently found. Literature, in itself, is but a trifling matter; and is merely valuable as being the armory in which the weapons of the human mind are laid up, and from which, when required, they can be quickly drawn. But he would be a sorry reasoner, who, on that account, should propose to sacrifice the end, that he might obtain the means; who should hope to defend the armory by giving up the weapons, and who should destroy the treasure, in order to improve the magazine in which the treasure is kept.

Yet this is what many persons are apt to do. From literary men, in particular, we hear too much of the necessity of protecting and rewarding literature, and we hear too little of the necessity of that freedom and boldness, in the absence of which the most splendid literature is altogether worthless. Indeed, there is a general tendency, not to exaggerate the advantages of knowledge,—for that is impossible,—but to misunderstand what that is in which knowledge really consists. Real knowledge, the knowledge on which all civilization is based, solely consists in an acquaintance with the relations which things and ideas bear to each other and to themselves; in other words, in an acquaintance with physical and mental laws. If the time should ever come when all these laws are known, the circle of human knowledge will then be complete; and, in the interim, the value of literature depends upon the extent to which it communicates either a knowledge of the laws, or the materials by which the laws may be discovered. The business of education is to accelerate this great movement, and thus increase the fitness and aptitude of men, by increasing the resources which they possess. Towards this purpose, literature, so far as it is auxiliary, is highly useful. But to look upon an acquaintance with literature as one of the objects of education, is to mistake the order of events, and to make the end subservient to the means. It is because this is done, that we often find what are called highly educated men, the progress of whose knowledge has been actually retarded by the activity of their education. We often find them burdened by prejudices, which their reading, instead of dissipating, has rendered more inveterate.[35] For literature, being the depository of the thoughts of mankind, is full, not only of wisdom, but also of absurdities. The benefit, therefore, which is derived from literature, will depend, not so much upon the literature itself, as upon the skill with which it is studied, and the judgment with which it is selected. These are the preliminary conditions of success; and if they are not obeyed, the number and the value of the books in a country become a matter quite unimportant. Even in an advanced stage of civilization, there is always a tendency to prefer those parts of literature which favour ancient prejudices, rather than those which oppose them; and in cases where this tendency is very strong, the only effect of great learning will be, to supply the materials which may corroborate old errors, and confirm old superstitions. In our time such instances are not uncommon; and we frequently meet with men whose erudition ministers to their ignorance, and who the more they read, the less they know. There have been states of society in which this disposition was so general, that literature has done far more harm than good. Thus, for example, in the whole period from the sixth to the tenth centuries, there were not in all Europe more than three or four men who dared to think for themselves; and even they were obliged to veil their meaning in obscure and mystical language. The remaining part of society was, during these four centuries, sunk in the most degrading ignorance. Under these circumstances, the few who were able to read, confined their studies to works which encouraged and strengthened their superstition, such as the legends of the saints, and the homilies

---

[35] Locke has noticed this 'learned ignorance,' for which many men are remarkable. See a fine passage in the *Essay on Human Understanding*, book iii. chap. x. in *Locke's Works*, vol. ii. p. 27, and similar remarks in his *Conduct of the Understanding*, vol. ii. pp. 350, 364, 365, and in his *Thoughts on Education*, vol. viii. pp. 84-87. If this profound writer were now alive what a war he would wage against our great universities and public schools, where innumerable things are still taught which no one is concerned to understand, and which few will take the trouble to remember. Compare *Condorcet, Vie de Turgot*, pp. 255, 256 note.

of the fathers. From these sources they drew those lying and impudent fables, of which the theology of that time is principally composed.³⁶ These miserable stories were widely circulated, and were valued as solid and important truths. The more the literature was read, the more the stories were believed; in other words, the greater the learning, the greater the ignorance.³⁷ And I entertain no doubt, that if, in the seventh and eighth centuries, which were the worst part of that period,³⁸ all knowledge of the alphabet had for a while been lost, so that men could no longer read the books in which they delighted, the subsequent progress of Europe would have been more rapid than it really was. For when the progress began, its principal antagonist was that credulity which the literature had fostered. It was not that better books were wanting, but it was that the relish for such books was extinct. There was the literature of Greece and Rome, which the monks not only preserved, but even occasionally looked into and copied. But what could that avail such readers as they? So far from recognizing the merit of the ancient writers, they were unable to feel even the beauties of their style, and they trembled at the boldness of their inquiries. At the first glimpse of the light, their eyes were blinded.

---

³⁶ The statistics of this sort of literature would prove a curious subject for inquiry. No one, I believe, has thought it worth while to sum them up; but M. Guizot has made an estimate that the Bollandist collection contains more than twenty-five thousand lives of saints; 'à en juger par approximation, ils contiennent plus de 25,000 vies de saints.' *Guizot, Histoire de la Civilisation en France*, vol. ii. p. 32. It is said (*Ledwich's Antiquities of Ireland*, p. 62) that of St. Patrick alone there were sixty-six biographers before Jocelin.

³⁷ For, as Laplace observes, in his remarks on the sources of error in connexion with the doctrine of probabilities, 'C'est à l'influence de l'opinion de ceux que la multitude juge les plus instruits, et à qui elle a coutume de donner sa confiance sur les plus importants objets de la vie, qu'est due la propagation de ces erreurs qui, dans les temps d'ignorance, ont couvert la face du monde.' *Bouillaud, Philosophie Médicale*, p. 218.

³⁸ M. Guizot (*Civilisation en France*, vol. ii. pp. 171, 172) thinks that, on the whole, the seventh was even worse than the eighth; but it is difficult to choose between them.

They never turned the leaves of a pagan author without standing aghast at the risk they were running; and they were in constant fear, lest by imbibing any of his opinions, they should involve themselves in a deadly sin. The result was, that they willingly laid aside the great master-pieces of antiquity; and in their place they substituted those wretched compilations, which corrupted their taste, increased their credulity, strengthened their errors, and prolonged the ignorance of Europe, by embodying each separate superstition in a written and accessible form, thus perpetuating its influence, and enabling it to enfeeble the understanding even of a distant posterity.

It is in this way that the nature of the literature possessed by a people is of very inferior importance, in comparison with the disposition of the people by whom the literature is to be read. In what are rightly termed the Dark Ages, there was a literature in which valuable materials were to be found; but there was no one who knew how to use them. During a considerable period, the Latin language was a vernacular dialect;[39] and, if men had chosen, they might have studied the great Latin authors. But to do this, they must have been in a state of society very different from that in which they actually lived. They, like every other people, measured merit by the standard commonly received in their own age; and, according to their standard, the dross was better than the gold. They, therefore, rejected the gold, and hoarded up the dross. What took place then is, on a smaller scale, taking place now. Every literature contains something that is true, and much that is false; and the effect it produces will chiefly depend upon the skill with which the truth is discriminated from the falsehood. New ideas, and new discoveries, possess prospectively an importance difficult to exag-

---

[39] Some of the results of Latin being colloquially employed by the monks are judiciously stated in *Herder's Ideen zur Geschichte der Menschheit*, vol. iv. pp. 202, 203. The remarks on this custom by Dugald Stewart refer to a later period. *Stewart's Philosophy of the Mind*, vol. iii. pp. 110, 111.

gerate; but until the ideas are received, and the discoveries adopted, they exercise no influence, and, therefore, work no good. No literature can ever benefit a people, unless it finds them in a state of preliminary preparation. In this respect, the analogy with religious opinions is complete. If the religion and the literature of a country are unsuited to its wants, they will be useless, because the literature will be neglected, and the religion will be disobeyed. In such cases, even the ablest books are unread, and the purest doctrines despised. The works fall into oblivion; the faith is corrupted by heresy.

The other opinion to which I have referred is, that the civilization of Europe is chiefly owing to the ability which has been displayed by the different governments, and to the sagacity with which the evils of society have been palliated by legislative remedies. To any one who has studied history in its original sources, this notion must appear so extravagant, as to make it difficult to refute it with becoming gravity. Indeed, of all the social theories which have ever been broached, there is none so utterly untenable, and so unsound in all its parts, as this. In the first place, we have the obvious consideration, that the rulers of a country have, under ordinary circumstances, always been the inhabitants of that country; nurtured by its literature, bred to its traditions, and imbibing its prejudices. Such men are, at best, only the creatures of the age, never its creators. Their measures are the result of social progress, not the cause of it. This may be proved, not only by speculative arguments, but also by a practical consideration, which any reader of history can verify for himself. No great political improvement, no great reform, either legislative or executive, has ever been originated in any country by its rulers. The first suggesters of such steps have invariably been bold and able thinkers, who discern the abuse, denounce it, and point out how it is to be remedied. But long after this is done, even the most enlightened governments continue to uphold the abuse, and reject the remedy. At length, if circumstances are favourable, the pressure from without becomes so strong, that the government is obliged to give way; and, the reform being accomplished, the people are expected to admire the wisdom of their rulers, by whom all this has been done. That this is the course of political improvement, must be well known to whoever has studied the law-books of different countries in connexion with the previous progress of their knowledge. Full and decisive evidence of this will be brought forward in the present work; but, by way of illustration, I may refer to the abolition of the corn-laws, undoubtedly one of the most remarkable facts in the history of England during this century. The propriety, and, indeed, the necessity, of their abolition, is now admitted by every one of tolerable information; and the question arises, as to how it was brought about. Those Englishmen who are little versed in the history of their country will say, that the real cause was the wisdom of Parliament; while others, attempting to look a little further, will ascribe it to the activity of the Anti-Corn-Law League, and the consequent pressure put upon Government. But whoever will minutely trace the different stages through which this great question successively passed, will find, that the Government, the Legislature, and the League, were the unwitting instruments of a power far greater than all other powers put together. They were simply the exponents of that march of public opinion, which on this subject had begun nearly a century before their time. The steps of this vast movement I shall examine on another occasion; at present it is enough to say, that soon after the middle of the eighteenth century, the absurdity of protective restrictions on trade was so fully demonstrated by the political economists, as to be admitted by every man who understood their arguments, and had mastered the evidence connected with them. From this moment, the repeal of the corn-laws became a matter, not of party, nor of expediency, but merely of knowledge. Those who knew the facts, opposed the laws; those who were ignorant of the facts, favoured the laws. It was, therefore, clear, that whenever the diffusion of knowledge reached a certain point, the laws must fall. The merit of the League was, to assist this diffusion; the merit of the Parliament was, to yield to it. It is, however, certain, that the members both of League and Legislature could at best only slightly hasten what the progress of knowledge rendered inevitable. If they had lived a century earlier, they would have been altogether powerless, because the age would not have been ripe for their labours. They were the creatures of a movement which began long before any of them were born; and the utmost they could do was, to put into operation what others had taught, and repeat, in louder tones, the lessons they had learned from their masters. For, it was not pretended, they did not even pretend themselves, that there was anything new in the doctrines which they preached from the hustings, and disseminated in every part of the kingdom. The discoveries had long since been made, and were gradually doing their work; encroaching upon old errors, and making proselytes in all directions. The reformers of our time swam with the stream: they aided what it would have been impossible long to resist. Nor is this to be deemed a slight or grudging praise of the services they undoubtedly rendered. The opposition they had to encounter was still immense; and it should always be remembered, as a proof of the backwardness of political knowledge, and of the incompetence of political legislators, that although the principles of free trade had been established for nearly a century by a chain of arguments as solid as those on which the truths of mathematics are based, they were to the last moment strenuously resisted; and it was only with the greatest difficulty that Parliament was induced to grant what the people were determined to have, and the necessity of which had been proved by the ablest men during three successive generations.

I have selected this instance as an illustration, because the facts connected with it are undisputed, and, indeed, are fresh in the memory of us all. For it was not concealed at the time, and posterity ought to know, that this great measure, which, with the exception of the Reform Bill, is by far the most important ever passed by a British parliament, was, like the Reform Bill, extorted from the legislature by a pressure from without; that it was conceded, not cheerfully, but with fear; and that it was carried by statesmen who had spent their lives in opposing what they now suddenly advocated. Such was the history of these events; and such likewise has been the history of all those improvements which are important enough to rank as epochs in the history of modern legislation.

Besides this, there is another circumstance worthy the attention of those writers who ascribe a large part of European civilization to measures originated by European governments. This is, that every great reform which has been effected, has consisted, not in doing something new, but in undoing something old. The most valuable additions made to legislation have been enactments destructive of preceding legislation; and the best laws which have been passed, have been those by which some former laws were repealed. In the case just mentioned, of the corn-laws, all that was done was to repeal the old laws, and leave trade to its natural freedom. When this great reform was accomplished, the only result was, to place things on the same footing as if legislators had never interfered at all. Precisely the same remark is applicable to another leading improvement in modern legislation, namely, the decrease of religious persecution. This is unquestionably an immense boon; though, unfortunately, it is still imperfect, even in the most civilized countries. But it is evident that the concession merely consists in this: that legislators have retraced their own steps, and undone their own work. If we examine the policy of the most humane and enlightened governments, we shall find this to be the course they have pursued. The whole scope and tendency of modern legislation is, to restore things to that natural channel from which the ignorance of preceding legislation has driven them. This is one of the great works of the present age; and if legislators do it well, they will deserve the gratitude of mankind. But though we may thus be grateful to individual lawgivers, we owe no thanks to lawgivers, considered as a class. For since the most valuable improvements in legislation are those which subvert preceding legislation, it is clear that the balance of good cannot be on their side. It is clear, that the progress of civilization cannot be due to those who, on the most important subjects, have done so much harm, that their successors are considered benefactors, simply because they reverse their policy, and thus restore affairs to the state in which they would have remained, if politicians had allowed them to run on in the course which the wants of society required.

Indeed, the extent to which the governing classes have interfered, and the mischiefs which that interference has produced, are so remarkable, as to make thoughtful men wonder how civilization could advance, in the face of such repeated obstacles. In some of the European countries, the obstacles have, in fact, proved insuperable, and the national progress is thereby stopped. Even in England, where, from causes which I shall presently relate, the higher ranks have for some centuries been less powerful than elsewhere, there has been inflicted an amount of evil, which, though much smaller than that incurred in other countries, is sufficiently serious to form a melancholy chapter in the history of the human mind. To sum up these evils would be to write a history of English legislation; for it may be broadly stated, that, with the exception of certain necessary enactments respecting the preservation of order, and the punishment of crime, nearly everything which has been done, has been done amiss. Thus, to take only such conspicuous facts as do not admit of controversy, it is certain that all the most important interests have been grievously damaged by the attempts of legislators to aid them. Among the accessories of modern civilization, there is none of greater moment than trade, the spread of which has probably done more than any other single agent to increase the comfort and happiness of man. But every European government which has legislated respecting trade, has acted as if its main object were to suppress the trade, and ruin the traders. Instead of leaving the national industry to take its own course, it has been troubled by an interminable series of regulations, all intended for its good, and all inflicting serious harm. To such a height has this been carried, that the commercial reforms which have distinguished England during the last twenty years, have solely consisted in undoing this mischievous and intrusive legislation. The laws formerly enacted on this subject, and too many of which are still in force, are marvellous to contemplate. It is no exaggeration to say, that the history of the commercial legislation of Europe presents every possible contrivance for hampering the energies of commerce. Indeed, a very high authority, who has maturely studied this subject, has recently declared, that if it had not been for smuggling, trade could not have been conducted, but must have perished, in consequence of this incessant interference.[40] However paradoxical this assertion may appear, it will be denied by no one who knows how feeble trade once was, and how strong the obstacles were which opposed it. In every quarter, and at every moment, the hand of government was felt. Duties on importation, and duties on exportation; bounties to raise up a losing trade, and taxes to pull down a remunerative one; this branch of industry forbidden, and that branch of industry encouraged; one article of commerce must not be grown, because it was grown in the colonies; another article might be grown and bought, but not sold again, while a third article might be bought and sold, but not leave the country. Then, too, we find laws to regulate wages; laws to regulate prices; laws to regulate profits; laws to regulate the interest of money; custom-house arrangements of the most vexatious

---

[40] 'C'est à la contrebande que le commerce doit de n'avoir pas péri sous l'influence du régime prohibitif; tandis que ce régime condamnait les peuples à s'approvisionner aux sources les plus éloignées, la contrebande rapprochait les distances, abaissait les prix, et neutralisait l'action funeste des monopoles.' *Blanqui, Histoire de l'Economie Politique en Europe*, Paris, 1845, vol. ii. pp. 25, 26.

kind, aided by a complicated scheme, which was well
called the sliding-scale,—a scheme of such perverse
ingenuity, that the duties constantly varied on the
same article, and no man could calculate beforehand
what he would have to pay. To this uncertainty, itself
the bane of all commerce, there was added a severity of
exaction, felt by every class of consumers and producers.
The tolls were so onerous, as to double and often quad-
ruple the cost of production. A system was organized,
and strictly enforced, of interference with markets,
interference with manufactories, interference with
machinery, interference even with shops. The towns
were guarded by excisemen, and the ports swarmed
with tide-waiters, whose sole business was to inspect
nearly every process of domestic industry, peer into
every package, and tax every article; while, that absurdity might be carried to its extreme height, a large
part of all this was by way of protection: that is to
say, the money was avowedly raised, and the inconvenience suffered, not for the use of the government,
but for the benefit of the people; in other words, the
industrious classes were robbed, in order that industry
might thrive.

Such are some of the benefits which European trade
owes to the paternal care of European legislators. But
worse still remains behind. For the economical evils,
great as they were, have been far surpassed by the
moral evils which this system produced. The first
inevitable consequence was, that, in every part of
Europe, there arose numerous and powerful gangs of
armed smugglers, who lived by disobeying the laws
which their ignorant rulers had imposed. These men,
desperate from the fear of punishment,[41] and accus-

---

[41] The 19 Geo. II. c. 34, made 'all forcible acts of smuggling, carried on in defiance of the laws, or *even in disguise to evade them*, felony without benefit of clergy.' *Blackstone's Commentaries*, vol. iv. p. 155. Townsend, who travelled through France in 1786, says, that when any of the numerous smugglers were taken, 'some of them are hanged, some are broken upon the wheel, and some are burnt alive.' *Townsend's Spain*, vol. i. p. 85, edit. 1792. On the general operation of the French laws against

tomed to the commission of every crime, contaminated the surrounding population; introduced into peaceful villages vices formerly unknown; caused the ruin of entire families; spread, wherever they came, drunkenness, theft, and dissoluteness; and familiarized their associates with those coarse and swinish debaucheries which were the natural habits of so vagrant and lawless a life.[42] The innumerable crimes arising from this,[43] are directly chargeable upon the European governments by whom they were provoked. The offences were caused by the laws; and now that the laws are repealed, the offences have disappeared. But it will hardly be pretended, that the interests of civilization have been advanced by such a policy as this. It will

---

[42] smugglers in the eighteenth century, compare *Tucker's Life of Jefferson*, vol. i. pp. 213, 214, with *Parliamentary History*, vol. ix. p. 1240.

[43] In a work of considerable ability, the following account is given of the state of things in England and France so late as the year 1824: 'While this was going forward on the English coast, the smugglers on the opposite shore were engaged, with much more labour, risk, and expense, in introducing English woollens, by a vast system of fraud and lying, into the towns, past a series of custom-houses. In both countries, there was an utter dissoluteness of morals connected with these transactions. Cheating and lying were essential to the whole system; drunkenness accompanied it; contempt for all law grew up under it; honest industry perished beneath it; and it was crowned with murder.' *Martineau's History of England during Thirty Years' Peace*, vol. i. p. 341, 8vo. 1849.

[a] For evidence of the extraordinary extent to which smuggling was formerly carried, and that not secretly, but by powerful bodies of armed men, see *Parliamentary History*, vol. ix. pp. 243, 247, 1290, 1345, vol. x. pp. 394, 405, 530, 532, vol. xi. p. 935. And on the number of persons engaged in it, compare *Tomline's Life of Pitt*, vol. i. p. 359: see also *Sinclair's History of the Public Revenue*, vol. iii. p. 232; *Otter's Life of Clarke*, vol. i. p. 391. In France, the evil was equally great. M. Lemontey says, that early in the eighteenth century, 'la contrebande devenait une profession ouverte, et des compagnies de cavalerie désertèrent tout entières leurs étendards pour suivre contre le fisc cette guerre populaire.' Lemontey, *Essai sur l'Etablissement monarchique de Louis XIV*, p. 430. According to Townsend, there were, in 1780, 'more than 1500 smugglers in the Pyrenees.' *Townsend's Journey through Spain*, vol. i. p. 84.

hardly be pretended, that we owe much to a system which, having called into existence a new class of criminals, at length retraces its steps; and, though it thus puts an end to the crime, only destroys what its own acts had created.

It is unnecessary to say, that these remarks do not affect the real services rendered to society by every tolerably organized government. In all countries, a power of punishing crime, and of framing laws, must reside somewhere; otherwise the nation is in a state of anarchy. But the accusation which the historian is bound to bring against every government which has hitherto existed is, that it has overstepped its proper functions, and, at each step, has done incalculable harm. The love of exercising power has been found to be so universal, that no class of men who have possessed authority have been able to avoid abusing it. To maintain order, to prevent the strong from oppressing the weak, and to adopt certain precautions respecting the public health, are the only services which any government can render to the interests of civilization. That these are services of immense value, no one will deny; but it cannot be said, that by them civilization is advanced, or the progress of Man accelerated. All that is done is, to afford the opportunity of progress; the progress itself must depend upon other matters. And that this is the sound view of legislation, is, moreover, evident from the fact, that as knowledge is becoming more diffused, and as an increasing experience is enabling each successive generation better to understand the complicated relations of life; just in the same proportion are men insisting upon the repeal of those protective laws, the enactment of which was deemed by politicians to be the greatest triumph of political foresight.

Seeing, therefore, that the efforts of government in favour of civilization are, when most successful, altogether negative; and seeing too, that when those efforts are more than negative, they become injurious,—it clearly follows, that all speculations must be erroneous which ascribe the progress of Europe to the wisdom of its rulers. This is an inference which rests not only on the arguments already adduced, but on facts which might be multiplied from every page of history. For no government having recognized its proper limits, the result is, that every government has inflicted on its subjects great injuries; and has done this nearly always with the best intentions. The effects of its protective policy in injuring trade, and, what is far worse, in increasing crime, have just been noticed; and to these instances, innumerable others might be added. Thus, during many centuries, every government thought it was its bounden duty to encourage religious truth, and discourage religious error. The mischief this has produced is incalculable. Putting aside all other considerations, it is enough to mention its two leading consequences; which are, the increase of hypocrisy, and the increase of perjury. The increase of hypocrisy is the inevitable result of connecting any description of penalty with the profession of particular opinions. Whatever may be the case with individuals, it is certain that the majority of men find an extreme difficulty in long resisting constant temptation. And when the temptation comes to them in the shape of honour and emolument, they are too often ready to profess the dominant opinions, and abandon, not indeed their belief, but the external marks by which that belief is made public. Every man who takes this step is a hypocrite; and every government which encourages this step to be taken, is an abettor of hypocrisy and a creator of hypocrites. Well, therefore, may we say, that when a government holds out as a bait, that those who profess certain opinions shall enjoy certain privileges, it plays the part of the tempter of old, and, like the Evil One, basely offers the good things of this world to him who will change his worship and deny his faith. At the same time, and as a part of this system, the increase of perjury has accompanied the increase of hypocrisy. For legislators, plainly seeing that proselytes thus obtained could not be relied upon, have met the danger by the most extraordinary precautions; and compelling men to confirm their belief by repeated oaths, have thus sought to protect the old creed against the new converts. It is this suspicion as to the motives of others, which has given rise to oaths of every kind and in every direction. In England, even the boy at college is forced to swear about matters which he cannot understand, and which far riper minds are unable to master. If he afterwards goes into Parliament, he must again swear about his religion; and at nearly every stage of political life he must take fresh oaths; the solemnity of which is often strangely contrasted with the trivial functions to which they are the prelude. A solemn adjuration of the Deity being thus made at every turn, it has happened, as might have been expected, that oaths, enjoined as a matter of course, have at length degenerated into a matter of form. What is lightly taken, is easily broken. And the best observers of English society,—observers too whose characters are very different, and who hold the most opposite opinions,—are all agreed on this, that the perjury habitually practised in England, and of which government is the immediate creator, is so general, that it has become a source of national corruption, has diminished the value of human testimony, and shaken the confidence which men naturally place in the word of their fellow-creatures.⁴⁴

The open vices, and, what is much more dangerous,

---

⁴⁴ Archbishop Whately says, what hardly any thinking man will now deny, 'If oaths were abolished—leaving the penalties for false witness (no unimportant part of our security) unaltered—I am convinced that, on the whole, testimony would be more trustworthy than it is.' *Whately's Elements of Rhetoric*, 8vo. 1850, p. 47. See also on the amount of perjury caused by English legislation, *Jeremy Bentham's Works*, edit. Bowring, vol. ii. p. 210, vol. v. pp. 191-229, 454-466, vol. vi. pp. 314, 315; *Orme's Life of Owen*, p. 195; *Locke's Works*, vol. iv. p. 6; *Berkeley's Works*, vol. ii. p. 196; *Whiston's Memoirs*, pp. 83, 411-413; *Hamilton's Discussions on Philosophy and Literature*, pp. 454, 522, 527, 528. Sir W. Hamilton sums up: 'But if the perjury of England stands pre-eminent in the world, the perjury of the English Universities, and of Oxford in particular, stands pre-eminent in England.' p. 528. Compare *Priestley's Memoirs*, vol. i. p. 374 and *Baker's Life of Sir Thomas Bernard*, 1819, pp. 188, 189.

the hidden corruption, thus generated in the midst of society by the ignorant interference of Christian rulers, is indeed a painful subject; but it is one which I could not omit in an analysis of the causes of civilization. It would be easy to push the inquiry still further, and to show how legislators, in every attempt they have made to protect some particular interests, and uphold some particular principles, have not only failed, but have brought about results diametrically opposite to those which they proposed. We have seen that their laws in favour of industry have injured industry; that their laws in favour of religion have increased hypocrisy; and that their laws to secure truth have encouraged perjury. Exactly in the same way, nearly every country has taken steps to prevent usury, and keep down the interest of money; and the invariable effect has been to increase usury, and raise the interest of money. For, since no prohibition, however stringent, can destroy the natural relation between demand and supply, it has followed, that when some men want to borrow, and other men want to lend, both parties are sure to find means of evading a law which interferes with their mutual rights.[44] If the two parties were left to adjust their own bargain undisturbed, the usury would depend on the circumstances of the loan; such as the amount of security, and the chance of repayment. But this natural arrangement has been complicated by the interference of government.[45] A certain risk being always

---

[44] 'L'observation rigoureuse de ces loix seroit destructive de tout commerce; aussi ne sont-elles pas observées rigoureusement.' *Mémoires sur les Prêts d'Argent*, sec. xiv., in *Œuvres de Turgot*, vol. v. pp. 278, 279. Compare *Ricardo's Works*, pp. 178, 179, with *Condorcet, Vie de Turgot*, pp. 53, 54, 228.

[45] Aided by the church. Ecclesiastical councils contain numerous regulations against usury; and, in 1179, Pope Alexander ordered that usurers were not to be buried: 'Quia in omnibus ferè locis crimen usurarum invaluit; ut multi negotiis prætermissis quasi licitè usuras exerceant; et qualiter utriusque testamenti pagina condemnetur, non attendunt: ideò constituimus, ut usurarii manifesti nec ad communionem recipiantur altaris, nec Christianam, si in hoc peccato decesserint, accipiant sepulturam, sed nec oblationem eorum quisquam

incurred by those who disobey the law, the usurer, very properly, refuses to lend his money unless he is also compensated for the danger he is in from the penalty hanging over him. This compensation can only be made by the borrower, who is thus obliged to pay what in reality is a double interest: one interest for the natural risk on the loan, and another interest for the extra risk from the law. Such, then, is the position in which every European legislature has placed itself. By enactments against usury, it has increased what it wished to destroy; it has passed laws, which the imperative necessities of men compel them to violate; while, to wind up the whole, the penalty for such violation falls on the borrowers; that is, on the very class in whose favour the legislators interfered.[47]

In the same meddling spirit, and with the same mistaken notions of protection, the great Christian governments have done other things still more injurious. They have made strenuous and repeated efforts to destroy the liberty of the press, and prevent men from expressing their sentiments on the most important questions in politics and religion. In nearly every country, they, with the aid of the church, have organized a vast system of literary police; the sole object of which is, to abrogate the undoubted right of every citizen to lay his opinions before his fellow-citizens. In the very few countries where they have stopped short of these extreme steps, they have had recourse to others less violent, but equally unwarrantable. For even where they have not openly forbidden the free dissemination

---

accipist.' *Rog. de Hoved. Annal. in Rerum Anglicarum Scriptores post Bedam*, p. 335, Lond. 1596, folio. In Spain, the Inquisition took cognizance of usury. See Llorente, *Histoire de l'Inquisition*, vol. i. p. 339. Compare *Ledwich's Antiquities of Ireland*, p. 133.

[47] The whole subject of the usury laws has been treated by Bentham in so complete and exhaustive a manner, that I cannot do better than refer the reader to his admirable 'Letters.' A part only of the question is discussed, and that very imperfectly, in *Rey's Science Sociale*, vol. iii. pp. 61, 65. On the necessity of usury to mitigate the effects of a commercial panic, see *Mill's Principles of Political Economy*, vol. ii. p. 185.

of knowledge, they have done all that they could to check it. On all the implements of knowledge, and on all the means by which it is diffused, such as paper, books, political journals, and the like, they have imposed duties so heavy, that they could hardly have done worse if they had been the sworn advocates of popular ignorance. Indeed, looking at what they have actually accomplished, it may be emphatically said, that they have taxed the human mind. They have made the very thoughts of men pay toll. Whoever wishes to communicate his ideas to others, and thus do what he can to increase the stock of our acquirements, must first pour his contributions into the imperial exchequer. That is the penalty inflicted on him for instructing his fellow-creatures. That is the blackmail which government extorts from literature; and on receipt of which it accords its favour, and agrees to abstain from further demands. And what causes all this to be the more insufferable, is the use which is made of these and similar exactions, wrung from every kind of industry, both bodily and mental. It is truly a frightful consideration, that knowledge is to be hindered, and that the proceeds of honest labour, of patient thought, and sometimes of profound genius, are to be diminished, in order that a large part of their scanty earnings may go to swell the pomp of an idle and ignorant court, minister to the caprice of a few powerful individuals, and too often supply them with the means of turning against the people resources which the people called into existence.

These, and the foregoing statements, respecting the effects produced on European society by political legislation, are not doubtful or hypothetical inferences, but are such as every reader of history may verify for himself. Indeed, some of them are still acting in England; and, in one country or another, the whole of them may be seen in full force. When put together, they compose an aggregate so formidable, that we may well wonder how, in the face of them, civilization has been able to advance. That, under such circumstances, it has advanced, is a decisive proof of the extraordinary energy of Man; and justifies a confident belief, that as the pressure

of legislation is diminished, and the human mind less
hampered, the progress will continue with accelerated
speed. But it is absurd, it would be a mockery of all
sound reasoning, to ascribe to legislation any share in
the progress ; or to expect any benefit from future legislators, except that sort of benefit which consists in undoing the work of their predecessors. This is what the
present generation claims at their hands ; and it should
be remembered that what one generation solicits as a
boon, the next generation demands as a right. And,
when the right is pertinaciously refused, one of two
things has always happened : either the nation has re-
trograded, or else the people have risen. Should the
government remain firm, this is the cruel dilemma in
which men are placed. If they submit, they injure
their country ; if they rebel, they may injure it still
more. In the ancient monarchies of the East, their
usual plan was to yield ; in the monarchies of Europe,
it has been to resist. Hence those insurrections and
rebellions which occupy so large a space in modern
history, and which are but repetitions of the old story,
the undying struggle between oppressors and oppressed.
It would, however, be unjust to deny, that in one
country the fatal crisis has now for several generations
been successfully averted. In one European country,
and in one alone, the people have been so strong and
the government so weak, that the history of legislation,
taken as a whole, is, notwithstanding a few aberrations,
the history of slow, but constant concession : reforms
which would have been refused to argument, have been
yielded from fear ; while from the steady increase of
democratic opinions, protection after protection, and
privilege after privilege, have, even in our time, been
torn away ; until the old institutions, though they
retain their former name, have lost their former vigour,
and there no longer remains a doubt as to what their
fate must ultimately be. Nor need we add, that in this
same country, where, more than in any other of Europe,
legislators are the exponents and the servants of the
popular will, the progress has, on this account, been
more undeviating than elsewhere ; there has been

neither anarchy nor revolution; and the world has been made familiar with the great truth, that one main condition of the prosperity of a people is, that its rulers shall have very little power, that they shall exercise that power very sparingly, and that they shall by no means presume to raise themselves into supreme judges of the national interests, or deem themselves authorized to defeat the wishes of those for whose benefit alone they occupy the post entrusted to them.

CHAPTER VI.

ORIGIN OF HISTORY, AND STATE OF HISTORICAL LITERATURE DURING THE MIDDLE AGES.

I HAVE now laid before the reader an examination of those conspicuous circumstances to which the progress of civilization is commonly ascribed; and I have proved that such circumstances, so far from being the cause of civilization, are at best only its effects; and that although religion, literature, and legislation do, undoubtedly, modify the condition of mankind, they are still more modified by it. Indeed, as we have clearly seen, they, even in their most favourable position, can be but secondary agents; because, however beneficial their apparent influence may be, they are themselves the product of preceding changes, and their results will vary according to the variations of the society on which they work.

It is thus that, by each successive analysis, the field of the present inquiry has been narrowed, until we have found reason to believe that the growth of European civilization is solely due to the progress of knowledge, and that the progress of knowledge depends on the number of truths which the human intellect discovers, and on the extent to which they are diffused. In support of this proposition, I have, as yet, only brought forward such general arguments as establish a very strong probability; which, to raise to a certainty, will require an appeal to history in the widest sense of the term. Thus to verify speculative conclusions by an exhaustive enumeration of the most important particular facts, is the task which I purpose to execute so far as my powers will allow; and in the preceding chapter I have briefly stated the method according to which the investigation will be conducted. Besides this, it has appeared to me that the principles which I have laid down may also be tested by a mode of proceeding which I have not yet mentioned, but which is intimately connected with the subject now before us. This is, to incorporate with an inquiry into the progress of the history of Man, another inquiry into the progress of History itself. By this means, great light will be thrown on the movements of society; since there must always be a connexion between the way in which men contemplate the past, and the way in which they contemplate the present; both views being in fact different forms of the same habits of thought, and therefore presenting, in each age, a certain sympathy and correspondence with each other. It will, moreover, be found, that such an inquiry into what I call the history of history, will establish two leading facts of considerable value. The first fact is, that during the last three centuries, historians, taken as a class, have shown a constantly increasing respect for the human intellect, and an aversion for those innumerable contrivances by which it was formerly shackled. The second fact is, that during the same period, they have displayed a growing tendency to neglect matters once deemed of paramount importance, and have been more willing to attend to subjects connected with the condition of the people and the diffusion of knowledge. These two facts will be decisively established in the present Introduction; and it must be admitted, that their existence corroborates the principles which I have propounded. If it can be ascertained, that as society has improved, historical literature has constantly tended in one given direction, there arises a very strong probability in favour of the truth of those views towards which it is manifestly approaching. Indeed, it is a probability of this sort which makes it so important for the student of any particular science to be acquainted with its history; because there is always a fair presumption that when general knowledge is advancing, any single department of it, if studied by competent men, is also advancing, even when the results may have been so small as to seem unworthy of attention. Hence it becomes highly important to observe the way in which, during successive ages, historians have shifted their ground; since we shall find that such changes have in the long-run always pointed to the same quarter, and are, in reality, only part of that vast movement by which the human intellect, with infinite difficulty, has vindicated its own rights, and slowly emancipated itself from those inveterate prejudices which long impeded its action.

With a view to these considerations, it seems advisable that, when examining the different civilizations into which the great countries of Europe have diverged, I should also give an account of the way in which history has been commonly written in each country. In the employment of this resource, I shall be mainly guided by a desire to illustrate the intimate connexion between the actual condition of a people and their opinions respecting the past; and, in order to keep this connexion in sight, I shall treat the state of historical literature, not as a separate subject, but as forming part of the intellectual history of each nation. The present volume will contain a view of the principal characteristics of French civilization until the great Revolution; and with that there will be incorporated an account of the French historians, and of the remarkable improvements they introduced into their own departments of knowledge. The relation which these improvements bore to the state of society from which they proceeded, is very striking, and will be examined at some length; while, in the next volume, the civilization and the historical literature of the other leading countries will be treated in a similar manner. Before, however, entering into these different subjects, it has occurred to me, that a preliminary inquiry into the origin of European history would be interesting, as supplying information respecting matters which are little known, and also as enabling the reader to understand the extreme difficulty with which history has reached its present advanced, but still very imperfect, state. The materials for studying the earliest condition of Europe have long since perished; but the extensive information we now possess concerning barbarous nations will supply us with a useful resource, because they have all much in common; the opinions of extreme ignorance being, indeed, every where the same, except when modified by the differences which nature presents in various countries. I have, therefore, no hesitation in employing the evidence which has been collected by competent travellers, and drawing inferences from it respecting that period of the European mind, of which we have no direct knowledge. Such conclusions will, of course, be speculative; but, during the last thousand years, we are quite independent of them, inasmuch as every great country has had chroniclers of its own since the ninth century, while the French have an uninterrupted series since the sixth century. In the present chapter, I intend to give specimens of the way in which, until the sixteenth century, history was habitually written by the highest European authorities. Its subsequent improvement during the seventeenth and eighteenth centuries, will be related under the separate heads of the countries where the progress was made; and as history, previous to the improvement, was little else than a tissue of the grossest errors, I will, in the first place, examine the leading causes of its universal corruption, and indicate the steps by which it was so disfigured that, during several centuries, Europe did not possess a single man who had critically studied the past, or who was even able to record with tolerable accuracy the events of his own time.

At a very early period in the progress of a people, and long before they are acquainted with the use of letters, they feel the want of some resource, which in peace may amuse their leisure, and in war may stimulate their courage. This is supplied to them by the invention of ballads; which form the groundwork of all historical knowledge, and which, in one shape or another, are found among some of the rudest tribes of the earth. They are, for the most part, sung by a class of men whose particular business it is thus to preserve the stock of traditions. Indeed, so natural is this curiosity as to past events, that there are few nations to whom these bards or minstrels are unknown. Thus, to select a few instances, it is they who have preserved the popular traditions, not only of Europe,[1] but also of China, Tibet, and Tartary;[2] likewise of India,[3] of Scinde,[4] of Belochistan,[5] of Western Asia,[6] of the islands

---

[1] For an account of the ancient bards of Gaul, see the *Benedictine Hist. Lit. de la France*, vol. i. part i. pp. 25-28. Those of Scotland are noticed in *Barry's Hist. of the Orkney Islands*, p. 89; and for a modern instance in the island of Col, near Mull, see *Otter's Life of Clarke*, vol. i. p. 307. As to the Irish bards in the seventh century, see *Sharon Turner's Hist. of England*, vol. iii. p. 571. Spenser's account of them in the sixteenth century (*Somers Tracts*, vol. i. pp. 590, 591) shows that the order was then falling into contempt; and in the seventeenth century this is confirmed by Sir William Temple; *Essay on Poetry*, in *Temple's Works*, vol. iii. pp. 431, 432. But it was not till the eighteenth century that they became extinct; for Mr. Prior (*Life of Goldsmith*, vol. i. pp. 36, 57) says, that Carolan, 'the last of the ancient Irish bards,' died in 1738. Without them the memory of many events would have been entirely lost; since, even at the end of the seventeenth century, there being no registers in Ireland, the ordinary means of recording facts were so little known, that parents often took the precaution of having the names and ages of children marked on their arms with gunpowder. See *Kirkman's Memoirs of Charles Macklin*, 8vo. 1799,

vol. i. pp. 144, 145, a curious book. Compare, respecting Carolan, *Nichols's Illustrations of the Eighteenth Century*, vol. vii. pp. 688-694.

[2] On these Toolholos, as they are called, see *Huc's Travels in Tartary, Thibet, and China*, vol. i. pp. 65-67. Huc says, p. 67, 'These poet-singers, who remind us of the minstrels and rhapsodists of Greece, are also very numerous in China; but they are, probably, no where so numerous or so popular as in Thibet.'

[3] On the bards of the Deccan, see *Wilks's History of the South of India*, 4to. 1810, vol. i. pp. 20, 21, and *Transac. of the Bombay Soc.* vol. i. p. 162. For those of other parts of India, see *Heber's Journey*, vol. ii. pp. 452-455; *Burnes on the North-west Frontier of India*, in *Journal of Geog. Soc.* vol. iv. pp. 110, 111; *Prinsep*, in *Journal of Asiat. Soc.* vol. viii. p. 395; *Forbes's Oriental Memoirs*, vol. i. pp. 376, 377, 543; and *Asiatic Researches*, vol. ix. p. 78. They are mentioned in the oldest Veda, which is also the oldest of all the Indian books. See *Rig Veda Sanhita*, vol. i. p. 158.

[4] See *Burton's Sindh*, p. 56, 8vo. 1851.

[5] *Burton's Sindh*, p. 59.

[6] *Burnes's Travels into Bokhara*, 8vo. 1834, vol. ii. pp. 107, 115, 116.

of the Black Sea,[7] of Egypt,[8] of Western Africa,[9] of North America,[10] of South America,[11] and of the islands in the Pacific.[12]

In all these countries, letters were long unknown; and, as a people in that state have no means of perpetuating their history except by oral tradition, they select the form best calculated to assist their memory; and it will, I believe, be found that the first rudiments of knowledge consist always of poetry, and often of rhyme.[13] The jingle pleases the ear of the barbarian, and affords a security that he will hand it down to his children in the unimpaired state in which he received it.[14] This

---

[7] *Clarke's Travels*, 8vo. 1816, vol. ii. p. 101.

[8] Compare *Wilkinson's Ancient Egyptians*, vol. ii. p. 304, with *Bunsen's Egypt*, vol. i. p. 96, vol. ii. p. 92.

[9] I have mislaid my note on the bards of Western Africa, and can only refer to a hasty notice in *Mungo Park's Travels*, vol. i. p. 70. 8vo. 1817.

[10] *Buchanan's Sketches of the North-American Indians*, p. 337.

[11] *Prescott's History of Peru*, vol. i. pp. 31, 32, 117.

[12] *Ellis, Polynesian Researches*, vol. i. pp. 85, 109, 411; *Ellis, Tour through Hawaii*, p. 91. Compare *Cook's Voyages*, vol. v. p. 237, with *Beechey's Voyage to the Pacific*, vol. ii. p. 106. Some of these ballads have been collected, but, I believe, not published. See *Cheever's Sandwich Islands*, 8vo. 1851, p. 181.

[13] It is a singular proof of the carelessness with which the history of barbarous nations has been studied, that authors constantly assert rhyme to be a comparatively recent contrivance; and even Pinkerton, writing to Laing in 1799, says, 'Rhyme was not known in Europe till about the ninth century.' *Pinkerton's Literary Correspondence*, vol. ii. p. 92. The truth is, that rhyme was not only known to the ancient Greeks and Romans, but was used, long before the date Pinkerton mentions, by the Anglo-Saxons, by the Irish, by the Welsh, and, I believe, by the Bretons. See *Mure's Hist. of the Literature of Greece*, vol. ii. p. 113; *Hallam's Lit. of Europe*, vol. i. p. 31; *Villemarqué, Chants Populaires de la Bretagne*, vol. i pp. lviii. lix. compared with *Sue vêtre, les Derniers Bretons*, p. 143; *Turner's Hist. of England*, vol. iii. pp. 383. 643, vol. vii. pp. 324, 328, 330. Rhyme is also used by the Fantees (*Bowdich, Mission to Ashantee*, p. 368); by the Persians (*Transac. of Bombay Soc.* vol. ii. p. 82); by the Chinese (*Transac. of Asiatic Soc.* vol. ii. pp. 407, 409, and *Davis's Chinese*, vol. ii. p. 269); by the Malays (*Asiatic Researches*, vol. x. pp. 176, 196); by the Javanese (*Crawfurd's Hist. of the Indian Archipelago*, vol. ii. pp. 19, 20); and by the Siamese (*Transac. of Asiatic Soc.* vol. iii. p. 299).

[14] The habit thus acquired,

guarantee against error increases still further the value of these ballads; and instead of being considered as a mere amusement, they rise to the dignity of judicial authorities.[14] The allusions contained in them, are satisfactory proofs to decide the merits of rival families, or even to fix the limits of those rude estates which such a society can possess. We therefore find, that the professed reciters and composers of these songs are the recognized judges in all disputed matters; and as they are often priests, and believed to be inspired, it is probably in this way that the notion of the divine origin of poetry first arose.[15] These ballads will, of course, vary, according to

long survives the circumstances which made it necessary. During many centuries, the love of versification was so widely diffused, that works in rhyme were composed on nearly all subjects, even in Europe; and this practice, which marks the ascendency of the imagination, is, as I have shown, a characteristic of the great Indian civilization, where the understanding was always in abeyance. On early French historians who wrote in rhyme, see *Monteil, Hist. des divers Etats*, vol. vi. p. 147. Montucla (*Hist. des Mathémat.* vol. i. p. 506) mentions a mathematical treatise, written in the thirteenth century, 'en vers techniques.' Compare the remarks of Matter (*Hist. de l'Ecole d'Alexandrie*, vol. ii. pp. 179-183) on the scientific poetry of Aratus; and on that of Hygin. p. 260. Thus, too, we find an Anglo-Norman writing 'the Institutes of Justinian in verse;' *Turner's Hist. of England*, vol. vii. p. 307: and a Polish historian composing 'his numerous works on genealogy and heraldry mostly in rhyme.' *Talvi's Language and Literature of the Slavic Nations*, 8vo. 1850, p. 246.

Compare *Origines du Droit Français*, in *Œuvres de Michelet*, vol. ii. p. 310.

[15] Mr. Ellis, a missionary in the South-Sea Islands, says of the inhabitants, 'Their traditionary ballads were a kind of standard, or classical authority, to which they referred for the purpose of determining any disputed fact in their history.' And when doubts arose, 'as they had no records to which they could at such times refer, they could only oppose one oral tradition to another; which unavoidably involved the parties in protracted, and often obstinate debates.' *Ellis, Polynesian Researches*, vol. i. pp. 202, 203. Compare *Elphinstone's Hist. of India*, p. 66; *Laing's Heimskringla*, 8vo. 1844, vol. i. pp. 50, 51; *Twell's Life of Pocock*, edit. 1816, p. 143.

[16] The inspiration of poetry is sometimes explained by its spontaneousness (*Cousin, Hist. de la Philosophie*, IIe série, vol. i. pp. 135, 136); and there can be no doubt that one cause of the reverence felt for great poets, is the necessity they seem to experience of pouring out their thoughts without reference to

the customs and temperaments of the different nations, and according to the climate to which they are accustomed. In the south they assume a passionate and voluptuous form; in the north they are rather remarkable for their tragic and warlike character.[17] But, notwithstanding these diversities, all such productions have one feature in common. They are not only founded on truth, but making allowance for the colourings of poetry, they are all strictly true. Men who are constantly repeating songs which they constantly hear, and who appeal to the authorized singers of them as final umpires in disputed questions, are not likely to be mistaken on matters, in the accuracy of which they have so lively an interest.[18]

This is the earliest, and most simple, of the various stages through which history is obliged to pass. But,

---

their own wishes. Still, it will, I believe, be found, that the notion of poetry being a divine art is most rife in those states of society in which knowledge is monopolised by the bards, and in which the bards are both priests and historians. On this combination of pursuits, compare a note in *Malcolm's Hist. of Persia*, vol. i. p. 90, with *Mure's Hist. of the Lit. of Greece*, vol. i. p. 148, vol. ii. p. 228, and *Petrie's* learned work, *Ecclesiastical Architecture of Ireland*, Dublin, 1845, p. 354. For evidence of the great respect paid to bards, see *Mallet's Northern Antiquities*, pp. 234–236; *Wheaton's Hist. of the Northmen*, pp. 50, 51; *Wright's Biog. Brit. Lit.* vol. i. p. 3; *Warton's Hist. of English Poetry*, 1840 vol. i. pp. xxvi, xl.; *Grote's Hist of Greece*, vol. ii. p. 182, 1st edit.; and on their important duties, see the laws of Moelmund, Villemarqué, *Chants Populaires de la Bretagne*, 1846, vol. i. pp. v. and vi.; *Thirlwall's Hist. of Greece*, vol. i. p. 229; and *Origines du Droit*, in *Œuvres de Michelet*, vol. ii. p. 372.

[17] *Villemarqué, Chants Populaires*, vol. i. p. lv.

[18] As to the general accuracy of the early ballads, which has been rashly attacked by several writers, and among others by Sir Walter Scott, see *Villemarqué, Chants Populaires*, vol. i. pp. xxv.-xxxi., and *Talvi's Slavic Nations*, p. 150. On the tenacity of oral tradition, compare *Niebuhr's History of Rome*, 1847, vol. i. p. 230, with *Laing's Denmark*, pp. 197, 198, 350; *Wheaton's Hist. of the Northmen*, pp. 38, 39, 57–59. Another curious illustration of this is, that several barbarous nations continue to repeat the old traditions in the old words, for so many generations, that at length the very language becomes unintelligible to the majority of those who recite them. See *Mariner's Account of the Tonga Islands*, vol. i. p. 158, vol. ii. p. 217, and *Catlin's North American Indians*, vol. i. p. 126.

in the course of time, unless unfavourable circumstances intervene, society advances, and, among other changes, there is one in particular of the greatest importance: I mean the introduction of the art of writing, which, before many generations are passed, must effect a complete alteration in the character of the national traditions. The manner in which this occurs has, so far as I am aware, never been pointed out; and it will, therefore, be interesting to attempt to trace some of its details.

The first, and perhaps the most obvious consideration, is that the introduction of the art of writing gives permanence to the national knowledge, and thus lessens the utility of that oral information, in which all the acquirements of an unlettered people must be contained. Hence it is, that as a country advances, the influence of tradition diminishes, and traditions themselves become less trustworthy.[19] Besides this, the preservers of these traditions lose, in this stage of society, much of their former reputation. Among a perfectly unlettered people, the singers of ballads are, as we have already seen, the sole depositories of those historical facts on which the fame, and often the property, of their chieftains principally depend. But, when this same nation becomes acquainted with the art of writing, it grows unwilling to intrust these matters to the memory of itinerant singers, and avails itself of its new art to preserve them in a fixed and material form. As soon as this is effected, the importance of those who repeat the national traditions is sensibly diminished. They gradually sink into an inferior class, which, having lost its old reputation, no longer consists of those superior men to whose abilities it owed its former fame.[20] Thus we see, that although, without letters, there can be no knowledge of much importance, it is nevertheless true, that their intro-

---

[19] That the invention of letters would at first weaken the memory, is noticed in Plato's Phædrus, chap. 135 (*Platonis Opera*, vol. i. p. 187, edit. Bekker, Lond. 1826); where, however, the argument is pushed rather too far.

[20] This inevitable decline in the ability of the bards is noticed, though, as it appears to me, from a wrong point of view, in *Mure's Literat. of Greece*, vol. ii. p. 230.

duction is injurious to historical traditions in two distinct ways: first by weakening the traditions, and secondly by weakening the class of men whose occupation it is to preserve them.

But this is not all. Not only does the art of writing lessen the number of traditionary truths, but it directly encourages the propagation of falsehoods. This is effected by what may be termed a principle of accumulation, to which all systems of belief have been deeply indebted. In ancient times, for example, the name of Hercules was given to several of those great public robbers who scourged mankind, and who, if their crimes were successful, as well as enormous, were sure after their death to be worshipped as heroes.[21] How this appellation originated is uncertain; but it was probably bestowed at first on a single man, and afterwards on those who resembled him in the character of their achievements.[22] This mode of extending the use of a single name is natural to a barbarous people;[23] and would cause little or no confusion, as long as the traditions of the country remained local and unconnected. But as soon as these traditions became fixed by a written language, the collectors of them, deceived by the similarity of name, assembled the scattered facts, and, ascribing to a single man these accumulated

---

[21] Varro mentions forty-four of these vagabonds, who were all called Hercules. See a learned article in *Smith's Biog. and Mythology*, vol. ii. p. 401, 8vo. 1846. See also *Mackay's Religious Development of the Greeks and Hebrews*, vol. ii. pp. 71–79. On the relation between Hercules and Melcarth, compare *Matter, Hist. du Gnosticisme*, vol. i. p. 257, with *Heeren's Asiatic Nations*, vol. L. p. 295, 8vo. 1846. And as to the Hercules of Egypt, *Prichard's Analysis of Egyptian Mythology*, 1838, pp. 109, 115–119. As to the confusion of the different Hercules by the Dorians, see *Thirlwall's Hist. of Greece*, vol. i. p. 257; and compare p. 130.

[22] This appears to be the opinion of Frederick Schlegel; *Schlegel's Lectures on the History of Literature*, Edinb. 1818, vol. I. p. 260.

[23] The habit of generalizing names precedes that more advanced state of society in which men generalize phenomena. If this proposition is universally true, which I take it to be, it will throw some light on the history of disputes between the nominalists and the realists.

exploits, degraded history to the level of a miraculous mythology.[24] In the same way, soon after the use of letters was known in the North of Europe, there was drawn up by Saxo Grammaticus the life of the celebrated Ragnar Lodbrok. Either from accident or design, this great warrior of Scandinavia, who had taught England to tremble, had received the same name as another Ragnar, who was prince of Jutland about a hundred years earlier. This coincidence would have caused no confusion, as long as each district preserved a distinct and independent account of its own Ragnar. But, by possessing the resource of writing, men became able to consolidate the separate trains of events, and, as it were, fuse two truths into one error. And this was what actually happened. The credulous Saxo put together the different exploits of both Ragnars, and, ascribing the whole of them to his favourite hero, has involved in obscurity one of the most interesting parts of the early history of Europe.[25]

The annals of the North afford another curious instance of this source of error. A tribe of Finns, called Quœns, occupied a considerable part of the eastern coast of the Gulf of Bothnia. Their country was known as Quœnland; and this name gave rise to a belief that, to the north of the Baltic, there was a nation of Amazons. This would easily have been corrected by local knowledge; but, by the use of writing, the flying rumour was at once fixed; and the existence of such a

---

[24] We may form an idea of the fertility of this source of error from the fact, that in Egypt there were fifty-three cities bearing the same name: 'L'auteur du Kamous nous apprend qu'il y a en Egypte cinquante-trois villes du nom de Schobra: en effet, j'ai retrouvé tous ces noms dans les deux dénombremens déjà cités.' *Quatremère, Recherches sur la Langue et la Littérature de l'Egypte*, p. 199.

[25] On this confusion respecting Ragnar Lodbrok, see *Geijer's History of Sweden*, part i. pp. 13, 14; *Lappenberg's Anglo-Saxon Kings*, vol. ii. p. 31; *Wheaton's Hist. of the Northmen*, p. 150; *Mallet's Northern Antiquities*, p. 383; *Crichton's Scandinavia*, vol. i. p. 116. A comparison of these passages will justify the sarcastic remark of Koch on the history of Swedish and Danish heroes; *Koch, Tableau des Révolutions*, vol. i. p. 67 note.

ORIGIN OF HISTORICAL LITERATURE.   299

people is positively affirmed in some of the earliest European histories.[26] Thus, too, Abo, the ancient capital of Finland, was called Turku, which, in the Swedish language, means a market-place. Adam of Bremen, having occasion to treat of the countries adjoining the Baltic,[27] was so misled by the word Turku, that this celebrated historian assures his readers that there were Turks in Finland.[28]

To these illustrations many others might be added, showing how mere names deceived the early historians, and gave rise to relations which were entirely false, and might have been rectified on the spot; but which, owing to the art of writing, were carried into distant countries, and thus placed beyond the reach of contradiction. Of such cases, one more may be mentioned, as it concerns the history of England. Richard I., the most barbarous of our princes, was known to his contemporaries as the Lion; an appellation conferred upon him on account of his fearlessness, and the ferocity of his temper.[29] Hence it was said that he had

---

[26] *Prichard's Physical Hist. of Mankind*, vol. iii. p. 273. The Norwegians still give to the Finlanders the name of Quæner. See *Dillon's Lapland and Iceland*, 8vo. 1840, vol. ii. p. 221. Compare *Laing's Sweden*, pp. 45, 47. The Amazon river in South America owes its name to a similar fable. *Henderson's Hist. of Brazil*, p. 453; *Southey's Hist. of Brazil*, vol. i. p. 112; *M'Culloh's Researches concerning America*, pp. 407, 408; and *Journal of Geog. Soc.* vol. xv. p. 96, for an account of the wide diffusion of this error.

[27] Sharon Turner (*Hist. of England*, vol. iv. p. 30) calls him 'the Strabo of the Baltic;' and it was from him that most of the geographers in the Middle Ages derived their knowledge of the North.

[28] 'It was called in Finnish *Turku*, from the Swedish word *torg*, which signifies a market-place. The sound of this name misled Adam of Bremen into the belief that there were Turks in Finland.' *Cooley's Hist. of Maritime and Inland Discovery*, London, 1830, vol. i. p. 211.

[29] The chronicler of his crusade says, that he was called Lion on account of his never pardoning an offence: 'Nihil injuriarum reliquit inultum: unde et unus (*i.e.* the King of France) dictus est Agnus a Griffonibus, alter Leonis nomen accepit.' *Chronicon Ricardi Divisiensis de Rebus gestis Ricardi Primi*, edit. Stevenson, Lond. 1838, p. 18. Some of the Egyptian kings received the name of Lion 'from their heroic exploits.' *Vyse on the Pyramids*, vol. iii. p. 110.

the heart of a lion; and the title Cœur de Lion not only became indissolubly connected with his name, but actually gave rise to a story, repeated by innumerable writers, according to which he slew a lion in single combat.[90] The name gave rise to the story; the story confirmed the name; and another fiction was added to that long series of falsehoods of which history mainly consisted during the Middle Ages.

The corruptions of history, thus naturally brought about by the mere introduction of letters, were, in Europe, aided by an additional cause. With the art of writing, there was, in most cases, also communicated a knowledge of Christianity; and the new religion not only destroyed many of the Pagan traditions, but falsified the remainder, by amalgamating them with monastic legends. The extent to which this was carried would form a curious subject for inquiry; but one or two instances of it will perhaps be sufficient to satisfy the generality of readers.

Of the earliest state of the great Northern nations we have little positive evidence; but several of the lays in which the Scandinavian poets related the feats of their ancestors, or of their contemporaries, are still preserved; and, notwithstanding their subsequent corruption, it is admitted by the most competent judges that they embody real and historical events. But in the ninth and tenth centuries, Christian missionaries found their way across the Baltic, and introduced a knowledge of their religion among the inhabitants of Northern Europe.[31] Scarcely was this effected, when

---

[90] See Price's learned Preface to Warton's *History of English Poetry*, vol. i. p. 21; and on the similar story of Henry the Lion, see Maury, *Légendes du Moyen Age*, p. 160. Compare the account of Duke Godfrey's conflict with a bear, in *Matthæi Paris Historia Major*, p. 29, Lond. 1684, folio. I should not be surprised if the story of Alexander and the Lion (Thirlwall's *History of Greece*, vol. vi. p. 305) were equally fabulous.

[31] The first missionary was Ebbo, about the year 822. He was followed by Anschar, who afterwards pushed his enterprise as far as Sweden. The progress was, however, slow; and it was not till the latter half of the 11th century that Christianity was established firmly in the North. See Neander's *Hist. of*

the sources of history began to be poisoned. At the end of the eleventh century, Sæmund Sigfusson, a Christian priest, gathered the popular, and hitherto unwritten, histories of the North into what is called the Elder Edda; and he was satisfied with adding to his compilation the corrective of a Christian hymn.[52] A hundred years later, there was made another collection of the native histories; but the principle which I have mentioned, having had a longer time to operate, now displayed its effects still more clearly. In this second collection, which is known by the name of the Younger Edda, there is an agreeable mixture of Greek, Jewish, and Christian fables; and, for the first time in the Scandinavian annals, we meet with the widely diffused fiction of a Trojan descent.[53]

If, by way of further illustration, we turn to other parts of the world, we shall find a series of facts confirming this view. We shall find that, in those countries where there has been no change of religion, history is more trustworthy and connected than in those countries where such a change has taken place. In India, Brahmanism, which is still supreme, was established at so early a period, that its origin is lost in the remotest antiquity.[54] The consequence is, that the native annals

---

the Church, vol. v. pp. 373, 374, 379, 380, 400–402; *Mosheim's Eccles. Hist.* vol. i. pp. 188, 215, 216; *Barry's Hist. of the Orkney Islands*, p. 125. It is often supposed that some of the Danes in Ireland were Christians as early as the reign of Ivar I.; but this is a mistake, into which Ledwich fell by relying on a coin, which in reality refers to Ivar II. *Petrie's Ecclesiastical Architecture of Ireland*, p. 225; and *Ledwich's Antiquities of Ireland*, p. 159.

[52] Mr. Wheaton (*History of Northmen*, p. 60) says, that Sæmund 'merely added one song of his own composition, of a moral and Christian religious tendency; so as thereby to consecrate and leaven, as it were, the whole mass of Paganism.'

[53] *Wheaton's Hist. of the Northmen*, pp. 89, 90; *Mallet's Northern Antiquities*, pp. 377, 378, 435; *Schlegel's Lectures on the History of Literature*, vol. i. p. 285. Indeed, these interpolations are so numerous, that the earlier German antiquaries believed the Edda to be a forgery by the northern monks,—a paradox which Müller refuted more than forty years ago. Note in *Wheaton*, p. 61. Compare *Palgrave's English Commonwealth, Anglo-Saxon Period*, vol. i. p. 135.

[54] As is evident from the con-

have never been corrupted by any new superstition; and the Hindus are possessed of historic traditions more ancient than can be found among any other Asiatic people.³⁵ In the same way, the Chinese have for upwards of 2000 years preserved the religion of Fo, which is a form of Buddhism.³⁶ In China, therefore, though the civilization has never been equal to that of India, there is a history, not, indeed, as old as the natives would wish us to believe, but still stretching back to several centuries before the Christian era, from whence it has been brought down to our own times in an uninterrupted succession.³⁷ On the other hand, the Persians,

---

flicting statements made by the best orientalists, each of whom has some favourite hypothesis of his own respecting its origin. It is enough to say, that we have no account of India existing without Brahmanism; and as to its real history, nothing can be understood, until more steps have been taken towards generalizing the laws which regulate the growth of religious opinions.
³⁵ Dr. Prichard (*Physical Hist. of Mankind*, vol. iv. pp. 101–105) thinks that the Hindus have a history beginning B.C. 1391. Compare *Works of Sir W. Jones*, vol. i. pp. 311, 312. Mr. Wilson says, that even the genealogies in the Puranas are, 'in all probability, much more authentic than has been sometimes supposed.' Wilson's note in *Mill's Hist. of India*, vol. i. pp. 161, 162. See also his preface to the *Vishnu Purana*, p. lxv.; and *Asiatic Researches*, vol. v. p. 244.
³⁶ *Journal of Asiatic Soc.* vol. vi. p. 251; Herder, *Ideen sur Geschichte*, vol. iv. p. 70; *Works of Sir W. Jones*, vol. i. p. 104. I learn from a note in *Erman's Siberia*, vol. ii. p. 306, that one of the missionaries gravely suggests that 'Buddhism originated in the errors of the Manichæans, and is therefore but an imitation of Christianity.'
³⁷ M. Bunsen says, that the Chinese have 'a regular chronology, extending back 3000 years B.C.' *Bunsen's Egypt*, vol. i. p. 240. See also *Humboldt's Cosmos*, vol. ii. p. 475, vol. iv. p. 455; *Renouard, Hist. de la Médecine*, vol. i. pp. 47, 48; and the statements of Klaproth and Rémusat, in *Prichard's Physical Hist.* vol. iv. pp. 476, 477. The superior exactness of the Chinese annals is sometimes ascribed to their early knowledge of printing, with which they claim to have been acquainted in B.C. 1100. *Meidinger's Essay*, in *Journal of Statistical Society*, vol. iii. p. 163. But the fact is, that printing was unknown in China till the ninth or tenth century after Christ, and moveable types were not invented before 1041. *Humboldt's Cosmos*, vol. ii. p. 623; *Transac. of Asiatic Society*, vol. i. p. 7;

ORIGIN OF HISTORICAL LITERATURE. 303

whose intellectual development was certainly superior to that of the Chinese, are nevertheless without any authentic information respecting the early transactions of their ancient monarchy.[38] For this I can see no possible reason, except the fact, that Persia, soon after the promulgation of the Koran, was conquered by the Mohammedans, who completely subverted the Parsee religion, and thus interrupted the stream of the national traditions.[39] Hence it is that, putting aside the myths of the Zendavesta, we have no native authorities for Persian history of any value, until the appearance, in the eleventh century, of the Shah Nameh; in which, however, Ferdousi has mingled the miraculous relations of those two religions by which his country had been successively subjected.[40] The result is, that if it were

---

Journal Asiatique, vol. i. p. 137, Paris, 1822; *Davis's Chinese*, vol. i. pp. 174, 178, vol. iii. p. 1. There are some interesting papers on the early history of China in *Journal of Asiat. Soc.* vol. i. pp. 57-86, 213-222, vol. ii. pp. 166-171, 276-287.

[39] 'From the death of Alexander (323 B.C.) to the reign of Ardeshir Babegan (Artaxerxes), the founder of the Sassanian dynasty (200 A.D.), a period of more than five centuries, is almost a blank in the Persian history.' *Troyer's Preliminary Discourse to the Dabistan*, 8vo. 1843, vol. i. pp. lv. lvi. See to the same effect *Erskine on the Zend-Avesta*, in *Transac. of Soc. of Bombay*, vol. ii. pp. 303-305; and *Malcolm's Hist. of Persia*, vol. i. p. 68. The ancient Persian traditions are said to have been Pehlvi; *Malcolm*, vol. i. pp. 501-505; but if so, they have all perished, p. 555: compare Rawlinson's note in *Journal of Geog. Soc.* vol. x. p. 82.

[40] On the antagonism between Mohammedanism and the old Persian history, see a note in *Grote's Hist. of Greece*, vol. i. p. 623. Even at present, or, at all events, during this century, the best education in Persia consisted in learning the elements of Arabic grammar, 'logic, jurisprudence, the traditions of their prophet, and the commentaries on the Koran.' *Vans Kennedy on Persian Literature*, in *Transac. of Bombay Society*, vol. ii. p. 62. In the same way the Mohammedans neglected the old history of India, and would, no doubt, have destroyed or corrupted it; but they never had anything like the hold of India that they had of Persia, and, above all, they were unable to displace the native religion. However, their influence, so far as it went, was unfavourable; and Mr. Elphinstone (*Hist. of India*, p. 468) says, that till the sixteenth century there was no instance of a Mussulman carefully studying Hindu literature.

[40] On the Shah Nameh, see *Works of Sir W. Jones*, vol. iv.

not for the various discoveries which have been made, of monuments, inscriptions, and coins, we should be compelled to rely on the scanty and inaccurate details in the Greek writers for our knowledge of the history of one of the most important of the Asiatic monarchies.[41]

Even among more barbarous nations, we see the same principle at work. The Malayo-Polynesian race is well known to ethnologists, as covering an immense series of islands, extending from Madagascar to within 2000 miles of the western coast of America.[42] The religion

---

pp. 544, 545, vol. v. p. 594; *Mill's Hist. of India*, vol. ii. pp. 64, 65; *Journal of Asiatic Society*, vol. iv. p. 225. It is supposed by a very high authority that the Persian cuneiform inscriptions 'will enable us, in the end, to introduce something like chronological accuracy and order into the myths and traditions embodied in the Shah Nameh.' *Rawlinson on the Inscriptions of Assyria and Babylonia*, in *Journal of Asiat. Soc.* vol. xii. p. 446.

[41] On the ignorance of the Greeks respecting Persian history, see Vans Kennedy, in *Transac. of Soc. of Bombay*, vol. ii. pp. 119, 127-129, 136. Indeed, this learned writer says (p. 138) he is 'inclined to suspect that no Greek author ever derived his information from any native of Persia Proper, that is, of the country to the east of the Euphrates.' See also on the perplexities in Persian chronology, *Grote's Hist. of Greece*, vol. vi. p. 496, vol. ix. p. 3, vol. x. p. 405; and *Donaldson's New Cratylus*, 1839, p. 87 note. As to the foolish stories which the Greeks relate respecting Achæmenes, compare *Malcolm's Hist. of Persia*, vol. i. p. 18, with *Heeren's Asiatic Nations*, vol. i.

p. 243. Even Herodotus, who is invaluable in regard to Egypt, is not to be relied upon for Persia; as was noticed long ago by Sir W. Jones, in the preface to his *Nader Shah* (*Jones's Works*, vol. v. p. 540), and is partly admitted by Mr. Mure (*History of the Literature of Ancient Greece*, vol. iv. p. 338, 8vo. 1853).

[42] That is, to Easter Island, which appears to be its furthest boundary (*Prichard's Phys. Hist.* vol. v. p. 6); and of which there is a good account in *Beechey's Voyage to the Pacific*, vol. i. pp. 43-58, and a notice in *Jour. of Geog. Society*, vol. i. p. 195. The language of Easter Island has been long known to be Malayo-Polynesian; for it was understood by a native of the Society Islands, who accompanied Cook (*Cook's Voyages*, vol. iii. pp. 294, 308; and *Prichard*, vol. v. p. 147: compare *Marsden's History of Sumatra*, p. 164). Ethnologists have not usually paid sufficient honour to this great navigator, who was the first to remark the similarity between the different languages in Polynesia Proper. *Cook's Voyages*, vol. ii. pp. 60, 61, vol. iii. pp. 230, 280, 290, vol. iv. p. 305, vol. vi. p. 230, vol. vii. p. 115. As to Madagascar being the

of these widely scattered people was originally Polytheism, of which the purest forms were long preserved in the Philippine Islands.[43] But in the fifteenth century, many of the Polynesian nations were converted to Mohammedanism;[44] and this was followed by a process precisely the same as that which I have pointed out in other countries. The new religion, by changing the current of the national thoughts, corrupted the purity of the national history. Of all the islands in the Indian Archipelago, Java was the one which reached the highest civilization.[45] Now, however, the Javanese have not only lost their historical traditions, but even those lists of their kings which are extant are interpolated with the names of Mohammedan saints.[46] On the other hand, we find that in the

---

western limit of this vast race of people, see *Asiatic Researches*, vol. iv. p. 222; *Reports on Ethnology by Brit. Assoc. for* 1847, pp. 154, 216, 250; and *Ellis's Hist. of Madagascar*, vol. i. p. 133.

[43] Also the seat of the Tagala language; which, according to William Humboldt, is the most perfect of all the forms of the Malayo-Polynesian. *Prichard's Physical Hist.* vol. v. pp. 36, 51, 52.

[44] *Marsden's History of Sumatra*, p. 281. De Thou (*Hist. Univ.* vol. xiii. p. 59) supposes that the Javanese did not become Mohammedans till late in the sixteenth century; but it is now known that their conversion took place at least a hundred years earlier, the old religion being finally abolished in 1478. See *Crawfurd's Hist. of the Indian Archipelago*, vol. ii. p. 312; *Low's Sarawak*, p. 96; and *Raffles' Hist. of Java*, vol. i. pp. 309, 349, vol. ii. pp. 1, 66, 254. The doctrines of Mohammed spread quickly; and the Malay pilgrims enjoy the reputation, in modern times, of being among the most scrupulously religious of those who go to the Hadj. *Burckhardt's Arabia*, vol. ii. pp. 96, 97.

[45] The Javanese civilization is examined at great length by William Humboldt, in his celebrated work, *Ueber die Kawi Sprache*, Berlin, 1836. From the evidence supplied by some early Chinese writings, which have only recently been published, there are good grounds for believing that the Indian Colonies were established in Java in the first century after Christ. See *Wilson on the Foe Kue Ki*, in *Journal of Asiat. Soc.* vol. v. p. 137; compare vol. vi. p. 320.

[46] *Crawfurd's Hist. of the Indian Archipelago*, vol. ii. p. 297. Compare with this the exactness with which, even in the island of Celebes, the dates were preserved 'before the introduction of Mahomedanism.' *Crawfurd*, vol. i. p. 306. For similar

adjacent island of Bali, where the old religion is still preserved,[47] the legends of Java are remembered and cherished by the people.[48]

It would be useless to adduce further evidence respecting the manner in which, among an imperfectly civilized people, the establishment of a new religion will always affect the accuracy of their early history. I need only observe, that in this way the Christian priests have obscured the annals of every European people they converted, and have destroyed or corrupted the traditions of the Gauls,[49] of the Welsh, of the Irish,[50] of the Anglo-Saxons,[51] of the Sclavonic nations,[52] of the Finns,[53] and even of the Icelanders.[54]

---

instances of royal genealogies being obscured by the introduction into them of the names of gods, see Kemble's *Saxons in England*, vol. i. pp. 27, 335.

[47] *Asiatic Researches*, vol. x. p. 191, vol. xiii. p. 128. In the Appendix to Raffles' *Hist. of Java*, vol. ii. p. cxlii., it is said, that 'in Bali not more than one in two hundred, if so many, are Mahomedans.' See also p. 65, and vol. i. p. 530.

[48] Indeed, the Javanese appear to have no other means of acquiring the old Kawi traditions than by learning them from natives of Bali. See note to an Essay on the Island of Bali, in *Asiatic Researches*, vol. xiii. p. 162, Calcutta, 1820, 4to. Sir Stamford Raffles (*Hist. of Java*, vol. i. p. 400) says, 'It is chiefly to Bali that we must look for illustrations of the ancient state of the Javans.' See also p. 414.

[49] Respecting the corruption of Druidical traditions in Gaul by Christian priests, see Villemarqué, *Chants Populaires de la Bretagne*, Paris, 1846, vol. i. pp. xviii. xix.

[50] The injury done to the traditions handed down by Welsh and Irish bards, is noticed in Dr. Prichard's valuable work, *Physical Hist. of Mankind*, vol. iii. p. 184, 8vo, 1841. See also Warton's *Hist. of English Poetry*, vol. i. p. xxxvii. note.

[51] See the remarks on Beowulf, in Wright's *Biog. Brit. Lit.* vol. i. p. 7, 8vo, 1842. See also pp. 13, 14: and compare Kemble's *Saxons in England*, vol. i. p. 331.

[52] Talvi's *Language and Literature of the Slavic Nations*, 8vo, 1850, p. 231. The Pagan songs of the Slovaks, in the north-west of Hungary, were for a time preserved; but even they are now lost. Talvi, p. 216.

[53] The monkish chroniclers neglected the old Finnish traditions; and allowing them to perish, preferred the inventions of Saxo and Johannes Magnus. Prichard's *Physical Hist.* vol. iii. pp. 284, 285.

[54] For an instance in which the monks have falsified the old Icelandic traditions, see Mr. Keightley's learned book on *Fairy Mythology*, 8vo, 1850, p. 159.

Besides all this, there occurred other circumstances tending in the same direction. Owing to events which I shall hereafter explain, the literature of Europe, shortly before the final dissolution of the Roman Empire, fell entirely into the hands of the clergy, who were long venerated as the sole instructors of mankind. For several centuries, it was extremely rare to meet with a layman who could read or write; and of course it was still rarer to meet with one able to compose a work. Literature, being thus monopolized by a single class, assumed the peculiarities natural to its new masters.[55] And as the clergy, taken as a body, have always looked on it as their business to enforce belief, rather than encourage inquiry, it is no wonder if they displayed in their writings the spirit incidental to the habits of their profession. Hence, as I have already observed, literature, during many ages, instead of benefiting society, injured it, by increasing credulity, and thus stopping the progress of knowledge. Indeed, the aptitude for falsehood became so great, that there was nothing men were unwilling to believe. Nothing came amiss to their greedy and credulous ears. Histories of omens, prodigies, apparitions, strange portents, monstrous appearances in the heavens, the wildest and most incoherent absurdities, were repeated from mouth to mouth, and copied from book to book, with as much care as if they were the choicest treasures of human wisdom.[56] That Europe should ever have emerged

---

[55] The Rev. Mr. Dowling, who looks back with great regret to this happy period, says, 'Writers were almost universally ecclesiastical. Literature was scarcely anything but a religious exercise; for everything that was studied, was studied with a reference to religion. The men, therefore, who wrote history, wrote ecclesiastical history.' *Dowling's Introduction to the Critical Study of Ecclesiastical History*, 8vo, 1838, p. 56; a work of some talent, but chiefly interesting as a manifesto by an active party.

[56] Thus, for instance, a celebrated historian, who wrote at the end of the twelfth century, says of the reign of William Rufus: 'Ejusdem regis tempore, ut ex parte supradictum est, in sole, luna, et stellis multa signa visa sunt, mare quoque littus persæpe egrediebatur, et homines et animalia submersit, villas et domos quamplures subvertit.

from such a state, is the most decisive proof of the extraordinary energy of Man, since we cannot even conceive a condition of society more unfavourable to his progress. But it is evident, that until the emancipation was effected, the credulity and looseness of thought which were universal, unfitted men for habits of investigation, and made it impossible for them to engage in a successful study of past affairs, or even record with accuracy what was taking place around them.[57]

If, therefore, we recur to the facts just cited, we may say that, omitting several circumstances altogether subordinate, there were three leading causes of the corruption of the history of Europe in the Middle Ages. The first cause was, the sudden introduction of the art of writing, and the consequent fusion of different local traditions, which, when separate, were accurate, but when united were false. The second cause was, the change of religion; which acted in two ways, producing not merely an interruption of the old traditions, but also an interpolation of them. And the third cause, probably the most powerful of all, was, that history became monopolized by a class of men whose professional habits made them quick to believe, and who, moreover, had a direct interest in increasing the general credulity, since it was the basis upon which their own authority was built.

'In pago qui Barukeshire nominatur, ante occisionem regis sanguis de fonte tribus septimanis emanavit. Multis etiam Normannis diabolus in horribili specie se frequenter in silvis ostandens, plura cum eis de rege et Ranulfo, et quibusdam aliis locutus est. Nec mirum, nam illorum tempore ferè omnis legum siluit justitia, cansisque justitia subpositis, sola in principibus imperabat pecunia.' *Rog. de Houden Annal. in Scriptores post Bedam,* p. 268. See also the same work, pp. 356–358; and compare *Matthæi Westmonast. Flores Historiarum,* part i. pp. 266, 269, part ii. p. 298.

[57] Even the descriptions of natural objects which historians attempted in the Middle Ages, were marked by the same carelessness. See some good observations by Dr. Arnold, on Bede's account of the Solent Sea. *Arnold's Lectures on Modern History,* pp. 102, 103.

By the operation of these causes, the history of Europe became corrupted to an extent for which we can find no parallel in any other period. That there was, properly speaking, no history, was the smallest part of the inconvenience; but, unhappily, men, not satisfied with the absence of truth, supplied its place by the invention of falsehood. Among innumerable instances of this, there is one species of inventions worth noticing, because they evince that love of antiquity, which is a marked characteristic of those classes by whom history was then written. I allude to fictions regarding the origin of different nations, in all of which the spirit of the Middle Ages is very discernible. During many centuries, it was believed by every people that they were directly descended from ancestors who had been present at the siege of Troy. That was a proposition which no one thought of doubting.[58] The only question was, as to the details of so illustrious a lineage. On this, however, there was a certain unanimity of opinion; since, not to mention inferior

---

[58] In *Le Long's Bibliothèque Historique de la France*, vol. ii. p. 8, it is said, that the descent of the kings of France from the Trojans was universally believed before the sixteenth century: 'Cette descendance a été crue véritable près de huit cents ans, et soutenue par tous les écrivains de notre histoire; la fausseté n'en a été reconnue qu'au commencement du seizième siècle.' Polydore Vergil, who died in the middle of the sixteenth century, attacked this opinion in regard to England, and thereby made his history unpopular. See *Ellis's Preface to Polydore Vergil*, p. xx. 4to, 1844, published by the Camden Society. 'He discarded Brute, as an unreal personage.' In 1128, Henry I., king of England, inquired from a learned man respecting the early history of France. The answer is preserved by an historian of the thirteenth century: 'Regum potentissime, inquiens, sicut pleræque gentes Europæ, ita Franci a Trojanis originem duxerunt.' *Matthæi Paris Hist. Major*, p. 59. See also *Rog. de Hov. in Scriptores post Bedam*, p. 274. On the descent of the Britons from Priam and Æneas, see *Matthæi Westmonast. Flores Historiarum*, part i. p. 66. Indeed, at the beginning of the fourteenth century, their Trojan origin was stated as a notorious fact, in a letter written to Pope Boniface by Edward I., and signed by the English nobility. See *Warton's Hist. of English Poetry*, vol. i. pp. 131, 132; and *Campbell's Lives of the Chancellors*, vol. i. p. 165.

countries, it was admitted that the French were descended from Francus, whom everybody knew to be the son of Hector; and it was also known that the Britons came from Brutus, whose father was no other than Æneas himself.[59]

Touching the origin of particular places, the great historians of the Middle Ages are equally communicative. In the accounts they give of them, as well as in the lives they write of eminent men, the history usually begins at a very remote period; and the events relating to their subject are often traced back, in an unbroken series, from the moment when Noah left the ark, or even when Adam passed the gates of Paradise.[60] On other occasions, the antiquity they assign is somewhat less; but the range of their information is always extraordinary. They say, that the capital of France is called after Paris, the son of Priam, because he fled there when Troy was overthrown.[61] They also mention

---

[59] The general opinion was, that Brutus, or Brute, was the son of Æneas; but some historians affirmed that he was the great-grandson. See *Turner's Hist. of England*, vol. i. p. 63, vol. vii. p. 220.

[60] In the *Notes to a Chronicle of London from 1089 to 1483*, pp. 183-187, edit. 4to, 1827, there is a pedigree, in which the history of the bishops of London is traced back, not only to the migration of Brutus from Troy, but also to Noah and Adam. Thus, too, Goropius, in his history of Antwerp, written in the sixteenth century: 'Vand zoowell de Nederlandsche taal als de Wysbegeerte van Orpheus in de ark van Noach.' *Van Kampen, Geschiedenis der Letteren*, 8vo, 1821, vol. i. p. 91; see also p. 86. In the thirteenth century, Mathew Paris (*Historia Major*, p. 352) says of Alfred, 'Hujus genealogia in Anglorum historiis perducitur usque ad Adam primum parentem.' See, to the same effect, *Matthæi Westmonast. Flores Historiarum*, part i. pp. 323, 324, 415. In William of Malmesbury's Chronicle (*Scriptores post Bedam*, p. 22 rev.) the genealogy of the Saxon kings is traced back to Adam. For other, and similar, instances, see a note in *Lingard's History of England*, vol. i. p. 403. And Mr. Ticknor (*History of Spanish Literature*, vol. i. p. 509) mentions that the Spanish chroniclers present 'an uninterrupted succession of Spanish kings from Tubal, a grandson of Noah.'

[61] Monteil, in his curious book, *Histoire des divers Etats*, vol. v. p. 70, mentions the old belief 'que les Parisiens sont du sang des rois des anciens Troyens, par Paris, fils de Priam.' Even in the seventeenth century this

that Tours owed its name to being the burial-place of Turonus, one of the Trojans;[62] while the city of Troyes was actually built by the Trojans, as its etymology clearly proves.[63] It was well ascertained that Nuremberg was called after the Emperor Nero;[64] and Jerusalem after King Jebus,[65] a man of vast celebrity in the Middle Ages, but whose existence later historians have not been able to verify. The river Humber received its name because, in ancient times, a king of the Huns had been drowned in it.[66] The Gauls derived their origin, according to some, from Galathia, a female descendant of Japhet; according to others, from Gomer, the son of Japhet.[67] Prussia was called after Prussus,

---

idea was not extinct; and Coryat, who travelled in France in 1608, gives another version of it. He says, 'As for her name of Paris, she hath it (as some write) from Paris, the eighteenth king of Gallia Celtica, whom some write to have been lineally descended from Japhet, one of the three sons of Noah, and to have founded this city.' *Coryat's Crudities,* 1611, reprinted 1776, vol. i. pp. 27, 28.

[62] 'Erat ibi quidam Tros nomine Turonus Bruti nepos... De nomine ipsius prædicta civitas Turonis vocabulum nacta est; quia ibidem sepultus fuit.' *Galfredi Monumet. Hist. Briton.* lib. i. cap. xv. p. 19. And Mathew of Westminster, who wrote in the fourteenth century, says (*Flores Historiarum,* part i. p. 17): 'Tros nomine Turnus... De nomine verò ipsius Turonorum civitas vocabulum traxit, quis ibidem, ut testatur Homerus, sepultus fuit.'

[63] 'On convient bien que les Troyens de notre Troyes sont du sang des anciens Troyens.' *Monteil, Divers Etats,* vol. v. p. 69.

[64] Monconys, who was in Nuremberg in 1663, found this opinion still held there; and he seems himself half inclined to believe it; for, in visiting a castle, he observes, 'Mais je ne sçai si c'est un ouvrage de Néron, comme l'on le dit, et que même le nom de Nuremberg en vient.' *Voyages de Monconys,* vol. iv. p. 141, edit. Paris, 1695.

[65] 'Deinceps regnante in ea Jebusæo, dicta Jebus, et sic ex Jebus et Salem dicta est Jebusalem. Unde post dempta b litterà et addita r, dicta est Hierusalem.' *Matthæi Paris Historia Major,* p. 43. This reminds me of another great writer, who was one of the fathers, and was moreover a saint, and who, says M. Matter, 'dérive les Samaritains du roi Samarius, fils de Canaan.' *Matter, Hist. du Gnosticisme,* vol. l. p. 41.

[66] 'Humber rex Hunnorum ... ad flumen diffugiens, submersus est intra ipsum, et nomen suum flumini reliquit.' *Matthæi Westmonast. Flores Historiarum,* part i. p. 19.

[67] These two opinions, which

a brother of Augustus.[68] This was remarkably modern; but Silesia had its name from the prophet Elisha—from whom, indeed, the Silesians descended;[69] while as to the city of Zurich, its exact date was a matter of dispute, but it was unquestionably built in the time of Abraham.[70] It was likewise from Abraham and Sarah that the gipsies immediately sprung.[71] The blood of the Saracens was less pure, since they were only descended from Sarah—in what way it is not mentioned; but she probably had them by another marriage, or, may be, as the fruit of an Egyptian intrigue.[72] At all events, the Scotch certainly came from Egypt; for they were originally the issue of Scota, who was a daughter of Pharaoh, and who bequeathed to them her name.[73] On sundry similar matters, the Middle Ages

---

[68] long divided the learned world, are stated in *Le Long, Bibliothèque Historique de la France*, vol. ii. pp. 5, 49.

[69] See a curious allusion to this in *De Thou, Hist. Univ.* vol. viii. p. 160; where, however, it is erroneously supposed to be a Russian invention.

[70] 'The Silesians are not without voluminous writers upon their antiquities; and one of them gravely derives the name and descent of his country from the prophet Elisha.' *Adams's Letters on Silesia*, p. 267, Lond. 8vo, 1804.

[71] In 1608, Coryat, when in Zurich, was 'told by the learned Hospinian that their city was founded in the time of Abraham.' *Coryat's Crudities*, vol. i. Epistle to the Reader, sig. D. I always give the most recent instance I have met with, because, in the history of the European intellect, it is important to know how long the spirit of the Middle Ages survived in different countries.

[72] They were 'seuls enfants légitimes' of Abraham and Sarah. *Monteil, Divers Ftats,* vol. v. p. 19.

[73] Mathew Paris, who is apprehensive lest the reputation of Sarah should suffer, says, 'Saraceni perversè se putant ex Sara dici; sed verius Agareni dicuntur ab Agar; et Ismaelitæ, ab Ismaele filio Abrahæ.' *Hist. Major*, p. 357. Compare a similar passage in *Mezeray, Histoire de France*, vol. i. p. 127: 'Sarrasins, ou de la ville de Sarai, ou de Sara femme d'Abraham, dnquel ils se disent faussement légitimes héritiers.' After this, the idea, or the fear of the idea, soon died away; and Beausobre (*Histoire Critique de Manichée*, vol. i. p. 24) says: 'On dérive vulgairement le nom de Sarrasins du mot arabe Sarah, ou Sarak, qui signifie effectivement voleur.' A good example of a secular turn given to a theological etymology. For a similar case in northern history, see *Whitelocke's Journal of the Swedish Embassy*, vol. i. pp. 190, 191.

[73] Early in the fourteenth cen-

ORIGIN OF HISTORICAL LITERATURE.   313

possessed information equally valuable. It was well
known that the city of Naples was founded on eggs;[74]
and it was also known, that the order of St. Michael
was instituted in person by the archangel, who was
himself the first knight, and to whom, in fact, chivalry
owes its origin.[75] In regard to the Tartars, that people,
of course, proceeded from Tartarus; which some theologians said was an inferior kind of hell, but others
declared to be hell itself.[76] However this might be,
the fact of their birth-place being from below was
indisputable, and was proved by many circumstances

---

tury, this was stated, in a letter to the Pope, as a well-known historical fact. See *Lingard's Hist. of England*, vol. ii. p. 187: 'They are sprung from Scota the daughter of Pharaoh, who landed in Ireland, and whose descendants wrested, by force of arms, the northern half of Britain from the progeny of Brute.'

[74] Mr. Wright (*Narratives of Sorcery*, 8vo, 1851, vol. i. p. 115) says, 'The foundation of the city of Naples upon eggs, and the egg on which its fate depended, seem to have been legends generally current in the Middle Ages;' and he refers to Montfaucon, *Monumens de la Mon. Fr.* vol. ii. p. 329, for proof, that by the statutes of the order of the Saint Esprit, 'a chapter of the knights was appointed to be held annually in castello ovi incantati in mirabili periculo.'

[75] 'The order of Saint Michael, in France, pretends to the possession of a regular descent from Michael the Archangel, who, according to the enlightened judgment of French antiquarians, was the premier chevalier in the world; and it was he, they say, who established the earliest chivalric order in Paradise itself.' *Mills's Hist. of Chivalry*, vol. i. pp. 363, 364.

[76] The etymology of Tartars from Tartarus is ascribed to the piety of Saint Louis in *Prichard's Physical History*, vol. iv. p. 278; but I think that I have met with it before his time, though I cannot now recover the passage. The earliest instance I remember is in 1241, when the saint was twenty-six years old. See a letter from the emperor Frederick, in *Matthæi Paris Historia Major*, p. 497: 'Pervenissent dicti Tartari (imo Tartarei),' &c.; and on the expression of Louis, see p. 496: 'Quos vocamus Tartaros ad suas Tartareas sedes.' Since the thirteenth century, the subject has attracted the attention of English divines; and the celebrated theologian Whiston mentions 'my last famous discovery, or rather my revival of Dr. Giles Fletcher's famous discovery, that the Tartars are no other than the ten tribes of Israel, which have been so long sought for in vain.' *Memoirs of the Life and Writings of William Whiston*, p. 575. Compare, on the opinions held respecting the Tartars, *Journal Asiatique*, I° série, vol. vi. p. 374, Paris, 1825.

which showed the fatal and mysterious influence they were able to exercise. For the Turks were identical with the Tartars; and it was notorious, that since the Cross had fallen into Turkish hands, all Christian children had ten teeth less than formerly; a universal calamity, which there seemed to be no means of repairing.[77]

Other points relating to the history of past events were cleared up with equal facility. In Europe during many centuries, the only animal food in general use was pork; beef, veal, and mutton, being comparatively unknown.[78] It was, therefore, with no small astonish-

---

[77] Peignot (*Dict. des Livres*, vol. ii. p. 69, Paris, 1806) says, that Rigord, in his history of Philip Augustus, assures his readers 'que depuis que la vraie croix a été prise par les Turcs, les enfans n'ont plus que 20 ou 23 dents, au lieu qu'ils en avaient 30 ou 32 auparavant.' Even in the fifteenth century, it was believed that the number of teeth had diminished from 32 to 22, or at most 24. See *Sprengel, Hist. de la Médecine*, vol. ii. pp. 481, 482, Paris, 1815. Compare *Hecker on the Black Death*, pp. 31, 32, in his learned work, *Epidemics of the Middle Ages*, published by the Sydenham Society.

[78] In the sacred books of the Scandinavians, pork is represented as the principal food, even in heaven. See *Mallet's Northern Antiquities*, p. 105. It was the chief food of the Irish in the twelfth century: *Ledwich, Antiquities of Ireland*, Dublin, 1804, p. 370; and also of the Anglo-Saxons at an earlier period: *Turner's Hist. of England*, vol. iii. p. 22. In France it was equally common, and Charlemagne kept in his forests immense droves of pigs. *Note in Esprit des Lois*, in *Œuvres de Montesquieu*, p. 513. In Spain those who did not like pork were tried by the Inquisition as suspected Jews: *Llorente, Hist. de l'Inquisition*, vol. i. pp. 269, 442, 445. Late in the sixteenth century, there was a particular disease, said to be caused by the quantity of it eaten in Hungary. *Sprengel, Hist. de la Médecine*, vol. iii. p. 93; and even at present, the barbarous Lettes are passionately fond of it. *Kohl's Russia*, pp. 386, 387. In the middle of the sixteenth century, I find that Philip II., when in England, generally dined on bacon; of which he ate so much, as frequently to make himself very ill. See *Ambassades de Messieurs de Noailles en Angleterre*, vol. v. pp. 240, 241, edit. 1763. The ambassador writes, that Philip was 'grand mangeur oultre mesure,' and used to consume large quantities 'de lard, dont il faict le plus souvent son principal repas.' In the Middle Ages, 'les Thuringiens payaient leur tribut en porcs, la denrée la plus précieuse de leur pays.' *Œuvres de Michelet*, vol. ii. p. 389

ment that the crusaders, on returning from the East, told their countrymen that they had been among a people who, like the Jews, thought pork unclean, and refused to eat it. But the feelings of lively wonder which this intelligence excited, were destroyed as soon as the cause of the fact was explained. The subject was taken up by Mathew Paris, the most eminent historian during the thirteenth century, and one of the most eminent during the Middle Ages.[79] This celebrated writer informs us, that the Mohammedans refuse to eat pork on account of a singular circumstance which happened to their prophet. It appears that Mohammed, having, on one occasion, gorged himself with food and drink till he was in a state of insensibility, fell asleep on a dunghill, and, in this disgraceful condition, was seen by a litter of pigs. The pigs attacked the fallen prophet, and suffocated him to death; for which reason his followers abominate pigs, and refuse to partake of their flesh.[80] This striking fact explains one great peculiarity of the Mohammedans;[81] and another fact,

---

[79] Sismondi (*Hist. des Français*, vol. vii. pp. 325, 326) passes a high eulogy upon him; and Mosheim (*Ecclesiast. History*, vol. i. p. 313) says: 'Among the historians (of the thirteenth century), the first place is due to Mathew Paris; a writer of the highest merit, both in point of knowledge and prudence.'

[80] *Matthæi Paris Historia Major*, p. 362. He concludes his account by saying, 'Unde adhuc Saraceni sues præ cæteris animalibus exosas habent et abominabiles.' Mathew Paris obtained his information from a clergyman, 'quendam magni nominis celebrem prædicatorem,' p. 360 According to Mathew of Westminster, the pigs not only suffocated Mohammed, but actually ate the greater part of him: 'In maxima parte a porcis corrosum invenerunt.' *Matthæi Westmonast. Flores Historiarum*, part i. p. 215.

[81] By a singular contradiction, the African Mohammedans now 'believe that a great enmity subsists between hogs and Christians.' *Mungo Park's Travels*, vol. i. p. 185. Many medical authors have supposed that pork is peculiarly unwholesome in hot countries; but this requires confirmation: and it is certain, that it is recommended by Arabian physicians, and is more generally eaten both in Asia and in Africa than is usually believed. Comp. *Sprengel, Hist. de la Médecine*, vol. ii. p. 323; *Volney, Voyage en Syrie*, vol. i. p. 449; *Buchanan's Journey through the Mysore*, vol. ii. p. 88, vol. iii. p. 57; *Raffles' Hist. of Java*, vol. ii. p. 5; *Ellis's Hist. of Madagascar*,

equally striking, explains how it was that their sect came into existence. For it was well known, that Mohammed was originally a cardinal, and only became a heretic because he failed in his design of being elected pope.[42]

In regard to the early history of Christianity, the great writers of the Middle Ages were particularly inquisitive; and they preserved the memory of events, of which otherwise we should have been entirely ignorant. After Froissart, the most celebrated historian of the fourteenth century, was certainly Mathew of Westminster, with whose name, at least, most readers are familiar. This eminent man directed his attention, among other matters, to the history of Judas, in order to discover the circumstances under which the character of that arch-apostate was formed. His researches seem to have been very extensive; but their principal results were, that Judas, when an infant, was deserted by his parents, and exposed on an island called Scarioth, from whence he received the name of Judas Iscariot. To this the historian adds, that after Judas grew up, he, among other enormities, slew his own father, and then married his own mother.[43] The same writer, in another part of his history, mentions a fact interesting to those who study the antiquities of the Holy See. Some questions had been raised as to the propriety of kissing the

---

vol. i. pp. 201, 403, 416; *Cook's Voyages*, vol. ii. p. 265; *Burnes's Travels into Bokhara*, vol. iii. p. 141. As facts of this sort are important physiologically and socially, it is advisable that they should be collected; and I therefore add, that the North-American Indians are said to have 'a disgust for pork.' *Journal of the Geog. Society*, vol. xv. p. 30; and that Dobell (*Travels*, vol. ii. p. 260, 8vo, 1830) says, 'I believe there is more pork eaten in China than in all the rest of the world put together.'

[42] This idea, which was a favourite one in the Middle Ages, is said to have been a Rabbinical invention. See *Lettres de Gui Patin*, vol. iii. p. 127: 'que Mahomet, le faux prophète, avait été cardinal; et que, par dépit de n'avoir été pape, il s'étoit fait hérésiarque.'

[43] See the ample details in *Matthæi Westmonast. Flores Historiarum*, part i. pp. 86, 87; and at p. 88, 'Judas matrem suam uxorem duxerat, et quod patrem suum occiderat.'

pope's toe, and even theologians had their doubts
touching so singular a ceremony. But this difficulty
also was set at rest by Mathew of Westminster, who
explains the true origin of the custom. He says, that
formerly it was usual to kiss the hand of his holiness;
but that towards the end of the eighth century, a certain lewd woman, in making an offering to the pope,
not only kissed his hand, but also pressed it. The
pope—his name was Leo—seeing the danger, cut off
his hand, and thus escaped the contamination to which
he had been exposed. Since that time, the precaution
has been taken of kissing the pope's toe instead of his
hand; and lest any one should doubt the accuracy of
this account, the historian assures us that the hand,
which had been cut off five or six hundred years before, still existed in Rome, and was indeed a standing
miracle, since it was preserved in the Lateran in its
original state, free from corruption.[84] And as some
readers might wish to be informed respecting the
Lateran itself, where the hand was kept, this also is
considered by the historian, in another part of his
great work, where he traces it back to the emperor
Nero. For it is said that this wicked persecutor of
the faith, on one occasion, vomited a frog covered with
blood, which he believed to be his own progeny, and
therefore caused to be shut up in a vault, where it
remained hidden for some time. Now, in the Latin
language, *latente* means hidden, and *rana* means a
frog; so that, by putting these two words together,
we have the origin of the Lateran, which, in fact, was
built where the frog was found.[85]

---

[84] This took place in the year 798. *Matthæi Westmonast. Flores Historiarum*, part i. p. 293. The historian thus concludes his relation: 'Et statutum est nunc quòd nunquam extunc manus Papæ ab offerentibus deoscularetur, sed pes. Cùm ante fuerat consuetudo quòd manus, non pes, deoscularetur. In hujus miraculi memoriam reservatur adhuc manus abscissa in thesauro lateranensi, quam dominus custodit incorruptam ad laudem matris suæ.'

[85] '... Ita ut Nero se puero gravidum existimaret.... Tandem dolore nimio vexatus, medicis ait: Accelerate tempus partus, quia languore vix anhelitum habeo respirandi. Tunc ipsum ad vomitum impotiona-

318   ORIGIN OF HISTORICAL LITERATURE.

It would be easy to fill volumes with similar notions; all of which were devoutly believed in those ages of darkness, or, as they have been well called, Ages of Faith. Those, indeed, were golden days for the ecclesiastical profession, since the credulity of men had reached a height which seemed to ensure to the clergy a long and universal dominion. How the prospects of the church were subsequently darkened, and how the human reason began to rebel, will be related in another part of this Introduction, where I shall endeavour to trace the rise of that secular and sceptical spirit to which European civilization owes its origin. But, before closing the present chapter, it may be well to give a few more illustrations of the opinions held in the Middle Ages; and, for this purpose, I will select the two historical accounts, which, of all others, were the most popular, exercised most influence, and were most universally believed.

The histories to which I refer, are those of Arthur and Charlemagne; both of which bear the names of dignitaries of the church, and were received with the respect due to their illustrious authors. That concerning Charlemagne is called the Chronicle of Turpin, and purports to be written by Turpin, archbishop of Rheims, a friend of the emperor and his companion in war.[86] From some passages it contains, there is reason to think that it was really composed at the beginning of the twelfth century;[87] but, in the Middle Ages,

---

verunt, et ranam visu terribilem, humoribus infectam, et sanguine edidit cruentatam. . . . Unde et pars illa civitatis, ut aliqui dicunt, ubi rana latuerat, Lateranum, à latente rana, nomen accepit.' *Matthæi Westmonast.* part i. p. 98. Compare the account given by Roger of Hoveden, of a woman who vomited two toads. *Script. post Bedam,* p. 457 rev. In the Middle Ages there were many superstitions respecting these animals, and they appear to have been used by heralds as marks of degradation. See *Lankester's Memorials of Ray,* p. 197.

[86] '. . . Ego Turpinus in valle Caroli loco præfato, astante rege,' &c. *De Vita Caroli Magni,* p. 74, edit. Ciampi.

[87] Turner (*History of England,* vol. vii. pp. 256–268) has attempted to prove that it was written by Calixtus II.; but his arguments, though ingenious and learned, are not decisive. Warton

men were not nice in these matters, and no one was likely to dispute its authenticity. Indeed, the name of an archbishop of Rheims was sufficient recommendation; and we find accordingly, that in the year 1122 it received the formal approbation of the pope;[88] and that Vincent de Beauvais, one of the most celebrated writers in the thirteenth century, and tutor to the sons of Louis IX., mentions it as a work of value, and as being the principal authority for the reign of Charlemagne.[89]

A book thus generally read, and sanctioned by such competent judges, must be a tolerable standard for testing the knowledge and opinions of those times. On this account, a short notice of it will be useful for our present purpose, as it will enable us to understand the extreme slowness with which history has improved, and the almost imperceptible steps by which it advanced, until fresh life was breathed into it by the great thinkers of the eighteenth century.

In the Chronicle of Turpin, we are informed that the invasion of Spain by Charlemagne took place in consequence of the direct instigation of St. James, the brother of St. John.[90] The apostle, being the cause of the attack, adopted measures to secure its success. When Charlemagne besieged Pamplona, that city made an obstinate resistance; but as soon as prayers were offered up by the invaders, the walls suddenly fell to the ground.[91] After this, the emperor rapidly overran

---

(*Hist. Eng. Poetry*, vol. i. p. 128) says it was composed about 1110.

[88] The pope 'statuit historiam Sancti Caroli descriptam a beato Turpino Remensi Archiepiscopo esse authenticam.' *Note in Turner*, vol. vii. p. 250.

[89] In his famous Speculum, 'il recommande spécialement les études historiques, dont il paraît que la plupart de ses contemporains méconnaissaient l'utilité; mais lorsqu'il indique les sources où il puisera ce genre d'instruction, c'est Turpin qu'il désigne comme le principal historien de Charlemagne.' *Histoire Littéraire de la France*, vol. xviii. p. 474, Paris, 1835, 4to; see also p. 517; and on its influence in Spain, see *Ticknor's History of Spanish Literature*, vol. i. pp. 222, 223.

[90] *Caroli Magni Historia*, edit. Ciampi, pp. 3-5.

[91] '... Muri collapsi funditus corruerunt.' *De Vita Caroli*, p. 5. On this, Ciampi, in his notes on

the whole country, almost annihilated the Mohammedans, and built innumerable churches.[92] But, the resources of Satan are inexhaustible. On the side of the enemy, a giant now appeared, whose name was Fenacute, and who was descended from Goliath of old.[93] This Fenacute was the most formidable opponent the Christians had yet encountered. His strength was equal to that of forty men;[94] his face measured one cubit; his arms and legs four cubits; his total height was twenty cubits. Against him Charlemagne sent the most eminent warriors; but they were easily discomfited by the giant; of whose prodigious force some idea may be formed from the fact, that the length even of his fingers was three palms.[95] The Christians were filled with consternation. In vain did more than twenty chosen men advance against the giant; not one returned from the field; Fenacute took them all under his arms, and carried them off into captivity.[96] At length the celebrated Orlando came forward, and challenged him to mortal combat. An obstinate fight ensued; and the Christian, not meeting with the success he expected, engaged his adversary in a theological discussion.[97] Here the pagan was easily defeated; and Orlando, warmed by the controversy, pressed on his enemy, smote the giant with his sword, and dealt him a fatal

---

Turpin, gravely says (pp. 94, 95): 'Questo fatto della presa di Pamplona è reso maraviglioso per la subitanea caduta delle mura, a somiglianza delle mura di Gerico.' This reminds me of a circumstance mentioned by Monconys, who, on visiting Oxford in 1663, was shown a horn which was preserved in that ancient city, because it was said to be made in the same way as that by which the walls of Jericho were blown down: 'Les Juifs tiennent que leurs ancêtres se servirent de parailles pour abbattre les murailles de Jérico.' *Voyages de Monconys*, vol. iii. p. 95, edit. Paris, 1695.

[92] *De Vita Caroli*, cap. v. pp. 11, 12; is headed 'De ecclesiis quas Carolus fecit.'
[93] 'Gigas nomine Fenacutus, qui fuit de genere Goliat.' *De Vita Caroli*, p. 39.
[94] 'Vim xl. fortium possidebat.' p. 39.
[95] 'Erat enim statura ejus quasi cubitis xx., facies erat longa quasi unius cubiti, et nasus illius unius palmi mensurali, et brachia et crura ejus quatuor cubitorum erant, et digiti ejus tribus palmis.' p. 40.
[96] *De Vita Caroli*, p. 40.
[97] Ibid. pp. 43–47.

ORIGIN OF HISTORICAL LITERATURE. 321

wound. After this, the last hope of the Mohammedans was extinct; the Christian arms had finally triumphed, and Charlemagne divided Spain among those gallant followers who had aided him in effecting its conquest.[98]

On the history of Arthur, the Middle Ages possessed information equally authentic. Different accounts had been circulated respecting this celebrated king;[99] but their comparative value was still unsettled, when, early in the twelfth century, the subject attracted the attention of Geoffrey, the well-known Archdeacon of Monmouth. This eminent man, in A.D. 1147, published the result of his inquiries, in a work which he called *History of the Britons*.[100] In this book, he takes a comprehensive view of the whole question; and not only relates the life of Arthur, but also traces the circumstances which prepared the way for the appearance of that great conqueror. In regard to the actions of Arthur, the historian was singularly fortunate, inasmuch as the materials necessary for that part of his subject were collected by Walter Archdeacon of Oxford, who was a friend of Geoffrey, and who, like him, took great interest in the study of history.[101] The work is, therefore, the joint composition of the two archdeacons; and is entitled to respect, not only on this account, but also because it was one of the most popular of all the productions of the Middle Ages.

---

[98] *De Vita Caroli*, p. 52. On the twelve peers of Charlemagne, in connexion with Turpin, see Sismondi, *Hist. des Français*, vol. v. pp. 246, 537, 538, vol. vi. p. 534.

[99] The Welsh, however, accused Gildas of having thrown his history 'into the sea.' Palgrave's *Anglo-Saxon Commonwealth*, vol. i. p. 453. The industrious Sharon Turner (*Hist. of England*, vol. i. pp. 282-295) has collected a great deal of evidence respecting Arthur; of whose existence he, of course, entertains no doubt. Indeed, at p. 292, he gives us an account of the discovery, in the twelfth century, of Arthur's body!

[100] In Turner's *Hist. of England*, vol. vii. pp. 269, 270, it is said to have appeared in 1128; but Mr. Wright (*Biog. Brit. Lit.* vol. ii. p. 144) seems to have proved that the real date is 1147.

[101] Geoffrey says, 'A Gualtero Oxinefordensi in multis historiis peritissimo viro audivit'

The earlier part of this great history is occupied with the result of those researches which the Archdeacon of Monmouth had made into the state of Britain before the accession of Arthur. With this we are not so much concerned; though it may be mentioned, that the archdeacon ascertained that, after the capture of Troy, Ascanius fled from the city, and begat a son, who became father to Brutus.[102] In those days, England was peopled by giants, all of whom were slain by Brutus; who, having extirpated the entire race, built London, settled the affairs of the country, and called it, after himself, by the name of Britain.[103] The archdeacon proceeds to relate the actions of a long line of kings who succeeded Brutus, most of whom were remarkable for their abilities, and some were famous for the prodigies which occurred in their time. Thus, during the government of Rivallo, it rained blood for three consecutive days;[104] and when Morvidus was on the throne, the coasts were infested by a horrid sea-monster, which, having devoured innumerable persons, at length swallowed the king himself.[105]

These and similar matters are related by the Arch-

(i. e. *ille* Geoffrey) 'vili licet stylo, breviter tamen propalabit, quæ prælia inclytus ille rex post victoriam istam, in Britanniam reversus, cum nepote suo commiserit.' *Galfredi Monumentensis Historia Britonum*, lib. xi. sec. l. p. 200. And in the dedication to the Earl of Gloucester, p. 1, he says, 'Walterus Oxinefordensis archidiaconus, vir in oratoria arte atque in exoticis historiis eruditus.' Compare *Matthæi Westmonast. Flores Historiarum*, part i. p. 248.

[102] *Galfredi Historia Britonum*, pp. 3, 4.

[103] 'Erat tunc nomen insulæ Albion, quæ a nemine, exceptis paucis gigantibus, inhabitabatur. . . . Denique Brutus de nomine suo insulam Britanniam, sociosque suos Britones appellat.' *Galf. Hist. Britonum*, p. 20.

[104] 'In tempore ejus tribus diebus cecidit pluvia sanguinea, et muscarum affluentia; quibus homines moriebantur.' *Hist. Brit*. p. 36.

[105] 'Advenerat namque ex partibus Hibernici maris inauditæ feritatis bellua, quæ incolas maritimos sine intermissione devorabat. Cumque fama aures ejus attigisset, accessit ipse ad illam, et solus cum sola congressus est. At cum omnia tela sua in illam in vanum consumpsisset, acceleravit monstrum illud, et apertis faucibus ipsum velut pisciculum devoravit.' *Hist. Brit*. p. 51.

deacon of Monmouth as the fruit of his own inquiries; but in the subsequent account of Arthur, he was aided by his friend the Archdeacon of Oxford. The two archdeacons inform their readers, that King Arthur owed his existence to a magical contrivance of Merlin, the celebrated wizard; the particulars of which they relate with a minuteness which, considering the sacred character of the historians, is rather remarkable.[106] The subsequent actions of Arthur did not belie his supernatural origin. His might nothing was able to withstand. He slew an immense number of Saxons; he overran Norway, invaded Gaul, fixed his court at Paris, and made preparations to effect the conquest of all Europe.[107] He engaged two giants in single combat, and killed them both. One of these giants, who inhabited the Mount of St. Michael, was the terror of the whole country, and destroyed all the soldiers sent against him, except those he took prisoners, in order to eat them while they were yet alive.[108] But he fell a victim to the prowess of Arthur; as also did another giant, named Ritho, who was, if possible, still more formidable. For Ritho, not content with warring on men of the meaner sort, actually clothed himself in furs which were entirely made of the beards of the kings he had killed.[109]

Such were the statements which, under the name of history, were laid before the world in the twelfth century; and that, too, not by obscure writers, but by high dignitaries of the church. Nor was anything

---

[106] The particulars of the intrigue are in *Galf. Hist. Brit.* pp. 151, 152. For information respecting Merlin, see also *Matthaei Westmonast. Flores Historiarum*, part i. pp. 161, 162; and *Naudé, Apologie pour les Grands Hommes*, pp. 308, 309, 318, 319, edit. Amsterdam, 1712.

[107] *Hist. Britonum*, pp. 167–170; a brilliant chapter.

[108] 'Sed et plures cupiebat quos semivivos devorabat.' *Hist. Brit.* p. 181.

[109] 'Hic namque ex barbis regum quos peremerat, fecerat sibi pelles, et mandaverat Arturo ut barbam suam diligenter excoriaret, atque excoriatam sibi dirigeret: ut quemadmodum ipse ceteris præerat regibus, ita quoque in honorem ejus ceteris barbis ipsam superponeret.' *Galf. Hist. Brit.* p. 184.

wanting by which the success of the work might be ensured. Its vouchers were the Archdeacon of Monmouth, and the Archdeacon of Oxford; it was dedicated to Robert Earl of Gloucester, the son of Henry I.; and it was considered so important a contribution to the national literature, that its principal author was raised to the bishopric of Asaph,—a preferment which he is said to owe to his success in investigating the annals of English history.[110] A book thus stamped with every possible mark of approbation, is surely no bad measure of the age in which it was admired. Indeed, the feeling was so universal, that, during several centuries, there are not more than two or three instances of any critic suspecting its accuracy.[111] A Latin abridgment of it was published by the well-known historian, Alfred of Beverley;[112] and, in order that it might be more generally known, it was translated into English by Layamon,[113] and into Anglo-Norman, first by

---

[110] 'It was partly, perhaps, the reputation of this book, which procured its author the bishopric of St. Asaph.' *Life of Geoffrey of Monmouth*, in *Wright's Biog. Brit. Lit.* vol. ii. p. 144, 8vo, 1846. According to the Welsh writers, he was Bishop of Llandaff. See *Stephens's Literature of the Kymry*, 8vo, 1849, p. 323.

[111] Mr. Wright (*Biog. Brit. Lit.* vol. ii. p. 146) says: "Within a century after its first publication, it was generally adopted by writers on English history; and during several centuries, only one or two rare instances occur of persons who ventured to speak against its veracity.' And Sir Henry Ellis says of Polydore Vergil, who wrote early in the sixteenth century, 'For the repudiation of Geoffrey of Monmouth's history, Polydore Vergil was considered almost as a man deprived of reason. Such were the prejudices of the time.' *Polydore Vergil's English Hist.* vol. i. p. x. edit. Ellis, 1846, 4to. See also, on its popularity, *Lappenberg's Hist. of the Anglo-Saxon Kings*, vol. i. p. 102. In the seventeenth century, which was the first sceptical century in Europe, men began to open their eyes on these matters; and Boyle, for example, classes together 'the fabulous labours of Hercules, and exploits of Arthur of Britain.' *Boyle's Works*, vol. iv. p. 425.

[112] *Wright's Biog. Brit. Lit.* vol. ii. p. 156; *Turner's Hist. of England*, vol. vii. p. 282.

[113] According to Mr. Wright (*Biog. Brit.* vol. ii. p. 439), it was translated through the medium of Wace. But it would be more correct to say, that Layamon made the absurdities of Geoffrey the basis of his work, rather than translated them; for

Gaimar, and afterwards by Wace;[114] zealous men, who were anxious that the important truths it contained should be diffused as widely as circumstances would allow.

It will hardly be necessary that I should adduce further evidence of the way in which history was written during the Middle Ages; for the preceding specimens have not been taken at random, but have been selected from the ablest and most celebrated authors; and as such present a very favourable type of the knowledge and judgment of Europe in those days. In the fourteenth and fifteenth centuries, there appeared, for the first time, faint signs of an approaching change;[115] but this improvement was not very marked until late in the sixteenth century, or even early in the seventeenth. The principal steps of this interesting movement will be traced in another part of the Introduction, when I shall show, that although in the seventeenth century the progress was unmistakeable, there was no attempt to take a comprehensive view of history until nearly the middle of the eighteenth century; when the subject was studied, first by the great French thinkers, then by one or two of the Scotch, and, some years later, by the Germans. This reformation of history was connected, as I shall point out, with other intellectual

---

[114] he amplifies 15,000 lines of Wace's *Brut* into 32,000 of his own jargon. See Sir F. Madden's *Preface to Layamon's Brut*, 8vo, 1847, vol. i. p. xiii. I cannot refrain from bearing testimony to the great philological value of this work of Layamon's, by the publication of which its accomplished editor has made an important contribution towards the study of the history of the English language. So far, however, as Layamon is concerned, we can only contemplate with wonder an age of which he was considered an ornament.

[114] *Wright's Biog. Brit. Lit.* vol. ii. pp. 151, 207; *Hallam's Literature of Europe*, vol. i. p. 35.

[115] Of which Froissart is the earliest instance; since he is the first who took a secular view of affairs, all the preceding historians being essentially theological. In Spain, too, we find, late in the fourteenth century, a political spirit beginning to appear among historians. See the remarks on Ayala, in *Ticknor's Hist. of Spanish Lit.* vol. i. pp. 165, 166; where, however, Mr. Ticknor represents Froissart as more unworldly than he really was.

changes, which corresponded to it, and which affected the social relations of all the principal countries of Europe. But, without anticipating what will be found in another part of this volume, it is sufficient to say, that not only was no history written before the end of the sixteenth century, but that the state of society was such as to make it impossible for one to be written. The knowledge of Europe was not yet ripe enough to enable it to be successfully applied to the study of past events. For we are not to suppose that the deficiencies of the early historians were caused by a lack of natural abilities. The average intellect of men is probably always the same; but the pressure exercised on them by society is constantly varying. It was, therefore, the general condition of society, which, in former days, compelled even the ablest writers to believe the most childish absurdities. Until that condition was altered, the existence of history was impossible, because it was impossible to find any one who knew what was most important to relate, what to reject, and what to believe.

The consequence was, that even when history was studied by men of such eminent abilities as Macchiavelli and Bodin, they could turn it to no better account than to use it as a vehicle for political speculations; and in none of their works do we find the least attempt to rise to generalizations large enough to include all the social phenomena. The same remark applies to Comines, who, though inferior to Macchiavelli and Bodin, was an observer of no ordinary acuteness, and certainly displays a rare sagacity in his estimation of particular characters. But this was due to his own intellect; while the age in which he lived made him superstitious, and, for the larger purposes of history, miserably shortsighted. His shortsightedness is strikingly shown in his utter ignorance of that great intellectual movement, which, in his own time, was rapidly overthrowing the feudal institutions of the Middle Ages; but to which he never once alludes, reserving his attention for those trivial political intrigues in the relation of which he believed history to consist.[116] As to his superstition, it would be idle to give many instances of that; since no man could live in the fifteenth century without having his mind enfeebled by the universal credulity. It may, however, be observed, that though he was personally acquainted with statesmen and diplomatists, and had, therefore, the fullest opportunity of seeing how enterprises of the fairest promise are constantly ruined, merely by the incapacity of those who undertake them, he, on all important occasions, ascribes such failure, not to the real cause, but to the immediate interference of the Deity. So marked, and so irresistible, was the tendency of the fifteenth century, that this eminent politician, a man of the world, and well skilled in the arts of life, deliberately asserts that battles are lost, not because the army is ill supplied, nor because the campaign is ill conceived, nor because the general is incompetent; but because the people or their prince are wicked, and Providence seeks to punish them. For, says Comines, war is a great mystery; and being used by God as the means of accomplishing his wishes, He gives victory, sometimes to one side, sometimes to the other.[117] Hence, too,

---

[116] On this, Arnold says, truly enough, 'Comines's Memoirs are striking from their perfect unconsciousness: the knell of the Middle Ages had been already sounded, yet Comines has no other notions than such as they had tended to foster; he describes their events, their characters, their relations, as if they were to continue for centuries.' *Arnold's Lectures on Modern History*, p. 118. To this I may add, that whenever Comines has occasion to mention the lower classes, which is very rarely the case, he speaks of them with great contempt. See two striking instances in *Mémoires de* *Philippe de Comines*, vol. ii. pp. 277, 287, edit. Paris, 1826.

[117] He says, that a field of battle is 'un des accomplissemens des œuvres que Dieu a commencées aucunes fois par petites mouvetes et occasions, et en donnant la victoire aucunes fois à l'un, et aucunes fois à l'autre: et est cecy mystère si grand, que les royaumes et grandes seigneuries en prennent aucunes fois fins et désolations, et les autres accroissement, et commencement de régner.' *Mém. de Comines*, vol. l. pp. 361, 362. Respecting the wanton invasion of Italy, he says, that the expedition might have been easily

disturbances occur in the state, solely by divine disposition; and they never would happen, except that princes or kingdoms, having become prosperous, forget the source from which their prosperity proceeded.[118]

Such attempts as these, to make politics a mere branch of theology,[119] are characteristic of the time; and they are the more interesting, as the work of a man of great ability, and of one, too, who had grown old in the experience of public life. When views of this sort were advocated, not by a monk in his cloister, but by a distinguished statesman, well versed in public affairs, we may easily imagine what was the average intellectual condition of those who were every way his inferiors. It is but too evident, that from them nothing could be expected; and that many steps had yet to be taken, before Europe could emerge from the superstition in-

---

ruined if the enemy had thought of poisoning the wells or the food: 'mais ils n'y eussent point failly, s'ils y eussent voulu essayer; mais il est de croire que nostre sauveur et rédempteur Jésus-Christ leur ostoit leur vouloir.' vol. iii. p. 154. So, he adds, p. 155, 'pour conclure l'article, semble que nostre seigneur Jésus-Christ ait voulu que toute la gloire du voyage ait esté attribuée à luy.' Compare the *Institutes of Timour*, p. 7; an instructive combination of superstition and ferocity.

[119] 'Mais mon advis est que cela ne se fait que par disposition divine; car quand les princes ou royaumes ont esté en grande prosperité ou richesses, et ils ont mesconnoissance dont procède telle grâce, Dieu leur dresse un ennemi ou ennemie, dont nul ne se douteroit, comme vous pouvez voir par les rois nommez en la Bible, et par ce que puis peu d'années en avez veu en cette Angleterre, et en cette maison de Bourgogne et autres lieux que avez veu et voyez tous les jours.' *Mém. de Comines*, vol. i. pp. 388, 389. See also his remarks on the Duke of Burgundy, vol. ii. p. 179; and in particular, his extraordinary digression, livre v. chap. xviii. vol. ii. pp. 290–298.

[119] Dr. Lingard (*Hist. of England*, vol. i. p. 357) says, 'From the doctrine of a superintending providence, the piety of our ancestors had drawn a rash but very convenient inference, that success is an indication of the Divine will, and that, of course, to resist a victorious competitor, is to resist the judgment of heaven;' see also p. 114. The last vestige of this once universal opinion is the expression, which is gradually falling into disuse, of 'appealing to the God of Battles.'

which it was sunk, and break through those grievous impediments which hindered its future progress.

But, though much remained to be done, there can be no doubt that the movement onward was uninterrupted, and that, even while Comines was writing, there were unequivocal symptoms of a great and decisive change. Still, they were only indications of what was approaching; and about a hundred years elapsed, after his death, before the progress was apparent in the whole of its results. For, though the Protestant Reformation was a consequence of this progress, it was for some time unfavourable to it, by encouraging the ablest men in the discussion of questions inaccessible to human reason, and thus diverting them from subjects in which their efforts would have been available for the general purposes of civilization. Hence we find, that little was really accomplished until the end of the sixteenth century, when, as we shall see in the next two chapters, the theological fervour began to subside in England and France, and the way was prepared for that purely secular philosophy, of which Bacon and Descartes were the exponents, but by no means the creators.[130] This epoch belongs to the seventeenth century, and from it we may date the intellectual regeneration of Europe; just as from the eighteenth century we may date its

---

[130] See *Guizot, Civilisation en Europe*, p. 166; the best passage in that able, but rather unequal work: 'Parcourez l'histoire du v⁰ au xvi⁰ siècle; c'est la théologie qui possède et dirige l'esprit humain; toutes les opinions sont empreintes de théologie; les questions philosophiques, politiques, historiques, sont toujours considérées sous un point de vue théologique. L'église est tellement souveraine dans l'ordre intellectuel, que même les sciences mathématiques et physiques sont tenues de se soumettre à ses doctrines. L'esprit théologique est en quelque sorte le sang qui a coulé dans les veines du monde européen jusqu'à Bacon et Descartes. Pour la première fois, Bacon en Angleterre, et Descartes en France, ont jeté l'intelligence hors des voies de la théologie.' A noble passage, and perfectly true: but what would have been the effect produced by Bacon and Descartes, if, instead of living in the seventeenth century, they had lived in the seventh? Would their philosophy have been equally secular; or, being equally secular, would it have been equally successful?

social regeneration. But during the greater part of the sixteenth century, the credulity was still universal, since it affected not merely the lowest and most ignorant classes, but even those who were best educated. Of this innumerable proofs might be given; though, for the sake of brevity, I will confine myself to two instances, which are particularly striking, from the circumstances attending them, and from the influence they exercised over men who might be supposed little liable to similar delusions.

At the end of the fifteenth, and early in the sixteenth century, Stoeffler, the celebrated astronomer, was professor of mathematics at Tubingen. This eminent man rendered great services to astronomy, and was one of the first who pointed out the way of remedying the errors in the Julian calendar, according to which time was then computed.[121] But neither his abilities nor his knowledge could protect him against the spirit of his age. In 1524, he published the result of some abstruse calculations, in which he had been long engaged, and by which he had ascertained the remarkable fact, that in that same year the world would again be destroyed by a deluge. This announcement, made by a man of such eminence, and made, too, with the utmost confidence, caused a lively and universal alarm.[122] News of the approaching event was rapidly circulated, and Europe was filled with consternation. To avoid the first shock, those who had houses by the sea, or on rivers, abandoned them;[123] while others, perceiving that

---

[121] Compare *Biog. Univ.* vol. xliii. p. 577, with *Montucla, Hist. des Mathématiques*, vol. i. p. 678.

[122] Naudé mentions, that in France it drove many persons almost mad: 'In Gallia parum afuit quin ad insaniam homines non paucos periculi metu (diluvium) adegerit.' *Bayle*, in voce *Stofflerus*, note B.

[123] 'Nam Petrus Cirvellus Hispanorum omnium sui temporis doctissimus, cum theologiae, in almo Complutensi gymnasio, lectoris munere fungeretur, et vero multos, ut ipsemet inquit, fluviis vel mari finitimos populos, jam stupido metu perculsos, domicilia ac sedes mutare vidisset, ac praedia, supellectilem, bonaque omnia, contra justum valorem sub actione distrahere, ac alia loca vel altitudine, vel siccitate magis secura requirere, sui officii esse putavit, in publica

such measures could only be temporary, adopted more active precautions. It was suggested that, as a preliminary step, the Emperor Charles V. should appoint inspectors to survey the country, and mark those places which, being least exposed to the coming flood, would be most likely to afford a shelter. That this should be done, was the wish of the imperial general, who was then stationed at Florence, and by whose desire a work was written recommending it.[124] But the minds of men were too distracted for so deliberate a plan; and besides, as the height of the flood was uncertain, it was impossible to say whether it would not reach the top of the most elevated mountains. In the midst of these and similar schemes, the fatal day drew near, and nothing had yet been contrived on a scale large enough to meet the evil. To enumerate the different proposals which were made and rejected, would fill a long chapter. One proposal is, however, worth noticing, because it was carried into effect with great zeal, and is, moreover, very characteristic of the age. An ecclesiastic of the name of Auriol, who was then professor of canon law at the University of Toulouse, revolved in his own mind various expedients by which this universal disaster might be mitigated. At length it occurred to him that it was practicable to imitate the course which, on a similar emergency, Noah had adopted with eminent success. Scarcely was the idea conceived, when it was put into execution. The inhabitants of Toulouse lent their aid; and an ark was built, in the hope that some part, at least, of the human species might be preserved, to continue their race, and repeople the earth, after the waters should have subsided, and the land again become dry.[125]

---

illa consternatione, quam de nihilo excitare persuasum non habebat,' &c. *Bayle,* note B.

[124] Ibid.

[125] In addition to the account in Bayle, the reader may refer to *Biog. Univ.* vol. iii. p. 88, vol. xxxi. p. 283, vol. xliii. pp. 577, 678; *Sprengel, Hist. de la Méde-*cine, vol. iii. p. 251; *Delambre, Hist. de l'Astronomie du Moyen Age,* Paris, 1819, 4to, p. 376; *Montucla, Hist. des Mathématiques,* vol. i. p. 622; *Dict. Philosoph.,* article *Astrologie,* in *Œuvres de Voltaire,* vol. xxxvii. pp. 148, 149.

About seventy years after this alarm had passed away, there happened another circumstance, which for a time afforded occupation to the most celebrated men in one of the principal countries of Europe. At the end of the sixteenth century, terrible excitement was caused by a report that a golden tooth had appeared in the jaw of a child born in Silesia. The rumour, on being investigated, turned out to be too true. It became impossible to conceal it from the public; and the miracle was soon known all over Germany, where, being looked on as a mysterious omen, universal anxiety was felt as to what this new thing might mean. Its real import was first unfolded by Dr. Horst. In 1595, this eminent physician published the result of his researches, by which it appears that, at the birth of the child, the sun was in conjunction with Saturn, at the sign Aries. The event, therefore, though supernatural, was by no means alarming. The golden tooth was the precursor of a golden age, in which the emperor would drive the Turks from Christendom, and lay the foundations of an empire that would last for thousands of years. And this, says Horst, is clearly alluded to by Daniel, in his well-known second chapter, where the prophet speaks of a statue with a golden head.[126]

---

[126] This history of the golden tooth is partly related by De Thou: see his *Hist. Univ.* vol. xi. pp. 634, 635. And on the controversy to which it gave rise, compare *Hist. des Oracles*, chap. iv., in *Œuvres de Fontenelle*, vol. ii. pp. 219, 220, ed. Paris, 1766; Sprengel, *Hist. de la Médecine*, vol. iii. pp. 247-249; *Biog. Univ.* vol. xx. p. 579.

CHAPTER VII.

OUTLINE OF THE HISTORY OF THE ENGLISH INTELLECT FROM THE MIDDLE OF THE SIXTEENTH TO THE END OF THE EIGHTEENTH CENTURY.

It is difficult for an ordinary reader, living in the middle of the nineteenth century, to understand, that only three hundred years before he was born, the public mind was in the benighted state disclosed in the preceding chapter. It is still more difficult for him to understand that the darkness was shared not merely by men of an average education, but by men of considerable ability, men in every respect among the foremost of their age. A reader of this sort may satisfy himself that the evidence is indisputable; he may verify the statements I have brought forward, and admit that there is no possible doubt about them; but even then he will find it hard to conceive that there ever was a state of society in which such miserable absurdities were welcomed as sober and important truths, and were supposed to form an essential part of the general stock of European knowledge.

But a more careful examination will do much to dissipate this natural astonishment. In point of fact, so far from wondering that such things were believed, the wonder would have been if they were rejected. For in those times, as in all others, every thing was of a piece. Not only in historical literature, but in all kinds of literature, on every subject—in science, in religion, in legislation—the presiding principle was a blind and unhesitating credulity. The more the history of Europe anterior to the seventeenth century is studied, the more completely will this fact be verified. Now and then a great man arose, who had his doubts respecting the universal belief; who whispered a suspicion as to the existence of giants thirty feet high, of dragons with wings, and of armies flying through the air; who thought that astrology might be a cheat, and necromancy a bubble; and who even went so far as to raise a question respecting the propriety of drowning every witch and burning every heretic. A few such men there undoubtedly were; but they were despised as mere theorists, idle visionaries, who, unacquainted with the practice of life, arrogantly opposed their own reason to the wisdom of their ancestors. In the state of society in which they were born, it was impossible that they should make any permanent impression. Indeed, they had enough to do to look to themselves, and provide for their own security; for, until the latter part of the sixteenth century, there was no country in which a man was not in great personal peril if he expressed open doubts respecting the belief of his contemporaries.

Yet it is evident, that until doubt began, progress was impossible. For, as we have clearly seen, the advance of civilization solely depends on the acquisitions made by the human intellect, and on the extent to which those acquisitions are diffused. But men who are perfectly satisfied with their own knowledge, will never attempt to increase it. Men who are perfectly convinced of the accuracy of their opinions, will never take the pains of examining the basis on which they are built. They look always with wonder, and often with horror, on views contrary to those which they inherited from their fathers; and while they are in this state of mind, it is impossible that they should receive any new truth which interferes with their foregone conclusions.

On this account it is, that although the acquisition of fresh knowledge is the necessary precursor of every step in social progress, such acquisition must itself be preceded by a love of inquiry, and therefore by a spirit of doubt; because without doubt there will be no inquiry, and without inquiry there will be no knowledge. For knowledge is not an inert and passive principle, which comes to us whether we will or no; but it must be sought before it can be won; it is the product of great labour and therefore of great sacrifice. And it is absurd to suppose that men will incur the labour, and make the sacrifice, for subjects respecting which they are already perfectly content. They who do not feel the darkness, will never look for the light. If on any point we have attained to certainty, we make no further inquiry on that point; because inquiry would be useless, or perhaps dangerous. The doubt must intervene, before the investigation can begin. Here, then, we have the act of doubting as the originator, or, at all events, the necessary antecedent, of all progress. Here we have that scepticism, the very name of which is an abomination to the ignorant; because it disturbs their lazy and complacent minds; because it troubles their cherished superstitions; because it imposes on them the fatigue of inquiry; and because it rouses even sluggish understandings to ask if things are as they are commonly supposed, and if all is really true which they from their childhood have been taught to believe.

The more we examine this great principle of scepticism, the more distinctly shall we see the immense part it has played in the progress of European civilization. To state in general terms, what in this Introduction will be fully proved, it may be said, that to scepticism we owe that spirit of inquiry, which, during the last two centuries, has gradually encroached on every possible subject; has reformed every department of practical and speculative knowledge; has weakened the authority of the privileged classes, and thus placed liberty on a surer foundation; has chastized the despotism of princes; has restrained the arrogance of the nobles; and has even diminished the prejudices of the clergy. In a word, it is this which has remedied the three fundamental errors of the olden time: errors which made the people, in politics too confiding; in science too credulous; in religion too intolerant.

This rapid summary of what has actually been effected, may perhaps startle those readers to whom such large investigations are not familiar. The importance, however, of the principle at issue is so great, that I purpose in this Introduction to verify it by an examination of all the prominent forms of European civilization. Such an inquiry will lead to the remarkable conclusion, that no single fact has so extensively affected the different nations as the duration, the amount, and above all the diffusion, of their scepticism. In Spain, the church, aided by the Inquisition, has always been strong enough to punish sceptical writers, and prevent, not indeed the existence, but the promulgation of sceptical opinions.[1] By this means the spirit of doubt being quenched, knowledge has for several centuries remained almost stationary; and civilization, which is the fruit of knowledge, has also been stationary. But in England and France, which, as we shall presently see, are the countries where scepticism first openly appeared, and where it has been most diffused, the results are altogether different; and the love of inquiry being encouraged, there has arisen that constantly-progressive knowledge to which these two great nations owe their prosperity. In the remaining part of this volume, I shall trace the history of this principle in France and England, and examine the different forms under which it has appeared, and the way in which those forms have affected the national interests. In the order of the investigation, I shall give the precedence to England; because, for the reasons already stated, its civilization must be deemed more normal than that of France; and therefore, notwithstanding its numerous deficiencies, it approaches the natural type more closely than its great

---

[1] On the influence of the French literature, which, late in the eighteenth century, crept into Spain in spite of the church, and diffused a considerable amount of scepticism among the most educated classes, compare *Llorente, Hist. de l'Inquisition*, vol. i. p. 322, vol. ii. p. 543, vol. iv. pp. 98, 99, 102, 148; *Doblado's Letters from Spain*, pp. 115, 119, 120, 133, 231, 232; *Lord Holland's Foreign Reminiscences*, edit. 1850, p. 76; *Southey's Hist. of Brasil*, vol. iii. p. 607; and an imperfect statement of the same fact in *Alison's Hist. of Europe*, vol. x. p. 8. In regard to the Spanish colonies, compare *Humboldt, Nouv. Espagne*, vol. ii. p. 818, with *Ward's Mexico*, vol. i. p. 83.

neighbour has been able to do. But as the fullest details respecting English civilization will be found in the body of the present work, I intend in the Introduction to devote merely a single chapter to it, and to consider our national history simply in reference to the immediate consequences of the sceptical movement; reserving for a future occasion those subsidiary matters which, though less comprehensive, are still of great value. And as the growth of religious toleration is undoubtedly the most important of all, I will, in the first place, state the circumstances under which it appeared in England in the sixteenth century; and I will then point out how other events, which immediately followed, were part of the same progress, and were indeed merely the same principles acting in different directions.

A careful study of the history of religious toleration will prove, that in every Christian country where it has been adopted, it has been forced upon the clergy by the authority of the secular classes.[2] At the present day, it is still unknown to those nations among whom the ecclesiastical power is stronger than the temporal power; and as this, during many centuries, was the general condition, it is not wonderful that, in the early history of Europe, we should find scarcely a trace of so wise and benevolent an opinion. But at the moment when Elizabeth mounted the throne of England, our country was about equally divided between two hostile

[2] Nearly two hundred years ago, Sir William Temple observed that in Holland the clergy possessed less power than in other countries; and that, therefore, there existed an unusual amount of toleration. *Observations upon the United Provinces*, in *Temple's Works*, vol. i. pp. 157-162. About seventy years later, the same inference was drawn by another acute observer, Le Blanc, who, after mentioning the liberality which the different sects displayed towards each other in Holland, adds, 'La grande raison d'une harmonie si parfaite est que tout s'y règle par les séculiers de chacune de ces religions, et qu'on n'y souffriroit pas des ministres, dont le zèle imprudent pourroit détruire cette heureuse correspondance.' *Le Blanc, Lettres d'un Français*, vol. i. p. 73. I merely give these as illustrations of an important principle, which I shall hereafter prove.

creeds; and the queen, with remarkable ability, contrived during some time so to balance the rival powers, as to allow to neither a decisive preponderance. This was the first instance which had been seen in Europe of a government successfully carried on without the active participation of the spiritual authority; and the consequence was, that for several years the principle of toleration, though still most imperfectly understood, was pushed to an extent which is truly surprising for so barbarous an age.³ Unhappily, after a time, various circumstances, which I shall relate in their proper place, induced Elizabeth to change a policy which she, even with all her wisdom, perhaps considered to be a dangerous experiment, and for which the knowledge of the country was as yet hardly ripe. But although she now allowed the Protestants to gratify their hatred against the Catholics, there was, in the midst of the sanguinary scenes which followed, one circumstance very worthy of remark. Although many persons were most unquestionably executed merely for their religion, no one ventured to state their religion as the cause of their execution.⁴ The most barbarous punishments were inflicted upon them; but they were told that they might escape the punishment by renouncing certain principles which were said to be injurious to the safety of the state.⁵ It is true, that many of these principles

---

³ 'In the first eleven years of her reign, not one Roman Catholic was prosecuted capitally for religion.' *Neal's Hist. of the Puritans*, vol. i. p. 444; and the same remark in *Collier's Eccles. Hist.* vol. vii. p. 252, edit. 1840.

⁴ Without quoting the impudent defence which Chief-Justice Popham made, in 1606, for the barbarous treatment of the Catholics (*Campbell's Chief Justices*, vol. i. p. 225), I will give the words of the two immediate successors of Elizabeth. James I. says: 'The truth is, according to my owne knowledge, the late queene of famous memory never punished any Papist for religion.' *Works of King James*, London, 1616, folio, p. 252. And Charles I. says: 'I am informed, neither Queen Elizabeth nor my father did ever avow that any priest in their times was executed merely for religion.' *Parl. Hist.* vol. ii. p. 713.

⁵ This was the defence set up in 1583, in a work called *The Execution of Justice in England*, and ascribed to Burleigh. See *Hallam's Const. Hist.* vol. i. pp. 146, 147; and *Somers Tracts*,

were such as no Catholic could abandon without at the same time abandoning his religion, of which they formed an essential part. But the mere fact that the spirit of persecution was driven to such a subterfuge, showed that a great progress had been made by the age. A most important point, indeed, was gained when the bigot became a hypocrite; and when the clergy, though willing to burn men for the good of their souls, were obliged to justify their cruelty by alleging considerations of a more temporal, and, as they considered, a less important character.[6]

A remarkable evidence of the change that was then taking place, is found in the two most important theological works which appeared in England during the reign of Elizabeth. *Hooker's Ecclesiastical Polity* was published at the end of the sixteenth century,[7] and is

---

vol. i. pp. 189–208: 'a number of persons whom they term as martyrs.' p. 195; and at p. 202, the writer attacks those who have 'entitled certain that have suffered for treason to be martyrs for religion.' In the same way, the opponents of Catholic Emancipation in our time, found themselves compelled to abandon the old theological ground, and to defend the persecution of the Catholics rather by political arguments than by religious ones. Lord Eldon, who was by far the most influential leader of the intolerant party, said, in a speech in the House of Lords, in 1810, that 'the enactments against the Catholics were meant to guard, not against the abstract opinions of their religion, but against the political dangers of a faith which acknowledged a foreign supremacy.' *Twiss's Life of Eldon*, vol. i. p. 435; see also pp. 483, 501, 577–580. Compare *Alison's Hist.* vol. vi. pp. 379 seq., a summary of the debate in 1805.

[6] Mr. Sewell seems to have this change in view in his *Christian Politics*, 8vo, 1844, p. 277. Compare Coleridge's note in *Southey's Life of Wesley*, vol. i. p. 270. An able writer says of the persecutions which, in the seventeenth century, the Church of England directed against her opponents: 'This is the stale pretence of the clergy in all countries, after they have solicited the government to make penal laws against those they call hereticks or schismaticks, and prompted the magistrates to a vigorous execution, then they lay all the odium on the civil power for whom they have no excuse to allege, but that such men suffered, not for religion, but for disobedience to the laws.' *Somers Tracts*, vol. xii. p. 534. See also *Butler's Mem. of the Catholics*, vol. i. p. 389, and vol. ii. pp. 44–46.

[7] The first four books, which are in every point of view the most important, were published

still considered one of the greatest bulwarks of our national church. If we compare this work with *Jewel's Apology for the Church of England*, which was written thirty years before it,* we shall at once be struck by the different methods these eminent writers employed. Both Hooker and Jewel were men of learning and genius. Both of them were familiar with the Bible, the Fathers, and the Councils. Both of them wrote with the avowed object of defending the Church of England; and both of them were well acquainted with the ordinary weapons of theological controversy. But here the resemblance stops. The men were very similar; their works are entirely different. During the thirty years which had elapsed, the English intellect had made immense progress; and the arguments which in the time of Jewel were found perfectly satisfactory, would not have been listened to in the time of Hooker. The work of Jewel is full of quotations from the Fathers and the Councils, whose mere assertions, when they are uncontradicted by Scripture, he seems to regard as positive proofs. Hooker, though he shows much respect to the Councils, lays little stress upon the Fathers, and evidently considered that his readers would not pay much attention to their unsupported opinions. Jewel inculcates the importance of faith; Hooker insists upon the exercise of reason.* The first

in 1594. *Walton's Life of Hooker*, in *Wordsworth's Ecclesiast. Biog.* vol. iii. p. 509. The sixth book is said not to be authentic; and doubts have been thrown upon the seventh and eighth books; but Mr. Hallam thinks that they are certainly genuine. *Literature of Europe*, vol. ii. pp. 24, 25.

* *Jewel's Apology* was written in 1561 or 1562. See *Wordsworth's Eccles. Biog.* vol. iii. p. 313. This work, the Bible, and *Fox's Martyrs*, were ordered, in the reign of Elizabeth, 'to be fixed in all parish churches, to be read by the people.' *Aubrey's Letters*, vol. ii. p. 42. The order, in regard to Jewel's *Defence*, was repeated by James I. and Charles I. *Butler's Mem. of the Catholics*, vol. iv. p. 413.

* 'Wherefore the natural measure whereby to judge our doings is, the sentence of Reason determining and setting down what is good to be done.' *Eccl. Polity*, book i. sec. viii. in *Hooker's Works*, vol. i. p. 99. He requires of his opponents, 'not to exact at our hands for every action the knowledge of some place of Scripture out of which we stand

employs all his talents in collecting the decisions of antiquity, and in deciding upon the meaning which they may be supposed to bear. The other quotes the ancients, not so much from respect for their authority, as with the view of illustrating his own arguments. Thus, for instance, both Hooker and Jewel assert the undoubted right of the sovereign to interfere in ecclesiastical affairs. Jewel, however, fancied that he had proved the right, when he had pointed out that it was exercised by Moses, by Joshua, by David, and by Solomon.[10] On the other hand, Hooker lays down

bound to deduce it, as by divers testimonies they seek to enforce: but rather, as the truth is, so to acknowledge, that *it sufficeth if such actions be framed according to the law of reason.*' Book ii. sec. i. *Works*, vol. i. p. 151. 'For men to be tied and led by authority, as it were with a kind of captivity of judgment, and, though there be reason to the contrary, not to listen unto it, but to follow, like beasts, the first in the herd, they know not nor care not whither: this were brutish. Again, that authority of men should prevail with men, either against or above Reason, is no part of our belief. Companies of learned men, be they never so great and reverend, are to yield unto Reason.' Book ii. sec. vii. vol. i. pp. 182, 183. In book v. sec. viii. vol. ii. p. 23, he says, that even 'the voice of the church' is to be held inferior to reason. See also a long passage in book vii. sec. xi. vol. iii. p. 152; and on the application of reason to the general theory of religion, see vol. i. pp. 220–223, book iii. sec. viii. Again, at p. 226: 'Theology, what is it, but the science of things divine? What science can be attained

unto, without the help of natural discourse and Reason?' And he indignantly asks those who insist on the supremacy of faith, 'May we cause our faith without Reason to appear reasonable in the eyes of men?' vol. i. p. 230.

[10] After referring to Isaiah, he adds: 'Præter, inquam, hæc omnia, ex historiis et optimorum temporum exemplis videmus pios principes procurationem ecclesiarum ab officio suo nunquam putasse alienam.

'Moses civilis magistratus, ac ductor populi, omnem religionis, et sacrorum rationem, et accepit a Deo, et populo tradidit, et Aaronem episcopum de aureo vitulo, et de violata religione, vehementer et graviter castigavit. Josue, etsi non aliud erat, quàm magistratus civilis, tamen cùm primùm inauguraretur et præficeretur populo, accepit mandata nominatim de religione, deque colendo Deo.

'David rex, cùm omnis jam religio, ab impio rege Saule prorsus esset dissipata, reduxit arcam Dei, hoc est, religionem restituit: nec tantùm adfuit ut admonitor aut hortator operis, sed etiam psalmos et hymnos dedit, et classes disposuit, et pompam

that this right exists, not because it is ancient, but
because it is advisable; and because it is unjust to suppose
that men who are not ecclesiastics will consent to
be bound by laws which ecclesiastics alone have framed.[11]
In the same opposite spirit do these great writers conduct
their defence of their own church. Jewel, like all
the authors of his time, had exercised his memory
more than his reason; and he thinks to settle the
whole dispute by crowding together texts from the
Bible, with the opinions of the commentators upon
them.[11] But Hooker, who lived in the age of Shake-

instituit, et quodammodo præfuit
sacerdotibus.
 'Salomon rex ædificavit templum
Domino, quod ejus pater
David animo tantùm destinaverat:
et postremò orationem egregiam
habuit ad populum de
religione, et cultu Dei; et Abiatharum
episcopum postea summovit,
et in ejus locum Sadocem
surrogavit.' *Apolog. Eccles.
Anglic.* pp. 161, 162.
 [11] He says that, although the
clergy may be supposed more
competent than laymen to regulate
ecclesiastical matters, this
will practically avail them nothing:
'It were unnatural not to
think the pastors and bishops of
our souls a great deal more fit
than men of secular trades and
callings; howbeit, when all which
the wisdom of all sorts can do
is done, for the devising of laws
in the church, it is the general
consent of all that giveth them
the form and vigour of laws;
without which they could be no
more unto us than the counsels
of physicians to the sick.' *Ecclesiastical
Polity,* book viii. sec. vi.
vol. iii. p. 303. He adds, p. 326:
'Till it be proved that some
special law of Christ hath for
ever annexed unto the clergy
alone the power to make ecclesiastical
laws, we are to hold it a
thing most *consonant with equity
and reason,* that no ecclesiastical
laws be made in a Christian commonwealth,
without consent as
well of the laity as of the clergy,
but least of all without consent
of the highest power.'
 [12] 'Quòd si docemus sacrosanctum
Dei evangelium, et
veteres episcopos, atque ecclesiam
primitivam nobiscum facere.'
If this be so, then, indeed,
'speramus, neminem illorum'
(his opponents) 'ita negligentem
fore salutis suæ, quin ut velit
aliquando cogitationem suscipere,
ad utros potiùs se adjungat.'
Apolog. Eccles. Anglic. p. 17.
At p. 53, he indignantly asks if
any one will dare to impeach the
Fathers: 'Ergo Origenes, Ambrosius,
Augustinus, Chrysostomus,
Gelasius, Theodoretus erant
desertores fidei catholicæ? Ergo
tot veterum episcoporum et doctorum
virorum tanta consensio
nihil aliud erat quàm conspiratio
hæreticorum? Aut quod tum
laudabatur in illis, id nunc damnatur
in nobis? Quodque in
illis erat catholicum, id nunc
mutatis tantùm hominum voluntatibus,
repentè factum est

speare and Bacon, found himself constrained to take
views of a far more comprehensive character. His
defence rests neither upon tradition nor upon commentators, nor ever upon revelation; but he is content that
the pretensions of the hostile parties shall be decided
by their applicability to the great exigencies of society,
and by the ease with which they adapt themselves to
the general purposes of ordinary life.[13]

It requires but little penetration to see the immense
importance of the change which these two great works
represent. As long as an opinion in theology was
defended by the old dogmatic method, it was impossible

---

schismaticum? Aut quod olim erat verum, nunc statim, quia istis non placet, erit falsum?' His work is full of this sort of eloquent, but, as it appears to our age, pointless declamation.

[13] This large view underlies the whole of the *Ecclesiastical Polity*. I can only afford room for a few extracts, which will be illustrations rather than proofs: the proof will be obvious to every competent reader of the work itself. 'True it is, the ancienter the better ceremonies of religion are; howbeit not absolutely true and without exception; *but true only so far forth as those different ages do agree* in the state of those things for which, at the first, those rites, orders, and ceremonies were instituted.' vol. i. p. 36. 'We count those things perfect which want nothing requisite for the end whereto they were instituted.' vol. i. p. 191. 'Because when a thing doth cease to be available unto the end which gave it being, the continuance of it must then of necessity appear superfluous.' And even of the laws of God, he boldly adds: 'Notwithstanding the authority of their Maker, the mutability of that end for which they are made doth also make them changeable.' vol. i. p. 236. 'And therefore laws, though both ordained of God himself, and the end for which they were ordained continuing, may notwithstanding cease, if by alteration of persons or times they be found unsufficient to attain unto that end.' vol. i. p. 238. At p. 240: 'I therefore conclude, that neither God's being Author of laws for government of his church, nor his committing them unto Scripture, is any reason sufficient wherefore all churches should for ever be bound to keep them without change.' See, too, vol. iii. p. 169, on 'the exigence of necessity.' Compare pp. 182, 183, and vol. i. p. 323, vol. ii. pp. 273, 424. Not a vestige of such arguments can be found in Jewel; who, on the contrary, says (*Apologia*, p. 114), 'Certè in religionem Dei nihil gravius dici potest, quàm si ea accusetur novitatis. Ut enim in Deo ipso, ita in ejus cultu nihil oportet esse novum.'

to assail it without incurring the imputation of heresy.
But when it was chiefly defended by human reasoning,
its support was seriously weakened. For by this means
the element of uncertainty was let in. It might be
alleged, that the arguments of one sect are as good as
those of another; and that we cannot be sure of the
truth of our principles, until we have heard what is to
be said on the opposite side. According to the old
theological theory, it was easy to justify the most
barbarous persecution. If a man knew that the only
true religion was the one which he professed, and if he
also knew that those who died in a contrary opinion
were doomed to everlasting perdition—if he knew
these things beyond the remotest possibility of a doubt,
he might fairly argue, that it is merciful to punish the
body in order to save the soul, and secure to immortal
beings their future salvation, even though he employed
so sharp a remedy as the halter or the stake.[14] But if
this same man is taught to think that questions of religion are to be settled by reason as well as by faith, he
can scarcely avoid the reflection, that the reason even
of the strongest minds is not infallible, since it has led
the ablest men to the most opposite conclusions. When
this idea is once diffused among a people, it cannot fail
to influence their conduct. No one of common sense
and common honesty will dare to levy upon another, on
account of his religion, the extreme penalty of the law,
when he knows it possible that his own opinions may
be wrong, and that those of the man he has punished
may be right. From the moment when questions of
religion begin to evade the jurisdiction of faith, and
submit to the jurisdiction of reason, persecution becomes
a crime of the deepest dye. Thus it was in England in
the seventeenth century. As theology became more
reasonable, it became less confident, and therefore more
merciful. Seventeen years after the publication of the

---

[14] Archbishop Whately has made some very good remarks on this. See his *Errors of Romanism traced to their Origin in Human Nature*, pp. 237, 238.

great work of Hooker, two men were publicly burned by the English bishops, for holding heretical opinions.[15] But this was the last gasp of expiring bigotry; and since that memorable day, the soil of England has never been stained by the blood of a man who has suffered for his religious creed.[16]

We have thus seen the rise of that scepticism which in physics must always be the beginning of science, and in religion must always be the beginning of toleration. There is, indeed, no doubt that in both cases individual thinkers may, by a great effort of original genius, emancipate themselves from the operation of this law. But in the progress of nations no such emancipation is possible. As long as men refer the movements of the comets to the immediate finger of God, and as long as they believe that an eclipse is one of the modes by which the Deity expresses his anger, they will never be guilty of the blasphemous presumption of attempting to predict such supernatural appearances. Before they could dare to investigate the causes of these mysterious phenomena, it is necessary that they should believe, or at all events that they should suspect, that the phenomena themselves were capable of being explained by the human mind. In the same way, until men are content in some degree to bring their religion before the bar of their own reason, they never can understand how it is that there should be a diversity of creeds, or how any one can differ from themselves

---

[15] Their names were Legat and Wightman, and they suffered in 1611: see the contemporary account in *Somers Tracts*, vol. ii. pp. 400-408. Compare *Blackstone's Comment.* vol. iv. p. 49; *Harris's Lives of the Stuarts*, vol. i. pp. 143, 144; and note in *Burton's Diary*, vol. i. p. 118. Of these martyrs to their opinions, Mr. Hallam says: 'The first was burned by King, bishop of London; the second by Neyle, of Litchfield.' *Const. Hist.* vol. i. pp. 611, 612.

[16] It should be mentioned, to the honour of the Court of Chancery, that late in the sixteenth, and early in the seventeenth century, its powers were exerted against the execution of those cruel laws, by which the Church of England was allowed to persecute men who differed from its own views. See *Campbell's Chancellors*, vol. ii. pp. 135, 176, 231.

without being guilty of the most enormous and unpardonable crime.[17]

If we now continue to trace the progress of opinions in England, we shall see the full force of these remarks. A general spirit of inquiry, of doubt, and even of insubordination, began to occupy the minds of men. In physics, it enabled them, almost at a blow, to throw off the shackles of antiquity, and give birth to sciences founded not on notions of old, but on individual observations and individual experiments.[18] In politics, it stimulated them to rise against the government, and eventually bring their king to the scaffold. In religion, it vented itself in a thousand sects, each of which proclaimed, and often exaggerated, the efficiency of private judgment.[19] The details of this vast movement form

---

[17] 'To tax any one, therefore, with want of reverence, because he pays no respect to what we venerate, is either irrelevant, or is a mere confusion. The fact, so far as it is true, is no reproach, but an honour; because to reverence all persons and all things is absolutely wrong: reverence shown to that which does not deserve it, is no virtue; no, nor even an amiable weakness, but a plain folly and sin. But if it be meant that he is wanting in proper reverence, not respecting what is really to be respected, that is assuming the whole question at issue, because what we call divine, he calls an idol; and as, supposing that we are in the right, we are bound to fall down and worship, so, supposing him to be in the right, he is no less bound to pull it to the ground and destroy it.' *Arnold's Lectures on Modern History*, pp. 210, 211. Considering the ability of Dr. Arnold, considering his great influence, and considering his profession, his antecedents, and the character of the university in which he was speaking, it must be allowed that this is a remarkable passage, and one well worthy the notice of those who wish to study the tendencies of the English mind during the present generation.

[18] On the connexion between the rise of the Baconian philosophy and the change in the spirit of theologians, compare *Comte, Philosophie Positive*, vol. v. p. 701, with *Whately on Dangers to Christian Faith*, pp. 148, 149. It favoured, as Tennemann (*Gesch. der Philos.* vol. x. p. 14) says, the 'Belebung der selbstthätigen Kraft des menschlichen Geistes:' and hence the attack on the inductive philosophy in *Newman's Development of Christian Doctrine*, pp. 179-183. But Mr. Newman does not seem to be aware how irrevocably we are now pledged to the movement which he seeks to reverse.

[19] The rapid increase of heresy in the middle of the seventeenth century is very remarkable, and

one of the most interesting parts of the history of England: but without anticipating what I must hereafter relate, I will at present mention only one instance, which, from the circumstances attending it, is very characteristic of the age. The celebrated work by Chillingworth on the *Religion of Protestants*, is generally admitted to be the best defence which the Reformers have been able to make against the Church of Rome.[20] It was published in 1637,[21] and the position of the author would induce us to look for the fullest display of bigotry that was consistent with the spirit of his time. Chillingworth had recently abandoned the creed which he now came forward to attack; and he, therefore, might be expected to have that natural inclination to dogmatize with which apostasy is usually accompanied. Besides this, he was the godson and the intimate friend of Laud,[22] whose memory is still loathed, as the meanest, the most cruel, and the most narrow-

it greatly aided civilization in England by encouraging habits of independent thought. In Feb. 1646-7, Boyle writes from London, 'There are few days pass here, that may not justly be accused of the brewing or branching of some new opinion. Nay, some are so studiously changling in that particular, they esteem an opinion as a diurnal, after a day or two scarce worth the keeping. If any man have lost his religion, let him repair to London, and I'll warrant him he shall find it: I had almost said too, and if any man has a religion, let him but come hither now, and he shall go near to lose it.' *Birch's Life of Boyle*, in *Boyle's Works*, vol. i. pp. 20, 21. See also *Bates's Account of the late Troubles*, edit. 1685, part ii. p. 219, on 'that unbridled licentiousness of hereticks which grew greater and greater daily.' Compare to the same effect *Carlyle's Cromwell*, vol. i. p. 289; *Hallam's Const. Hist.* vol. i. p. 608; and *Carwithen's Hist. of the Church of England*, vol. ii. p. 203: 'sectaries began to swarm.'

[20] Not to quote the opinions of inferior men respecting Chillingworth, it is enough to mention, that Lord Mansfield said he was 'a perfect model of argumentation.' *Butler's Reminiscences*, vol. i. p. 126. Compare a letter from Warburton, in *Nichols's Illustrations of the Eighteenth Century*, vol. iv. p. 849.

[21] *Des Maizeaux, Life of Chillingworth*, p. 141.

[22] *Aubrey's Letters and Lives*, vol. ii. p. 285; *Des Maizeaux, Life of Chillingworth*, pp. 2, 9. The correspondence between Laud and Chillingworth is supposed to be lost. *Des Maizeaux*, p. 12. Carwithen (*Hist. of the Church of England*, vol. ii. p. 214) says, 'Laud was the godfather of Chillingworth.'

minded man who ever sat on the episcopal bench.[22]
He was, moreover, a fellow of Oxford, and was a constant resident at that ancient university, which has always been esteemed as the refuge of superstition, and which has preserved to our own day its unenviable fame.[24] If now we turn to the work that was written under those auspices, we can scarcely believe that it was produced in the same generation, and in the same country, where, only twenty-six years before, two men had been publicly burned because they advocated opinions different to those of the established church. It is, indeed, a most remarkable proof of the prodigious energy of that great movement which was now going on, that its pressure should be felt under circumstances the most hostile to it which can possibly be conceived; and that a friend of Laud, and a fellow of Oxford, should, in a grave theological treatise, lay down principles utterly subversive of that theological spirit which for many centuries had enslaved the whole of Europe.

In this great work, all authority in matters of religion is openly set at defiance. Hooker, indeed, had appealed from the jurisdiction of the Fathers to the jurisdiction of reason; he had, however, been careful to add, that the reason of individuals ought to bow before that of the church, as we find it expressed in great Councils, and in the general voice of ecclesiastical tradition.[26] But Chillingworth would hear of none of these things. He would admit of no reservations which

---

[22] The character of Laud is now well understood and generally known. His odious cruelties made him so hated by his contemporaries, that after his condemnation, many persons shut up their shops, and refused to open them till he was executed. This is mentioned by Walton, an eye-witness. See *Walton's Life of Sanderson*, in *Wordsworth's Eccles. Biog.* vol. iv. p. 429.

[24] A modern writer suggests, with exquisite simplicity, that Chillingworth derived his liberal principles *from* Oxford: 'the very same college which nursed the high intellect and tolerant principles of Chillingworth.' *Bowles's Life of Bishop Ken*, vol. i. p. xxi.

[26] Hooker's undue respect for the Councils of the Church is noticed by Mr. Hallam, *Const. Hist.* vol. i. p. 213. Compare the hesitating remarks in *Coleridge's Literary Remains*, vol. iii. pp. 35, 36.

tended to limit the sacred right of private judgment. He not only went far beyond Hooker in neglecting the Fathers,[26] but he even ventured to despise the Councils. Although the sole object of his work was to decide on the conflicting claims of the two greatest sects into which the Christian Church has broken, he never quotes as authorities the Councils of that very church respecting which the disputes were agitated.[27] His strong and subtle intellect, penetrating the depths of the subject, despised that sort of controversy which had long busied the minds of men. In discussing the points upon which the Catholics and Protestants were at issue, he does not inquire whether the doctrines in question met the approval of the early church, but he asks if they are in accordance with human reason; and he does not hesitate to say that, however true they may be, no man is bound to believe them if he finds that they are repugnant to the dictates of his own understanding. Nor will he consent that faith should supply the absence of authority. Even this favourite principle of theologians is by Chillingworth made to yield to the supremacy of the human reason.[28] Reason, he says,

---

[26] Reading the Fathers he contemptuously calls travelling on a 'north-west discovery.' *Chillingworth's Religion of Protestants*, p. 366. Even to Augustine, who was probably the ablest of them, Chillingworth pays no deference. See what he says at pp. 196, 333, 376; and as to the authority of the Fathers in general, see pp. 252, 346. Chillingworth observed, happily enough, that churchmen 'account them fathers when they are for them, and children when they are against them.' *Calamy's Life*, vol. i. p. 253.

[27] As to the supposed authority of Councils, see *Religion of Protestants*, pp. 132, 463. It affords curious evidence of the slow progress of theologians to observe the different spirit in which some of our clergy consider these matters. See, for instance, Palmer *on the Church*, 1839, vol. ii. pp. 150-171. In no other branch of inquiry do we find this obstinate determination to adhere to theories which all thinking men have rejected for the last two centuries.

[28] Indeed, he attempts to fasten the same doctrine upon the Catholics; which, if he could have done, would of course have ended the controversy. He says, rather unfairly, 'Your church you admit, because you think you have reason to do so; so that by you, as well as Protestants, all is finally resolved into your own reason.' *Relig. of Protest.* p. 134.

gives us knowledge; while faith only gives us belief, which is a part of knowledge, and is, therefore, inferior to it. It is by reason, and not by faith, that we must discriminate in religious matters; and it is by reason alone that we can distinguish truth from falsehood. Finally, he solemnly reminds his readers, that in religious matters no one ought to be expected to draw strong conclusions from imperfect premises, or to credit improbable statements upon scanty evidence; still less, he says, was it ever intended that men should so prostitute their reason, as to believe with infallible faith that which they are unable to prove with infallible arguments.[29]

No one of ordinary reflection can fail to perceive the manifest tendency of these opinions. But what is more important to observe is, the process through which, in the march of civilization, the human mind had been obliged to pass before it could reach such elevated views. The Reformation, by destroying the dogma of an infallible church, had of course weakened the reverence which was paid to ecclesiastical antiquity. Still, such was the force of old associations, that our countrymen long continued to respect what they had ceased to

---

[29] 'God desires only that we believe the conclusion, as much as the premises deserve; that the strength of our faith be equal or proportionable to the credibility of the motives to it.' *Relig. of Protest.* p. 66. 'For my part, I am certain that God hath given us our reason to discern between truth and falsehood; and he that makes not this use of it, but believes things he knows not why, I say it is by chance that he believes the truth, and not by choice; and I cannot but fear that God will not accept of this sacrifice of fools.' p. 133. 'God's spirit, if he please, may work more,—a certainty of adherence beyond a certainty of evidence; but neither God doth, nor man may, require of us, as our duty, to give a greater assent to the conclusion than the premises deserve; to build an infallible faith upon motives that are only highly credible and not infallible; as it were a great and heavy building upon a foundation that hath not strength proportionate.' p. 149. 'For faith is not knowledge, no more than three is four, but eminently contained in it; so that he that knows, believes, and something more; but he that believes many times does not know—nay, if he doth barely and merely believe, he doth never know.' p. 412. See also p. 417.

venerate. Thus it was, that Jewel, though recognizing the supreme authority of the Bible, had, in cases where it was silent or ambiguous, anxiously appealed to the early church, by whose decision he supposed all difficulties could be easily cleared. He, therefore, only used his reason to ascertain the discrepancies which existed between Scripture and tradition; but when they did not clash, he paid what is now considered a superstitious deference to antiquity. Thirty years after him came Hooker;[30] who made a step in advance, and laying down principles from which Jewel would have shrunk with fear, did much to weaken that which it was reserved for Chillingworth utterly to destroy. Thus it is, that these three great men represent the three distinct epochs of the three successive generations in which they respectively lived. In Jewel, reason is, if I may so say, the superstructure of the system; but authority is the basis upon which the superstructure is built. In Hooker, authority is only the superstructure, and reason is the basis.[31] But in Chillingworth, whose writings were harbingers of the coming storm, authority entirely disappears, and the whole fabric of religion is made to rest upon the way in which the unaided reason of man shall interpret the decrees of an omnipotent God.

---

[30] On the connexion between the Reformation and the views advocated in the *Ecclesiastical Polity*, compare *Newman's Development of Christian Doctrine*, p. 47, with some able remarks by Locke, in *King's Life of Locke*, vol. ii. pp. 99–101. Locke, who was anything but a friend to the church, was a great admirer of Hooker, and in one place calls him 'the arch-philosopher.' *Essay on Government*, in *Locke's Works*, vol. iv. p. 380.

[31] The opposition between Jewel and Hooker was so marked, that some of the opponents of Hooker quoted against him Jewel's Apology. See *Wordsworth's Eccl. Biog.* vol. iii. p. 513. Dr. Wordsworth calls this 'curious;' but it would be much more curious if it had not happened. Compare the remarks made by the Bishop of Limerick (*Parr's Works*, vol. ii. p. 470, *Notes on the Spital Sermon*), who says, that Hooker 'opened that fountain of reason,' &c.; language which will hardly be considered too strong by those who have compared the *Ecclesiastical Polity* with the theological works previously produced by the English church.

The immense success of this great work of Chillingworth, must have aided that movement of which it is itself an evidence.³² It formed a decisive vindication of religious dissent;³³ and thus justified the breaking up of the Anglican church, which the same generation lived to witness. Its fundamental principle was adopted by the most influential writers of the seventeenth century,—such as Hales, Owen, Taylor, Burnet, Tillotson, Locke, and even the cautious and time-serving Temple; all of whom insisted upon the authority of private judgment, as forming a tribunal from which no one had the power of appeal. The inference to be drawn from this seems obvious.³⁴ If the ultimate test of truth is individual judgment, and if no one can affirm that the judgments of men, which are often contradictory, can ever be infallible, it follows of necessity that there is no decisive criterion of religious truth. This is a melancholy, and, as I firmly believe, a most inaccurate conclusion; but it is one which every nation must entertain, before it can achieve that great work of toleration, which, even in our own country, and in our own time, is not yet consummated. It is necessary that men should learn to doubt, before they begin to tolerate; and that they should recognize the fallibility of their own opinions, before they respect the opinions of their opponents.³⁵

---

³² Des Maizeaux (*Life of Chillingworth*, pp. 220, 221) says: 'His book was received with a general applause; and, what perhaps never happened to any other controversial work of that bulk, two editions of it were published within less than five months. . . . The quick sale of a book, and especially of a book of controversy, in folio, is a good proof that the author hit the taste of his time.' See also *Biographia Britannica*, edit. Kippis, vol. iii. pp. 511, 512.

³³ Or, as Calamy cautiously puts it, Chillingworth's work 'appeared to me to go a great way towards the justifying of moderate conformity.' *Calamy's Life*, vol. i. p. 234. Compare *Palmer on the Church*, vol. i. pp. 267, 268; and what is probably an allusion to Chillingworth in *Doddridge's Correspond. and Diary*, vol. ii. p. 81. See also the opinion of Hobbes, in *Aubrey's Letters and Lives*, vol. ii. pp. 268, 629.

³⁴ A short but able view of the aspect which the English mind now began to assume, will be found in Stäudlin, *Geschichte der theologischen Wissenschaften*, vol. ii. pp. 95 seq.

³⁵ In *Whately's Dangers to*

This great process is far from being yet completed in any country; and the European mind, barely emerged from its early credulity, and from an overweening confidence in its own belief, is still in a middle, and, so to say, a probationary stage. When that stage shall be finally passed, when we shall have learned to estimate men solely by their character and their acts, and not at all by their theological dogmas, we shall then be able to form our religious opinions by that purely transcendental process, of which in every age glimpses have been granted to a few gifted minds. That this is the direction in which things are now hastening, must be clear to every one who has studied the progress of modern civilization. Within the short space of three centuries, the old theological spirit has been compelled, not only to descend from its long-established supremacy, but to abandon those strongholds to which, in the face of advancing knowledge, it has vainly attempted to secure a retreat. All its most cherished pretensions it has been forced gradually to relinquish.[36] And although in England a temporary prominence has recently been given to certain religious controversies, still the circumstances attending them show the alteration in the character of the age. Disputes which, a century ago, would have set the whole kingdom in a flame, are now regarded with indifference by the vast

Christian Faith, pp. 186–198, there is a perspicuous statement of the arguments now commonly received against coercing men for their religious opinions. But the most powerful of these arguments are based entirely upon expediency, which would have insured their rejection in an age of strong religious convictions. Some, and only some, of the theological difficulties respecting toleration, are noticed in *Coleridge's Lit. Remains*, vol. i. pp. 312–315; and in another work (*The Friend*, vol. i. p. 78), he mentions, what is the real fact, 'that same indifference which makes toleration so easy a virtue with us.' See also *Archdeacon Hare's Guesses at Truth*, 2nd series, 1848, p. 278; and *Nichols's Illustrations of Lit. Hist.* vol. v. p. 817: 'a spirit of mutual toleration and forbearance has appeared (at least one good consequence of religious indifference).'

[36] It would be idle to offer proofs of so notorious a fact; but the reader will be interested by some striking remarks in *Capefigue, Hist. de la Réforme*, vol. i. pp. 228, 229.

majority of educated men. The complications of modern society, and the immense variety of interests into which it is divided, have done much to distract the intellect, and to prevent it from dwelling upon subjects which a less-occupied people would deem of paramount importance. Besides this, the accumulations of science are far superior to those of any former age, and offer suggestions of such surpassing interest, that nearly all our greatest thinkers devote to them the whole of their time, and refuse to busy themselves with matters of mere speculative belief. The consequence is, that what used to be considered the most important of all questions, is now abandoned to inferior men, who mimic the zeal, without possessing the influence of those really great divines whose works are among the glories of our early literature. These turbulent polemics have, indeed, distracted the church by their clamour, but they have not made the slightest impression upon the great body of English intellect; and an overwhelming majority of the nation is notoriously opposed to that monastic and ascetic religion which it is now vainly attempted to reconstruct. The truth is, that the time for these things has gone by. Theological interests have long ceased to be supreme; and the affairs of nations are no longer regulated according to ecclesiastical views.[37] In

---

[37] A writer intimately acquainted with the social condition of the great European countries, says: 'Ecclesiastical power is almost extinct as an active element in the political or social affairs of nations or of individuals, in the cabinet or in the family circle; and a new element, literary power, is taking its place in the government of the world.' *Laing's Denmark*, 1852, p. 82. On this natural tendency in regard to legislation, see Meyer, *Esprit des Institut. Judiciaires*, vol. i. p. 267 note; and a good summary in Stäudlin, *Gesch. der theolog. Wissenschaften*, vol. ii. pp. 304, 305. It is not surprising to find that many of the clergy complain of a movement so subversive of their own power. Compare *Ward's Ideal of a Christian Church*, pp. 40, 108–111, 388; *Sewell's Christian Politics*, pp. 276, 277, 279; *Palmer's Treatise on the Church*, vol. ii. p. 361. It is thus that everything is tending to confirm the remarkable prediction of Sir James Mackintosh, that 'church-power (unless some revolution, auspicious to priestcraft, should replunge Europe in ignorance) will certainly not survive the nineteenth century.' *Mem. of Mackintosh*, vol. i. p. 67.

England, where the march has been more rapid than elsewhere, this change is very observable. In every other department we have had a series of great and powerful thinkers, who have done honour to their country, and have won the admiration of mankind. But for more than a century, we have not produced a single original work in the whole field of controversial theology. For more than a century, the apathy on this subject has been so marked, that there has been made no addition of value to that immense mass of divinity which, among thinking men, is in every successive generation losing something of its former interest.[36]

[36] 'The "divines" in England at the present day, her bishops, professors, and prebendaries, are not theologians. They are logicians, chemists, skilled in the mathematics, historians, poor commentators upon Greek poets.' *Theodore Parker's Critical and Miscellaneous Writings*, 1848, p. 302. At p. 33, the same high authority says: 'But, within the present century, what has been written in the English tongue, in any department of theological scholarship, which is of value and makes a mark on the age? The *Bridgewater Treatises*, and the new edition of *Paley*,—we blush to confess it,—are the best things.' Sir William Hamilton (*Discussions on Philosophy*, 1852, p. 699) notices the decline of 'British theology,' though he appears ignorant of the cause of it. The Rev. Mr. Ward (*Ideal of a Christian Church*, p. 405) remarks, that 'we cannot wonder, however keenly we may mourn, at the decline and fall of dogmatic theology.' See also Lord Jeffrey's *Essays*, vol. iv. p. 337: 'Warburton, we think, was the last of our great divines. . . . The days of the Cudworths and Barrows, the Hookers and Taylors, are long gone by.' Dr. Parr was the only English theologian since Warburton who possessed sufficient learning to retrieve this position; but he always refused to do so, being, unconsciously to himself, held back by the spirit of his age. Thus, we find him writing to Archbishop Magee, in 1823: 'As to myself, I long ago determined not to take any active part in polemical theology.' *Parr's Works*, vol. vii. p. 11.

In the same way, since the early part of the eighteenth century, hardly any one has carefully read the Fathers, except for mere historical and secular purposes. The first step was taken about the middle of the seventeenth century, when the custom of quoting them in sermons began to be abandoned. *Burnet's Own Time*, vol. i. pp. 329, 330; *Orme's Life of Owen*, p. 184. After this they rapidly fell into contempt; and the Rev. Mr. Dowling (*Study of Ecclesiast. History*, p. 195) asserts, that 'Waterland, who died in 1740, was the last of our great

These are only some of the innumerable signs, which must be discerned by every man who is not blinded by the prejudices of an imperfect education. An immense majority of the clergy,—some from ambitious feelings, but the greater part, I believe, from conscientious motives,—are striving to check the progress of that scepticism which is now gathering in upon us from every quarter.[29] It is time that these well-intentioned,

patristical scholars.' To this I may add, that nine years subsequent to the death of Waterland, the obvious decay of professional learning struck Warburton, afterwards Bishop of Gloucester, so much, that he wrote to Jortin, somewhat roughly, 'anything makes a divine among our parsons.' See his *Letter*, written in 1749, in *Nichols's Illustrations of Lit. Hist.* vol. ii. p. 173; and for other evidence of the neglect by the clergy of their ancient studies, see *Jones's Memoirs of Horne, Bishop of Norwich*, pp. 68, 184; and the complaint of Dr. Knowler, in 1766, in *Nichols's Lit. Anec.* vol. ii. p. 130. Since then, attempts have been made at Oxford to remedy this tendency; but such attempts, being opposed by the general march of affairs, have been, and must be, futile. Indeed, so manifest is the inferiority of these recent efforts, that one of the most active cultivators in that field frankly admits, that, in point of knowledge, his own party has effected nothing; and he even asserts, with great bitterness, that 'it is melancholy to say it, but the chief, perhaps the only, English writer who has any claim to be considered an ecclesiastical historian, is the infidel Gibbon.' *Newman on the Develop. of Christ. Doct.* p. 5.

[29] As some writers, moved by their wishes rather than by their knowledge, seek to deny this, it may be well to observe, that the increase of scepticism since the latter part of the eighteenth century is attested by an immense mass of evidence, as will appear to whoever will compare the following authorities: *Whately's Dangers to Christian Faith*, p. 87; *Kay's Social Condition of the People*, vol. ii. p. 506; *Tocqueville, de la Démocratie*, vol. iii. p. 72; *J. H. Newman on Development*, pp. 28, 29; *F. W. Newman's Natural History of the Soul*, p. 197; *Parr's Works*, vol. ii. p. 5, vol. iii. pp. 688, 689; *Felkin's Moral Statistics*, in *Journal of Statist. Soc.* vol. i. p. 541; *Watson's Observations on the Life of Wesley*, pp. 155, 194; *Matter, Hist. du Gnosticisme*, vol. ii. p. 485; *Ward's Ideal of a Christian Church*, pp. 266, 267, 404; *Turner's Hist. of England*, vol. ii. pp. 129, 142, vol. iii. p. 509; *Priestley's Memoirs*, vol. i. pp. 127, 128, 446, vol. ii. p. 751; *Cappe's Memoirs*, p. 367; *Nichols's Lit. Anec. of Eighteenth Century*, vol. iv. p. 671, vol. viii. p. 473; *Nichols's Illust. of Lit. Hist.* vol. v. p. 640; *Combe's Notes on the United States*, vol. ii. pp. 171, 172, 183.

though mistaken, men should see the delusion under which they labour. That by which they are so much alarmed, is the intermediate step which leads from superstition to toleration. The higher order of minds have passed through this stage, and are approaching what is probably the ultimate form of the religious history of the human race. But the people at large, and even some of those who are commonly called educated men, are only now entering that earlier epoch in which scepticism[40] is the leading feature of the mind. So far, therefore, from our apprehensions being excited by this rapidly-increasing spirit, we ought rather to do everything in our power to encourage that which, though painful to some, is salutary to all; because by it alone can religious bigotry be effectually destroyed. Nor ought we to be surprised that, before this can be done, a certain degree of suffering must first intervene.[41] If one age believes too much, it is

[40] It has been suggested to me by an able friend, that there is a class of persons who will misunderstand this expression; and that there is another class who, without misunderstanding it, will intentionally misrepresent its meaning. Hence, it may be well to state distinctly what I wish to convey by the word 'scepticism.' By scepticism I merely mean hardness of belief; so that an increased scepticism is an increased perception of the difficulty of proving assertions; or, in other words, it is an increased application, and an increased diffusion, of the rules of reasoning, and of the laws of evidence. This feeling of hesitation and of suspended judgment has, in every department of thought, been the invariable preliminary to all the intellectual revolutions through which the human mind has passed; and without it, there could be no progress, no change, no civilization. In physics, it is the necessary precursor of science; in politics, of liberty; in theology, of toleration. These are the three leading forms of scepticism; it is, therefore, clear, that in religion the sceptic steers a middle course between atheism and orthodoxy, rejecting both extremes, because he sees that both are incapable of proof.

[41] What a learned historian has said of the effect which the method of Socrates produced on a very few Greek minds, is applicable to that state through which a great part of Europe is now passing: 'The Socratic dialectics, clearing away from the mind its mist of fancied knowledge, and laying bare the real ignorance, produced an immediate effect, like the touch of the torpedo. The newly-created consciousness

but a natural reaction that another age should believe too little. Such are the imperfections of our nature, that we are compelled, by the very laws of its progress, to pass through those crises of scepticism and of mental distress, which to a vulgar eye are states of national decline and national shame; but which are only as the fire by which the gold must be purged before it can leave its dross in the pot of the refiner. To apply the imagery of the great allegorist, it is necessary that the poor pilgrim, laden with the weight of accumulated superstitions, should struggle through the Slough of Despond and the Valley of Death, before he can reach that glorious city, glittering with gold and with jewels, of which the first sight is sufficient recompense for his toils and his fears.

During the whole of the seventeenth century, this double movement of scepticism and of toleration continued to advance; though its progress was constantly checked by the two successors of Elizabeth, who in every thing reversed the enlightened policy of the great queen. These princes exhausted their strength in struggling against the tendencies of an age they were unable to understand; but, happily, the spirit which they wished to quench had reached a height that

---

of ignorance was alike unexpected, painful, and humiliating, —a season of doubt and discomfort, yet combined with an internal working and yearning after truth, never before experienced. Such intellectual quickening, which could never commence until the mind had been disabused of its original illusion of false knowledge, was considered by Socrates not merely as the index and precursor, but as the indispensable condition of future progress.' *Grote's Hist. of Greece*, vol. viii. pp. 614, 615, 8vo, 1851. Compare *Kritik der reinen Vernunft*, in *Kant's Werke*, vol. ii. pp. 572, 577.

'So ist der Skeptizismus ein Ruheplatz für die menschliche Vernunft, da sie sich über ihre dogmatische Wanderung besinnen und den Entwurf von der Gegend machen kann, wo sie sich befindet, um ihren Weg fernerhin mit mehrerer Sicherheit wählen zu können, aber nicht ein Wohnplatz zum beständigen Aufenthalte. . . . So ist das skeptische Verfahren zwar an sich selbst für die Vernunftfragen nicht befriedigend, aber doch vorübend, um ihre Vorsichtigkeit zu erwecken und auf gründliche Mittel zu weisen, die sie in ihren rechtmässigen Besitzen sichern können.'

mocked their control. At the same time, the march of
the English mind was still further aided by the nature
of those disputes which, during half a century, divided
the country. In the reign of Elizabeth, the great
contest had been between the church and its opponents;
between those who were orthodox, and those who were
heretical. But in the reigns of James and Charles,
theology was for the first time merged in politics. It
was no longer a struggle of creeds and dogmas; but
it was a struggle between those who favoured the
crown, and those who supported the parliament. The
minds of men, thus fixed upon matters of real importance, neglected those inferior pursuits that had engrossed the attention of their fathers.[43] When, at
length, public affairs had reached their crisis, the hard
fate of the king, which eventually advanced the interests of the throne, was most injurious to those of the
church. There can, indeed, be no doubt that the
circumstances connected with the execution of Charles,
inflicted a blow upon the whole system of ecclesiastical

---

[43] Dr. Arnold, whose keen eye noted this change, says (*Lectures on Modern History*, p. 232), 'What strikes us predominantly, is, that what, in Elizabeth's time, was a controversy between divines, was now a great political contest between the crown and the parliament.' The ordinary compilers, such as Sir A. Alison (*Hist. of Europe*, vol. i. p. 51), and others, have entirely misrepresented this movement; an error the more singular, because the eminently political character of the struggle was recognized by several contemporaries. Even Cromwell, notwithstanding the difficult game he had to play, distinctly stated, in 1655, that the origin of the war was not religious. See *Carlyle's Cromwell*, vol. iii. p. 103; and corroborative evidence in *Walker's History of Independency*, part i. p. 132. James I. also saw that the Puritans were more dangerous to the state than to the church: 'do not so far differ from us in points of religion, as in their confused form of policy and parity; being ever discontented with the present government, and impatient to suffer any superiority; which maketh their sects insufferable in any well-governed commonwealth.' *Speech of James I.*, in *Parl. Hist.* vol. i. p. 982. See also the observations ascribed to De Foe, in *Somers Tracts*, vol. ix. p. 572: 'The king and parliament fell out about matters of civil right; .... the first difference between the king and the English parliament did not respect religion, but civil property.'

authority, from which, in this country, it has never been able to recover. The violent death of the king excited the sympathies of the people; and by thus strengthening the hands of the royalists, hastened the restoration of the monarchy.[43] But the mere name of that great party which had risen to power, was suggestive of the change that, in a religious point of view, was taking place in the national mind. It was, indeed, no light thing, that England should be ruled by men who called themselves Independents; and who, under that title, not only beat back the pretensions of the clergy, but professed an unbounded contempt for all those rites and dogmas which the clergy had, during many centuries, continued to amass.[44]

---

[43] See *Clarendon's Hist. of the Rebellion*, p. 716. Sir W. Temple, in his *Memoirs*, observes, that the throne of Charles II. was strengthened by 'what had passed in the last reign.' *Temple's Works*, vol. ii. p. 344. This may be illustrated by the remarks of M. Lamartine on the execution of Louis XVI. *Hist. des Girondins*, vol. v. pp. 86–7: 'Sa mort, au contraire, aliénait de la cause française cette partie immense des populations qui ne juge les événements humains que par le cœur. La nature humaine est pathétique; la république l'oublia, elle donna à la royauté quelque chose du martyre, à la liberté quelque chose de la vengeance. Elle prépara ainsi une réaction contre la cause républicaine, et mit du côté de la royauté la sensibilité, l'intérêt, les larmes d'une partie des peuples.'

[44] The energy with which the House of Commons, in 1646, repelled the pretensions of 'the Assembly of Divines,' is one of many proofs of the determination of the predominant party not to allow ecclesiastical encroachments. See the remarkable details in *Parl. Hist.* vol. iii. pp. 459–463; see also p. 1305. As a natural consequence, the Independents were the first sect which, when possessed of power, advocated toleration. Compare *Orme's Life of Owen*, pp. 63–75, 102–111; *Somers Tracts*, vol. xii. p. 542; *Walker's Hist. of Independency*, part ii. pp. 50, 157, part iii. p. 22; *Clarendon's Hist. of the Rebellion*, pp. 610, 640. Some writers ascribe great merit to Jeremy Taylor for his advocacy of toleration (*Heber's Life of Taylor*, p. xxvii.; and *Parr's Works*, vol. iv. p. 417); but the truth is that when he wrote the famous *Liberty of Prophesying*, his enemies were in power; so that he was pleading for his own interests. When, however, the Church of England again obtained the upper hand, Taylor withdrew the concessions which he had made in the season of adversity. See the indignant remarks of Coleridge (*Lit. Remains*, vol. iii. p. 250), who,

SIXTEENTH TO THE EIGHTEENTH CENTURY. 361

True it is, that the Independents did not always push to their full extent the consequences of their own doctrines.⁴⁵ Still, it was a great matter to have those doctrines recognized by the constituted authorities of the state. Besides this, it is important to remark, that the Puritans were more fanatical than superstitious.⁴⁶ They were so ignorant of the real principles of government, as to direct penal laws against private vices; and to suppose that immorality could be stemmed by legislation.⁴⁷ But, notwithstanding this serious error,

---

though a great admirer of Taylor, expresses himself strongly on this dereliction: see also a recently published *Letter to Percy, Bishop of Dromore*, in *Nichols's Illustrations of Lit. History*, vol. vii. p. 464.

⁴⁵ However, Bishop Short (*History of the Church of England*, 8vo, 1847, pp. 452, 458) says, what is undoubtedly true, that the hostility of Cromwell to the church was not theological, but political. The same remark is made by Bishop Kennet. *Note in Burton's Diary*, vol. ii. p. 479. See also *Vaughan's Cromwell*, vol. i. p. xcvii.; and on the generally tolerant spirit of this great man, see *Hallam's Const. Hist.* vol. ii. p. 14; and the evidence in *Harris's Lives of the Stuarts*, vol. iii. pp. 37–47. But the most distinct recognition of the principle, is in a *Letter from Cromwell to Major-General Crawford*, recently printed in *Carlyle's Cromwell*, vol. i. pp. 201, 202, 8vo, 1846. In it Cromwell writes, 'Sir, the state, in choosing men to serve it, takes no notice of their opinions; if they be willing faithfully to serve it— that satisfies.' See additional proof in *Carwithen's Hist. of the Church of Engl.* vol. ii. pp. 245, 249.

⁴⁶ No one can understand the real history of the Puritans, who does not take this into consideration. In the present Introduction, it is impossible to discuss so large a subject; and I must reserve it for the future part of this work, in which the history of England will be specially treated. In the mean time, I may mention, that the distinction between fanaticism and superstition is clearly indicated, but not analyzed, by Archbishop Whately, in his *Errors of Romanism traced to their Origin in Human Nature*, p. 40. This should be compared with *Hume's Philosophical Works*, vol. iii. pp. 81–89, Edinb. 1826, on the difference between enthusiasm and superstition; a difference which is noticed, but, as it appears to me, misunderstood, by Maclaine, in his *Additions to Mosheim's Ecclesiast. Hist.* vol. ii. p. 38.

⁴⁷ Compare *Barrington's Observations on the Statutes*, p. 143, with *Burton's Diary of the Parliaments of Cromwell*, vol. i. pp. xcviii. 145, 392, vol. ii. pp. 35, 229. In 1650, a second conviction of fornication was made felony, without benefit of clergy; but, after the Restoration, Charles II. and his friends found this law

they always resisted the aggressions even of their own clergy; and the destruction of the old episcopal hierarchy, though perhaps too hastily effected, must have produced many beneficial results. When the great party by whom these things were accomplished, was at length overthrown, the progress of events still continued to tend in the same direction. After the Restoration, the church, though reinstated in her ancient pomp, had evidently lost her ancient power.⁴⁸ At the same time, the new king, from levity, rather than from reason, despised the disputes of theologians, and treated questions of religion with what he considered a philosophic indifference.⁴⁹ The courtiers followed his example, and thought they could not err in imitating him, whom they regarded as the Lord's anointed. The results were such as must be familiar even to the most superficial readers of English literature. That grave and measured scepticism, by which the Independents had been characterized, lost all its decorum when it was transplanted into the ungenial atmosphere of a court. The men by whom the king was surrounded, were unequal to the difficulties of suspense; and they attempted to fortify their doubts by the blasphemous expression of a wild and desperate infidelity. With scarcely an excep-

---

rather inconvenient; so it was repealed. See *Blackstone's Commentaries*, vol. iv. p. 65.

⁴⁸ See *Life of Ken, by a Layman*, edit. 1854, vol. i. p. 61. At p. 129, the same writer says, with sorrow, 'The church recovered much of her temporal possessions, but not her spiritual rule.' The power of the bishops was abridged 'by the destruction of the court of high-commission.' *Short's Hist. of the Church of England*, p. 595. See also, on the diminished influence of the Church-of-England clergy after the Restoration, *Southey's Life of Wesley*, vol. i. pp. 278, 279; and *Watson's Observations on the Life of Wesley*, pp. 129-131.

⁴⁹ Buckingham and Halifax, the two men who were perhaps best acquainted with Charles II., both declared that he was a deist. Compare *Lingard's Hist. of Engl.* vol. viii. p. 127, with *Harris's Lives of the Stuarts*, vol. v. p. 65. His subsequent conversion to Catholicism is exactly analogous to the increased devotion of Louis XIV. during the later years of his life. In both cases, superstition was the natural refuge of a worn-out and discontented libertine, who had exhausted all the resources of the lowest and most grovelling pleasures.

tion, all those writers who were most favoured by Charles, exhausted the devices of their ribald spirit, in mocking a religion, of the nature of which they were profoundly ignorant. These impious buffooneries would, by themselves, have left no permanent impression on the age; but they deserve attention, because they were the corrupt and exaggerated representatives of a more general tendency. They were the unwholesome offspring of that spirit of disbelief, and of that daring revolt against authority, which characterized the most eminent Englishmen during the seventeenth century. It was this which caused Locke to be an innovator in his philosophy, and an Unitarian in his creed. It was this which made Newton a Socinian; which forced Milton to be the great enemy of the church, and which not only turned the poet into a rebel, but tainted with Arianism the *Paradise Lost*. In a word, it was the same contempt for tradition, and the same resolution to spurn the yoke, which, being first carried into philosophy by Bacon, was afterwards carried into politics by Cromwell; and which, during that very generation, was enforced in theology by Chillingworth, Owen, and Hales; in metaphysics by Hobbes and Glanvil; and in the theory of government by Harrington, Sydney, and Locke.

The progress which the English intellect was now making towards shaking off ancient superstitions,[50] was

---

[50] One of the most curious instances of this may be seen in the destruction of the old notions respecting witchcraft. This important revolution in our opinions was effected, so far as the educated classes are concerned, between the Restoration and the Revolution; that is to say, in 1660, the majority of educated men still believed in witchcraft; while in 1688, the majority disbelieved it. In 1665, the old orthodox view was stated by Chief-Baron Hale, who, on a trial of two women for witchcraft, said to the jury: 'That there are such creatures as witches, I make no doubt at all; for, first, the Scriptures have affirmed so much; secondly, the wisdom of all nations hath provided laws against such persons, which is an argument of their confidence of such a crime.' Campbell's *Lives of the Chief Justices*, vol. i. pp. 565, 566. This reasoning was irresistible, and the witches were hung; but the change in public opinion began to affect

still further aided by the extraordinary zeal displayed in the cultivation of the physical sciences. This, like all great social movements, is clearly traceable to the events by which it was preceded. It was partly cause, and partly effect, of the increasing incredulity of the age. The scepticism of the educated classes made them dissatisfied with those long-established opinions, which only rested on unsupported authority; and this gave rise to a desire to ascertain how far such notions might be verified or refuted by the real condition of

---

even the judges, and after this melancholy exhibition of the Chief-Baron, such scenes became gradually rarer; though Lord Campbell is mistaken in supposing (p. 563) that this was 'the last capital conviction in England for the crime of bewitching.' So far from this, three persons were executed at Exeter for witchcraft in 1682. See *Hutchinson's Historical Essay concerning Witchcraft*, 1720, pp. 56, 57. Hutchinson says: 'I suppose these are the last three that have been hanged in England.' If, however, one may rely upon a statement made by Dr. Parr, two witches were hung at Northampton in 1705; and in '1712, five other witches suffered the same fate at the same place.' *Parr's Works*, vol. iv. p. 182, 8vo, 1828. This is the more shameful, because, as I shall hereafter prove, from the literature of that time, a disbelief in the existence of witches had become almost universal among educated men; though the old superstition was still defended on the judgment-seat and in the pulpit. As to the opinions of the clergy, compare *Cudworth's Intellect. Syst.* vol. iii. pp. 345, 348; *Vernon Correspond.* vol. ii. pp. 302, 303; *Burt's Letters from the North of Scotland*, vol. i. pp. 220, 221; *Wesley's Journals*, pp. 602, 713. Wesley, who had more influence than all the bishops put together, says: 'It is true, likewise, that the English in general, and, indeed, most of the men of learning in Europe, have given up all accounts of witches and apparitions as mere old wives' fables. I am sorry for it. . . . The giving up witchcraft is, in effect, giving up the Bible. . . . But I cannot give up, to all the Deists in Great Britain, the existence of witchcraft, till I give up the credit of all history, sacred and profane.'

However, all was in vain. Every year diminished the old belief; and in 1736, a generation before Wesley had recorded these opinions, the laws against witchcraft were repealed, and another vestige of superstition effaced from the English statute-book. See *Barrington on the Statutes*, p. 407; *Note* in *Burton's Diary*, vol. i. p. 26; *Harris's Life of Hardwicke*, vol. i. p. 307.

To this it may be interesting to add, that in Spain a witch was burned so late as 1781. *Ticknor's Hist. of Spanish Literature*, vol. iii. p. 238.

things. A curious instance of the rapid progress of this spirit may be found in the works of an author who was one of the most eminent among the mere literary men of his time. While the Civil War was barely decided, and three years before the execution of the king, Sir Thomas Browne published his celebrated work, called *Inquiries into Vulgar and Common Errors*.[51] This able and learned production has the merit of anticipating some of those results which more modern inquirers have obtained;[52] but it is chiefly remarkable, as being the first systematic and deliberate onslaught ever made in England upon those superstitious fancies which were then prevalent respecting the external world. And what is still more interesting is, that the circumstances under which it appeared make it evident, that while the learning and genius of the author belonged to himself, the scepticism which he displayed respecting popular belief was forced on him by the pressure of the age.

In or about 1633, when the throne was still occupied by a superstitious prince; when the Church of England was at the height of her apparent power; and when men were incessantly persecuted for their religious opinions—this same Sir Thomas Browne wrote his *Religio Medici*,[53] in which we find all the qualities of his later work, except the scepticism. Indeed, in the *Religio Medici*, there is shown a credulity that must have secured the sympathy of those classes which were then dominant. Of all the prejudices which at that time were deemed an essential part of the popular creed, there was not one which Browne ventured to deny. He announces his belief in the philosopher's stone;[54] in spirits, and tutelary angels;[55] and in

---

[51] The first edition was published in 1646. *Works of Sir Thomas Browne*, vol. ii. p. 163.

[52] See the notes in Mr. Wilkin's edition of *Browne's Works*, Lond. 1836, vol. ii. pp. 284, 360, 361.

[53] The precise date is unknown; but Mr. Wilkin supposes that it was written 'between the years 1633 and 1635.' Preface to *Religio Medici*, in *Browne's Works*, vol. ii. p. 4.

[54] Ibid. vol. ii. p. 58.

[55] Ibid. vol. ii. p. 47.

palmistry.⁵⁶ He not only peremptorily affirms the reality of witches, but he says that those who deny their existence are not merely infidels, but atheists.⁵⁷ He carefully tells us that he reckons his nativity, not from his birth, but from his baptism; for before he was baptized, he could not be said to exist.⁵⁸ To these touches of wisdom, he moreover adds, that the more improbable any proposition is, the greater his willingness to assent to it; but that when a thing is actually impossible, he is on that very account prepared to believe it.⁵⁹

Such were the opinions put forth by Sir Thomas Browne in the first of the two great works he presented to the world. But in his *Inquiries into Vulgar Errors*, there is displayed a spirit so entirely different, that if it were not for the most decisive evidence, we could hardly believe it to be written by the same man. The truth, however, is, that during the twelve years which elapsed between the two works, there was completed that vast social and intellectual revolution, of which the overthrow of the church and the execution of the king were but minor incidents. We know from the literature, from the private correspondence, and from the public acts of that time, how impossible it was, even for the strongest minds, to escape the effects of the general intoxication. No wonder, then, that Browne, who certainly was inferior to several of his

---

⁵⁶ Or, as he calls it, 'chiromancy.' *Religio Medici*, in *Browne's Works*, vol. ii. p. 89.

⁵⁷ 'For my part, I have ever believed, and do now know, that there are witches. They that doubt of these, do not only deny them, but spirits; and are obliquely, and upon consequence, a sort, not of infidels, but atheists.' Ibid. vol. ii. pp. 43, 44.

⁵⁸ 'From this I do compute or calculate my nativity.' Ibid. vol. ii. p. 64.

⁵⁹ *Religio Medici*, sec. ix. in *Browne's Works*, vol. ii. pp. 13, 14: unfortunately too long to extract. This is the 'credo quia impossibile est,' originally one of Tertullian's absurdities, and once quoted in the House of Lords by the Duke of Argyle, as 'the ancient religious maxim.' *Parl. Hist.* vol. xi. p. 802. Compare the sarcastic remark on this maxim in the *Essay concerning Human Understanding*, book iv. chap. xviii. *Locke's Works*, vol. ii. p. 271. It was the spirit embodied in this sentence which supplied Celsus with some formidable arguments against the Fathers. *Neander's Hist. of the Church*, vol. i. pp. 227, 228.

contemporaries, should have been affected by a movement which they were unable to resist. It would have been strange, indeed, if he alone had remained uninfluenced by that sceptical spirit, which, because it had been arbitrarily repressed, had now broken all bounds, and in the reaction soon swept away those institutions which vainly attempted to stop its course.

It is in this point of view that a comparison of the two works becomes highly interesting, and, indeed, very important. In this, his later production, we hear no more about believing things because they are impossible; but we are told of 'the two great pillars of truth, experience and solid reason.'[60] We are also reminded that one main cause of error is 'adherence unto authority;'[61] that another is, 'neglect of inquiry;'[62] and, strange to say, that a third is 'credulity.'[63] All this was not very consistent with the old theological spirit; and we need not, therefore, be surprised that Browne not only exposes some of the innumerable blunders of the Fathers,[64] but, after speaking of errors in general, curtly adds: 'Many others there are, which we resign unto divinity, and perhaps deserve not controversy.'[65]

The difference between these two works is no bad measure of the rapidity of that vast movement which, in the middle of the seventeenth century, was seen in every branch of practical and speculative life. After the death of Bacon, one of the most distinguished Englishmen was certainly Boyle, who, if compared with his contemporaries, may be said to rank immediately below Newton, though, of course, very inferior to him as an original thinker.[66] With the additions he

---

[60] *Inquiries into Vulgar and Common Errors*, book iii. chap. xxviii. in *Browne's Works*, vol. ii. p. 534.
[61] Ibid book i. chap. vii. vol. ii. p. 225.
[62] 'A supinity, or neglect of inquiry.' Ibid. book i. chap. v. vol. ii. p. 211.
[63] 'A third cause of common errors is the credulity of men.' Book i. chap. v. vol. ii. p. 208.
[64] See two amusing instances in vol. ii. pp. 267, 438.
[65] *Vulgar and Common Errors*, book vii. chap. xi., in *Browne's Works*, vol. iii. p. 326.
[66] Monk (*Life of Bentley*, vol. i. p. 37) says, that Boyle's discoveries 'have placed his name

made to our knowledge we are not immediately concerned; but it may be mentioned, that he was the first who instituted exact experiments into the relation between colour and heat;[67] and by this means, not only ascertained some very important facts, but laid a foundation for that union between optics and thermotics, which, though not yet completed, now merely waits for some great philosopher to strike out a generalization large enough to cover both, and thus fuse the two sciences into a single study. It is also to Boyle, more than to any other Englishman, that we owe the science of hydrostatics, in the state in which we now possess it.[68] He is the original discoverer of that beautiful law, so fertile in valuable results, according to which the elasticity of air varies as its density.[69] And, in the opinion of one

---

in a rank second only to that of Newton;' and this, I believe, is true, notwithstanding the immense superiority of Newton.

[67] Compare *Powell on Radiant Heat* (*Brit. Assoc.* vol. i. p. 287), with *Lloyd's Report on Physical Optics*, 1834, p. 338. For the remarks on colours, see *Boyle's Works*, vol. ii. pp. 1–40; and for the account of his experiments, pp. 41–80; and a slight notice in *Brewster's Life of Newton*, vol. i. pp. 155, 156, 236. It is, I think, not generally known, that Power is said to be indebted to Boyle for originating some of his experiments on colours. See a letter from Hooke, in *Boyle's Works*, vol. v. p. 533.

[68] Dr. Whewell (*Bridgewater Treatise*, p. 266) well observes, that Boyle and Pascal are to hydrostatics what Galileo is to mechanics, and Copernicus, Kepler, and Newton to astronomy. See also on Boyle, as the founder of hydrostatics, *Thomson's Hist. of the Royal Society*, pp. 397,

398; and his *Hist. of Chemistry*, vol. i. p. 204.

[69] This was discovered by Boyle about 1650, and confirmed by Mariotte in 1676. See *Whewell's Hist. of the Inductive Sciences*, vol. ii. pp. 557, 588; *Thomson's Hist. of Chemistry*, vol. i. p. 215; *Turner's Chemistry*, vol. i. pp. 41, 200; *Brande's Chemistry*, vol. i. p. 363. This law has been empirically verified by the French Institute, and found to hold good for a pressure even of twenty-seven atmospheres. See *Challis on the Mathematical Theory of Fluids*, in *Sixth Report of Brit. Assoc.* p. 226; and *Herschel's Nat. Philos.* p. 231. Although Boyle preceded Mariotte by a quarter of a century, the discovery is rather unfairly called the law of Boyle and Mariotte; while foreign writers, refining on this, frequently omit the name of Boyle altogether, and term it the law of Mariotte! See, for instance, *Liebig's Letters on Chemistry*, p. 126; *Monteil*,

of the most eminent modern naturalists, it was Boyle who opened up those chemical inquiries, which went on accumulating until, a century later, they supplied the means by which Lavoisier and his contemporaries fixed the real basis of chemistry, and enabled it for the first time to take its proper stand among those sciences that deal with the external world.[70]

The application of these discoveries to the happiness of Man, and particularly to what may be called the material interests of civilization, will be traced in another part of this work; but what I now wish to observe, is the way in which such investigations harmonized with the movement I am attempting to describe. In the whole of his physical inquiries, Boyle constantly insists upon two fundamental principles: namely, the importance of individual experiments, and the comparative unimportance of the facts which, on these subjects, antiquity has handed down.[71] These are the

---

Divers États, vol. viii. p. 122; *Kaemtz's Meteorology*, p. 236; *Comte, Philos. Pos.* vol. i. pp. 583, 645, vol. ii. pp. 484, 615; *Pouillet, Élémens de Physique*, vol. i. p. 339, vol. ii. pp. 58, 183.

[70] 'L'un des créateurs de la physique expérimentale, l'illustre Robert Boyle, avait aussi reconnu, dès le milieu du dix-septième siècle, une grande partie des faits qui servent aujourd'hui de base à cette chimie nouvelle.' *Cuvier, Progrès des Sciences*, vol. i. p. 30. The 'aussi' refers to Rey. See also *Cuvier, Hist. des Sciences Naturelles*, part ii. pp. 322, 346-349. A still more recent writer says, that Boyle 'stood, in fact, on the very brink of the pneumatic chemistry of Priestley; he had in his hand the key to the great discovery of Lavoisier.' *Johnston on Dimorphous Bodies*, in *Reports of Brit. Assoc.* vol. vi. p. 163. See further respecting Boyle, *Robin et Verdeil, Chimie Anatomique*, Paris, 1853, vol. i. pp. 576, 577, 579, vol. ii. p. 24; and *Sprengel, Hist. de la Médecine*, vol. iv. p. 177.

[71] This disregard of ancient authority appears so constantly in his works, that it is difficult to choose among innumerable passages which might be quoted. I will select one which strikes me as well expressed, and is certainly very characteristic. In his *Free Inquiry into the vulgarly received Notion of Nature*, he says (*Boyle's Works*, vol. iv. p. 359), 'For I am wont to judge of opinions as of coins: I consider much less, in any one that I am to receive, whose inscription it bears, than what metal it is made of. It is indifferent enough to me whether it was stamped many years or ages

two great keys to his method: they are the views which he inherited from Bacon, and they are also the views which have been held by every man who, during the last two centuries, has added anything of moment to the stock of human knowledge. First to doubt,[72] then to inquire, and then to discover, has been the process universally followed by our great teachers. So strongly did Boyle feel this, that though he was an eminently religious man,[73] he gave to the most popular of his scientific works the title of *The Sceptical Chemist*; meaning to intimate, that until men were sceptical concerning the chemistry of their own time, it would be impossible that they should advance far in the career which lay before them. Nor can we fail to observe that this remarkable work, in which such havoc was made with old notions, was published in 1661,[74] the year after the accession of Charles II., in whose reign

since, or came but yesterday from the mint.' In other places he speaks of the 'schoolmen' and 'gownsmen' with a contempt not much inferior to that expressed by Locke himself.

[72] In his *Considerations touching Experimental Essays*, he says (*Boyle's Works*, vol. i. p. 197), ' Perhaps you will wonder, Pyrophilus, that in almost every one of the following essays I should speak so doubtingly, and use so often *perhaps*, *it seems*, *it is not improbable*, and such other expressions as argue a diffidence of the truth of the opinions I incline to,' &c. Indeed, this spirit is seen at every turn. Thus his *Essay on Crystals*, which, considering the then state of knowledge, is a remarkable production, is entitled ' Doubts and Experiments touching the curious Figures of Salts.' *Works*, vol. ii. p. 488. It is, therefore, with good reason that M. Humboldt terms him ' the cautious and doubting Robert Boyle.' *Humboldt's Cosmos*, vol. ii. p. 730.

[73] On the sincere Christianity of Boyle, compare *Burnet's Lives and Characters*, edit. Jebb, 1833, pp. 351–360; *Life of Ken*, by a Layman, vol. i. pp. 32, 33; *Whewell's Bridgewater Treatise*, p. 273. He made several attempts to reconcile the scientific method with the defence of established religious opinions. See one of the best instances of this, in *Boyle's Works*, vol. v. pp. 38, 39.

[74] The *Sceptical Chemist* is in *Boyle's Works*, vol. i. pp. 290–371. It went through two editions in the author's lifetime, an unusual success for a book of that kind. *Boyle's Works*, vol. i. p. 375, vol. iv. p. 89, vol. v. p. 345. I find from a letter written in 1696 (*Fairfax Correspondence*, vol. iv. p. 344), that Boyle's works were then becoming scarce, and that there was an intention of reprinting the whole of them. In regard

the spread of incredulity was indeed rapid, since it was seen not only among the intellectual classes, but even among the nobles and personal friends of the king. It is true, that in that rank of society, it assumed an offensive and degenerate form. But the movement must have been one of no common energy which, in so early a stage, could thus penetrate the recesses of the palace, and excite the minds of the courtiers; a lazy and feeble race, who from the frivolity of their habits are, under ordinary circumstances, predisposed to superstition, and prepared to believe whatever the wisdom of their fathers has bequeathed to them.

In everything this tendency was now seen. Everything marked a growing determination to subordinate old notions to new inquiries. At the very moment when Boyle was prosecuting his labours, Charles II. incorporated the Royal Society, which was formed with the avowed object of increasing knowledge by direct experiment.[75] And it is well worthy of remark, that the charter now first granted to this celebrated institution declares that its object is the extension of natural knowledge, as opposed to that which is supernatural.[76]

---

to the *Sceptical Chemist*, it was so popular, that it attracted the attention of Monconys, a French traveller, who visited London in 1663, and from whom we learn that it was to be bought for four shillings, 'pour quatre chelins.' *Voyages de Monconys*, vol. iii. p. 67, edit. 1695; a book containing some very curious facts respecting London in the reign of Charles II.; but, so far as I am aware, not quoted by any English historian. In *Sprengel's Hist. de la Médecine*, vol. v. pp. 78-9, there is a summary of the views advocated in the *Sceptical Chemist*, respecting which Sprengel says, ' Ce fut cependant aussi en Angleterre que s'élevèrent les premiers doutes sur l'exactitude des explications chimiques.'

[75] ' From the nature and constitution of the Royal Society, the objects of their attention were necessarily unlimited. The physical sciences, however, or those which are promoted by experiment, were their declared objects; and experiment was the method which they professed to follow in accomplishing their purpose.' *Thomson's Hist. of the Royal Society*, p. 6. When the society was first instituted, experiments were so unusual, that there was a difficulty of finding the necessary workmen in London. See a curious passage in *Weld's Hist. of the Royal Society*, 1848, vol. ii. p. 88.

[76] Dr. Paris (*Life of Sir H. Davy*, 1831, vol. ii. p. 178) says, 'The charter of the Royal Society states, that it was estab-

It is easy to imagine with what terror and disgust these things were viewed by those inordinate admirers of antiquity who, solely occupied in venerating past ages, are unable either to respect the present or hope for the future. These great obstructors of mankind played, in the seventeenth century, the same part as they play in our own day, rejecting every novelty, and therefore opposing every improvement. The angry contest which arose between the two parties, and the hostility directed against the Royal Society, as the first institution in which the idea of progress was distinctly embodied, are among the most instructive parts of our history, and on another occasion I shall relate them at considerable length. At present it is enough to say, that the reactionary party, though led by an overwhelming majority of the clergy, was entirely defeated; as, indeed, was to be expected, seeing that their opponents had on their side nearly all the intellect of the country, and were moreover reinforced by such aid as the court could bestow. The progress was, in truth, so rapid as to carry away with it some of the ablest members even of the ecclesiastical profession; their love of knowledge proving too strong for the old traditions in which they had been bred. But these were exceptional cases, and, speaking generally, there is no doubt that in the reign of Charles II. the antagonism between physical science and the theological spirit was such as to induce nearly the whole of the clergy to array them-

---

lished for the improvement of *natural* science. This epithet *natural* was originally intended to imply a meaning, of which very few persons, I believe, are aware. At the period of the establishment of the society, the arts of witchcraft and divination were very extensively encouraged; and the word *natural* was therefore introduced in contradistinction to *supernatural*.' The charters granted by Charles II. are printed in Weld's *History of the Royal Society*, vol. ii. pp. 481–521. Evelyn (*Diary*, 13 *Aug*. 1662, vol. ii. p. 195) mentions, that the object of the Royal Society was 'natural knowledge.' See also *Aubrey's Letters and Lives*, vol. ii. p. 358; *Pulteney's Hist. of Botany*, vol. ii. pp. 97, 98; and on the distinction thus established in the popular mind between natural and supernatural, compare *Boyle's Works*, vol. ii. p. 455, vol. iv. pp. 286, 359.

selves against the science, and seek to bring it into discredit. Nor ought we to be surprised that they should have adopted this course. That inquisitive and experimental spirit which they wished to check was not only offensive to their prejudices, but it was also detrimental to their power. For, in the first place, the mere habit of cultivating physical science taught men to require a severity of proof which it was soon found that the clergy were, in their own department, unable to supply. And, in the second place, the additions made to physical knowledge opened new fields of thought, and thus tended still further to divert attention from ecclesiastical topics. Both these effects would of course be limited to the comparatively few persons who were interested in scientific inquiries: it is, however, to be observed, that the ultimate results of such inquiries must have been extended over a far wider surface. This may be called their secondary influence; and the way in which it operated is well worth our attention, because an acquaintance with it will go far to explain the reason of that marked opposition which has always existed between superstition and knowledge.

It is evident, that a nation perfectly ignorant of physical laws will refer to supernatural causes all the phenomena by which it is surrounded.[77] But so soon

---

[77] The speculative view of this tendency has been recently illustrated in the most comprehensive manner by M. Auguste Comte, in his *Philosophie Positive*; and his conclusions in regard to the earliest stage of the human mind are confirmed by everything we know of barbarous nations; and they are also confirmed, as he has decisively proved, by the history of physical science. In addition to the facts he has adduced, I may mention, that the history of geology supplies evidence analogous to that which he has collected from other departments.

A popular notion of the working of this belief in supernatural causation may be seen in a circumstance related by Combe. He says, that in the middle of the eighteenth century the country west of Edinburgh was so unhealthy, 'that every spring the farmers and their servants were seized with fever and ague.' As long as the cause of this was unknown, 'these visitations were believed to be sent by Providence;' but after a time the

as natural science begins to do its work, there are introduced the elements of a great change. Each successive discovery, by ascertaining the law that governs certain events, deprives them of that apparent mystery in which they were formerly involved."¹ The love of the marvellous becomes proportionably diminished; and when any science has made such progress as to enable those who are acquainted with it to foretell the events with which it deals, it is clear that the whole of those events are at once withdrawn from the jurisdiction of supernatural, and brought under the authority

---

land was drained, the ague disappeared, and the inhabitants perceived that what they had believed to be supernatural was perfectly natural, and that the cause was the state of the land, not the intervention of the Deity. *Combe's Constitution of Man*, Edinb. 1847, p. 156.

" I say apparent mystery, because it does not at all lessen the real mystery. But this does not affect the accuracy of my remark, inasmuch as the people at large never enter into such subtleties as the difference between Law and Cause; a difference, indeed, which is so neglected, that it is often lost sight of even in scientific books. All that the people know is, that events which they once believed to be directly controlled by the Deity, and modified by Him, are not only foretold by the human mind, but are altered by human interference. The attempts which Paley and others have made to solve this mystery by rising from the laws to the cause, are evidently futile, because to the eye of reason the solution is as incomprehensible as the problem; and the arguments of the natural theologians, in so far as they are arguments, must depend on reason. As Mr. Newman truly says, 'A God uncaused and existing from eternity, is to the full as incomprehensible as a world uncaused and existing from eternity. We must not reject the latter theory as incomprehensible; for so is every other possible theory.' *Newman's Natural History of the Soul*, 1849, p. 36. The truth of this conclusion is unintentionally confirmed by the defence of the old method, which is set up by Dr. Whewell in his *Bridgewater Treatise*, pp. 262–5; because the remarks made by that able writer refer to men who, from their vast powers, were most likely to rise to that transcendental view of religion which is slowly but steadily gaining ground among us. Kant, probably the deepest thinker of the eighteenth century, clearly saw that no arguments drawn from the external world could prove the existence of a First Cause. See, among other passages, two particularly remarkable in *Kritik der reinen Vernunft*, *Kant's Werke*, vol. ii. pp. 478, 481, on 'der physikotheologische Beweis.'

of natural powers.[79] The business of physical philosophy is, to explain external phenomena with a view to their prediction; and every successful prediction which is recognised by the people causes a disruption of one of those links which, as it were, bind the imagination to the occult and invisible world. Hence it is that, supposing other things equal, the superstition of a nation must always bear an exact proportion to the extent of its physical knowledge. This may be in some degree verified by the ordinary experience of mankind. For if we compare the different classes of society, we shall find that they are superstitious in proportion as the phenomena with which they are brought in contact have or have not been explained by natural laws. The credulity of sailors is notorious, and every literature contains evidence of the multiplicity of their superstitions, and of the tenacity with which they cling to them.[80] This is perfectly explicable by the principle I have laid down. Meteorology has not yet been raised to a science; and the laws which regulate winds and storms being in consequence still unknown, it naturally follows, that the class of men most exposed to their

---

[79] This is tersely expressed by M. Lamennais: 'Pourquoi les corps gravitent-ils les uns vers les autres? Parceque Dieu l'a voulu, disaient les anciens. Parceque les corps s'attirent, dit la science.' Maury, Légendes du Moyen Age, p. 38. See to the same effect Mackay's Religious Development, 1850, vol. i. pp. 5, 30, 31, and elsewhere. See also a partial statement of the antithesis in Copleston's Inquiry into Necessity and Predestination, p. 49; an ingenious but overrated book.

[80] I much regret that I did not collect proof of this at an earlier period of my reading. But having omitted taking the requisite notes, I can only refer, on the superstition of sailors to Heber's Journey through India, vol. i. p. 423; Richardson's Travels in the Sahara, vol. i. p 11; Burckhardt's Travels in Arabia, vol. ii. p. 347; Davis's Chinese, vol. iii. pp. 16, 17; Travels of Ibn Batuta in the Fourteenth Century, p. 43; Journal of Asiat. Soc. vol. i. p. 9; Works of Sir Thomas Browne, vol. i. p. 130; Alison's Hist. of Europe, vol. iv. p. 566; Burnes's Travels into Bokhara, vol. iii. p. 53; Leigh Hunt's Autobiography, 1850, vol. ii. p. 255; Cumberland's Memoirs, 1807, vol. i. pp. 422-425; Walsh's Brazil, vol. i. pp. 96, 97; Richardson's Arctic Expedition, vol. i. p. 93; Holcroft's Memoirs, vol. i. p. 207, vol. iii. p. 197.

dangers should be precisely the class which is most superstitious.[61] On the other hand, soldiers live upon an element much more obedient to man, and they are less liable than sailors to those risks which defy the calculations of science. Soldiers, therefore, have fewer inducements to appeal to supernatural interference; and it is universally observed, that as a body they are less superstitious than sailors. If, again, we compare agriculturists with manufacturers, we shall see the operation of the same principle. To the cultivators of land, one of the most important circumstances is the weather, which, if it turn out unfavourable, may at once defeat all their calculations. But science not having yet succeeded in discovering the laws of rain, men are at present unable to foretell it for any considerable period; the inhabitant of the country is, therefore, driven to believe that it is the result of supernatural agency, and we still see the extraordinary spectacle of prayers offered up in our churches for dry weather or for wet weather; a superstition which to future ages will appear as childish as the feelings of pious awe with which our fathers regarded the presence of a comet, or the approach of an eclipse. We are now acquainted with the laws which determine the movements of comets and eclipses; and as we are able to predict their appearance, we have ceased to pray that we may be preserved from them.[62]

[61] Andokides, when accused before the dikastery at Athens, said, 'No, dikasts; the dangers of accusation and trial are human, but the dangers encountered at sea are divine.' *Grote's Hist. of Greece*, vol. xi. p. 252. Thus, too, it has been observed, that the dangers of the whale-fishery stimulated the superstition of the Anglo-Saxons. See *Kemble's Saxons in England*, vol. i. pp. 390, 391. Erman, who mentions the dangerous navigation of the Lake of Baikal, says, 'There is a saying at Irkutsk, that it is only upon the Baikal, in the autumn, that a man learns to pray from his heart.' *Erman's Travels in Siberia*, vol. ii. p. 186.

[62] In Europe, in the tenth century, an entire army fled before one of those appearances, which would now scarcely terrify a child: 'Toute l'armée d'Othon se dispersa subitement à l'apparition d'une éclipse de soleil, qui la remplit de terreur, et qui fut regardée comme l'annonce du malheur qu'on attendait depuis longtemps.' *Sprengel, Hist. de la Médecine*, vol. ii. p. 368. The terror inspired by eclipses was

But because our researches into the phenomena of rain happen to have been less successful,[43] we resort to the

not finally destroyed before the eighteenth century; and in the latter half of the seventeenth century they still caused great fear both in France and in England. See *Evelyn's Diary*, vol. ii. p. 52, vol. iii. p. 372; *Carlyle's Cromwell*, vol. ii. p. 366; *Lettres de Patin*, vol. iii. p. 36. Compare *Voyages de Monconys*, vol. v. p. 104, with *Hare's Guesses at Truth*, 2nd series, pp. 194, 195. There probably never has been an ignorant nation whose superstition has not been excited by eclipses. For evidence of the universality of this feeling, see *Symes's Embassy to Ava*, vol. ii. p. 298; *Raffles' Hist. of Java*, vol. i. p. 530; *Southey's Hist. of Brazil*, vol. i. p. 354, vol. ii. p. 371; *Marsden's Hist. of Sumatra*, p. 169; *Niebuhr, Description de l'Arabie*, p. 105; *Moffat's Southern Africa*, p. 337; *Mungo Park's Travels*, vol. i. p. 414; *Moorcroft's Travels in the Himalayan Provinces*, vol. ii. p. 4; *Crawfurd's Hist. of the Indian Archipelago*, vol. i. p. 305; *Ellis's Polynesian Researches*, vol. i. p. 331; *Mackay's Religious Development*, vol. i. p. 425; *Works of Sir W. Jones*, vol. iii. p. 176, vol. vi. p. 16; *Wilson's Note* in the *Vishnu Purana*, p. 140; *Wilson's Theatre of the Hindus*, vol. i. part ii. p. 00; *Montucla, Hist. des Mathématiques*, vol. i. p. 444; *Asiatic Researches*, vol. xii. p. 464; *Ward's View of the Hindoos*, vol. i. p. 101; *Prescott's Hist. of Peru*, vol. i. p. 123; *Kohl's Russia*, p. 374; *Thirlwall's Hist. of Greece*, vol. iii. p. 440, vol. vi. p. 216; *Murray's Life of Bruce*, p. 103; *Turner's Embassy to Tibet*, p. 289; *Grote's Hist. of Greece*, vol. vii. p. 432, vol. xii. pp. 205, 557; *Journal Asiatique*, 1ᵉ série, vol. iii. p. 202, Paris, 1823; *Clot-Bey, de la Peste*, Paris, 1840, p. 224.

In regard to the feelings inspired by comets, and the influence of Bayle in removing those superstitions late in the seventeenth century, compare *Tennemann, Gesch. der Philosoph.*, vol. xi. p. 252; *Le Vassor, Hist. de Louis XIII*, vol. iii. p. 415; *Lettres de Sevigné*, vol. iv. p. 336; *Autobiography of Sir S. D'Ewes*, edit. Halliwell, vol. i. pp. 122, 123, 136.

[44] On the peculiar complications which have retarded meteorology, and thus prevented us from accurately predicting the weather, compare *Forbes on Meteorology*, in *Second Report of British Association*, pp. 249-251; *Cuvier, Progrès des Sciences*, vol. i. pp. 69, 248; *Kaemtz's Meteorology*, pp. 2-4; *Prout's Bridgewater Treatise*, pp. 290-295; *Somerville's Physical Geog.* vol. ii. pp. 18, 19. But all the best authorities are agreed that this ignorance cannot last long; and that the constant advance which we are now making in physical science will eventually enable us to explain even these phenomena. Thus, for instance, Sir John Leslie says, 'It cannot be disputed, however, that all the changes which happen in the mass of our atmosphere, involved, capricious, and irregular

impious contrivance of calling in the aid of the Deity to supply those deficiencies in science which are the result of our own sloth; and we are not ashamed, in our public churches, to prostitute the rites of religion by using them as a cloak to conceal an ignorance we ought frankly to confess.[64] The agriculturist is thus

---

as they may appear, are yet the necessary results of principles as fixed, and perhaps as simple, as those which direct the revolutions of the solar system. Could we unravel the intricate maze, we might trace the action of each distinct cause, and hence deduce the ultimate effects arising from their combined operation. With the possession of such data, we might safely predict the state of the weather at any future period, as we now calculate an eclipse of the sun or moon, or foretell a conjunction of the planets.' *Leslie's Natural Philosophy*, p. 405: see also p. 185, and the remarks of Mr. Snow Harris (*Brit. Assoc. for 1844*, p. 241), and of Mr. Hamilton (*Journal of Geog. Soc.* vol. xix. p. xci.) Thus, too, Dr. Whewell (*Bridgewater Treatise*, p. 3) says, that 'the changes of winds and skies are produced by causes, of whose rules "no philosophical mind" will doubt the fixity.'

[64] This connexion between ignorance and devotion is so clearly marked, that many nations have a separate god for the weather, to whom they say their prayers. In countries where men stop short of this, they ascribe the changes to witchcraft, or to some other supernatural power. See *Mariner's Tonga Islands*, vol. ii. pp. 7, 108; *Tuckey's Expedit. to the Zaire*, pp. 214, 215; *Ellis's Hist. of Madagascar*, vol. ii. p. 354; *Asiatic Researches*, vol. vi. pp. 193, 194, 297, vol. xvi. pp. 223, 342; *Southey's Hist. of Brazil*, vol. iii. p. 187; *Davis's Chinese*, vol. ii. p. 154; *Beausobre, Hist. de Manichée*, vol. ii. p. 394; *Cudworth's Intellect Syst.* vol. ii. p. 539. The Hindus refer rain to supernatural causes in the *Rig Veda*, which is the oldest of their religious books; and they have held similar notions ever since. *Rig Veda Sanhita*, vol. i. pp. xxx. 10, 19, 26, 145, 175, 205, 224, 225, 265, 266, vol. ii. pp. 28, 41, 62, 110, 153, 158, 164, 166, 192, 199, 231, 258, 268, 293, 329; *Journal of Asiatic Soc.* vol. iii. p. 91; *Coleman's Mythol. of the Hindus*, p. 111; *Ward's View of the Hindoos*, vol. i. p. 36. See further two curious passages in the *Dabistan*, vol. i. p. 115, vol. ii. p. 337; and on the 'Rain-makers,' compare *Catlin's North-American Indians*, vol. i. pp. 134–140, with *Buchanan's North-American Indians*, pp. 256, 260: also a precisely similar class in Africa (*Moffat's Southern Africa*, pp. 305–325), and in Arabia (*Niebuhr, Desc. de l'Arabie*, pp. 237, 238).

Coming to a state of society nearer our own, we find that in the ninth century it was taken for granted in Christian countries that wind and hail were the work of wizards (*Neander's Hist. of the Church*, vol. vi. pp. 118, 139);

taught to ascribe to supernatural agency the most important phenomena with which he is concerned;[85] and there can be no doubt that this is one of the causes of those superstitious feelings by which the inhabitants of the country are unfavourably contrasted with those of the town.[86] But the manufacturer, and, indeed, nearly every one engaged in the business of cities, has employments, the success of which being regulated by his own abilities, has no connexion with those unexplained events that perplex the imagination of the cultivators of the earth. He who, by his ingenuity, works up the raw material, is evidently less affected by uncontrollable occurrences, than he by whom the raw material is originally grown. Whether it is fair, or whether it is wet, he pursues his labours with equal success, and learns to rely solely upon his own energy, and the cunning of his own arm. As the sailor is naturally more superstitious than the soldier, because he has to deal with a more unstable element; just in the same way is the agriculturist more superstitious than the mechanic, because he is more frequently and more

---

that similar views passed on to the sixteenth century, and were sanctioned by Luther (*Maury, Légendes Pieuses*, pp. 18, 19); and finally, that when Swinburne was in Spain, only eighty years ago, he found the clergy on the point of putting an end to the opera, because they 'attributed the want of rain to the influence of that ungodly entertainment.' *Swinburne's Travels through Spain in 1775 and 1776*, vol. i. p. 177, 2nd edit. London, 1787.

[86] See some remarks by the Rev. Mr. Ward, which strike me as rather incautious, and which certainly are dangerous to his own profession, as increasing the hostility between it and science, in *Ward's Ideal of a Christian Church*, p. 278. What Coleridge has said, is worth attending to: see *The Friend*, vol. iii. pp. 222, 223.

[86] M. Kohl, whose acuteness as a traveller is well known, has found that the agricultural classes are the 'most blindly ignorant and prejudiced' of all. *Kohl's Russia*, p. 365. And Sir R. Murchison, who has enjoyed extensive means of observation, familiarly mentions the 'credulous farmers.' *Murchison's Siluria*, p. 61. In Asia, exactly the same tendency has been noticed: see *Marsden's Hist. of Sumatra*, p. 63. Some curious evidence of agricultural superstitions respecting the weather may be seen in *Monteil, Hist. des divers Etats*, vol. iii. pp. 31, 39.

seriously affected by events which the ignorance of some men makes them call capricious, and the ignorance of other men makes them call supernatural.

It would be easy, by an extension of these remarks, to show how the progress of manufactures, besides increasing the national wealth, has done immense service to civilization, by inspiring Man with a confidence in his own resources;[87] and how, by giving rise to a new class of employments, it has, if I may so say, shifted the scene in which superstition is most likely to dwell. But to trace this would carry me beyond my present limits; and the illustrations already given are sufficient to explain how the theological spirit must have been diminished by that love of experimental science, which forms one of the principal features in the reign of Charles II.[88]

I have now laid before the reader what I conceive to be the point of view from which we ought to estimate a period whose true nature seems to me to have been grievously misunderstood. Those political writers who judge events without regard to that intellectual development of which they are but a part, will find much to condemn, and scarcely anything to approve, in the reign of Charles II. By such authors, I shall be censured for having travelled out of that narrow path in which history has been too often confined. And yet I

---

[87] In this point of view, the opposite tendencies of agriculture and manufactures are judiciously contrasted by Mr. Porter, at the end of his essay on the *Statistics of Agriculture, Journal of the Statist. Soc.* vol. ii. pp. 295, 296.

[88] Indeed, there never has been a period in England in which physical experiments were so fashionable. This is merely worth observing as a symptom of the age, since Charles II. and the nobles were not likely to add, and did not add, anything to our knowledge; and their patronage of science, such as it was, degraded it rather than advanced it. Still, the prevalence of the taste is curious; and in addition to the picture drawn by Mr. Macaulay (*Hist. of England*, 1st edit. vol. i. pp. 408–412), I may refer the reader to *Monconys' Voyages*, vol. iii. p. 31; *Sorbiere's Voyage to England*, pp. 32, 33; *Evelyn's Diary*, vol. ii. pp. 199, 286; *Pepys' Diary*, vol. i. p. 375, vol. ii. p. 34, vol. iii. p. 85, vol. iv. p. 229; *Burnet's Own Time*, vol. i. pp. 171, 322, vol. ii. p. 275; *Burnet's Lives*, p. 144; *Campbell's Chief-Justices*, vol. i. p. 592.

am at a loss to perceive how it is possible, except by the adoption of such a course, to understand a period which, on a superficial view, is full of the grossest inconsistencies. This difficulty will be rendered very obvious, if we compare for a moment the nature of the government of Charles with the great things which, under that government, were peaceably effected. Never before was there such a want of apparent connexion between the means and the end. If we look only at the characters of the rulers, and at their foreign policy, we must pronounce the reign of Charles II. to be the worst that has ever been seen in England. If, on the other hand, we confine our observations to the laws which were passed, and to the principles which were established, we shall be obliged to confess that this same reign forms one of the brightest epochs in our national annals. Politically and morally, there were to be found in the government all the elements of confusion, of weakness, and of crime. The king himself was a mean and spiritless voluptuary, without the morals of a Christian, and almost without the feelings of a man.[89] His ministers, with the exception of Clarendon, whom he hated for his virtues, had not one of the attributes of statesmen, and nearly all of them were pensioned by the crown of France.[90] The weight

---

[89] His treatment of his young wife immediately after marriage is perhaps the worst thing recorded of this base and contemptible prince. *Lister's Life of Clarendon*, vol. ii. pp. 145–153. This is matter of proof; but Burnet (*Own Time*, vol. i. p. 522, and vol. ii. p. 467) whispers a horrible suspicion, which I cannot believe to be true, even of Charles II., and which Harris, who has collected some evidence of his astounding profligacy, does not mention, though he quotes one of the passages in Burnet. *Harris's Lives of the Stuarts*, vol. v. pp. 36–43. However, as Dr.

Parr says, in reference to another accusation against him, 'There is little occasion to blacken the memory of that wicked monarch, Charles II., by the aid of invidious conjectures.' *Notes on James II.* in *Parr's Works*, vol. iv. p. 477. Compare *Fox's History of James II.* p. 71.

[90] Even Clarendon has been charged with receiving bribes from Louis XIV.; but for this there appears to be no good authority. Compare *Hallam's Const. Hist.* vol. ii. pp. 66, 67 note, with *Campbell's Chancellors*, vol. iii. p. 213.

of taxation was increased,[91] while the security of the
kingdom was diminished.[92] By the forced surrender
of the charters of the towns, our municipal rights were
endangered.[93] By shutting the exchequer, our national
credit was destroyed.[94] Though immense sums were
spent in maintaining our naval and military power, we
were left so defenceless, that when a war broke out,
which had long been preparing, we seemed suddenly to
be taken by surprise. Such was the miserable incapacity of the government, that the fleets of Holland were
able, not only to ride triumphant round our coasts, but
to sail up the Thames, attack our arsenals, burn our
ships, and insult the metropolis of England.[95] Yet,
notwithstanding all these things, it is an undoubted
fact, that in this same reign of Charles II. more steps
were taken in the right direction than had been taken,
in any period of equal length, during the twelve cen-

---

[91] *Lister's Life of Clarendon*, vol. ii. p. 377; *Harris's Lives of the Stuarts*, vol. iv. pp. 340–344.

[92] Immediately after the Restoration, the custom began of appointing to naval commands incompetent youths of birth, to the discouragement of those able officers who had been employed under Cromwell. Compare *Burnet's Own Time*, vol. i. p. 290, with *Pepys' Diary*, vol. ii. p. 413, vol. iii. pp. 68, 72.

[93] *Harris's Lives of the Stuarts*, vol. v. pp. 323–328. The court was so bent on abrogating the charter of the city of London, that Saunders was made chief-justice for the express purpose. See *Campbell's Chief-Justices*, vol. ii. p. 59. Roger North says (*Lives of the Norths*, vol. ii. p. 67), 'Nothing was accounted at court so meritorious as the procuring of charters, as the language then was.' Compare *Bulstrode's Memoirs*, pp. 379, 388.

[94] The panic caused by this scandalous robbery is described by De Foe; *Wilson's Life of De Foe*, vol. i. p. 52. See also *Calamy's Life of Himself*, vol. i. p. 78; *Parker's Hist. of his Own Time*, pp. 141–143. The amount stolen by the king is estimated at 1,328,526l. *Sinclair's Hist. of the Revenue*, vol. i. p. 315. According to Lord Campbell, 'nearly a million and a half.' *Lives of the Chancellors*, vol. iv. p. 113.

[95] There is a very curious account in *Pepys' Diary*, vol. iii. pp. 242–264, of the terror felt by the Londoners on this occasion. Pepys himself buried his gold (p. 261 and pp. 376–379). Evelyn (*Diary*, vol. ii. p. 267) says: 'The alarme was so greate, that it put both country and citty into a paniq, feare, and consternation, such as I hope I shall never see more; every body was flying, none knew why or whither.'

turies we had occupied the soil of Britain. By the mere force of that intellectual movement, which was unwittingly supported by the crown, there were effected, in the course of a few years, reforms which changed the face of society.[96] The two great obstacles by which the nation had long been embarrassed, consisted of a spiritual tyranny and a territorial tyranny: the tyranny of the church and the tyranny of the nobles. An attempt was now made to remedy these evils; not by palliatives, but by striking at the power of the classes who did the mischief. For now it was that a law was placed on the statute-book, taking away that celebrated writ, which enabled the bishops or their delegates to cause those men to be burned whose religion was different to their own.[97] Now it was that the clergy were deprived of the privilege of taxing themselves, and were forced to submit to an assessment made by the ordinary legislature.[98] Now, too, there was enacted a

---

[96] The most important of these reforms were carried, as is nearly always the case, in opposition to the real wishes of the ruling classes. Charles II. and James II. often said of the Habeas Corpus Act, 'that a government could not subsist with such a law.' *Dalrymple's Memoirs*, vol. ii. p. 104. Lord-Keeper Guilford was even opposed to the abolition of military tenures. 'He thought,' says his brother, 'the taking away of the tenures a desperate wound to the liberties of the people of England.' *Lives of the Norths*, vol. ii. p. 82. These are the sort of men by whom great nations are governed. A passage in *Life of James, by Himself*, edit. Clarke, vol. ii. p. 621, confirms the statement in Dalrymple, so far as James is concerned. This should be compared with a letter from Louis XIV., in the Barillon correspondence. *Appendix to Fox's James II.* p. cxxiv.

[97] *Blackstone's Commentaries*, vol. iv. p. 48; *Campbell's Chancellors*, vol. iii. p. 431. This destruction of the writ *De Heretico comburendo* was in 1677. It is noticed in *Palmer's Treatise on the Church*, vol. i. p. 500; and in *Collier's Ecclesiast. Hist.* vol. viii. p. 478.

[98] This was in 1664. See the account of it in *Collier's Ecclesiast. Hist.* vol. viii. pp. 463-466. Collier, who is evidently displeased by the change, says: 'The consenting, therefore, to be taxed by the temporal Commons, makes the clergy more dependent on a foreign body, takes away the right of disposing of their own money, and lays their estates in some measure at discretion.' See also, on the injury this has inflicted on the church,

law forbidding any bishop, or any ecclesiastical court, to tender the *ex-officio* oath, by which the church had hitherto enjoyed the power of compelling a suspected person to criminate himself.[99] In regard to the nobles, it was also during the reign of Charles II. that the House of Lords, after a sharp struggle, was obliged to abandon its pretensions to an original jurisdiction in civil suits; and thus lost for ever an important resource for extending its own influence.[100] It was in the same reign that there was settled the right of the people to be taxed entirely by their representatives; the House of Commons having ever since retained the sole power of proposing money bills, and regulating the amount of imposts, merely leaving to the Peers the form of consenting to what has been already determined.[101] These were the attempts which were made to bridle the clergy and the nobles. But there were also effected

---

[99] *Lathbury's Hist. of Convocation*, pp. 259, 260. And Coleridge (*Literary Remains*, vol. iv. pp. 152, 153) points this out as characterizing one of the three 'grand evil epochs of our present church.' So marked, however, was the tendency of that time, that this most important measure was presumably effected by an arrangement between Sheldon and Clarendon. See the notes by Onslow in *Burnet's Own Time*, vol. i. p. 340, vol. iv. pp. 508, 509. Compare Lord Camden's statement (*Parl. Hist.* vol. xvi. p. 169) with the speech of Lord Bathurst (vol. xxii. p. 77); and of Lord Temple on Tooke's case (vol. xxxv. p. 1357). Mr. Carwithen (*Hist. of the Church of England*, vol. ii. p. 354, Oxford, 1849) grieves over 'this deprivation of the liberties of the English clergy.'

[99] 13 Car. II. c. 12. Compare *Stephens's Life of Tooke*, vol. i. pp. 169, 170, with *Blackstone's Commentaries*, vol. iii. p. 101. Mr. Hallam (*Const. Hist.* vol. i. pp. 197, 198) has adduced evidence of the way in which the clergy were accustomed to injure their opponents by the *ex-officio* oath.

[100] This was the issue of the famous controversy respecting Skinner, in 1669; and 'from this time,' says Mr. Hallam, 'the Lords have tacitly abandoned all pretensions to an original jurisdiction in civil suits.' *Const. Hist.* vol. ii. p. 184. There is an account of this case of Skinner, which was connected with the East-India Company, in *Mill's Hist. of India*, vol. l. pp. 102, 103.

[101] *Hallam's Const. Hist.* vol. ii. pp. 189–192; and *Eccleston's English Antiquities*, p. 326. The disputes between the two houses respecting taxation, are noticed very briefly in *Parker's Hist. of his Own Time*, pp. 135, 136.

other things of equal importance. By the destruction of the scandalous prerogatives of Purveyance and Preemption, a limit was set to the power of the sovereign to vex his refractory subjects.[102] By the Habeas Corpus Act, the liberty of every Englishman was made as certain as law could make it; it being guaranteed to him, that if accused of crime, he, instead of languishing in prison, as had often been the case, should be brought to a fair and speedy trial.[103] By the Statute of Frauds and Perjuries, a security hitherto unknown was conferred upon private property.[104] By the

---

[102] The 'famous rights of purveyance and pre-emption' were abolished by 12 Car. II. c. 24. *Hallam's Const. Hist.* vol. ii. p. 11. Burke, in his magnificent speech on Economical Reform, describes the abuses of the old system of purveyance. *Burke's Works,* vol. i. p. 239. See also *Kemble's Saxons in England,* vol. ii. p. 66, note; *Barrington on the Statutes,* pp. 183–185, 237; *Lingard's Hist. of England,* vol. ii. pp. 338, 339; *Sinclair's Hist. of the Revenue,* vol. i. p. 232; *Parl. Hist.* vol. iii. p. 1299. These passages will give an idea of the iniquities practised under this 'right,' which, like most gross injustices, was one of the good old customs of the British constitution, being at least as ancient as Canute. See *Allen on the Royal Prerogative,* p. 152. Indeed, a recent writer of considerable learning (*Spence, Origin of the Laws of Europe,* p. 319) derives it from the Roman law. A bill had been brought in to take it away in 1656. See *Burton's Cromwellian Diary,* vol. i. p. 81. When Adam Smith wrote, it still existed in France and Germany. *Wealth of Nations,* book iii. chap. ii. p. 161.

[103] On the Habeas Corpus Act, which became law in 1679, see *Campbell's Chancellors,* vol. iii. pp. 345–347; *Mackintosh, Revolution of 1688,* p. 49; and *Lingard's Hist. of England,* vol. viii. p. 17. The peculiarities of this law, as compared with the imitations of it in other countries, are clearly stated in *Meyer, Esprit des Institutions Judiciaires,* vol. ii. p. 283. Mr. Lister (*Life of Clarendon,* vol. ii. p. 454) says: 'Imprisonment in gaols beyond the seas was not prevented by law till the passing of the Habeas Corpus Act, in 1679.'

[104] Blackstone (*Commentaries,* vol. iv. p. 439) calls this 'a great and necessary security to private property;' and Lord Campbell (*Chancellors,* vol. iii. p. 423) terms it 'the most important and most beneficial piece of juridical legislation of which we can boast.' On its effects, compare Jones's valuable *Commentary on Isaeus* (*Works of Sir W. Jones,* vol. iv. p. 239) with *Story's Conflict of Laws,* pp. 521, 522, 627, 684; and *Tayler on Statute Law,* in *Journal of Statistical Society,* vol. xvii. p. 150.

abolition of general impeachments, an end was put to a great engine of tyranny, with which powerful and unscrupulous men had frequently ruined their political adversaries.[105] By the cessation of those laws which restricted the liberty of printing, there was laid the foundation of that great Public Press, which, more than any other single cause, has diffused among the people a knowledge of their own power, and has thus, to an almost incredible extent, aided the progress of English civilization.[106] And, to complete this noble picture, there were finally destroyed those feudal incidents, which our Norman conquerors had imposed,—the military tenures; the court of wards; the fines for alienation; the right of forfeiture for marriage by reason of tenure; the aids, the homages, the escuages, the primer seisins; and all those mischievous subtleties, of which the mere names sound in modern ears as a wild and barbarous jargon, but which pressed upon our ancestors as real and serious evils.[107]

---

[105] Lord Campbell (*Lives of the Chancellors*, vol. iii. p. 247) says, that the struggle in 1667 'put an end to general impeachments.'

[106] Printing at first was regulated by royal proclamations; then by the Star-chamber; and afterwards by the Long Parliament. The decrees of the Star-chamber were taken as the basis of 13 and 14 Car. II. c. 33; but this act expired in 1679, and was not renewed during the reign of Charles II. Compare *Blackstone's Comment.* vol. iv. p. 152, with *Hunt's Hist. of Newspapers*, vol. i. p. 154, and *Fox's Hist. of James II.* p. 146.

[107] The fullest account I have seen in any history, of this great Revolution, which swept away the traditions and the language of feudalism, is that given in *Harris's Lives of the Stuarts*, vol. iv. pp. 369–378. But Harris, though an industrious collector, was a man of slender ability, and not at all aware of the real nature of a change, of which the obvious and immediately practical results formed the smallest part. The true point of view is, that it was a formal recognition by the legislature that the Middle Ages were extinct, and that it was necessary to inaugurate a more modern and innovating policy. Hereafter I shall have occasion to examine this in detail, and show how it was merely a symptom of a revolutionary movement. In the meantime the reader may refer to the very short notices in *Dalrymple's Hist. of Feudal Property*, p. 69; *Blackstone's Comment.* vol. ii. pp. 76, 77; *Hallam's Const. Hist.* vol. ii. p. 11; *Parl. Hist.* vol. iv. pp. 53, 167, 168; *Meyer, Institutions Judiciaires*, vol. ii. p. 58.

These were the things which were done in the reign of Charles II.; and if we consider the miserable incompetence of the king, the idle profligacy of his court, the unblushing venality of his ministers, the constant conspiracies to which the country was exposed from within, and the unprecedented insults to which it was subjected from without; if we, moreover, consider that to all this there were added two natural calamities of the most grievous description,—a Great Plague, which thinned society in all its ranks, and scattered confusion through the kingdom, and a Great Fire, which, besides increasing the mortality from the pestilence, destroyed in a moment those accumulations of industry by which industry itself is nourished;—if we put all these things together, how can we reconcile inconsistencies apparently so gross? How could so wonderful a progress be made in the face of these unparalleled disasters? How could such men, under such circumstances, effect such improvements? These are questions which our political compilers are unable to answer; because they look too much at the peculiarities of individuals, and too little at the temper of the age in which those individuals live. Such writers do not perceive that the history of every civilized country is the history of its intellectual development, which kings, statesmen, and legislators are more likely to retard than to hasten; because, however great their power may be, they are at best the accidental and insufficient representatives of the spirit of their time; and because, so far from being able to regulate the movements of the national mind, they themselves form the smallest part of it, and, in a general view of the progress of Man, are only to be regarded as the puppets who strut and fret their hour upon a little stage; while, beyond them, and on every side of them, are forming opinions and principles which they can scarcely perceive, but by which alone the whole course of human affairs is ultimately governed.

The truth is, that the vast legislative reforms, for which the reign of Charles II. is so remarkable, merely form a part of that movement, which, though traceable to a much earlier period, had only for three generations been in undisguised operation. These important improvements were the result of that bold, sceptical, inquiring, and reforming spirit, which had now seized the three great departments of Theology, of Science, and of Politics. The old principles of tradition, of authority, and of dogma, were gradually becoming weaker; and of course, in the same proportion, there was diminished the influence of the classes by whom those principles were chiefly upheld. As the power of particular sections of society thus declined, the power of the people at large increased. The real interests of the nation began to be perceived, so soon as the superstitions were dispersed by which those interests had long been obscured. This, I believe, is the real solution of what at first seems a curious problem,—namely, how it was that such comprehensive reforms should have been accomplished in so bad, and in many respects so infamous, a reign. It is, no doubt, true, that those reforms were essentially the result of the intellectual march of the age; but, so far from being made in spite of the vices of the sovereign, they were actually aided by them. With the exception of the needy profligates who thronged his court, all classes of men soon learned to despise a king who was a drunkard, a libertine, and a hypocrite; who had neither shame nor sensibility; and who, in point of honour, was unworthy to enter the presence of the meanest of his subjects. To have the throne filled for a quarter of a century by such a man as this, was the surest way of weakening that ignorant and indiscriminate loyalty, to which the people have often sacrificed their dearest rights. Thus, the character of the king, merely considered from this point of view, was eminently favourable to the growth of national liberty.[108] But the

---

[108] Mr. Hallam has a noble passage on the services rendered to English civilization by the vices of the English court: 'We are, however, much indebted to the memory of Barbara Duchess of Cleveland, Louisa Duchess of Portsmouth, and Mrs. Eleanor Gwyn. We owe a tribute of gratitude to the Mays, the Killigrews, the Chiffinches, and the Grammonts. They played a ser-

advantage did not stop there. The reckless debaucheries of Charles made him abhor everything approaching to restraint; and this gave him a dislike to a class, whose profession, at least, pre-supposes a conduct of more than ordinary purity. The consequence was, that he, not from views of enlightened policy, but merely from a love of vicious indulgence, always had a distaste for the clergy; and, so far from advancing their power, frequently expressed for them an open contempt.[109] His most intimate friends directed against them those coarse and profligate jokes which are preserved in the literature of the time; and which, in the opinion of the courtiers, were to be ranked among the noblest specimens of human wit. From men of this sort the church had, indeed, little to apprehend; but their language, and the favour with which it was received, are part of the symptoms by which we may study the temper of that age. Many other illustrations will occur to most readers; I may, however, mention one, which is interesting on account of the eminence of the philosopher

---

viceable part in ridding the kingdom of its besotted loyalty. They saved our forefathers from the Star-chamber and the High-commission court; they laboured in their vocation against standing armies and corruption; they pressed forward the great ultimate security of English freedom —the expulsion of the House of Stuart.' *Hallam's Const. Hist.* vol. ii. p. 50.

[109] Burnet (*Own Time*, vol. i. p. 448) tells us that, in 1667, the king, even at the council-board, expressed himself against the bishops, and said, that the clergy 'thought of nothing but to get good benefices, and to keep a good table.' See also, on his dislike to the bishops, vol. ii. p. 22; and *Pepys' Diary*, vol. iv. p. 2. In another place, vol iv. p. 42, Pepys writes: 'And I believe the hierarchy will in a little time be shaken, whether they will or no; the king being offended with them, and set upon it, as I hear.' Evelyn, in a conversation with Pepys, noticed with regret such conduct of Charles, 'that a bishop shall never be seen about him, as the king of France hath always.' *Pepys*, vol. iii. p. 201. Evelyn, in his benevolent way, ascribes this to 'the negligence of the clergy;' but history teaches us that the clergy have never neglected kings, except when the king has first neglected them. Sir John Reresby gives a curious account of a conversation Charles II. held with him respecting 'mitred heads,' in which the feeling of the king is very apparent. *Reresby's Travels and Memoirs*, p. 238.

concerned in it. The most dangerous opponent of
the clergy in the seventeenth century, was certainly
Hobbes, the subtlest dialectician of his time; a writer,
too, of singular clearness, and, among British metaphysicians, inferior only to Berkeley. This profound
thinker published several speculations very unfavourable to the church, and directly opposed to principles
which are essential to ecclesiastical authority. As a
natural consequence, he was hated by the clergy; his
doctrines were declared to be highly pernicious; and
he was accused of wishing to subvert the national
religion, and corrupt the national morals.[110] So far did
this proceed, that, during his life, and for several years
after his death, every man who ventured to think for
himself was stigmatized as a Hobbist, or, as it was
sometimes called, a Hobbian.[111] This marked hostility
on the part of the clergy was a sufficient recommendation to the favour of Charles. The king, even before
his accession, had imbibed many of his principles;[112]

---

[110] On the animosity of the clergy against Hobbes, and on the extent to which he recipro- cated it, compare *Aubrey's Letters and Lives*, vol. ii. pp. 632, 631; *Tennemann, Gesch. der Philos.* vol. x. p. 111; with the angry language of Burnet (*Own Time*, vol. i. p. 322), and of Whiston (*Memoirs*, p. 251). See also *Wood's Athenæ Oxonienses*, edit. Bliss, vol. iii. p. 1211. Mon- conys, who was in London in 1663, says of Hobbes, ' Il me dit l'aversion que tous les gens d'église tant catholiques que pro- testans avoient pour lui.' *Mon- conys' Voyages*, vol. iii. p. 43; and p. 115, 'M. Hobbes, que je trouvai toujours fort ennemi des prêtres catholiques et des protestans.' About the same time, Sorbiere was in London; and he writes respecting Hobbes: 'I know not how it comes to pass, the clergy are afraid of him, and so are the Oxford mathematicians and their adhe- rents; wherefore his majesty (Charles II.) was pleased to make a very good comparison when he told me, he was like a bear, whom they baited with dogs to try him.' *Sorbiere's Voyage to England*, p. 40.

[111] This was a common ex- pression for whoever attacked established opinions late in the seventeenth, and even early in the eighteenth century. For in- stances of it, see *Baxter's Life of Himself*, folio, 1696, part iii. p. 48; *Boyle's Works*, vol. v. pp. 505, 510; *Monk's Life of Bentley*, vol. i. p. 41; *Vernon Correspond.* vol. iii. p. 13; *King's Life of Locke*, vol. i. p. 191; *Brewster's Life of Newton*, vol. ii. p. 149.

[112] Burnet says, they 'made

and, after the Restoration, he treated the author with what was deemed a scandalous respect. He protected him from his enemies; he somewhat ostentatiously hung up his portrait in his own private room at Whitehall;[113] and he even conferred a pension on this, the most formidable opponent who had yet appeared against the spiritual hierarchy.[114]

If we look for a moment at the ecclesiastical appointments of Charles, we shall find evidence of the same tendency. In his reign, the highest dignities in the church were invariably conferred upon men who were deficient either in ability or in honesty. It would perhaps be an over-refinement to ascribe to the king a deliberate plan for lowering the reputation of the episcopal bench; but it is certain, that if he had such a plan, he followed the course most likely to effect his purpose. For it is no exaggeration to say, that, during his life, the leading English prelates were, without exception, either incapable or insincere; they were unable to defend what they really believed, or else they did not believe what they openly professed. Never before were the interests of the Anglican church so feebly guarded. The first Archbishop of Canterbury appointed by Charles was Juxon, whose deficiencies were notorious; and of whom his friends could only say, that his want of ability was compensated by the goodness of his intentions.[115] When he died, the king raised up as his successor Sheldon, whom he had previously made Bishop of London; and who not only brought discredit on his order by acts of gross intolerance,[116]

---

deep and lasting impressions on the king's mind.' *Own Time*, vol. i. p. 172.

[113] A likeness, by Cooper. See *Wood's Athenæ Oxonienses*, edit. Bliss, vol. iii. p. 1208.

[114] *Sorbiere's Voyage to England*, p. 39; *Wood's Athenæ Oxonienses*, vol. iii. p. 1208. On the popularity of the works of Hobbes in the reign of Charles II. compare *Pepys' Diary*, vol. iv. p. 164, with *Lives of the Norths*, vol. iii. p. 339.

[115] Bishop Burnet says of him, at his appointment: 'As he was never a great divine, so he was now superannuated.' *Own Time*, vol. i. p. 303.

[116] Of which his own friend, Bishop Parker, gives a specimen. See *Parker's History of his own Time*, pp. 31–33. Compare Neal's *Hist. of the Puritans*, vol. iv.

but who was so regardless of the common decencies of his station, that he used to amuse his associates, by having exhibitions in his own house, imitating the way in which the Presbyterians delivered their sermons.[117] After the death of Sheldon, Charles appointed to the archbishopric Sancroft; whose superstitious fancies exposed him to the contempt even of his own profession, and who was as much despised as Sheldon had been hated.[118] In the rank immediately below this, we find the same principle at work. The three Archbishops of York, during the reign of Charles II., were Frewen, Stearn, and Dolben; who were so utterly devoid of ability, that notwithstanding their elevated position, they are altogether forgotten, not one reader out of a thousand having ever heard their names.[119]

Such appointments as these are indeed striking; and what makes them more so, is, that they were by no means necessary; they were not forced on the king by

---

p. 429; *Wilson's Mem. of De Foe*, vol. i. p. 46.

[117] In 1669, Pepys was at one of these entertainments, which took place not only at the house, but in the presence of the archbishop. See the scandalous details in *Pepys' Diary*, vol. iv. pp. 321, 322; or in *Wilson's De Foe*, vol. i. pp. 44, 45.

[118] Burnet, who knew Sancroft, calls him 'a poor-spirited and fearful man' (*Own Time*, vol. iii. p. 354); and mentions (vol. iii. p. 138) an instance of his superstition, which will be easily believed by whoever has read his ridiculous sermons, which D'Oyly has wickedly published. See Appendix to *D'Oyly's Sancroft*, pp. 339–420. Dr. Lake says that everybody was amazed when it was known that Sancroft was to be archbishop. *Lake's Diary*, 30th Dec. 1677, p. 18, in vol. i. of the *Camden Miscellany*, 1847,

4to. His character, so far as he had one, is fairly drawn by Dr. Birch: 'slow, timorous, and narrow-spirited, but at the same time a good, honest, and wellmeaning man.' *Birch's Life of Tillotson*, p. 151. See also respecting him, *Macaulay's Hist. of England*, vol. ii. p. 616, vol. iii. p. 77, vol. iv. pp. 40–42.

[119] Frewen was so obscure a man, that there is no life of him either in *Chalmers' Biographical Dictionary*, or in Rose's more recent, but inferior work. The little that is known of Stearn, or Sterne, is unfavourable. Compare *Burnet*, vol. ii. p. 427, with *Baxter's Life of Himself*, folio, 1696, part ii. p. 338. And of Dolben I have been unable to collect anything of interest, except that he had a good library. See the traditional account in *Jones's Memoirs of Bishop Horne*, p. 60.

court intrigue, nor was there a lack of more competent men. The truth seems to be, that Charles was unwilling to confer ecclesiastical promotion upon any one who had ability enough to increase the authority of the church, and restore it to its former pre-eminence. At his accession, the two ablest of the clergy were undoubtedly Jeremy Taylor and Isaac Barrow. Both of them were notorious for their loyalty; both of them were men of unspotted virtue; and both of them have left a reputation which will hardly perish while the English language is remembered. But Taylor, though he had married the king's sister,[120] was treated with marked neglect; and, being exiled to an Irish bishopric, had to pass the remainder of his life in what, at that time, was truly called a barbarous country.[121] As to Barrow, who, in point of genius, was probably superior to Taylor,[122] he had the mortification of seeing the most incapable men raised to the highest posts in the church, while he himself was unnoticed; and, notwithstanding that his family had greatly suffered in the royal cause,[123] he received no sort of preferment until five years before his death, when the king conferred on him the mastership of Trinity College, Cambridge.[124]

---

[120] His wife was Joanna Bridges, a bastard of Charles I. Compare *Notes and Queries*, vol. vii. p. 305, with *Heber's Life of Jeremy Taylor*, in *Taylor's Works*, vol. i. p. xxxiv. Bishop Heber, p. xxxv. adds, 'But, notwithstanding the splendour of such an alliance, there is no reason to believe that it added materially to Taylor's income.'

[121] Coleridge (*Lit. Remains*, vol. iii. p. 208) says, that this neglect of Jeremy Taylor by Charles 'is a problem of which perhaps his virtues present the most probable solution.'

[122] Superior, certainly, in comprehensiveness, and in the range of his studies; so that it is aptly said by a respectable authority, that he was at once 'the great precursor of Sir Isaac Newton, and the pride of the English pulpit.' *Wordsworth's Ecclesiast. Biog.* vol. iv. p. 344. See also, respecting Barrow, *Montucla, Hist. des Mathémat.* vol. ii. pp. 88, 89, 359, 300, 504, 505, vol. iii. pp. 436-438.

[123] 'His father having suffered greatly in his estate by his attachment to the royal cause.' *Chalmers' Biog. Dict.* vol. iv. p. 39.

[124] Barrow, displeased at not receiving preferment after the Restoration, wrote the lines:

'Te magis optavit rediturum Carole nemo ;
Et nemo sensit arcus te rediisse minus.'

It is hardly necessary to point out how all this must have tended to weaken the church, and accelerate that great movement for which the reign of Charles II. is remarkable.[125] At the same time, there were many other circumstances which, in this preliminary sketch, it is impossible to notice, but which were stamped with the general character of revolt against ancient authority. In a subsequent volume, this will be placed in a still clearer light, because I shall have an opportunity of bringing forward evidence which, from the abundance of its details, would be unsuited to the present Introduction. Enough, however, has been stated, to indicate the general march of the English mind, and supply the reader with a clue by which he may understand those still more complicated events, which, as the seventeenth century advanced, began to thicken upon us.

A few years before the death of Charles II., the clergy made a great effort to recover their former power by reviving those doctrines of Passive Obedience and Divine Right, which are obviously favourable to the progress of superstition.[126] But as the English in-

---

Hamilton's Life of Barrow, in Barrow's Works, Edinb. 1845, vol. i. p. xxiii.

[125] Everything Mr. Macaulay has said on the contempt into which the clergy fell in the reign of Charles II. is perfectly accurate; and from evidence which I have collected, I know that this very able writer, of whose immense research few people are competent judges, has rather understated the case than overstated it. On several subjects I should venture to differ from Mr. Macaulay; but I cannot refrain from expressing my admiration of his unwearied diligence, of the consummate skill with which he has arranged his materials, and of the noble love of liberty which animates his entire work. These are qualities which will long survive the aspersions of his puny detractors, — men who, in point of knowledge and ability, are unworthy to loosen the shoe-latchet of him they foolishly attack.

[126] *Hallam's Const. Hist.* vol. ii. pp. 142, 143, 153–156; from which it appears that this movement began about 1681. The clergy, as a body, are naturally favourable to this doctrine; and the following passage, published only twelve years ago, will give the reader an idea of the views that some of them entertain. The Rev. Mr. Sewell (*Christian Politics*, Lond. 1844, p. 157) says, that the reigning prince is 'a being armed with supreme physical power by the hand and permission of Providence; as such, the lord of our property,

tellect was now sufficiently advanced to reject such dogmas, this futile attempt only increased the opposition between the interests of the people as a body, and the interests of the clergy as a class. Scarcely had this scheme been defeated, when the sudden death of Charles placed on the throne a prince whose most earnest desire was to restore the Catholic church, and reinstate among us that mischievous system which openly boasts of subjugating the reason of Man. This change in affairs was, if we consider it in its ultimate results, the most fortunate circumstance which could have happened to our country. In spite of the difference of their religion, the English clergy had always displayed an affection towards James, whose reverence for the priesthood they greatly admired; though they were anxious that the warmth of his affections should be lavished on the Church of England and not on the Church of Rome. They were sensible of the advantages which would accrue to their own order, if his piety could be turned into a new channel.[127] They saw that it was for his interest to abandon his religion; and they thought that to a man so cruel and so vicious, his own interest

---

the master of our lives, the fountain of honour, the dispenser of law, before whom each subject must surrender his will and conform his actions. . . . Who, when he errs, errs as a man, and not as a king, and is responsible, not to man, but to God.' And at p. 111, the same writer informs us that the church, 'with one uniform, unhesitating voice, has proclaimed the duty of "passive obedience."' See also on this slavish tenet, as upheld by the church, Wordsworth's *Ecclesiast. Biog.* vol. iv. p. 668; *Life of Ken, by a Layman,* vol. ii. p. 523; *Lathbury's Hist. of Convocation,* p. 228; *Lathbury's Nonjurors,* pp. 50, 135, 197; and a letter from Nelson, author of the *Fasts and Festivals,* in *Nichols's Lit. Anec.* vol. iv. p. 216. With good reason, therefore, did Fox tell the House of Commons, that ' by being a good churchman, a person might become a bad citizen.' *Parl. Hist.* vol. xxix. p. 1377.

[127] The Archbishop of Canterbury, in 1678, was engaged in an attempt to convert James; and in a letter to the Bishop of Winchester, he notices the 'happy consequences' which would result from his success. See this characteristic letter in *Clarendon Corresp.* vol. ii. pp. 465, 466. See also the motives of the bishops, candidly but broadly stated, in Mr. Wilson's valuable work, *Life of De Foe,* vol. i. p. 74.

would be the sole consideration.[128] The consequence was, that in one of the most critical moments of his life, they made in his favour a great and successful effort; and they not only used all their strength to defeat the bill by which it was proposed to exclude him from the succession, but when the measure was rejected, they presented an address to Charles, congratulating him on the result.[129] When James actually mounted the throne, they continued to display the same spirit. Whether they still hoped for his conversion, or whether, in their eagerness to persecute the dissenters, they overlooked the danger to their own church, is uncertain; but it is one of the most singular and unquestionable facts in our history, that for some time there existed a strict alliance between a Protestant hierarchy and a Popish king.[130] The terrible crimes which were the result of this compact are but too notorious. But what is more worthy of attention is, the circumstance that caused the dissolution of this conspiracy between the crown and the church. The ground of the quarrel was an attempt made by the king to effect, in some degree, a religious toleration. By the celebrated Test and Corporation Acts, it had been ordered, that all persons who were employed by government should be compelled, under a heavy penalty, to receive the sacrament according to the rites of the English church. The offence of James was, that he

---

[128] In a high-church pamphlet, published in 1682, against the Bill of Exclusion, the cause of James is advocated; but the inconvenience he would suffer by remaining a Catholic is strongly insisted upon. See the wily remarks in *Somers Tracts*, vol. viii. pp. 258, 259.

[129] *Wordsworth's Ecclesiast. Biog.* vol. iv. p. 665. On their eagerness against the bill, see *Harris's Lives of the Stuarts*, vol. v. p. 181; *Burnet's Own Time*, vol. ii. p. 216; *Somers Tracts*, vol. x. pp. 216, 253; *Campbell's Chancellors*, vol. iii. p. 353; *Carwithen's Hist. of the Church of England*, vol. ii. p. 431.

[130] At the accession of James II. 'the pulpits throughout England resounded with thanksgivings; and a numerous set of addresses flattered his Majesty, in the strongest expressions, with assurances of unshaken loyalty and obedience, without limitation or reserve.' *Neal's Hist. of the Puritans*, vol. v. p. 2. See also *Calamy's Life*, vol. i. p. 118.

now issued what was called a Declaration of Indulgence, in which he announced his intention of suspending the execution of these laws.[131] From this moment, the position of the two great parties was entirely changed. The bishops clearly perceived that the statutes which it was thus attempted to abrogate, were highly favourable to their own power; and hence, in their opinion, formed an essential part of the constitution of a Christian country. They had willingly combined with James, while he assisted them in persecuting men who worshipped God in a manner different from themselves.[132] So long as this compact held good, they were indifferent as to matters which they considered to be of minor importance. They looked on in silence, while the king was amassing the materials with which he hoped to turn a free government into an absolute monarchy.[133] They saw Jeffreys and Kirke torturing their fellow-subjects; they saw the gaols crowded with

---

[131] On the 18th March, 1687, the king announced to the Privy Council that he had determined ' to grant, by his own authority, entire liberty of conscience to all his subjects.' On the 4th April appeared the memorable Declaration of Indulgence.' *Macaulay's Hist. of England*, vol. ii. p. 211; and see *Life of James II.*, edited by Clarke, vol. ii. p. 112. There is a summary of the Declaration in *Neal's Hist. of the Puritans*, vol. v. pp. 30, 31. As to the second Declaration, see *Macaulay*, vol. ii. pp. 344, 345; *Clarendon Correspond.* vol. ii. p. 170.

[132] It was in the autumn of 1685, that the clergy and the government persecuted the dissenters with the greatest virulence. See *Macaulay's Hist.* vol. i. pp. 667, 668. Compare *Neal's Hist. of the Puritans*, vol. v. pp. 4-12, with a letter from Lord Clarendon, dated 21st December 1685, in *Clarendon Correspond.* vol. i. p. 192. It is said (*Burnet's Own Time*, vol. iii. pp. 175, 176), that on many occasions the church party made use of the ecclesiastical courts to extort money from the Nonconformists; and for confirmation of this, see *Mackintosh's Revolution of 1688*, pp. 173, 640.

[133] It appears from the accounts in the War Office, that James, even in the first year of his reign, had a standing army of nearly 20,000 men. *Mackintosh's Revolution*, pp. 3, 77, 688: 'A disciplined army of about 20,000 men was, for the first time, established during peace in this island.' As this naturally inspired great alarm, the king gave out that the number did not exceed 15,000. *Life of James II.*, edited by Clarke, vol. ii. pp. 52, 57.

prisoners, and the scaffold streaming with blood.[134] They were well pleased that some of the best and ablest men in the kingdom should be barbarously persecuted; that Baxter should be thrown into prison, and that Howe should be forced into exile. They witnessed with composure the most revolting cruelties, because the victims of them were the opponents of the English church. Although the minds of men were filled with terror and with loathing, the bishops made no complaint. They preserved their loyalty unimpaired, and insisted on the necessity of humble submission to the Lord's anointed.[135] But the moment James proposed to protect against persecution those who were hostile to the church; the moment he announced his intention of breaking down that monopoly of offices and of honours which the bishops had long secured for their own party;—the moment this took place, the hierarchy became alive to the dangers with which the country was threatened from the violence of so arbitrary a prince.[136] The king had laid his hand on the ark, and the guardians of the temple flew to arms. How could

---

[134] Compare *Burnet*, vol. iii. pp. 55–62, with *Dalrymple's Memoirs*, vol. i. part i. book ii. pp. 198–203. Ken, so far as I remember, was the only one who set his face against these atrocities. He was a very humane man, and did what he could to mitigate the sufferings of the prisoners in Monmouth's rebellion; but it is not mentioned that he attempted to stop the persecutions directed against the innocent Nonconformists, who were barbarously punished, not because they rebelled, but because they dissented. *Life of Ken, by a Layman*, vol. i. p. 298.

[135] 'From the conduct of the clergy in this and the former reign, it is quite clear, that if the king had been a Protestant, of the profession of the Church of England, or even a quiet, submissive Catholic, without any zeal for his religion,—confining himself solely to matters of state, and having a proper respect for church property,—he might have plundered other Protestants at his pleasure, and have trampled upon the liberties of his country, without the danger of resistance.' *Wilson's Life of De Foe*, vol. i. p. 138. Or, as Fox says, 'Thus, as long as James contented himself with absolute power in civil matters, and did not make use of his authority against the church, everything went smooth and easy.' *Fox's Hist. of James II.*, p. 105.

[136] Compare *Neal's Hist. of the Puritans*, vol. v. p. 58, with *Life of James II.*, edit. Clarke, vol. ii. p. 70; where it is well said, that

they tolerate a prince who would not allow them to persecute their enemies? How could they support a sovereign who sought to favour those who differed from the national church? They soon determined on the line of conduct it behoved them to take. With an almost unanimous voice, they refused to obey the order by which the king commanded them to read in their churches the edict for religious toleration.[137] Nor did they stop there. So great was their enmity against him they had recently cherished, that they actually applied for aid to those very dissenters whom, only a few weeks before, they had hotly persecuted; seeking by magnificent promises to win over to their side men they had hitherto hunted even to the death.[138] The most eminent of the Nonconformists

the clergy of the Church of England 'had preached prerogative and the sovereign power to the highest pitch, while it was favourable to them; but when they apprehended the least danger from it, they cried out as soon as the shoe pinched, though it was of their own putting on.' See also pp. 113, 164. What their servility was to the crown, while they thought that the crown was with them, may be estimated from the statement of De Foe: 'I have heard it publicly preached, that if the king commanded my head, and sent his messengers to fetch it, I was bound to submit, and stand while it was cut off.' *Wilson's Life of De Foe*, vol. i. p. 118.

[137] D'Oyly (*Life of Sancroft*, p. 164) says, 'On the whole, it is supposed that not more than 200 out of the whole body of clergy, estimated at 10,000, complied with the king's requisition.' 'Only seven obeyed in the city of London, and not above 200 all England over.' *Burnet's Own Time*, vol. iii. p. 218. On Sunday, 20th May 1688, Lord Clarendon writes: 'I was at St. James's church; in the evening I had an account that the Declaration was read only in four churches in the city and liberties.' *Clarendon Corresp.* vol. ii. pp. 172, 173. When this conduct became known, it was observed that the church 'supported the crown only so long as she dictated to it; and became rebellious at the moment when she was forbidden to be intolerant.' *Mackintosh's Revolution of* 1688, p. 255.

[138] The first advances were made when the Declaration of the king in favour of 'liberty of conscience' was on the point of being issued, and immediately after the proceedings at Oxford had shown his determination to break down the monopoly of offices possessed by the church. 'The clergy at the same time prayed and entreated the dissenters to appear on their side, and stand by the Establishment, making large promises of favour

were far from being duped by this sudden affection.[129] But their hatred of Popery, and their fear of the ulterior designs of the king, prevailed over every other consideration; and there arose that singular combination between churchmen and dissenters, which has never since been repeated. This coalition, backed by the general voice of the people, soon overturned the throne, and gave rise to what is justly deemed one of the most important events in the history of England.

Thus it was, that the proximate cause of that great revolution which cost James his crown, was the publication by the king of an edict of religious toleration, and the consequent indignation of the clergy at seeing so audacious an act performed by a Christian prince. It is true, that if other things had not conspired, this alone could never have effected so great a change. But it was the immediate cause of it, because it was the cause of the schism between the church and the throne, and of the alliance between the church and the dissenters. This is a fact never to be forgotten. We ought never to forget, that the first and only time the Church of England has made war upon the crown, was when the crown had declared its intention of tolerating, and in some degree protecting, the rival religions of the

---

and brotherly affection if ever they came into power.' Neal's *Hist. of the Puritans*, vol. v. p. 29. See also, at pp. 58, 59, the conciliating letter from the Archbishop of Canterbury after the Declaration. 'Such,' says Neal, 'such was the language of the church in distress!' Compare Birch's *Life of Tillotson*, p. 153; Ellis's *Correspond.* vol. ii. p. 63; Ellis's *Orig. Letters*, 2nd series, vol. iv. p. 117; Mackintosh's *Revolution*, p. 286; *Somers Tracts*, vol. ix. p. 132; Macaulay's *Hist. of England*, vol. ii. pp. 218, 219.

[129] See the indignant language of De Foe (Wilson's *Life of De Foe*, vol. l. pp. 130, 131, 133, 134; and a *Letter from a Dissenter to the Petitioning Bishops*, in *Somers Tracts*, vol. ix. pp. 117, 118. The writer says: 'Pray, my lords, let me ask you a question. Suppose the king, instead of his Declamation, had issued out a proclamation, commanding justices of the peace, constables, informers, and all other persons, to be more rigorous, if possible, against dissenters, and do their utmost to the perfect quelling and destroying them; and had ordered this to be read in your churches in the time of divine service,— would you have made any scruple of that?'

country.[140] There is no doubt that the Declaration which was then issued was illegal, and that it was conceived in an insidious spirit. But declarations equally illegal, equally insidious, and much more tyrannical, had on other occasions been made by the sovereign, without exciting the anger of the clergy.[141] These are things which it is good for us to ponder. These are lessons of inestimable value for those to whom it is given, not, indeed, to direct, but in some degree to modify, the march of public opinion. As to the people in general, it is impossible for them to exaggerate the obligations which they and all of us owe to the Revolution of 1688. But let them take heed that superstition does not mingle with their gratitude. Let them admire that majestic edifice of national liberty, which stands alone in Europe like a beacon in the midst of the waters; but let them not think that they owe anything to men who, in contributing to its erection, sought the gratification of their own selfishness, and the consolidation of that spiritual power which by it they fondly hoped to secure.

---

[140] That this was the immediate cause, so far as the head of the church-party was concerned, is unblushingly avowed by the biographer and defender of the then Archbishop of Canterbury. 'The order published from the king in council, May 4th, 1688, directing the archbishops and bishops to send to the clergy in their respective dioceses the Declaration for Liberty of Conscience, to be publicly read in all the churches of the kingdom, made it impossible for the Archbishop of Canterbury to abstain any longer from engaging in an open and declared opposition to the counsels under which the king was now unhappily acting.' *D'Oyly's Life of Sancroft*, p. 151.

[141] Some writers have attempted to defend the clergy, on the ground that they thought it illegal to publish a declaration of this kind. But such a defence is incompatible with their doctrine of passive obedience; and besides this, it was contradicted by precedents and decisions of their own. Jeremy Taylor, in his *Ductor Dubitantium*, their great work of authority, asserts that 'the unlawful proclamations and edicts of a true prince may be published by the clergy in their several charges.' *Heber's Life of Taylor*, p. cclxxxvi. Heber adds: 'I wish I had not found this in Taylor; and I thank Heaven that the principle was not adopted by the English clergy in 1687.' But why was it not adopted in 1687? Simply because in 1687 the king attacked the monopoly enjoyed by the clergy; and therefore the

It is, indeed, difficult to conceive the full amount of the impetus given to English civilization by the expulsion of the House of Stuart. Among the most immediate results, may be mentioned the limits that were set to the royal prerogative;[142] the important steps that were taken towards religious toleration;[143] the remarkable and permanent improvement in the administration of justice;[144] the final abolition of a censorship over the press;[145] and, what has not excited sufficient attention,

clergy forgot their principle, that they might smite their enemy. And what makes the motives of this change still more palpable is, that as late as 1681, the Archbishop of Canterbury caused the clergy to read a Declaration issued by Charles II.; and that in a revised copy of the Liturgy he had also added to the rubric to the same effect. See *Neal's Hist. of the Puritans*, vol. v. p. 56. Compare *Calamy's Own Life*, vol. i. pp. 199, 200; *Mackintosh's Revolution*, pp. 242, 243; *D'Oyly's Life of Sancroft*, p. 152; *King's Life of Locke*, vol. i. p. 259; *Life of James II.*, edit. Clarke, vol. ii. p. 156.

[143] They are summed up in a popular pamphlet ascribed to Lord Somers, and printed in *Somers Tracts*, vol. x. pp. 263, 264. The diminished respect felt for the crown after 1688 is judiciously noticed in *Mahon's Hist. of England*, vol. i. p. 9.

[143] The Toleration Act was passed in 1689. A copy of it is given by the historians of the dissenters, who call it their Magna Charta. See *Bogue and Bennett's History of the Dissenters*, vol. i. pp. 187–198. The historian of the Catholics equally allows that the reign of William III. is 'the era from which their enjoyment of religious toleration may be dated.' *Butler's Memoirs of the Catholics*, vol. iii. pp. 122, 139. This is said by Mr. Butler in regard, not to the Protestant dissenters, but to the Catholics; so that we have the admission of both parties as to the importance of this epoch. Even the shameful act forced upon William in 1700 was, as Mr. Hallam truly says, evaded in its worst provisions. *Const. Hist.* vol. ii. pp. 332, 333.

[144] *Campbell's Chancellors*, vol. iv. pp. 102, 355, and his *Chief-Justices*, vol. ii. pp. 95, 116, 118, 136, 142, 143. See also *Barrington's Observations on the Statutes*, pp. 23, 102, 558; and even *Alison's Hist. of Europe*, vol. i. p. 236, vol. ix. p. 243; an unwary concession from such an enemy to popular liberty.

[145] This was effected before the end of the seventeenth century. See *Campbell's Chancellors*, vol. iv. pp. 121, 122. Compare Lord Camden on Literary Property, in *Parl. Hist.* vol. xvii. p. 994; *Hunt's History of Newspapers*, vol. i. pp. 161, 162; *Somers Tracts*, vol. xiii. p. 555; and a more detailed account in *Macaulay's Hist. of England*, vol. iv. pp. 348 seq. 540 seq.; though Mr. Macaulay in ascribing, p. 353, so much to the influence of Blount, has not, I think, suffi-

the rapid growth of those great monetary interests by which, as we shall hereafter see, the prejudices of the superstitious classes have in no small degree been counterbalanced.[146] These are the main characteristics of the reign of William III.; a reign often aspersed, and little understood,[147] but of which it may be truly said, that, taking its difficulties into due consideration, it is the most successful and the most splendid recorded in the history of any country. But these topics rather belong to the subsequent volumes of this work; and at present we are only concerned in tracing the effects of the Revolution upon that ecclesiastical power by which it was immediately brought about.

Scarcely had the clergy succeeded in expelling James, when the greater number of them repented of their own act.[148] Indeed, even before he was driven

---

[146] Mr. Cooke (*Hist. of Party*, vol. ii. pp. 5, 143) notices this remarkable rise of the monied classes early in the eighteenth century; but he merely observes, that the consequence was to strengthen the Whig party. Though this is undoubtedly true, the ultimate results, as I shall hereafter point out, were far more important than any political or even economical consequences. It was not till 1694 that the Bank of England was established; and this great institution at first met with the warmest opposition from the admirers of old times, who thought it must be useless because their ancestors did without it. See the curious details in *Sinclair's Hist. of the Revenue*, vol. iii. pp. 6–9; and on the connexion between it and the Whigs, see *Macaulay's Hist. of England*, vol. iv. p. 502. There is a short account of its origin and progress in *Smith's Wealth of Nations*, book ii. chap. ii. p. 130.

[147] Frequently misunderstood, even by those who praise it. Thus, for instance, a living writer informs us that, 'great as have been the obligations which England owes, in many different views, to the Revolution, it is beyond all question the greatest, that it brought in a sovereign instructed in the art of overcoming the ignorant impatience of taxation which is the invariable characteristic of free communities; and thus gave it a government capable of turning to the best account the activity and energy of its inhabitants, at the same time that it had the means given it of maintaining their independence.' *Alison's Hist. of Europe*, vol. vii. p. 5. This, I should suppose, is the most eccentric eulogy ever passed on William III.

[148] On their sudden repentance, and on the causes of it, see Neal's *Hist. of the Puritans*, vol. v. p. 71.

from the country, several things had occurred to make them doubt the policy of the course they were pursuing. During the last few weeks that he was allowed to reign, he had shown symptoms of increasing respect for the English hierarchy. The archbishopric of York had so long been vacant, as to cause a belief that it was the intention of the crown either to appoint to it a Catholic, or else to seize its revenues.[149] But James, to the delight of the church, now filled up this important office by nominating Lamplugh, who was well known to be a stanch churchman and a zealous defender of episcopal privileges.[150] Just before this, the king also rescinded the order by which the Bishop of London had been suspended from the exercise of his functions.[151] To the bishops in general he made great promises of future favour;[152] some of them, it was said, were to be called

---

[149] *Mackintosh's Revolution of 1688*, pp. 81, 191. After the death of Archbishop Dolben, 'the see was kept vacant for more than two years,' and Cartwright hoped to obtain it. See *Cartwright's Diary*, by Hunter, 4to, 1843, p. 45. In the same way, we find from a letter to the Archbishop of Canterbury (*Clarendon Corresp.* vol. i. p. 409) that in May 1686 uneasiness was felt because the Irish bishoprics were not filled up. Compare Burnet, vol. iii. p. 103. Curwithen (*Hist. of the Ch. of England*, vol. ii. p. 492) says, that James had intended to raise the Jesuit Petre to the archbishopric.

[150] Lamplugh was translated from the bishopric of Exeter to the archbishopric of York in November 1688. See the contemporary account in the *Ellis Correspondence*, vol. ii. p. 303, and *Ellis's Original Letters*, second series, vol. iv. p. 151. He was a most orthodox man; and not only hated the dissenters, but showed his zeal by persecuting them. *Wilson's Life of De Foe*, vol. i. pp. 94, 95. Compare an anecdote of him in *Baxter's Life of Himself*, folio, 1696, part iii. pp. 178, 179.

[151] In a letter, dated London, 29th September 1688 (*Ellis Correspondence*, vol. ii. p. 224, and *Ellis's Orig. Letters*, second series, vol. iv. p. 128), it is stated, that the Bishop of London's 'suspension is taken off.' See also *Somers Tracts*, vol. ix. p. 215. This is the more observable, because, according to Johnstone, there was an intention, in December 1687, of depriving him. *Mackintosh's Revolution*, pp. 211, 212.

[152] This disposition on the part of the king again to favour the bishops and the church became a matter of common remark in September 1688. See *Ellis Correspond.* vol. ii. pp. 201, 202, 209, 219, 224, 225, 226, 227; *Clarendon Correspond.* vol. ii. pp. 188, 192. Sir John Reresby,

to his privy council; and, in the meantime, he cancelled that ecclesiastical commission which, by limiting their power, had excited their anger.[153] Besides this, there occurred some other circumstances which the clergy now had to consider. It was rumoured, and it was generally believed, that William was no great admirer of ecclesiastical establishments; and that, being a friend to toleration, he was more likely to diminish the power than increase the privileges of the English hierarchy.[154] It was also known that he favoured the Presbyterians, whom the Church not unreasonably regarded as her bitterest enemies.[155] And when, in addition to all this,

who was then in London, writes, in October 1688, that James 'begins again to court the Church of England.' *Reresby's Memoirs*, p. 357. Indeed, the difficulties of James were now becoming so great, that he had hardly any choice.

[153] *Ellis Correspond.* vol. ii. p. 213; *Life of James II.*, edit. Clarke, vol. ii. p. 189.

[154] In November 1687, it was said that he wished the dissenters to have 'entire liberty for the full exercise of their religion,' and to be freed 'from the severity of the penal laws.' *Somers Tracts*, vol. ix. p. 184. This is the earliest distinct notice I have seen of William's desire to deprive the church of the power of punishing nonconformists; but after he arrived in England his intentions became obvious. In January 1688-9 the friends of the church complained 'that the countenance he gave the dissenters gave too much cause of jealousy to the Church of England.' *Clarendon Correspond.* vol. ii. p. 238. Compare *Neal's Hist. of the Puritans*, vol. v. p. 81; *Bogue and Bennett's Hist. of the Dissenters*, vol. ii. p. 318; *Birch's Life of Tillotson*, pp. 156, 157; *Somers Tracts*, vol. x. p. 341, vol. xi. p. 108. Burnet, in his summary of the character of William, observes that, 'his indifference as to the forms of church-government, and his being zealous for toleration, together with his cold behaviour towards the clergy, gave them generally very ill impressions of him.' *Own Time*, vol. iv. p. 550. At p. 192 the bishop says, 'He took no notice of the clergy, and seemed to have little concern in the matters of the church or of religion.'

[155] Sir John Reresby, who was an attentive observer of what was going on, says, 'The prince, upon his arrival, seemed more inclined to the Presbyterians than to the members of the church; which startled the clergy.' *Reresby's Memoirs*, p. 375: see also pp. 399, 405: 'the church-people hated the Dutch, and had rather turn Papists than receive the Presbyterians among them.' Compare *Evelyn's Diary*, vol. iii. p. 281: 'the Presbyterians, our now governors.'

William, on mere grounds of expediency, actually abolished episcopacy in Scotland, it became evident that, by thus repudiating the doctrine of divine right, he had directed a great blow against those opinions on which, in England, ecclesiastical authority was based.[156]

While these things were agitating the public mind, the eyes of men were naturally turned upon the bishops, who, though they had lost much of their former power, were still respected by a large majority of the people as the guardians of the national religion. But at this critical moment they were so blinded, either by their ambition or by their prejudices, that they adopted a course which of all others was the most injurious to their reputation. They made a sudden attempt to reverse that political movement of which they were themselves the principal originators. Their conduct on this occasion amply confirms that account of their motives which I have already given. If, in aiding those preliminary measures by which the Revolution was effected, they had been moved by a desire of relieving the nation from despotism, they would have eagerly welcomed that great man at whose approach the despot took to flight. This is what the clergy would have done, if they had loved their country better than they loved their order. But they pursued a precisely opposite course; because they preferred the petty interests of their own class to the

---

[156] Burnet (*Own Time*, vol. iv. p. 50) says of the clergy in 1689: 'The king was suspected by them, by reason of the favour showed to dissenters; but chiefly for his abolishing episcopacy in Scotland, and his consenting to the setting up presbytery there.' On this great change, compare Bogue and Bennett's *History of Dissenters*, vol. ii. pp. 379–384; Barry's *Hist. of the Orkney Islands*, p. 257; Neal's *Hist. of the Puritans*, vol. v. pp. 85, 86: and on the indignation felt by the Anglican clergy at the abolition of episcopacy in Scotland, see a contemporary pamphlet in *Somers Tracts*, vol. ix. pp. 510, 516, where fears are expressed lest William should effect a similar measure in England. The writer very fairly observes, p. 522, 'For if we give up the *jus divinum* of episcopacy in Scotland, we must yield it also as to England. And then we are wholly precarious.' See also vol. x. pp. 341, 503; Lathbury's *Hist. of Convocation*, pp. 277, 278; and Macpherson's *Original Papers*, vol. i. p. 509.

welfare of the great body of the people, and because they would rather that the country should be oppressed than that the church should be humbled. Nearly the whole of the bishops and clergy had, only a few weeks before, braved the anger of their sovereign sooner than read in their churches an edict for religious toleration, and seven of the most influential of the episcopal order had, in the same cause, willingly submitted to the risk of a public trial before the ordinary tribunals of the land. This bold course they professed to have adopted, not because they disliked toleration, but because they hated tyranny. And yet when William arrived in England, and when James stole away from the kingdom like a thief in the night, this same ecclesiastical profession pressed forward to reject that great man, who, without striking a blow, had by his mere presence saved the country from the slavery with which it was threatened. We shall not easily find in modern history another instance of such gross inconsistency, or rather, let us say, of such selfish and reckless ambition. For this change of plan, far from being concealed, was so openly displayed, and the causes of it were so obvious, that the scandal was laid bare before the whole country. Within the space of a few weeks the apostasy was consummated. The first in the field was the Archbishop of Canterbury, who, anxious to retain his office, had promised to wait upon William. But when he saw the direction things were likely to take, he withdrew his promise, and would not recognize a prince who showed such indifference to the sacred order.[167] Indeed, so great was his anger, that he sharply rebuked his chaplain for presuming to pray for William and Mary, although they had been proclaimed with the full consent

---

[167] *Burnet's Own Time*, vol. iii. p. 340. Burnet, who had the best means of information, says, 'Though he had once agreed to it, yet would not come.' Lord Clarendon, in his *Diary*, 3rd January 1688-9, writes, that the archbishop expressed to him on that day his determination neither to call on William nor even to send to him (*Clarendon Correspond.* vol. ii. p. 240); and this resolution appears to have been taken deliberately: 'he was careful not to do it, for the reasons he formerly gave me.'

of the nation, and although the crown had been delivered to them by the solemn and deliberate act of a public convention of the estates of the realm.[158] While such was the conduct of the primate of England, his brethren were not wanting to him in this great emergency of their common fate. The oath of allegiance was refused not only by the Archbishop of Canterbury, but also by the Bishop of Bath and Wells, by the Bishop of Chester, by the Bishop of Chichester, by the Bishop of Ely, by the Bishop of Gloucester, by the Bishop of Norwich, by the Bishop of Peterborough, and by the Bishop of Worcester.[159] As to the inferior clergy, our information is less precise; but it is said that about six hundred of them imitated their superiors in declining to recognize for their king him whom the country had elected.[160] The other members of this turbulent faction were unwilling, by so bold a measure, to incur that deprivation of their livings with which William would probably have visited them. They, therefore, preferred a safer and more inglorious opposition, by which they could embarrass the government without injuring themselves, and could gain the reputation of orthodoxy without incurring the pains of martyrdom.

The effect which all this produced on the temper of the nation may be easily imagined. The question was now narrowed to an issue which every plain man could

---

[158] See the account given by his chaplain Wharton, in *D'Oyly's Life of Sancroft*, p. 259, where it is stated that the archbishop was very irate ('vehementer excandescens'), and told him, 'that he must thenceforward desist from offering prayers for the new king and queen, or else from performing the duties of his chapel.' See also *Birch's Life of Tillotson*, p. 144. Thus too the Bishop of Norwich declared 'that he would not pray for King William and Queen Mary.' *Clarendon Correspond.* vol. ii. p. 263. The same spirit was universal among the high-church clergy; and when public prayers were offered up for the king and queen, they were called by the nonjurors 'the immoral prayers,' and this became a technical and recognized expression. *Life of Ken, by a Layman*, vol. ii. pp. 648, 650.

[159] *Lathbury's Hist. of the Nonjurors*, p. 45; *D'Oyly's Sancroft*, p. 260.

[160] Nairne's Papers mention, in 1693, 'six hundred ministers who have not taken the oaths.' *Macpherson's Orig. Papers*, vol. i. p. 459.

at once understand. On the one side, there was an overwhelming majority of the clergy.[161] On the other side there was all the intellect of England, and all her dearest interests. The mere fact that such an opposition could exist without kindling a civil war, showed how the growing intelligence of the people had weakened the authority of the ecclesiastical profession. Besides this, the opposition was not only futile, but it was also injurious to the class that made it.[162] For it was now seen that the clergy only cared for the people as long as the people cared for them. The violence with which these angry men [163] set themselves against the

---

[161] The only friends William possessed among the clergy were the low-churchmen, as they were afterwards called; and it is supposed that they formed barely a tenth of the entire body in 1689: 'We should probably overrate their numerical strength, if we were to estimate them at a tenth part of the priesthood.' *Macaulay's Hist. of England*, vol. iii. p. 74.

[162] The earliest allusion I have seen to the injury the clergy were inflicting on the church, by their conduct after the arrival of William, is in *Evelyn's Diary*, vol. iii. p. 273, — a curious passage, gently hinting at the 'wonder of many,' at the behaviour of 'the Archbishop of Canterbury, and some of the rest.' With Evelyn, who loved the church, this was an unpleasant subject; but others were less scrupulous; and in parliament, in particular, men did not refrain from expressing what must have been the sentiments of every impartial observer. In the celebrated debate, in January 1688-9, when the throne was declared vacant, Pollexfen said:

'Some of the clergy are for one thing, some for another; I think they scarce know what they would have.' *Parl. Hist.* vol. v p. 56. In February, Maynard, one of the most influential members, indignantly said: 'I think the clergy are out of their wits; and' I believe, if the clergy should have their wills, few or none of us should be here again.' *Ibid.* vol. v. p. 129. The clergy were themselves bitterly sensible of the general hostility; and one of them writes, in 1694: 'The people of England, who were so excessively enamoured of us when the bishops were in the tower, that they hardly forbore to worship us, are now, I wish I could say but cool and very indifferent towards us.' *Somers Tracts*, vol. ix. p. 526. The growing indignation against the clergy, caused by their obvious desire to sacrifice the country to the interests of the church, is strikingly displayed in a letter from Sir Roland Gwyne, written in 1710, and printed in *Macpherson's Orig. Papers*, vol. ii. p. 207.

[163] They are so called by

interests of the nation clearly proved the selfishness of that zeal against James, of which they had formerly made so great a merit. They continued to hope for his return, to intrigue for him, and in some instances to correspond with him; although they well knew that his presence would cause a civil war, and that he was so generally hated that he dared not show his face in England unless protected by the troops of a foreign and hostile power.[164]

But this was not the whole of the damage which, in those anxious times, the church inflicted upon herself. When the bishops refused to take the oaths to the new government, measures were adopted to remove them from their sees; and William did not hesitate to eject by force of law the Archbishop of Canterbury and five of his brethren.[165] The prelates, smarting under the insult, were goaded into measures of unusual activity. They loudly proclaimed that the powers of the church, which had long been waning, were now extinct.[166] They denied the right of the legislature to pass a law against them. They denied the right of the sovereign to put that law into execution.[167] They not only con-

---

Burnet: 'these angry men, that had raised this flame in the church.' *Own Time*, vol. v. p. 17.

[164] Indeed, the high-church party, in their publications, distinctly intimated, that if James were not recalled, he should be reinstated by a foreign army. *Somers Tracts*, vol. x. pp. 377, 405, 457, 462. Compare *Mahon's Hist. of England*, vol. ii. p. 138. Burnet (*Own Time*, vol. iv. pp. 361, 362) says, they were 'confounded' when they heard of the peace of 1697; and Calamy (*Life of Himself*, vol. ii. p. 322) makes the same remark on the death of Louis XIV.: 'It very much puzzled the counsels of the Jacobites, and spoiled their projects.'

[165] *D'Oyly's Life of Sancroft*, p. 266; *Wordsworth's Eccl. Biog.* iv. p. 683.

[166] Sancroft, on his death-bed, in 1693, prayed for the 'poor suffering church, which, by this revolution, is almost destroyed.' *D'Oyly's Sancroft*, p. 311; and *Macpherson's Original Papers*, vol. i. p. 280. See also *Remarks*, published in 1693 (*Somers Tracts*, vol. x. p. 504) where it is said, that William had, 'as far as possible he could, dissolved the true old Church of England;' and that, 'in a moment of time, her face was so altered, as scarce to be known again.'

[167] 'Ken, though deprived, never admitted in the secular power the right of deprivation; and it is well known that he

SIXTEENTH TO THE EIGHTEENTH CENTURY. 411

tinued to give themselves the title of bishops, but they made arrangements to perpetuate the schism which their own violence had created. The Archbishop of Canterbury, as he insisted upon being called, made a formal renunciation of his imaginary right into the hands of Lloyd,[168] who still supposed himself to be Bishop of Norwich, although William had recently expelled him from his see. The scheme of these turbulent priests was then communicated to James, who willingly supported their plan for establishing a permanent feud in the English church.[169] The result of this conspiracy between the rebellious prelates and the pretended king, was the appointment of a series of men who gave themselves out as forming the real episcopacy, and who received the homage of every one who preferred the claims of the church to the authority of the state.[170] This mock succession of imaginary bishops

---

studiously retained his title.' Bowles's *Life of Ken*, vol. ii. p. 225. Thus, too, Lloyd, so late as 1703, signs himself, 'Wm. Nor.' (*Life of Ken, by a Layman*, vol. ii. p. 720); though, having been legally deprived, he was no more bishop of Norwich than he was emperor of China. And Sancroft, in the last of his letters, published by D'Oyly (*Life*, p. 303), signs 'W. C.'

[169] The strange document, by which he appointed Dr. Lloyd his vicar-general, is printed in Latin, in *D'Oyly's Sancroft*, p. 295, and in English, in *Life of Ken, by a Layman*, vol. ii. pp. 640.

[169] Lathbury's *Hist. of the Nonjurors*, p. 96; *Life of Ken, by a Layman*, vol. ii. pp. 641, 642.

[170] The struggle between James and William was essentially a struggle between ecclesiastical interests and secular interests; and this was seen as early as 1689, when, as we learn from Burnet, who was much more a politician than a priest, 'the church was as the word given out by the Jacobite party, under which they might more safely shelter themselves.' *Own Time*, vol. iv. p. 57. See also, on this identification of the Jacobites with the church, *Birch's Life of Tillotson*, p. 222; and the argument of Dodwell, pp. 246, 247, in 1691. Dodwell justly observed, that the successors of the deprived bishops were schismatical, in a spiritual point of view; and that, 'if they should pretend to lay authority as sufficient, they would overthrow the being of a church as a society.' The bishops appointed by William were evidently intruders, according to church principles; and as their intrusion could only be justified according to lay principles, it followed that the

continued for more than a century;[171] and, by dividing the allegiance of churchmen, lessened the power of the church.[172] In several instances, the unseemly spectacle was exhibited of two bishops for the same place; one nominated by the spiritual power, the other nominated by the temporal power. Those who considered the church as superior to the state, of course attached themselves to the spurious bishops; while the appointments of William were acknowledged by that rapidly increasing party, who preferred secular advantages to ecclesiastical theories.[173]

---

success of the intrusion was the triumph of lay principles over church ones. Hence it is, that the fundamental idea of the rebellion of 1688, is the elevation of the state above the church; just as the fundamental idea of the rebellion of 1642, is the elevation of the commons above the crown.

[171] According to Dr. D'Oyly (*Life of Sancroft*, p. 297), Dr. Gordon 'died in London, November 1779, and is supposed to have been the last nonjuring bishop.' In *Short's Hist. of the Church of England*, p. 583, Lond. 1847, it is also stated, that 'this schism continued till 1779.' But Mr. Hallam (*Const. Hist.* vol. ii. p. 404) has pointed out a passage in the *State Trials*, which proves that another of the bishops, named Cartwright, was still living at Shrewsbury in 1793; and Mr. Lathbury (*Hist. of the Nonjurors*, Lond. 1845, p. 412) says, that he died in 1799.

[172] Calamy (*Own Life*, vol. i. pp. 328–330, vol. ii. pp. 338, 357, 358) gives an interesting account of these feuds within the church, consequent upon the revolution. Indeed, their bitterness was such, that it was necessary to coin names for the two parties; and, between 1700 and 1702, we, for the first time, hear the expressions, high-church and low-church. See *Burnet's Own Time*, vol. iv. p. 447, vol. v. p. 70. Compare *Wilson's Life of De Foe*, vol. ii. p. 26; *Parl. Hist.* vol. vi. pp. 162, 498. On the difference between them, as it was understood in the reign of Anne, see *Somers Tracts*, vol. xii. p. 532, and *Macpherson's Orig. Papers*, vol. ii. p. 166. On the dawning schism in the church, see the speech of Sir T. Littleton, in 1690, *Parl. Hist.* vol. v. p. 593. Hence many complained that they could not tell which was the real church. See curious evidence of this perplexity in *Somers Tracts*, vol. ix. pp. 477–481.

[173] The alternative is fairly stated in a letter written in 1691 (*Life of Ken, by a Layman*, vol. ii. p. 599): 'If the deprived bishop be the only lawful bishop, then the people and clergy of his diocese are bound to own him, and no other; then all the bishops who own the authority of a new archbishop, and live in communion with him, are schis-

Such were some of the events which, at the end of the seventeenth century, widened the breach that had long existed between the interests of the nation and the interests of the clergy.[174] There was also another circumstance which considerably increased this alienation. Many of the English clergy, though they retained their affection for James, did not choose to brave the anger of the government, or risk the loss of their livings. To avoid this, and to reconcile their conscience with their interest, they availed themselves of a supposed distinction between a king by right and a king in possession.[175] The consequence was, that while with their lips they took an oath of allegiance to William, they in their hearts paid homage to James; and, while they prayed for one king in their churches, they were bound to pray for another in their closets.[176]

---

matics; and the clergy who live in communion with schismatical bishops are schismatics themselves; and the whole Church of England now established by law is schismatical.'

[174] Lord Mahon (*Hist. of England*, vol. ii. p. 245) notices, what he terms, the 'unnatural alienation between the church and state,' consequent upon the Revolution of 1688: and on the diminished power of the church caused by the same event, see *Phillimore's Mem. of Lyttleton*, vol. i. p. 352.

[175] The old absurdity of *de facto* and *de jure*; as if any man could retain a right to a throne which the people would not allow him to occupy!

[176] In 1715, Leslie, by far the ablest of them, thus states their position: 'You are now driven to this dilemma,—swear, or swear not; if you swear, you kill the soul; and if you swear not, you kill the body, in the loss of your bread.' *Somers Tracts*, vol. xiii. p. 686. The result of the dilemma was what might have been expected; and a high-church writer, in the reign of William III., boasts (*Somers Tracts*, vol. x. p. 344) that the oaths taken by the clergy were no protection to the government: 'not that the government receives any security from oaths.' Whiston, too, says in his *Memoirs*, p. 30: 'Yet do I too well remember that the far greatest part of those of the university and clergy that then took the oaths to the government, seemed to me to take them with a doubtful conscience, if not against its dictates.' This was in 1693; and, in 1710, we find: 'There are now circumstances to make us believe that the Jacobite clergy have the like instructions to take any oaths, to get possession of a pulpit for the service of the cause, to bellow out the hereditary right, the pretended title of the Pretender.' *Somers Tracts*, vol. xii. p. 641. A

By this wretched subterfuge, a large body of the clergy were at once turned into concealed rebels; and we have it on the authority of a contemporary bishop, that the prevarication of which these men were notoriously guilty was a still further aid to that scepticism, the progress of which he bitterly deplores.[177]

As the eighteenth century advanced, the great movement of liberation rapidly proceeded. One of the most important of the ecclesiastical resources had formerly been Convocation; in which the clergy, by meeting in a body, were able to discountenance in an imposing manner whatever might be hostile to the church; and had, moreover, an opportunity, which they sedulously employed, of devising schemes favourable to the spiritual authority.[178] But, in the progress of the age, this weapon also was taken from them. Within a very few years after the Revolution, Convocation fell into general contempt;[179] and, in 1717, this celebrated

---

knowledge of this fact, or, at all events, a belief of it, was soon diffused; and, eight years later, the celebrated Lord Cowper, then lord chancellor, said, in the House of Lords, 'that his majesty had also the best part of the landed, and all the trading interest; *that as to the clergy, he would say nothing—but that it was notorious that the majority of the populace had been poisoned, and that the poison was not yet quite expelled.*' Parl. Hist. vol. vii. p. 641; also given, but not quite verbatim, in Campbell's Chancellors, vol. iv. p. 365.

[177] 'The prevarication of too many in so sacred a matter contributed not a little to fortify the growing atheism of the present age.' Burnet's Own Time, vol. iii. p. 381. See also, to the same effect, vol. iv. pp. 176, 177; and a remarkable passage in Somers Tracts, vol. xii. p. 673. I need hardly add, that it was then usual to confuse scepticism with atheism; though the two things are not only different, but incompatible. In regard to the quibble respecting *de facto* and *de jure*, and the use made of it by the clergy, the reader should compare Wilson's Mem. of De Foe, vol. i. pp. 171, 172; Somers Tracts, vol. ix. p. 631; Campbell's Chancellors, vol. iv. p. 409; and a letter from the Rev. Francis Jessop, written in 1717, in Nichols's Lit. Illustrations, vol. iv. pp. 120–123.

[178] Among which must be particularly mentioned the practice of censuring all books that encouraged free inquiry. In this respect, the clergy were extremely mischievous. See Lathbury's Hist. of Convocation, pp. 124, 280, 338, 351; and Wilson's Life of De Foe, vol. ii. p. 170.

[179] In 1704, Burnet (Own

SIXTEENTH TO THE EIGHTEENTH CENTURY. 415

assembly was finally prorogued by an act of the crown, it being justly considered that the country had no further occasion for its services.[180] Since that period, this great council of the English church has never been allowed to meet for the purpose of deliberating on its own affairs, until a few years ago, when, by the connivance of a feeble government, it was permitted to reassemble. So marked, however, has been the change in the temper of the nation, that this once formidable body does not now retain even a semblance of its ancient influence; its resolutions are no longer feared, its discussions are no longer studied; and the business of the country continues to be conducted without regard to those interests which, only a few generations ago, were considered by every statesman to be of supreme importance.[181]

Indeed, immediately after the Revolution, the tendency of things became too obvious to be mistaken, even by the most superficial observers. The ablest men in the country no longer flocked into the church, but preferred those secular professions in which ability was more likely to be rewarded.[182] At the same time, and

---

[180] *Time*, vol. v. p. 138) says of Convocation, 'but little opposition was made to them, as very little regard was had to them.' In 1700, there was a squabble between the upper and lower house of Convocation for Canterbury; which, no doubt, aided these feelings. See *Life of Archbishop Sharp*, edited by Newcome, vol. i. p. 348, where this wretched feud is related with great gravity.

[180] Charles Butler (*Reminiscences*, vol. ii. p. 95) says, that the final prorogation was in 1720; but, according to all the other authorities I have met with, it was in 1717. See *Hallam's Const. Hist.* vol. ii. p. 305; Lathbury's *Hist. of Convocation*, p. 385; *Mahon's Hist. of England*, vol. i. p. 302; *Monk's Life of Bentley*, vol. ii. p. 350.

[181] A letter, written by the Rev. Thomas Clayton in 1727, is worth reading, as illustrating the feelings of the clergy on this subject. He asserts, that one of the causes of the obvious degeneracy of the age is, that, owing to Convocation not being allowed to meet, 'bold and impious books appear barefaced to the world without any public censure.' See this letter in *Nichols's Illustrations of the Eighteenth Century*, vol. iv. pp. 414–416; and compare with it, *Letters between Warburton and Hurd*, pp. 310–312.

[182] On the decline of ability

as a natural part of the great movement, the clergy saw all the offices of power and emolument, which they had been used to hold, gradually falling out of their hands. Not only in the dark ages, but even so late as the fifteenth century, they were still strong enough to monopolize the most honourable and lucrative posts in the empire.[183] In the sixteenth century, the tide began to turn against them, and advanced with such steadiness, that, since the seventeenth century, there has been no instance of any ecclesiastic being made lord

---

in ecclesiastical literature, see note 38 in this chapter. In 1685, a complaint was made that secular professions were becoming more sought after than ecclesiastical ones. See *England's Wants*, sec. lvi. in *Somers Tracts*, vol. ix. p. 231, where the writer mournfully states, that in his time 'physic and law, professions ever acknowledged in all nations to be inferior to divinity, are generally embraced by gentlemen, and sometimes by persons nobly descended, and *preferred much above the divine's profession*.' This preference was, of course, most displayed by young men of intellect; and a large amount of energy being thus drawn off from the church, gave rise to that decay of spirit and of general power which has been already noticed; and which is also indicated by Coleridge, in his remarks on the 'apologising theology' which succeeded the Revolution. *Coleridge's Lit. Remains*, vol. iii. pp. 51, 52, 116, 117, 119. Compare *Stephen's Essays on Ecclesiast. Biog.* 2d edit. 1850, vol. ii. p. 66, on 'this depression of theology;' and *Hare's Mission of the Comforter*, 1850, p. 264, on the 'intellectually feebler age.' Evelyn, in 1691, laments the diminished energy then beginning to be observed among 'young preachers.' *Evelyn's Diary*, vol. iii. p. 309; and for another notice, in 1696, of this 'dead and lifeless way of preaching,' see *Life of Cudworth*, p. 35, in vol. i. of *Cudworth's Intellect Syst.*

[183] Sharon Turner, describing the state of things in England in the fifteenth century, says, 'Clergymen were secretaries of government, the privy seals, cabinet councillors, treasurers of the crown, ambassadors, commissioners to open parliament, and to Scotland; presidents of the king's council, supervisors of the royal works, chancellors, keepers of the records, the masters of the rolls, and even the physicians, both to the king and to the duke of Gloucester, during the reign of Henry VI. and afterwards.' *Turner's Hist. of England*, vol. vi. p. 132. On their enormous wealth, see *Eccleston's English Antiquities*, p. 146: 'In the early part of the fourteenth century, it is calculated that very nearly one-half of the soil of the kingdom was in the hands of the clergy.'

chancellor;[184] and, since the beginning of the eighteenth century, there has been no instance of one receiving any diplomatic appointment, or, indeed, holding any important office in the state.[185] Nor has this increasing ascendency of laymen been confined to the executive government. On the contrary, we find in both Houses of Parliament the same principle at work. In the early and barbarous periods of our history, one half of the House of Lords consisted of temporal peers; the other half of spiritual ones.[186] By the beginning of the eighteenth century, the spiritual peers, instead of forming one-half of the upper house, had dwindled away to one-eighth;[187] and, in the middle of the nineteenth century, they have still further shrunk to one-fourteenth:[188] thus supplying a striking numerical instance of that diminution of ecclesiastical power which is an essential requisite of modern civilization. Precisely in

---

[184] In 1625, Williams bishop of Lincoln was dismissed from his office of lord-keeper; and Lord Campbell observes (*Lives of the Chancellors*, vol. ii. p. 492): 'This is the last time that an ecclesiastic has held the great seal of England; and, notwithstanding the admiration in some quarters of mediæval usages, I presume the experiment is not likely to be soon repeated.'

[185] Monk (*Life of Bentley*, vol. i. p. 222) says, that Dr. John Robinson, bishop of Bristol, was 'lord privy seal, and plenipotentiary at the treaty of Utrecht; and is the last ecclesiastic in England who has held any of the high offices of state.' A high-church writer, in 1712, complains of the efforts that were being made to 'thrust the churchmen out of their places of power in the government.' *Somers Tracts*, vol. xiii. p. 211.

[186] In and after the reign of Henry III. 'the number of archbishops, bishops, abbots, priors, and ecclesiastical persons was for the most part equal to, and very often far exceeded, the number of the temporal lords and barons.' *Parry's Parliaments and Councils of England*, London, 1839, p. xvii. Of this Mr. Parry gives several instances; the most remarkable of which is, that 'in 49 Henry III., 120 prelates, and only 23 temporal lords, were summoned.' This, of course, was an extreme case.

[187] See an analysis of the House of Lords, in 1713, in *Mahon's Hist. of England*, vol. i. pp. 43-45; from which it appears that the total was 207, of whom 26 were spiritual. This includes the Catholics.

[188] By the returns in Dod for 1854, I find that the House of Lords contains 436 members, of whom 30 belong to the episcopal bench.

the same way, more than fifty years have elapsed since any clergyman has been able to take his seat as a representative of the people; the House of Commons having, in 1801, formally closed their doors against a profession which, in the olden time, would have been gladly admitted, even by the proudest and most exclusive assembly.[189] In the House of Lords, the bishops still retain their seats; but their precarious tenure is everywhere remarked, and the progress of public opinion is constantly pointing to a period, which cannot now be far distant, when the Peers will imitate the example set by the Commons, and will induce the legislature to relieve the upper house of its spiritual members; since they, by their habits, their tastes, and their traditions, are evidently unfitted for the profane exigencies of political life.[190]

While the fabric of superstition was thus tottering from internal decay, and while that ecclesiastical authority which had formerly played so great a part was gradually yielding to the advance of knowledge, there suddenly occurred an event which, though it might naturally have been expected, evidently took by surprise even those whom it most interested. I allude, of course, to that great religious revolution, which was a fitting supplement to the political revolution which

---

[189] For different accounts, and of course different views, of this final expulsion of the clergy from the House of Commons, see *Pellew's Life of Sidmouth*, vol. i. pp. 419, 420; *Stephens's Mem. of Tooke*, vol. ii. pp. 247–260; *Holland's Mem. of the Whig Party*, vol. i. pp. 178–180; *Campbell's Chancellors*, vol. vii. p. 148; *Twiss's Life of Eldon*, vol. i. p. 263; *Adolphus's Hist. of George III.*, vol. vii. p. 487.

[190] That the banishment of the clergy from the lower house was the natural prelude to the banishment of the bishops from the upper, was hinted at the time, and with regret, by a very keen observer. In the discussion 'on the Bill to prevent Persons in Holy Orders from sitting in the House of Commons,' Lord Thurlow 'mentioned the tenure of the bishops at this time, and said, if the bill went to disfranchise the lower orders of the clergy, it might go the length of *striking at the right of the reverend bench opposite to seats in that house*; though he knew it had been held that the reverend prelates sat, in the right of their baronies, as temporal peers.' *Parl. Hist.* vol. xxxv. p. 1542.

preceded it. The dissenters, who were strengthened by the expulsion of James, had by no means forgotten those cruel punishments which the Church of England, in the days of her power, had constantly inflicted upon them; and they felt that the moment had now come when they could assume towards her a bolder front than that on which they had hitherto ventured.[191] Besides this, they had in the mean time received fresh causes of provocation. After the death of our great king William III., the throne was occupied by a foolish and ignorant woman, whose love for the clergy would, in a more superstitious age, have led to dangerous results.[192] Even as it was, a temporary reaction took place, and during her reign the church was treated with a deference which William had disdained to show.[193] The

---

[191] It is impossible now to ascertain the full extent to which the Church of England, in the seventeenth century, persecuted the dissenters; but Jeremy White is said to have had a list of sixty thousand of these sufferers between 1660 and 1688, of whom no less than five thousand died in prison. *Bogue and Bennett's Hist. of the Dissenters*, vol. i. p. 108. On the cruel spirit which the clergy displayed in the reign of Charles II. compare *Harris's Lives of the Stuarts*, vol. v. p. 106; *Orme's Life of Owen*, p. 344; *Somers Tracts*, vol. xii. p. 531. Indeed, Harwood frankly said in the House of Commons, in 1672, 'Our aim is to bring all dissenting men into the Protestant church, and he that is not willing to come into the church should not have ease.' *Parl. Hist.* vol. iv. p. 530. On the zeal with which this principle was carried out, see an account, written in 1671, in *Somers Tracts*, vol. vii. pp. 586–

615; and the statement of De Foe, in *Wilson's Life of De Foe*, vol. ii. pp. 443–444.

[192] Besides the correspondence which the Duchess of Marlborough preserved for the instruction of posterity, we have some materials for estimating the abilities of Anne in the letters published in *Dalrymple's Memoirs*. In one of them Anne writes, soon after the Declaration for Liberty of Conscience was issued, 'It is a melancholy prospect that all we of the Church of England have. All the sectaries may now do what they please. Every one has the free exercise of their religion, on purpose, no doubt, to ruin us, which I think to all impartial judges is very plain.' *Dalrymple's Memoirs*, appendix to book v. vol. ii. p. 173.

[193] See a notable passage in *Somers Tracts*, vol. xii. p. 658, which should be compared with *Wilson's Life of De Foe*, vol. iii. p. 372.

natural consequence immediately followed. New measures of persecution were devised, and fresh laws were passed against those Protestants who did not conform to the doctrines and discipline of the English church.[194] But after the death of Anne the dissenters quickly rallied; their hopes revived,[195] their numbers continued to increase, and in spite of the opposition of the clergy, the laws against them were repealed.[196] As by these means they were placed more on a level with their opponents, and as their temper was soured by the injuries they had recently received, it was clear that a great struggle between the two parties was inevitable.[197]

---

[194] *Bogue and Bennett's History of the Dissenters*, vol. i. pp. 228–230, 237, 260–277; and *Hallam's Const. Hist.* vol. ii. pp. 396, 397. Mr. Hallam says, 'It is impossible to doubt for an instant, that if the queen's life had preserved the Tory government for a few years, every vestige of the toleration would have been effaced.' It appears from the *Vernon Correspond.* vol. iii. p. 228, Lond. 1841, that soon after the accession of Anne, there was a proposal 'to debar dissenters of their votes in elections;' and we know from Burnet (*Own Time*, vol. v. pp. 108, 136, 137, 218) that the clergy would have been glad if Anne had displayed even more zeal against them than she really did.

[195] *Bogue and Bennett's Hist. of the Dissenters*, vol. iii. p. 118. In Ivimey's *History of the Baptists*, it is said that the death of Anne was an 'answer to the dissenters' prayers.' *Southey's Commonplace Book*, third series, p. 135; see also p. 147, on the joy of the dissenters at the death of this troublesome woman.

[196] Two of the worst of them, 'the act against occasional conformity, and that restraining education, were repealed in the session of 1719.' *Hallam's Const. Hist.* vol. ii. p. 398. The repeal of the act against occasional conformity was strenuously opposed by the archbishops of York and of Canterbury (*Bogue and Bennett's Hist. of the Dissenters*, vol. iii. p. 132); but their opposition was futile; and when the Bishop of London, in 1726, wished to strain the Act of Toleration, he was prevented by Yorke, the attorney-general. See the pithy reply of Yorke, in *Harris's Life of Hardwicke*, vol. i. pp. 193, 194.

[197] At the end of the seventeenth century, great attention was excited by the way in which the dissenters were beginning to organize themselves into societies and synods. See, in the *Vernon Correspond.* vol. ii. pp. 128–130, 133, 156, some curious evidence of this, in letters written by Vernon, who was then secretary of state; and on the apprehensions caused by the increase of their schools, and by their systematic interference in elections,

SIXTEENTH TO THE EIGHTEENTH CENTURY. 421

For by this time the protracted tyranny of the English clergy had totally destroyed those feelings of respect which, even in the midst of hostility, often linger in the mind; and by the influence of which, if they had still existed, the contest might perhaps have been averted. But such motives of restraint were now despised; and the dissenters, exasperated by incessant persecution,[198] determined to avail themselves of the declining power of the church. They had resisted her when she was strong; it was hardly to be expected that they would spare her when she was feeble. Under two of the most remarkable men of the eighteenth century, Whitefield, the first of theological orators,[199] and Wesley, the first of theological statesmen,[200] there was

---

see *Life of Archbishop Sharp*, edited by Newcome, vol. i. pp. 125, 358. The church was eager to put down all dissenters' schools; and in 1705, the Archbishop of York told the House of Lords that he 'apprehended danger from the increase of dissenters, and particularly from the many academies set up by them.' *Parl. Hist.* vol. vi. pp. 492, 493. See also, on the increase of their schools, pp. 1351, 1352.

[198] In *Somers Tracts*, vol. xii. p. 684, it is stated, that in the reign of Charles II. 'this hard usage had begotten in the dissenters the utmost animosity against the persecuting churchmen.' Their increasing discontent, in the reign of Anne, was observed by Calamy. See *Calamy's Own Life*, vol. ii. pp. 244, 253, 274, 284, 285.

[199] If the power of moving the passions be the proper test by which to judge an orator, we may certainly pronounce Whitefield to be the greatest since the apostles. His first sermon was delivered in 1736 (*Nichols's Lit. Anec.* vol. ii. pp. 102, 122); his field-preaching began in 1739 (*Southey's Life of Wesley*, vol. i. pp. 196, 197); and the eighteen thousand sermons which he is said to have poured forth during his career of thirty-four years (*Southey's Wesley*, vol. ii. p. 531) produced the most astonishing effects on all classes, educated and uneducated. For evidence of the excitement caused by this marvellous man, and of the eagerness with which his discourses were read as well as heard, see *Nichols's Lit. Anec.* vol. ii. pp. 546, 547, and his *Illustrations*, vol. iv. pp. 302-304; *Mem. of Franklin, by Himself*, vol. i. pp. 161-167; *Doddridge's Correspond.* vol. iv. p. 55; *Stewart's Philos. of the Mind*, vol. iii. pp. 291, 292; *Lady Mary Montagu's Letters*, in her Works, 1803, vol. iv. p. 162; *Correspond. between Ladies Pomfret and Hartford*, 2nd edit. 1806, vol. i. pp. 138, 160-162; *Marchmont Papers*, vol. ii. p. 377.

[200] Of whom Mr. Macaulay

organized a great system of religion, which bore the
same relation to the Church of England that the Church
of England bore to the Church of Rome. Thus, after
an interval of two hundred years, a second spiritual
Reformation was effected in our country. In the
eighteenth century the Wesleyans were to the Bishops
what, in the sixteenth century, the Reformers were to
the Popes.[201] It is indeed true, that the dissenters from
the Church of England, unlike the dissenters from the
Church of Rome, soon lost that intellectual vigour for
which at first they were remarkable. Since the death
of their great leaders, they have not produced one man
of original genius; and since the time of Adam Clarke,
they have not had among them even a single scholar
who has enjoyed an European reputation. This mental
penury is perhaps owing, not to any circumstances
peculiar to their sect, but merely to that general decline
of the theological spirit, by which their adversaries have
been weakened as well as themselves.[202] Be this as it
may, it is at all events certain, that the injury they have
inflicted on the English church is far greater than is
generally supposed, and, I am inclined to think, is
hardly inferior to that which in the sixteenth century
Protestantism inflicted upon Popery. Setting aside the
actual loss in the number of its members,[203] there can

---

has said (*Essays*, vol. i. p. 221, 3rd edit.), that his 'genius for government was not inferior to that of Richelieu;' and strongly as this is expressed, it will hardly appear an exaggeration to those who have compared the success of Wesley with his difficulties.

[201] It was in 1739 that Wesley first openly rebelled against the church, and refused to obey the Bishop of Bristol, who ordered him to quit his diocese. *Southey's Life of Wesley*, vol. i. pp. 226, 243. In the same year he began to preach in the fields. See the remarkable entry in his *Journals*, p. 78, 29th March, 1739.

[202] They frankly confess that 'indifference has been another enemy to the increase of the dissenting cause.' *Bogue and Bennett's Hist. of the Dissenters*, vol. iv. p. 320. In *Newman's Development of Christian Doctrine*, pp. 39–40, there are some remarks on the diminished energy of Wesleyanism, which Mr. Newman seems to ascribe to the fact that the Wesleyans have reached that point in which 'order takes the place of enthusiasm.' p. 43. This is probably true; but I still think that the larger cause has been the more active one.

[203] Walpole, in his sneering

SIXTEENTH TO THE EIGHTEENTH CENTURY. 423

be no doubt that the mere formation of a Protestant faction, unopposed by the government, was a dangerous precedent; and we know from contemporary history that it was so considered by those who were most interested in the result.²⁰⁴ Besides this, the Wesleyans

way, mentions the spread of Methodism in the middle of the eighteenth century (*Walpole's Letters*, vol. ii. pp. 268, 272); and Lord Carlisle, in 1775, told the House of Lords (*Parl. Hist.* vol. xviii. p. 634) 'that Methodism was daily gaining ground, particularly in the manufacturing towns;' while, to come down still later, it appears from a letter by the Duke of Wellington to Lord Eldon (*Twiss's Life of Eldon*, vol. ii. p. 35) that about 1808 it was making proselytes in the army.

These statements, though accurate, are somewhat vague; but we have other and more precise evidence respecting the rapid growth of religious dissent. According to a paper found in one of the chests of William III., and printed by Dalrymple (*Memoirs*, vol. ii. part ii., appendix to chapter i. p. 40), the proportion in England of conformists to nonconformists was as 22¾ to 1. Eighty-four years after the death of William, the dissenters, instead of comprising only a twenty-third, were estimated at 'a fourth part of the whole community.' Letter from Watson to the Duke of Rutland, written in 1786, in *Life of Watson, Bishop of Llandaff*, vol. i. p. 246. Since then, the movement has been uninterrupted; and the returns recently published by government disclose the startling fact, that on Sunday, 31st March 1851, the members of the Church of England who attended morning service only exceeded by one-half the Independents, Baptists, and Methodists who attended at their own places of worship. See the Census Table, in *Journal of Statist. Soc.* vol. xviii. p. 151. If this rate of decline continues, it will be impossible for the Church of England to survive another century the attacks of her enemies.

²⁰⁴ The treatment which the Wesleyans received from the clergy, many of whom were magistrates, shows what would have taken place if such violence had not been discouraged by the government. See *Southey's Life of Wesley*, vol. i. pp. 395–406. Wesley has himself given many details, which Southey did not think proper to relate, of the calumnies and insults to which he and his followers were subjected by the clergy. See *Wesley's Journals*, pp. 114, 145, 178, 181, 198, 235, 256, 275, 375, 562, 619, 637, 646. Compare *Watson's Observations on Southey's Wesley*, pp. 173, 174; and for other evidence of the treatment of those who differed from the church, see *Correspondence and Diary of Doddridge*, vol. ii. p. 17, vol. iii. pp. 108, 131, 132, 144, 145, 156. Grosley, who visited England in 1765, says of Whitefield, 'The ministers of the established religion did their utmost to baffle the new preacher; they preached against him, representing him to

displayed an organization so superior to that of their predecessors the Puritans, that they soon became a centre round which the enemies of the church could conveniently rally. And, what is perhaps still more important, the order, regularity, and publicity, by which their proceedings have usually been marked, distinguished them from other sects; and by raising them as it were to the dignity of a rival establishment, have encouraged the diminution of that exclusive and superstitious respect which was once paid to the Anglican hierarchy.[203]

But these things, interesting as they are, only formed a single step of that vast process by which the ecclesiastical power was weakened, and our countrymen thus enabled to secure a religious liberty, imperfect indeed, but far superior to that possessed by any other people. Among the innumerable symptoms of this great movement, there were two of peculiar importance. These were, the separation of theology, first from morals, and

---

the people as a fanatic, a visionary, &c. &c.; in fine, they opposed him with so much success, that they caused him to be pelted with stones in every place where he opened his mouth to the public.' *Grosley's Tour to London*, Lond. 1772, vol. i. p. 356.

[206] That Wesleyanism encouraged dissent by imparting to it an orderly character, which in some degree approximated to church-discipline, is judiciously observed in *Bogue and Bennett's History of the Dissenters*, vol. iii. pp. 165, 166. But these writers deal rather too harshly with Wesley; though there is no doubt that he was a very ambitious man, and over-fond of power. At an early period of his career he began to aim at objects higher than those attempted by the Puritans, whose efforts, particularly in the sixteenth century, he looked at somewhat contemptuously. Thus, for instance, in 1747, only eight years after he had revolted against the church, he expresses in his Journal his wonder 'at the weakness of those holy confessors' (the Elizabethan Puritans), 'many of whom spent so much of their time and strength in disputing about surplice and hoods, or kneeling at the Lord's Supper!' *Journals*, p. 249, March 13th, 1747. Such warfare as this would have ill satisfied the soaring mind of Wesley; and from the spirit which pervades his voluminous Journals, as well as from the careful and far-seeing provisions which he made for managing his sect, it is evident that this great schismatic had larger views than any of his predecessors, and that he wished to organize a system capable of rivalling the established church.

then from politics. The separation from morals was effected late in the seventeenth century; the separation from politics before the middle of the eighteenth century. And it is a striking instance of the decline of the old ecclesiastical spirit, that both of these great changes were begun by the clergy themselves. Cumberland, bishop of Peterborough, was the first who endeavoured to construct a system of morals without the aid of theology.[206] Warburton, bishop of Gloucester, was the first who laid down that the state must consider religion in reference, not to revelation, but to expediency; and that it should favour any particular creed, not in proportion to its truth, but solely with a view to its general utility.[207] Nor were these mere

---

[206] Mr. Hallam (*Lit. of Europe*, vol. iii. p. 390) says, that Cumberland 'seems to have been the first Christian writer who sought to establish systematically the principles of moral right independently of revelation.' See also, on this important change, *Whewell's Hist. of Moral Philosophy in England*, pp. 12, 54. The dangers always incurred by making theology the basis of morals are now pretty well understood; but by no writer have they been pointed out more clearly than by M. Charles Comte: see the able exposition in his *Traité de Législation*, vol. i. pp. 223–247. There is a short and unsatisfactory account of Cumberland's book in *Mackintosh's Ethical Philosophy*, pp. 134–137. He was a man of considerable learning, and is noticed by M. Quatremère as one of the earliest students of Coptic. *Quatremère sur la Langue et la Littérature de l'Egypte*, p. 89. He was made a bishop in 1691, having published the *De Legibus* in 1672. *Chalmers's Biog. Dict.* vol. xi. pp. 133, 135.

[207] This was in his work entitled *The Alliance between Church and State*, which first appeared, according to Hurd (*Life of Warburton*, 1794, 4to. p. 13), in 1736, and, as may be supposed, caused great scandal. The history of its influence I shall trace on another occasion; in the mean time, the reader should compare, respecting its tendency, *Palmer on the Church*, vol. ii. pp. 313, 322, 323; *Parr's Works*, vol. i. pp. 657, 665, vol. vii. p. 128; *Whateley's Dangers to Christian Faith*, p. 190; and *Nichols's Lit. Anec.* vol. iii. p. 18. In January 1739–40, Warburton writes to Stukeley (*Nichols's Illustrations*, vol. ii. p. 53): 'But you know how dangerous new roads in theology are, by the clamour of the bigots against me.' See also some letters which passed between him and the elder Pitt in 1762, on the subject of expediency, printed in *Chatham Correspond.* vol. ii. pp. 184 seq. Warburton writes, p. 190, 'My opinion is, and ever was, that the state has nothing at all to do

barren principles, which subsequent inquirers were unable to apply. The opinions of Cumberland, pushed to their furthest extent by Hume,[208] were shortly afterwards applied to practical conduct by Paley,[209] and to speculative jurisprudence by Bentham and Mill;[210] while the opinions of Warburton, spreading with still greater rapidity, have influenced our legislative policy, and are now professed, not only by advanced thinkers, but even by those ordinary men, who, if they had lived fifty years earlier, would have shrunk from them with undissembled fear.[211]

---

with errors in religion, nor the least right so much as to attempt to repress them.' To make such a man a bishop was a great feat for the eighteenth century, and would have been an impossible one for the seventeenth.

[208] The relation between Cumberland and Hume consists in the entirely secular plan according to which both investigated ethics; in other respects, there is great difference between their conclusions; but if the anti-theological method is admitted to be sound, it is certain that the treatment of the subject by Hume is more consequential from the premisses, than is that by his predecessor. It is this which makes Hume a continuator of Cumberland; though with the advantage, not only of coming half a century after him, but of possessing a more comprehensive mind. The ethical speculations of Hume are in the third book of his *Treatise of Human Nature* (*Hume's Philosophical Works*, Edin. 1826, vol. ii. pp. 219 seq.), and in his *Inquiry concerning the Principles of Morals*, ibid. vol. iv. pp. 237–365.

[209] The moral system of Paley, being essentially utilitarian, completed the revolution in that field of inquiry; and as his work was drawn up with great ability, it exercised immense influence in an age already prepared for its reception. His *Moral and Political Philosophy* was published in 1785; in 1786 it became a standard book at Cambridge; and by 1805 it had 'passed through fifteen editions.' *Meadley's Memoirs of Paley*, pp. 127, 145. Compare *Whewell's Hist. of Moral Philosophy*, p. 176.

[210] That the writings of these two eminent men form part of the same scheme, is well known to those who have studied the history of the school to which they belong; and on the intellectual relation they bore to each other, I cannot do better than refer to a very striking letter by James Mill himself, in *Bentham's Works*, edit. Bowring, vol. x. pp. 481, 482.

[211] The repeal of the Test Act, the admission of Catholics into Parliament, and the steadily increasing feeling in favour of the admission of the Jews, are the leading symptoms of this great movement. On the gradual diffusion among us of the doctrine of expediency, which, on all subjects not yet raised to sciences,

Thus it was that, in England, theology was finally severed from the two great departments of ethics and of government. As, however, this important change was at first not of a practical, but solely of an intellectual character, its operation was, for many years, confined to a small class, and has not yet produced the whole of those results which we have every reason to anticipate. But there were other circumstances which tended in the same direction, and which, being known to all men of tolerable education, produced effects more immediate, though perhaps less permanent. To trace their details, and point out the connexion between them, will be the business of part of the future volumes of this work: at present, I can only glance at the leading features. Of these, the most prominent were: The great Arian controversy, which, rashly instigated by Whiston, Clarke, and Waterland, disseminated doubts among nearly all classes;[312] the Bangorian controversy, which, involving matters of ecclesiastical discipline hitherto untouched, led to discussions dangerous to the power of the church;[313] the great work of

---

ought to be the sole regulator of human actions, see a remarkable, but a mournful letter, written in 1812, in the *Life of Wilberforce*, vol. iv. p. 28. See also the speech of Lord Eldon in 1828, in *Twiss's Life of Eldon*, vol. ii. p. 203.

[313] From a curious passage in *Hutton's Life of Himself*, p. 27, we learn that, in 1739, the scepticism of the Anti-Trinitarians had penetrated among the tradesmen at Nottingham. Compare, respecting the spread of this heresy, *Nichols's Lit. Anec.* vol. viii. p. 375; *Priestley's Memoirs*, vol. i. pp. 25, 26, 53; *Doddridge's Correspond. and Diary*, vol. ii. p. 477, note; and on Peirce, who took an active part, and whom Whiston boasts of having corrupted, see *Whiston's Memoirs*, pp. 143, 144.

Sharp, who was Archbishop of York when the controversy began, foresaw its dangerous consequences. *Life of Sharp*, edited by Newcome, vol. ii. pp. 7, 8, 135, 136. See further *Maclaine's* note in *Mosheim's Ecclesiast. Hist.* vol. ii. pp. 293, 294; *Lathbury's Hist. of Convocation*, pp. 338, 342, 351; and a note in *Butler's Reminisc.* vol. i. pp. 206, 207.

[810] Mr. Butler (*Mem. of the Catholics*, vol. iii. pp. 182–184, 347–350) notices with evident pleasure the effect of this famous controversy in weakening the Anglican Church. Compare *Bogue and Bennett's Hist. of the Dissenters*, vol. iii. pp. 135–141. Whiston (*Memoirs*, p. 244) says: 'And, indeed, this Bangorian controversy seemed for a great while to engross the attention of

Blackburne on the Confessional, which at one moment almost caused a schism in the Establishment itself;[214] the celebrated dispute respecting miracles between Middleton, Church, and Dodwell, continued, with still larger views, by Hume, Campbell, and Douglas;[215] the exposure of the gross absurdities of the Fathers, which,

[214] the public.' See more about it in *Lathbury's Hist. of Convocation*, pp. 372–383; *Nichols's Lit. Anec.* vol. I. p. 152, vol. ix. pp. 433, 434, 516; *Nichols's Illustrations*, vol. i. p. 840; *Bishop Newton's Life of Himself*, pp. 177, 178.

[214] *The Confessional*, a most able attack on the subscription of creeds and articles, was published in 1766; and, according to a contemporary observer, 'it excited a general spirit of inquiry.' *Cappe's Memoirs*, pp. 147, 148. The consequence was, that in 1772 a society was instituted by Blackburne and other clergy of the Church of England, with the avowed object of doing away with all subscriptions in religion. *Nichols's Lit. Anec.* vol. i. p. 570; *Illustrations*, vol. vi. p. 654. A petition against the Articles was at once drawn up, signed by 200 clergy (*Adolphus's George III.* vol. i. p. 506), and brought before the House of Commons. In the animated debate which followed, Sir William Meredith said that 'the Thirty-nine Articles of the Church of England were framed when the spirit of free inquiry, when liberal and enlarged notions, were yet in their infancy.' *Parl. Hist.* vol. xvii. p. 246. He added, p. 247: 'Several of the Articles are absolutely unintelligible, and, indeed, contradictory and absurd.' Lord George Germain said: 'In my apprehension, some of the Articles are incomprehensible, and some self-contradictory;' p. 265. Mr. Sawbridge declared that the Articles are 'strikingly absurd;' Mr. Salter that they are 'too absurd to be defended;' and Mr. Dunning that they are 'palpably ridiculous,' p. 294. For further information on this attempt at reform, see *Disney's Life of Jebb*, pp. 31–36; *Meadley's Mem. of Paley*, pp. 68–94; *Hodgson's Life of Porteus*, pp. 38–40; *Memoirs of Priestley*, vol. ii. p. 582; and a characteristic notice in *Palmer's Treatise on the Church*, vol. i. pp. 270, 271.

[215] Hume says, that on his return from Italy in 1749, he found 'all England in a ferment on account of Dr. Middleton's *Free Inquiry*.' *Hume's Life of Himself*, in his *Works*, vol. i. p. 7. See also, on the excitement caused by this masterly attack, *Nichols's Illustrations of the Eighteenth Century*, vol. ii. p. 176; which should be compared with *Doddridge's Correspond.* vol. iv. pp. 536, 537: and on the 'miraculous controversy' in general, see *Porteus's Life of Secker*, 1797, p. 38; *Phillimore's Mem. of Lyttleton*, vol. i. p. 161; *Nichols's Lit. Anec.* vol. ii. pp. 440, 527, vol. iii. pp. 535, 750, vol. v. pp. 417, 418, 600; *Hull's Letters*, 1778, vol. i. p. 109; *Warburton's Letters to Hurd*, pp. 49, 50.

SIXTEENTH TO THE EIGHTEENTH CENTURY. 429

already begun by Daillé and Barbeyrac, was followed up by Cave, Middleton, and Jortin; the important and unrefuted statements of Gibbon, in his fifteenth and sixteenth chapters; the additional strength conferred on those chapters by the lame attacks of Davis, Chelsum, Whitaker, and Watson;[216] while, not to mention inferior matters, the century was closed amid the confusion caused by that decisive controversy between Porson and Travis, respecting the text of the Heavenly Witnesses, which excited immense attention,[217] and was immediately accompanied by the discoveries of geologists, in which, not only was the fidelity of the Mosaic cosmogony impugned, but its accuracy was shown to be impossible.[218] These things, following each other in

---

[216] *Gibbon's Decline and Fall* has now been jealously scrutinized by two generations of eager and unscrupulous opponents; and I am only expressing the general opinion of competent judges when I say, that by each successive scrutiny it has gained fresh reputation. Against his celebrated fifteenth and sixteenth chapters, all the devices of controversy have been exhausted; but the only result has been, that while the fame of the historian is untarnished, the attacks of his enemies are falling into complete oblivion. The work of Gibbon remains; but who is there who feels any interest in what was written against him?

[217] On the effect produced by these matchless letters of Porson, see *Harford's Life of Bishop Burgess*, p. 374; and as to the previous agitation of the question in England, see *Calamy's Own Life*, vol. ii. pp. 442, 443; *Monk's Life of Bentley*, vol. ii. pp. 16–19, 146, 286–289; *Butler's Reminiscences*, vol. i. p. 211. Compare *Somers Tracts*, vol. xii. p. 137, vol. xiii. p. 456.

[218] The sceptical character of geology was first clearly exhibited during the last thirty years of the eighteenth century. Previously, the geologists had, for the most part, allied themselves with the theologians; but the increasing boldness of public opinion now enabled them to institute independent investigations, without regard to doctrines hitherto received. In this point of view, much was effected by the researches of Hutton, whose work, says Sir Charles Lyell, contains the first attempt 'to explain the former changes of the earth's crust by reference exclusively to natural agents.' *Lyell's Principles of Geology*, p. 60. To establish this method was, of course, to dissolve the alliance with the theologians; but an earlier symptom of the change was seen in 1773, that is, fifteen years before Hutton wrote: see a letter in *Watson's Life of Himself*, vol. i. p. 402,

rapid and startling succession, perplexed the faith of
men, disturbed their easy credulity, and produced effects
on the public mind, which can only be estimated by
those who have studied the history of that time in its
original sources. Indeed, they cannot be understood,
even in their general bearings, except by taking into
consideration some other circumstances with which the
great progress was intimately connected.

For, in the mean time, an immense change had begun,
not only among speculative minds, but also among the
people themselves. The increase of scepticism stimulated their curiosity; and the diffusion of education
supplied the means of gratifying it. Hence, we find
that one of the leading characteristics of the eighteenth
century, and one which pre-eminently distinguished it
from all that preceded, was a craving after knowledge
on the part of those classes from whom knowledge had
hitherto been shut out. It was in that great age, that
there were first established schools for the lower orders
on the only day they had time to attend them,[219] and

---

where it is stated that the 'free-
thinkers' attacked the 'Mosaic
account of the world's age,
especially since the publication of
Mr. Brydone's *Travels Through
Sicily and Malta.*' According to
Lowndes(*Bibliographer's Manual*,
vol. i. p. 279), Brydone's book
was published in 1773; and in
1784 Sir William Jones notices
the tendency of these inquiries:
see his *Discourse on the Gods of
Greece, Italy, and India*, in which
he observes (*Works*, vol. i. p. 233)
with regret, that he lived in 'an
age when some intelligent and
virtuous persons are inclined to
doubt the authenticity of the
accounts delivered by Moses
concerning the primitive world.'
Since then, the progress of geology has been so rapid, that the
historical value of the writings
of Moses is abandoned by all

enlightened men, even among the
clergy themselves. I need only
refer to what has been said by
two of the most eminent of that
profession, Dr. Arnold and Mr.
Baden Powell. See the observations of Arnold in *Newman's
Phases of Faith*, p. 111 (compare
pp. 122, 123); and the still more
decisive remarks in *Powell's Sermons on Christianity without
Judaism*, 1856, pp. 38, 39. For
other instances, see *Lyell's Second
Visit to the United States*, 1849,
vol. i. pp. 219, 220.

[219] It is usually supposed that
Sunday-schools were begun by
Raikes, in 1781; but, though he
appears to have been the first to
organise them on a suitable scale,
there is no doubt that they were
established by Lindsey, in or
immediately after 1765. See
Capps's Memoir's, pp. 118, 122;

newspapers on the only day they had time to read them.²²⁰ It was then that there were first seen, in our country, circulating libraries;²²¹ and it was then, too, that the art of printing, instead of being almost confined to London, began to be generally practised in country-towns.²²² It was also in the eighteenth cen-

---

Harford's *Life of Burgess*, p. 92; *Nichols's Lit. Anec.* vol. iii. pp. 430, 431, vol. ix. p. 540; *Chalmers's Biog. Dict.* vol. xxv. p. 185; *Journ. of Stat. Soc.* vol. x. p. 196, v. xiii. p. 265; *Hodgson's Life of Porteus*, p. 92. It is said, in *Spencer's Social Statics*, p. 343, that the clergy of the Church of England were, as a body, opposed to the establishment of Sunday-schools. (Compare *Watson's Observations on Southey's Wesley*, p. 149.) At all events, they increased rapidly, and by the end of the century had become common. See *Nichols's Lit. Anec.* vol. v. pp. 678, 679; *Nichols's Illustrations*, vol. i. p. 460; *Life of Wilberforce*, vol. i. p. 180, vol. ii. p. 296; *Wesley's Journals*, pp. 806, 807.

²²⁰ Mr. Hunt (*Hist. of Newspapers*, vol. i. p. 273) makes no mention of Sunday newspapers earlier than a notice by Crabbe in 1785; but in 1799, Lord Belgrave said, in the House of Commons, that they first appeared 'about the year 1780.' *Parl. Hist.* vol. xxxiv. p. 1006. In 1799, Wilberforce tried to have a law enacted to suppress them. *Life of Wilberforce*, vol. ii. pp. 338, 424.

²²¹ When Franklin came to London, in 1725, there was not a single circulating library in the metropolis. See *Franklin's Life of Himself*, vol. i. p. 64; and, in 1807, 'the only library in London which approached the nature of a public library was that of Sion College, belonging to the London clergy.' *Ellis's Letters of Literary Men*, p. 245. The exact date of the earliest circulating library I have not yet ascertained; but, according to Southey (*The Doctor*, edit. Warter, 1848, p. 271), the first set up in London was about the middle of the eighteenth century, by Samuel Fancourt. Hutton (*Life of Himself*, p. 279) says, 'I was the first who opened a circulating library in Birmingham, in 1751.' Other notices of them, during the latter half of the century, will be found in *Coleridge's Biographia Literaria*, vol. ii. p. 329, edit. 1847; *Leigh Hunt's Autobiography*, vol. i. p. 260; *Nichols's Lit. Anec.* vol. iii. pp. 648, 682; *Nichols's Illustrations*, vol. i. p. 424; *Whewell's Hist. of Moral Philosophy*, p. 190; *Sinclair's Correspond.* vol. i. p. 143. Indeed, they increased so rapidly, that some wise men proposed to tax them, 'by a licence, at the rate of 2s. 6d. per 100 volumes per annum.' *Sinclair's Hist. of the Revenue*, vol. iii. p. 268.

²²² In 1746, Gent, the well-known printer, wrote his own life. In this curious work, he states, that in 1714 there were 'few printers in England, except London, at that time; none then, I am sure, at Chester, Liverpool,

tury, that the earliest systematic efforts were made to popularize the sciences, and facilitate the acquisition of their general principles, by writing treatises on them in an easy and untechnical style:[222] while, at the same

---

Whitehaven, Preston, Manchester, Kendal, and Leeds, as for the most part now abound.' *Life of Thomas Gent*, pp. 20, 21. (Compare a list of country printing-houses, in 1724, in *Nichols's Lit. Anec.* vol. i. p. 289.) How this state of things was remedied, is a most important inquiry for the historian; but in this note I can only give a few illustrations of the condition of different districts. The first printing-office in Rochester was established by Fisher, who died in 1786 (*Nichols's Lit. Anec.* vol. iii. p. 675); the first in Whitby, was in 1770 (*Illustrations*, vol. iii. p. 787); and Richard Greene, who died in 1793, 'was the first who brought a printing-press to Lichfield' (*Ibid.* vol. vi. p. 320). In the reign of Anne, there was not a single bookseller in Birmingham (*Southey's Commonplace Book*, 1st series, 1849, p. 568); but, in 1749, we find a printer established there (*Hull's Letters*, Lond. 1778, vol. i. p. 92); and, in 1774, there was a printer even in Falkirk (*Parl. Hist.* vol. xvii. p. 1099). In other parts the movement was slower; and we are told that, about 1780, 'there was scarcely a bookseller in Cornwall.' *Life of Samuel Drew, by his Son*, 1834, pp. 40, 41.

[222] Desaguliers and Hill were the two first writers who gave themselves up to popularizing physical truths. At the beginning of the reign of George I. Desaguliers was 'the first who read lectures in London on experimental philosophy.' *Southey's Commonplace Book*, 3d series, 1850, p. 77. See also *Penny Cyclopædia*, vol. viii. p. 430; and, on his elementary works, compare *Nichols's Lit. Anec.* vol. vi. p. 81. As to Hill, he is said to have set the example of publishing popular scientific works in numbers; a plan so well suited to that inquisitive age, that, if we believe Horace Walpole, he 'earned fifteen guineas a week.' *Letter to Henry Zouch*, January 3rd, 1761, in *Walpole's Letters*, vol. iv. p. 117, edit. 1840.

In the latter half of the eighteenth century, the demand for books on the natural sciences rapidly increased (see, among many other instances which might be quoted, a note in *Pulteney's Hist. of Botany*, vol. ii. p. 180); and, early in the reign of George III., Priestley began to write popularly on physical subjects. (*Memoirs of Priestley*, vol. i. pp. 288, 289.) Goldsmith did something in the same direction (*Prior's Life of Goldsmith*, vol. i. pp. 414, 469, vol. ii. p. 198); and Pennant, whose earliest work appeared in 1766, was 'the first who treated the natural history of Britain in a popular and interesting style.' *Swainson on the Study of Natural History*, p. 50. In the reign of George II., publishers began to encourage elementary works on chemistry. *Nichols's Lit. Anec.* vol. ix. p. 763.

time, the invention of Encyclopædias enabled their results to be brought together, and digested in a form more accessible than any hitherto employed.[224] Then, too, we first meet with literary periodical reviews; by means of which large bodies of practical men acquired information, scanty indeed, but every way superior to their former ignorance.[225] The formation of societies for purchasing books now became general;[226] and, before the close of the century, we hear of clubs instituted by reading men among the industrious classes.[227] In every department, the same eager curiosity was shown. In the middle of the eighteenth century, debating societies sprung up among tradesmen;[228] and

---

[224] In 1704, 1708, and 1710, Harris published his *Dictionary of Arts and Sciences;* and from this, according to *Nichols's Lit. Anec.* vol. ix. pp. 770, 771, has 'originated all the other dictionaries and cyclopædias that have since appeared.' Compare vol. v. p. 659; and *Bogue and Bennett's Hist. of the Dissenters,* vol. iv. p. 500.

[225] Late in the seventeenth century, an attempt was first made in England to establish literary journals. *Hallam's Lit. of Europe,* vol. iii. p. 539; and *Dibdin's Bibliomania,* 1842, p. 16. But reviews, as we now understand the word, meaning a critical publication, were unknown before the accession of George II.; but, about the middle of his reign, they began to increase. Compare *Wright's England under the House of Hanover,* 1848, vol. i. p. 304, with *Nichols's Lit. Anec.* vol. iii. pp. 507, 508. At an earlier period, the functions of reviews were performed, as Monk says, by pamphlets. *Monk's Life of Bentley,* vol. i. p. 112.

[226] As we find from many casual notices of book clubs and book societies. See, for example, *Doddridge's Correspond.* vol. ii. pp. 57, 119; *Jesse's Life of Selwyn,* vol. ii. p. 23; *Nichols's Illustrations of the Eighteenth Century,* vol. v. pp. 164, 824, 825; *Wakefield's Life of Himself,* vol. i. p. 526; *Memoirs of Sir J. E. Smith,* vol. i. p. 8; *Life of Roscoe, by his Son,* vol. i. p. 228 (though this last was perhaps a circulating library).

[227] 'Numerous associations or clubs, composed principally of reading men of the lower ranks.' *Life of Dr. Currie, by his Son,* vol. i. p. 175.

[228] Of which the most remarkable was that called the Robin Hood Society; respecting which the reader should compare *Campbell's Lives of the Chancellors,* vol. vi. p. 373; *Grosley's London,* vol. i. p. 150; *Parl. Hist.* vol. xvii. p. 301; *Southey's Commonplace Book,* 4th series, p. 339; *Forster's Life of Goldsmith,* vol. i. p. 310; *Prior's Life of Goldsmith,* vol. i. pp. 419, 420; *Prior's Life of Burke,* p. 75; *Nichols's Lit. Anec.* vol. iii. p. 164.

this was followed by a still bolder innovation, for, in 1769, there was held the first public meeting ever assembled in England, the first in which it was attempted to enlighten Englishmen respecting their political rights.[229] About the same time, the proceedings in our courts of law began to be studied by the people, and communicated to them through the medium of the daily press.[230] Shortly before this, political newspapers arose,[231] and a sharp struggle broke out between them

---

[229] 'From the summer of 1769 is to be dated the first establishment of public meetings in England.' *Albemarle's Mem. of Rockingham*, vol. ii. p. 93. 'Public meetings, ... through which the people might declare their newly-acquired consciousness of power, ... cannot be distinctly traced higher than the year 1769; but they were now (i.e. in 1770) of daily occurrence.' *Cooke's Hist. of Party*, vol. iii. p. 187. See also *Hallam's Const. Hist.* vol. ii. p. 420.

[230] The most interesting trials were first noticed in newspapers towards the end of the reign of George II. *Campbell's Chancellors*, vol. v. p. 52, vol. vi. p. 54.

[231] In 1696, the only newspapers were weekly; and the first daily paper appeared in the reign of Anne. Compare *Simmonds's Essay on Newspapers*, in *Journal of Statist. Society*, vol. iv. p. 113, with *Hunt's Hist. of Newspapers*, vol. i. pp. 167, 175, vol. ii. p. 90; and *Nichols's Lit. Anec.* vol. iv. p. 80. In 1710, they, instead of merely communicating news, as heretofore, began to take part in 'the discussion of political topics' (*Hallam's Const. Hist.* vol. ii. p. 443); and, as this change had been preceded a very few years by the introduction of cheap political pamphlets (see a curious passage in *Wilson's Life of De Foe*, vol. ii. p. 29), it become evident that a great movement was at hand in regard to the diffusion of such inquiries. Within twenty years after the death of Anne, the revolution was completed; and the press, for the first time in the history of the world, was made an exponent of public opinion. The earliest notice of this new power which I have met with, in parliament, is in a speech delivered by Danvers, in 1738; which is worth quoting, both because it marks an epoch, and because it is characteristic of that troublesome class to which the man belonged. 'But I believe,' says this distinguished legislator,—'but I believe the people of Great Britain are governed by a power that never was heard of, as a supreme authority, in any age or country before. This power, sir, does not consist in the absolute will of the prince, in the direction of parliament, in the strength of an army, in the influence of the clergy; neither, sir, is it a petticoat government: but, sir, it is the government of the press. The stuff which our weekly newspapers are filled with, is

and the two Houses of Parliament touching the right of publishing the debates; the end of which was, that both houses, though aided by the crown, were totally defeated; and, for the first time, the people were able to study the proceedings of the national legislature, and thus gain some acquaintance with the national affairs.[232] Scarcely was this triumph completed, when fresh stimulus was given by the promulgation of that great political doctrine of personal representation,[233] which must eventually carry all before it; and the germ of

---

received with greater reverence than acts of parliament; and the sentiments of one of these scribblers have more weight with the multitude than the opinion of the best politician in the kingdom.' *Parl. Hist.* vol. x. p. 448.

[232] This great contest was brought to a close in 1771 and 1772; when, as Lord Campbell says, 'the right of publishing parliamentary debates was substantially established.' *Campbell's Chancellors*, vol. v. p. 511, vol. vi. p. 90. For further information respecting this important victory, see *Cooke's Hist. of Party*, vol. iii. pp. 179-184; *Almon's Correspond. of Wilkes*, 1805, vol. v. p. 63; *Stephens's Mem. of Tooke*, vol. i. pp. 329-351; *Mahon's Hist. of England*, vol. v. p. 290; and, on its connexion with *Junius's Letters*, see *Forster's Life of Goldsmith*, vol. ii. pp. 183, 184.

George III, always consistent and always wrong, strenuously opposed this extension of the popular rights. In 1771, he wrote to Lord North: 'It is highly necessary that this strange and lawless method of publishing debates in the papers should be put a stop to. But is not the House of Lords the best court to bring such miscreants before; as it can fine, as well as imprison, and has broader shoulders to support the odium of so salutary a measure?' *App. to Mahon*, vol. v. p. xlviii.; and *note* in *Walpole's George III.* vol. iv. p. 280, where the words, 'in the papers,' are omitted; but I copy the letter, as printed by Lord Mahon. In other respects, both versions are the same; so that we now know the idea George III. had of what constituted a miscreant.

[233] Lord John Russell, in his work on the *History of the English Constitution*, says: 'Dr. Jebb, and after him Mr. Cartwright, broached the theory of personal representation;' but this appears to be a mistake, since the theory is said to have been first put forward by Cartwright, in 1776. Compare *Russell on the Constitution*, 1821, pp. 240, 241, with *Life and Corresp. of Cartwright*, 1826, vol. i. pp. 91, 92. A letter in the *Life of Dr. Currie*, vol. ii. pp. 307-314, shows the interest which even sober and practical men were beginning to feel in the doctrine before the end of the century.

which may be traced late in the seventeenth century, when the true idea of personal independence began to take root and flourish.[234] Finally, it was reserved for the eighteenth century to set the first example of calling on the people to adjudicate upon those solemn questions of religion in which hitherto they had never been consulted, although it is now universally admitted that to their growing intelligence these, and all other matters, must ultimately be referred.[235]

In connexion with all this, there was a corresponding change in the very form and make of our literature. The harsh and pedantic method, which our great writers had long been accustomed to employ, was ill suited to an impetuous and inquisitive generation, thirsting after knowledge, and therefore intolerant of obscurities formerly unheeded. Hence it was that, early in the eighteenth century, the powerful, but cumbrous, language, and the long, involved sentences, so natural to

---

[234] On this I have a philological remark of some interest,—namely, that there is reason to believe that 'the word "independence," in its modern acceptation,' does not occur in our language before the early part of the eighteenth century. See *Hare's Guesses at Truth*, 2nd series, 1848, p. 262. A similar change, though at a later period, took place in France. See the observations on the word 'Individualisme,' in *Tocqueville, Démocratie en Amérique*, vol. iv. p. 156; and in the later work, by the same author, *L'Ancien Régime*, Paris, 1856, pp. 148, 149.

[235] Archbishop Whately (*Dangers to Christian Faith*, pp. 76, 77) says: 'Neither the attacks on our religion, nor the evidences in its support, were, to any great extent, brought forward in a popular form, till near the close of the last century. On both sides, the learned (or those who professed to be such) seem to have agreed in this,—that the mass of the people were to acquiesce in the decision of their superiors, and neither should, nor could, exercise their own minds on the question.' This is well put, and quite true; and should be compared with the complaint in *Wakefield's Life of Himself*, vol. ii. p. 21; *Nichols's Lit. Anec. of the Eighteenth Century*, vol. viii. p. 144; and *Hodgson's Life of Bishop Porteus*, pp. 73, 74, 122, 125, 126. See also a speech by Mansfield, in 1761 (*Parl. Hist.* vol. xxii. p. 265), when an attempt was made to put down the 'Theological Society.' The whole debate is worth reading; not on account of its merits, but because it supplies evidence of the prevailing spirit.

our ancient authors, were, notwithstanding their beauty, suddenly discarded, and were succeeded by a lighter and simpler style, which, being more rapidly understood, was better suited to the exigencies of the age.[236]

The extension of knowledge being thus accompanied by an increased simplicity in the manner of its communication, naturally gave rise to a greater independence in literary men, and a greater boldness in literary inquiries. As long as books, either from the difficulty

---

[236] Coleridge (*Lit. Remains*, vol. i. pp. 230 seq.) has made some interesting remarks on the vicissitudes of English style; and he justly observes, p. 238, that, 'after the Revolution, the spirit of the nation became much more commercial than it had been before; a learned body, or clerisy, as such, gradually disappeared; and literature in general began to be addressed to the common, miscellaneous public.' He goes on to lament this change; though, in that, I disagree with him. See also *The Friend*, vol. i. p. 19, where he contrasts the modern style with 'the stately march and difficult evolutions' of the great writers of the seventeenth century. Compare, on this alteration, the preface to Nader Shah, in *Works of Sir W. Jones*, vol. v. p. 544. See also, in *Harford's Life of Burgess*, pp. 40, 41, a curious letter from Monboddo, the last of our really great pedants, mourning over this characteristic of modern composition. He terms it contemptuously a 'short cut of a style;' and wishes to return to 'the true ancient taste,' with plenty of 'parentheses'!

The truth is, that this movement was merely part of that tendency to approximate the different classes of society which was first clearly seen in the eighteenth century, and which influenced not only the style of author, but also their social habits. Hume observes that, in the 'last age,' learned men had separated themselves too much from the world; but that, in his time, they were becoming more 'conversible.' *Essay V.*, in *Hume's Philosophical Works*, vol. iv. pp. 539, 540. That 'philosophers' were growing men of the world, is also noticed in a curious passage in *Alciphron*, dial. i., in *Berkeley's Works*, vol. i. p. 312; and, respecting the general social amalgamation, see a letter to the Countess of Bute, in 1753, in *Works of Lady Mary Montagu*, edit.1803, vol. iv. pp. 194, 195. As to the influence of Addison, who led the way in establishing the easy, and therefore democratic, style, and who, more than any single writer, made literature popular, compare *Aikin's Life of Addison*, vol. ii. p. 65, with *Turner's Hist. of England*, vol. ii. p. 7. Subsequently a reaction was attempted by Johnson, Gibbon, and Parr; but this, being contrary to the spirit of the age, was short-lived.

of their style, or from the general incuriosity of the people, found but few readers, it was evident that authors must rely upon the patronage of public bodies, or of rich and titled individuals. And, as men are always inclined to flatter those upon whom they are dependent, it too often happened that even our greatest writers prostituted their abilities by fawning upon the prejudices of their patrons. The consequence was that literature, so far from disturbing ancient superstitions, and stirring up the mind to new inquiries, frequently assumed a timid and subservient air, natural to its subordinate position. But now all this was changed. Those servile and shameful dedications;[237] that mean and crouching spirit; that incessant homage to mere rank and birth; that constant confusion between power and right; that ignorant admiration for

---

[237] And the servility was, for the most part, well paid; indeed, rewarded far more than it was worth. During the sixteenth, seventeenth, and early part of the eighteenth century, a sum of money was invariably presented to the author in return for his dedication. Of course, the grosser the flattery, the larger the sum. On the relation thus established between authors and men of rank, and on the eagerness with which even eminent writers looked to their patrons for gratuities, varying from 40s. to 100l., see *Drake's Shakespeare and his Times*, 1817, 4to. vol. ii. p. 225; *Monk's Life of Bentley*, vol. i. pp. 194, 309; *Whiston's Memoirs*, p. 203; *Nichols's Illustrations*, vol. ii. p. 709; *Harris's Life of Hardwicke*, vol. iii. p. 36; *Bunbury's Life of Hanmer*, p. 81. Compare a note in *Burton's Diary*, vol. iii. p. 52; and as to the importance of fixing on a proper person to whom to dedicate, see *Ellis's Letters Lit. Men*, pp. 231–234; and the matter-of-fact remark in *Bishop Newton's Life*, p. 14; also, *Hughes's Letters*, edit. 1773, vol. iii. p. xxxi. appendix.

About the middle of the eighteenth century was the turning-point of this deplorable condition; and Watson, for instance, in 1769, laid it down as a rule, 'never to dedicate to those from whom I expected favours.' *Watson's Life of Himself*, vol. i. p. 54. So, too, Warburton, in 1758, boasts that his dedication was not, as usual, 'occupied by trifles or falsehoods.' See his letter, in *Chatham Correspond.* vol. i. p. 315. Nearly at the same period, the same change was effected in France, where D'Alembert set the example of ridiculing the old custom. See *Brougham's Men of Letters*, vol. ii. pp. 439, 440; *Correspond. de Madame Dudeffand*, vol. ii. p. 148; and *Œuvres de Voltaire*, vol. xl. p. 41, vol. lxi. p. 285.

everything which is old, and that still more ignorant contempt for everything which is new:—all these features became gradually fainter: and authors, relying upon the patronage of the people, began to advocate the claims of their new allies with a boldness upon which they could not have ventured in any previous age.[238]

From all these things there resulted consequences of vast importance. From this simplification, independence, and diffusion[239] of knowledge, it necessarily happened, that the issue of those great disputes to which I have alluded became, in the eighteenth century, more generally known than would have been possible in any preceding century. It was now known that theological and political questions were being constantly agitated, in which genius and learning were on one side, and orthodoxy and tradition on the other. It became known that the points which were mooted were not only as to the credibility of particular facts, but also as to the truth of general principles, with which

---

[238] When Le Blanc visited England, in the middle of the reign of George II., the custom of authors relying upon the patronage of individuals was beginning to die away, and the plan of publishing by subscription had become general. See the interesting details in *Le Blanc, Lettres d'un Français*, vol. i. pp. 305–308; and for the former state of things, see vol. ii. pp. 148–153. Burke, who came to London in 1750, observes, with surprise, that 'writers of the first talents are left to the capricious patronage of the public. Notwithstanding discouragement, literature is cultivated to a high degree.' *Prior's Life of Burke*, p. 21. This increasing independence also appears from the fact that, in 1762, we find the first instance of a popular writer attacking public men by name; authors having previously confined themselves 'to the initials only of the great men whom they assailed.' *Mahon's Hist. of England*, vol. v. p. 19. The feud between literature and rank may be further illustrated by an entry in Holcroft's Diary for 1798, *Mem. of Holcroft*, vol. iii. p. 28.

[239] In England, the marked increase in the number of books took place during the latter half of the eighteenth century, and particularly after 1756. See some valuable evidence in *Journal of the Statistical Society*, vol. iii. pp. 383, 384. To this I may add, that between 1753 and 1792, the circulation of newspapers was more than doubled. *Hunt's Hist. of Newspapers*, vol. i. p. 252.

the interests and happiness of Man were intimately concerned. Disputes which had hitherto been confined to a very small part of society began to spread far and wide, and suggest doubts that served as materials for national thought. The consequence was, that the spirit of inquiry became every year more active, and more general; the desire for reform constantly increased; and if affairs had been allowed to run on in their natural course, the eighteenth century could not have passed away without decisive and salutary changes both in the church and the state. But soon after the middle of this period, there unfortunately arose a series of political combinations which disturbed the march of events, and eventually produced a crisis so full of danger, that, among any other people, it would certainly have ended either in a loss of liberty or in a dissolution of government. This disastrous reaction, from the effects of which England has, perhaps, barely recovered, has never been studied with anything like the care its importance demands; indeed, it is so little understood, that no historian has traced the opposition between it and that great intellectual movement of which I have just sketched an outline. On this account, as also with the view of giving more completeness to the present chapter, I intend to examine its most important epochs, and point out, so far as I am able, the way in which they are connected with each other. According to the scheme of this Introduction, such an inquiry must, of course, be very cursory, as its sole object is to lay a foundation for those general principles, without which history is a mere assemblage of empirical observations, unconnected, and therefore unimportant. It must likewise be remembered, that as the circumstances about to be considered were not social, but political, we are the more liable to err in our conclusions respecting them; and this partly because the materials for the history of a people are more extensive, more indirect, and therefore less liable to be garbled, than are those for the history of a government; and partly because the conduct of small bodies of men, such as ministers and kings, is always more capricious, that is to say, less

SIXTEENTH TO THE EIGHTEENTH CENTURY. 441

regulated by known laws, than is the conduct of those large bodies collectively called society, or a nation.[240] With this precautionary remark, I will now endeavour to trace what, in a mere political point of view, is the reactionary and retrogressive period of English history.

It must be considered as a most fortunate circumstance, that after the death of Anne,[241] the throne should be occupied for nearly fifty years by two princes, aliens in manners and in country, of whom one spoke our language but indifferently, and the other knew it not at all.[242] The immediate predecessors of George III. were, indeed, of so sluggish a disposition, and were so profoundly ignorant of the people they undertook to govern,[243] that, notwithstanding their arbitrary temper, there was no danger of their organizing a party to

---

[240] The apparent caprice and irregularity in small numbers arise from the perturbations produced by the operation of minor and usually unknown laws. In large numbers, these perturbations have a tendency to balance each other; and this I take to be the sole foundation of the accuracy obtained by striking an average. If we could refer all phenomena to their laws, we should never use averages. Of course, the expression *capricious* is, strictly speaking, inaccurate, and is merely a measure of our ignorance.

[241] The temporary political reaction under Anne is well related by Lord Cowper, in his *Hist. of Parties*, printed in appendix to *Campbell's Lives of the Chancellors*, vol. iv. p. 411, 412. This able work of Lord Campbell's, though rather inaccurate for the earlier period, is particularly valuable for the history of the eighteenth century.

[242] See *Reminiscences of the Courts of George I. and George II.* by Horace Walpole, pp. lv. xciv.; and *Mahon's Hist. of England*, vol. i. pp. 100, 235. The fault of George II. was in his bad pronunciation of English; but George I. was not even able to pronounce it badly, and could only converse with his minister, Sir Robert Walpole, in Latin. The French court saw this state of things with great pleasure; and in December 1714, Madame de Maintenon wrote to the Princesse des Ursins (*Lettres inédites de Maintenon*, vol. iii. p. 157): 'On dit que le nouveau roi d'Angleterre se dégoûte de ses sujets, et que ses sujets sont dégoûtés de lui. Dieu veuille remettre le tout en meilleur ordre !' On the effect this produced on the language spoken at the English court, compare *Le Blanc, Lettres d'un Français*, vol. i. p. 159.

[243] In 1715, Leslie writes respecting George I., that he is 'a stranger to you, and altogether ignorant of your language, your laws, customs, and constitution.' *Somers Tracts*, vol. xiii. p. 703.

extend the boundaries of the royal prerogative.³⁴⁴ And as they were foreigners, they never had sufficient sympathy with the English church to induce them to aid the clergy in their natural desire to recover their former power.³⁴⁵ Besides this, the fractious and disloyal conduct of many of the hierarchy must have tended to alienate the regard of the sovereign, as it had already cost them the affection of the people.³⁴⁶

---

³⁴⁴ Great light has been thrown upon the character of George II. by the recent publication of *Lord Hervey's Memoirs*; a curious work, which fully confirms what we know from other sources respecting the king's ignorance of English politics. Indeed, that prince cared for nothing but soldiers and women; and his highest ambition was to combine the reputation of a great general with that of a successful libertine. Besides the testimony of Lord Hervey, it is certain, from other authorities, that George II. was despised as well as disliked, and was spoken of contemptuously by observers of his character, and even by his own ministers. See the *Marchmont Papers*, vol. i. pp. 29, 181, 187.

In reference to the decline of the royal authority, it is important to observe, that since the accession of George I. none of our sovereigns have been allowed to be present at state deliberations. See *Bancroft's American Revolution*, vol. ii. p. 47, and *Campbell's Chancellors*, vol. iii. p. 191.

³⁴⁵ See the remarks said to be written by Bishop Atterbury, in *Somers Tracts*, vol. xiii. p. 534, contrasting the affection Anne felt for the church with the coldness of George I. The whole of the pamphlet (pp. 521-541) ought to be read. It affords a curious picture of a baffled churchman.

³⁴⁶ The ill-feeling which the Church of England generally bore against the government of the two first Georges was openly displayed, and was so pertinacious as to form a leading fact in the history of England. In 1722, Bishop Atterbury was arrested, because he was known to be engaged in a treasonable conspiracy with the Pretender. As soon as he was seized, the church offered up prayers for him. 'Under the pretence,' says Lord Mahon,—'under the pretence of his being afflicted with the gout, he was publicly prayed for in most of the churches of London and Westminster.' *Mahon's Hist. of England*, vol. ii. p. 36. See also *Parl. Hist.* vol. vii. p. 988, and vol. viii. p. 347.

At Oxford, where the clergy have long been in the ascendant, they made such efforts to instil their principles as to call down the indignation of the elder Pitt, who, in a speech in Parliament in 1754, denounced that university, which he said had for many years 'been raising a succession of treason—there never was such a seminary!' *Walpole's Mem. of George II.* vol. i. p. 413. Com-

Those circumstances, though in themselves they may be considered trifling, were in reality of great importance, because they secured to the nation the progress of that spirit of inquiry, which, if there had been a coalition between the crown and the church, it would have been attempted to stifle. Even as it was, some attempts were occasionally made; but they were comparatively speaking rare, and they lacked the vigour which they would have possessed, if there had been an intimate alliance between the temporal and spiritual authorities. Indeed, the state of affairs was so favourable, that the old Tory faction, pressed by the people and abandoned by the crown, was unable for more than forty years to take any share in the government.[247] At the same time, considerable progress, as we shall hereafter see, was made in legislation; and our statute-book, during that period, contains ample evidence of the decline of the powerful party by which England had once been entirely ruled.

---

pare the *Bedford Correspondence*, vol. i. pp. 594, 595, with *Harris's Life of Hardwicke*, vol. ii. p. 383; and on the temper of the clergy generally after the death of Anne, *Parl. Hist.* vol. vii. pp. 541, 542; *Bowles's Life of Ken*, vol. ii. pp. 188, 189; *Monk's Life of Bentley*, vol. i. pp. 370, 426.

The immediate consequence of this was very remarkable. For the government and the dissenters, being both opposed by the church, naturally combined together: the dissenters using all their influence against the Pretender, and the government protecting them against ecclesiastical prosecutions. See evidence of this in *Doddridge's Correspond. and Diary*, vol. i. p. 30, vol. ii. p. 321, vol. iii. pp. 110, 125, vol. iv. pp. 428, 436, 437; *Hutton's Life of Himself*, pp. 159, 160; *Parl. Hist.* vol. xxviii. pp. 11, 303, vol. xxix. pp. 1434, 1463; *Memoirs of Priestley*, vol. ii. p. 506; *Life of Wakefield*, vol. i. p. 220.

[247] 'The year 1762 forms an era in the history of the two factions, since it witnessed the destruction of that monopoly of honours and emoluments which the Whigs had held for forty-five years.' *Cooke's Hist. of Party*, vol. ii. p. 406. Compare *Albemarle's Memoirs of Rockingham*, vol. ii. p. 92. Lord Bolingbroke clearly foresaw what would happen in consequence of the accession of George I. Immediately after the death of Anne, he wrote to the Bishop of Rochester: 'But the grief of my soul is this, I see plainly that the Tory party is gone.' *Macpherson's Original Papers*, vol. ii. p. 631.

But by the death of George II. the political aspect was suddenly changed, and the wishes of the sovereign became once more antagonistic to the interests of the people. What made this the more dangerous was, that, to a superficial observer, the accession of George III. was one of the most fortunate events that could have occurred. The new king was born in England, spoke English as his mother tongue,[248] and was said to look upon Hanover as a foreign country, whose interests were to be considered of subordinate importance.[249] At the same time, the last hopes of the House of Stuart were now destroyed;[250] the Pretender himself was languishing in Italy, where he shortly after died: and his son, a slave to vices which seemed hereditary in that family, was consuming his life in an unpitied and ignominious obscurity.[251]

---

[248] Grosley, who visited England only five years after the accession of George III., mentions the great effect produced upon the English when they heard the king pronounce their language without 'a foreign accent.' *Grosley's Tour to London*, vol. ii. p. 106. It is well known that the king, in his first speech, boasted of being a Briton; but what is, perhaps, less generally known is, that the honour was on the side of the country: 'What a lustre,' said the House of Lords in their address to him, —'what a lustre does it cast upon the name of Briton when you, sir, are pleased to esteem it amongst your glories!' *Parl. Hist.* vol. xv. p. 986.

[249] *Parl. Hist.* vol. xxix. p. 955; *Walpole's Mem. of George III.* vol. i. pp. 4, 110.

[250] The accession of George III. is generally fixed on as the period when English Jacobinism became extinct. See *Butler's Reminiscences*, vol. ii. p. 92. At the first court held by the new king, it was observed, says Horace Walpole, that 'the Earl of Litchfield, Sir Walter Bagot, and the principal Jacobites went to court.' *Walpole's Mem. of George III.* vol. i. p. 14. Only three years earlier the Jacobites had been active; and in 1757, Rigby writes to the Duke of Bedford: 'Fox's election at Windsor is very doubtful. There is a Jacobite subscription of 5,000*l.* raised against him, with Sir James Dashwood's name at the head of it.' *Bedford Correspond.* vol. ii. p. 261.

[251] Charles Stuart was so stupidly ignorant, that at the age of twenty-five he could hardly write, and was altogether unable to spell. *Mahon's Hist. of England*, vol. iii. pp. 165, 106, and appendix, p. ix. After the death of his father, in 1766, this abject creature, who called himself king of England, went to Rome, and took to drinking. *Ibid.* vol. iii. pp. 351–353. In 1779, Swinburne

And yet these circumstances, which appeared so favourable, did of necessity involve the most disastrous consequences. The fear of a disputed succession being removed, the sovereign was emboldened to a course on which he otherwise would not have ventured.[251] All those monstrous doctrines respecting the rights of kings, which the Revolution was supposed to have destroyed, were suddenly revived.[253] The clergy, abandoning the now hopeless cause of the Pretender, displayed the same zeal for the House of Hanover which they had formerly displayed for the House of Stuart. The pulpits resounded with praises of the new king, of his domestic virtues, of his piety, but above all of his dutiful attachment to the English church. The result was, the establishment of an alliance between the two parties more intimate than any that had been seen in England since the time of Charles I.[254] Under their

saw him at Florence, where he used to appear every night at the opera, perfectly drunk. *Swinburne's Courts of Europe*, vol. i. pp. 253–255; and in 1787, only the year before he died, he continued the same degrading practice. See a letter from Sir J. E. Smith, written from Naples in March 1787, in *Smith's Correspond.* vol. i. p. 208. Another letter, written as early as 1761 (*Grenville Papers*, vol. i. p. 366), describes 'the young Pretender always drunk.'

[252] On the connexion between the decline of the Stuart interest and the increased power of the crown under George III., compare *Thoughts on the Present Discontents*, in *Burke's Works*, vol. i. pp. 127, 128, with *Watson's Life of Himself*, vol. i. p. 136; and for an intimation that this result was expected, see *Grosley's London*, vol. ii. p. 252.

[253] *Campbell's Chancellors*, vol. v. p. 245: 'The divine inde-feasible right of kings became the favourite theme—in total forgetfulness of its incompatibility with the parliamentary title of the reigning monarch.' Horace Walpole (*Mem. of George III.* vol. i. p. 16) says, that in 1760 'prerogative became a fashionable word.'

[254] The respect George III. always displayed for church-ceremonies formed of itself a marked contrast with the indifference of his immediate predecessors; and the change was gratefully noticed. Compare *Mahon's Hist. of England*, vol. v. pp. 54, 55, with the extract from Archbishop Secker, in *Bancroft's American Revolution*, vol. i. p. 440. For other evidence of the admiration both parties felt and openly expressed for each other, see an address from the bishop and clergy of St. Asaph (*Parr's Works*, vol. vii. p. 352), and a letter from the king to Pitt (*Russell's Memorials of Fox*,

auspices, the old Tory faction rapidly rallied, and were soon able to dispossess their rivals of the management of the government. This reactionary movement was greatly aided by the personal character of George III.; for he, being despotic as well as superstitious, was equally anxious to extend the prerogative, and strengthen the church. Every liberal sentiment, everything approaching to reform, nay, even the mere mention of inquiry, was an abomination in the eyes of that narrow and ignorant prince. Without knowledge, without taste, without even a glimpse of one of the sciences, or a feeling for one of the fine arts, education had done nothing to enlarge a mind which nature had more than usually contracted.[255] Totally ignorant of the history and resources of foreign countries, and barely knowing their geographical position, his information was scarcely more extensive respecting the people over whom he was called to rule. In that immense mass of evidence now extant, and which consists of every description of private correspondence, records of private conversation and of public acts, there is not to be found the slightest proof that he knew any one of those numerous things which the governor of a country ought to know; or, indeed, that he was acquainted with a single duty of his position, except that mere mechanical routine of ordinary business, which might have been effected by the lowest clerk in the meanest office in his kingdom.

The course of proceeding which such a king as this was likely to follow could be easily foreseen. He gathered round his throne that great party, who, clinging to the tradition of the past, have always made it their boast to check the progress of their age. During the sixty years of his reign, he, with the sole exception of Pitt, never willingly admitted to his councils a single

---

vol. iii. p. 251), which should be compared with *Priestley's Memoirs*, vol. i. pp. 137, 138.

[255] The education of George III. had been shamefully neglected; and when he arrived at manhood he never attempted to repair its deficiencies, but remained during his long life in a state of pitiable ignorance. Compare *Brougham's Statesmen*, vol. i. pp. 13–15; *Walpole's Mem. of George III.* vol. i. p. 55; *Mahon's Hist. of England*, vol. iv. pp. 54, 207.

man of great ability;[256] not one whose name is associated with any measure of value either in domestic or in foreign policy. Even Pitt only maintained his position in the state by forgetting the lessons of his illustrious father, and abandoning those liberal principles in which he had been educated, and with which he entered public life. Because George III. hated the idea of reform, Pitt not only relinquished what he had before declared to be absolutely necessary,[257] but did not hesitate to persecute to the death the party with whom he had once associated in order to obtain it.[258] Because George III. looked upon slavery as one of those good old customs which the wisdom of his ancestors had consecrated, Pitt did not dare to use his power for procuring its abolition, but left to his successors the glory of destroying that infamous trade, on the preservation

---

[256] See some good remarks by Lord John Russell in his Introduction to the *Bedford Correspondence*, vol. iii. p. lxii.

[257] In a motion for reform in Parliament in 1782, he declared that it was 'essentially necessary.' See his speech, in *Parl. Hist.* vol. xxii. p. 1416. In 1784 he mentioned 'the necessity of a parliamentary reform,' vol. xxiv. p. 349; see also pp. 998, 999. Compare *Disney's Life of Jebb*, p. 209. Nor is it true, as some have said, that he afterwards abandoned the cause of reform because the times were unfavourable to it. On the contrary, he, in a speech delivered in 1800, said (*Parl. Hist.* vol. xxxv. p. 47): 'Upon this subject, sir, I think it right to state the inmost thoughts of my mind; I think it right to declare my most decided opinion, that, *even if the times were proper for experiments, any, even the slightest, change in such a constitution must be considered as an evil.*' It is remarkable that, even as early as 1783, Paley appears to have suspected the sincerity of Pitt's professions in favour of reform. See *Meadley's Memoirs of Paley*, p. 121.

[258] In 1794 Grey taunted him with this in the House of Commons: 'William Pitt, the reformer of that day, was William Pitt, the prosecutor, ay and persecutor too, of reformers now.' *Parl. Hist.* vol. xxxi. p. 532; compare vol. xxxiii. p. 659. So too Lord Campbell (*Chief-Justices*, vol. ii. p. 544): 'He afterwards tried to hang a few of his brother reformers who continued steady in the cause.' See further, on this damning fact in the career of Pitt, *Campbell's Chancellors*, vol. vii. p. 106; *Brougham's Statesmen*, vol. ii. p. 21; *Belsham's History*, vol. ix. pp. 79, 242; *Life of Cartwright*, vol. i. p. 198; and even a letter from the mild and benevolent Roscoe, in *Life of Roscoe, by his Son*, vol. i. p. 113.

of which his royal master had set his heart.[259] Because
George III. detested the French, of whom he knew as
much as he knew of the inhabitants of Kamtchatka or
of Tibet, Pitt, contrary to his own judgment, engaged
in a war with France by which England was seriously
imperilled, and the English people burdened with a
debt that their remotest posterity will be unable to
pay.[260] But, notwithstanding all this, when Pitt, only
a few years before his death, showed a determination to
concede to the Irish some small share of their undoubted
rights, the king dismissed him from office; and the
king's friends, as they were called,[261] expressed their

---

[259] Such was the king's zeal in favour of the slave-trade, that in 1770 'he issued an instruction under his own hand commanding the governor (of Virginia), upon pain of the highest displeasure, to assent to no law by which the importation of slaves should be in any respect prohibited or obstructed.' Bancroft's *American Revolution*, vol. iii. p. 456: so that, as Mr. Bancroft indignantly observes, p. 469, while the courts of law had decided ' that as soon as any slave set his foot on English ground he becomes free, the king of England stood in the path of humanity, and made himself the pillar of the colonial slave-trade.' The shuffling conduct of Pitt in this matter makes it hard for any honest man to forgive him. Compare *Brougham's Statesmen*, vol. ii. pp. 14, 103–105; *Russell's Mem. of Fox*, vol. iii. pp. 131, 278, 279; *Belsham's Hist. of Great Britain*, vol. x. pp. 34, 35; *Life of Wakefield*, vol. i. p. 197; *Porter's Progress of the Nation*, vol. iii. p. 426; *Holland's Mem. of the Whig Party*, vol. ii. p. 157; and the striking remarks of Francis, in *Parl. Hist.* vol. xxxii. p. 949.

[260] That Pitt wished to remain at peace, and was hurried into the war with France by the influence of the court, is admitted by the best-informed writers, men in other respects of different opinions. See, for instance, *Brougham's Statesmen*, vol. ii. p. 9; *Rogers's Introduction to Burke's Works*, p. lxxxiv.; *Nicholls's Recollections*, vol. ii. pp. 155, 200.

[261] The mere existence of such a party, with such a name, shows how, in a political point of view, England was receding during this period from the maxims established at the Revolution. Respecting this active faction, compare the indignant remarks of Burke (*Works*, vol. i. p. 133) with *Albemarle's Rockingham*, vol. i. pp. 5, 307; *Buckingham's Mem. of George III.* vol. i. p. 284, vol. ii. p. 154; *Russell's Mem. of Fox*, vol. i. pp. 61, 120, vol. ii. pp. 50, 77; *Bedford Correspond.* vol. iii. p. xlv.; *Parr's Works*, vol. viii. p. 513; *Butler's Reminiscences*. vol. i. p. 74; *Burke's Correspond.* vol. i. p. 352; *Walpole's George III.* vol. iv. p. 316; *The Grenville Papers*, vol. ii. pp. 33, 34,

indignation at the presumption of a minister who could oppose the wishes of so benign and gracious a master.[262] And when, unhappily for his own fame, this great man determined to return to power, he could only recover office by conceding that very point for which he had relinquished it; thus setting the mischievous example of the minister of a free country sacrificing his own judgment to the personal prejudices of the reigning sovereign.

As it was hardly possible to find other ministers, who to equal abilities would add equal subservience, it is not surprising that the highest offices were constantly filled by men of notorious incapacity.[263] Indeed, the king seemed to have an instinctive antipathy to everything great and noble. During the reign of George II. the elder Pitt had won for himself a reputation which covered the world, and had carried to an unprecedented height the glories of the English name.[264] He, however,

---

vol. iii. p. 57, vol. iv. p. 79, 152, 219, 303; *Parl. Hist.* vol. xvi. pp. 841, 973, vol. xviii. pp. 1005, 1246, vol. xix. pp. 435, 856, vol. xxii. pp. 650, 1173.

[262] See an extraordinary passage in *Pellew's Life of Sidmouth*, vol. i. p. 334.

[263] This decline in the abilities of official men was noticed by Burke, in 1770, as a necessary consequence of the new system. Compare *Thoughts on the Present Discontents* (*Burke's Works*, vol. i. p. 149) with his striking summary (*Parl. Hist.* vol. xvi. p. 879) of the degeneracy during the first nine years of George III. 'Thus situated, the question at last was not, who could do the public business best, but who would undertake to do it at all. Men of talents and integrity would not accept of employments where they were neither allowed to exercise their judgment nor display the rectitude of their hearts. In 1780, when the evil had become still more obvious, the same great observer denounced it in his celebrated address to his Bristol constituents. 'At present,' he says, 'it is the plan of the court to make its servants insignificant.' *Burke's Works*, vol. i. p. 257. See further *Parr's Works*, vol. iii. pp. 258, 260, 261.

[264] The military success of his administration is related in very strong language, but not unfairly, in *Mahon's Hist. of England*, vol. iv. pp. 108, 185, 186, and see the admirable summary in *Brougham's Statesmen*, vol. i. pp. 33, 34: and for evidence of the fear with which he inspired the enemies of England, compare *Mahon*, vol. v. p. 165 note; *Bedford Correspond.* vol. iii. pp. 87, 246, 247; *Walpole's Letters to Mann*, vol. i. p. 304, edit. 1843; *Walpole's Mem. of George III.*

as the avowed friend of popular rights, strenuously opposed the despotic principles of the court; and for this reason he was hated by George III. with a hatred that seemed barely compatible with a sane mind.[265] Fox was one of the greatest statesmen of the eighteenth century, and was better acquainted than any other with the character and resources of those foreign nations with which our own interests were intimately connected.[266] To this rare and important knowledge he added a sweetness and an amenity of temper which extorted the praises even of his political opponents.[267] But he, too, was the steady supporter of civil and religious liberty; and he, too, was so detested by George III., that the king, with his own hand, struck his name out of the list of privy councillors,[268] and

---

vol. ii. p. 232; and the reluctant admission in *Georgel, Mémoires*, vol. i. pp. 79, 80.

[265] Lord Brougham (*Sketches of Statesmen*, vol. i. pp. 22, 33) has published striking evidence of what he calls 'the truly savage feelings' with which George III. regarded Lord Chatham (compare *Russell's Mem. of Fox*, vol. i. p. 129). Indeed, the sentiments of the king were even displayed in the arrangements at the funeral of the great minister. *Note in Adolphus's Hist. of George III.* vol. ii. p. 568; and for other evidence of ill-will, see two notes from the king to Lord North, in *Mahon's Hist. of England*, vol. vi. appendix, pp. lii. liv.; *The Grenville Papers*, vol. ii. p. 386; *Bancroft's American Revolution*, vol. i. p. 438.

[266] Lord Brougham (*Sketches of Statesmen*, vol. i. p. 219) says: 'It may be questioned if any politician, in any age, ever knew so thoroughly the various interests and the exact position of all the countries with which his own had dealings to conduct or relations to maintain.' See also *Parr's Works*, vol. iv. pp. 14, 15; *Russell's Mem. of Fox*, vol. i. pp. 320, 321, vol. ii. pp. 91, 243; *Bisset's Life of Burke*, vol. i. p. 338.

[267] Burke, even after the French Revolution, said, that Fox 'was of the most artless, candid, open, and benevolent disposition, disinterested in the extreme; of a temper mild and placable even to a fault, without one drop of gall in his whole constitution.' Speech on the Army Estimates in 1790, in *Parl. Hist.* vol. xxviii. p. 356. For further evidence, compare *Alison's Hist. of Europe*, vol. vii. p. 171; *Holland's Mem. of the Whig Party*, vol. i. pp. 3, 273; *Trotter's Mem. of Fox*, pp. xi. xii, 24, 178, 415.

[268] *Adolphus's Hist. of George III.* vol. vi. p. 692. A singular circumstance connected with this wanton outrage is related in the *Mem. of Holcroft*, vol. iii. p. 60.

declared that he would rather abdicate the throne than admit him to a share in the government.²⁶⁹

While this unfavourable change was taking place in the sovereign and ministers of the country, a change equally unfavourable was being effected in the second branch of the imperial legislature. Until the reign of George III., the House of Lords was decidedly superior to the House of Commons in the liberality and general accomplishments of its members. It is true, that in both houses there prevailed a spirit which must be called narrow and superstitious, if tried by the larger standard of the present age. But among the peers such feelings were tempered by an education that raised them far above those country gentlemen and ignorant fox-hunting squires of whom the lower house was then chiefly composed. From this superiority in their knowledge, there naturally followed a larger and more liberal turn of thought than was possessed by those who were called the representatives of the people. The result was, that the old Tory spirit, becoming gradually weaker in the upper house, took refuge in the lower; where, for about sixty years after the Revolution, the high-church party and the friends of the Stuarts formed a dangerous faction.²⁷⁰ Thus, for instance, the two men who rendered the most eminent services to the Hanoverian dynasty, and therefore to the liberties of

---

²⁶⁹ Compare *Adolphus's Hist. of George III.* vol. iv. pp. 107, 108, with *Russell's Mem. of Fox*, vol. i. pp. 101, 287, 288, vol. ii. p. 44. Dutens, who had much intercourse with English politicians, heard of the threat of abdication in 1784. *Dutens' Mémoires*, vol. iii. p. 104. Lord Holland says, that during the fatal illness of Fox, 'the king had watched the progress of Mr. Fox's disorder. He could hardly suppress his indecent exultation at his death.' *Holland's Mem. of the Whig Party*, vol. ii. p. 40.

²⁷⁰ In 1725, the Duke of Wharton, in a letter to the Pretender, after mentioning some proceedings in the Commons, adds, 'In the House of Lords our number is so small, that any behaviour there will be immaterial.' *Mahon's Hist. of England*, vol. ii. appendix, p. xxiii. See also, respecting the greater strength of the Tories in the House of Commons, *Somers Tracts*, vol. xi. p. 242, vol. xiii. pp. 624, 631; *Campbell's Chancellors*, vol. iv. p. 158; *Campbell's Chief-Justices*, vol. ii. p. 150.

England, were undoubtedly Somers and Walpole. Both of them were remarkable for their principles of toleration, and both of them owed their safety to the interference of the House of Lords. Somers, early in the eighteenth century, was protected by the peers from the scandalous prosecution instituted against him by the other house of parliament.[271] Forty years after this, the Commons, who wished to hunt Walpole to the death, carried up a bill encouraging witnesses to appear against him by remitting to them the penalties to which they might be liable.[272] This barbarous measure had been passed through the lower house without the least difficulty; but in the Lords it was rejected by a preponderance of nearly two to one.[273] In the same way the Schism Act, by which the friends of the church subjected the dissenters to a cruel persecution,[274] was hurried through the Commons by a large and eager majority.[275] In the Lords, however, the votes were nearly balanced; and although the bill was passed, amendments were added by which the violence of its provisions was in some degree softened.[276]

---

[271] Compare *Vernon Correspond.* vol. iii. p. 149, with *Burnet's Own Time,* vol. iv. p. 504. Burnet says, 'All the Jacobites joined to support the pretensions of the Commons.' The Commons complained that the Lords had shown 'such an indulgence to the person accused as is not to be paralleled in any parliamentary proceedings.' *Parl. Hist.* vol. v. p. 1294. See also their angry remonstrance, pp. 1314, 1315.

[272] Mahon's *Hist. of England,* vol. iii. p. 122.

[273] 'Content, 47; non-content, 92.' *Parl. Hist.* vol. xii. p. 711. Mr. Phillimore (*Mem. of Lyttelton,* vol. i. p. 213) ascribes this to the exertions of Lord Hardwicke; but the state of parties in the upper house is sufficient explanation; and even in 1735 it was said that 'the Lords were betwixt the devil and the deep sea,' the devil being Walpole. *Marchmont Papers,* vol. ii. p. 59. Compare *Bishop Newton's Life of Himself,* p. 60.

[274] See an account of some of its provisions in Mahon's *Hist. of England,* vol. i. pp. 80, 81. The object of the bill is frankly stated in *Parl. Hist.* vol. vi. p. 1349, where we are informed that 'as the farther discouragement and even ruin of the dissenters was thought necessary for accomplishing this scheme, it was begun with the famous Schism Bill.'

[275] By 237 to 126. *Parl. Hist.* vol. vi. p. 1351.

[276] Mahon's *Hist. of England,* vol. i. p. 83; *Bunbury's Correspond. of Hanmer,* p. 48. The

This superiority of the upper house over the lower was, on the whole, steadily maintained during the reign of George II.;[277] the ministers not being anxious to strengthen the high-church party in the Lords, and the king himself so rarely suggesting fresh creations as to cause a belief that he particularly disliked increasing their numbers.[278]

It was reserved for George III., by an unsparing use of his prerogative, entirely to change the character of the upper house, and thus lay the foundation for that disrepute into which since then the peers have been constantly falling. The creations he made were numerous beyond all precedent; their object evidently being to neutralize the liberal spirit hitherto prevailing, and thus turn the House of Lords into an engine for resisting the popular wishes, and stopping the progress of reform.[279] How completely this plan succeeded, is well known to the readers of our history; indeed, it was sure to be successful, considering the character of the men who were promoted. They consisted almost entirely of two classes: of country gentlemen, remarkable for nothing but their wealth, and the number of votes their wealth enabled them to control;[280] and of mere lawyers, who had risen to judicial appointments partly from their professional learning, but

---

bill was carried in the Lords by 77 against 72.

[277] 'If we scrutinize the votes of the peers from the period of the revolution to the death of George II., we shall find a very great majority of the old English nobility to have been the advocates of Whig principles.' *Cooke's Hist. of Party*, vol. iii. p. 363.

[278] Compare *Harris's Life of Hardwicke*, vol. iii. p. 519, with the conversation between Sir Robert Walpole and Lord Hervey, in *Hervey's Mem. of George II.* vol. ii. p. 251, edit. 1848.

[279] *Cooke's Hist. of Party*, vol. iii. pp. 363, 364, 365, 463; *Parl. Hist.* vol. xviii. p. 1418, vol. xxiv. p. 493, vol. xxvii. p. 1069, vol. xxix. pp. 1334, 1494, vol. xxxiii. pp. 90, 602, 1315.

[280] This was too notorious to be denied; and in the House of Commons, in 1800, Nicholls taunted the Government with 'holding out a peerage, or elevation to a higher rank in the peerage, to every man who could procure a nomination to a certain number of seats in parliament.' *Parl. Hist.* vol. xxxv. p. 762. So too Sheridan, in 1792, said (vol. xxix. p. 1333), 'In this country peerages had been bartered for election interest.'

chiefly from the zeal with which they repressed the popular liberties, and favoured the royal prerogative.²⁶¹ That this is no exaggerated description, may be ascertained by any one who will consult the lists of the new peers made by George III. Here and there we find an eminent man, whose public services were so notorious that it was impossible to avoid rewarding them; but, putting aside those who were in a manner forced upon the sovereign, it would be idle to deny that the remainder, and of course the overwhelming majority, were marked by a narrowness and illiberality of sentiment which, more than anything else, brought the whole order into contempt.²⁶² No great thinkers; no great writers; no great orators; no great statesmen; none of the true nobility of the land,—were to be found among the spurious nobles created by George III. Nor were the material interests of the country better represented in this strange composition. Among the most important men in England, those engaged in banking and commerce held a high place: since the end of the seventeenth century their influence had rapidly in-

---

²⁶¹ On this great influx of lawyers into the House of Lords, most of whom zealously advocated arbitrary principles, see Belsham's *Hist. of Great Britain*, vol. vii. pp. 266, 267; *Adolphus's Hist. of George III.* vol. iii. p. 363; *Parl. Hist.* vol. xxxv. p. 1523.

²⁶² It was foretold at the time, that the effect of the numerous creations made during Pitt's power would be to lower the House of Lords. Compare *Butler's Reminiscences*, vol. i. p. 76, with Erskine's speech in *Parl. Hist.* vol. xxix. p. 1330; and see Sheridan's speech, vol. xxxiii. p. 1197. But their language, indignant as it is, was restrained by a desire of not wholly breaking with the court. Other men, who were more independent in their position, and cared nothing for the chance of future office, expressed themselves in terms such as had never before been heard within the walls of Parliament. Rolle, for instance, declared that 'there had been persons created peers during the present minister's power, who were not fit to be his grooms.' *Parl. Hist.* vol. xxvii. p. 1198. Out of doors, the feeling of contempt was equally strong; see *Life of Cartwright*, vol. i. p. 278; and see the remark even of the courtly Sir W. Jones, on the increasing disregard for learning shown by 'the nobles of our days.' *Preface to Persian Grammar*, in *Jones's Works*, vol. ii. p. 125.

creased; while their intelligence, their clear, methodical habits, and their general knowledge of affairs, made them every way superior to those classes from whom the upper house was now recruited. But in the reign of George III. claims of this sort were little heeded; and we are assured by Burke, whose authority on such a subject no one will dispute, that there never had been a time in which so few persons connected with commerce were raised to the peerage.[283]

It would be endless to collect all the symptoms which mark the political degeneracy of England during this period; a degeneracy the more striking, because it was opposed to the spirit of the time, and because it took place in spite of a great progress, both social and intellectual. How that progress eventually stopped the political reaction, and even forced it to retrace its own steps, will appear in another part of this work; but there is one circumstance which I cannot refrain from noticing at some length, since it affords a most interesting illustration of the tendency of public affairs, while at the same time it exhibits the character of one of the greatest men, and, Bacon alone excepted, the greatest thinker, who has ever devoted himself to the practice of English politics.

The slightest sketch of the reign of George III. would indeed be miserably imperfect if it were to omit the name of Edmund Burke. The studies of this extraordinary man not only covered the whole field of political inquiry,[284] but extended to an immense variety of

---

[283] In his *Thoughts on French Affairs*, written in 1791, he says, 'At no period in the history of England have so few peers been taken out of trade, or from families newly created by commerce.' *Burke's Works*, vol. i. p. 506. Indeed, according to Sir Nathaniel Wraxall (*Posthumous Memoirs*, vol. i. pp. 66, 67, Lond. 1836), the only instance when George III. broke this rule was when Smith the banker was made Lord Carrington. Wraxall is an indifferent authority, and there may be other cases; but they were certainly very few, and I cannot call any to mind.

[284] Nicholls, who knew him, says, 'The political knowledge of Mr. Burke might be considered almost as an encyclopædia; every man who approached him received instruction from his stores.' *Nicholls's Recollections*, vol. i. p. 20.

subjects, which, though apparently unconnected with politics, do in reality bear upon them as important adjuncts; since, to a philosophic mind, every branch of knowledge lights up even those that seem most remote from it. The eulogy passed upon him by one who was no mean judge of men,[265] might be justified, and more than justified, by passages from his works, as well as by the opinions of the most eminent of his contemporaries.[266] Thus it is, that while his insight into the philosophy of jurisprudence has gained the applause of lawyers,[267] his acquaintance with the whole range and theory of the fine arts has won the admiration of artists;[268] a striking combination of two pursuits, often,

---

[265] 'The excursions of his genius are immense. His imperial fancy has laid all nature under tribute, and has collected riches from every scene of the creation, and every walk of art.' *Works of Robert Hall,* London, 1846, p. 196. So, too, Wilberforce says of him, 'He had come late into Parliament, and had had time to lay in vast stores of knowledge. The field from which he drew his illustrations was magnificent. Like the fabled object of the fairy's favours, whenever he opened his mouth pearls and diamonds dropped from him.' *Life of Wilberforce,* vol. i. p. 150.

[266] Lord Thurlow is said to have declared, what I suppose is now the general opinion of competent judges, that the fame of Burke would survive that of Pitt and Fox. *Butler's Reminiscences,* vol. i. p. 169. But the noblest eulogy on Burke was pronounced by a man far greater than Thurlow. In 1790, Fox stated in the House of Commons, 'that if he were to put all the political information which he had learnt from books, all which he had gained from science, and all which any knowledge of the world and its affairs had taught him, into one scale, and the improvement which he had derived from his right hon. friend's instruction and conversation were placed in the other, he should be at a loss to decide to which to give the preference.' *Parl. Hist.,* vol. xxviii. p. 363.

[267] Lord Campbell (*Lives of the Chief-Justices,* vol. ii. p. 443) says, 'Burke, a philosophic statesman, deeply imbued with the scientific principles of jurisprudence.' See also, on his knowledge of law, *Butler's Reminiscences,* vol. i. p. 131; and *Bisset's Life of Burke,* vol. i. p. 230.

[268] Barry, in his celebrated Letter to the Dilettanti Society, regrets that Burke should have been diverted from the study of the fine arts into the pursuit of politics, because he had one of those 'minds of an admirable expansion and catholicity, so as to embrace the whole concerns of art, ancient as well as modern, domestic as well as foreign.'

though erroneously, held to be incompatible with each other. At the same time, and notwithstanding the occupations of political life, we know on good authority, that he had paid great attention to the history and filiation of languages;[239] a vast subject, which within the last thirty years has become an important resource for the study of the human mind, but the very idea of which had, in its large sense, only begun to dawn upon a few solitary thinkers. And, what is even more remarkable, when Adam Smith came to London full of those discoveries which have immortalized his name, he found to his amazement that Burke had anticipated conclusions the maturing of which cost Smith himself many years of anxious and unremitting labour.[240]

To these great inquiries, which touch the basis of social philosophy, Burke added a considerable acquaintance with physical science, and even with the practice and routine of mechanical trades. All this was so digested and worked into his mind, that it was ready on every occasion; not, like the knowledge of ordinary politicians, broken and wasted in fragments, but blended into a complete whole, fused by a genius that gave life even to the dullest pursuits. This, indeed, was the

---

[239] *Barry's Works*, vol. ii. p. 538, 4to, 1809. In the *Annual Register* for 1798, p. 329, 2nd edit., it is stated that Sir Joshua Reynolds 'deemed Burke the best judge of pictures that he ever knew.' See further *Works of Sir J. Reynolds*, Lond. 1846, vol. i. p. 155; and *Bisset's Life of Burke*, vol. ii. p. 257. A somewhat curious conversation between Burke and Reynolds, on a point of art, is preserved in *Holcroft's Memoirs*, vol. ii. pp. 276, 277.

[240] See a letter from Winstanley, the Camden Professor of Ancient History, in *Bisset's Life of Burke*, vol. ii. pp. 390, 391, and in *Prior's Life of Burke*, p. 427. Winstanley writes, 'It would have been exceedingly difficult to have met with a person who knew more of the philosophy, the history, and filiation of languages, or of the principles of etymological deduction, than Mr. Burke.'

[240] Adam Smith told Burke, 'after they had conversed on subjects of political economy, that he was the only man who, without communication, thought on these topics exactly as he did.' *Bisset's Life of Burke*, vol. ii. p. 429; and see *Prior's Life of Burke*, p. 58; and on his knowledge of political economy, *Brougham's Sketches of Statesmen*, vol. i. p. 205.

characteristic of Burke, that in his hands nothing was
barren. Such was the strength and exuberance of his
intellect, that it bore fruit in all directions, and could
confer dignity upon the meanest subjects, by showing
their connexion with general principles and the part
they have to play in the great scheme of human affairs.

But what has always appeared to me still more
remarkable in the character of Burke, is the singular
sobriety with which he employed his extraordinary
acquirements. During the best part of his life, his
political principles, so far from being speculative, were
altogether practical. This is particularly striking, because
he had every temptation to adopt an opposite
course. He possessed materials for generalization far
more ample than any politician of his time, and he had
a mind eminently prone to take large views. On many
occasions, and indeed whenever an opportunity occurred,
he showed his capacity as an original and speculative
thinker. But the moment he set foot on political
ground, he changed his method. In questions connected
with the accumulation and distribution of wealth
he saw that it was possible, by proceeding from a few
simple principles, to construct a deductive science
available for the commercial and financial interests of
the country. Further than this he refused to advance,
because he knew that, with this single exception, every
department of politics was purely empirical, and was
likely long to remain so. Hence it was, that he recognized
in all its bearings that great doctrine, which even
in our own days is too often forgotten, that the aim
of the legislator should be, not truth, but expediency.
Looking at the actual state of knowledge, he was forced
to admit, that all political principles have been raised
by hasty induction from limited facts; and that, therefore,
it is the part of a wise man, when he adds to the
facts, to revise the induction, and, instead of sacrificing
practice to principles, modify the principles that he may
change the practice. Or, to put this in another way,
he lays it down that political principles are at the best
but the product of human reason; while political practice
has to do with human nature and human passions,

of which reason forms but a part;[291] and that, on this account, the proper business of a statesman is, to contrive the means by which certain ends may be effected, leaving it to the general voice of the country to determine what those ends shall be, and shaping his own conduct, not according to his own principles, but according to the wishes of the people for whom he legislates, and whom he is bound to obey.[292]

---

[291] 'Politics ought to be adjusted, not to human reasonings, but to human nature; of which the reason is but a part, and by no means the greatest part.' *Observations on a late State of the Nation*, in *Burke's Works*, vol. i. p. 113. Hence the distinction he had constantly in view between the generalizations of philosophy, which ought to be impregnable, and those of politics, which must be fluctuating; and hence in his noble work, *Thoughts on the Cause of the present Discontents*, he says (vol. i. p. 136), 'No lines can be laid down for civil or political wisdom. They are a matter incapable of exact definition.' See also p. 151, on which he grounds his defence of the spirit of party; it being evident that if truth were the prime object of the political art, the idea of party, as such, would be indefensible. Compare with this the difference between 'la vérité en soi' and 'la vérité sociale,' as expounded by M. Rey in his *Science Sociale*, vol. ii. p. 322, Paris, 1842.

[292] In 1780 he plainly told the House of Commons that 'the people are the masters. They have only to express their wants at large and in gross. We are the expert artists; we are the skilful workmen, to shape their desires into perfect form, and to fit the utensil to the use. They are the sufferers, they tell the symptoms of the complaint; but we know the exact seat of the disease, and how to apply the remedy according to the rules of art. How shocking would it be to see us pervert our skill into a sinister and servile dexterity, for the purpose of evading our duty, and *defrauding our employers, who are our natural lords*, of the object of their just expectations!' *Burke's Works*, vol. i. p. 254. In 1777, in his *Letter to the Sheriffs of Bristol* (*Works*, vol. i. p. 216), 'In effect, to follow, not to force, the public inclination; to give a direction, a form, a technical dress, and a specific sanction, to the general sense of the community,—is the true end of legislature.' In his *Letter on the Duration of Parliament* (vol. ii. p. 430), 'It would be dreadful, indeed, if there was any power in the nation capable of resisting its unanimous desire, or even the desire of any very great and decided majority of the people. The people may be deceived in their choice of an object. *But I can scarcely conceive any choice they can make to be so very mischievous, as the existence of any human force capable of resisting it.*' So,

It is these views, and the extraordinary ability with which they were advocated, which make the appearance of Burke a memorable epoch in our political history.[293] We had, no doubt, other statesmen before him, who denied the validity of general principles in politics; but their denial was only the happy guess of ignorance, and they rejected theories which they had never taken the pains to study. Burke rejected them because he knew them. It was his rare merit that, notwithstanding every inducement to rely upon his own generalizations, he resisted the temptation; that, though rich in all the varieties of political knowledge, he made his opinions subservient to the march of events; that he recognized as the object of government, not the preservation of particular institutions, nor the propagation of particular tenets, but the happiness of the people at large; and, above all, that he insisted upon an obedience to the popular wishes, which no statesman before him had paid, and which too many statesmen since him have forgotten. Our country, indeed, is still full of those vulgar politicians, against whom Burke raised his voice; feeble and shallow men, who, having spent their little force in resisting the progress of reform,

---

too, he says (vol. i. pp. 125, 214), that when government and the people differ, government is generally in the wrong: compare pp. 217, 218, 276, vol. ii. p. 440. And to give only one more instance, but a very decisive one, he, in 1772, when speaking on a Bill respecting the Importation and Exportation of Corn, said, 'On this occasion I give way to the present Bill, not because I approve of the measure in itself, but because I think it prudent to yield to the spirit of the times. *The people will have it so; and it is not for their representatives to say nay.* I cannot, however, help entering my protest against the general principles of policy on which it is supported, because I think them extremely dangerous.' *Parl. Hist.* vol. xvii. p. 480.

[293] The effect which Burke's profound views produced in the House of Commons, where, however, few men were able to understand them in their full extent, is described by Dr. Hay, who was present at one of his great speeches; which, he says, 'formed a kind of new political philosophy.' *Burke's Correspond.* vol. i. p. 103. Compare a letter from Lee, written in the same year, 1766, in *Forster's Life of Goldsmith*, vol. ii. pp. 38, 39; and in *Duubury's Correspond. of Hanmer*, p. 456.

find themselves at length compelled to yield; and then, so soon as they have exhausted the artifices of their petty schemes, and, by their tardy and ungraceful concessions, have sown the seed of future disaffection, they turn upon the age by which they have been baffled; they mourn over the degeneracy of mankind; they lament the decay of public spirit; and they weep for the fate of a people, who have been so regardless of the wisdom of their ancestors, as to tamper with a constitution already hoary with the prescription of centuries.

Those who have studied the reign of George III. will easily understand the immense advantage of having a man like Burke to oppose these miserable delusions; delusions which have been fatal to many countries, and have more than once almost ruined our own.[294] They will also understand that, in the opinion of the king, this great statesman was, at best, but an eloquent declaimer, to be classed in the same category with Fox and Chatham; all three ingenious men, but unsafe, unsteady, quite unfit for weighty concerns, and by no means calculated for so exalted an honour as admission into the royal councils. In point of fact, during the thirty years Burke was engaged in public life, he never once held an office in the cabinet;[295] and the

---

[294] Burke was never weary of attacking the common argument, that, because a country has long flourished under some particular custom, therefore the custom must be good. See an admirable instance of this in his speech on the power of the attorney-general to file informations *ex officio;* where he likens such reasoners to the father of Scriblerus, who 'venerated the rust and canker which exalted a brazen pot-lid into the shield of a hero.' He adds: 'But, sir, we are told that the time during which this power existed, is the time during which monarchy most flourished: and what, then, can no two things subsist together but as cause and effect? May not a man have enjoyed better health during the time that he walked with an oaken stick, than afterwards, when he changed it for a cane, without supposing, like the Druids, that there are occult virtues in oak, and that the stick and the health were cause and effect?' *Parl. Hist.* vol. xvi. pp. 1190, 1191.

[295] This, as Mr. Cooke truly says, is an instance of aristocratic prejudice; but it is certain that a hint from George III. would have remedied the shameful

only occasions on which he occupied even a subordinate post, were in those very short intervals when the fluctuations of politics compelled the appointment of a liberal ministry.

Indeed the part taken by Burke in public affairs must have been very galling to a king who thought everything good that was old, and everything right that was established.²⁹⁶ For, so far was this remarkable man in advance of his contemporaries, that there are few of the great measures of the present generation which he did not anticipate, and zealously defend. Not only did he attack the absurd laws against forestalling and regrating,²⁹⁷ but, by advocating the freedom of trade, he struck at the root of all similar prohibitions.²⁹⁸ He supported those just claims of the Catholics,²⁹⁹ which,

---

neglect. *Cooke's Hist. of Party*, vol. iii. p. 277, 278.

²⁹⁶ It is easy to imagine how George III. must have been offended by such sentiments as these: 'I am not of the opinion of those gentlemen who are against disturbing the public repose; I like a clamour whenever there is an abuse. The fire-ball at midnight disturbs your sleep, but it keeps you from being burnt in your bed. The hue and cry alarms the county, but preserves all the property of the province.' Burke's speech on Prosecutions for Libels, in 1771, in *Parl. Hist.* vol. xvii. p. 54.

²⁹⁷ He moved their repeal. *Parl. Hist.* vol. xxvi. p. 1169. Even Lord Chatham issued, in 1766, a proclamation against forestallers and regraters, very much to the admiration of Lord Mahon, who says, 'Lord Chatham acted with characteristic energy.' *Mahon's Hist. of England*, vol. v. p. 166. More than thirty years later, and after Burke's death, Lord Kenyon, then chief-justice, eulogised these preposterous laws. *Holland's Mem. of the Whig Party*, vol. i. p. 167. Compare *Adolphus's Hist. of George III.* vol. vii. p. 406; and *Cockburn's Memorials of his Time*, Edinb. 1856, p. 73.

²⁹⁸ 'That liberality in the commercial system, which, I trust, will one day be adopted.' *Burke's Works*, vol. i. p. 223. And, in his letter to Burgh (*Ibid.* vol. ii. p. 409), 'But that to which I attached myself the most particularly, was to fix the principle of a free trade in all the ports of these islands, as founded in justice, and beneficial to the whole; but principally to this, the seat of the supreme power.'

²⁹⁹ *Prior's Life of Burke*, p. 467; *Burke's Works*, vol. i. pp. 263-271, 537-561, vol. ii. pp. 431-447. He refutes (vol. i. p. 548) the notion that the coronation oath was intended to bind the crown in its legislative capacity. Compare *Mem. of Mackintosh*, vol. i. pp. 170, 171,

during his lifetime, were obstinately refused; but which were conceded, many years after his death, as the only means of preserving the integrity of the empire. He supported the petition of the Dissenters, that they might be relieved from the restrictions to which, for the benefit of the Church of England, they were subjected.[300] Into other departments of politics he carried the same spirit. He opposed the cruel laws against insolvents,[301] by which, in the time of George III., our statute-book was still defaced; and he vainly attempted to soften the penal code,[302] the increasing severity of which was one of the worst features of that bad reign.[303] He wished to abolish the old plan of enlisting soldiers for life;[304] a barbarous and impolitic practice, as the English legislature began to perceive several years later.[305] He attacked the slave-trade;[306] which, being an ancient usage, the king wished to preserve, as

---

with *Butler's Reminiscences*, vol. i. p. 134.

[300] *Parl. Hist.* vol. xvii. pp. 435, 436, vol. xx. p. 306. See also *Burke's Correspondence*, vol. ii. pp. 17, 18; and *Prior's Life of Burke*, p. 143.

[301] *Burke's Works*, vol. i. pp. 261, 262, part of his speech at Bristol.

[302] *Prior's Life of Burke*, p. 317. See also his admirable remarks, in *Works*, vol. ii. p. 417; and his speech, in *Parl. Hist.* vol. xxviii. p. 146.

[303] On this increasing cruelty of the English laws, compare *Parr's Works*, vol. iv. pp. 150, 259, with *Parl. Hist.* vol. xxii. p. 271, vol. xxiv. p. 1222, vol. xxvi. p. 1037, vol. xxviii. p. 143; and, in regard to the execution of them, see *Life of Romilly, by Himself*, vol. i. p. 65; and *Alison's Hist. of Europe*, vol. ix. p. 620.

[304] In one short speech (*Parl. Hist.* vol. xx. pp. 150, 151), he has almost exhausted the arguments against enlistment for life.

[305] In 1806, that is nine years after the death of Burke, parliament first authorized enlistment for a term of years. See an account of the debates in *Alison's Hist. of Europe*, vol. vii. pp. 380–391. Compare *Nichols's Illustrations of the Eighteenth Century*, vol. v. p. 475; and *Holland's Mem. of the Whig Party*, vol. ii. p. 116.

[306] *Prior's Life of Burke*, p. 316; *Parl. Hist.* vol. xxvii. p. 502, vol. xxviii. pp. 69, 96; and *Life of Wilberforce*, vol. i. pp. 152, 171, contain evidence of his animosity against the slave-trade, and a more than sufficient answer to the ill-natured, and, what is worse, the ignorant, remark about Burke, in the *Duke of Buckingham's Mem. of George III.* vol. i. p. 350.

part of the British constitution.³⁰⁷ He refuted,³⁰⁸ but, owing to the prejudices of the age, was unable to subvert, the dangerous power exercised by the judges, who, in criminal prosecutions for libel, confined the jury to the mere question of publication; thus taking the real issue into their own hands, and making themselves the arbiters of the fate of those who were so unfortunate as to be placed at their bar.³⁰⁹ And, what many will think not the least of his merits, he was the first in that long line of financial reformers to whom we are deeply indebted.³¹⁰ Notwithstanding the difficulties thrown in his way, he carried through Parliament a series of bills, by which several useless places were entirely abolished, and, in the single office of paymaster-general, a saving effected to the country of 25,000*l.* a year.³¹¹

These things alone are sufficient to explain the ani-

---

³⁰⁷ On the respect which George III. felt for the slave-trade, see note 259 to this chapter. I might also have quoted the testimony of Lord Brougham: 'The court was decidedly against abolition. George III. always regarded the question with abhorrence, as savouring of innovation.' *Brougham's Statesmen*, vol. ii. p. 104. Compare *Combe's North America*, vol. i. p. 332.

³⁰⁸ *Burke's Works*, vol. ii. pp. 490–496; *Parl. Hist.* vol. xvii. pp. 44–55, a very able speech, delivered in 1771. Compare a letter to Dowdeswell, in *Burke's Correspond.* vol. i. pp. 251, 252.

³⁰⁹ The arguments of Burke anticipated, by more than twenty years, Fox's celebrated Libel Bill, which was not passed till 1792; although, in 1752, juries had begun, in spite of the judges, to return general verdicts on the merits. See *Campbell's Chancellors*, vol. v. pp. 238, 243, 341–345, vol. vi. p. 210; and *Meyer, Institutions Judiciaires*, vol. ii. pp. 204, 205, Paris, 1823.

³¹⁰ Mr. Farr, in his valuable essay on the statistics of the civil service (in *Journal of Statist. Soc.* vol xii. pp. 103–125), calls Burke 'one of the first and ablest financial reformers in parliament,' p. 104. The truth, however, is, that he was not only one of the first, but the first. He was the first man who laid before parliament a general and systematic scheme for diminishing the expenses of government; and his preliminary speech on that occasion is one of the finest of all his compositions.

³¹¹ *Prior's Life of Burke*, pp. 206, 234. See also, on the retrenchments he effected, *Sinclair's Hist. of the Revenue*, vol. ii. pp. 84, 85; *Burke's Correspond.* vol. iii. p. 14; and *Bisset's Life of Burke*, vol. ii. pp. 57–60.

mosity of a prince whose boast it was, that he would bequeath the government to his successor in the same state as that in which he had received it. There was, however, another circumstance by which the royal feelings were still further wounded. The determination of the king to oppress the Americans was so notorious that, when the war actually broke out, it was called the 'king's war,' and those who opposed it were regarded as the personal enemies of their sovereign.[312] In this, however, as in all other questions, the conduct of Burke was governed, not by traditions and principles, such as George III. cherished, but by large views of general expediency. Burke, in forming his opinions respecting this disgraceful contest, refused to be guided by arguments respecting the right of either party.[313] He would not enter into any discussion as to whether a mother country has the right to tax her colonies, or whether the colonies have a right to tax themselves. Such points he left to be mooted by those politicians

---

[312] In 1768, Lord Rockingham said, in the House of Lords, 'Instead of calling the war, the war of parliament, or of the people, it was called the king's war, his majesty's favourite war.' *Parl. Hist.* vol. xix. p. 857. Compare *Cooke's Hist. of Party,* vol. iii. p. 235, with the pungent remarks in *Walpole's George III.* vol. iv. p. 114. Nicholls (*Recollections,* vol. i. p. 35) says: 'The war was considered as the war of the king personally. Those who supported it were called the king's friends; while those who wished the country to pause, and reconsider the propriety of persevering in the contest, were branded as disloyal.'

[313] 'I am not here going into the distinction of rights, nor attempting to mark their boundaries. I do not enter into these metaphysical distinctions; I hate the very sound of them. Speech on American taxation in 1774, in *Burke's Works,* vol. i. p. 173. In 1775 (vol. i. p. 192): 'But my consideration is narrow, confined, and wholly limited to the policy of the question.' At p. 183: 'we should act in regard to America, not 'according to abstract ideas of right, by no means according to mere general theories of government; the resort to which appears to me, in our present situation, no better than arrant trifling.' In one of his earliest political pamphlets, written in 1769, he says, that the arguments of the opponents of America 'are conclusive; conclusive as to right; but the very reverse as to policy and practice,' vol. i. p. 112. Compare a letter, written in 1775, in *Burke's Correspond.* vol. ii. p. 12.

who, pretending to be guided by principles, are, in reality, subjugated by prejudice.[814] For his own part he was content to compare the cost with the gain. It was enough for Burke that, considering the power of our American colonies, considering their distance from us, and considering the probability of their being aided by France, it was not advisable to exercise the power; and it was, therefore, idle to talk of the right. Hence he opposed the taxation of America, not because it was unprecedented, but because it was inexpedient. As a natural consequence he likewise opposed the Boston-Port Bill, and that shameful bill, to forbid all intercourse with America, which was not inaptly called the starvation plan; violent measures, by which the king hoped to curb the colonies, and break the spirit of those noble men, whom he hated even more than he feared.[815]

It is certainly no faint characteristic of those times, that a man like Burke, who dedicated to politics abilities equal to far nobler things, should, during thirty years, have received from his prince neither favour nor reward. But George III. was a king whose delight it was to raise the humble and exalt the meek. His reign,

---

[814] In 1766, George III. writes to Lord Rockingham (*Albemarle's Rockingham*, vol. i. pp. 271, 272): 'Talbot is as right as I can desire, in the Stamp Act; strong for our declaring our right, but willing to repeal!' In other words, willing to offend the Americans, by a speculative assertion of an abstract right, but careful to forego the advantage which that right might produce.

[815] The intense hatred with which George III. regarded the Americans, was so natural to such a mind as his, that one can hardly blame his constant exhibition of it during the time that the struggle was actually impending. But what is truly disgraceful is, that, after the war was over, he displayed this rancour on an occasion when, of all others, he was bound to suppress it. In 1786, Jefferson and Adams were in England officially, and, as a matter of courtesy to the king, made their appearance at court. So regardless, however, was George III. of the common decencies of his station, that he treated these eminent men with marked incivility, although they were then paying their respects to him in his own palace. See *Tucker's Life of Jefferson*, vol. i. p. 220; and *Mem. and Corresp. of Jefferson*, vol. i. p. 54.

indeed, was the golden age of successful mediocrity; an age in which little men were favoured, and great men depressed; when Addington was cherished as a statesman, and Beattie pensioned as a philosopher; and when, in all the walks of public life, the first conditions of promotion were, to fawn upon ancient prejudices, and support established abuses.

This neglect of the most eminent of English politicians is highly instructive; but the circumstances which followed, though extremely painful, have a still deeper interest, and are well worth the attention of those whose habits of mind lead them to study the intellectual peculiarities of great men.

For, at this distance of time, when his nearest relations are no more, it would be affectation to deny that Burke, during the last few years of his life, fell into a state of complete hallucination. When the French Revolution broke out, his mind, already fainting under the weight of incessant labour, could not support the contemplation of an event so unprecedented, so appalling, and threatening results of such frightful magnitude. And, when the crimes of that great revolution, instead of diminishing, continued to increase, then it was that the feelings of Burke finally mastered his reason; the balance tottered; the proportions of that gigantic intellect were disturbed. From this moment, his sympathy with present suffering was so intense, that he lost all memory of the tyranny by which the sufferings were provoked. His mind, once so steady, so little swayed by prejudice and passion, reeled under the pressure of events which turned the brains of thousands.[316] And whoever will compare the spirit of his

---

[316] All great revolutions have a direct tendency to increase insanity, as long as they last, and probably for some time afterwards: but in this, as in other respects, the French revolution stands alone in the number of its victims. On the horrible, but curious subject of madness caused by the excitement of the events which occurred in France late in the eighteenth century, compare *Prichard on Insanity in relation to Jurisprudence*, 1842, p. 90; his *Treatise on Insanity*, 1835, pp. 161, 183, 230, 339; *Esquirol, Maladies Mentales*, vol. i. pp. 43, 53, 54, 66, 211,

latest works with the dates of their publication, will
see how this melancholy change was aggravated by
that bitter bereavement, from which he never rallied,
and which alone was sufficient to prostrate the understanding of one in whom the severity of the reason
was so tempered, so nicely poised, by the warmth of the
affections. Never, indeed, can there be forgotten those
touching, those exquisite allusions to the death of that
only son, who was the joy of his soul, and the pride of
his heart, and to whom he fondly hoped to bequeath
the inheritance of his imperishable name. Never can
we forget that image of desolation under which the
noble old man figured his immeasurable grief 'I live
in an inverted order. They who ought to have succeeded me, have gone before me. They who should
have been to me as posterity, are in the place of ancestors. . . . The storm has gone over me, and I lie
like one of those old oaks which the late hurricane has
scattered about me. I am stripped of all my honours;
I am torn up by the roots, and lie prostrate on the
earth.'[317]

It would, perhaps, be displaying a morbid curiosity,
to attempt to raise the veil, and trace the decay of so
mighty a mind.[318] Indeed, in all such cases, most of
the evidence perishes; for those who have the best

---

[317] 447, vol. ii. pp. 193, 726; *Feuchtersleben's Medical Psychology*, p. 254; *Georget, De la Folie*, p. 156; *Pinel, Traité sur l'Aliénation Mentale*, pp. 30, 108, 109, 177, 178, 185, 207, 215, 257, 349, 392, 457, 481; *Alison's Hist. of Europe*, vol. iii. p. 112.

[317] *Burke's Works*, vol. ii. p. 268.

[318] The earliest unmistakable instances of those violent out-breaks which showed the pre-sence of disease, were in the debates on the regency bill, in February 1789, when Sir Richard Hill, with brutal candour, hinted at Burke's madness, even in his presence. *Parl. Hist.* vol. xxvii. p. 1240. Compare a letter from Sir William Young, in *Buckingham's Mem. of George III.* 1853, vol. ii. p. 73; 'Burke finished his wild speech in a manner next to madness.' This was in December 1788; and, from that time until his death, it became every year more evident that his intellect was disordered. See a melancholy description of him in a letter, written by Dr. Currie in 1792 (*Life of Currie*, vol. ii. p. 150); and, above all, see his own incoherent letter, in 1796, in his *Correspond. with Laurence*, p. 67.

opportunities of witnessing the infirmities of a great man, are not those who most love to relate them. But it is certain, that the change was first clearly seen immediately after the breaking out of the French Revolution; that it was aggravated by the death of his son; and that it became progressively worse till death closed the scene.[319] In his *Reflections on the French Revolution*; in his *Remarks on the Policy of the Allies*: in his *Letter to Elliot*; in his *Letter to a Noble Lord*; and in his *Letters on a Regicide Peace*, we may note the consecutive steps of an increasing, and at length an uncontrollable, violence. To the single principle of hatred of the French Revolution, he sacrificed his oldest associations and his dearest friends. Fox, as is well known, always looked up to Burke as to a master, from whose lips he had gathered the lessons of political wisdom.[320] Burke, on his side, fully recognized the vast abilities of his friend, and loved him for that affectionate disposition, and for those winning manners, which, it has often been said, none who saw them could ever resist. But now, without the slightest pretence of a personal quarrel, this long intimacy[321] was rudely severed. Because Fox would not abandon that love of popular liberty which they had long cherished in common, Burke, publicly, and in his place in parliament, declared that their friendship was at an end; for that he would never more hold communion with a man who lent his support to the French people.[322] At the same

---

[319] His son died in August 1794 (*Burke's Correspond.* vol. iv. p. 224); and his most violent works were written between that period and his own death, in July 1797.

[320] 'This disciple, as he was proud to acknowledge himself.' *Brougham's Statesmen*, vol. i. p. 218. In 1791, Fox said, that Burke 'had taught him everything he knew in politics.' *Parl. Hist.* vol. xxix. p. 379. See also *Adolphus's Hist. of George III.*

vol. iv. pp. 472, 610; and a letter from Fox to Parr, in *Parr's Works*, vol. vii. p. 287.

[321] It had begun in 1766, when Fox was only seventeen. *Russell's Mem. of Fox*, vol. i. p. 26.

[322] On this painful rupture, compare with the *Parliamentary History*, *Holland's Mem. of the Whig Party*, vol. i. pp. 10, 11; *Prior's Life of Burke*, pp. 375–379; *Tomline's Life of Pitt*, vol. ii. pp. 385–395. The complete change in Burke's feelings

time, and indeed the very evening on which this occurred, Burke, who had hitherto been remarkable for the courtesy of his manners,[323] deliberately insulted another of his friends, who was taking him home in his carriage; and, in a state of frantic excitement, insisted on being immediately set down, in the middle of the night, in a pouring rain, because he could not, he said, remain seated by 'a friend to the revolutionary doctrines of the French.'[324]

Nor is it true, as some have supposed, that this mania of hostility was solely directed against the criminal part of the French people. It would be difficult, in that or in any other age, to find two men of more active, or indeed enthusiastic benevolence, than Condorcet and La Fayette. Besides this, Condorcet was one of the most profound thinkers of his time, and will be remembered as long as genius is honoured among us.[325] La Fayette was no doubt inferior to Condorcet in point of ability; but he was the intimate friend of Washington, on whose conduct he modelled his own,[326] and by whose side he had fought for the liberties of America: his integrity was, and still is, unsullied; and his character had a chivalrous and noble

---

towards his old friend also appears in a very intemperate letter, written to Dr. Laurence in 1797. *Burke's Correspond. with Laurence*, p. 152. Compare *Parr's Works*, vol. iv. pp. 67–80, 84–90, 109.

[323] Which used to be contrasted with the bluntness of Johnson; these eminent men being the two best talkers of their time. See *Bisset's Life of Burke*, vol. i. p. 127.

[324] *Rogers's Introduction to Burke's Works*, p. xliv.; *Prior's Life of Burke*, p. 384.

[325] There is an interesting account of the melancholy death of this remarkable man in *Lamartine, Hist. des Girondins*, vol. viii. pp. 76–80; and a contemporary relation in *Musset-Pathay, Vie de Rousseau*, vol. ii. pp. 42–47.

[326] This is the honourable testimony of a political opponent; who says, that after the dissolution of the Assembly 'La Fayette se conforma à la conduite de Washington, qu'il avait pris pour modèle.' *Cassagnac, Révolution Française*, vol. iii. pp. 370, 371. Compare the grudging admission of his enemy Bouillé, *Mém. de Bouillé*, vol. i. p. 125; and for proofs of the affectionate intimacy between Washington and La Fayette, see *Mém. de Lafayette*, vol. i. pp. 16, 21, 29, 44, 55, 83, 92, 111, 165, 197, 204, 395, vol. ii. p. 123.

turn, which Burke, in his better days, would have been the first to admire.[327] Both, however, were natives of that hated country whose liberties they vainly attempted to achieve. On this account, Burke declared Condorcet to be guilty of 'impious sophistry;'[328] to be a 'fanatic atheist, and furious democratic republican;'[329] and to be capable of 'the lowest, as well as the highest and most determined villainies.'[330] As to La Fayette, when an attempt was made to mitigate the cruel treatment he was receiving from the Prussian government, Burke not only opposed the motion made for that purpose in the House of Commons, but took the opportunity of grossly insulting the unfortunate captive, who was then languishing in a dungeon.[331] So dead had he become

---

[327] The Duke of Bedford, no bad judge of character, said in 1794, that La Fayette's 'whole life was an illustration of truth, disinterestedness, and honour.' *Parl. Hist.* vol. xxxi. p. 664. So, too, the continuator of Sismondi (*Hist. des Français*, vol. xxx. p. 355), 'La Fayette, le chevalier de la liberté d'Amérique;' and Lamartine (*Hist. des Girondins*, vol. iii. p. 200), 'Martyr de la liberté après en avoir été le héros.' Ségur, who was intimately acquainted with him, gives some account of his noble character, as it appeared when he was a boy of nineteen. *Mém. de Ségur*, vol. i. pp. 106, 107. Forty years later, Lady Morgan met him in France; and what she relates shows how little he had changed, and how simple his tastes and the habits of his mind still were. *Morgan's France*, vol. ii. pp. 285–312. Other notices, from personal knowledge, will be found in *Life of Roscoe*, vol. ii. p. 178; and in *Trotter's Mem. of Fox*, pp. 319 seq.

[328] 'The impious sophistry of Condorcet.' *Letter to a Noble Lord*, in *Burke's Works*, vol. ii. p. 273.

[329] *Thoughts on French Affairs* in *Burke's Works*, vol. i. p. 574.

[330] 'Condorcet (though no marquis, as he styled himself before the Revolution) is a man of another sort of birth, fashion, and occupation from Brissot; but in every principle and every disposition, to the lowest as well as the highest and most determined villainies, fully his equal.' *Thoughts on French Affairs*, in *Burke's Works*, vol. i. p. 579.

[331] 'Groaning under the most oppressive cruelty in the dungeons of Magdeburg.' *Belsham's Hist. of Great Brit.* vol. ix. p. 151. See the afflicting details of his sufferings, in *Mém. de Lafayette*, vol. i. p. 479, vol. ii. pp. 75, 77, 78, 80, 91, 92; and on the noble equanimity with which he bore them, see *De Staël, Rév. Française*, Paris, 1820, vol. ii. p. 103.

on this subject, even to the common instincts of our nature, that, in his place in parliament, he could find no better way of speaking of this injured and high-souled man, than by calling him a ruffian: 'I would not,' says Burke,—' I would not debase my humanity by supporting an application in behalf of such a horrid ruffian.'[332]

As to France itself, it is 'Cannibal Castle;'[333] it is 'the republic of assassins;'[334] it is 'a hell;'[335] its government is composed of 'the dirtiest, lowest, most fraudulent, most knavish, of chicaners;'[336] its National Assembly are 'miscreants;'[337] its people are 'an allied army of Amazonian and male cannibal Parisians;'[338] they are 'a nation of murderers;'[339] they are 'the basest of mankind;'[340] they are 'murderous atheists;'[341] they are 'a gang of robbers;'[342] they are 'the prostitute outcasts of mankind;'[343] they are 'a desperate gang of plunderers, murderers, tyrants, and atheists.'[344] To make the slightest concessions to such a country in order to preserve peace, is offering victims 'on the altars of blasphemed regicide;'[345] even to enter into negotiations is 'exposing our lazar sores at the door of every proud servitor of the French republic, where the court-dogs will not deign to lick them.'[346] When our ambassador

---

[332] It is hardly credible that such language should have been applied to a man like La Fayette; but I have copied it from the *Parliamentary History*, vol. xxxi. p. 51, and from *Adolphus*, vol. v. p. 593. The only difference is, that in Adolphus the expression is 'I would not debase my humanity;' but in the *Parl. Hist.*, 'I would not debauch my humanity.' But both authorities are agreed as to the term 'horrid ruffian' being used by Burke. Compare *Burke's Correspondence with Laurence*, pp. 91, 99.

[333] *Burke's Works*, vol. ii. p. 319. In every instance I quote the precise words employed by Burke.

[334] *Ibid.* vol. ii. p. 279.
[335] Burke's speech, in *Parl. Hist.* vol. xxxi. p. 379.
[336] *Burke's Works*, vol. ii. p. 335.
[337] *Burke's Corresp.* vol. iii. p. 140.
[338] *Burke's Works*, vol. ii. p. 322.
[339] *Parl. Hist.* vol. xxx. p. 115.
[340] *Ibid.* p. 112.
[341] *Ibid.* p. 188.
[342] *Ibid.* p. 435.
[343] *Ibid.* p. 646; the concluding sentence of one of Burke's speeches in 1793.
[344] *Ibid.* vol. xxxi. p. 426.
[345] *Burke's Works*, vol. ii. p. 320.
[346] *Ibid.* p. 286.

was actually in Paris, he 'had the honour of passing his mornings in respectful attendance at the office of a regicide pettifogger;'[347] and we were taunted with having sent a 'peer of the realm to the scum of the earth.'[348] 'France has no longer a place in Europe; it is expunged from the map; its very name should be forgotten.'[349] Why, then, need men travel in it? Why need our children learn its language? and why are we to endanger the morals of our ambassadors? who can hardly fail to return from such a land with their principles corrupted, and with a wish to conspire against their own country.'[350]

This is sad, indeed, from such a man as Burke once was; but what remains, shows still more clearly how the associations and composition of his mind had been altered. He who, with humanity not less than with wisdom, had strenuously laboured to prevent the American war, devoted the last few years of his life to kindle a new war, compared to which that with America

---

[347] *Ibid.* p. 322.
[348] *Ibid.* p. 318.
[349] *Parl. Hist.* vol. xxviii. p. 353, vol. xxx. p. 390; *Adolphus*, vol. iv. p. 467.
[350] In the *Letters on a Regicide Peace*, published the year before he died, he says, 'These ambassadors may easily return as good courtiers as they went: but can they ever return from that degrading residence loyal and faithful subjects; or with any true affection to their master, or true attachment to the constitution, religion, or laws of their country? There is great danger that they who enter smiling into this Tryphonian cave, will come out of it sad and serious conspirators; and such will continue as long as they live.' *Burke's Works*, vol. ii. p. 282. He adds in the same work, p. 361, 'Is it for this benefit we open "the usual relations of peace and amity?" Is it for this our youth of both sexes are to form themselves by travel? Is it for this that with expense and pains we form their lisping infant accents to the language of France? . . . . . Let it be remembered, that no young man can go to any part of Europe without taking this place of pestilential contagion in his way; and, whilst the less active part of the community will be debauched by this travel, whilst children are poisoned at these schools, our trade will put the finishing hand to our ruin. No factory will be settled in France, that will not become a club of complete French Jacobins. The minds of young men of that description will receive a taint in their religion, their morals, and their politics, which they will in a short time communicate to the whole kingdom.'

was a light and trivial episode. In his calmer moments,
no one would have more willingly recognized that the
opinions prevalent in any country are the inevitable
results of the circumstances in which that country had
been placed. But now he sought to alter those opinions
by force. From the beginning of the French Revolution, he insisted upon the right, and indeed upon the
necessity, of compelling France to change her principles;[351] and, at a later period, he blamed the allied sovereigns for not dictating to a great people the government
they ought to adopt.[352] Such was the havoc circumstances had made in his well-ordered intellect, that to this
one principle he sacrificed every consideration of justice,
of mercy, and of expediency. As if war, even in its mildest
form, were not sufficiently hateful, he sought to give to
it that character of a crusade[353] which increasing knowledge had long since banished: and loudly proclaiming
that the contest was religious rather than temporal, he
revived old prejudices in order to cause fresh crimes.[354]
He also declared that the war should be carried on for
revenge as well as for defence, and that we must never
lay down our arms until we had utterly destroyed the

---

[351] In *Observations on the Conduct of the Minority*, 1793, he says, that during four years he had wished for 'a general war against jacobins and jacobinism.' *Burke's Works*, vol. i. p. 611.

[352] For, in the first place, the united sovereigns very much injured their cause by admitting that they had nothing to do with the interior arrangements of France.' *Heads for Consideration on the Present State of Affairs*, written in November 1792, in *Burke's Works*, vol. i. p. 583. And that he knew that this was not merely a question of destroying a faction, appears from the observable circumstance, that even in January 1791 he wrote to Trevor respecting war, 'France is weak indeed, divided and deranged; but God knows, when the things came to be tried, whether the invaders would not find that their enterprise *was not to support a party, but to conquer a kingdom*.' *Burke's Correspond.* vol. iii. p. 184.

[353] As Lord J. Russell truly calls it, *Mem. of Fox*, vol. iii. p. 34. See also *Schlosser's Eighteenth Century*, vol. ii. p. 93, vol. v. p. 109, vol. vi. p. 291; *Nicholls's Recollections*, vol. i. p. 300; *Parr's Works*, vol. iii. p. 242.

[354] 'We cannot, if we would, delude ourselves about the true state of this dreadful contest. *It is a religious war*.' *Remarks on the Policy of the Allies*, in *Burke's Works*, vol. i. p. 600.

men by whom the Revolution was brought about.[445] And, as if these things were not enough, he insisted that this, the most awful of all wars, being begun, was not to be hurried over; although it was to be carried on for revenge as well as for religion, and the resources of civilized men were to be quickened by the ferocious passions of crusaders, still it was not to be soon ended; it was to be durable; it must have permanence; it must, says Burke, in the spirit of a burning hatred, be protracted in a long war: 'I speak it emphatically, and with a desire that it should be marked, in a *long* war.'[446]

It was to be a war to force a great people to change their government. It was to be a war carried on for the purpose of punishment. It was also to be a religious war. Finally, it was to be a long war. Was there ever any other man who wished to afflict the human race with such extensive, searching, and protracted calamities? Such cruel, such reckless, and yet such deliberate opinions, if they issued from a sane mind, would immortalize even the most obscure statesman, because they would load his name with imperishable infamy. For where can we find, even among the most ignorant or most sanguinary politicians, sentiments like these? Yet they proceed from one who, a very few years before, was the most eminent political philosopher England has ever possessed. To us it is only given to mourn over so noble a wreck. More than this no one should do. We may contemplate with reverence the mighty ruin; but the mysteries of its decay let no man presume to invade, unless, to use the language of the

---

[445] See the long list of proscriptions in *Burke's Works*, vol. i. p. 604. And the principle of revenge is again advocated in a letter written in 1793, in *Burke's Correspond.* vol. iv. p. 163. And in 1794, he told the House of Commons that 'the war must no longer be confined to the vain attempt of raising a barrier to the lawless and savage power of France; but must be directed to the only rational end it can pursue; namely, the entire destruction of the desperate horde which gave it birth.' *Parl. Hist.* vol. xxxi. p. 427.

[446] *Letters on a Regicide Peace*, in *Burke's Works*, vol. ii. p. 291. In this horrible sentence, perhaps the most horrible ever penned by an English politician, the italics are not my own; they are in the text.

greatest of our masters, he can tell how to minister to a diseased mind, pluck the sorrows which are rooted in the memory, and raze out the troubles that are written in the brain.

It is a relief to turn from so painful a subject, even though we descend to the petty, huckstering politics of the English court. And truly, the history of the treatment experienced by the most illustrious of our politicians, is highly characteristic of the prince under whom he lived. While Burke was consuming his life in great public services, labouring to reform our finances, improve our laws, and enlighten our commercial policy,—while he was occupied with these things, the king regarded him with coldness and aversion.[357] But when the great statesman degenerated into an angry brawler; when, irritated by disease, he made it the sole aim of his declining years to kindle a deadly war between the two first countries of Europe, and declared that to this barbarous object he would sacrifice all other questions of policy, however important they might be;[358]—then it was that a perception of his vast abilities began to dawn upon the mind of the king. Before this, no one had been bold enough to circulate in the palace even a whisper of his merits. Now, however, in the successive, and eventually the rapid decline of his powers, he had fallen almost to the level of the royal intellect; and now he was first warmed by the beams of the royal favour. Now he was a man after the king's own heart.[359] Less than two years

---

[357] 'I know,' said Burke, in one of those magnificent speeches which mark the zenith of his intellect,—'I know the map of England as well as the noble lord, or as any other person; and I know that the way I take is not the road to preferment.' *Parl. Hist.* vol. xvii. p. 1269.

[358] See, among many other instances, an extraordinary passage on 'Jacobinism,' in his *Works*, vol. ii. p. 449, which should be compared with a letter he wrote in 1792, respecting a proposed coalition ministry, *Corresppond.* vol. iii. pp. 519, 520: 'But my advice was, that as a foundation of the whole, the political principle must be settled as the preliminary, namely, "a total hostility to the French system, at home and abroad."'

[359] The earliest evidence I have met with of the heart of George III. beginning to open towards

before his death, there was settled upon him, at the express desire of George III., two considerable pensions;[260] and the king even wished to raise him to the peerage, in order that the House of Lords might benefit by the services of so great a counsellor.[261]

This digression respecting the character of Burke has been longer than I had anticipated; but it will not, I hope, be considered unimportant; for, in addition to the intrinsic interest of the subject, it illustrates the feelings of George III. towards great men, and it shows what the opinions were which in his reign it was thought necessary to hold. In the sequel of this work, I shall trace the effect of such opinions upon the interests of the country, considered as a whole; but for the object of the present Introduction, it will be sufficient to point out the connexion in one or two more of those prominent instances, the character of which is too notorious to admit of discussion.

Of these leading and conspicuous events, the American war was the earliest, and for several years it almost entirely absorbed the attention of English politicians. In the reign of George II. a proposal had been made to increase the revenue by taxing the colonies; which, as the Americans were totally unrepresented in parliament, was simply a proposition to tax an entire people without even the form of asking their consent. This scheme of public robbery was rejected by that able and

---

Burke, is in August 1791; see in *Burke's Correspondence*, vol. iii. p. 278, an exquisitely absurd account of his reception at the levee. Burke must have been fallen, indeed, before he could write such a letter.

[260] 'Said to have originated in the express wish of the king.' *Prior's Life of Burke*, p. 489. Mr. Prior estimates these pensions at 3,700l. a-year; but if we may rely on Mr. Nicholls, the sum was even greater: 'Mr. Burke was rewarded with two pensions, estimated to be worth 40,000l.' *Nicholls's Recollections*, vol. i. p. 136. Burke was sixty-five; and a pension of 3,700l. a-year would not be worth 40,000l., as the tables were then calculated. The statement of Mr. Prior is, however, confirmed by Wansey, in 1794. See *Nicholls' Lit. Anec. of the Eighteenth Century*, vol. iii. p. 81.

[261] *Prior's Life of Burke*, p. 400; *Nicholls's Lit. Anec.* vol. iii. p. 81; *Bisset's Life of Burke*, vol ii. p. 414.

moderate man who was then at the head of affairs; and
the suggestion, being generally deemed impracticable,
fell to the ground, and seems, indeed, hardly to have
excited attention.[361] But what was deemed by the
government of George II. to be a dangerous stretch
of arbitrary power, was eagerly welcomed by the
government of George III. For the new king, having
the most exalted notion of his own authority, and being,
from his miserable education, entirely ignorant of public affairs, thought that to tax the Americans for the
benefit of the English, would be a masterpiece of policy.
When, therefore, the old idea was revived, it met with
his cordial acquiescence; and when the Americans
showed their intention of resisting this monstrous injustice, he was only the more confirmed in his opinion
that it was necessary to curb their unruly will. Nor
need we be surprised at the rapidity with which such
angry feelings broke out. Indeed, looking, on the one
hand, at the despotic principles which, for the first
time since the Revolution, were now revived at the
English court; and looking, on the other hand, at the
independent spirit of the colonists,—it was impossible to
avoid a struggle between the two parties; and the only
questions were, as to what form the contest would take,
and towards which side victory was most likely to
incline.[362]

---

[361] 'It had been proposed to Sir Robert Walpole to raise the revenue by imposing taxes on America; but that minister, who could foresee beyond the benefit of the actual moment, declared it must be a bolder man than himself who should venture on such an expedient.' *Walpole's George III* vol. ii. p. 70. Compare *Phillimore's Mem. of Lyt-telton*, vol. ii. p. 662; *Bancroft's American Revolution*, vol. i p. 96; *Belsham's Hist. of Great Britain*, vol. v. p. 102.

[362] That some sort of rupture was unavoidable, must, I think, be admitted; but we are not bound to believe the assertion of Horace Walpole, who says (*Mem. of George II.* vol. i. p. 397) that in 1754 he predicted the American rebellion. Walpole, though a keen observer of the surface of society, was not the man to take a view of this kind; unless, as is hardly probable, he heard an opinion to that effect expressed by his father. Sir Robert Walpole may have said something respecting the increasing love of liberty in the colonies; but it was impossible for him to foresee how that love would be fostered by the arbitrary proceedings of the government of George III.

SIXTEENTH TO THE EIGHTEENTH CENTURY. 479

On the part of the English government, no time was lost. Five years after the accession of George III., a bill was brought into parliament to tax the Americans;[364] and so complete had been the change in political affairs, that not the least difficulty was found in passing a measure which, in the reign of George II., no minister had dared to propose. Formerly, such a proposal, if made, would certainly have been rejected; now the most powerful parties in the state were united in its favour. The king, on every occasion, paid a court to the clergy, to which, since the death of Anne, they had been unaccustomed; he was, therefore, sure of their support, and they zealously aided him in every attempt to oppress the colonies.[365] The aristocracy, a few leading Whigs alone excepted, were on the same side, and looked to the taxation of America as a means of lessening their own contributions.[366] As to George III., his feelings on the subject were notorious;[367] and

---

[364] The general proposition was introduced in 1764; the bill itself early in 1765. See *Mahon's Hist. of England*, vol. v. pp. 82, 85; and *Grenville Papers*, vol. ii. pp. 373, 374. On the complete change of policy which this indicated, see *Brougham's Polit. Philos.* part iii. p. 328.

[365] The correspondence of that time contains ample proof of the bitterness of the clergy against the Americans. Even in 1777, Burke wrote to Fox: 'The Tories do universally think their power and consequence involved in the success of this American business. The clergy are astonishingly warm in it; and what the Tories are when embodied and united with their natural head, the crown, and animated by their clergy, no man knows better than yourself.' *Burke's Works*, vol. ii. p. 390. Compare *Bishop Newton's Life of Himself*, pp. 134, 157.

[366] 'The overbearing aristocracy desired some reduction of the land tax, at the expense of America.' *Bancroft's Hist. of the American Revolution*, vol. ii. p. 414. The merchants, on the other hand, were opposed to these violent proceedings. See, on this contrast between the landed and commercial interests, a letter from Lord Shelburne, in 1774, and another from Lord Camden, in 1775, in *Chatham Correspond.* vol. iv. pp. 341, 401. See also the speeches of Trecothick and Vyner, in *Parl. Hist.* vol. xvi. p. 507, vol. xviii. p. 1361.

[367] It was believed at the time, and it is not improbable, that the king himself suggested the taxation of America, to which Grenville at first objected. Compare *Wraxall's Mem. of his own Time*, vol. ii. pp. 111, 112, with *Nicholls's Recollections*, vol. i. pp. 208, 386. This may have been merely a rumour; but it is quite consistent with everything we know of the character of George III., and there can, at all events, be no

the more liberal party not having yet recovered from the loss of power consequent on the death of George II., there was little fear of difficulties from the cabinet; it being well known that the throne was occupied by a prince whose first object was to keep ministers in strict dependence on himself, and who, whenever it was practicable, called into office such weak and flexible men as would yield unhesitating submission to his wishes.³⁶⁸

Everything being thus prepared, there followed those events which were to be expected from such a combination. 'Without stopping to relate details which are known to every reader, it may be briefly mentioned that, in this new state of things, the wise and forbearing policy of the preceding reign was set at naught, and the national councils guided by rash and ignorant

---

doubt as to his feelings respecting the general question. It is certain that he over-persuaded Lord North to engage in the contest with America, and induced that minister to go to war, and to continue it even after success had become hopeless. See Bancroft's *American Revolution*, vol. iii. pp. 307, 308; *Russell's Mem. of Fox*, vol. i. pp. 247, 254; and the *Bedford Correspond.* vol. iii. p. li. See also, in regard to the repeal of the Stamp Act, the *Grenville Papers*, vol. iii. p. 373; a curious passage, with which Lord Mahon, the last edition of whose history was published in the same year (1853), appears to have been unacquainted. *Mahon's Hist. of England*, vol. v. p. 139. In America the sentiments of the king were well known. In 1775, Jefferson writes from Philadelphia: 'We are told, and everything proves it true, that he is the bitterest enemy we have.' *Jefferson's Correspond.* vol. i. p. 153. And in 1782 Franklin writes to Livingston, 'The king hates us most cordially.' *Life of Franklin*, vol. ii. p. 126.

³⁶⁹ 'A court,' as Lord Albemarle observes,—'a court that required ministers to be, not the public servants of the state, but the private domestics of the sovereign.' *Albemarle's Mem. of Rockingham*, vol. i. p. 248. Compare *Bancroft's American Revolution*, vol. ii. p. 109. In the same way, Burke, in 1767, writes: 'His majesty never was in better spirits. He has got a ministry weak and dependant; and, what is better, willing to continue so.' *Burke's Correspond.* vol. i. p. 133. Ten years later, Lord Chatham openly taunted the king with this disgraceful peculiarity: 'Thus to pliable men, not capable men, was the government of this once glorious empire intrusted.' *Chatham's Speech in 1777*, in *Adolphus*, vol. ii. pp. 499, 500.

men, who soon brought the greatest disasters upon the country, and within a few years actually dismembered the empire. In order to enforce the monstrous claim of taxing a whole people without their consent, there was waged against America a war ill-conducted, unsuccessful, and, what is far worse, accompanied by cruelties disgraceful to a civilized nation.[369] To this may be added, that an immense trade was nearly annihilated; every branch of commerce was thrown into confusion;[370] we were disgraced in the eyes of Europe;[371] we incurred an expense of 140,000,000*l*.;[372]

---

[369] For some evidence of the ferocity with which this war was conducted by the English, see *Tucker's Life of Jefferson*, vol. i. pp. 138, 139, 160; *Jefferson's Mem. and Correspond.* vol. i. pp. 352, 429, vol. ii. pp. 336, 337; *Almon's Corrrspond. of Wilkes*, vol. v. pp. 229–232, edit. 1805; *Adolphus's Hist. of George III.* vol. ii. pp. 362, 391. These horrible cruelties were frequently mentioned in parliament, but without producing the least effect on the king or his ministers. See *Parl. Hist.* vol. xix. pp. 371, 403, 423, 424, 432, 436, 440, 477, 487, 488, 489, 567, 573, 579, 685, 972, 1393, 1394, vol. xx. p. 43. Among the expenses of the war which government laid before parliament, one of the items was for 'five gross of scalping knives.' *Parl. Hist.* vol. xix. pp. 971, 972. See further *Mém. de Lafayette*, vol. i. pp. 23, 25, 99.

[370] In Manchester, 'in consequence of the American troubles, nine in ten of the artisans in that town had been discharged from employment.' This was stated in 1766, by no less an authority than Conway. *Mahon's Hist. of England*, vol. v. p. 135. As the struggle became more obstinate the evil was more marked, and ample evidence of the enormous injury inflicted on England will be found by comparing *Franklin's Correspondence*, vol. i. p. 352, *Adolphus's Hist. of George III.* vol. ii. p. 261; *Burke's Works*, vol. i. p. 111; *Parl. Hist.* vol. xviii. pp. 734, 951, 963, 964, vol. xix. pp. 259, 341, 710, 711, 1072; *Walpole's Mem. of George III.* vol. ii. p. 218.

[371] Even Mr. Adolphus, in his Tory history, says, that in 1782 'the cause of Great Britain seemed degraded to the lowest state; ill success and the prevalent opinion of mismanagement rendered the espousal of it among the selfish powers of the continent almost disreputable.' *Hist. of George III.* vol. iii. pp. 391, 392. For proof of the opinions held in foreign countries respecting this, I cannot do better than refer to *Mém. de Ségur*, vol. iii. pp. 184, 185; *Œuvres de Turgot*, vol. ix. p. 377; *Soulavie, Mém. de Louis XVI.* vol. iv. pp. 353, 354; *Koch, Tableau des Révolutions*, vol. ii. pp. 190–194; *Mem. of Mallet du Pan*, vol. i. p. 37.

[372] Sir John Sinclair, in his *Hist. of the Revenue*, vol. ii. p. 114, says 139,171,876*l*.

and we lost by far the most valuable colonies any nation has ever possessed.

Such were the first fruits of the policy of George III. But the mischief did not stop there. The opinions which it was necessary to advocate in order to justify this barbarous war, recoiled upon ourselves. In order to defend the attempt to destroy the liberties of America, principles were laid down which, if carried into effect, would have subverted the liberties of England. Not only in the court, but in both houses of parliament, from the episcopal bench, and from the pulpits of the church-party, there were promulgated doctrines of the most dangerous kind—doctrines unsuited to a limited monarchy, and, indeed, incompatible with it. The extent to which this reaction proceeded is known to very few readers, because the evidence of it is chiefly to be found in the parliamentary debates, and in the theological literature, particularly the sermons of that time, none of which are now much studied. But, not to anticipate matters belonging to another part of this work, it is enough to say that the danger was so imminent as to make the ablest defenders of popular liberty believe that everything was at stake; and that if the Americans were vanquished, the next step would be to attack the liberties of England, and endeavour to extend to the mother-country the same arbitrary government which by that time would have been established in the colonies.[373]

---

[373] Dr. Jebb, an able observer, thought that the American war 'must be decisive of the liberties of both countries.' *Disney's Life of Jebb*, p. 92. So, too, Lord Chatham wrote in 1777, 'poor England will have fallen upon her own sword.' *The Grenville Papers*, vol. iv. p. 573. In the same year, Burke said of the attempt made to rule the colonies by military force, 'that the establishment of such a power in America will utterly ruin our finances (though its certain effect), is the smallest part of our concern. It will become an apt, powerful, and certain engine for the destruction of our freedom here.' *Burke's Works*, vol. ii. p. 399. Compare vol. i. pp. 189, 210; *Parl. Hist.* vol. xvi. pp. 104, 107, 651, 652, vol. xix. pp. 11, 1056, vol. xx. p. 119, vol. xxi. p. 907. Hence it was that Fox wished the Americans to be victorious (*Russell's Mem. of Fox*, vol. i. p. 143); for which some writers have actually accused him of want of patriotism!

Whether or not these fears were exaggerated, is a question of considerable difficulty; but after a careful study of that time, and a study too from sources not much used by historians, I feel satisfied that they who are best acquainted with the period will be the most willing to admit that, though the danger may have been overrated, it was far more serious than men are now inclined to believe. At all events, it is certain that the general aspect of political affairs was calculated to excite great alarm. It is certain, that during many years, the authority of the crown continued to increase, until it reached a height of which no example had been seen in England for several generations. It is certain that the Church of England exerted all her influence in favour of those despotic principles which the king wished to enforce. It is also certain that, by the constant creation of new peers, all holding the same views, the character of the House of Lords was undergoing a slow but decisive change; and that, whenever a favourable opportunity arose, high judicial appointments and high ecclesiastical appointments were conferred upon men notorious for their leaning towards the royal prerogative. These are facts which cannot be denied; and, putting them together, there remains, I think, no doubt, that the American war was a great crisis in the history of England, and that if the colonists had been defeated, our liberties would have been for a time in considerable jeopardy. From that risk we were saved by the Americans, who with heroic spirit resisted the royal armies, defeated them at every point, and at length, separating themselves from the mother-country, began that wonderful career, which, in less than eighty years, has raised them to an unexampled prosperity, and which to us ought to be deeply interesting, as showing what may be effected by the unaided resources of a free people.

Seven years after this great contest had been brought to a successful close, and the Americans, happily for the interests of mankind, had finally secured their independence, another nation rose up and turned against its rulers. The history of the

causes of the French Revolution will be found in
another part of this volume; at present we have only
to glance at the effects it produced upon the policy of
the English government. In France, as is well known,
the movement was extremely rapid; the old institutions, which were so corrupted as to be utterly unfit
for use, were quickly destroyed; and the people,
frenzied by centuries of oppression, practised the most
revolting cruelties, saddening the hour of their triumph
by crimes that disgraced the noble cause for which
they struggled.

All this, frightful as it was, did nevertheless form a
part of the natural course of affairs; it was the old
story of tyranny exciting revenge, and revenge blind-
ing men to every consequence except the pleasure of
glutting their own passions. If, under these circumstances, France had been left to herself, the Revolution,
like all other revolutions, would soon have subsided,
and a form of government have arisen suited to the
actual condition of things. What the form would
have been, it is impossible now to say; that, however,
was a question with which no foreign country had the
slightest concern. Whether it should be an oligarchy,
or a despotic monarchy, or a republic, it was for
France to decide; but it was evidently not the
business of any other nation to decide for her. Still
less was it likely that, on so delicate a point, France
would submit to dictation from a country which had
always been her rival, and which not unfrequently
had been her bitter and successful enemy.

But these considerations, obvious as they are, were
lost upon George III., and upon those classes which
were then in the ascendant. The fact that a great
people had risen against their oppressors disquieted
the consciences of men in high places. The same evil
passions, and indeed the same evil language, which a
few years before were directed against the Americans,
were now turned against the French; and it was but
too clear that the same results would follow.[274] In

---

[274] In 1792, and therefore before the war broke out, Lord
Lansdowne, one of the extremely
few peers who escaped from the
prevailing corruption, said, 'The
present instance recalled to his

defiance of every maxim of sound policy, the English ambassador was recalled from France simply because that country chose to do away with the monarchy, and substitute a republic in its place. This was the first decisive step towards an open rupture, and it was taken, not because France had injured England, but because France had changed her government.[375] A few months later, the French, copying the example of the English in the preceding century,[376] brought their king to a public trial, sentenced him to die, and struck off his head in the midst of his own capital. It must be allowed that this act was needless, that it was cruel, and that it was grossly impolitic. But it is palpably evident that they who consented to the execution were responsible only to God and their country; and that any notice of it from abroad, which bore the appearance of a threat, would rouse the spirit of France, would unite all parties into one, and would induce the nation to adopt as its own a crime of which it might otherwise have repented, but which it could not now abjure without incurring the shame of having yielded to the dictation of a foreign power.

In England, however, as soon as the fate of the king was known, the government, without waiting for explanation, and without asking for any guarantee as to the future, treated the death of Louis as an offence against itself, and imperiously ordered the French residents to quit the country:[377] thus wantonly

---

memory the proceedings of this country previous to the American war. The same abusive and degrading terms were applied to the Americans that were now used to the National Convention,—*the same consequences might follow.*' *Parl. Hist.* vol. xxx. p. 155.

[376] Compare *Belsham's Hist. of Great Britain*, vol. viii. p. 490, with *Tomline's Life of Pitt*, vol. ii. p. 548. The letter to Lord Gower, the English minister in Paris, is printed in *Parl. Hist.* vol. xxx. pp. 143, 144. Its date is 17th August, 1792.

[376] Just before the Revolution, Robert de Saint-Vincent pertinently remarked, by way of caution, that the English 'have dethroned seven of their kings, and beheaded the eighth.' *Mem. of Mallet du Pan*, vol. i. p. 146; and we are told in *Alison's Europe* (vol. ii. pp. 199, 296, 315), that in 1792 Louis ' anticipated the fate of Charles I.' Compare *Williams's Letters from France*, 2nd edit. 1796, vol. iv. p. 2.

[377] Belsham (*Hist. of Great Britain*, vol. viii. p. 525) supposes, and probably with reason,

originating a war which lasted twenty years, cost the
lives of millions, plunged all Europe into confusion, and,
more than any other circumstance, stopped the march
of civilization, by postponing for a whole generation
those reforms, which, late in the eighteenth century,
the progress of affairs rendered indispensable.

The European results of this, the most hateful, the
most unjust, and the most atrocious war, England has
ever waged against any country, will be hereafter
considered;[378] at present I confine myself to a short
summary of its leading effects on English society.

What distinguishes this sanguinary contest from all
preceding ones, and what gives to it its worst feature,
is, that it was eminently a war of opinions,—a war
which we carried on, not with a view to territorial
acquisitions, but with the object of repressing that
desire for reforms of every kind, which had now become
the marked characteristic of the leading countries of
Europe.[379] As soon, therefore, as hostilities began the

---

[378] that the English government was bent upon war even before the death of Louis; but it appears (*Tomline's Pitt*, vol. ii. p. 599) that it was not until the 24th of January 1793, that Chauvelin was actually ordered to leave England, and that this was in consequence of 'the British ministers having received information of the execution of the king of France.' Compare *Belsham*, vol. viii. p. 530. The common opinion, therefore, seems correct, that the proximate cause of hostilities was the execution of Louis. See *Alison's Hist.* vol. ii. p. 522, vol. v. p. 249, vol. vi. p.656; and *Newmarch*, in *Journal of Statist. Soc.* vol. xviii. p. 108.

[378] Lord Brougham (*Sketches of Statesmen*, vol. i. p. 79) rightly says of this war, that 'the youngest man living will not survive the fatal effects of this flagrant political crime.' So eager, however, was George III. in its favour, that when Wilberforce separated himself from Pitt on account of the war, and moved an amendment on the subject in the House of Commons, the king showed his spite by refusing to take any notice of Wilberforce the next time he appeared at court. *Life of Wilberforce*, vol. ii. pp. 10, 72.

[379] In 1793 and subsequently, it was stated both by the opposition, and also by the supporters of government, that the war with France was directed against doctrines and opinions, and that one of its main objects was to discourage the progress of democratic institutions. See, among many other instances, *Parl. Hist.* vol. xxx. pp. 413, 417, 1077, 1199, 1200, 1263, vol. xxxi. pp. 466, 592, 649, 880, 1036, 1047, vol. xxxiii. pp. 603, 604; *Nicholls's Recollections*, vol. ii. pp. 156, 187.

English government had a twofold duty to perform—it had to destroy a republic abroad, and it had to prevent improvement at home. The first of these duties it fulfilled by squandering the blood and the treasure of England, till it had thrown nearly every family into mourning, and reduced the country to the verge of national bankruptcy. The other duty it attempted to execute by enacting a series of laws intended to put an end to the free discussion of political questions, and stifle that spirit of inquiry which was every year becoming more active. These laws were so comprehensive, and so well calculated to effect their purpose, that if the energy of the nation had not prevented their being properly enforced, they would either have destroyed every vestige of popular liberty, or else have provoked a general rebellion. Indeed, during several years the danger was so imminent, that, in the opinion of some high authorities, nothing could have averted it, but the bold spirit with which our English juries, by their hostile verdicts, resisted the proceedings of government, and refused to sanction laws which the crown had proposed, and to which a timid and servile legislature had willingly consented.[360]

We may form some idea of the magnitude of the crisis by considering the steps which were actually taken against the two most important of all our

---

[360] Lord Campbell (*Lives of the Chancellors*, vol. vi. p. 449) says, that if the laws passed in 1794 had been enforced, 'the only chance of escaping servitude would have been civil war.' Compare *Brougham's Statesmen*, vol. i. p. 237, vol. ii. pp. 63, 64, on our 'escape from proscription and from arbitrary power . . . during the almost hopeless struggle from 1793 to 1801.' Both these writers pay great and deserved honour to the successful efforts of Erskine with juries. Indeed the spirit of our jurors was so determined, that in 1794, at Tooke's trial, they only consulted eight minutes before bringing in a verdict of acquittal. *Stephen's Mem. of Horne Tooke*, vol. ii. p. 147; see also, on this crisis, *Life of Cartwright*, vol. i. p. 210. The people sympathised throughout with the victims; and while the trial of Hardy was pending, the attorney-general, Scott, was always mobbed when he left the court, and on one occasion his life was in danger. *Twiss's Life of Eldon*, vol. i. pp. 185, 186. Compare *Holcroft's Memoirs*, vol. ii. pp. 180, 181.

institutions, namely, the freedom of the public press, and the right of assembling in meetings for the purpose of public discussion. These are, in a political point of view, the two most striking peculiarities which distinguish us from every other European people. As long as they are preserved intact, and as long as they are fearlessly and frequently employed, there will always be ample protection against those encroachments on the part of government which cannot be too jealously watched, and to which even the freest country is liable. To this may be added, that these institutions possess other advantages of the highest order. By encouraging political discussion, they increase the amount of intellect brought to bear upon the political business of the country. They also increase the total strength of the nation, by causing large classes of men to exercise faculties which would otherwise lie dormant, but which by these means are quickened into activity, and become available for other purposes of social interest.

But in the period we are now considering, it was deemed advisable that the influence of the people should be lessened; it was, therefore, thought improper that they should strengthen their abilities by exercising them. To relate the details of that bitter war, which, late in the eighteenth century, the English government carried on against every kind of free discussion, would lead me far beyond the limits of this Introduction; and I can only hastily refer to the vindictive prosecutions, and, whenever a verdict was obtained, the vindictive punishments, of men like Adams, Bonney, Crossfield, Frost, Gerald, Hardy, Holt, Hodson, Holcroft, Joyce, Kidd, Lambert, Margarot, Martin, Muir, Palmer, Perry, Skirving, Stannard, Thelwall, Tooke, Wakefield, Wardle, Winterbotham: all of whom were indicted, and many of whom were fined, imprisoned, or transported, because they expressed their sentiments with freedom, and because they used language such as in our time is employed with perfect impunity, by speakers at public meetings, and by writers in the public press.

As, however, juries in several cases refused to con-

SIXTEENTH TO THE EIGHTEENTH CENTURY. 489

vict men who were prosecuted for these offences, it was determined to recur to measures still more decisive. In 1795, a law was passed, by which it was manifestly intended to put an end for ever to all popular discussions either on political or religious matters. For by it every public meeting was forbidden, unless notice of it were inserted in a newspaper five days beforehand;[361] such notice to contain a statement of the objects of the meeting, and of the time and place where it was to assemble. And, to bring the whole arrangement completely under the supervision of government, it was ordered, that not only should the notice, thus published, be signed by householders, but that the original manuscript should be preserved, for the information of the justices of the peace, who might require a copy of it: a significant threat, which, in those days, was easily understood.[362] It was also enacted that, even after these precautions had been taken, any single justice might compel the meeting to disperse, if, in his opinion, the language held by the speakers was calculated to bring the sovereign or the government into contempt; while, at the same time, he was authorized to arrest those whom he considered to be the offenders.[363] The power of dissolving a public meeting, and of seizing its leaders, was thus conferred upon a common magistrate, and conferred too without the

---

[361] 'Five days at least.' *Stat.* 36 *George III.* c. 8, § 1. This applied to meetings 'holden for the purpose or on the pretext of considering of or preparing any petition, complaint, remonstrance, or declaration, or other address to the king, or to both houses, or either house, of parliament, for alteration of matters established in church or state, or for the purpose or on the pretext of deliberating upon any grievance in church or state.' The only exceptions allowed were in the case of meetings called by magistrates, officials, and the majority of the grand jury.

[362] The insertor of the notice in the newspaper 'shall cause such notice and authority to be carefully preserved, ... and cause a true copy thereof (if required) to be delivered to any justice of the peace for the county, city, town, or place where such person shall reside, or where such newspaper shall be printed, and who shall require the same.' 36 *George III.* c. 8, § 1.

[363] C. 8, §§ 6 and 7, referring to 'meetings on notice;' and to persons holding language which shall even 'tend to incite.' These two sections are very remarkable.

slightest provision against its abuse. In other words, the right of putting an end to all public discussions on the most important subjects, was lodged in the hands of a man appointed by the crown, and removable by the crown at its own pleasure. To this it was added, that if the meeting should consist of twelve, or upwards of twelve persons, and should remain together for one hour after being ordered to separate,—in such case, the penalty of death was to be inflicted, even if only twelve disobeyed this the arbitrary command of a single and irresponsible magistrate.[384]

In 1799, another law was passed, forbidding any open field, or place of any kind, to be used for lecturing, or for debating, unless a specific license for such place had been obtained from the magistrates. It was likewise enacted, that all circulating-libraries, and all reading-rooms, should be subject to the same provision; no person, without leave from the constituted authorities, being permitted to lend on hire in his own house, newspapers, pamphlets, or even books of any kind.[385] Before shops of this sort could be opened, a license must first be obtained from two justices of the peace; which, however, was to be renewed at least once a year, and might be revoked at any intermediate period.[386] If a man lent books without the permission of the magistrates, or if he allowed lectures or debates, 'on any subject whatever,' to be held under his roof, then, for such grievous crime, he was to be fined 100*l.* a-day; and every person who aided him, either by presiding over the discussion, or by supplying a book, was for each offence to be fined 20*l.* The proprietor of so

---

[384] ' It shall be adjudged,' says the Act, ' felony without benefit of clergy; and the offenders therein shall be adjudged felons, and shall suffer death as in case of felony without benefit of clergy.' 36 *George III.* c. 8, § 6.

[385] *Stat.* 39 *George III.* c. 79, § 15.

[386] The license ' shall be in force for the space of one year and no longer, or for any less space of time therein to be specified; and which license it shall be lawful for the justices of the peace' &c. ' to revoke and declare void, and no longer in force, by any order of such justices; .... and thereupon such license shall cease and determine, and be thenceforth utterly void and of no effect.' 39 *George III.* c. 79, § 18.

pernicious an establishment was not only to suffer from these ruinous fines, but was declared liable to still further punishment as the keeper of a disorderly house.[267]

To modern ears it sounds somewhat strange, that the owner of a public reading-room should not only incur extravagant fines, but should also be punished as the keeper of a disorderly house; and that all this should happen to him, simply because he opened his shop without asking permission from the local magistrates. Strange, however, as this appears, it was, at all events, consistent, since it formed part of a regular plan for bringing, not only the actions of men, but even their opinions, under the direct control of the executive government. Thus it was that the laws, now for the first time passed, against newspapers, were so stringent, and the prosecution of authors so unrelenting, that there was an evident intention to ruin every public writer who expressed independent sentiments.[268]

---

[267] Such things are so incredible, that I must again quote the words of the Act: 'Every house, room, or place, which shall be opened or used as a place of meeting for the purpose of reading books, pamphlets, newspapers, or other publications, and to which any person shall be admitted by payment of money' (if not regularly licensed by the authorities), ...'shall be deemed a disorderly house;' and the person opening it shall 'be otherwise punished as the law directs in case of disorderly houses.' 39 *George III.* c. 79, § 15. The germ of this law may be found in 36 *George III.* c. 8, § § 12, 13, 14, 15, 16. Nowhere are the weakest parts of the human mind more clearly seen than in the history of legislation.

[268] See the particulars in *Hunt's Hist. of Newspapers*, vol. i. pp. 281–4. Mr. Hunt says, p. 284: 'In addition to all these laws, directed solely towards the press, other statutes were made to bear upon it, for the purpose of repressing the free expression of popular opinion.' In 1793, Dr. Currie writes: 'The prosecutions that are commenced by government all over England against printers, publishers, &c. would astonish you; and most of these are for offences committed many months ago. The printer of the *Manchester Herald* has had seven different indictments preferred against him for paragraphs in his paper; and six *different* indictments for selling or disposing of six different copies of Paine,—all previous to the *trial* of Paine. The man was opulent, supposed worth 20,000*l.*; but these different actions will ruin him, as they were intended to do.' *Currie's Life*, vol. i. pp. 185, 186. See also a letter from Roscoe to Lord

These measures, and others of a similar character, which will hereafter be noticed, excited such alarm, that, in the opinion of some of the ablest observers, the state of public affairs was becoming desperate, perhaps irretrievable. The extreme despondency with which, late in the eighteenth century, the best friends of liberty looked to the future, is very observable, and forms a striking feature in their private correspondence.[369] And although comparatively few men venture to express such sentiments in public, Fox, whose fearless temper made him heedless of risk, openly stated what would have checked the government, if anything could have done so. For this eminent statesman, who had been minister more than once, and was afterwards minister again, did not hesitate to say, from

---

Lansdowne, in *Life of Roscoe*, vol. i. p. 124; and *Mem. of Holcroft*, vol. ii. pp. 151, 152: 'Printers and booksellers all over the kingdom were hunted out for prosecution.' See further, *Life of Cartwright*, vol. i. pp. 199, 200; *Adolphus's Hist. of George III*. vol. v. pp. 525, 526; *Mem. of Wakefield*, vol. ii. p. 69.

[370] In 1793, Dr. Currie, after mentioning the attempts made by government to destroy the liberty of the press, adds: 'For my part, I foresee troubles, and conceive the nation was never in such a dangerous crisis.' *Currie's Mem.* vol. i. p. 186. In 1795, Fox writes (*Russell's Mem. of Fox*, vol. iii. pp. 124, 125): 'There appears to me to be no choice at present, but between an absolute surrender of the liberties of the people and a vigorous exertion, attended, I admit, with considerable hazard, at a time like the present. My view of things is, I own, very gloomy; and I am convinced that, in a very few years, this government will become completely absolute, or that confusion will arise of a nature almost as much to be deprecated as despotism itself.' In the same year, Dr. Raine writes (*Parr's Works*, vol. vii. p. 533): 'The mischievous conduct of men in power has long made this country an uneasy dwelling for the moderate and peaceful man; their present proceedings render our situation alarming, and our prospects dreadful.' See also p. 530. In 1796, the Bishop of Llandaff writes (*Life of Watson*, vol. ii. pp. 36, 37): 'The malady which attacks the constitution (influence of the crown) is without remedy; violent applications might be used; their success would be doubtful, and I, for one, never wish to see them tried.' Compare vol. i. p. 222. And, in 1799, Priestley dreaded a revolution; but, at the same time, thought there was 'no longer any hope of a peaceable and gradual reform.' *Mem. of Priestley*, vol. i. pp. 198, 199.

his place in parliament, in 1795, that if these, and other shameful laws which were proposed, should be actually passed, forcible resistance to the government would be merely a question of prudence; and that the people, if they felt themselves equal to the conflict, would be justified in withstanding the arbitrary measures by which their rulers sought to extinguish their liberties.[320]

Nothing, however, could stop the government in its headlong career. The ministers, secure of a majority in both houses of parliament, were able to carry their measures in defiance of the people, who opposed them by every mode short of actual violence.[321] And as the object of these new laws was, to check the spirit of

---

[320] In this memorable declaration, Fox said, that 'he had a right to hope and expect that these bills, which positively repealed the Bill of Rights, and cut up the whole of the constitution by the roots, by changing our limited monarchy into an absolute despotism, would not be enacted by parliament against the declared sense of a great majority of the people. If, however, ministers were determined, by means of the corrupt influence they possessed in the two houses of parliament, to pass the bills in direct opposition to the declared sense of a great majority of the nation, and they should be put in force with all their rigorous provisions, if his opinion were asked by the people as to their obedience, he should tell them, that it was no longer a question of moral obligation and duty, but of prudence. It would, indeed, be a case of extremity alone which could justify resistance; and the only question would be, whether that resistance was prudent.' *Parl. Hist.* vol. xxxii. p. 383. On this, Windham remarked, and Fox did not deny, that 'the meaning obviously was, that the right hon. gentleman would advise the people, whenever they were strong enough, to resist the execution of the law;' and to this both Sheridan and Grey immediately assented. p. 385–387.

[321] 'Never had there appeared, in the memory of the oldest man, so firm and decided a plurality of adversaries to the ministerial measures, as on this occasion (*i.e.* in 1795): the interest of the public seemed so deeply at stake, that individuals, not only of the decent, but of the most vulgar professions, gave up a considerable portion of their time and occupations in attending the numerous meetings that were called in every part of the kingdom, to the professed intent of counteracting this attempt of the ministry.' *Note in Parl. History*, vol. xxxii. p. 381. It was at this period that Fox made the declaration which I have quoted in the previous note.

inquiry, and prevent reforms, which the progress of society rendered indispensable, there were also brought into play other means subservient to the same end. It is no exaggeration to say, that for some years England was ruled by a system of absolute terror.[392] The ministers of the day, turning a struggle of party into a war of proscription, filled the prisons with their political opponents, and allowed them, when in confinement, to be treated with shameful severity.[393] If a man was known to be a reformer, he was constantly in danger of being arrested; and if he escaped that, he was watched at every turn, and his private letters were opened as they passed through the post-office.[394] In such cases, no scruples were allowed. Even the confidence of domestic life was violated. No opponent of government was safe under his own roof, against the tales of eavesdroppers and the gossip of servants. Discord was introduced into the bosom of families, and schisms caused between parents and their children.[395] Not

---

[392] It was called at the time the 'Reign of Terror;' and so indeed it was for every opponent of government. See *Campbell's Chancellors*, vol. vi. p. 441; *Mem. of Wakefield*, vol. ii. p. 67; and *Trotter's Mem. of Fox*, p. 10.

[393] 'The iniquitous system of secret imprisonment, under which Pitt and Dundas had now filled all the gaols with parliamentary reformers; men who were cast into dungeons without any public accusation, and from whom the habeas-corpus suspension act had taken every hope of redress.' *Cooke's Hist. of Party*, vol. iii. p. 447. On the cruelty with which these political opponents of government were treated when in prison, see *Stephens's Mem. of Tooke*, vol ii. pp. 121, 125, 423; *Parl. Hist.* vol. xxxiv. pp. 112, 113, 126, 129, 170, 515, vol. xxxv. pp. 742, 743; *Cloncurry's Recollections*, pp. 46, 86, 87, 140, 226.

[394] *Life of Currie*, vol. ii. p. 160; *Stephens's Mem. of Tooke*, vol. ii. pp. 118, 119.

[395] In 1793, Roscoe writes: 'Every man is called on to be a spy upon his brother.' *Life of Roscoe*, vol. i. p. 127. Compare Fox's statement (*Parl. Hist.* vol. xxx. p. 21), that what government had done was, 'to erect every man, not merely into an inquisitor, but into a judge, a spy, an informer,—to set father against father, brother against brother; and in this way you expect to maintain the tranquillity of the country.' See also vol. xxx. p. 1529; and a remarkable passage in *Coleridge's Biog. Lit.* (vol. i. p. 192), on the extent of 'secret defamation,' in and after 1793. For further evidence of this horrible state of society, see *Mem. of Holcroft*, vol. ii. pp. 150, 151; *Stephens's Mem. of Horne Tooke*, vol. ii. pp. 115, 116.

only were the most strenuous attempts made to silence the press, but the booksellers were so constantly prosecuted that they did not dare to publish a work if its author were obnoxious to the court.[396] Indeed, whoever opposed the government was proclaimed an enemy to his country.[397] Political associations and public meetings were strictly forbidden. Every popular leader was in personal danger; and every popular assemblage was dispersed, either by threats or by military execution. That hateful machinery, familiar to the worst days of the seventeenth century, was put into motion. Spies were paid; witnesses were suborned; juries were packed.[398] The coffee-houses, the inns, and the clubs, were filled with emissaries of the government, who reported the most hasty expressions of common conversation.[399] If, by these means, no sort

---

[396] There was even considerable difficulty in finding a printer for Tooke's great philological work, *The Diversions of Purley.* See *Stephens's Mem. of Tooke,* vol. ii. pp. 345–348. In 1798, Fox wrote to Cartwright (*Life of Cartwright,* vol. i. p. 248): 'The decision against Wakefield's publisher appears to me decisive against the liberty of the press; and, indeed, after it, one can hardly conceive how any prudent tradesman can venture to publish anything that can, in any way, be disagreeable to the ministers.'

[397] Those who opposed the slave-trade were called jacobins, and 'enemies to the ministers;' and the celebrated Dr. Currie was pronounced to be a jacobin, and an 'enemy to his country,' because he remonstrated against the shameful manner in which the English government, in 1800, allowed the French prisoners to be treated. *Life of Currie,* vol. i. pp. 330, 332; *Life of Wilberforce,* vol. i. pp. 342–344, vol. ii. pp. 18, 133; *Parl. Hist.* vol. xxx. p. 654, vol. xxxi. p. 467, vol. xxxiii. p. 1387, vol. xxxiv. pp. 1119, 1485.

[398] *Life of Cartwright,* vol. i. p. 209; *Hunt's Hist. of Newspapers,* vol. ii. p. 104; *Belsham's Hist.* vol. ix. p. 227; *Adolphus's Hist.* vol. vi. p. 264; *Annual Register for 1795,* pp. 156, 160; *Stephens's Mem. of Tooke,* vol. ii. p. 118; *Life of Currie,* vol. i. p. 172; *Campbell's Chancellors,* vol. vi. p. 316, vol. vii. p. 316; *Life of Wilberforce,* vol. iv. pp. 369, 377; *Parl. Hist.* vol. xxxi. pp. 543, 667, 668, 1067, vol. xxxii. pp. 296, 302, 366, 367, 374, 664, vol. xxxv. pp. 1538, 1540; *Holcroft's Memoirs,* vol. ii. p. 190.

[399] In addition to the passages referred to in the preceding note, compare *Hutton's Life of Himself,* p. 209, with *Campbell's Chancellors,* vol. vi. p. 441, vol. vii. p. 104, and *Adolphus's Hist. of George III.* vol. vi. p. 45. In 1798, Caldwall wrote to Sir

of evidence could be collected, there was another resource, which was unsparingly used. For, the habeas-corpus act being constantly suspended, the crown had the power of imprisoning without inquiry, and without limitation, any person offensive to the ministry, but of whose crime no proof was attempted to be brought.[400]

Such was the way in which, at the end of the eighteenth century, the rulers of England, under pretence of protecting the institutions of the country, oppressed the people, for whose benefit alone those institutions ought to exist. Nor was even this the whole of the injury they actually inflicted. Their attempts to stop the progress of opinions were intimately connected with that monstrous system of foreign policy, by which there has been entailed upon us a debt of unexampled magnitude. To pay the interest of this, and to meet the current expenses of a profuse and reckless administration, taxes were laid upon nearly every product of industry and of nature. In the vast majority of cases, these taxes fell upon the great body of the people,[401] who were thus placed in a position of singular hardship.

James Smith (*Correspondence of Sir J. E. Smith*, vol. ii. p. 143): 'The power of the crown is become irresistible. The new scheme of inquisition into every man's private circumstances is beyond any attempt I have ever heard of under Louis XIV.'

[400] In 1794, Fox said, in his speech on the habeas-corpus suspension bill: 'Every man who talked freely, every man who detested, as he did from his heart, this war, might be, and would be, in the hands and at the mercy of ministers. Living under such a government, and being subject to insurrection, comparing the two evils, he confessed, he thought the evil they were pretending to remedy, was less than the one they were going to inflict by the remedy itself.'

Parl. Hist. vol. xxxi. p. 509. In 1800, Lord Holland stated, in the House of Lords, that, of 'the seven years of the war, the habeas-corpus act had been suspended five; and, of the multitudes who had been imprisoned in virtue of that suspension, few had been brought to trial, and only one convicted.' vol. xxxiv. pp. 1488. See also vol. xxxv. p. 609, 610. On the effect of the suspension of the habeas-corpus act upon literature, see *Life of Currie*, vol. i. p. 506.

[401] See decisive evidence of this, in *Porter's Progress of the Nation*, vol. ii. pp. 283–295; and, on the enormous increase of expense and taxation, see *Pellew's Life of Sidmouth*, vol. i. p. 358, vol. ii. p. 47.

For the upper classes not only refused to the rest of the nation the reforms which were urgently required, but compelled the country to pay for the precautions which, in consequence of the refusal, it was thought necessary to take. Thus it was that the government diminished the liberties of the people, and wasted the fruit of their industry, in order to protect that very people against opinions which the growth of their knowledge had irresistibly forced upon them.

It is not surprising that, in the face of these circumstances, some of the ablest observers should have despaired of the liberties of England, and should have believed that, in the course of a few years, a despotic government would be firmly established. Even we, who, looking at these things half a century after they occurred, are able to take a calmer view, and who moreover possess the advantages of a larger knowledge, and a riper experience, must nevertheless allow that, so far as political events were concerned, the danger was more imminent than at any moment since the reign of Charles I. But what was forgotten then, and what is too often forgotten now, is, that political events form only one of the many parts which compose the history of a great country. In the period we have been considering, the political movement was, no doubt, more threatening than it had been for several generations. On the other hand, the intellectual movement was, as we have seen, highly favourable, and its influence was rapidly spreading. Hence it was that, while the government of the country tended in one direction, the knowledge of the country tended in another; and while political events kept us back, intellectual events urged us forward. In this way, the despotic principles that were enforced were, in some degree, neutralized; and although it was impossible to prevent them from causing great suffering, still the effect of that suffering was to increase the determination of the people to reform a system under which such evils could be inflicted. For while they felt the evils, the knowledge which they had obtained made them see the remedy. They saw that the men who were at the head of affairs

were despotic; but they saw, too, that the system must
be wrong, which could secure to such men such authority. This confirmed their dissatisfaction, and justified
their resolution to effect some fresh arrangement, which
should allow their voices to be heard in the councils of
the state.[401] And that resolution, I need hardly add,
grew stronger and stronger, until it eventually produced
those great legislative reforms which have already
signalized the present century, have given a new tone
to the character of public men, and changed the structure of the English parliament.

It is thus that, in the latter part of the eighteenth
century, the increase and diffusion of knowledge were
in England, directly antagonistic to the political events
which occurred during the same period. The extent
and the nature of that antagonism I have endeavoured
to explain, as clearly as the complexity of the subject,
and the limits of this Introduction, enable me to do.
We have seen that, looking at our country as a whole,
the obvious tendency of affairs was to abridge the
authority of the church, the nobles, and the crown, and
thus give greater play to the power of the people.
Looking, however, at the country, not as a whole, but
looking merely at its political history, we find that the
personal peculiarities of George III., and the circumstances under which he came to the throne, enabled
him to stop the great progress, and eventually cause a
dangerous reaction. Happily for the fortunes of England, those principles of liberty which he and his
supporters wished to destroy, had before his reign
become so powerful, and so widely diffused, that they

---

[401] A careful observer of what was going on late in the eighteenth century, expresses what, early in the nineteenth century, was becoming the conviction of most men of plain, sound understanding, who had no interest in the existing corruption: 'Immoderate taxation, the result of the unnecessary wars of the reign of George III., is the cause of our embarrassments; and that immoderate taxation has been occasioned by the House of Commons being composed of men not interested to protect the property of the people.'—*Nicholls's Recollections*, vol. i. p. 213.

not only resisted this political reaction, but seemed to
gain fresh strength from the contest. That the struggle
was arduous, and at one time extremely critical, it is
impossible to deny. Such, however, is the force of
liberal opinions, when they have once taken root in
the popular mind, that notwithstanding the ordeal to
which they were exposed, and notwithstanding the
punishments inflicted on their advocates, it was found
impossible to stifle them; it was found impossible
even to prevent their increase. Doctrines subversive of every principle of freedom were personally
favoured by the sovereign, openly avowed by the
government, and zealously defended by the most
powerful classes; and laws in accordance with these
doctrines were placed on our statute-book, and enforced
in our courts. All, however, was in vain. In a few
years that generation began to pass away; a better one
succeeded in its place; and the system of tyranny fell
to the ground. And thus it is, that in all countries
which are even tolerably free, every system must fall
if it opposes the march of opinions, and gives
shelter to maxims and institutions repugnant to the
spirit of the age. In this sort of contest, the ultimate
result is never doubtful. For the vigour of an arbitrary government depends merely on a few individuals,
who, whatever their abilities may be, are liable, after
their death, to be replaced by timid and incompetent
successors. But the vigour of public opinion is not
exposed to these casualties; it is unaffected by the laws
of mortality; it does not flourish to-day and decline
to-morrow; and so far from depending on the lives of
individual men, it is governed by large general causes,
which, from their very comprehensiveness, are in short
periods scarcely seen, but on a comparison of long
periods, are found to outweigh all other considerations,
and reduce to insignificance those little stratagems by
which princes and statesmen think to disturb the order
of events, and mould to their will the destinies of a
great and civilized people.

These are broad and general truths, which will
hardly be questioned by any man who, with a competent

knowledge of history, has reflected much on the nature and conditions of modern society. But during the period we have been considering, they were utterly neglected by our political rulers, who not only thought themselves able to check the growth of opinions, but entirely mistook the very end and object of government. In those days, it was believed that government is made for the minority, to whose wishes the majority are bound humbly to submit. It was believed that the power of making laws must always be lodged in the hands of a few privileged classes; that the nation at large has no concern with those laws, except to obey them;[403] and that it is the duty of a wise government to secure the obedience of the people by preventing them from being enlightened by the spread of knowledge.[404] We may surely deem it a remarkable circumstance, that these notions, and the schemes of legislation founded upon them, should, within half a century, have died away so completely, that they are no longer advocated, even by men of the most ordinary abilities. What is still more remarkable is, that this great change should have been effected, not by any external event, nor by a sudden insurrection of the people, but by the unaided action of moral force,—the silent, though overwhelming pressure of public opinion. This has always seemed to me a decisive proof of the natural, and, if I may so say, the healthy march of English civilization. It is a proof of an elasticity, and yet a sobriety of spirit, such as no other nation has ever

---

[403] Bishop Horsley, the great champion of the existing state of things, said in the House of Lords, in 1795, that he 'did not know what the mass of the people in any country had to do with the laws, but to obey them.' *Cooke's Hist. of Party*, vol. iii. p. 435. Compare *Godwin on Population*, p. 669.

[404] Lord Cockburn (*Life of Jeffrey*, 1852, vol. i. pp. 67, 68) says: 'If there was any principle that was reverenced as indisputable by almost the whole adherents of the party in power sixty, or even fifty, or perhaps even forty years ago, it was that the ignorance of the people was necessary for their obedience to the law.' One argument was, 'that to extend instruction, would be to multiply the crime of forgery!' *Porter's Progress of the Nation*, vol. iii. p. 205.

displayed. No other nation could have escaped from such a crisis, except by passing through a revolution, of which the cost might well have exceeded the gain. The truth, however, is, that in England the course of affairs, which I have endeavoured to trace since the sixteenth century, had diffused among the people a knowledge of their own resources, and a skill and independence in the use of them, imperfect, indeed, but still far superior to that possessed by any other of the great European countries. Besides this, other circumstances, which will be hereafter related,[405] had, so early as the eleventh century, begun to affect our national character, and had assisted in imparting to it that sturdy boldness, and, at the same time, those habits of foresight, and of cautious reserve, to which the English mind owes its leading peculiarities. With us, therefore, the love of liberty has been tempered by a spirit of prudence, which has softened its violence, without impairing its strength. It is this which, more than once, has taught our countrymen to bear even considerable oppression rather than run the risk of rising against their oppressors. It has taught them to stay their hands; it has taught them to husband their force until they can use it with irresistible effect. To this great and valuable habit we owe the safety of England late in the eighteenth century. If the people had risen, they would have staked their all; and what the result of that desperate game would have been, no man can say. Happily for them, and for their posterity, they were content to wait yet a little; they were willing to bide their time, and watch the issue of things. Of this noble conduct their descendants reap the reward. After the lapse of a few years, the political crisis began to subside, and the people re-entered on their former rights. For although their rights had been in abeyance, they were not destroyed, simply because the spirit still existed by which they were originally won. Nor can any one doubt that, if those evil days had been prolonged, that same spirit which had animated their

---

[405] See chapters ix. and x., on the history of the protective spirit.

fathers in the reign of Charles I. would have again broken forth, and society have been convulsed by a revolution, the bare idea of which is frightful to contemplate. In the mean time, all this was avoided; and although popular tumults did arise in different parts of the country, and although the measures of government caused a disaffection of the most serious kind,[406] still the people, taken as a whole, remained firm, and patiently reserved their force till a better time, when, for their benefit, a new party was organized in the state, by whom their interests were successfully advocated even within the walls of parliament.

This great and salutary reaction began early in the present century; but the circumstances which accompanied it are so extremely complicated, and have been so little studied, that I cannot pretend in this Introduction to offer even a sketch of them. It is sufficient to say, what must be generally known, that for nearly fifty years the movement has continued with unabated speed. Everything which has been done, has increased the influence of the people. Blow after blow has been directed against those classes which were once the sole depositaries of power. The Reform Bill, the Emancipation of the Catholics, and the Repeal of the Corn-laws, are admitted to be the three greatest political achievements of the present generation. Each of these vast measures has depressed a powerful party. The extension of the suffrage has lessened the influence of hereditary rank, and has broken up that great oligarchy of landowners, by which the House of Commons had long been ruled. The abolition of Protection has still further enfeebled the territorial aristocracy; while those superstitious feelings by which the ecclesiastical order is mainly upheld, received a severe shock, first by the repeal of the Test and Corporation Acts, and afterwards by the admission of Catholics into the

---

[406] Sir A. Alison notices in his *History*, (vol. iv. p. 213) ' how widely the spirit of discontent was diffused in 1796; and the only wonder is, that the people were able to keep it in bounds. That, however, is a question which writers of his stamp never consider.

legislature; steps which are with reason regarded as supplying precedents of mischievous import for the interests of the Established Church.[407] These measures, and others which are now obviously inevitable, have taken, and will continue to take, power from particular sections of society, in order to confer it upon the people at large. Indeed, the rapid progress of democratic opinions is a fact which no one in the present day ventures to deny. Timid and ignorant men are alarmed at the movement; but that there is such a movement is notorious to all the world. No one now dares to talk of bridling the people, or of resisting their united wishes. The utmost that is said is, that efforts should be made to inform them as to their real interests, and enlighten public opinion; but every one allows that, so soon as public opinion is formed, it can no longer be withstood. On this point all are agreed; and this new power, which is gradually superseding every other, is now obeyed by those very statesmen who, had they lived sixty years ago, would have been the first to deny its authority, ridicule its pretensions, and, if possible, extinguish its liberty.

Such is the great gap which separates the public men of our time from those who flourished under that bad system which George III. sought to perpetuate. And it is evident, that this vast progress was brought about rather by destroying the system, than by improving the men. It is also evident, that the system

---

[407] Bishop Burgess, in a letter to Lord Melbourne, bitterly complained that Catholic emancipation was 'the extinction of the purely Protestant character of the British legislature.' *Harford's Life of Burgess*, p. 506: see also pp. 238, 239, 369, 370. There can be no doubt that the bishop rightly estimated the danger to his own party; and as to the Corporation and Test Acts, which, says another bishop (*Tomline's Life of Pitt*, vol. ii. p. 604), 'were justly regarded as the firmest bulwarks of the British constitution,' the feeling was so strong, that at an episcopal meeting in 1787, there were only two members who were willing to repeal these persecuting laws. See *Bishop Watson's Life of Himself*, vol. i. p. 262. Lord Eldon, who to the last stood up for the church, pronounced the bill for repealing these acts to be a 'revolutionary bill.' *Twiss's Life of Eldon*, vol. ii. p. 202.

perished because it was unsuited to the age; in other words, because a progressive people will never tolerate an unprogressive government. But it is a mere matter of history, that our legislators, even to the last moment, were so terrified by the idea of innovation, that they refused every reform until the voice of the people rose high enough to awe them into submission, and forced them to grant what, without such pressure, they would by no means have conceded.

These things ought to serve as a lesson to our political rulers. They ought also to moderate the presumption of legislators, and teach them that their best measures are but temporary expedients, which it will be the business of a later and riper age to efface. It would be well if such considerations were to check the confidence, and silence the loquacity, of those superficial men, who, raised to temporary power, think themselves bound to guarantee certain institutions, and uphold certain opinions. They ought clearly to understand, that it does not lie within their function thus to anticipate the march of affairs, and provide for distant contingencies. In trifling matters, indeed, this may be done without danger; though, as the constant changes in the laws of every country abundantly prove, it is also done without benefit. But in reference to those large and fundamental measures which bear upon the destiny of a people, such anticipation is worse than useless,— it is highly injurious. In the present state of knowledge, politics, so far from being a science, is one of the most backward of all the arts; and the only safe course for the legislator is, to look upon his craft as consisting in the adaptation of temporary contrivances to temporary emergencies.[406] His business is to follow the

---

[406] Sir C. Lewis, though in his learned work he over-estimates the resources possessed by politicians, does nevertheless allow that they are rarely able to anticipate the manner in which their measures will work. *Lewis on the Methods of Observation and Reasoning in Politics*, 1852, vol. ii. pp. 360–362. A writer of repute, M. Flassan, says (*Hist. de la Diplomatie*, vol. i. p. 19): 'On doit être très-indulgent sur les erreurs de la politique, à cause de la facilité qu'il y a à en commettre, erreurs auxquelles la

age, and not at all to attempt to lead it. He should be satisfied with studying what is passing around him; and should modify his schemes, not according to the notions he has inherited from his fathers, but according to the actual exigencies of his own time. For he may rely upon it, that the movements of society have now become so rapid, that the wants of one generation are no measure of the wants of another; and that men, urged by a sense of their own progress, are growing weary of idle talk about the wisdom of their ancestors, and are fast discarding those trite and sleepy maxims which have hitherto imposed upon them, but by which they will not consent to be much longer troubled.

---

sagesse même quelquefois entraîne.' The first part of this sentence is true enough; but it conveys a truth which ought to repress that love of interfering with the natural march of affairs which still characterises politicians, even in the freest countries.

END OF THE FIRST VOLUME.

LONDON: PRINTED BY
SPOTTISWOODE AND CO., NEW-STREET SQUARE
AND PARLIAMENT STREET

HENRY THOMAS BUCKLE'S LITERARY REMAINS.

Just published, in THREE VOLUMES, 8vo. price 52s. 6d.

MISCELLANEOUS
AND
POSTHUMOUS WORKS

OF THE LATE

HENRY THOMAS BUCKLE.

Edited, with a Biographical Notice, by HELEN TAYLOR.

Mr. BUCKLE's great work on the History of Civilization in England is a colossal fragment; but it is obvious that even thus much of a vast design could not have been achieved if the Author had not brought together an immense store of materials for his work generally. He was, it is well known, an insatiable reader, and his method was equal to his industry. Throughout the wide range of subjects which came under his hand, it had been, from his earlier years, his constant practice to transcribe from the authors whose works he read all passages which appeared to be either important in themselves, or likely in any way to bear upon his own task, interweaving with them his own remarks, and adding such references as his reading and his memory suggested to him. So abundant are these references that a very large proportion of the articles in his Common Place Books may be regarded as a key to the whole literature on the topic in question. But, not content with making such extracts, annotations, and references, he was in the habit of throwing into rough form for his great work such portions of the subject as were forced prominently on his attention; and thus he had ready to his hand many blocks or masses of stone to be worked into the great fabric which he was raising. These blocks are but rough hewn, and would probably have assumed forms more or less different had he lived to carry out his design further; but it has been thought that, for historical students, there is probably not one which would be altogether devoid of interest, while in many cases the interest may be even increased by the fragmentary form which shows the working of the author's mind, and the growth of his mature convictions. It seemed, therefore, to be a matter of question whether any attempt should be made to present in a more connected order that which Mr. BUCKLE had been compelled to leave unfinished; and the Editor determined accordingly that the last work which the world would receive from his pen should appear precisely as he had left it.

Of the three volumes containing these Remains, the first comprises his Miscellaneous Works published during his lifetime, and his Fragments. The former, consisting of a Paper on the Influence of Women on the Progress of Knowledge, a Letter on POOLEY's Case, and a Review of Mr. MILL's Work on Liberty, may now have a greater interest than they had when first published, as throwing light on the deepest and strongest beliefs of the Author on subjects of universal and paramount importance. The Fragments consist of some passages on the reign of Queen Elizabeth, published in Fraser's Magazine, about five years after the Author's death; while among the rest, now for the first time published, will be found papers on matters his treatment of which is likely to be especially characteristic—as, for instance, on the Spanish and the Scotch, on the Triumph of Intellectual over Physical Laws, on the History of Witchcraft, on the Influence of the Clergy upon Civilization, and of German Literature on the Literature of this country. With these will be found papers on those real or supposed changes or developments in society on which he was disposed to form his estimate of the present, and to build his hopes for the future.

The contents of his Common Place Books, contained in the second and third volumes, it would be absolutely impossible to classify in the space of a few paragraphs. It may be enough to say that the reader will here find the quarries among which the Author patiently worked with a systematic exactness which left no room for confusion. These Articles have been printed precisely as they were left by the Author, a few only having been omitted on account of the subjects of which they treated. The numbering has, however, been carried on as in the original, chiefly because the Index to the Common Place Books was made by the Author himself, and has been printed *verbatim*, and therefore contains references to the omitted articles; partly because these articles are referred to by numbers in other places; and also because it was thought right that they who care to do so may see where omissions have occurred.

A large proportion of the Common Place Books, even when substantially extracted from other writers, is in Mr. BUCKLE's own words, especially towards the latter part. On this account it has been thought best to make as few alterations as possible in them as they originally stood, although the reader may observe many mistakes which the Author would probably have corrected had he himself given the books to the press. But they have been left unaltered, because some statements which may appear mistakes to the editor or reader might have proved to be deliberate opinions of the writer, which he might have been able to substantiate; while the alteration or omission of others about which there seems no room for doubt, would have diminished the autobiographical value of the Remains—a great part of their value to the general reader.

But generally, it may be said that so much of the Common Place Books is original while so much of the Fragments consists of little more than abstracts of books, that the difference of character between the two is not very great. The Fragments are necessarily disjointed; but it was felt that even to alter the words in which they are thrown together would often have involved a risk of substantially misrepresenting the Author's ideas. The originality of his mind was shewn in a great degree in the arrangement of his materials; and it would be both rash and presumptuous for anyone else to disturb the order in which he has placed even the most apparently disconnected facts. This order may be in many cases accidental, but it also may be the result of some of the writer's most characteristic powers, destined, had he lived, to throw new light on the relations of history. To disturb it, therefore, might be unfair not only to Mr. BUCKLE, but to the studious among his readers, to whom the apparently accidental order of some of the great heap of facts and ideas here thrown together may be like a flash of light, and may lead the way to new combinations. To have meddled with this order might have been to destroy their chief value to kindred minds.

In the BIOGRAPHICAL MEMOIR prefixed to these volumes the Editor has endeavoured to exhibit the man as he appeared among those who knew him intimately, and the conditions which determined the direction of his work. His life was uneventful; but on the few among whom he lived he left an impression not to be effaced; and for those who are familiar with his writings this sketch, slight though it be, of his mental and moral growth, must, it is thought, have a permanent interest.

London: LONGMANS, GREEN, and CO. Paternoster Row.

JANUARY 1877.

GENERAL LIST OF WORKS

PUBLISHED BY

Messrs. LONGMANS, GREEN, AND CO.

PATERNOSTER ROW, LONDON.

History, Politics, Historical Memoirs, &c.

The **HISTORY of ENGLAND** from the Accession of James the Second. By Lord MACAULAY.
    STUDENT'S EDITION, 2 vols. crown 8vo. 12s.
    PEOPLE'S EDITION, 4 vols. crown 8vo. 16s.
    CABINET EDITION, 8 vols. post 8vo. 48s.
    LIBRARY EDITION, 5 vols. 8vo. £4.

LORD MACAULAY'S WORKS. Complete and Uniform Library Edition. Edited by his Sister, Lady TREVELYAN. 8 vols. 8vo. with Portrait price £5. 5s. cloth, or £8. 8s. bound in tree-calf by Rivière.

The **HISTORY of ENGLAND** from the Fall of Wolsey to the Defeat of the Spanish Armada. By JAMES ANTHONY FROUDE, M.A. late Fellow of Exeter College, Oxford.
    LIBRARY EDITION, Twelve Volumes, 8vo. price £8. 18s.
    CABINET EDITION, Twelve Volumes, crown 8vo. price 72s.

The **ENGLISH in IRELAND** in the **EIGHTEENTH CENTURY.** By JAMES ANTHONY FROUDE, M.A. late Fellow of Exeter College, Oxford. 3 vols. 8vo. price 48s.

JOURNAL of the **REIGNS** of **KING GEORGE IV.** and **KING WILLIAM IV.** By the late CHARLES C. F. GREVILLE, Esq. Edited by HENRY REEVE, Esq. Fifth Edition. 3 vols. 8vo. 36s.

RECOLLECTIONS and SUGGESTIONS, 1813-1873. By JOHN Earl RUSSELL, K.G. New Edition, revised and enlarged. 8vo. 16s.

On **PARLIAMENTARY GOVERNMENT** in **ENGLAND**; its Origin, Development, and Practical Operation. By ALPHEUS TODD, Librarian of the Legislative Assembly of Canada. 2 vols. 8vo. price £1. 17s.

The **CONSTITUTIONAL HISTORY** of **ENGLAND**, since the Accession of George III. 1760—1860. By Sir THOMAS ERSKINE MAY, K.C.B. D.C.L. The Fifth Edition, thoroughly revised. 3 vols. crown 8vo. price 18s.

DEMOCRACY in **EUROPE**; a History. By Sir THOMAS ERSKINE MAY, K.C.B. D.C.L. 2 vols. 8vo. [*In the press.*]

The **NEW REFORMATION,** a Narrative of the Old Catholic Movement, from 1870 to the Present Time; with an Historical Introduction. By THEODORUS. 8vo. price 12s.

A

NEW WORKS PUBLISHED BY LONGMANS AND CO.

The **OXFORD REFORMERS** — John Colet, Erasmus, and Thomas More; being a History of their Fellow-work. By FREDERIC SEEBOHM. Second Edition, enlarged. 8vo. 14s.

LECTURES on the **HISTORY of ENGLAND**, from the Earliest Times to the Death of King Edward II. By WILLIAM LONGMAN, F.S.A. With Maps and Illustrations. 8vo. 15s.

The **HISTORY** of the **LIFE** and **TIMES** of **EDWARD** the **THIRD**. By WILLIAM LONGMAN, F.S.A. With 9 Maps, 8 Plates, and 16 Woodcuts. 2 vols. 8vo. 28s.

INTRODUCTORY LECTURES on **MODERN HISTORY**. Delivered in Lent Term, 1842; with the Inaugural Lecture delivered in December 1841. By the Rev. THOMAS ARNOLD, D.D. 8vo. price 7s. 6d.

WATERLOO LECTURES; a Study of the Campaign of 1815. By Colonel CHARLES C. CHESNEY, R.E. Third Edition. 8vo. with Map, 10s. 6d.

HISTORY of ENGLAND under the **DUKE of BUCKINGHAM** and **CHARLES** the **FIRST**, 1624-1628. By SAMUEL RAWSON GARDINER, late Student of Ch. Ch. 2 vols. 8vo. with two Maps, price 24s.

The **SIXTH ORIENTAL MONARCHY**; or, the Geography, History, and Antiquities of PARTHIA. By GEORGE RAWLINSON, M.A. Professor of Ancient History in the University of Oxford. Maps and Illustrations. 8vo. 16s.

The **SEVENTH GREAT ORIENTAL MONARCHY**; or, a History of the SASSANIANS: with Notices, Geographical and Antiquarian. By G. RAWLINSON, M.A. Map and numerous Illustrations. 8vo. price 28s.

A **HISTORY of GREECE**. By the Rev. GEORGE W. COX, M.A. late Scholar of Trinity College, Oxford. VOLS. I. & II. (to the Close of the Peloponnesian War). 8vo. with Maps and Plans, 36s.

GENERAL HISTORY of GREECE to the Death of Alexander the Great; with a Sketch of the Subsequent History to the Present Time. By the Rev. GEORGE W. COX, M.A. With 11 Maps. Crown 8vo. 7s. 6d.

The **GREEKS** and the **PERSIANS**. By the Rev. GEORGE W. COX, M.A. (*Epochs of Ancient History, I.*) With 4 Coloured Maps. Fcp. 8vo. price 2s. 6d.

The **TALE** of the **GREAT PERSIAN WAR**, from the Histories of Herodotus. By GEORGE W. COX, M.A. New Edition. Fcp. 3s. 6d.

The **HISTORY of ROME**. By WILLIAM IHNE. VOLS. I. and II. 8vo. price 30s. The Third Volume is in the press.

GENERAL HISTORY OF ROME from the Foundation of the City to the Fall of Augustulus, B.C. 753—A.D. 476. By the Very Rev. C. MERIVALE, D.D. Dean of Ely. With Five Maps. Crown 8vo. 7s. 6d.

HISTORY of the ROMANS under the EMPIRE. By the Very Rev. C. MERIVALE, D.D. Dean of Ely. 8 vols. post 8vo. 48s.

The **FALL of the ROMAN REPUBLIC**; a Short History of the Last Century of the Commonwealth. By the same Author. 12mo. 7s. 6d.

The **STUDENT'S MANUAL** of the **HISTORY** of **INDIA**, from the Earliest Period to the Present. By Colonel MEADOWS TAYLOR, M.R.A.S. M.R.I.A. Second Thousand. Crown 8vo. with Maps, 7s. 6d.

The **HISTORY of INDIA**, from the Earliest Period to the close of Lord Dalhousie's Administration. By J. C. MARSHMAN. 3 vols. crown 8vo. 22s. 6d.

The **NATIVE STATES** of **INDIA** in **SUBSIDIARY ALLIANCE** with the BRITISH GOVERNMENT; an Historical Sketch. By Colonel G. B. MALLESON, C.S.I. With 6 Coloured Maps. 8vo. 15s.

INDIAN POLITY; a View of the System of Administration in India. By Lieutenant-Colonel GEORGE CHESNEY, Fellow of the University of Calcutta. New Edition, revised; with Map. 8vo. price 21s.

The **BRITISH ARMY** in **1875**; with Suggestions on its Administration and Organisation. By JOHN HOLMS, M.P. New and Enlarged Edition, with 4 Diagrams. Crown 8vo. price 4s. 6d.

The **HISTORY** of **PRUSSIA**, from the Earliest Times to the Present Day; tracing the Origin and Development of her Military Organisation. By Captain W. J. WYATT. Vols. I. and II. A.D. 700 to A.D. 1525. 8vo. 36s.

POPULAR HISTORY of **FRANCE**, from the Earliest Times to the Death of Louis XIV. By ELIZABETH M. SEWELL, Author of 'Amy Herbert' &c. With 8 Coloured Maps. Crown 6vo. 7s. 6d.

STUDIES from **GENOESE HISTORY**. By Colonel G. B. MALLESON, C.S.I. Guardian to His Highness the Maharájá of Mysore. Crown 8vo. 10s. 6d.

LORD MACAULAY'S CRITICAL and **HISTORICAL ESSAYS**. CHEAP EDITION, authorised and complete. Crown 8vo. 3s. 6d.

CABINET EDITION, 4 vols. post 8vo. 24s. | LIBRARY EDITION, 3 vols. 8vo. 36s.
PEOPLE'S EDITION, 2 vols. crown 8vo. 8s. | STUDENT'S EDITION, 1 vol. cr. 8vo. 6s.

HISTORY of **EUROPEAN MORALS**, from Augustus to Charlemagne By W. E. H. LECKY, M.A. Second Edition. 2 vols. 8vo. price 28s.

HISTORY of the **RISE** and **INFLUENCE** of the **SPIRIT** of **RATIONALISM** in **EUROPE**. By W. E. H. LECKY, M.A. Cabinet Edition, being the Fourth. 2 vols. crown 8vo. price 16s.

The **HISTORY** of **PHILOSOPHY**, from Thales to Comte. By GEORGE HENRY LEWES. Fourth Edition. 2 vols. 8vo. 32s.

The **HISTORY** of the **PELOPONNESIAN WAR**. By THUCYDIDES. Translated by R. CRAWLEY, Fellow of Worcester College, Oxford. 8vo. 10s. 6d.

The **MYTHOLOGY** of the **ARYAN NATIONS**. By GEORGE W. COX, M.A. late Scholar of Trinity College, Oxford, 2 vols. 8vo. 28s.

TALES of **ANCIENT GREECE**. By GEORGE W. COX, M.A. late Scholar of Trin. Coll. Oxon. Crown 8vo. price 6s. 6d.

HISTORY of **CIVILISATION** in England and France, Spain and Scotland. By HENRY THOMAS BUCKLE. New Edition of the entire Work, with a complete INDEX. 3 vols. crown 8vo. 24s.

SKETCH of the **HISTORY** of the **CHURCH** of **ENGLAND** to the Revolution of 1688. By the Right Rev. T. V. SHORT, D.D. Lord Bishop of St. Asaph. Eighth Edition. Crown 8vo. 7s. 6d.

MAUNDER'S HISTORICAL TREASURY; General Introductory Outlines of Universal History, and a series of Separate Histories. Latest Edition, revised by the Rev. G. W. COX, M.A. Fcp. 8vo. 6s. cloth, or 10s. 6d. calf.

CATES' and WOODWARD'S ENCYCLOPÆDIA of CHRONOLOGY, HISTORICAL and BIOGRAPHICAL. 8vo. price 42s.

The **ERA** of the **PROTESTANT REVOLUTION**. By F. SEEBOHM. With 4 Coloured Maps and 12 Diagrams on Wood. Fcp. 8vo. 2s. 6d.

The **CRUSADES.** By the Rev. G. W. Cox, M.A. late Scholar of Trinity College, Oxford. With Coloured Map. Fcp. 8vo. 2s. 6d.

The **THIRTY YEARS' WAR, 1618-1648.** By Samuel Rawson Gardiner, late Student of Christ Church. With Coloured Map. Fcp. 8vo. 2s. 6d.

The **HOUSES of LANCASTER and YORK**; with the Conquest and Loss of France. By James Gairdner, of the Public Record Office. With Five Coloured Maps. Fcp. 8vo. 2s. 6d.

EDWARD the THIRD. By the Rev. W. Warburton, M.A. late Fellow of All Souls College, Oxford. With 3 Coloured Maps and 5 Genealogical Tables. Fcp. 8vo. 2s. 6d.

The **AGE of ELIZABETH.** By the Rev. M. Creighton, M.A. late Fellow and Tutor of Merton College, Oxford. With 5 Maps and 4 Genealogical Tables. Fcp. 8vo. 2s. 6d.

The **FALL of the STUARTS**; and Western Europe from 1678 to 1697. By the Rev. E. Hale, M.A. Assistant-Master, Eton. With 11 Maps and Plans. Fcp. 8vo. 2s. 6d.

The **FIRST TWO STUARTS and the PURITAN REVOLUTION,** 1603-1660. By Samuel Rawson Gardiner, late Student of Christ Church. With 4 Coloured Maps. Fcp. 8vo. 2s. 6d.

The **WAR of AMERICAN INDEPENDENCE, 1775-1783.** By John Malcolm Ludlow, Barrister-at-Law. With 4 Coloured Maps. Fcp. 8vo. 2s. 6d.

REALITIES of IRISH LIFE. By W. Stuart Trench, late Land Agent in Ireland to the Marquess of Lansdowne, the Marquess of Bath, and Lord Digby. Cheaper Edition. Crown 8vo. price 2s. 6d.

Biographical Works.

The **LIFE and LETTERS of LORD MACAULAY.** By his Nephew, G. Otto Trevelyan, M.P. 2 vols. 8vo. with Portrait, price 36s.

The **LIFE of SIR WILLIAM FAIRBAIRN,** Bart. F.R.S. Corresponding Member of the National Institute of France, &c. Partly written by himself; edited and completed by William Pole, F.R.S. 8vo. Portrait. 18s.

ARTHUR SCHOPENHAUER, his LIFE and his PHILOSOPHY. By Helen Zimmern. Post 8vo. with Portrait, 7s. 6d.

MEMOIRS of BARON STOCKMAR. By his Son, Baron E. Von Stockmar. Translated from the German by G. A. M. Edited by F. Max Müller, M.A. 2 vols. crown 8vo. 21s.

AUTOBIOGRAPHY. By John Stuart Mill. 8vo. price 7s. 6d.

The **LIFE of NAPOLEON III.** derived from State Records, Unpublished Family Correspondence, and Personal Testimony. By Blanchard Jerrold. 4 vols. 8vo. with numerous Portraits and Facsimiles. Vols. I. and II. price 18s. each. The Third Volume is in the press.

LIFE and LETTERS of Sir GILBERT ELLIOT, First EARL of MINTO. Edited by the Countess of Minto. 3 vols. 8vo. 31s. 6d.

ESSAYS in MODERN MILITARY BIOGRAPHY. By Charles Cornwallis Chesney, Lieutenant-Colonel in the Royal Engineers. 8vo. 12s. 6d.

The **MEMOIRS of SIR JOHN RERESBY,** of Thrybergh, Bart. M.P. for York, &c. 1634-1689. Written by Himself. Edited from the Original Manuscript by James J. Cartwright, M.A. 8vo. price 21s.

ISAAC CASAUBON, 1559-1614. By MARK PATTISON, Rector of
Lincoln College, Oxford. 8vo. 18s.

LORD GEORGE BENTINCK; a Political Biography. By the Right
Hon. BENJAMIN DISRAELI, M.P. Crown 8vo. price 6s.

LEADERS of PUBLIC OPINION in IRELAND; Swift, Flood,
Grattan, and O'Connell. By W. E. H. LECKY, M.A. New Edition, revised and
enlarged. Crown 8vo. price 7s. 6d.

DICTIONARY of GENERAL BIOGRAPHY; containing Concise
Memoirs and Notices of the most Eminent Persons of all Countries, from the
Earliest Ages. By W. L. R. CATES. New Edition, extended in a Supplement
to the Year 1876. Medium 8vo. price 25s.

LIFE of the DUKE of WELLINGTON. By the Rev. G. R. GLEIG,
M.A. Popular Edition, carefully revised; with copious Additions. Crown 8vo.
with Portrait, 5s.

MEMOIRS of SIR HENRY HAVELOCK, K.C.B. By JOHN CLARK
MARSHMAN. Cabinet Edition, with Portrait. Crown 8vo. price 3s. 6d.

VICISSITUDES of FAMILIES. By Sir J. BERNARD BURKE, C.B.
Ulster King of Arms. New Edition, enlarged. 2 vols. crown 8vo. 21s.

The RISE of GREAT FAMILIES, other Essays and Stories. By Sir
J. BERNARD BURKE, C.B. Ulster King of Arms. Crown 8vo. price 12s. 6d.

ESSAYS in ECCLESIASTICAL BIOGRAPHY. By the Right Hon.
Sir J. STEPHEN, LL.D. Cabinet Edition. Crown 8vo. 7s. 6d.

MAUNDER'S BIOGRAPHICAL TREASURY. Latest Edition, re-
constructed, thoroughly revised, and in great part rewritten; with 1,500 additional Memoirs and Notices, by W. L. R. CATES. Fcp. 8vo. 6s. cloth; 10s. 6d. calf.

LETTERS and LIFE of FRANCIS BACON, including all his Occasional Works. Collected and edited, with a Commentary, by J. SPEDDING,
Trin. Coll. Cantab. Complete in 7 vols. 8vo. £4. 4s.

The LIFE, WORKS, and OPINIONS of HEINRICH HEINE. By
WILLIAM STIGAND. 2 vols. 8vo. with Portrait of Heine, price 28s.

BIOGRAPHICAL and CRITICAL ESSAYS, reprinted from Reviews,
with Additions and Corrections. Second Edition of the Second Series. By A.
HAYWARD, Q.C. 2 vols. 8vo. price 28s. THIRD SERIES, in 1 vol. 8vo. price 14s.

Criticism, Philosophy, Polity, &c.

The LAW of NATIONS considered as INDEPENDENT POLITICAL
COMMUNITIES; the Rights and Duties of Nations in Time of War. By
Sir TRAVERS TWISS, D.C.L., F.R.S. New Edition, revised; with an Intro-
ductory Juridical Review of the Results of Recent Wars, and an Appendix of
Treaties and other Documents. 8vo. 21s.

CHURCH and STATE: their relations Historically Developed. By
T. HEINRICH GEFFCKEN, Professor of International Law at the University of
Strasburg. Translated from the German by E. FAIRFAX TAYLOR. 2 vols. 8vo. 42s.

A SYSTEMATIC VIEW of the SCIENCE of JURISPRUDENCE.
By SHELDON AMOS, M.A. Professor of Jurisprudence to the Inns of Court,
London. 8vo. price 18s.

A PRIMER of the ENGLISH CONSTITUTION and GOVERNMENT.
By SHELDON AMOS, M.A. Professor of Jurisprudence to the Inns of Court.
Second Edition, revised. Crown 8vo. 6s.

OUTLINES of CIVIL PROCEDURE. Being a General View of the Supreme Court of Judicature and of the whole Practice in the Common Law and Chancery Divisions under all the Statutes now in force. By EDWARD STANLEY ROSCOE, Barrister-at-Law. 12mo. price 3s. 6d.

The INSTITUTES of JUSTINIAN; with English Introduction, Translation and Notes. By T. C. SANDARS, M.A. Sixth Edition. 8vo. 18s.

SOCRATES and the SOCRATIC SCHOOLS. Translated from the German of Dr. E. ZELLER, with the Author's approval, by the Rev. OSWALD J. REICHEL, M.A. Crown 8vo. 8s. 6d.

The STOICS, EPICUREANS, and SCEPTICS. Translated from the German of Dr. E. ZELLER, with the Author's approval, by OSWALD J. REICHEL, M.A. Crown 8vo. price 14s.

PLATO and the OLDER ACADEMY. Translated from the German of Dr. EDUARD ZELLER by S. FRANCES ALLEYNE and ALFRED GOODWIN, B.A. Fellow of Balliol College, Oxford. Crown 8vo. 18s.

The ETHICS of ARISTOTLE, with Essays and Notes. By Sir A. GRANT, Bart. M.A. LL.D. Third Edition. 2 vols. 8vo. 32s.

The POLITICS of ARISTOTLE; Greek Text, with English Notes. By RICHARD CONGREVE, M.A. New Edition, revised. 8vo. 18s.

The NICOMACHEAN ETHICS of ARISTOTLE newly translated into English. By R. WILLIAMS, B.A. Fellow and late Lecturer of Merton College, and sometime Student of Christ Church, Oxford. New Edition. 8vo. 7s. 6d.

PICTURE LOGIC; an Attempt to Popularise the Science of Reasoning by the combination of Humorous Pictures with Examples of Reasoning taken from Daily Life. By A. SWINBOURNE, B.A. With Woodcut Illustrations from Drawings by the Author. Second Edition. Fcp. 8vo. price 5s.

ELEMENTS of LOGIC. By R. WHATELY, D.D. late Archbishop of Dublin. New Edition. 8vo. 10s. 6d. crown 8vo. 4s. 6d.

Elements of Rhetoric. By the same Author. New Edition. 8vo. 10s. 6d. crown 8vo. 4s. 6d.

English Synonymes. By E. JANE WHATELY. Edited by Archbishop WHATELY. Fifth Edition. Fcp. 8vo. price 3s.

On the INFLUENCE of AUTHORITY in MATTERS of OPINION. By the late Sir GEORGE CORNEWALL LEWIS, Bart. New Edition. 8vo. 14s.

COMTE'S SYSTEM of POSITIVE POLITY, or TREATISE upon SOCIOLOGY. Translated from the Paris Edition of 1851-1854, and furnished with Analytical Tables of Contents. In Four Volumes, 8vo. each forming in some degree an independent Treatise:—

Vol. I. General View of Positivism and its Introductory Principles. Translated by J. H. BRIDGES, M.B. Price 21s.

Vol. II. Social Statics, or the Abstract Laws of Human Order. Translated by F. HARRISON, M.A. Price 14s.

Vol. III. Social Dynamics, or the General Laws of Human Progress (the Philosophy of History). Translated by Professor E. S. BEESLY, M.A. 8vo. 21s.

Vol. IV. Synthesis of the Future of Mankind. Translated by R. CONGREVE, M.D.; and an Appendix, containing the Author's Minor Treatises, translated by H. D. Hutton, M.A. *[In the press.*

DEMOCRACY in AMERICA. By ALEXIS DE TOCQUEVILLE. Translated by HENRY REEVE, Esq. New Edition. 2 vols. crown 8vo. 16s.

ORDER and PROGRESS: Part I. Thoughts on Government; Part II. Studies of Political Crises. By FREDERIC HARRISON, M.A. of Lincoln's Inn. 8vo. price 14s.

BACON'S ESSAYS with ANNOTATIONS. By R. WHATELY, D.D. late Archbishop of Dublin. New Edition, 8vo. price 10s. 6d.

LORD BACON'S WORKS, collected and edited by J. SPEDDING, M.A. R. L. ELLIS, M.A. and D. D. HEATH. 7 vols. 8vo. price £3. 13s. 6d.

On REPRESENTATIVE GOVERNMENT. By JOHN STUART MILL. Crown 8vo. price 2s.

On LIBERTY. By JOHN STUART MILL. New Edition. Post 8vo. 7s. 6d. Crown 8vo. price 1s. 4d.

PRINCIPLES of POLITICAL ECONOMY. By JOHN STUART MILL. Seventh Edition. 2 vols. 8vo. 30s. Or in 1 vol. crown 8vo. price 5s.

ESSAYS on SOME UNSETTLED QUESTIONS of POLITICAL ECONOMY. By JOHN STUART MILL. Second Edition. 8vo. 6s. 6d.

UTILITARIANISM. By JOHN STUART MILL. New Edition. 8vo. 5s

DISSERTATIONS and DISCUSSIONS: Political, Philosophical, and Historical. By JOHN STUART MILL. New Editions. 4 vols. 8vo. price £2. 6s. 6d.

EXAMINATION of Sir W. HAMILTON'S PHILOSOPHY, and of the Principal Philosophical Questions discussed in his Writings. By JOHN STUART MILL. Fourth Edition. 8vo. 16s.

An OUTLINE of the NECESSARY LAWS of THOUGHT; a Treatise on Pure and Applied Logic. By the Most Rev. W. THOMSON, Lord Archbishop of York, D.D. F.R.S. New Edition. Crown 8vo. price 6s.

PRINCIPLES of ECONOMICAL PHILOSOPHY. By HENRY DUNNING MACLEOD, M.A. Barrister-at-Law. Second Edition. In Two Volumes. VOL. I. 8vo. price 15s. VOL. II. PART I. price 12s. VOL. II. PART II. just ready.

A SYSTEM of LOGIC, RATIOCINATIVE and INDUCTIVE. By JOHN STUART MILL. Ninth Edition. Two vols. 8vo. 25s.

SPEECHES of the RIGHT HON. LORD MACAULAY, corrected by Himself. People's Edition, crown 8vo. 3s. 6d.

The ORATION of DEMOSTHENES on the CROWN. Translated by the Right Hon. Sir R. P. COLLIER. Crown 8vo. price 5s.

FAMILIES of SPEECH: Four Lectures delivered before the Royal Institution of Great Britain. By the Rev. F. W. FARRAR, D.D. F.R.S. New Edition. Crown 8vo. 5s. 6d.

CHAPTERS on LANGUAGE. By the Rev. F. W. FARRAR, D.D. F.R.S. New Edition. Crown 8vo. 5s.

HANDBOOK of the ENGLISH LANGUAGE. For the use of Students of the Universities and the Higher Classes in Schools. By R. G. LATHAM, M.A. M.D. The Ninth Edition. Crown 8vo. price 6s.

DICTIONARY of the ENGLISH LANGUAGE. By R. G. LATHAM, M.A. M.D. Abridged from Dr. Latham's Edition of Johnson's English Dictionary, and condensed into One Volume. Medium 8vo. price 24s.

A DICTIONARY of the ENGLISH LANGUAGE. By R. G. LATHAM, M.A. M.D. Founded on the Dictionary of Dr. SAMUEL JOHNSON, as edited by the Rev. H. J. TODD, with numerous Emendations and Additions. In Four Volumes, 4to. price £7.

THESAURUS of ENGLISH WORDS and PHRASES, classified and arranged so as to facilitate the Expression of Ideas, and assist in Literary Composition. By P. M. ROGET, M.D. New Edition. Crown 8vo. 10s. 6d.

LECTURES on the SCIENCE of LANGUAGE. By F. MAX MÜLLER, M.A. &c. The Eighth Edition. 2 vols. crown 8vo. 16s.

MANUAL of ENGLISH LITERATURE, Historical and Critical. By THOMAS ARNOLD, M.A. New Edition. Crown 8vo. 7s. 6d.

SOUTHEY'S DOCTOR, complete in One Volume. Edited by the Rev. J. W. WARTER, B.D. Square crown 8vo. 12s. 6d.

HISTORICAL and CRITICAL COMMENTARY on the OLD TESTAMENT; with a New Translation. By M. M. KALISCH, Ph.D. VOL. I. Genesis, 8vo. 18s. or adapted for the General Reader, 12s. VOL. II. Exodus, 15s. or adapted for the General Reader, 12s. VOL. III. Leviticus, PART I. 15s. or adapted for the General Reader, 8s. VOL. IV. Leviticus, PART II. 15s. or adapted for the General Reader, 8s.

A DICTIONARY of ROMAN and GREEK ANTIQUITIES, with about Two Thousand Engravings on Wood from Ancient Originals, Illustrative of the Industrial Arts and Social Life of the Greeks and Romans. By A. RICH, B.A. Third Edition, revised and improved. Crown 8vo. price 7s. 6d.

A LATIN-ENGLISH DICTIONARY. By JOHN T. WHITE, D.D. Oxon. and J. E. RIDDLE, M.A. Oxon. Fifth Edition. 1 vol. 4to. 28s.

WHITE'S COLLEGE LATIN-ENGLISH DICTIONARY (Intermediate Size), abridged for the use of University Students from the Parent Work (as above). Medium 8vo. Third Edition, 15s.

WHITE'S JUNIOR STUDENT'S COMPLETE LATIN-ENGLISH and ENGLISH-LATIN DICTIONARY. New Edition. Square 12mo. price 12s.

Separately { The ENGLISH-LATIN DICTIONARY, price 5s. 6d.
The LATIN-ENGLISH DICTIONARY, price 7s. 6d.

A LATIN-ENGLISH DICTIONARY, adapted for the Use of Middle-Class Schools. By JOHN T. WHITE, D.D. Oxon. Square fcp. 8vo. price 3s.

An ENGLISH-GREEK LEXICON, containing all the Greek Words used by Writers of good authority. By C. D. YONGE, M.A. 4to. price 21s.

Mr. YONGE'S NEW LEXICON, English and Greek, abridged from his larger work (as above). Revised Edition. Square 12mo. price 8s. 6d.

A GREEK-ENGLISH LEXICON. Compiled by H. G. LIDDELL, D.D. Dean of Christ Church, and R. SCOTT, D.D. Dean of Rochester. Sixth Edition. Crown 4to. price 36s.

A LEXICON, GREEK and ENGLISH, abridged from LIDDELL and SCOTT's Greek-English Lexicon. Fourteenth Edition. Square 12mo. 7s. 6d.

A PRACTICAL DICTIONARY of the FRENCH and ENGLISH LANGUAGES. By L. CONTANSEAU. Revised Edition. Post 8vo. 7s. 6d.

CONTANSEAU'S POCKET DICTIONARY, French and English, abridged from the above by the Author. New Edition. Square 18mo. 3s. 6d.

A NEW POCKET DICTIONARY of the GERMAN and ENGLISH LANGUAGES. By F. W. LONGMAN, Balliol College, Oxford. 18mo. 5s.

NEW PRACTICAL DICTIONARY of the GERMAN LANGUAGE; German-English and English-German. By the Rev. W. L. BLACKLEY, M.A. and Dr. CARL MARTIN FRIEDLÄNDER. Post 8vo. 7s. 6d.

The MASTERY of LANGUAGES; or, the Art of Speaking Foreign Tongues Idiomatically. By THOMAS PRENDERGAST. 8vo. 6s.

Miscellaneous Works and *Popular Metaphysics.*

LECTURES delivered in AMERICA in 1874. By CHARLES KINGSLEY, F.L.S. F.G.S. late Rector of Eversley. Crown 8vo. price 5s.

GERMAN HOME LIFE. Reprinted, with Revision and Additions, from *Fraser's Magazine.* Second Edition. Crown 8vo. 6s.

THE MISCELLANEOUS WORKS of THOMAS ARNOLD, D.D. Late Head Master of Rugby School and Regius Professor of Modern History in the University of Oxford, collected and republished. 8vo. 7s. 6d.

MISCELLANEOUS and POSTHUMOUS WORKS of the Late HENRY THOMAS BUCKLE. Edited, with a Biographical Notice, by HELEN TAYLOR. 3 vols. 8vo. price 52s. 6d.

MISCELLANEOUS WRITINGS of JOHN CONINGTON, M.A. late Corpus Professor of Latin in the University of Oxford. Edited by J. A. SYMONDS, M.A. With a Memoir by H. J. S. SMITH, M.A. 2 vols. 8vo. 28s.

ESSAYS, CRITICAL and BIOGRAPHICAL. Contributed to the *Edinburgh Review.* By HENRY ROGERS. New Edition, with Additions. 2 vols. crown 8vo. price 12s.

ESSAYS on some THEOLOGICAL CONTROVERSIES of the TIME. Contributed chiefly to the *Edinburgh Review.* By HENRY ROGERS. New Edition, with Additions. Crown 8vo. price 6s.

RECREATIONS of a COUNTRY PARSON. By A. K. H. B. FIRST and SECOND SERIES, crown 8vo. 3s. 6d. each.

The Common-place Philosopher in Town and Country. By A. K. H. B. Crown 8vo. price 3s. 6d.

Leisure Hours in Town; Essays Consolatory, Æsthetical, Moral, Social, and Domestic. By A. K. H. B. Crown 8vo. 3s. 6d.

The Autumn Holidays of a Country Parson; Essays contributed to *Fraser's Magazine,* &c. By A. K. H. B. Crown 8vo. 3s. 6d.

Seaside Musings on Sundays and Week-Days. By A. K. H. B. Crown 8vo. price 3s. 6d.

The Graver Thoughts of a Country Parson. By A. K. H. B. FIRST, SECOND, and THIRD SERIES, crown 8vo. 3s. 6d. each.

Critical Essays of a Country Parson, selected from Essays contributed to *Fraser's Magazine.* By A. K. H. B. Crown 8vo. 3s. 6d.

Sunday Afternoons at the Parish Church of a Scottish University City. By A. K. H. B. Crown 8vo. 3s. 6d.

Lessons of Middle Age; with some Account of various Cities and Men. By A. K. H. B. Crown 8vo. 8s. 6d.

Counsel and Comfort spoken from a City Pulpit. By A. K. H. B. Crown 8vo. price 3s. 6d.

Changed Aspects of Unchanged Truths; Memorials of St. Andrews Sundays. By A. K. H. B. Crown 8vo. 3s. 6d.

Present-day Thoughts; Memorials of St. Andrews Sundays. By A. K. H. B. Crown 8vo. 3s. 6d.

Landscapes, Churches, and Moralities. By A. K. H. B. Crown 8vo. price 3s. 6d.

SHORT STUDIES on GREAT SUBJECTS. By JAMES ANTHONY FROUDE, M.A. late Fellow of Exeter Coll. Oxford. 2 vols. crown 8vo. price 12s. or 2 vols. demy 8vo. price 24s. Vol. III. In the press.

SELECTIONS from the WRITINGS of LORD MACAULAY. Edited, with Occasional Explanatory Notes, by GEORGE OTTO TREVELYAN, M.P. Crown 8vo. price 6s.

LORD MACAULAY'S MISCELLANEOUS WRITINGS:—
LIBRARY EDITION. 2 vols. 8vo. Portrait, 21s.
PEOPLE'S EDITION. 1 vol. crown 8vo. 4s. 6d.

LORD MACAULAY'S MISCELLANEOUS WRITINGS and SPEECHES. STUDENT'S EDITION, in crown 8vo. price 6s.

The Rev. SYDNEY SMITH'S MISCELLANEOUS WORKS; including his Contributions to the *Edinburgh Review*. Crown 8vo. 6s.

The WIT and WISDOM of the Rev. SYDNEY SMITH; a Selection of the most memorable Passages in his Writings and Conversation. 16mo. 3s. 6d.

The ECLIPSE of FAITH; or, a Visit to a Religious Sceptic. By HENRY ROGERS. Latest Edition. Fcp. 8vo. price 5s.

Defence of the Eclipse of Faith, by its Author; a rejoinder to Dr. Newman's *Reply*. Latest Edition. Fcp 8vo. price 3s. 6d.

CHIPS from a GERMAN WORKSHOP; Essays on the Science of Religion, on Mythology, Traditions, and Customs, and on the Science of Language. By F. MAX MÜLLER, M.A. &c. 4 vols. 8vo. £2. 18s.

ANALYSIS of the PHENOMENA of the HUMAN MIND. By JAMES MILL. A New Edition, with Notes, Illustrative and Critical, by ALEXANDER BAIN, ANDREW FINDLATER, and GEORGE GROTE. Edited, with additional Notes, by JOHN STUART MILL. 2 vols. 8vo. price 28s.

An INTRODUCTION to MENTAL PHILOSOPHY, on the Inductive Method. By J. D. MORELL, M.A. LL.D. 8vo. 12s.

PHILOSOPHY WITHOUT ASSUMPTIONS. By the Rev. T. P. KIRKMAN, F.R.S. Rector of Croft, near Warrington. 8vo. 10s. 6d.

The SENSES and the INTELLECT. By ALEXANDER BAIN, M.D. Professor of Logic in the University of Aberdeen. Third Edition. 8vo. 15s.

The EMOTIONS and the WILL. By ALEXANDER BAIN, LL.D. Professor of Logic in the University of Aberdeen. Third Edition, thoroughly revised, and in great part re-written. 8vo. price 15s.

MENTAL and MORAL SCIENCE: a Compendium of Psychology and Ethics. By the same Author. Third Edition. Crown 8vo. 10s. 6d. Or separately: PART I. *Mental Science*, 6s. 6d. PART II. *Moral Science*, 4s. 6d.

LOGIC, DEDUCTIVE and INDUCTIVE. By ALEXANDER BAIN, LL.D. In TWO PARTS, crown 8vo. 10s. 6d. Each Part may be had separately:—
PART I. *Deduction*, 4s. PART II. *Induction*, 6s. 6d.

A BUDGET of PARADOXES. By AUGUSTUS DE MORGAN, F.R.A.S. and C.P.S. 8vo. 15s.

APPARITIONS; a Narrative of Facts. By the Rev. B. W. SAVILE, M.A. Author of 'The Truth of the Bible' &c. Crown 8vo. price 4s. 6d.

A TREATISE of HUMAN NATURE, being an Attempt to Introduce the Experimental Method of Reasoning into Moral Subjects; followed by Dialogues concerning Natural Religion. By DAVID HUME. Edited, with Notes, &c. by T. H. GREEN, Fellow and Tutor, Ball. Coll. and T. H. GROSE, Fellow and Tutor, Queen's Coll. Oxford. 2 vols. 8vo. 28s.

ESSAYS MORAL, POLITICAL, and LITERARY. By DAVID HUME. By the same Editors. 2 vols. 8vo. price 28s.

The PHILOSOPHY of NECESSITY; or, Natural Law as applicable to Mental, Moral, and Social Science. By CHARLES BRAY. 8vo. 9s.

UEBERWEG'S SYSTEM of LOGIC and HISTORY of LOGICAL DOCTRINES. Translated, with Notes and Appendices, by T. M. LINDSAY, M.A. F.R.S.E. 8vo. price 16s.

FRAGMENTARY PAPERS on SCIENCE and other Subjects. By the late Sir H. HOLLAND, Bart. Edited by his Son, the Rev. F. HOLLAND. 8vo. price 14s.

Astronomy, Meteorology, Popular Geography, &c.

BRINKLEY'S ASTRONOMY. Revised and partly re-written, with Additional Chapters, and an Appendix of Questions for Examination. By J. W. STUBBS, D.D. Fellow and Tutor of Trinity College, Dublin, and F. BRUNNOW, Ph.D. Astronomer Royal of Ireland. Crown 8vo. price 6s.

OUTLINES of ASTRONOMY. By Sir J. F. W. HERSCHEL, Bart. M.A. Latest Edition, with Plates and Diagrams. Square crown 8vo. 12s.

ESSAYS on ASTRONOMY, a Series of Papers on Planets and Meteors, the Sun and Sun-surrounding Space, Stars and Star-Cloudlets; with a Dissertation on the Transit of Venus. By R. A. PROCTOR, B.A. With Plates and Woodcuts. 8vo. 12s.

THE TRANSITS of VENUS; a Popular Account of Past and Coming Transits, from the first observed by Horrocks A.D. 1639 to the Transit of A.D. 2012. By R. A. PROCTOR, B.A. Second Edition, with 20 Plates (12 coloured) and 38 Woodcuts. Crown 8vo. 8s. 6d.

The UNIVERSE and the COMING TRANSITS: Presenting Researches into and New Views respecting the Constitution of the Heavens; together with an Investigation of the Conditions of the Coming Transits of Venus. By R. A. PROCTOR, B.A. With 22 Charts and 22 Woodcuts. 8vo. 16s.

The MOON; her Motions, Aspect, Scenery, and Physical Condition. By R. A. PROCTOR, B.A. With Plates, Charts, Woodcuts, and Three Lunar Photographs. Crown 8vo. 15s.

The SUN; RULER, LIGHT, FIRE, and LIFE of the PLANETARY SYSTEM. By R. A. PROCTOR, B.A. Third Edition, with 10 Plates (7 coloured) and 107 Figures on Wood. Crown 8vo. 14s.

OTHER WORLDS THAN OURS; the Plurality of Worlds Studied under the Light of Recent Scientific Researches. By R. A. PROCTOR, B.A. Third Edition, with 14 Illustrations. Crown 8vo. 10s. 6d.

The ORBS AROUND US; Familiar Essays on the Moon and Planets, Meteors and Comets, the Sun and Coloured Pairs of Stars. By R. A. PROCTOR, B.A. Second Edition, with Charts and 4 Diagrams. Crown 8vo. price 7s. 6d.

SATURN and its SYSTEM. By R. A. PROCTOR, B.A. 8vo. with 14 Plates, 14s.

The MOON, and the Condition and Configurations of its Surface. By EDMUND NEISON, Fellow of the Royal Astronomical Society, &c. With 26 Maps and 5 Plates. Medium 8vo. 31s. 6d.

A NEW STAR ATLAS, for the Library, the School, and the Observatory, in Twelve Circular Maps (with Two Index Plates). Intended as a Companion to 'Webb's Celestial Objects for Common Telescopes.' With a Letterpress Introduction on the Study of the Stars, illustrated by 9 Diagrams. By R. A. PROCTOR, B.A. Crown 8vo. 5s.

SCHELLEN'S SPECTRUM ANALYSIS, in its application to Terrestrial Substances and the Physical Constitution of the Heavenly Bodies. Translated by JANE and C. LASSELL; edited, with Notes, by W. HUGGINS, LL.D. F.R.S. With 13 Plates (6 coloured) and 223 Woodcuts. 8vo. price 28s.

CELESTIAL OBJECTS for COMMON TELESCOPES. By the Rev. T. W. WEBB, M.A. F.R.A.S. Third Edition, revised and enlarged; with Maps, Plate, and Woodcuts. Crown 8vo. price 7s. 6d.

AIR and RAIN; the Beginnings of a Chemical Climatology. By ROBERT ANGUS SMITH, Ph.D. F.R.S. F.C.S. With 8 Illustrations. 8vo. 24s.

AIR and its RELATIONS to LIFE; being, with some Additions, the Substance of a Course of Lectures delivered at the Royal Institution of Great Britain. By W. N. HARTLEY, F.C.S. Demonstrator of Chemistry at King's College, London. Second Edition, with 66 Woodcuts. Small 8vo. 6s.

NAUTICAL SURVEYING, an INTRODUCTION to the PRACTICAL and THEORETICAL STUDY of. By J. K. LAUGHTON, M.A. Small 8vo. 6s.

DOVE'S LAW of STORMS, considered in connexion with the Ordinary Movements of the Atmosphere. Translated by R. H. SCOTT, M.A. 8vo. 10s. 6d.

KEITH JOHNSTON'S GENERAL DICTIONARY of GEOGRAPHY, Descriptive, Physical, Statistical, and Historical; forming a complete Gazetteer of the World. New Edition, revised and corrected. 8vo. price 42s.

The PUBLIC SCHOOLS ATLAS of MODERN GEOGRAPHY. In 31 Coloured Maps, exhibiting clearly the more important Physical Features of the Countries delineated, and Noting all the Chief Places of Historical, Commercial, or Social Interest. Edited, with an Introduction, by the Rev. G. BUTLER, M.A. Imperial 8vo. or Imperial 4to. 5s. cloth.

The PUBLIC SCHOOLS MANUAL of MODERN GEOGRAPHY. By the Rev. GEORGE BUTLER, M.A. Principal of Liverpool College; Editor of 'The Public Schools Atlas of Modern Geography.' *[In preparation.*

The PUBLIC SCHOOLS ATLAS of ANCIENT GEOGRAPHY, in 25 Coloured Maps. Edited by the Rev. GEORGE BUTLER, M.A. Principal of Liverpool College. Imperial 8vo. or Imperial 4to. 7s. 6d. cloth.

MAUNDER'S TREASURY of GEOGRAPHY, Physical, Historical, Descriptive, and Political. Edited by W. HUGHES, F.R.G.S. Revised Edition, with 7 Maps and 16 Plates. Fcp. 6s. cloth, or 10s. 6d. bound in calf.

Natural History and *Popular Science.*

TEXT-BOOKS of SCIENCE, MECHANICAL and PHYSICAL, adapted for the use of Artisans and of Students in Public and Science Schools.

The following Text-Books in this Series may now be had:—
- ANDERSON's Strength of Materials, small 8vo. 3s. 6d.
- ARMSTRONG's Organic Chemistry, 3s. 6d.
- BARRY's Railway Appliances, 3s. 6d.
- BLOXAM's Metals, 3s. 6d.
- GOODEVE's Elements of Mechanism, 3s. 6d.
- ——— Principles of Mechanics, 3s. 6d.
- GRIFFIN's Algebra and Trigonometry, 3s. 6d. Notes, 3s. 6d.
- JENKIN's Electricity and Magnetism, 3s. 6d.
- MAXWELL's Theory of Heat, 3s. 6d.
- MERRIFIELD's Technical Arithmetic and Mensuration, 3s. 6d. Key, 3s. 6d.
- MILLER's Inorganic Chemistry, 3s. 6d.
- PREECE & SIVEWRIGHT's Telegraphy, 3s. 6d.
- SHELLEY's Workshop Appliances, 3s. 6d.
- THOME's Structural and Physiological Botany, 6s.
- THORPE's Quantitative Chemical Analysis, 4s. 6d.
- THORPE & MUIR's Qualitative Analysis, 3s. 6d.
- TILDEN's Chemical Philosophy, 3s. 6d.
- WATSON's Plane and Solid Geometry, 3s. 6d.

*** Other Text-Books in extension of this Series are in active preparation.

ELEMENTARY TREATISE on PHYSICS, Experimental and Applied. Translated and edited from GANOT's *Éléments de Physique* by E. ATKINSON, Ph.D. F.C.S. Seventh Edition, revised and enlarged; with 4 Coloured Plates and 758 Woodcuts. Post 8vo. 15s.

NATURAL PHILOSOPHY for GENERAL READERS and YOUNG PERSONS; being a Course of Physics divested of Mathematical Formulæ expressed in the language of daily life. Translated from GANOT's *Cours de Physique* and by E. ATKINSON, Ph.D. F.C.S. Second Edition, with 2 Plates and 429 Woodcuts. Crown 8vo. price 7s. 6d.

HELMHOLTZ'S POPULAR LECTURES on SCIENTIFIC SUBJECTS. Translated by E. ATKINSON, Ph.D. F.C.S. Professor of Experimental Science, Staff College. With an Introduction by Professor TYNDALL. 8vo. with numerous Woodcuts, price 12s. 6d.

On the SENSATIONS of TONE as a Physiological Basis for the Theory of Music. By HERMANN L. F. HELMHOLTZ, M.D. Professor of Physics in the University of Berlin. Translated, with the Author's sanction, from the Third German Edition, with Additional Notes and an Additional Appendix, by ALEXANDER J. ELLIS, F.R.S. &c. 8vo. price 36s.

The HISTORY of MODERN MUSIC, a Course of Lectures delivered at the Royal Institution of Great Britain. By JOHN HULLAH, Professor of Vocal Music in Queen's College and Bedford College, and Organist of Charterhouse. New Edition. 8vo. 8s. 6d.

The TRANSITION PERIOD of MUSICAL HISTORY; a Second Course of Lectures on the History of Music from the Beginning of the Seventeenth to the Middle of the Eighteenth Century, delivered at the Royal Institution. By JOHN HULLAH. New Edition. 8vo. 10s. 6d.

SOUND. By JOHN TYNDALL, LL.D. D.C.L. F.R.S. Third Edition, including Recent Researches on Fog-Signalling; Portrait and Woodcuts. Crown 8vo. 10s. 6d.

HEAT a MODE of MOTION. By JOHN TYNDALL, LL.D. D.C.L. F.R.S. Fifth Edition. Plate and Woodcuts. Crown 8vo. 10s. 6d.

CONTRIBUTIONS to MOLECULAR PHYSICS in the DOMAIN of RADIANT HEAT. By J. TYNDALL, LL.D. D.C.L. F.R.S. With 2 Plates and 31 Woodcuts. 8vo. 16s.

RESEARCHES on DIAMAGNETISM and MAGNE-CRYSTALLIC ACTION; including the Question of Diamagnetic Polarity. By J. TYNDALL, M.D. D.C.L. F.R.S. With 6 plates and many Woodcuts. 8vo. 14s.

NOTES of a COURSE of SEVEN LECTURES on ELECTRICAL PHENOMENA and THEORIES, delivered at the Royal Institution, A.D. 1870. By JOHN TYNDALL, LL.D., D.C.L., F.R.S. Crown 8vo. 1s. sewed; 1s. 6d. cloth.

SIX LECTURES on LIGHT delivered in America in 1872 and 1873. By JOHN TYNDALL, LL.D. D.C.L. F.R.S. Second Edition, with Portrait, Plate, and 59 Diagrams. Crown 8vo. 7s. 6d.

NOTES of a COURSE of NINE LECTURES on LIGHT delivered at the Royal Institution, A.D. 1869. By JOHN TYNDALL, LL.D. D.C.L. F.R.S. Crown 8vo. price 1s. sewed, or 1s. 6d. cloth.

FRAGMENTS of SCIENCE. By JOHN TYNDALL, LL.D. D.C.L. F.R.S. Third Edition, with a New Introduction. Crown 8vo. 10s. 6d.

LIGHT SCIENCE for LEISURE HOURS; a Series of Familiar Essays on Scientific Subjects, Natural Phenomena, &c. By R. A. PROCTOR, B.A. First and Second Series. Crown 8vo. 7s. 6d. each.

A TREATISE on MAGNETISM, General and Terrestrial. By HUMPHREY LLOYD, D.D. D.C.L., Provost of Trinity College, Dublin. 8vo. 10s. 6d.

ELEMENTARY TREATISE on the WAVE-THEORY of LIGHT. By HUMPHREY LLOYD, D.D. D.C.L. Provost of Trinity College, Dublin. Third Edition, revised and enlarged. 8vo. price 10s. 6d.

The CORRELATION of PHYSICAL FORCES. By the Hon. Sir W. R. GROVE, M.A. F.R.S. one of the Judges of the Court of Common Pleas. Sixth Edition, with other Contributions to Science. 8vo. price 15s.

The COMPARATIVE ANATOMY and PHYSIOLOGY of the VERTEBRATE ANIMALS. By RICHARD OWEN, F.R.S. D.C.L. With 1,472 Woodcuts. 3 vols. 8vo. £3. 13s. 6d.

PRINCIPLES of ANIMAL MECHANICS. By the Rev. S. HAUGHTON, F.R.S. Fellow of Trin. Coll. Dubl. M.D. Dubl. and D.C.L. Oxon. Second Edition, with 111 Figures on Wood. 8vo. 21s.

ROCKS CLASSIFIED and DESCRIBED. By BERNHARD VON COTTA. English Edition, by P. H. LAWRENCE; with English, German, and French Synonymes. Post 8vo. 14s.

The ANCIENT STONE IMPLEMENTS, WEAPONS, and ORNAMENTS of GREAT BRITAIN. By JOHN EVANS, F.R.S. F.S.A. With 2 Plates and 476 Woodcuts. 8vo. price 28s.

The NATIVE RACES of the PACIFIC STATES of NORTH AMERICA. By HUBERT HOWE BANCROFT. 5 vols. 8vo. with Maps, £6. 5s.

The ORIGIN of CIVILISATION and the PRIMITIVE CONDITION of MAN; Mental and Social Condition of Savages. By Sir JOHN LUBBOCK, Bart. M.P. F.R.S. Third Edition, with 25 Woodcuts. 8vo. 16s.

BIBLE ANIMALS; being a Description of every Living Creature mentioned in the Scriptures, from the Ape to the Coral. By the Rev. J. G. WOOD, M.A. F.L.S. With about 112 Vignettes on Wood. 8vo. 14s.

HOMES WITHOUT HANDS; a Description of the Habitations of Animals, classed according to their Principle of Construction. By the Rev. J. G. Wood, M.A. F.L.S. With about 140 Vignettes on Wood. 8vo. 14s.

INSECTS AT HOME; a Popular Account of British Insects, their Structure, Habits, and Transformations. By the Rev. J. G. Wood, M.A. F.L.S. With upwards of 700 Illustrations. 8vo. price 14s.

INSECTS ABROAD; a Popular Account of Foreign Insects, their Structure, Habits, and Transformations. By J. G. Wood, M.A. F.L.S. Printed and illustrated uniformly with 'Insects at Home.' 8vo. price 21s.

STRANGE DWELLINGS; a description of the Habitations of Animals, abridged from 'Homes without Hands.' By the Rev. J. G. Wood, M.A. F.L.S. With about 60 Woodcut Illustrations. Crown 8vo. price 7s. 6d.

OUT of DOORS; a Selection of original Articles on Practical Natural History. By the Rev. J. G. Wood, M.A. F.L.S. With Eleven Illustrations from Original Designs engraved on Wood by G. Pearson. Crown 8vo. price 7s. 6d.

A FAMILIAR HISTORY of BIRDS. By E. Stanley, D.D. F.R.S. late Lord Bishop of Norwich. Seventh Edition, with Woodcuts. Fcp. 3s. 6d.

The SEA and its LIVING WONDERS. By Dr. George Hartwig. Latest revised Edition. 8vo. with many Illustrations, 10s. 6d.

The TROPICAL WORLD. By Dr. George Hartwig. With above 160 Illustrations. Latest revised Edition. 8vo. price 10s. 6d.

The SUBTERRANEAN WORLD. By Dr. George Hartwig. With 3 Maps and about 80 Woodcuts, including 8 full size of page. 8vo. price 10s. 6d.

The POLAR WORLD, a Popular Description of Man and Nature in the Arctic and Antarctic Regions of the Globe. By Dr. George Hartwig. With 8 Chromoxylographs, 3 Maps, and 85 Woodcuts. 8vo. 10s. 6d.

THE AERIAL WORLD. By Dr. G. Hartwig. New Edition, with 8 Chromoxylographs and 60 Woodcut Illustrations. 8vo. price 21s.

KIRBY and SPENCE'S INTRODUCTION to ENTOMOLOGY, or Elements of the Natural History of Insects. 7th Edition. Crown 8vo. 5s.

MAUNDER'S TREASURY of NATURAL HISTORY, or Popular Dictionary of Birds, Beasts, Fishes, Reptiles, Insects, and Creeping Things. With above 900 Woodcuts. Fcp. 8vo. price 6s. cloth, or 10s. 6d. bound in calf.

MAUNDER'S SCIENTIFIC and LITERARY TREASURY. New Edition, thoroughly revised and in great part rewritten, with above 1,000 new Articles, by J. Y. Johnson. Fcp. 8vo. 6s. cloth, or 10s. 6d. calf.

BRANDE'S DICTIONARY of SCIENCE, LITERATURE, and ART. Re-edited by the Rev. George W. Cox, M.A. late Scholar of Trinity College, Oxford; assisted by Contributors of eminent Scientific and Literary Acquirements. New Edition, revised. 3 vols. medium 8vo. 63s.

HANDBOOK of HARDY TREES, SHRUBS, and HERBACEOUS PLANTS, containing Descriptions, Native Countries, &c. of a Selection of the Best Species in Cultivation; together with Cultural Details, Comparative Hardiness, Suitability for Particular Positions, &c. By W. B. Hemsley. Based on Decaisne and Naudin's *Manuel de l'Amateur des Jardins*, and including the 264 Original Woodcuts. Medium 8vo. 21s.

A GENERAL SYSTEM of BOTANY DESCRIPTIVE and ANALYTICAL.
By E. Le Maout, and J. Decaisne, Members of the Institute of France. Translated by Mrs. Hooker. The Orders arranged after the Method followed in the Universities and Schools of Great Britain, its Colonies, America, and India; with an Appendix on the Natural Method, and other Additions, by J. D. Hooker, F.R.S. &c. Second Thousand, with 5,500 Woodcuts. Imperial 8vo. 31s. 6d.

The TREASURY of BOTANY, or Popular Dictionary of the Vegetable Kingdom; including a Glossary of Botanical Terms. Edited by J. Lindley, F.R.S. and T. Moore, F.L.S. assisted by eminent Contributors. With 274 Woodcuts and 20 Steel Plates. Two Parts, fcp. 8vo. 12s. cloth, or 21s. calf.

The ELEMENTS of BOTANY for FAMILIES and SCHOOLS.
Tenth Edition, revised by Thomas Moore, F.L.S. Fcp. 8vo. with 154 Woodcuts, 2s. 6d.

The ROSE AMATEUR'S GUIDE. By Thomas Rivers. Fourteenth Edition. Fcp. 8vo. 4s.

LOUDON'S ENCYCLOPÆDIA of PLANTS; comprising the Specific Character, Description, Culture, History, &c. of all the Plants found in Great Britain. With upwards of 12,000 Woodcuts. 8vo. 42s.

FOREST TREES and WOODLAND SCENERY, as described in Ancient and Modern Poets. By William Menzies, Deputy Surveyor of Windsor Forest and Parks, &c. With Twenty Chromo-lithographic Plates. Folio, price £5 5s.

Chemistry and Physiology.

A DICTIONARY of CHEMISTRY and the Allied Branches of other Sciences. By Henry Watts, F.R.S. assisted by eminent Contributors. Seven Volumes, medium 8vo. price £10. 16s. 6d.

ELEMENTS of CHEMISTRY, Theoretical and Practical. By W. Allen Miller, M.D. late Prof. of Chemistry, King's Coll. London. New Edition. 3 vols. 8vo. Part I. Chemical Physics, 15s. Part II. Inorganic Chemistry, 21s. Part III. Organic Chemistry, New Edition in the press.

SELECT METHODS in CHEMICAL ANALYSIS, chiefly INORGANIC. By William Crookes, F.R.S. With 22 Woodcuts. Crown 8vo. price 12s. 6d.

A PRACTICAL HANDBOOK of DYEING and CALICO PRINTING. By William Crookes, F.R.S. With 11 Page Plates, 48 Specimens of Dyed and Printed Fabrics, and 38 Woodcuts. 8vo. 42s.

OUTLINES of PHYSIOLOGY, Human and Comparative. By John Marshall, F.R.C.S. Surgeon to the University College Hospital. 2 vols. crown 8vo. with 172 Woodcuts, 32s.

HEALTH in the HOUSE; a Series of Lectures on Elementary Physiology in its application to the Daily Wants of Man and Animals, delivered to the Wives and Children of Working Men in Leeds and Saltaire. By Catherine M. Buckton. New Edition, revised. Small 8vo. Woodcuts, 2s.

The Fine Arts, and Illustrated Editions.

A DICTIONARY of ARTISTS of the ENGLISH SCHOOL: Painters, Sculptors, Architects, Engravers, and Ornamentists; with Notices of their Lives and Works. By S. REDGRAVE. 8vo. 16s.

MOORE'S IRISH MELODIES, with 161 Steel Plates from Original Drawings by D. MACLISE, R.A. Super-royal 8vo. 31s.

LORD MACAULAY'S LAYS of ANCIENT ROME. With 90 Illustrations on Wood, from the Antique, from Drawings by G. SCHARF. Fcp. 4to. 21s.

Miniature Edition of Lord Macaulay's Lays of Ancient Rome, with the Illustrations (as above) reduced in Lithography. Imp. 16mo. 10s. 6d.

POEMS. By WILLIAM B. SCOTT. I. Ballads and Tales. II. Studies from Nature. III. Sonnets &c. Illustrated by 17 Etchings by W. B. SCOTT (the Author) and L. ALMA TADEMA. Crown 8vo. price 15s.

HALF-HOUR LECTURES on the HISTORY and PRACTICE of the FINE and ORNAMENTAL ARTS. By WILLIAM B. SCOTT. Third Edition, with 50 Woodcuts. Crown 8vo. 8s. 6d.

The THREE CATHEDRALS DEDICATED to ST. PAUL, in LONDON; their History from the Foundation of the First Building in the Sixth Century to the Proposals for the Adornment of the Present Cathedral. By WILLIAM LONGMAN, F.A.S. With numerous Illustrations. Square crown 8vo. 21s.

IN FAIRYLAND; Pictures from the Elf-World. By RICHARD DOYLE. With a Poem by W. ALLINGHAM. With Sixteen Plates, containing Thirty-six Designs printed in Colours. Second Edition. Folio, price 15s.

The NEW TESTAMENT, illustrated with Wood Engravings after the Early Masters, chiefly of the Italian School. Crown 4to. 63s. cloth, gilt top; or £5 5s. elegantly bound in morocco.

SACRED and LEGENDARY ART. By MRS. JAMESON.

Legends of the Saints and Martyrs. New Edition, with 19 Etchings and 187 Woodcuts. 2 vols. square crown 8vo. 31s. 6d.

Legends of the Monastic Orders. New Edition, with 11 Etchings and 88 Woodcuts. 1 vol. square crown 8vo. 21s.

Legends of the Madonna. New Edition, with 27 Etchings and 165 Woodcuts. 1 vol. square crown 8vo. 21s.

The History of Our Lord, with that of his Types and Precursors. Completed by Lady EASTLAKE. Revised Edition, with 31 Etchings and 281 Woodcuts. 2 vols. square crown 8vo. 42s.

The Useful Arts, Manufactures, &c.

GWILT'S ENCYCLOPÆDIA of ARCHITECTURE, with above 1,600 Engravings on Wood. New Edition, revised and enlarged by WYATT PAPWORTH. 8vo. 52s. 6d.

HINTS on HOUSEHOLD TASTE in FURNITURE, UPHOLSTERY, and other Details. By CHARLES L. EASTLAKE, Architect. Third Edition, with about 90 Illustrations. Square crown 8vo. 14s.

INDUSTRIAL CHEMISTRY; a Manual for Manufacturers and for use in Colleges or Technical Schools. Being a Translation of Professors Stohmann and Engler's German Edition of PAYEN'S *Précis de Chimie Industrielle*, by Dr. J. D. BARRY. Edited and supplemented by B. H. PAUL, Ph.D. 8vo. with Plates and Woodcuts. [*In the press.*

URE'S DICTIONARY of ARTS, MANUFACTURES, and MINES. Seventh Edition, rewritten and enlarged by ROBERT HUNT, F.R.S. assisted by numerous Contributors eminent in Science and the Arts, and familiar with Manufactures. With above 2,100 Woodcuts. 3 vols. medium 8vo. £5 5s.

HANDBOOK of PRACTICAL TELEGRAPHY. By R. S. CULLEY, Memb. Inst. C.E. Engineer-in-Chief of Telegraphs to the Post Office. Sixth Edition, with 144 Woodcuts and 5 Plates. 8vo. price 16s.

TELEGRAPHY. By W. H. PREECE, C.E. Divisional Engineer, P.O. Telegraphs; and J. SIVEWRIGHT, M.A. Superintendent (Engineering Department) P.O. Telegraphs. Small 8vo. with 160 Woodcuts, 3s. 6d.

RAILWAY APPLIANCES; a Description of Details of Railway Construction subsequent to the completion of the Earthworks and Masonry, including a short Notice of Railway Rolling Stock. By J. W. BARRY, Member of the Institution of Civil Engineers. Small 8vo. with 207 Woodcuts, 4s. 6d.

ENCYCLOPÆDIA of CIVIL ENGINEERING, Historical, Theoretical, and Practical. By E. CRESY, C.E. With above 3,000 Woodcuts. 8vo. 42s.

OCCASIONAL PAPERS on SUBJECTS connected with CIVIL ENGINEERING, GUNNERY, and Naval Architecture. By MICHAEL SCOTT, Memb. Inst. C.E. & of Inst. N.A. 2 vols. 8vo. with Plates, 42s.

NAVAL POWERS and their POLICY, with Tabular Statements of British and Foreign Ironclad Navies, giving Dimensions, Armour, Details of Armament, Engines, Speed, &c. By JOHN C. PAGET. 8vo. 10s. 6d.

TREATISE on MILLS and MILLWORK. By Sir W. FAIRBAIRN, Bart. F.R.S. New Edition, with 18 Plates and 322 Woodcuts. 2 vols. 8vo. 32s.

USEFUL INFORMATION for ENGINEERS. By Sir W. FAIRBAIRN, Bart. F.R.S. Revised Edition, with Illustrations. 3 vols. crown 8vo. price 31s. 6d.

The APPLICATION of CAST and WROUGHT IRON to Building Purposes. By Sir W. FAIRBAIRN, Bart. F.R.S. Fourth Edition, enlarged; with 6 Plates and 118 Woodcuts. 8vo. price 16s.

The THEORY of STRAINS in GIRDERS and similar Structures, with Observations on the application of Theory to Practice, and Tables of the Strength and other Properties of Materials. By BINDON B. STONEY, M.A. M. Inst. C.E. New Edition, royal 8vo. with 5 Plates and 123 Woodcuts, 36s.

A TREATISE on the STEAM ENGINE, in its various Applications to Mines, Mills, Steam Navigation, Railways, and Agriculture. By J. BOURNE, C.E. Eighth Edition; with Portrait, 37 Plates, and 546 Woodcuts. 4to. 42s.

CATECHISM of the STEAM ENGINE, in its various Applications to Mines, Mills, Steam Navigation, Railways, and Agriculture. By the same Author. With 89 Woodcuts. Fcp. 8vo. 6s.

HANDBOOK of the STEAM ENGINE. By the same Author, forming a KEY to the Catechism of the Steam Engine, with 67 Woodcuts. Fcp. 9s.

BOURNE'S RECENT IMPROVEMENTS in the STEAM ENGINE in its various applications to Mines, Mills, Steam Navigation, Railways, and Agriculture. By JOHN BOURNE, C.E. New Edition, with 124 Woodcuts. Fcp. 8vo. 6s.

PRACTICAL TREATISE on METALLURGY, adapted from the last German Edition of Professor Kerl's *Metallurgy* by W. Crookes, F.R.S. &c. and E. Röhrig, Ph.D. M.E. With 625 Woodcuts. 3 vols. 8vo. price £4 19s.

MITCHELL'S MANUAL of PRACTICAL ASSAYING. Fourth Edition, for the most part rewritten, with all the recent Discoveries Incorporated, by W. Crookes, F.R.S. With 199 Woodcuts. 8vo. 31s. 6d.

LOUDON'S ENCYCLOPÆDIA of AGRICULTURE: comprising the Laying-out, Improvement, and Management of Landed Property, and the Cultivation and Economy of Agricultural Produce. With 1,100 Woodcuts. 8vo. 21s.

Loudon's Encyclopædia of Gardening: comprising the Theory and Practice of Horticulture, Floriculture, Arboriculture, and Landscape Gardening. With 1,000 Woodcuts. 8vo. 21s.

REMINISCENCES of FEN and MERE. By J. M. Heathcote. With 27 Illustrations and 3 Maps. Square crown 8vo. price 28s.

Religious and *Moral Works.*

CHRISTIAN LIFE, its COURSE, its HINDRANCES, and its HELPS; Sermons preached mostly in the Chapel of Rugby School. By the late Rev. Thomas Arnold, D.D. 8vo. 7s. 6d.

CHRISTIAN LIFE, its HOPES, its FEARS, and its CLOSE; Sermons preached mostly in the Chapel of Rugby School. By the late Rev. Thomas Arnold, D.D. 8vo. 7s. 6d.

SERMONS chiefly on the INTERPRETATION of SCRIPTURE. By the late Rev. Thomas Arnold, D.D. 8vo. price 7s. 6d.

SERMONS preached in the Chapel of Rugby School; with an Address before Confirmation. By the late Rev. Thomas Arnold, D.D. Fcp. 8vo. 3s. 6d.

THREE ESSAYS on RELIGION: Nature; the Utility of Religion; Theism. By John Stuart Mill. 8vo. price 10s. 6d.

INTRODUCTION to the SCIENCE of RELIGION. Four Lectures delivered at the Royal Institution; with Two Essays on False Analogies and the Philosophy of Mythology. By F. Max Müller, M.A. Crown 8vo. 10s. 6d.

SUPERNATURAL RELIGION; an Inquiry into the Reality of Divine Revelation. Sixth Edition, carefully revised, with Eighty Pages of New Preface. 2 vols. 8vo. 24s.

NOTES on the EARLIER HEBREW SCRIPTURES. By Sir G. B. Airy, K.C.B. 8vo. price 4s.

ISLAM under the ARABS. By Robert Durie Osborn, Major in the Bengal Staff Corps. 8vo. 12s.

RELIGION and SCIENCE, their Relations to each other at the Present Day; Three Essays on the Grounds of Religious Beliefs. By Stanley T. Gibson, B.D., late Fellow of Queen's College, Cambridge. 8vo. 10s. 6d.

The PRIMITIVE and CATHOLIC FAITH in Relation to the Church of England. By the Rev. B. W. Savile, M.A. Rector of Shillingford, Exeter, Author of 'Truth of the Bible' &c. 8vo. price 7s.

SYNONYMS of the OLD TESTAMENT, their BEARING on CHRISTIAN FAITH and PRACTICE. By the Rev. R. B. GIRDLESTONE, M.A. 8vo. 15s.

An INTRODUCTION to the THEOLOGY of the CHURCH of ENGLAND, in an Exposition of the Thirty-nine Articles. By the Rev. T. P. BOULTBEE, LL.D. New Edition, Fcp. 8vo. price 6s.

An EXPOSITION of the 39 ARTICLES, Historical and Doctrinal. By E. HAROLD BROWNE, D.D. Lord Bishop of Winchester. New Edit. 8vo. 16s.

The LIFE and EPISTLES of ST. PAUL. By the Rev. W. J. CONYBEARE, M.A., and the Very Rev. J. S. HOWSON, D.D. Dean of Chester:—
LIBRARY EDITION, with all the Original Illustrations, Maps, Landscapes on Steel, Woodcuts, &c. 2 vols. 4to. 42s.
INTERMEDIATE EDITION, with a Selection of Maps, Plates, and Woodcuts. 2 vols. square crown 8vo. 31s.
STUDENT'S EDITION, revised and condensed, with 46 Illustrations and Maps. 1 vol. crown 8vo. price 9s.

HISTORY of the REFORMATION in EUROPE in the TIME of CALVIN. By the Rev. J. H. MERLE D'AUBIGNÉ, D.D. Translated by W. L. R. CATES. 7 vols. 8vo. price £5. 11s.
*** Vol. VIII. completing the Work, is preparing for publication.

NEW TESTAMENT COMMENTARIES. By the Rev. W. A. O'CONOR, B.A. Rector of St. Simon and St. Jude, Manchester. Crown 8vo.
>Epistle to the Romans, price 3s. 6d.
>Epistle to the Hebrews, 4s. 6d.
>St. John's Gospel, 10s. 6d.

A CRITICAL and GRAMMATICAL COMMENTARY on ST. PAUL'S Epistles. By C. J. ELLICOTT, D.D. Lord Bishop of Gloucester and Bristol. 8vo.
>Galatians, Fourth Edition, 8s. 6d.
>Ephesians, Fourth Edition, 8s. 6d.
>Pastoral Epistles, Fourth Edition, 10s. 6d.
>Philippians, Colossians, and Philemon, Third Edition, 10s. 6d.
>Thessalonians, Third Edition, 7s. 6d.

HISTORICAL LECTURES on the LIFE of OUR LORD. By C. J. ELLICOTT, D.D. Bishop of Gloucester and Bristol. Sixth Edition. 8vo. 12s.

EVIDENCE of the TRUTH of the CHRISTIAN RELIGION derived from the Literal Fulfilment of Prophecy. By ALEXANDER KEITH, D.D. 37th Edition, with Plates, in square 8vo. 12s. 6d.; 39th Edition, in post 8vo. 6s.

HISTORY of ISRAEL. By H. EWALD, late Professor of the Univ. of Göttingen. Translated by J. E. CARPENTER, M.A., with a Preface by RUSSELL MARTINEAU, M.A. 5 vols. 8vo. 63s.

The ANTIQUITIES of ISRAEL. By HEINRICH EWALD, late Professor of the University of Göttingen. Translated from the German by HENRY SHAEN SOLLY, M.A. 8vo. price 12s. 6d.

The TREASURY of BIBLE KNOWLEDGE; being a Dictionary of the Books, Persons, Places, Events, and other matters of which mention is made in Holy Scripture. By Rev. J. AYRE, M.A. With Maps, 16 Plates, and numerous Woodcuts. Fcp. 8vo. price 6s. cloth, or 10s. 6d. neatly bound in calf.

LECTURES on the PENTATEUCH and the MOABITE STONE. By the Right Rev. J. W. COLENSO, D.D. Bishop of Natal. 8vo. 12s.

The PENTATEUCH and BOOK of JOSHUA CRITICALLY EXAMINED. By the Right Rev. J. W. COLENSO, D.D. Bishop of Natal. Crown 8vo. 6s.

An INTRODUCTION to the STUDY of the NEW TESTAMENT, Critical, Exegetical, and Theological. By the Rev. S. DAVIDSON, D.D. LL.D. 2 vols. 8vo. price 30s.

SOME QUESTIONS of the DAY. By the Author of 'Amy Herbert.' Crown 8vo. price 2s. 6d.

THOUGHTS for the AGE. By the Author of 'Amy Herbert,' &c. New Edition, revised. Fcp. 8vo. price 3s. 6d.

The DOCTRINE and PRACTICE of CONFESSION in the CHURCH of ENGLAND. By the Rev. W. E. JELF, B.D. 8vo. price 7s. 6d.

PREPARATION for the HOLY COMMUNION; the Devotions chiefly from the Works of JEREMY TAYLOR. By Miss SEWELL. 32mo. 3s.

LYRA GERMANICA, Hymns translated from the German by Miss C. WINKWORTH. Fcp. 8vo. price 5s.

SPIRITUAL SONGS for the SUNDAYS and HOLIDAYS throughout the Year. By J. S. B. MONSELL, LL.D. Ninth Thousand. Fcp. 8vo. 5s. 18mo. 2s.

ENDEAVOURS after the CHRISTIAN LIFE: Discourses. By the Rev. J. MARTINEAU, LL.D. Fifth Edition, carefully revised. Crown 8vo. 7s. 6d.

HYMNS of PRAISE and PRAYER, collected and edited by the Rev. J. MARTINEAU, LL.D. Crown 8vo. 4s. 6d. 32mo. 1s. 6d.

The TYPES of GENESIS, briefly considered as revealing the Development of Human Nature. By ANDREW JUKES. Third Edition. Crown 8vo. 7s. 6d.

The SECOND DEATH and the RESTITUTION of ALL THINGS; with some Preliminary Remarks on the Nature and Inspiration of Holy Scripture. By ANDREW JUKES. Fourth Edition. Crown 8vo. 3s. 6d.

WHATELY'S INTRODUCTORY LESSONS on the CHRISTIAN Evidences. 18mo. 6d.

BISHOP JEREMY TAYLOR'S ENTIRE WORKS. With Life by BISHOP HEBER. Revised and corrected by the Rev. C. P. EDEN. Complete in Ten Volumes, 8vo. cloth, price £5. 5s.

Travels, Voyages, &c.

The INDIAN ALPS, and How we Crossed them: being a Narrative of Two Years' Residence in the Eastern Himalayas, and Two Months' Tour into the Interior, towards Kinchinjunga and Mount Everest. By a Lady PIONEER. With Illustrations from Original Drawings made on the spot by the Authoress. Imperial 8vo. 42s.

TYROL and the TYROLESE; being an Account of the People and the Land, in their Social, Sporting, and Mountaineering Aspects. By W. A. BAILLIE GROHMAN. With numerous Illustrations from Sketches by the Author. Crown 8vo. 14s.

'The FROSTY CAUCASUS;' An Account of a Walk through Part of the Range, and of an Ascent of Elbruz in the Summer of 1874. By F. C. GROVE. With Eight Illustrations engraved on Wood by E. Whymper, from Photographs taken during the Journey, and a Map. Crown 8vo. price 15s.

A THOUSAND MILES up the NILE, being a JOURNEY through EGYPT and NUBIA to the SECOND CATARACT. By AMELIA B. EDWARDS. With Eighty Illustrations from Drawings by the Authoress, Two Maps, Plans, Facsimiles, &c. Imperial 8vo. price 42s.

OVER the SEA and FAR AWAY; being a Narrative of a Ramble round the World. By THOMAS WOODBINE HINCHLIFF, M.A. F.R.G.S. President of the Alpine Club, Author of 'Summer Months among the Alps.' With 14 full-page Illustrations, engraved on Wood from Photographs and Sketches. Medium 8vo. 21s.

THROUGH BOSNIA and the HERZEGOVINA on FOOT during the INSURRECTION, August and September 1875; with an Historical Review of Bosnia, and a Glimpse at the Croats, Slavonians, and the Ancient Republic of Ragusa. By A. J. EVANS, B.A. F.S.A. With Map and 58 Wood Engravings from Photographs and Sketches by the Author. 8vo. 18s.

DISCOVERIES at EPHESUS, including the Site and Remains of the Great Temple of Diana. By J. T. WOOD, F.S.A. With 27 Lithographic Plates and 42 Engravings on Wood from Original Drawings and Photographs. Imperial 8vo. price 63s.

MEMORIALS of the DISCOVERY and EARLY SETTLEMENT of the BERMUDAS or SOMERS ISLANDS, from 1515 to 1685. Compiled from the Colonial Records and other original sources. By Major-General J. H. LEFROY, R.A. C.B. F.R.S. &c. Governor of the Bermudas. 8vo. with Map.
[In the press.

ITALIAN ALPS; Sketches in the Mountains of Ticino, Lombardy, the Trentino, and Venetia. By DOUGLAS W. FRESHFIELD, Editor of 'The Alpine Journal.' Square crown 8vo. with Maps and Illustrations, price 15s.

The RIFLE and the HOUND in CEYLON. By Sir SAMUEL W. BAKER, M.A. F.R.G.S. New Edition, with Illustrations engraved on Wood by G. Pearson. Crown 8vo. 7s. 6d.

EIGHT YEARS in CEYLON. By Sir SAMUEL W. BAKER, M.A. F.R.G.S. New Edition, with Illustrations engraved on Wood, by G. Pearson. Crown 8vo. 7s. 6d.

TWO YEARS in FIJI, a Descriptive Narrative of a Residence in the Fijian Group of Islands; with some Account of the Fortunes of Foreign Settlers and Colonists up to the Time of the British Annexation. By LITTON FORBES, M.D. F.R.G.S. Crown 8vo. 8s. 6d.

MEETING the SUN; a Journey all round the World through Egypt, China Japan, and California. By WILLIAM SIMPSON, F.R.G.S. With 48 Heliotypes and Wood Engravings from Drawings by the Author. Medium 8vo. 24s.

UNTRODDEN PEAKS and UNFREQUENTED VALLEYS; a Midsummer Ramble among the Dolomites. By AMELIA B. EDWARDS. With a Map and 27 Wood Engravings. Medium 8vo. 21s.

The **DOLOMITE MOUNTAINS**; Excursions through Tyrol, Carinthia, Carniola, and Friuli, 1861-1863. By J. Gilbert and G. C. Churchill, F.R.G.S. With numerous Illustrations. Square crown 8vo. 21s.

The **ALPINE CLUB MAP of SWITZERLAND**, with parts of the Neighbouring Countries, on the Scale of Four Miles to an Inch. Edited by R. C. Nichols, F.S.A. F.R.G.S. In Four Sheets, price 42s. or mounted in a case, 52s. 6d. Each Sheet may be had separately, price 12s. or mounted in a case, 15s.

MAP of the **CHAIN** of **MONT BLANC**, from an Actual Survey in 1863-1864. By Adams-Reilly, F.R.G.S. M.A.C. Published under the Authority of the Alpine Club. In Chromolithography on extra stout drawing-paper 28in. x 17in. price 10s. or mounted on canvas in a folding case, 12s. 6d.

HOW to SEE NORWAY. By Captain J. R. Campbell. With Map and 5 Woodcuts. Fcp. 8vo. price 5s.

GUIDE to the **PYRENEES**, for the use of Mountaineers. By Charles Packe. With Map and Illustrations. Crown 8vo. 7s. 6d.

The **ALPINE GUIDE**. By John Ball, M.R.I.A. late President of the Alpine Club. 3 vols. post 8vo. Thoroughly Revised Editions, with Maps and Illustrations:—I. *Western Alps*, 6s. 6d. II. *Central Alps*, 7s. 6d. III. *Eastern Alps*, 10s. 6d. Or in Ten Parts, price 2s. 6d. each.

Introduction on Alpine Travelling in General, and on the Geology of the Alps, price 1s. Each of the Three Volumes or Parts of the *Alpine Guide* may be had with this INTRODUCTION prefixed, price 1s. extra.

Works of Fiction.

The **ATELIER du LYS**; or, an Art-Student in the Reign of Terror. By the Author of 'Mademoiselle Mori' Third Edition. 1 vol. crown 8vo. 6s.

NOVELS and **TALES.** By the Right Hon. B. Disraeli, M.P. Cabinet Edition, complete in Ten Volumes, crown 8vo. price £3.

Lothair, 6s.	Henrietta Temple, 6s.
Coningsby, 6s.	Contarini Fleming, &c. 6s.
Sybil, 6s.	Alroy, Ixion, &c. 6s.
Tancred, 6s.	The Young Duke, &c. 6s.
Venetia, 6s.	Vivian Grey 6s.

CABINET EDITION of STORIES and TALES by Miss Sewell:—

Amy Herbert, 2s. 6d.	Ivors, 2s. 6d.
Gertrude, 2s. 6d.	Katharine Ashton, 2s. 6d
The Earl's Daughter, 2s. 6d.	Margaret Percival, 3s. 6d.
Experience of Life, 2s. 6d.	Laneton Parsonage, 3s. 6d.
Cleve Hall, 2s. 6d.	Ursula, 3s. 6d.

BECKER'S GALLUS; or, Roman Scenes of the Time of Augustus: with Notes and Excursuses. New Edition. Post 8vo. 7s. 6d.

BECKER'S CHARICLES; a Tale illustrative of Private Life among the Ancient Greeks: with Notes and Excursuses. New Edition. Post 8vo. 7s. 6d.

HIGGLEDY-PIGGLEDY; or, Stories for Everybody and Everybody's Children. By the Right Hon. E. H. Knatchbull-Hugessen, M.P. With Nine Illustrations from Original Designs by R. Doyle, engraved on Wood by G. Pearson. Crown 8vo. price 6s.

WHISPERS from FAIRYLAND. By the Right Hon. E. H. Knatchbull-Hugessen, M.P. With Nine Illustrations from Original Designs engraved on Wood by G. Pearson. Crown 8vo. price 6s.

The MODERN NOVELIST'S LIBRARY. Each Work, in crown 8vo. complete in a Single Volume:—

ATHERSTONE PRIORY, 2s. boards; 2s. 6d. cloth.
MADEMOISELLE MORI, 2s. boards; 2s. 6d. cloth.
MELVILLE'S GLADIATORS, 2s boards; 2s. 6d. cloth.
——— GOOD FOR NOTHING, 2s. boards; 2s. 6d. cloth.
——— HOLMBY HOUSE, 2s. boards; 2s. 6d. cloth.
——— INTERPRETER, 2s. boards; 2s. 6d. cloth.
——— KATE COVENTRY, 2s. boards; 2s. 6d. cloth.
——— QUEEN'S MARIES, 2s. boards; 2s. 6d. cloth.
——— DIGBY GRAND, 2s. boards; 2s. 6d. cloth.
——— GENERAL BOUNCE, 2s. boards; 2s. 6d. cloth.
TROLLOPE'S WARDEN, 1s. 6d. boards; 2s. cloth.
——— BARCHESTER TOWERS, 2s. boards; 2s. 6d. cloth.
BRAMLEY-MOORE'S SIX SISTERS of the VALLEYS, 2s. boards; 2s. 6d. cloth.
The BURGOMASTER'S FAMILY, 2s. boards; 2s. 6d. cloth.
ELSA, a Tale of the Tyrolean Alps. Translated from the German of WILHELMINE VON HILLERN by Lady WALLACE. 2s. boards; 2s. 6d. cloth.

Poetry and *The Drama.*

POEMS. By WILLIAM B. SCOTT. I. Ballads and Tales. II. Studies from Nature. III. Sonnets &c. Illustrated by 17 Etchings by L. ALMA TADEMA and WILLIAM B. SCOTT. Crown 8vo. price 15s.

MOORE'S IRISH MELODIES, with 161 Steel Plates from Original Drawings by D. MACLISE, R.A. New Edition. Super-royal 8vo. 21s.

The LONDON SERIES of FRENCH CLASSICS. Edited by CH. CASSAL, LL.D. T. KARCHER, LL.B. and LÉONCE STIÉVENARD. In course of publication, in fcp. 8vo. volumes. The following Plays, in the Division of the Drama in this Series, are now ready:—

CORNEILLE'S LE CID, 1s. 6d.
CORNEILLE'S POLYEUCTE, 1s. 6d.
RACINE'S IPHIGÉNIE, 1s. 6d.
VOLTAIRE'S ZAIRE, 1s. 6d.

VOLTAIRE'S ALZIRE, 1s. 6d.
LAMARTINE'S TOUSSAINT LOUVERTURE 2s. 6d.
DE VIGNY'S CHATTERTON, 1s. 6d.

BALLADS and LYRICS of OLD FRANCE; with other Poems. By A. LANG, M.A. Late fellow of Merton College, Oxford. Square fcp. 8vo. 5s.

SOUTHEY'S POETICAL WORKS, with the Author's last Corrections and copyright Additions. Medium 8vo. with Portrait and Vignette, 14s.

LAYS of ANCIENT ROME; with IVRY and the ARMADA. By the Right Hon. Lord MACAULAY. 16mo. 3s. 6d.

LORD MACAULAY'S LAYS of ANCIENT ROME. With 90 Illustrations on Wood, from the Antique, from Drawings by G. SCHARF. Fcp. 4to. 21s.

Miniature Edition of Lord Macaulay's Lays of Ancient Rome, with the Illustrations (as above) reduced in Lithography. Imp. 16mo. 10s. 6d.

The ÆNEID of VIRGIL Translated into English Verse. By JOHN CONINGTON, M.A. New Edition. Crown 8vo. 9s.

HORATII OPERA. Library Edition, with Marginal References and English Notes. Edited by the Rev. J. E. Yonge, M.A. 8vo. 21s.

The LYCIDAS and EPITAPHIUM DAMONIS of MILTON. Edited, with Notes and Introduction (including a Reprint of the rare Latin Version of the Lycidas, by W. Hogg, 1694), by C. S. Jerram, M.A. Crown 8vo. 2s. 6d.

BOWDLER'S FAMILY SHAKSPEARE, cheaper Genuine Editions. Medium 8vo. large type, with 36 Woodcuts, price 14s. Cabinet Edition, with the same Illustrations, 6 vols. fcp. 8vo. price 21s.

POEMS. By Jean Ingelow. 2 vols. fcp. 8vo. price 10s.
First Series, containing 'Divided,' 'The Star's Monument,' &c. Sixteenth Thousand. Fcp. 8vo. price 5s.
Second Series, 'A Story of Doom,' 'Gladys and her Island,' &c. Fifth Thousand. Fcp. 8vo. price 5s.

POEMS by Jean Ingelow. First Series, with nearly 100 Illustrations, engraved on Wood by Dalziel Brothers. Fcp. 4to. 21s.

Rural Sports, &c.

DOWN the ROAD; Or, Reminiscences of a Gentleman Coachman. By C. T. S. Birch Reynardson. Second Edition, with Twelve Coloured Illustrations from Paintings by H. Alken. Medium 8vo. 21s.

ANNALS of the ROAD; Or, Notes on Mail and Stage Coaching in Great Britain. By Captain Malet, 18th Hussars. To which are added, Essays on the Road, by Nimrod. With 8 Woodcuts and 10 Illustrations in Chromolithography. Medium 8vo. 21s.

ENCYCLOPÆDIA of RURAL SPORTS; a complete Account, Historical, Practical, and Descriptive, of Hunting, Shooting, Fishing, Racing, and all other Rural and Athletic Sports and Pastimes. By D. P. Blaine. With above 600 Woodcuts (20 from Designs by John Leech). 8vo. 21s.

The FLY-FISHER'S ENTOMOLOGY. By Alfred Ronalds. With coloured Representations of the Natural and Artificial Insect. Sixth Edition, with 20 coloured Plates. 8vo. 14s.

A BOOK on ANGLING; a complete Treatise on the Art of Angling in every branch. By Francis Francis. New Edition, with Portrait and 15 other Plates, plain and coloured. Post 8vo. 15s.

WILCOCKS'S SEA-FISHERMAN; comprising the Chief Methods of Hook and Line Fishing, a Glance at Nets, and Remarks on Boats and Boating. New Edition, with 80 Woodcuts. Post 8vo. 12s. 6d.

HORSES and STABLES. By Colonel F. Fitzwygram, XV. the King's Hussars. With Twenty-four Plates of Illustrations, containing very numerous Figures engraved on Wood. 8vo. 10s. 6d.

The HORSE'S FOOT, and HOW to KEEP It SOUND. By W. Miles, Esq. Ninth Edition, with Illustrations. Imperial 8vo. 12s. 6d.

A PLAIN TREATISE on HORSE-SHOEING. By W. Miles, Esq. Sixth Edition. Post 8vo. with Illustrations, 2s. 6d.

STABLES and STABLE-FITTINGS. By W. MILES, ESQ. Imp. 8vo. with 13 Plates, 15s.

REMARKS on HORSES' TEETH, addressed to Purchasers. By W. MILES, Esq. Post 8vo. 1s. 6d.

The HORSE: with a Treatise on Draught. By WILLIAM YOUATT. New Edition, revised and enlarged. 8vo. with numerous Woodcuts, 12s. 6d.

The DOG. By WILLIAM YOUATT. 8vo. with numerous Woodcuts, 6s.

The DOG in HEALTH and DISEASE. By STONEHENGE. With 70 Wood Engravings. Square crown 8vo. 7s. 6d.

The GREYHOUND. By STONEHENGE. Revised Edition, with 25 Portraits of Greyhounds. Square crown 8vo. 15s.

The OX; his Diseases and their Treatment: with an Essay on Parturition in the Cow. By J. R. DOBSON. Crown 8vo. with Illustrations, 7s. 6d.

Works of Utility and General Information.

The THEORY and PRACTICE of BANKING. By H. D. MACLEOD, M.A. Barrister-at-Law. Third Edition, thoroughly revised. 2 vols. 8vo. price 26s.

The ELEMENTS of BANKING. By HENRY DUNNING MACLEOD, Esq. M.A. of Trinity College, Cambridge, and the Inner Temple, Barrister-at-Law. Crown 8vo. price 7s. 6d.

M'CULLOCH'S DICTIONARY, Practical, Theoretical, and Historical, of Commerce and Commercial Navigation. New and revised Edition. 8vo. 63s. Second Supplement, price 3s. 6d.

The CABINET LAWYER; a Popular Digest of the Laws of England, Civil, Criminal, and Constitutional; intended for Practical Use and General Information. Twenty-fifth Edition. Fcp. 8vo. price 9s.

BLACKSTONE ECONOMISED, a Compendium of the Laws of England to the Present time, in Four Books, each embracing the Legal Principles and Practical Information contained in their respective volumes of Blackstone, supplemented by Subsequent Statutory Enactments, Important Legal Decisions, &c. By D. M. AIRD, Barrister-at-Law. Revised Edition. Post 8vo. 7s. 6d.

PEWTNER'S COMPREHENSIVE SPECIFIER; a Guide to the Practical Specification of every kind of Building-Artificers' Work, with Forms of Conditions and Agreements. Edited by W. YOUNG. Crown 8vo. 6s.

WILLICH'S POPULAR TABLES for ascertaining according to the Carlisle Table of Mortality the Value of Lifehold, Leasehold, and Church Property, Renewal Fines, Reversions, &c.; also Interest, Legacy, Succession Duty, and various other useful Tables. Eighth Edition. Post 8vo. 10s.

HINTS to MOTHERS on the MANAGEMENT of their HEALTH during the Period of Pregnancy and in the Lying-in Room. By the late THOMAS BULL, M.D. New Edition, thoroughly revised and improved. Fcp. 8vo. 2s. 6d.

The **MATERNAL MANAGEMENT of CHILDREN in HEALTH** and Disease. By the late THOMAS BULL, M.D. New Edition, thoroughly revised and improved. Fcp. 8vo. 1s. 6d.

The **THEORY of the MODERN SCIENTIFIC GAME of WHIST**. By WILLIAM POLE, F.R.S. Seventh Edition, enlarged. Fcp. 8vo. 2s. 6d.

The **CORRECT CARD**; or, How to Play at Whist: a Whist Catechism. By Captain A. CAMPBELL-WALKER, F.R.G.S. late 79th Highlanders; Author of 'The Rifle, its Theory and Practice.' 32mo. 2s. 6d.

CHESS OPENINGS. By F. W. LONGMAN, Balliol College, Oxford. Second Edition revised. Fcp. 8vo. 2s. 6d.

THREE HUNDRED ORIGINAL CHESS PROBLEMS and STUDIES. By JAMES PIERCE, M.A. and W. T. PIERCE. With numerous Diagrams. Square fcp. 8vo. 7s. 6d. SUPPLEMENT, price 2s. 6d.

A SKETCH of the HISTORY of TAXES in ENGLAND from the Earliest Times to the Present Day. By STEPHEN DOWELL. Vol. I. to the Civil War 1642. 8vo. 10s. 6d.

The **NEW CODE** of the Education Department, with Notes, Analysis, Appendix, and Index, and a Sketch of the Administration of the Grants for Public Elementary Education (1839-1876). By H. J. GIBBS, and J. W. EDWARDS, Barrister-at-Law. Second Edition, revised and adapted to the New Code, 1876. Crown 8vo. 3s. 6d.

A PRACTICAL TREATISE on BREWING; with Formulæ for Public Brewers, and Instructions for Private Families. By W. BLACK. 8vo. 10s. 6d.

MODERN COOKERY for PRIVATE FAMILIES, reduced to a System of Easy Practice in a Series of carefully-tested Receipts. By ELIZA ACTON. Newly revised and enlarged; with 8 Plates and 150 Woodcuts. Fcp. 8vo. 6s.

MAUNDER'S TREASURY of KNOWLEDGE and LIBRARY of Reference; comprising an English Dictionary and Grammar, Universal Gazetteer, Classical Dictionary, Chronology, Law Dictionary, a synopsis of the Peerage useful Tables, &c. Revised Edition. Fcp. 8vo. 6s. cloth, or 10s. 6d. calf.

Knowledge for the *Young*.

The **STEPPING-STONE to KNOWLEDGE**; or upwards of 700 Questions and Answers on Miscellaneous Subjects, adapted to the capacity of Infant minds. New Edition, revised. 18mo. 1s.

SECOND SERIES of the STEPPING-STONE to KNOWLEDGE: Containing upwards of 800 Questions and Answers on Miscellaneous Subjects not contained in the FIRST SERIES. 18mo. 1s.

The **STEPPING-STONE to GEOGRAPHY**: Containing several Hundred Questions and Answers on Geographical Subjects. 18mo. 1s.

The **STEPPING-STONE to ENGLISH HISTORY**; Questions and Answers on the History of England. 18mo. 1s.

The **STEPPING-STONE to BIBLE KNOWLEDGE**; Questions and Answers on the Old and New Testaments. 18mo. 1s.

The **STEPPING-STONE to BIOGRAPHY**; Questions and Answers on the Lives of Eminent Men and Women. 18mo. 1s.

The **STEPPING-STONE to IRISH HISTORY**: Containing several Hundred Questions and Answers on the History of Ireland. 18mo. 1s.

The **STEPPING-STONE to FRENCH HISTORY**: Containing several Hundred Questions and Answers on the History of France. 18mo. 1s.

The **STEPPING-STONE to ROMAN HISTORY**: Containing several Hundred Questions and Answers on the History of Rome. 18mo. 1s.

The **STEPPING-STONE to GRECIAN HISTORY**: Containing several Hundred Questions and Answers on the History of Greece. 18mo. 1s.

The **STEPPING-STONE to ENGLISH GRAMMAR**: Containing several Hundred Questions and Answers on English Grammar. 18mo. 1s.

The **STEPPING-STONE to FRENCH PRONUNCIATION and CONVERSATION**: Containing several Hundred Questions and Answers. 18mo. 1s.

The **STEPPING-STONE to ASTRONOMY**: Containing several Hundred familiar Questions and Answers on the Earth and the Solar and Stellar Systems. 18mo. 1s.

The **STEPPING-STONE to MUSIC**: Containing several Hundred Questions on the Science; also a short History of Music. 18mo. 1s.

The **STEPPING-STONE to NATURAL HISTORY**: VERTEBRATE OR BACK-BONED ANIMALS. PART I. *Mammalia*; PART II. *Birds, Reptiles, and Fishes*. 18mo. 1s. each Part.

THE **STEPPING-STONE to ARCHITECTURE**; Questions and Answers explaining the Principles and Progress of Architecture from the Earliest Times. With 100 Woodcuts. 18mo. 1s.

INDEX.

Acton's Modern Cookery	27
Aird's Blackstone Economised	16
Airy's Notes on the Hebrew Scriptures	13
Alpine Club Map of Switzerland	22
Alpine Guide (The)	22
Amos's Jurisprudence	5
———— Primer of the Constitution	5
Anderson's Strength of Materials	13
Armstrong's Organic Chemistry	13
Arnold's (Dr.) Christian Life	13
———— Lectures on Modern History	2
———— Miscellaneous Works	9
———— Sermons	13
———— School Sermons	13
———— (T.) Manual of English Literature	5
Atelier du Lys (The)	20
Atherstone Priory	14
Autumn Holidays of a Country Parson	9
Ayre's Treasury of Bible Knowledge	19
Bacon's Essays, by Whately	7
———— Life and Letters, by Spedding	5
———— Works, edited by Spedding	7
Bain's Emotions and Will	10
———— Logic, Deductive and Inductive	11
———— Mental and Moral Science	10
———— on the Senses and Intellect	10
Baker's 2 works on Ceylon	22
Ball's Alpine Guide	22
Bancroft's Native Races of the Pacific	16
Barry on Railway Appliances	18
Becker's Charicles and Gallus	25
Black's Treatise on Brewing	27
Blackley's German-English Dictionary	9
Blaine's Rural Sports	25
Bloxam's Metals	13
Boultbee on 39 Articles	20
Bourne's Catechism of the Steam Engine	18
———— Handbook of Steam Engine	18
———— Improvements in the Steam Engine	18
———— Treatise on the Steam Engine	18
Bowdler's Family Shakspeare	26
Bramley-Moore's Six Sisters of the Valleys	24
Brande's Dictionary of Science, Literature, and Art	15
Bray's Philosophy of Necessity	11
Brinkley's Astronomy	11
Browne's Exposition of the 39 Articles	20

Buckle's History of Civilisation	2
Buckle's Miscellaneous Works	9
Buckton's Health in the House (Physiological Lectures)	5
Bull's Hints to Mothers	26
———— Maternal Management of Children	27
Burgomaster's Family (The)	24
Burke's Rise of Great Families	5
———— Vicissitudes of Families	5
Cabinet Lawyer	25
Campbell's Norway	23
Cates's Biographical Dictionary	5
———— and Woodward's Encyclopædia	3
Changed Aspects of Unchanged Truths	19
Chesney's Indian Polity	3
———— Modern Military Biography	4
———— Waterloo Campaign	2
Colenso (Bishop) on Pentateuch	21
———— on Moabite Stone, &c.	21
Commonplace Philosopher, by A.K.H.B.	9
Comte's Positive Philosophy	8
Congreve's Politics of Aristotle	5
Conington's Translation of the Æneid	24
———— Miscellaneous Writings	9
Contanseau's French Dictionaries	8
Conybeare and Howson's St. Paul	19
Cotton's (Bishop) Memoir	4
Counsel and Comfort from a City Pulpit	10
Cox's Aryan Mythology	3
———— Crusades	4
———— History of Greece	2
———— General ditto	2
———— Greeks and Persians	2
———— Tale of the Great Persian War	2
———— Tales of Ancient Greece	3
Crawley's Thucydides	3
Creighton's Age of Elizabeth	4
Cresy's Civil Engineering	18
Critical Essays of a Country Parson	9
Crookes's Chemical Analysis	15
———— Dyeing and Calico Printing	18
Cullen's Handbook of Telegraphy	18
D'Aubigné's Reformation	19
Davidson's Introduction to the New Testament	21
Decaisne and Le Maout's Botany	15
De Morgan's Budget of Paradoxes	11

DEMOSTHENES' Oration on the Crown,
  translated by COLLIER 7
DE TOCQUEVILLE'S Democracy in America .. 7
DISRAELI'S Lord George Bentinck 5
——— Novels and Tales 22
DOBSON on the Ox 14
DOVE on Storms 13
DOWELL'S History of Taxes 17
DOYLE'S Fairyland 17

EASTLAKE'S Hints on Household Taste 17
EDWARDS'S Journey of 1,000 Miles through
    Egypt and Nubia 20
——— Untrodden Peaks 22
Elements of Botany 15
ELLICOTT'S Commentary on Ephesians 20
——————— Galatians 20
——————— Pastoral Epist. 20
——————— Philippians, &c 20
——————— Thessalonians 20
——————— Lectures on the Life of Christ. 20
EVANS' (A. J.) Bosnia 22
——— (J.) Ancient Stone Implements 14
Elsa; a Tale of the Tyrolean Alps 24
EWALD'S Antiquities of Israel 20
——— History of Israel 20

FAIRBAIRN'S Applications of Iron 13
——————— Information for Engineers .. 13
——————— Life 4
——————— Mills and Millwork 13
FARRAR's Chapters on Language 7
——————— Families of Speech 7
FITZWYGRAM on Horses and Stables 23
FORBES'S Two Years in Fiji 22
FRANCIS'S Fishing Book 24
FRESHFIELD'S Italian Alps 22
FROUDE'S English in Ireland 1
——————— History of England 1
——————— Short Studies on Great Subjects 10

GAIRDNER'S Houses of Lancaster and York 4
——————— Puritan Revolution 4
GANOT'S Elementary Physics 13
——— Natural Philosophy 13
GARDINER'S Buckingham and Charles 3
——————— Thirty Years' War 4
GIFFEN on Church and State 5
German Home Life 9
GILLS & EDWARDS'S New Code 17
GIMSON'S Religion and Science 19
GILBERT and CHURCHILL'S Dolomites 22
GRIMSTON'S Bible Synonyms 15
GOODEVE'S Mechanism 13
——————— Mechanics 13
GRANT'S Ethics of Aristotle 6
Graver Thoughts of a Country Parson ... 9

GREVILLE'S Journal 3
GRIFFIN'S Algebra and Trigonometry 13
GROHMAN'S Tyrol and the Tyrolese 22
GROVE on Correlation of Physical Forces 14
——— 's (F. C.) Frosty Caucasus 22
GWILT'S Encyclopædia of Architecture .. 17

HALE'S Fall of the Stuarts 4
HARRISON'S Order and Progress 7
HARTLEY on the Air 12
HARTWIG'S Aerial World 15
——————— Polar World 15
——————— Sea and its Living Wonders 15
——————— Subterranean World 15
——————— Tropical World 15
HAUGHTON'S Animal Mechanics 14
HAYWARD'S Essays 9
HEATHCOTE'S Reminiscences of Fen and
    Mere 19
HEINE'S Life, Works, and Opinions, by
    STIGAND 5
HELMHOLTZ on Tone 15
——————— Popular Lectures 15
HENSLEY'S Handbook of Trees and Plants 15
HERSCHEL'S Outlines of Astronomy 11
HINCHLIFF'S Over the Sea and Far Away 22
HOLLAND'S Fragmentary Papers 11
HOLMS on the Army 3
HULLAH'S History of Modern Music 13
——————— Transition Period 13
HUME'S Essays 12
——— Treatise on Human Nature 11

INCE'S Roman History 3
Indian Alps (The), by a Lady Pioneer .. 21
LONGLOW'S Poems 26

JAMESON'S Saints and Martyrs 17
——————— Legends of the Madonna 17
——————— Monastic Orders 17
JAMESON and EASTLAKE'S Saviour 17
JELF on Confession in the English Church 21
JENKIN'S Electricity and Magnetism .. 13
JERRAM'S Lycidas of Milton 20
JERROLD'S Life of Napoleon 4
LORENTON'S Geographical Dictionary ... 10
JUKES'S Types of Genesis 21
——— on Second Death 21

KALISCH'S Commentary on the Bible 8
KAYE on Fulfilment of Prophecy 20
KERL'S Metallurgy 13
KINGSLEY'S Lectures delivered in America 10
KIRBY and SPENCE'S Entomology 15
KIRKMAN'S Philosophy 10
KNATCHBULL-HUGESSEN'S Higgledy-Piggledy 25
KNATCHBULL-HUGESSEN'S Whispers from
    Fairyland 25

Landscapes, Churches, and Moralities, by A. K. H. B. ... 12
LANG's Ballads and Lyrics ... 24
LATHAM's New English Dictionary ... 7
——— Johnson's Dictionary ... 8
——— Handbook of the English Language ... 7
LAUGHTON's Nautical Surveying ... 13
LAWRENCE on Rocks ... 14
LECKY's History of European Morals ... 3
——— Rationalism ... 3
——— Leaders of Public Opinion ... 4
LEFROY's Bermudas ... 27
Leisure Hours in Town, by A. K. H. B. ... 9
Lessons of Middle Age, by A. K. H. B. ... 10
LEWES' History of Philosophy ... 4
LEWIS on the Influence of Authority in Matters of Opinion ... 6
LIDDELL and SCOTT's Two Lexicons ... 8
LINDLEY and MOORE's Treasury of Botany ... 13
LLOYD's Magnetism ... 14
——— Wave-Theory of Light ... 14
London Series of French Classics ... 21
LONGMAN's (W.) Edward the Third ... 2
——— Lectures on History of England ... 2
——— Old and New St. Paul's ... 17
——— Chess Openings ... 27
——— (F. W.) German Dictionary ... 7
LOUDON's Agriculture ... 19
——— Gardening ... 19
——— Plants ... 14
LUDLOW's War of American Independence ... 4
LUBBOCK on Origin of Civilisation ... 11
Lyra Germanica ... 21

MACAULAY's (Lord) Essays ... 2
——— History of England ... 1
——— Lays of Ancient Rome ... 24
——— Life and Letters ... 4
——— Miscellaneous Writings ... 10
——— Speeches ... 7
——— Complete Works ... 1
MACLEOD's Economical Philosophy ... 7
——— Theory and Practice of Banking ... 25
——— Elements of Banking ... 25
McCULLOCH's Dictionary of Commerce ... 25
Mademoiselle Mori ... 22
MALET's Annals of the Road ... 27
MALLESON's Genoese Studies ... 3
——— Native States of India ... 3
MARSHALL's Physiology ... 12
MARSHMAN's Life of Havelock ... 4
——— History of India ... 2
MARTINEAU's Christian Life ... 21
——— Hymns ... 21
MAUNDER's Biographical Treasury ... 5
——— Geographical Treasury ... 12
——— Historical Treasury ... 3
——— Scientific and Literary Treasury ... 13
——— Treasury of Knowledge ... 27
——— Treasury of Natural History ... 14
MAXWELL's Theory of Heat ... 13

MAY's Constitutional History of England ... 1
——— History of Democracy ... 1
MELVILLE's Novels and Tales ... 24
MENZIES' Forest Trees ... 16
MERIVALE's Fall of the Roman Republic ... 8
——— General History of Rome ... 8
——— Romans under the Empire ... 8
MERRIFIELD's Arithmetic & Mensuration ... 14
MILES on Horse's Foot and Horseshoeing ... 25
——— Horses' Teeth and Stables ... 25
MILL (J.) on the Mind ... 10
MILL (J. S.) on Liberty ... 7
——— on Representative Government ... 7
——— on Utilitarianism ... 7
——— 's (J. S.) Autobiography ... 4
——— Dissertations and Discussions ... 7
——— Essays on Religion &c. ... 10
——— Political Economy ... 7
——— System of Logic ... 7
——— Hamilton's Philosophy ... 7
——— Unsettled Questions ... 7
MILLER's Elements of Chemistry ... 16
——— Inorganic Chemistry ... 13
MINTO's (Lord) Life and Letters ... 4
MITCHELL's Manual of Assaying ... 19
MONSELL's Spiritual Songs ... 21
MOORE's Irish Melodies ... 24
MORELL's Mental Philosophy ... 10
MÜLLER's (MAX) Chips from a German Workshop ... 10
——— Lectures on Language ... 8
——— Science of Religion ... 10

NELSON on the Moon ... 13
New Reformation, by THEODORE ... 1
New Testament, Illustrated Edition ... 17

O'CONOR's Commentary on Hebrews ... 20
——— Romans ... 20
——— St. John's Gospel ... 20
ODLING's Course of Practical Chemistry ... 15
OSBORN's Islam ... 19
OWEN's Comparative Anatomy and Physiology of Vertebrate Animals ... 11

PACKE's Guide to the Pyrenees ... 22
PAGET's Naval Powers ... 16
PATTISON's Casaubon ... 5
PAYEN's Industrial Chemistry ... 15
PEWTNER's Comprehensive Specifier ... 26
PIERCE's Chess Problems ... 27
POLE on Whist ... 27
PRENTICE and SIVEWRIGHT's Telegraphy ... 14
PRENDERGAST's Mastery of Languages ... 8
Present-Day Thoughts, by A. K. H. B. ... 10
PROCTOR's Astronomical Essays ... 11
——— Moon ... 11
——— New Star Atlas ... 12
——— Orbs Around Us ... 12
——— Plurality of Worlds ... 12

NEW WORKS PUBLISHED BY LONGMANS AND CO.

PROCTOR'S Saturn and its System 18
——— Scientific Essays 14
——— Sun 11
——— Transits of Venus 11
——— Universe 11
Public Schools Atlases (The) 13
——— Modern Geography 13

RAWLINSON'S Parthia 3
——— Sassanian Monarchy 3
Recreations of a Country Parson .... —
REDGRAVE'S Dictionary of Artists 17
REILLY'S Map of Mont Blanc 22
REMONT'S Memoirs 4
RICHARDSON'S Down the Road 20
RICH'S Dictionary of Antiquities 8
RIVERS' Rose Amateur's Guide 16
ROGERS'S Eclipse of Faith 19
——— Defence of ditto 19
——— Essays 8
ROGET'S English Thesaurus of Classified
Words and Phrases 8
RONALDS'S Fly-Fisher's Entomology ... 22
ROSCOE'S Outlines of Civil Procedure ... 4
RUSSELL'S (Lord) Recollections and Suggestions 1

SANDARS'S Justinian Institutes 4
SAVILE on Apparitions 10
——— on Primitive Faith 12
SCHELLEN'S Spectrum Analysis 12
SCOTT'S Lectures on the Fine Arts ... 17
——— Poems, Illustrated 17, 24
——— Papers on Engineering ... 12
Seaside Musings by A. K. H. B. 9
SEEBOHM'S Oxford Reformers of 1498 .. 3
——— Protestant Revolution ... 3
SEWELL'S Preparation for Communion ... 21
——— Questions of the Day ... 21
——— History of France 4
——— Tales and Stories 20
——— Thoughts for the Age ... 21
SHELLEY'S Workshop Appliances 12
SHORT'S Church History 3
SIMPSON'S Meeting the Sun 22
SMITH'S (SYDNEY) Essays 10
——— Wit and Wisdom 10
——— (Dr. R. A.) Air and Rain ... 12
SOUTHEY'S Doctor 9
——— Poetical Works 24
STANLEY'S History of British Birds ... 15
STEPHEN'S Ecclesiastical Biography ... —
Stepping Stones (the Series) 17, 20
STOCKMAR'S Memoirs 4
STONEHENGE on the Dog 22
——— on the Greyhound 22
STONEY on Strains 14
Sunday Afternoons, by A. K. H. B. 9
Supernatural Religion 13
SWINBOURNE'S Picture Logic 8

TAYLOR'S History of India 2
——— (Jeremy) Works, edited by EDEN 21
Text-Books of Science 12
THOMSON'S Laws of Thought 7
THORPE'S Quantitative Analysis 12
THORPE and MUIR'S Qualitative Analysis 12
TILDEN'S Chemical Philosophy 11
TODD (A.) on Parliamentary Government 1
TRENCH'S Realities of Irish Life 4
TREVELYAN'S Selections from MACAULAY'S Writings 10
TROLLOPE'S Barchester Towers 20
——— Warden 20
TWISS'S Law of Nations during the Time of War 5
TYNDALL on Diamagnetism 14
——— Electricity 14
——— Heat 13
——— Sound 13
——— American Lecture on Light 16
——— Fragments of Science ... 14
——— Lectures on Light 14
——— Molecular Physics 14

UEBERWEG'S System of Logic 11
URE'S Arts, Manufactures, and Mines ... 18

WALKER on Whist 22
WARBURTON'S Edward the Third 6
WATSON'S Geometry 12
WATTS'S Dictionary of Chemistry 14
WEBB'S Objects for Common Telescopes 13
WELLINGTON'S Life, by GLEIG 5
WHATELY'S English Synonymes 8
——— Christian Evidences ... 21
——— Logic 8
——— Rhetoric 8
WHITE'S Latin-English and English-Latin
Dictionaries 8
WILCOCKS'S Sea Fisherman 22
WILLIAMS'S Aristotle's Ethics 7
WILLICH'S Popular Tables 23
WOOD'S (J. G.) Bible Animals 14
——— Homes without Hands 14
——— Insects at Home 14
——— Abroad 14
——— Out of Doors 14
——— Strange Dwellings 14
——— (J. T.) Ephesus 2
WYATT'S History of Prussia 3

YONGE'S English-Greek Lexicon 8
——— Horace 20
YOUATT on the Dog 22
——— on the Horse 22

ZELLER'S Socrates 4
——— Stoics, Epicureans, and Sceptics 4
——— Plato 4
ZIMMERN'S Schopenhauer 4

Spottiswoode & Co., Printers, New-street Square, London.

www.ingramcontent.com/pod-product-compliance
Lightning Source LLC
Chambersburg PA
CBHW031935290426
44108CB00011B/565